D0918071

MORPHOLOGICAL
THEORY

Blackwell Textbooks in Linguistics

MORPHOLOGICAL THEORY

An Introduction to Word Structure in Generative Grammar

Andrew Spencer

BLACKWELL
Oxford UK & Cambridge USA

Copyright © Andrew Spencer 1991

First published 1991
Reprinted 1992

Blackwell Publishers
108 Cowley Road, Oxford, OX4 1JF, UK

238 Main Street, Suite 501
Cambridge, Massachusetts 02142, USA

All rights reserved. Except for the quotation of short passages for the purposes of criticism and review, no part of this publication may be reproduced, stored in a retrieval system, or transmitted, in any form or by any means, electronic, mechanical, photocopying, recording or otherwise, without the prior permission of the publisher.

Except in the United States of America, this book is sold subject to the condition that it shall not, by way of trade or otherwise, be lent, re-sold, hired out, or otherwise circulated without the publisher's prior consent in any form of binding or cover other than that in which it is published and without a similar condition including this condition being imposed on the subsequent purchaser.

British Library Cataloguing in Publication Data
A CIP catalogue record for this book is available from the British Library

Library of Congress Cataloging in Publication Data
Spencer, Andrew.
   Morphological theory : an introduction to word structure in
generative grammar / Andrew Spencer.
      p.   cm.
   Includes bibliographical references and index.
   ISBN 0–631–16143–0 (hardback) — ISBN 0–631–16144–9 (paperback)
   1. Grammar, Comparative and general—Morphology.   2. Generative
grammar.   I. Title.
P241.S64   1991
415—dc20   90–44350
                                                          CIP

Typeset in 10 on 12 pt Plantin
by Mathematical Composition Setters Ltd, Salisbury, Wilts

Printed in Great Britain by Cambridge University Press, Cambridge.

This book is printed on acid-free paper

for
FAY

Contents

Preface

This book is about morphology, that is, the structure of words. More importantly, it's about the kinds of *theories* that linguists have constructed to explain word structure. Although I hope the book will be useful in helping to develop the skills of morphological analysis, the primary goal is to show the reader how theories have been developed, criticized, and revised and why, in some cases, they've been abandoned.

Morphology is unusual amongst the subdisciplines of linguistics, in that much of the interest of the subject derives not so much from the facts of morphology themselves, but from the way that morphology interacts with and relates to other branches of linguistics, such as phonology and syntax. Indeed, the theme of the 'interface' between morphology and other components of grammar is one which runs through the whole book.

As the subtitle indicates, we'll be concerned with morphology in generative grammar. My aim has been to choose 'mainstream' trends and describe how morphology fits into those trends. Not everyone will agree with my choice of what counts as 'mainstream' generative grammar. In part, my decisions have been motivated by my personal interests and my particular (often rather limited) expertise. Among the topics which I've had to ignore are historical morphology (that is, morphology in language change), psycholinguistic research on morphology (in children and adults), and computational approaches. Nonetheless, I believe I've covered most of the key theoretical issues confronting contemporary linguists with an interest in morphology.

A variety of specialists have an interest in morphology and I hope this book will therefore prove useful to phonologists, syntacticians, historical linguists, descriptive linguists and others whose main interests lie outside morphological theory as such. In addition, psycholinguists and computer scientists working on language processing should find the book relates to their concerns. However, my primary audience is students of linguistics, and my intention is that the book should enable the student to tackle research articles relating to morphology in linguistic theory in the standard international journals, such as *Language*, *Linguistic Inquiry*, *Natural Language and Linguistic Theory*, *The Linguistic Review* and *Yearbook of Morphology*. In addition, such a reader should be able to make reasonable sense of the increasing numbers of theoretical monographs dealing with questions of morphology. In a sense, the book has been designed as a kind of graduated guidebook to such literature.

For the phonology interface, it has been relatively easy to determine what counts as 'mainstream' (though this won't immunize me from criticism!). The syntax interface presents a much richer assortment of theoretical approaches. I've chosen the framework which I personally find most congenial, namely, the so-called Government-Binding theory of Chomsky. This should not be taken as an indication that work in other frameworks should be neglected. On the contrary, specialists working on other theories (especially Lexical Functional Grammar and Generalized Phrase Structure Grammar) have had an extremely keen interest in morphology and the structure of the lexicon, and some of the better technical ideas which have worked their way into Government-Binding approaches have been 'borrowed' from those other frameworks. However, Government-Binding syntax is the framework with which students are most likely to be acquainted if they take courses in contemporary syntax. Moreover, the dominance of GB theory means that it tends to serve as the backdrop for theoretical discussion in any framework.

The importance of the 'interfaces' between morphology and the rest of linguistics has been responsible in large part for the revival of interest in morphology over the past fifteen years or so. Nowadays, it's simply not possible to do certain types of phonology or syntax without an appreciation of the implications for morphology. This puts a serious onus on the student of linguistics, however. Although the more elementary concepts in morphology can be grasped quite adequately without any real reference to the rest of linguistics, it's impossible to understand the full implications of contemporary research in morphology without a basic background in phonology and syntax. The book is written so as to be as autonomous as possible. For this reason I've been careful to explain as far as I can (even if very cursorily) the terms I use from outside morphology. The more important terms, whether from morphology or outside, are put in boldface at the first mention which includes a brief gloss.

It would, of course, be wrong to pretend that anyone can understand theory construction in morphology without a basic understanding of theoretical linguistics. Beyond part I especially, I assume some familiarity with such concepts as 'phoneme', 'distinctive feature', 'constituent structure', 'generative grammar'. However, linguistics courses vary immensely in what they cover, and, for this reason, I've added lists of textbooks and other introductory material for branches outside morphology to the Further Reading sections of the Notes to each chapter. These should provide more than sufficient background, especially in phonology and syntax.

It's perfectly possible to teach a complete course in morphology from this book, spanning, say, the last two years of a three-year degree in Linguistics. However, it's also possible to look upon the book as a sourcebook for instructors wishing to construct courses in morphology at various levels, as well as for students following such courses, or for those who wish to incorporate some discussion of morphology into more traditional linguistics teaching (say, phonology, syntax, or lexicology). For the more elementary courses (say, second-year undergraduate), one might use part I, the less advanced sections of part II, the first three sections of chapter 6 and then the more descriptive sections of the subsequent chapters. A more advanced course (say, second-semester postgraduate) might take part I as basic background reading and then use the book to concentrate on topics from parts II, III or IV. All the chapters except the last are furnished with exercises. Those marked with an asterisk (*) are problems I regard as more deep or advanced, and which are therefore more suited to postgraduate students or in many cases to larger-scale undergraduate assignments. Some of the exercises are effectively feedback exercises on the chapter itself and may have relatively straightforward answers. Others are problem sets illustrating the theoretical issues discussed in that chapter (and earlier chapters). Not infrequently, the exercises include data which are actually problematical for some of the theoretical proposals discussed in the chapter. In some cases, the exercises are simply meant to raise more general questions, often taken up again in later chapters. This means that the exercises are an integral part of the book. It also means that many of the exercises are open-ended and lack a 'correct answer', and for this reason even some of the elementary exercises will serve well as a starting point for more advanced discussion.

During the lengthy gestation period of this volume, I've had the benefit of considerable help, advice, criticism and support from friends and colleagues. Neil Smith deserves special thanks for suggesting the idea in the first place, and for reading most of the book and giving me extremely detailed comments, as well as much needed encouragement. Likewise, Dick Hayward and Iggy Roca read a large part of the manuscript and provided extremely helpful criticism. These three colleagues merit my special gratitude. Individual chapters received invaluable commentary from Bob Borsley, Andrew Carstairs-McCarthy, Grev Corbett, Nigel Fabb, Chris Lyons, and Matt Shibatani. In addition, I must thank Liliane Haegeman for inviting me to teach in Geneva for a year, where much of the book was written or prepared. Conversations with her and Ian Roberts did much to clarify my thinking in a variety of areas. In addition, Pavla Munch-Peterson, Ádám Nádasdy, Marek Piotrowski and Vlad Žegarac helped with some of the linguistic examples. I must also thank several generations of students in London and Geneva for being guinea pigs to my pedagogical experiments in morphology, and for test-driving some of the exercises with such good humour. Finally, special thanks to Fay Young, for much more than just proof-reading.

ACKNOWLEDGEMENTS

My thanks are due to the following for permission to reproduce figures from copyrighted material: Elsevier Publishing Co. (R. Beard 'Morpheme order in a Lexeme/Morpheme based morphology'), Foris Publications (H. Borer 'On the Parallelism Between Compounds and Constructs'), MIT Press (S. Anderson 'Where's Morphology?', G. Booij and J. Rubach 'Postcyclic versus Postlexical Rules in Lexical Phonology', M. Halle 'Prolegomena to a Theory of Morphology'), The Linguistic Society of America (A. Spencer 'Bracketing Paradoxes and the English Lexicon'), The Linguistic Society of America, M. Shibatani and T. Kageyama ('Word Formation in a Modular Theory of Grammar').

Abbreviations

Abs.	Absolutive (case)
Acc.	Accusative (case)
Act./ACT	active
Adj./ADJ	adjective
ADJP	adjective phrase
ADV	adverb
ADVP	adverb phrase
AFF	affix
Ag	Agent (theta role)
Agr	Agreement (GB theory)
All.	Allative (case)
AMR	Allomorphy Rule (Dressler)
AOG	Affix Ordering Generalization
AP	antipassive; adjective phrase
APF	Adjectival Passive Formation
APPL	applicative
ART	article
ASL	American Sign Language
Asp.	aspect
AUX	auxiliary (verb)
BEC	Bracket Erasure Convention
Ben	Benefactive (theta role)
BSL	British Sign Language
C	*see* Comp
CAOG	Compound Affix Ordering Generalization
CAUS	causative
CFPP	Case Frame Preservation Principle
cl	clitic
CL	classifier
Com.	Comitative (case)

Comp/COMP	Complementizer (node) (GB theory)
COND	conditional
COOP	Cooperative
CP	complementizer phrase (GB theory)
Dat.	Dative (case)
Det	determiner (GB theory)
dim.	diminutive
DIST	distributive
D.O.	direct object
duopl.	duoplural
DUR	durative
ec	empty category
ECM	Exceptional Case Marking
ECP	Empty Category Principle
El.	Elative (case)
E-language	externalized language
EMPH	emphatic
Erg.	Ergative (case)
Ev	Event (theta role)
EWP	Extended Word-and-Paradigm
Exp	Experiencer (theta role)
F/fem.	feminine
FOPC	First Order Projection Condition
FPC	Feature Percolation Convention
FSP	First Sister Principle
fut./FUT.	future
GB	Government-Binding
Gen.	Genitive (case)
Go	Goal (theta role)
GPSG	Generalized Phrase Structure Grammar
GTC	Government Transparency Corollary
H	high (tone)
HMC	Head Movement Constraint
I	*see* Infl
IA	Item-and-Arrangement
Ill.	Illative (case)
imm. fut.	immediate future
imper.	imperative
imperf.	imperfect
impfv.	imperfective
indic.	indicative
Iness.	Inessive (case)
INF	infinitive
Infl	Inflection (node) (GB theory)
Instr./INSTR	Instrumental (case)
I.O.	indirect object
IP	Item-and-Process; Infl phrase (GB theory)
IPA	International Phonetic Alphabet

IPM	Initial Phrase Marker
ITER	iterative
L	low (tone)
LCS	Lexico-conceptual structure
LF	Logical Form (GB theory)
LFG	Lexical Functional Grammar
Loc.	Locative (case, theta role)
LP	Lexical Phonology
l-s structure	logico-semantic structure (Marantz)
LSF	French Sign Language (Langue des Signes Française)
M/masc.	masculine
MID	middle
MPR	Morphonological Rule (Dressler)
MSC	Morpheme Structure Condition
N	neuter; noun
NEG	negative
neut.	neuter
NGP	Natural Generative Phonology
NI	noun incorporation
Nom.	Nominative (case)
NOM	Nominalization; nominative
NP	noun phrase
NVAP	No Vacuous Application Principle
Obj./OBJ	object
Obl./OBL	oblique
OM	object marker
OPT	optative
P	preposition
PAS	Predicate-argument structure
Pass./PASS	passive
PAST PT	past participle
Pat	Patient (theta role)
perfv.	perfective
PF	Phonological Form
PI	preposition incorporation
pl./PL	plural
P/N	person/number
Poss./POSS	possessive
PP	Prepositional Phrase
PR	Phonological Rule (Dressler)
Prep.	prepositional (case)
pres.	present
PRES PT	present participle
PROG	progressive
PSC	Paradigm Structure Condition
psg	phrase structure grammar
PTCL	particle
PTCPL	participle

Q	question
QR	Quantifier Raising
REC(IP)	reciprocal
refl./REFL	reflexive
RHR	Righthand Head Rule
S	subject; sentence
S_I	intransitive subject
S_T	transitive subject
SCC	Strict Cycle Condition
SDSP	System Defining Structural Property
SEMEL	semeliterative
sg./SG	singular
SM	subject marker
So	Source (theta role)
SPE	*The Sound Pattern of English* (Chomsky and Halle, 1968)
SR	surface representation
SUBJ	subject
subj.	subjunctive
T/A	tense/aspect
Th	Theme (theta role)
TOP	topic
TRANS	transitive
TSL	Trisyllabic Laxing
UBH	Unitary Base Hypothesis
UG	Universal Grammar
UR	underlying representation
UTAH	Universal Theta Assignment Hypothesis
V	verb
VP	verb phrase
WFR	word formation rule
WP	Word-and-Paradigm
W-syntax	Word syntax
1-AEX	1-Advancement Exclusiveness Law (Relational Grammar)
2VP	Second Velar Palatalization

PART I

Preliminaries

1

The Domain of Morphology

1.1 Word structure

All moderately literate speakers of English tend to know exactly two things about the word *antidisestablishmentarianism*. First, that it is the longest word in the English dictionary. Second, that it is comprised of separate components, such as *anti* (as in *anti-Soviet*, *anti-tank*), *dis* (as in *disconnect*, *disentangle*), *ment* (as in *deferment*, *containment*), *arian* (as *disciplinarian*, *parliamentarian*), *ism* (as in *Marxism-Leninism*). Characteristically, they tend to know nothing else about the word, for example, what it means.

The discipline of theoretical linguistics is concerned with providing a precise and explicit characterization of what it is that language users know when they know a language. However, not everything that a language user can be said to know about his or her language is of interest to the theoretical linguist. What linguistic theory aims to characterize is that knowledge which any speaker must possess in order to be regarded as a speaker of the language.

The 'fact' that *antidisestablishmentarianism* is the longest English word is something our language user has to learn (or be taught) explicitly. A speaker who believes such a thing believes it consciously, and could probably explain the basis of that belief (e.g. 'I checked the complete *OED* on my computer', 'My English teacher told me', 'Everybody knows that!' and so on). The idea that the word really is the longest in the language depends on the notion 'the English dictionary' (in the sense of some authoritative document recording every word in English). This notion is not essential to a characterization of English. English, and its speakers, existed before Dr Johnson set quill to paper. Finally, and crucially, anyone who happened not to know this fact (assuming that it is a fact, or even a coherent claim) could not be said on that basis not to be a speaker of English.

The second piece of knowledge is something which our language user was probably never taught and is probably not aware of knowing. Indeed, many people when confronted with the fact that our word is decomposable might retort 'How interesting!

I never knew that'. If you were to ask someone who hadn't been taught grammar or linguistics to decompose the word into its separate parts they might find it difficult or impossible. However, I would claim that all speakers (even illiterate ones) know these things. How can this be?

Although naive users of English (which includes almost anyone except trained linguists or grammarians) find it hard to articulate their knowledge of word structure, if you ask them the right questions, they can give you the evidence of their knowledge. Linguists tend not to like to perform real experiments, so we'll perform a thought experiment to illustrate this. Suppose someone hears the name of the current (1990) Soviet head of state for the first time by eavesdropping into the following snippet:

A: What do you think about Gorbachev?
B: Me, I'm anti-Gorbachev myself.

Given no other context our language user would probably have no idea what was meant by the term *Gorbachev*. A kind of cabbage soup, maybe, or the latest Soviet tank. Or perhaps a new American Secretary of State. However, he does know that whatever Gorbachev represents, speaker B is opposed to it/him/her/them. Likewise, without knowing what on earth it means, English speakers know that *antidisestablishmentarianism* is some kind of doctrine or stance or whatever (i.e. an 'ism'!). With a little ingenuity we can perform this thought experiment for all of the components I isolated earlier.

Here is another experiment (of the kind linguists do tend to perform). Ask your native speaker if he has ever heard the following, and, if he hasn't, whether they could be words in English: *disestablishmentarianism, establishmentarianism, disestablishmentarian, antidisestablishmentarian.* Likely as not his answers will be 'No, I haven't heard them' and 'Yes, they could be English words'. Now try the same for the following: *ismarianmentestablishdisanti, ismdisarianestablishantiment* and so on. (Practice saying these a few times before presenting them to your informant.) The answers here will be 'no' and 'no way!' These are simply not possible words of English. Moreover, any native speaker of the language can give you these judgements if you ask him or her in the right way.

This knowledge of word structure is in many respects of a kind with knowledge of sound structure and knowledge of sentence structure. It is part of what we have to know in order to be native speakers of English, and for that reason it is part of that knowledge of language which linguists regard as properly linguistic. Hence, it is something which linguistic theory has to account for, in the same way that it accounts for knowledge of phonological patterns or knowledge of syntactic structures. The branch of linguistics which concerns itself with these questions is morphology.

1.2   Morphemes, morphs and allomorphy

The components we isolated in the previous section are not words. They are called **morphemes**.[1] Admittedly, *anti* and *ism* tend to be used like words, and probably are words (in addition to being morphemes). The word *establish* is also a morpheme (in addition to being a word). What unites all of these entities is (i) that they seem to contribute some sort of meaning, or at least function, to the word of which they are a component, and (ii) that they can't themselves be decomposed into smaller morphemes. To be sure, we can split up morphemes like *anti-* into syllables and phonemes, but then we are entering a different domain of analysis, namely phonology. It is fairly clear that morphemes like *anti-* and *dis-* contribute a meaning. Likewise, we could say that a morpheme such as *-ism* means 'doctrine, set of beliefs, ...' or some such. We might be hard pressed to say exactly what *-ment* meant, though. However, it's easy to see that it fulfils a function, namely that of taking a verb, e.g. *establish*, and turning it into a noun, *establishment*. In the tradition of American structuralist linguistics established by Bloomfield (1933), a morpheme is generally defined as the 'minimal meaningful element'.

The fact that one and the same entity can be both a morpheme and a word (or, equivalently, that some words consist of just one morpheme, i.e. are monomorphemic) shouldn't worry us. However, it is useful to distinguish those morphemes which are also words in their own right from those which only appear as a proper subpart of a word. The former are called **free** morphemes and the latter **bound** morphemes.

Typically, a morphologically complex (or polymorphic) word will contain a central morpheme, which contributes the basic meaning, and a collection of other morphemes serving to modify this meaning in various ways. For instance, from the word *disagreements* we can dissect a basic morpheme *agree* and three bound morphemes, *dis-*, *-ment*, and *-s*. We call *agree* the **root** and the other (bound) morphemes **affixes**. The morphemes *-ment* and *-s*, which come to the right of the root, are **suffixes**, while *dis-*, which comes to the left, is a **prefix**. In the word *disagreements* we call the form *disagreement* the **stem**.

The fact that *disagreements* is the plural of *disagreement* (or just possibly its 'possessive' form, depending on how you spell it), is something which, again, all native speakers know. The difference obviously resides in the 's'. In the tradition of morphemic analysis established in Europe, the meaning of 'meaningful' in our definition of morpheme would be stretched to include the notion 'plural of a noun' (or, indeed, 'possessive form of a noun'). Some more morphological analysis is implicit in the Russian examples 1.1 (the 'š' is pronounced as in IPA[ʃ], 'j' as in IPA [j]:

1.1	a)	koška	'cat (used as subject of sentence)'
	b)	koški	'of a cat'
	c)	koške	'to/for a cat'
	d)	košku	'cat (used as direct object)'
	e)	koškoj	'by a cat'
	f) (o)	koške	'(about) a cat'

Anyone can tell that we have a unit *košk-*, with the basic meaning of 'cat', to which we add other units (like *-i*, *-e*, etc.). However, even those who know Russian will be hard put to say exactly, or even approximately, what these endings 'mean'. The best way of characterizing them is in terms of a mixture of meaning and grammatical function. The glosses I have provided are rudimentary to say the least, and a proper characterization of them would be a laborious task. For instance, it's an important fact about Russian noun morphology that form 1.1f, which happens in this example to coincide with 1.1c, is only ever used when the noun is governed by a preposition (though not just any old preposition). It's also important to know that the form 1.1e is used when the cat is the agent of a passive of sentence (*the mouse was eaten by a cat*), or when it forms the predicate with certain verbs (*this animal is a cat*).

So, some would call the endings of Russian nouns morphemes, and others would say they are something else. We will discuss this question in some detail later in this chapter and in other chapters.

One of the facts about morphemes which will be a recurrent theme throughout this book is that they have a physical (i.e. phonological and phonetic) form and also a meaning, or function, within the grammatical system. Morphemes, in other words, are at the front line of the 'double articulation' of language, that is the articulation into form (sound) and content (meaning or function), and much of morphological theory is given over to establishing just how the mapping between form and content is achieved.

Listen carefully to the plural endings of the words of 1.2:

1.2   a) cats   /kats/
         b) dogs   /dogz/
         c) horses   /ho:səz/
         d) cows   /kawz/

The regular plural ending (which we will regard as a morpheme) is found in precisely three different pronunciations, /s/, /z/, and /əz/.[2] Since these three elements all represent a morpheme they are called **morphs**. These are the **realizations** (i.e. alternative forms) of a single morpheme which we can represent as —Z. We say that the morphs /s z əz/ are **allomorphs** of −Z and that the plural morpheme exhibits **allomorphy**.[3]

The allomorphy illustrated in 1.2 is conditioned entirely by phonology. By this I mean that the choice of the allomorph for the plural suffix depends solely on the pronunciation of the stem. Some linguists don't count this kind of phonologically conditioned allomorphy as 'real' allomorphy. However, English displays allomorphic variation which is recognized as allomorphy by all linguists. Examine the roots of the words in 1.3 (the root in these cases is the word minus the ending):

1.3   a) index   indices   [indisi-z]
         b) house   houses   [hauz-əz]
         c) knife   knives   [naiv-z]

What is happening here is that the root used for the plural has a different phonological shape from that found in the singular form. In other words, the root exhibits allomorphy. Moreover, this is an idiosyncratic property of the words (or morphemes) of the type 'house' and 'knife'. It is not a property of the category of plural, for (i) it can occur in other forms of the same word, e.g. the verb *to house*; (ii) in general, words with a similar phonological shape don't display root allomorphy in the plural (e.g. *spouse*, *fife*, or even *indexes*).

Some allomorphy seems to be conditioned neither by phonology nor by the word to which a morpheme belongs or is attached, but by the presence of other mor-

phemes. There are a good many adjectives in English ending in a morpheme
-able/ible (both pronounced /əbl/). This morpheme assumes a different shape, however, whenever we attach the noun-forming suffix *-ity* to it:

1.4		
	possible	possibility
	credible	credibility
	probable	probability

Different suffixes which, like *-əbl*, surface with a schwa, [ə], have alternates with
vowels different from the /i/ of *-əbility*.[4]

1.5			
	musical	musicality	[mjuzikaliti]
	porous	porosity	[porositi]

Examples in which allomorphy is conditioned purely by another morpheme occur
in languages which form plurals of nouns in one of several relatively common and
productive ways, and in which different noun-forming suffixes take different plural
allomorphs. German is such a language. Any count noun formed from the suffix
-heit/keit will form its plural in *-en*, as in 1.6:

1.6		
	a) Schwachheit-en	weaknesses
	b) Spracheigentümlichkeit-en	idioms
	c) Flüssigkeit-en	fluids

However, in general a stem ending in, say, a vowel + /t/ might form its plural in any
of a number of ways (cf. 1.7):

1.7			
	a) Streit	Streit-e	quarrels
	b) Kraut	Kräut-er	plants
	c) Zeit	Zeit-en	times
	d) Braut	Bräut-e	brides

What we would want to say here is that the choice of the plural ending in 1.6 is
governed entirely by the *-heit/keit* morpheme.

A rich source of examples of allomorphy is provided by the ending *-ion* in English
which forms a noun from certain verbs (an 'abstract nominalization'). It has several
allomorphs, the commonest being *-ation* (as in *cite ~ citation*). However, after any
word which ends in the morpheme *-ceive* (e.g. *re-ceive, de-ceive, con-ceive*) we find
the allomorph *-ion: re-cept-ion, de-cept-ion, con-cept-ion*. These words (and others like
them with different bases) seem to have nothing in common except that they end in
the *-ceive/-cept-* morphemes.[5]

As we have seen with the *-ation ~ -ion* and *-ceive ~ -cept* allomorphy, variants of a
given morpheme may be phonologically very different from each other. When the
differences are relatively small and can be described by some sort of phonological process, linguists working within the generative paradigm have tried to assimilate the
allomorphy into phonology as far as possible. In some cases this might seem like a
hopeless task. For instance, the class of strong verbs in English provides examples

of pretty drastic allomorphy: *think ~ thought, bring ~ brought*. Nonetheless, in a fairly recent article on English phonology these alternations have been handled by sets of phonological rules (Halle and Mohanan, 1985). The extent to which this 'phonological' approach should be adopted is a matter of some controversy, which we shall be exploring in detail in part II.

However, there is a limit to phonological explanation in pretty well everyone's theory, and that limit is the phenomenon known as **suppletion**. This is illustrated by the type of alternation between *go* and its past tense form *went*. Here, there is absolutely no phonological connection between the two forms, so we have a case of **total suppletion**. Other standard examples from English are *good ~ better ~ best* and *good ~ well*. A less standard example is the nominalization of the verb *despise*. None of the usual ways of forming nouns from verbs work with this one: **despisal, *despisement, *dispission* (where the asterisk means 'ungrammatical form'). *Despite* used to be used but it means something else now. The real nominal is the suppletive form, *contempt*.

In other cases, the two allomorphs bear some phonological similarity. This is typically the result of one (or both) of two factors. The two allomorphs may be the consequence of a phonological change in the language which happened a long time ago and which has been overlain by yet more changes. This is the case with the *think ~ thought* cases. In other examples, we find that a morpheme (or strictly a word containing the morpheme) has been borrowed from another language at two different times and assimilated in two different forms, or, in more complex cases, we find the same morpheme has been borrowed from two different but related languages. For example, the word *France* was borrowed from Norman French (cf. modern French *France*). But English has also borrowed a morpheme *franco-* (as in *francophile, Franco-Prussian, francophone*) from Latin (though the Romans themselves got the word from Germanic). Historians use something closer to the original Germanic word when they use the term Frank and Frankish to refer to early periods of French history. Finally, the adjective from *France*, namely *French*, is another example of allomorphy, which cannot sensibly be explained by phonological rules of current (synchronic) English. The *France ~ French* alternation is a case of a morpheme changing shape through the ravages of historical sound changes. To the extent that we want to say that *France, French, Franco* and *Frank* are all allomorphs of some single morpheme we would have to say that we are dealing with suppletion here. But the variants still bear a fairly strong resemblance to each other. This type of suppletion would therefore be called **partial suppletion**.

1.3   Types of morphological operation

In this section I shall give an overview of the different ways in which the phonological form of words and morphemes can be mobilized to realize morphological categories. The morphological categories themselves will be discussed in more detail in the following section. Although our main concern will be simply to gain a feel for the variety of word and morpheme structure in the world's languages, we will also touch on some of the theoretical problems which arise when we try to describe this variety.

1.3.1 Inflection and derivation

Traditional grammarians usually distinguished between two main types of morphological operation, **inflection** (or **inflexion**) and **derivation**. The first was represented by example 1.1. There we saw that a noun in Russian appears in several different forms (called **cases**). The intuition here is that we have a single word, *koška*, 'a cat', and that it assumes several forms: *koški, koške, košku*, etc. (not to mention *koška* itself). In this way we speak of *koški* as 'the genitive singular (form) of the word *koška*'. On more homely territory we see the same thing when we say that *goes* is 'the third person singular present indicative of the verb *go*' or that *saw* is 'the past tense of the verb *see*'. Since inflected forms are just variants of one and the same word, inflecting a word shouldn't cause it to change its category. Moreover, even when a word can belong to more than one category, such as the innumerable English words which are both nouns and verbs, we inflect the word either as a noun or as a verb. For some theories it is a definition of inflection that it cannot cause a word to change its syntactic category.

The second type of operation, derivation, has also been illustrated already on a number of occasions. Let's take a straightforward example from English. The verb *institute* forms a noun *institution* by suffixation of *-ion*. From this I can form the adjective *institutional* which in turn yields a verb *institutionalize*. We have come in a spiral rather than a circle because the verb *institutionalize* doesn't mean the same as the verb *institute*. We can continue by deriving *institutionalization*. I can also say *institutionalizational*, another adjective, and, from this, form the adverb *institutionalizationally*. Now, there is no sense in which *institutionalizationally* is a 'form' of the word *institute*. We are dealing here with the creation of new words from old words, 'word formation' in a literal sense. As can be seen from my examples, derivation typically (though not necessarily) induces a change in syntactic category.

Put in these simple terms, it is not difficult to see why people might believe that inflectional morphology is the result of applying processes to words, while derivational morphology is the result of concatenating morphemes. As we shall see, things are not that simple, and it turns out to be extremely difficult to draw the line between inflection and derivation in such a way that it gives sensible answers for all languages.

There are two important notions associated with inflectional morphology: that of 'morphological class', and that of 'paradigm'.

If we look at languages that exhibit rich inflection (which excludes English) then we typically see that words of a given syntactic class don't necessarily all have the same inflections. Sometimes, the words fall into more or less arbitrary groupings which are associated with different sets of inflections. Such a grouping is called a **morphological class**.

All nouns in Russian belong to one of three groups, or **genders**, known as *masculine*, *feminine* and *neuter*. Although there is some correlation between the genders and sex, the correlation isn't perfect. The word *mužčina*, for example, takes the desinences (endings) of a feminine noun (like *koška*) but it means 'man'. Many names for things, qualities and so on are assigned to masculine, feminine or neuter genders on a semantically arbitrary basis, but the justification is *formal* (i.e. is determined by the shape, or form, of the word): roughly, if a noun ends in a (non-palatalized) consonant in its basic form it is masculine (e.g. *stol* 'table'), if it ends in

-a it is feminine (e.g. *lampa* 'lamp'), and if it ends in -o it is neuter (e.g. *okno* 'window').[6]

Gender systems of the Russian kind are frequent occurrences in the Indo-European languages, so that a similar distinction (sometimes with only two genders, masculine and feminine) is found in German, French, Italian, Spanish and Greek as well as the other Slavonic languages. However, gender systems and inflectional systems are in principle independent of each other. It is perfectly possible to have an inflectional system without any signs of gender (Finnish, Hungarian and many other Ural-Altaic languages manage this). On the other hand, it is perfectly possible to have gender without inflection. French has masculine and feminine gender but gender isn't represented formally on the nouns themselves (in most cases), for they have lost their case inflections. As a result, gender in French serves simply to differentiate between arbitrarily defined groups of words, or **lexical classes**, with no other morphological reflex. In Italian and Spanish the situation seems to be different. Here, too, the nouns have lost all their case desinences, and there are two genders, but masculine nouns tend to end in -o while feminine nouns tend to end in -a. So it looks as if the vestiges of a morphological class system have been retained, reflected solely in the desinences (though in fact this would be rather an oversimplification).

In some languages verbs are subclassified according to syntactic properties. One obvious distinction is between intransitive and transitive verbs. It is not uncommon in languages for intransitive verbs to have inflections indicating their subject while transitive verbs have inflections indicating both the subject and object (another example of *agreement*). For instance, in Chukchee (also spelt *Chukchi*), a paleosiberian language spoken in North East Siberia, we can tell from the form of the verb whether the subject and object are singular or plural, and 1st, 2nd or 3rd person, as can be seen from the examples in 1.8–9:

1.8   root *wakʔo* 'to sit down'
　a) tə-wakʔo-k   'I sat down'
　b)　wakʔo-gʔa   'he sat down'

1.9   root *pela* 'to leave (someone, something)'
　a) tə-pela-gət   'I left you (sg.)'
　b) tə-pela-gʔan   'I left him'
　c) ne-pela-gət   'he left you (sg.)'
　d)　pela-nen   'he left him'

In both the intransitive (1.8) and the transitive (1.9) examples the prefix *tə-* indicates 1st pers. sg. subject. However, in the transitive verb *pela-* we also see that the object is marked. In 1.9a, c the 2nd pers. sg. object is indicated by the suffix *-gət*. In 1.9b, d, the 3rd pers. sg. object is shown by two different suffixes, *-gʔan* and *-nen*. Neither of these suffixes appears on the intransitive verbs (though the *-gʔan* of 1.9b is rather similar in form to the 3rd pers. sg. subject marker *-gʔa* of 1.8b). Where we have this type of morphology, in which the endings of the two types of verb are different, we could speak of a 'transitive' class and an 'intransitive' class.

The gender-based or transitivity-based morphological class systems represent subclassifications which are motivated by syntactic considerations (agreement). For instance, in French the gender of the noun determines the form of the definite article in the singular, *le/la*: *le soleil* 'the sun', masculine, but *la table* 'the table', feminine. In the Chukchee verbs, we are specifying the person and number of the subject and object. But there are many languages in which the sole motivation for membership of a class is morphological: some words take one set of inflections and other words take another set. Often, this sort of system cuts across gender or other syntactically based subclassifications. When it happens in nouns we traditionally speak of **declensional classes** or **declensions**; with verbs we speak of **conjugational classes** or **conjugations**.

Russian provides an example of a conjugational system. Verbs inflect for person (1st, 2nd, 3rd) and number (singular and plural) in the non-past tense, and they also have an imperative, an infinitive and several participles. In the largest class a verb consists of a root morpheme followed by a conjugational marker (often referred to as a 'theme' or 'extension'). This surfaces variously as *-a-* or *-aj-*. The other main class of verbs is formed with a different theme, *-i-*. Examples of two typical verbs are given in 1.10 and 1.11:[7]

1.10   del-a-t' 'to do'
         Sg.   Pl.   Imperative
    1 del-aj-u   del-aj-em   Sg.: del-aj
    2 del-aj-eš   del-aj-ete   Pl.: del-aj-te
    3 del-aj-et   del-aj-ut
    Past participle active: del-a-l
    Past participle passive: del-a-n
    Present participle active: del-aj-uščij
    Present participle passive: del-aj-emyj

1.11   govor-i-t' 'to speak'
         Sg.   Pl.   Imperative
    1 govor-ju   govor-i-m   Sg.: govor-i
    2 govor-i-š   govor-i-te   Pl.: govor-i-te
    3 govor-i-t   govor-jat
    Past participle active: govor-i-l
    Past participle passive: govor-jo-n
    Present participle active: govor-jaščij
    Present participle passive: govor-i-myj

From these tables it is apparent that the ending which distinguish one form from another[8] are those to the right of the *-a(j)-* or *-i-* themes. On the other hand, if we compared the hundreds of verbs which belong to each of these groups we would find that they all had exactly the same theme intervening between the root and the desinences proper. This theme serves no other purpose than to help create a base to which to attach the inflectional desinences, and to define the separate morphological classes (conjugations). Again, this is a situation which is prevalent in inflecting Indo-European languages, and essentially the same phenomenon can be observed in the other Slavic languages, in the Romance languages, in Greek and so on.

The tabulations in 1.10 and 1.11 also illustrate the second notion connected with inflection, that of **paradigm**. A paradigm is the set of all the inflected forms which an individual word assumes. Sometimes the term refers to some specifiable subpart of the total paradigm. Thus, the list of word forms under 1.1 could be called 'the singular paradigm for the noun *koška*'. There is a feeling amongst many linguists that the notion of paradigm must be important, perhaps even in some sense primary. But it has proved extremely difficult to characterize the idea adequately, let along give it a formal definition, and in most contemporary theories of morphology the notion of 'paradigm' doesn't play any role. We will discuss this in rather more detail in chapters 2 and 6.[9]

1.3.2 Morphemes: things or rules?

A leitmotif of morphological theory is the interplay between a relatively abstract level of morphological analysis, at which a given morpheme can be thought of as a cover term for various relationships which hold between words, and a more concrete level at which words and morphemes are realized as sounds (or at least as phonemes). By 'abstract level' I mean a level at which, for instance, we can represent the idea of a past tense morpheme in English simply as an entity PAST of some sort, whose main property is that it is realized on verbs, and that it contrasts with a different property, i.e. PRESENT or NON-PAST. At the concrete level we find this category of PAST instantiated as the -*ed* ending of *walked* or the vowel of *sang* (as opposed to *sing*) or even the suppletion *went* (vis-à-vis *go*). The mere existence of the phenomenon of allomorphy shows that the mapping between these two levels is not trivial.

There are two persistent metaphors which are used by linguists to conceptualize this mapping. One is to regard morphemes as things which combine with each other to produce words. In this metaphor, a morpheme is a bit like a word, only smaller, and the morphology component of a grammar is a bit like syntax in that its primary function is to stick the morphemes together. The other metaphor regards morphemes as the end product of a process or rule or operation. Here, it is not the existence of the morphemes that counts but rather the system of relations or contrasts that morphemes create. On this view, morphology looks rather like generative phonology, because we take some underlying, basic form (say, a word), and perform some operation on it to derive a different form of that word, or a different word altogether.

1.3.3 Morphological formatives: morphemes as things

So far, we have witnessed the most typical examples of the type of morphology that is most readily interpreted as the concatenation of 'things', viz. affixation in which prefixes and suffixes are attached to a root.[10] Morphologists often identify two other sorts of affix: the **infix** and (more controversially) the **circumfix**.

An infix is an affix which is placed *inside* another morpheme (rather than beside a morpheme or between morphemes). In other words, it is capable of splitting up a single morpheme. A classic case of an infixing language is Tagalog, a major language of the Philippines. This uses the infixes -*um*- and -*in* in certain of its verb forms.[11] In the examples in 1.12 it is important to realize that the root *sulat* is a single morph: it can't be split up into two smaller morphemes such as *s*- and -*ulat*:

1.12   from monomorphemic root *sulat* 'writing':
a) sumulat 'to write' (subject focus)
b) sinulat (direct object focus)

In some languages a prefix and a suffix may attach to a base simultaneously to express a single meaning or category conjointly. Some morphologists regard such duets as a special kind of discontinuous affix, a circumfix. This type of affixation is also referred to as *parasynthesis*. For instance, it has been suggested that the German past participle is formed from a circumfix *ge ... t* as in *gewandert* 'wandered', from the verb base *wander-*. However, many linguists would argue that all cases of alleged circumfixation can be reduced (or must be reduced) to suffixation and concomitant prefixation. For instance, in the German case, the suffixal part of the circumfix always happens to be identical to the ending found in the past tense. There is thus no real need to appeal to a special affixal type. In some theories circumfixes are ruled out as impossible even in principle.[12]

One form of affixation is rather different from the standard prefixation and suffixation operations, so much so that it is not universally regarded as affixation. This is the phenomenon of **reduplication**, in which some part of a base is repeated, either to the left, or to the right, or, occasionally, in the middle. Tagalog, again, is a rich source of this type of morphology. In 1.13 we see the first syllable of a root is reduplicated:

1.13   a) Root *sulat* (as in example 1.12):
           future: susulat
      b) Root *basa* 'reading':
           prefixed infinitive: mambasa
           nominalization: mambabasa
      c) Root *sulat*:
           prefixed causative infinitive, 'to make (someone) write': magpasulat
           future: magpapasulat

Notice that in 1.13c the final syllable of the prefix has been reduplicated. In 1.14 we see an example of a whole root being reduplicated:

1.14   magsulatsulat 'to write intermittently'

For good measure, here are some examples in which reduplication interacts with infixation.

1.15   a) sumulat   'write'   infinitive
      b) sumusulat   present tense

1.16   a) bumasa   'read'   infinitive
      b) bumasabasa   'to read intermittently'

The interesting thing about reduplication is that it involves adding material, just like any other form of affixation, but the identity of the added material is partially or wholly determined by the base. Thus, we have a form of affixation which looks much more like some sort of process which is applied to the base rather than a simple concatenation of one morpheme with another. The phenomenon is of great theoretical interest for this reason, amongst others, and the whole of §5.2 will be devoted to it.[13]

Affixation is morphology *par excellence*. There are three other operations which affect word structure and which involve concatenation. They all lie on the margin of syntax, and in some theories are treated as syntactic operations: cliticization, compounding and incorporation.

Clitics, like affixes, are elements which cannot exist independently and can thus be regarded as a kind of bound morpheme. A typical clitic will attach itself to some other word or phrase (known as the **host**), and in straightforward cases the syntactic category of the host will be relatively unimportant (though, for instance, its position in the sentence may be crucial). Since clitics attach themselves to fully inflected words this means that, say, a pronominal clitic referring to the object of the verb might attach to the inflected NP subject of the sentence. For this reason we would be unwilling to think of the clitic as some kind of inflection. In this sense clitics are more like independent words.

Romance languages provide some of the best-studied examples of clitics (though in some respects their clitics are more like affixes than clitics in other languages). In French, object pronouns are clitics which attach themselves either before the verb (**proclitic**) or after it (**enclitic**). If there is more than one they follow a set order, which itself depends on whether they are procliticized, as in the indicative example 1.17a, or encliticized, as in the imperative example, 1.17b:

1.17   a) Il me   les   a   donné.
          he to-me them has given
          'He has given them to me.'
       b) Donnez-les   -moi
          give   -them-me
          'Give them to me.'

In many languages clitics attach to a word or phrase of any syntactic category provided it is in a particular position in the sentence, very commonly, sentence initial. Czech has clitic forms of object pronouns and of the auxiliary verb 'to be', used to form the past tense. Word order is very free, so any type of constituent can appear first in the sentence. However, the clitics must always come in second position, and like the French clitics they appear in a set order. All the sentences in 1.18 mean 'I saw him yesterday', where *jsem* and *ho* are the clitics. (The subject pronoun *já* 'I' is optional, being used only when special emphasis is put on the subject):

1.18   a) Viděl jsem   ho   včera.
          saw   AUX-1sg. him yesterday
       b) Včera jsem ho viděl.
       c) Já jsem ho viděl včera.
          'I saw him yesterday.'

Most languages exhibit some form of **compounding**. Indeed, in some languages (such as Chinese, Vietnamese) it is the only real evidence of morphological complexity. The archetypical case is the compounding of two nouns to produce a compound noun, of the type *morning coffee* or *coffee morning*. However, English also exhibits compounds consisting of Adjective-Noun (*blackbird*), Noun-Adjective (*cobalt blue*) and one or two cases of Verb-Noun (*swearword*). Some languages permit constructions which are not possible or which are unproductive in English. In Italian, as in other Romance languages, we can form what is generally regarded as a compound out of a verb with its object, as in *portalettere* 'postman', literally 'carries letters'. In some languages we seem to be able to create compound words out of whole phrases, as in the French *cessez-le-feu* 'cease fire' in which the noun *feu* 'fire' is modified by a definite article, and the verb component *cessez* 'cease' is in the imperative form.

One of the more intriguing phenomena in the world's morphologies is that of **incorporation**. We speak of incorporation when a word (typically a verb) forms a kind of compound with, say, its direct object, or adverbial modifiers, while retaining its original syntactic function. For true incorporation to occur, there must be a paraphrase using the same morphemes in which the incorporated roots surface as independent words. Chukchee provides a wealth of examples:

1.19   a) Tə-pelarkən qoraŋə.
        I -leave   reindeer
        'I'm leaving the reindeer.'
        b) Tə-qora-pelarkən.

In 1.19b, which means the same as 1.19a and uses the same roots, the root *qora* 'reindeer' has been incorporated by the verb to form a single word. This is evident from the fact that the 1st pers. sg. subject agreement prefix *tə-* precedes the root *qora*. The structure of the word is thus something like 'I-am-reindeer-leaving'. In other cases (e.g. in 1.20 below) we can tell that a root has been incorporated because it undergoes vowel harmony. This means that the vowels of certain roots will change under the influence of vowels of other morphemes. This process doesn't extend beyond the boundaries of a single word, so it serves as a phonological way of distinguishing between a word and a phrase. Much more complex examples are possible, in which a verb incorporates more than one root. In example 1.20, the roots *jaa*, *racwən* and *melgar*, as well as the verb root *maraw*, can all form independent words. (For good measure, the word *milger* which shows up here in a harmonized variant, *melgar*, is a noun-noun compound originally, meaning 'fire-bow'):

1.20   Tə-jaa   -racwəŋ -melgar-marawərkən.
        I -from a distance-compete-gun   -fight
        'I am fighting a duel.'

All three of these phenomena have excited the interest of theoretical linguists. I shall be discussing cliticization in some detail in chapter 9, and incorporation figures in chapter 7. The whole of chapter 8 is devoted to theories of compounding.

1.3.4 Morphological formatives: morphemes as rules

It is not uncommon to find that an affix conditions a phonological change in the base to which it attaches. On occasions we find that, as the language has evolved, the phonological form of the affix itself has withered away over time and left as its only trace the phonologically conditioned allomorphy of its base. When this happens, the **phonological alternation** (i.e. the change in shape shown by the base morpheme) takes over the function of the original affixation. Superficially, at least, a morpheme as a 'thing' has been replaced by a morpheme as a rule.

In this section we will look at five examples of morphemes which are realized as phonological alternations. The phonological processes they involve are stress (English), vowel length (Hausa), tone (Chicheŵa), **apophony**, or **ablaut**, i.e. a change in the vowels of the root (Arabic), and (**consonant) mutation**, i.e. word-initial alternations in consonants (Nivkh). We will then discuss a sixth case in which there is neither a surface morpheme nor a phonological change, *morphological conversion*.

Look at the data set in 1.21, in which an acute accent indicates position of main stress:

1.21   a) contrást   b) cóntrast
           incréase   íncrease
           impórt   ímport
           purpórt   púrport
           tormént   tórment
           transpórt   tránsport

All the (a) examples are verbs and all the (b) examples are nouns. What seems to be happening here is that position of stress is used as a derivational device to signal the syntactic category of the word. In the case of *perfect* we see the same thing happening with an adjective-verb pair.

Hausa, a Chadic language of Northern Nigeria, has elements, reminiscent of English auxiliaries, which appear before verbs to signal tense/aspect (i.e. the time at which and manner in which something takes place). The completive aspect markers are illustrated in 1.22 (doubled vowels are long, i.e. 'aa' = [a:]):

1.22   naa kaawoo   'I have brought'
        kaa kaawoo   'you (sg.) have brought'
        yaa kaawoo   'he has brought'
        taa kaawoo   'she has brought'
        an kaawoo   'one has brought'
        mun kaawoo   'we have brought'
        kun kaawoo   'you (pl.) have brought'
        sun kaawoo   'they have brought'

When these markers appear in relative clauses, in topicalized clauses, or after certain complementizers, however, they assume a special 'relative' form, shown in 1.23 (a grave accent indicates low tone and absence of accent indicates high tone):

1.23   abìn dà na kaawoo   'the thing which I have brought'
        abìn dà ka kaawoo   'the thing which you (sg.) ...'
        ...   ya kaawoo   etc.
                   ta kaawoo
                   akà kaawoo
                   mukà kaawoo
                   kukà kaawoo
                   sukà kaawoo

In the indefinite 3rd sg. form and the plural forms we see the aspect markers suffixed with -*n* in the normal form and with -*kà* in the relative form. But in the other person/number forms a long vowel alternates with a short vowel. These data suggest that for these forms it is the length of the vowel itself which indicates whether the markers are in the relative form.

Arabic verbs fall into a number of different classes (often referred to by the Hebrew term *binyanim*, singular *binyan*) based around a single triconsonantal root sequence. For instance, the sequence *k-t-b* forms the following eight classes of verb form, given their traditional numbering here (doubled constants are pronounced as geminates and doubled vowels are long; the alternations of length and the appearance of other consonants will be discussed in chapter 5:[14]

1.24	Binyan		
	I	katab	'write'
	II	kattab	'cause to write'
	III	kaatab	'correspond'
	IV	ʔaktab	'cause to write'
	VI	takaatab	'write to each other'
	VII	nkatab	'subscribe'
	VIII	ktatab	'write, be registered'
	X	staktab	'write, make write'

From the glosses it is clear that the basic meaning of the root is to do with writing. The different binyanim represent for the most part derivational classes (such as 'causative' or 'reciprocal'), though this is not systematic across all verbs.

Arabic also has a rich set of inflectional verbal classes. The table in 1.25 gives some of these for the eight binyanim of 1.24 ('Pftv.' = 'perfective', 'Impf.' = 'imperfective', 'Act.' = 'active', 'Pass.' = 'passive'; for present purposes it doesn't matter what these terms mean):

1.25		Pftv. Act.	Pftv. Pass.	Impf. Act.	Impf. Pass.
	I	katab	kutib	aktub	uktab
	II	kattab	kuttib	ukattib	ukattab
	III	kaatab	kuutib	ukaatib	ukaatab
	IV	ʔaktab	ʔuktib	uʔaktib	uʔaktab
	V	takattab	tukuttib	atakattab	utakattab
	VI	takaatab	tukuutib	atakaatab	utakaatab
	VII	nkatab	nkutib	ankatib	unkatab
	VIII	ktatab	ktutib	aktatib	uktatab

From 1.25 it is immediately apparent that the aspect (i.e. the Pftv. and Impf.) and voice (i.e. Act. and Pass.) categories are associated with different sequences of vowels (ignoring vowel length), given in 1.26:

1.26		
	Perfective Active	(a)-a-a
	Perfective Passive	(u)-u-i
	Imperfective Active	u-a-i or (a)-a-a-i
	Imperfective Passive	u-a-a-(a)

To be sure, not all the Imperfective Active forms fit the two schemas suggested, but for the other forms the fit is very good. Moreover, this impression is strengthened if other binyanim and other inflectional categories which I have omitted here are added.

Here, then, we have a morphological system in which the sequence of vowels represents a morphological category. Similar alternations between vowels in different morphological categories are found in Indo-European languages, including English. Thus, a miniature version of the Arabic pattern is shown by its translation (given in broad phonemic transcription in 1.27). The verb *sing* provides an extra dimension:

1.27   a) rait   rout   ritn̩   'write'
         b) siŋ   saŋ   sʌŋ   soŋ   'sing'

Chicheŵa, spoken predominantly in Malawi, is typical of the Bantu languages in that syllables may bear one of two tones, High (marked with an accent, ´) or Low (unmarked) (though some vowels may bear both at once, forming a falling tone, ˆ). Its verb morphology is also typical in that an intransitive verb form includes (amongst other things) a prefix agreeing with the subject and a tense/aspect marker. For instance, the form *ndi-ná-fótokoza* 'I explained' has the structure shown in 1.28:

1.28   ndi   -ná   fótokoza
         1sg.SUBJ-PAST-explain

There is a rich system of tenses and aspects in Chicheŵa. A sample is presented in 1.29 for the 1sg. form of the verb:

1.29   ndi-ná-fótokoza   simple past
         ndi-na-fótókoza   recent past
         ndí-nâ:-fótókoza   remote past
         ndi-ku-fótókoza   infinite/progressive
         ndí-ma-fotokózá   present habitual
         ndi-ma-fótókoza   past habitual
         ndí-dzá-fótokoza   future

As is evident, the tone pattern over the whole of the verb depends on the tense/aspect. In most cases this is accompanied by a change in the affix, but some forms, such as the simple and recent past, or the past habitual and future, are distinguished solely by tone. It appears that tone is therefore part of the tense/aspect morpheme (as Mtenje, 1987, from whom these data are taken, explicitly argues).

Nivkh (sometimes called Gilyak in the older literature) is a genetically isolated language of Siberia, spoken in the Amur basin and on the island of Sakhalin. The Nivkh consonant inventory includes voiced, voiceless and aspirated plosives, and voiced and voiceless fricatives. A number of grammatical and morphological relations are signalled (in part, at least) by consonant mutation. For instance, a voiceless plosive alternates with a voiced plosive and an aspirated plosive alternates with a voiceless fricative. Nouns can be formed from verb roots by suffixation, but this is also often accompanied by mutation, as in the examples of 1.30:[15]

1.30

	Verbs			Nouns
Rovd̦	'draw (e.g. water)'		qovs	'scoop'
rʌt̪t̪	'scrape'		tʌt̪s	'scraper'
vut̪id̦	'sweep'		put̪is	'broom'
xuvd̦	'hoop'		k'uvs	'hoop'
χad̦	'support'		q'as	'pillar'
fad̦	'put on knee-piece'		p'ad̦	'knee-piece'

A similar set of alternations is found within verbs: transitive and intransitive pairs will often be related solely by mutation, as in example 1.31:

1.31

	Transitive			Intransitive	
rʌŋzʌlʌd̦	'weigh'		tʌŋzʌlʌd̦	'weigh'	
χavud̦	'warm up'		q'avud̦	'warm up'	
γesqod̦	'burn something'		kesqod̦	'burn oneself'	
sʌud̦	'remove'		t̪'ʌud̦	'come off'	
vʌkzd̦	'lose'		pʌkzd̦	'get lost'	
rad̦	'bake'		t'ad̦	'bake'	
zod̦	'bend'		t̪od̦	'bend'	

The Nivkh case seems to be like that of other languages exhibiting mutation, in which the original set of alternations seems to have been the result of phonological changes induced by prefixation, compounding or whatever. The phonological aspect then becomes divorced from the morphological process (for example, by attrition of the conditioning prefix), leaving the phonological alternation as the sole vestige. Once the phonological alternation has been thus morphologized, however, it is free to assume an independent life of its own, and may be employed to express other morphological or grammatical relationships. This is true of Nivkh, in which, for example, mutation is found on nouns with a possessive affix, transitive verbs taking an overt direct object, heads of compound nouns, and in reduplication. Used with adjectives it can signify an intensive. As with other mutation languages, however, there remains a rather complex relation between purely grammatical conditioning factors and phonological conditioning factors.

The astute reader looking at the glosses to the examples of Nivkh transitive and intransitive verb pairs in 1.31 will have noticed that in English a lot of transitive and intransitive verb pairs have exactly the same form. This is not always true; for example, some verb pairs are related by ablaut similar to that illustrated for irregular verb forms in 1.27: *lie ~ lay, fall ~ fell* (a tree). Nonetheless, it is very frequently the case that a transitive and intransitive verb show no difference in shape. This phenomenon is actually more widespread in English. Consider the verb-noun and noun-verb pairs in 1.32:

1.32
a)
to cut	a cut
to run	a run
to stand	a stand
to ring	a ring
to walk	a walk

b) a hand   to hand
   an orbit   to orbit
   a ring   to ring
   a grandstand   to grandstand

It seems from these data that we can freely use a noun as a verb and vice versa despite the fact that English has a variety of affixes which do the same job.

Another instance of this occurs in the data of 1.33–5:

1.33   a) The chicken was killed (by Harriet).
          b) The chicken is freshly killed (*by Harriet).
          c) A freshly killed chicken.

1.34   a) This vase was broken (by Dick).
          b) This vase is completely broken (*by Dick).
          c) A completely broken vase.

1.35   a) The manuscript was written badly (by Tom).
          b) The manuscript is badly written (*by Tom).
          c) A badly written manuscript.

In these data we find that the passive participles which surface in the (a) examples are being used as adjectives in the (b, c) examples. Since the passive participle is generally regarded as an inflectional form of the verb we have another case of a word which shifts its allegiance from one syntactic category to another without undergoing any formal change.

There have been two approaches to the theoretical description of morphology of this sort. One is to say that we are allowed to 'convert' a noun to a verb or vice versa, or a participle to an adjective, by simply relabelling it. The other is to say that the change of category is the effect of attaching an affix, but that the affix happens to be phonologically null, a zero morpheme in other words. The first approach is referred to as (**morphological**) **conversion**, while the second is called **null** or **zero affixation**.

Morphological conversion is a kind of process, though not a phonological one. Here, the morpheme is a rule (usually formalized as a rule which changes the labelling from 'Noun' to 'Verb' or whatever). Zero affixation, on the other hand, is intended to be just like any other form of affixation. Here, the morpheme responsible is clearly a thing, though a ghostly one. These notions aren't incompatible with each other in general. It is possible for a grammatical theory to include both types of description. Indeed, one linguist (Lieber, 1981b) has argued that the data of 1.32 should be handled by morphological conversion, while the data of 1.33–5 illustrate zero affixation. However, it is possible to imagine a theory which was unable to countenance one or other of these possibilities, at least within one language.[16]

1.3.5 Summary

The examples of morphemes-as-things and morphemes-as-rules that I have given in §§1.3.3–4 are not meant to imply definitive analyses. Some linguists have claimed that all morphological operations should be regarded as rules; others have insisted that where possible, in cases in which it seems as though a rule is used as a morpheme, the data should be reanalysed in such a way that the underlying process is triggered by a morpheme-as-a-thing. For instance, confronted with initial consonant mutation, such a linguist might well propose that at some abstract underlying level there is a prefix or other formative which exerts its phonological influence and then disappears, leaving the mutation as its only trace. In that case, at the underlying level the morpheme would be represented by the 'abstract' prefix, and the phonological alternation would just be an example of phonologically conditioned allomorphy.

The moral is that a simple description of the surface facts doesn't necessarily constitute a full description, and so a superficial description doesn't always permit any theoretical inferences to be drawn. It is only in the context of an explicitly articulated theory of grammar that a set of data can reveal its full significance. More importantly, it is only within the framework of an explicit theory that we can hope to *explain* why the data pattern the way they do, by linking otherwise unconnected facts to each other, through a more abstract theoretical intermediary. This point will be illustrated on innumerable occasions throughout the book.

1.4   Functions of morphology – morphosyntax

In §1.3.1 we distinguished derivational morphology, by which new words are formed, from inflectional morphology. Derivational operations typically create a word of a different syntactic class from that of the base, but will also add further elements of meaning. For instance, the affixes *-er/-or* and *-ation* both turn verbs into nouns, but *-er/-or* creates nouns with the meaning of an agent or instrument, while *-ation* creates an abstract noun (cf. *creator, creation*). Inflectional operations leave untouched the syntactic category of the base, but they too add extra elements. These are elements of meaning (for example, tense, aspect, mood, negation and so on) and also grammatical function. For instance, an inflectional operation may turn an intransitive verb into a transitive one, or an active verb form into a passive one (though some morphologists would regard such alternations as derivational morphology). The two most widespread and important types of grammatical function served by inflection are **agreement** (or **concord**) and **government**.

In very many languages there are constructions in which inflectional morphology is used to show that two words or phrases belong to the same grammatical category. We have seen that, in Russian, nouns inflect for number, gender and case. An adjective modifying a noun has to *agree* with it for these categories. Some examples of this are given in 1.36–8 using the adjective *bol'šoj* 'large, big, grand', a masculine, feminine and neuter noun, and three of the twelve case/number categories:

1.36   teatr 'theatre' masculine
          a) bol'š-oj   teatr   nominative singular
          b) bol'š-omu teatr-u   dative singular
          c) bol'š-ix   teatr-ov   genitive plural

1.37   cerkov' 'church' feminine
          a) bol'š-aja   cerkov'   nom. sg.
          b) bol'š-oj   cerkvi   dat. sg.
          c) bol'š-ix   cerkvej   gen. pl.

1.38   mesto 'place' neuter
   a) bol'š-oje mest-o nom. sg.
   b) bol'š-omu mest-u dat. sg.
   c) bol'š-ix mest   gen. pl.

In a language in which nouns are marked for case we often find that some verbs have to be followed by an object in one case form while other verbs have to be followed by an object in a different case form. We say then that the verb *governs* a particular case. Prepositions, too, often govern a particular case, sometimes expressing slight differences of meaning by difference in case selection. Very commonly, a possessor phrase (like *the boy's* in *the boy's coat*) shows up in a special case (usually called the genitive). Russian provides some typical examples of these phenomena:

1.39 a) direktor zavod-a
     director factory-GENITIVE SG
     'the director of the factory'
     ... prinjal nov-yj kollektiv
      received new collective-ACCUSATIVE SG
     '... receive the new collective'
   b) ... pomogal nov-omu kollektiv-u
      helped new collective-DATIVE SG
     '... helped the new collective'
   c) ... rukovodil nov-ym kollektiv-om
         new collective-INSTRUMENTAL SG
     'supervised the new collective'

1.40 a) ot Ivan-a 'from Ivan – GENITIVE'
    b) k Ivan-u 'to(wards) Ivan – DATIVE'
    c) s Ivan-om 'with Ivan – INSTRUMENTAL'
    d) ob Ivan-e 'about Ivan – PREPOSITIONAL'

1.41 a) vojti v komnat-u 'to go in(to) the room-ACCUSATIVE'
    b) sidet' v komnat-e 'to sit in the room-PREPOSITIONAL'

While it is common for a possessor to appear in a genitive case form (or to be marked by a preposition, as in *the coat of the boy*), in a good many languages possession is marked by an agreement process. This means that the translation of *coat* (the possessed noun) in *the boy's coat* would be marked by means of inflections indicating, say, the person, number, or gender of the possessor (*the boy*). In some languages we see both types of marking simultaneously. This gives rise to constructions which read literally: *Tom his-brother* or *of-Tom his-brother*. Turkish (like many Ural-Altaic languages) provides examples of the construction. In 1.42 I have given the possessive inflection for a noun:

1.42 ev-im 'my room' ev-imiz 'our room'
    ev-in 'thy room' ev-iniz 'your room'
    ev-i   'his room' ev-leri 'their room'

In 1.43 we see a possessive phrase in which the possessed (*house*) agrees with the possessor (*director*) and the possessor is in the genitive case:

1.43   müdür-ün   ev-i
        director-GEN   house-POSS
        'the director's house'

Languages generally have ways of altering the relationship between a verb and its arguments (that is, its subject and its object(s)). These are grouped under the heading of **voice** or **valency changing** relationships in traditional grammar.[17] In many languages such relationships are signalled by inflections borne by the verb.

A common example is the **passive voice** (as opposed to the **active voice**). In English this is expressed by a mixture of syntax and morphology: a separate auxiliary is used (the verb *to be*) and a separate verb form, the passive (or past) participle (cf. the glosses in 1.45 below). In some languages, however, the passive patterns with the rest of the verbal inflectional paradigm, so that a verb in the passive has its own set of person and number inflections, distinct from the active voice. A classic example is Latin:

1.44   amāre 'to love'
        Active Present   Passive Present
        Sg.   Pl.   Sg.   Pl.
    1   amō   amāmus   amor   amāmur
    2   amās   amātis   amāris   amāminī
    3   amat   amant   amātur   amantur

1.45   a) Mīlitēs   puellam   amant.
           soldier-NOM pl. girl-ACC sg. love-3 pl.
           'The soldiers love the girl.'
        b) Puella   ā   mīlitibus   amātur.
           girl-NOM sg. by soldier-ABLATIVE pl. is-loved
           'The girl is loved by the solders.'

In many languages the marking of subjects and objects follows an **ergative** pattern. In this, one and the same marker (which might be a noun case ending or verb agreement) is used for the subject of an intransitive verb and for the direct object of a transitive verb, while a separate marker distinguishes the subject of a transitive verb. If case markers are used by the language, the first is called the Absolutive (ABS) and the second the Ergative (ERG). If we represent 'transitive subject' as S_T, 'intransitive subject' as S_I, and direct object as O, we can represent the distinction between nominative-accusative languages and ergative-absolutive languages schematically as in 1.46:[18]

1.46   a) NOM   ACC.   b) ERG   ABS
           S_T 0 S_T S_I
           S_I 0

Chukchee is an ergative language, as we can see from 1.47:

1.47   a) ətləg-e   ləunin ekək.
           father-ERG saw   son-ABS
           'The father saw the son.'
        b) Ekək   kətgəntatgʔe.
           son-ABS ran
           'The son ran.'

Now, the passive serves to promote the direct object to a subject and to demote the subject to an optional adjunct (or adverbial) marked by a preposition, or by an **oblique** case. (An oblique case in this book is any case which is not **direct**, i.e. which is not either Nominative or Accusative, or Ergative or Absolutive.) Ergative languages often have a voice in which the direct object is demoted to an optional adjunct in an oblique case while at the same time the S_T of the transitive construction becomes a S_I in the Absolutive. This is referred to as the **antipassive** construction. One way of doing this in Chukchee is by using the prefix *ine-*. The demoted direct object may appear in the Dative, Locative, or Instrumental case depending on the verb, as seen in 1.48–50:

1.48   Gəm t   -ine-tejk -ərkən (orw -etə).
        I-ABS 1 SG-AP-make-PRES (sledge—DAT)
        'I am making a sledge.'

1.49   ʔaacek-ət   ine-gənrit-ərkət   qaa-k
        boy   -ABS PL AP-guard-PRES PL reindeer-LOC
        'The boys are guarding the reindeer.'

1.50   Muri   mət -ine-ret -ərkən kimitʔ-e.
        we-ABS 1 PL-AP-carry-PRES load-INSTR
        'We are carrying the load.'

A good many languages have a morphological **causative**, a device for creating a verb form meaning 'to cause X to Verb' from a form 'X Verbs'.[19] Chukchee has a number of causative affixes, which regularly attach to intransitive verbs, and in a few cases to transitives. The commonest is the prefix *r-* (*rə-* before a consonant), often co-occurring with a suffix *-w*, *-et*, or *-ŋet*. In the examples given in 1.51–3 an intransitive verb, with markers showing agreement with the subject, becomes transitive, agreeing in addition with the object. In 1.54 a transitive verb has been causativized. These examples also show the effects of certain phonological rules, which are independent of the affixes themselves. The gloss '3sg./3sg.' means 'agreement with 3sg. subject and 3sg. object' (recall that verbs agree with their objects in Chukchee).

1.51   a) eret-gʔi   b) r-   eren -nin
           fall-3sg.   CAUSE-fall -3sg./3sg.
           'He fell.'   'He dropped it.'

1.52   a) pʔa-gʔe   b) rə-   pʔa -w   -nen
          dry-3sg.   CAUSE-dry-CAUSE-3sg./3sg.
          'It dried.'   'He dried it.'

1.53   a) cimet-gʔi   b) rə-   cime -w   -nin
          break-3sg.   CAUSE-break-CAUSE-3sg./3sg.
          'It broke.'   'He broke it.'

1.54   a) lʔu-nin   b) rə-   lʔu -nen   -nin
          see-3sg./3sg.   CAUSE-see-CAUSE-3sg./3sg.
          'He saw it.'   'He showed it.'

Since causatives are transitive, they can undergo antipassivization, as in 1.55:

1.55   rə-   lʔu -netə   -tku-gʔi
        CAUSE-see-CAUSE-AP-3sg.
        'He showed (something).'

In point of fact, this way of forming causatives is lexically restricted in Chukchee, and is not productive. (The productive way of forming causatives is to use a verb corresponding to the English 'make', as in 'to make someone do something'.) Nevertheless, in languages such as Turkish, Japanese, Malayalam and the Eskimo group of languages, pretty well any verb can form a morphological causative, and in many cases it is possible in theory freely to form causatives of causatives ('to make A make B do something').

The Malayo-Polynesian languages exhibit a great variety of voice type constructions, traditionally called *focus* constructions.[20] In these, direct objects, locatives or instrumentals become subjects. The different voices are marked by affixes on the verb, including infixes and reduplication (see §1.3.3), as well as particles marking NPs. Here are some examples from Tagalog (infixes are indicated by slashes as /INF/ in 1.56-8):

1.56   a) Ako ay   b-um-abasa   ang   aklat.
          I   PTCL read/INF/read PTCL book
          'I am reading the book.'
    b) Ang aklat ay   b-in-abasa   ko.
          PTCL book PTCL read/INF/read I
          (lit.: 'The book is being read by me.')

1.57   a) Siya'y   s-um-usulat   sa   akin. (from *sulat*)
          he-PTCL write/INF/write PTCL I
          'He is writing to me.'
    b) Ako ay   s-in-usulat-an   niya.
          I   PTCL write/INF/write-AFF he
          (lit.: 'I am being written to by him.')

1.58   a) Babayad ako ng   salapi
           pay-FUT I   PTCL money
           'I shall pay in cash.'
        b) I   -babayad ko an   salapi.
           AFF -pay-FUT I   PTCL money
           (lit.: 'Cash will be paid-in by me.')

The categories discussed so far tend to interact in fairly obvious ways with syntax. Other verbal inflectional categories have little or no syntactic function but encode grammaticalized aspects of meaning. The most common of these are the categories of **tense** and **aspect**, **mood**, and **modality**.[21]

Tense broadly means reference to the time of an event or state. English, for instance, distinguishes a past tense and a non-past tense. A common aspectual distinction is between an action that is completed (*completive* or *perfective* aspect) and one that is ongoing or unfinished or a state which has no end point (*imperfective*). Some of the Hausa and Arabic forms seen in the previous section express such categories. It is very common for tense and aspect to be combined into a single inflectional system (see, for instance, the Chicheŵa examples cited in 1.29).

In Indo-European languages, the term 'mood' usually refers to the categories of **indicative** mood (used to state facts of which the speaker is relatively confident), the **imperative** mood, used to issue commands, the **subjunctive** mood, used in questions or statements of which the speaker isn't so sure (for example, in subordinate clauses to verbs like *doubt* or *fear*), the **conditional** mood, for hypothetical propositions, and the **optative** mood, which indicates a wish. In some languages, however, there is a separate verb paradigm used in interrogative sentences, and many languages distinguish a variety of types of imperative (often referred to as **jussives**). Modality includes not only possibility, obligation, necessity and so on but also commonly **desideratives** (translating the English 'to want to do ...'). Many languages have rich sets of inflections for expressing different modalities and degrees of modality, of a kind conveyed by means of auxiliary verbs and adverbs in Indo-European languages. Many languages have verb inflections indicating the extent to which the speaker can personally vouch for the truth of his statement (**evidentiality**). It is not uncommon to find negation is an inflectional category of the verb. A number of languages of Asia and of MesoAmerica have a complex set of **honorifics** to express politeness and to indicate the speaker's perception of the relative social status of himself and his interlocutors.

The Japanese examples in 1.59 illustrate several of these categories:

1.59   Verb root *kak-/kai-* 'write'
        a) kak-u   present tense 'write, writes', etc.
        b) kak-e-ba   conditional 'would write'
        c) kak-oo   hortative 'let's write'
        d) kak-i-tai   desiderative 'want to write'
        e) kak-e-ru   potential 'can write'
        f) kak-a-nai   negative 'not write'
        g) kai-tara   conditional 'if someone writes'
        h) kak-i-soo   'look as if someone will write'
        i) kak-i-masu   honorific

This list by no means exhausts Japanese verbal inflection. Many of these affixes can be combined with each other to produce much more complex forms.

The richest and most involved inflectional systems are found with nouns and especially with verbs. In addition to these parts of speech, of course, many (though not all) languages have a category of adjective, which will often have similar inflectional properties to nouns. We have seen this for Russian: adjectives agree with their nouns for number, gender and case. An inflectional form peculiar to adjectives is frequently found, that indicating **comparison**, as in the **positive, comparative**, and **superlative** forms: *long–longer–longest*. This, however, is far from universal. Some languages have more complex comparison, including for example, special inflections for **equatives** (*as long as*).

The inflectional categories of nouns, verbs and adjectives we have seen so far are in a certain sense prototypical. However, it is extremely common for nouns to adopt what appear to be verbal inflections, verbs nominal inflections, and adjectives either sort of inflection. Several of these are of no little theoretical importance.

In English we can use nouns and adjectives along with verbs such as *be* or *become* to form predicates referring to the subject (as in *Tom is a linguist, Tom became drunk*). In Chukchee, when nouns and adjectives are used predicatively in this fashion, they agree in person and number with the subject of which they are predicated:

1.60   a) ənpənacgən   'old man'
         b) Muri ənpənacgə-more.
            we   old men   -1pl.
            'We are old men.'

1.61   Gəm n -ermej -gəm.
         I ADJ-strong-1sg.
         'I am strong.'

In Enets (and in other Samoyedic languages of northern Siberia) nominals used predicatively may also inflect for tense:

1.62   ɣ:ɜʔ   'I am a mother'   ɣ:ɜod'   'I was a mother'
         ɣ:d   'you are a mother'   ɣ:dos'   'you were a mother'
         ɣ: 'she is a mother'   ɣ:s'   'she was a mother'

The most important (and frequent) cases of inflectional categories appearing with the 'wrong' class of words are **participles** and **gerunds**. A participle is an adjectival form derived from a verb. In English we have a present participle (in *-ing*) and a past participle (the *-en* form), as in *a performing seal* or *a broken vase*. I have already illustrated participial forms for Russian verbs. The participles given in examples 1.10–11, §1.3.1, are all inflected like adjectives and the present participle active and the two passive participles can be used attributively (i.e. can modify a noun within a noun phrase, like *performing* and *broken* in the examples just cited). Other languages exploit a fuller range of verbal inflectional categories in their participles and in many cases participial constructions are the usual or only way of expressing the equivalent of an English relative clause (such as 'the house *that Jack built*').

A gerund is a verb inflected like a noun (and is often called a **verbal noun**). Its use in many languages is to form adverbial clauses and sentential complements (clauses used as direct objects to verbs such as *say* or *think*). Chukchee provides abundant exemplification.

Chukchee nouns appear in nine case forms. The declension of the singular of *kupren* 'net' is shown in 1.63 (notice that the Ablative, the Dative/Allative and the Comitative II cases condition vowel harmony):

1.63   Absolutive   kupre-n
          Ergative/Instrumental   kupre-te   by means of
          Locative   kupre-k   at, on, in, ...
          Ablative   kopra-jpə   from
          Allative   kopra-gtə   to/towards
          Orientative   kupre-gjit   according to
          Comitative I   ge-kupre-te   together with
          Comitative II   ga-kopra-ma   together with
          Designative   kupre-nu   in capacity of

Just as with Russian, these case forms are used where in English we would often have a preposition governing a noun, as implied by the glosses in 1.63.

Like the Russian case system, the Chukchee cases are also often used with a less concrete meaning for more-or-less grammaticalized function. For instance, the basic meaning of the Allative case is motion towards an object, but it is also used to mark the recipient (say, of a gift or of a communication). In this use it resembles the Dative case of Indo-European languages such as Russian. Even more abstractly, it can be used with the meaning 'for the purpose of'. This is the meaning of the case ending when it is attached to a verb stem rather than a noun. The result is a gerund of purpose, meaning 'to order to ...'. On the other hand, when we add the Ablative ending, whose basic meaning is 'away from', we form a causal gerund, 'because (of) ...'. (The semantic association is similar to that found in the causal use of *out of*, as in *He insulted her out of spite*).

Several of the other case endings appear equally with verb stems to form a variety of other gerunds. The examples 1.64–6 are of gerunds interpreted as cotemporaneous with the matrix verb:

1.64   Wakʔo-gtə,   tətaalgəlatək.
          sitting-down, I-looked-around
          'While I was sitting, I looked around.'

1.65   Qlawəlte   ətwətko-ma,   ŋewəsqetti nəmigciretqinet.
          the-men hunting,   the-women work
          aŋqacormək.
          on-the-shore
          'While the men are out (at sea) hunting, the women work on the shore.'

1.66   ətlon, ga-gəntaw-ma, kulilʔərʔugʔi.
          he   running   cried-out
          'As he was running, he cried out.'

In 1.67 the action expressed by the gerund precedes that of the main verb:

1.67   Rəjulʔət   pelqəntet-ək   ŋalwəlʔepə,   ŋewəsqetti
        the-herdsmen having-returned from-the-herd, the women
        cajpatgʔat.
        brewed-tea
        After the herdsmen returned from the herd, the women brewed the tea.'

In 1.68–70 the gerund has a causal interpretation, while in 1.71 it has the meaning 'to the extent that', 'in relation to':

1.68   ʔaacek opcatko-jpə   ermekwʔi.
        the-boy having-practised-weight-lifting became-strong
        'By practising weight-lifting, the boy became strong.'

1.69   Tumgətum pinkutku-te ejmekwʔi   rərkagtə.
        the-comrade by-jumping approached the-walrus
        'Jumping, the comrade approached the walrus.'

1.70   ətla   em-ʔelere-te   ŋaakagtə,
        the-mother, through-missing the-daughter,
        ləgiqupqetgʔi.
        greatly-became-thin
        'Through missing her daughter so much, the mother lost a lot of weight.'

1.71   ŋewəsqete rintə-gjit uttətʔul ʔəttʔən nəpenrətkoqen.
        the-woman throwing the-stick the-dog ran-off
        'Wherever the woman threw the stick, the dog ran after it.'

Example 1.72 is a minimal pair, in which the same Orientative case ending -*gjit* is attached to a noun stem 1.72a and a verb stem 1.72b:

1.72   a) Migcirə-gjit   nəməngəkwanmore.
           according-to-our-work they-pay-us
           'They pay us according to our work.'
        b) Migciretə-gjit   nəməngəkwanmore.
           according-to-the-way-we-work they-pay-us
           'They pay us according to the way we work.'

So far we have discussed the major lexical categories of noun, verb and adjective. In a few languages (for instance, the Celtic group) we find prepositions inflecting. Certain common prepositions in Welsh inflect for person and number, for instance, as can be seen from 1.73:[22]

1.73

	am 'about'	yn 'in'	gan 'with'
1sg.	amdanaf	ynof	gennyf
2sg.	amdanat	ynot	gennyt
3sg. masc.	amdano	ynddo	ganddo

3sg. fem.	amdani	ynddi	ganddi
1pl.	amdanom	ynom	gennym
2pl.	amdanoch	ynoch	gennych
3pl.	amdanynt	ynddynt	ganddynt

To round off our discussion, we'll note that in certain languages *complementizers* (often referred to by their more traditional name of *subordinating conjunction*) may inflect. In English (and other European languages) complementizers occur at the beginning of subordinate clauses, serving to indicate the type of subordinate clause. Thus, the word *that* in *Tom thinks that Dick loves Harriet* introduces the subordinate clause *Dick loves Harriet*, which functions as the complement (effectively the direct object) of the verb *think*.

West Flemish (a language spoken in Belgium, often regarded as a dialect of Dutch) has a complementizer *da(n)*, which is cognate to the English *that*. An example of its use is shown in 1.74:

1.74   Kpeinzen da   Valère goa moeten.
          I-think   that Valère go   look
          'I think that Valère will go and look.'

Unlike their English counterparts, however, the Flemish complementizers agree with the subject of their clause. Thus, we find examples such as 1.75 (taken from a grammar of West Flemish currently being prepared by Liliane Haegeman):

1.75   a) Kpeinzen dan-k (ik) goan moeten.
                   that-I (I)   go   look
          b)   da-j   (gie) goa moeten.
                   that-you (sg.) (you) go   look
          c)   da-se   (zie) goa moeten.
                   that-she (she) go   look
          d)   da-me   (wunder) goan moeten.
                   that-we (we)   go   look
          e)   da-j   (gunder) goa moeten.
                   that-you (pl.) (you)   go   look
          f)   dan-ze   (zunder) goan moeten.
                   that-they (they)   go   look
          g)   dan Valère en Pol   goan moeten.
                   that Valère and Paul go   look

Although the full pronoun forms (*ik*, *gie*, *zie*, and so on) are optional, the inflections on the complementizer are obligatory. Notice, too, that the complementizer shows agreement with the subject whether that subject is a pronoun, is left unexpressed, or is a full-noun phrase, as in 1.74 and 1.75g. In particular, notice that in 1.74, where we have a singular noun as subject, the complementizer is *da*, whereas when the subject is plural (as with the conjoined nouns in 1.75g) the complementizer is *dan*.

1.5   Summary

This completes our survey of the commoner morphological phenomena. We've seen that words have a readily identifiable structure, allowing us, in the simplest cases, to analyse words into their component morphemes. The morphemes themselves, however, appear in a variety of guises, and this variation is called allomorphy. Some types of allomorphy represent one of the main interfaces between morphology and the rest of grammar, namely, the morphology-phonology interface.

We then drew the traditional distinction between inflection, in which morphology alters the form of a given word, and derivation, in which we construct new words (typically on the basis of old ones). We surveyed the different ways in which morphology can manifest itself. Superficially, at least, there seem to be two types of morphological phenomenon. On the one hand morphology can be regarded as the concatenation of objects (as in affixation, compounding and cliticization). On the other hand we can sometimes view it as the operation of rules or processes, for instance, phonological process such as ablaut or consonant mutation, or morphosyntactic processes such as morphological conversion.

Finally, we surveyed the functions that morphology can typically subserve. Here we saw the second great interface, that between morphology and syntax.

It must be stressed that, although I have appealed to a number of traditional theoretical notions such as that of 'morpheme' or the distinction between inflection and derivation, some of these notions are currently the subject of intense debate. Moreover, there are some morphologists who regard all morphology as essentially the concatenation of things, and others who prefer to view it as essentially the operation of processes. Whether these distinctions are genuine or merely superficial will have to await further research. What I have presented here is a theoretically more-or-less neutral descriptive overview of the kind of categories which linguists often discuss. In the rest of the book we will see how linguists have attempted to construct general theories which seek to account for the great variety of morphological structures encountered in the world's languages and at the same time to develop a theory of the interface between morphology and the rest of grammar, that is, to account for the way that morphology interacts with other components, particularly the lexicon, phonology and syntax.

EXERCISES

1.1   Derivational affixes in English. Some derived words consist of an affix attached to a stem which is itself a word, i.e. a free morpheme (e.g. (i)). In other cases the stem is a bound morpheme (e.g. (ii)).

(i)   Word + affix $[[read]_V er]_N$
(ii) Root + affix $[[elektris]_A ity]_N$

(The root *electric-* never appears as a word on its own.)

For each of the nine relationships given below provide two affixes (prefixes *or* suffixes) which express that category relationship (other than the *-er* and *-ity* examples given above). Choose your affixes such that one attaches to free morpheme roots and the other to bound morpheme roots. For each affix give (at least) two words containing that affix with the given function. That is, provide 18 affixes and (at least) 36 words.

$$N \rightarrow V \quad V \rightarrow N \quad A \rightarrow N$$
$$N \rightarrow A \quad V \rightarrow A \quad A \rightarrow V$$
$$N \rightarrow N \quad V \rightarrow V \quad A \rightarrow A$$

[Note that not all of these are category changing]
[*Hint:* Try looking through a book or newspaper and analysing all the words you suspect of being derivationally complex. You might be surprised at how many there are.]

1.2a   Determine what conditions the allomorphy of the English -Z plural morpheme.

   Collect as many different examples of words taking each type of plural allomorph as you can and write them down in phonetic transcription. Then analyse your data to see what phonological properties of a word condition the choice of each allomorph.

1.2b   Determine the conditioning of the allomorphy which is shown by the past tense and 3 pers. sg. pres. indicative regular verb inflections of English and the allomorphy of the possessive marker ('apostrophe s').

*1.3   If you have followed a course in generative phonology, determine the underlying form of the -Z plural morpheme and write a series of rules to generate the three allomorphs. Do you need to appeal to extrinsic rule ordering?

1.4   There are about two hundred irregular ('strong') verbs in English. List as many of them as you can. On the basis of the allomorphy they exhibit and the kinds of affixes they take, determine what sort of subgroups they fall into.

1.5   Take a pocket-sized dictionary of English and collect all the words beginning with *im-/in-*. Check whether *im-/in-* is a morpheme for each of your words. For instance, comparing *input* with *output, throughput,* you should conclude that *in-* is a morpheme, whereas you should find it considerably harder to find evidence that *in-* is a morpheme in *inane*.

(i)   How many distinct (homonymous) *im-/in-* morphemes are there?
(ii)   Why is *input* misspelled (as *imput*) so often?

(iii) What other allomorphs of *im-/in-* are there? How do they relate to the different *im-/in-* morphemes you have already identified?

1.6   Consider carefully the words in (i–iii). To what extent do the words in a given list contain the same morpheme?

(i)   analysis, anabasis, anachronism, analogy, anaconda, anabaptist, anarchy, anarak.
(ii)   nominal, nominate, gnomic, nomic, nomenclature, noun,
(iii)   pedal, peduncle, pediform, p(a)ederast, p(a)edagogue, prop(a)edeutic, peddle, pedant.

*1.7   Phonaesthemes. Do the words in lists (i–ii) contain a common morpheme? If so, how are each of the words to be segmented; if not, why not?

(i)   glisten, glister, glitter, glimmer, glint, glare, glaze, gleam, glow.
(ii)   sneer, sneeze, sniff, sniffle, snoop, snooty, snore, snorkel, snot, snout.

*1.8   Outline arguments for and against analysing the following lists of words as all contain a common morpheme. [Use a dictionary which includes etymologies.]

(i)   nose, nostril, nasal, pince nez.
(ii)   host, hostel, hotel, table d'hôte, maître d'hôtel, ostler.
(iii)   morpheme, morphology, isomorphic, morphotropic, morphine.

*1.9   An important tool for the morphologist is a dictionary. As everyone knows, a dictionary is a list of words in alphabetical order, together with other information about each entry, such as its part of speech, its meaning, its pronunciation (if it isn't regular) and other bits of information (such as its etymology, if you're lucky). Using whatever reference books you can find, explain why this simple characterization is an oversimplification for languages such as the following. How does lexicographic practice in these languages overcome the problems posed?
    American (or British) Sign Language; Modern Standard Arabic; Palestinian Arabic (or Cairene, Lebanese, Moroccan, Tunisian, Gulf, etc.); (Mandarin) Chinese; Navajo; Swahili; Tagalog; Welsh (or Irish or Gaelic).

1.10   Aspect and 'Aktionsart' in the Naukan dialect of Asiatic Eskimo (Menovščikov, 1975). These Naukan words illustrate a complex set of grammaticalized distinctions between different types of action. Analyse each word into its component morphemes. [Pronunciation: as in IPA except that g = [ɣ], š = [ʃ]].

aglukata:quq	begins to work
agluqixta:quq	again begins to work
aglugjawxapixta:quq	begins to work intensively
ku:jma:quq	is swimming (towards something)
ku:jmaʁo:ʁaquq	swims (habitually)
qavałqaχtuq	suddenly fell asleep
łiŋaχtaquq	rings
łiŋaχtaga:taquq	rings intermittently
aglumsuxe:naquq	works constantly
agluka:quq	works with intermittent stoppages
tɨnluxpɨquq	knocks
tɨnluxpɨga:raqa:	taps incessantly (e.g. woodpecker)
aglukɨŋa:waquq	works for a long time
aglugaχquʁa:quq	works quickly
aqujgaquq	wanders about
aqujviluxtaquq	walks back and forth
ka:susaʁa:χłɨquq	will come early
ka:suqatamajaχtuq	he came more than once
agluŋura:quq	he works for the first time
qavavre:χtuq	he fell asleep again
aglufqara:quq	rarely works
qɨłpɨχta:quq	makes holes in something
qɨłpɨχquʁaquq	makes holes in various places
agluvrɨʁa:quq	works with difficulty
iglɨχtɨkša:ga:quq	walks very slowly
iglɨχtɨkjo:ʁaquq	scarcely drags oneself along
qavamse:quq	dozes
qavaχłɨqja:quq	sleeps fitfully
qavajaxtuq	almost fell asleep
qavato:χtuq	has fallen asleep at last
aglunani:ʁaquq	stops working
iglɨχtɨpixtaquq	walks a lot
qavaruga:quq	sleeps soundly
agluso:χaquq	does pretty good work
agluxtuga:quq	works carelessly
aglupa:quq	works in a haphazard manner

1.11   In (i–xii) you will find a set of sentences in Hungarian with an English translation. Identify the morphemes of Hungarian used in these examples and characterize their meaning or grammatical function. Certain of the grammatical morphemes exhibit allomorphy. Describe this allomorphy and describe what conditions it. [Assume the transcription is IPA.]

(i)   a nju:l a fy:ben yl.
       'The rabbit is sitting on the grass.'
(ii)   a la:nj a boltba medj.
       'The girl is going into the shop.'

(iii) braun u:r berlinbø:l be:tʃbe utazik.
       'Mr. Brown is travelling from Berlin to Vienna.'
(iv)   la:slo: a busban yl.
       'László is sitting in the bus.'
(v)   a vara:ʒlo: kives edj njulat a kalapbo:l.
       'The magician pulls a rabbit from the hat.'
(vi)   zolta:n megmadjara:zza a filmet a nø:nek.
       'Zoltán explains the film to the women.'
(vii) a katona ʃopronbo:l djø:rbe djalogol.
       'The soldier is marching from Sopron to Győr.'
(viii) petø:fi ja:noʃ a ko:rha:zban dolgozik.
       'János Petőfi works in the hospital.'
(ix)   a vara:ʒlo: megmutatja a njulat a djereknek
       'The magician shows the rabbit to the children.'
(x)   a kalap a sekre:njben van.
       'The hat is in the wardrobe.'
(xi)   gusta:v a pe:nzt a ne:met u:rnak adja.
       'Gustáv gives the money to the German gentleman.'
(xii) magda a boltbo:l jøn.
       'Magda is coming from the shop.'

*1.12   Esperanta tradukeksercico. Here are nine sentences in Esperanto (an Indo-European language created by Dr L. Zamenhof in the last century), together with a fairly free translation into English.

(a) Provide a short morpheme dictionary of Esperanto on the basis of the data, by listing all the morphemes you can find and giving their meaning or their grammatical function.

(b) Translate the five sentences of English numbered (i)–(v) into Esperanto.

It may help to know that Esperanto has *no* irregular morphology.

[Pronunciation guide: ĝ = [dʒ], c = [ts], ĉ = [tʃ], ĥ = [x], ŝ = [ʃ], ŭ = [w]; otherwise as in IPA]

1 La alta knabo malsaniĝis.
   'The tall boy fell ill.'
2 Ĉu li grandigis la grandecon de la dormejo?
   'Did he increase the size of the dormitory?'
3 Ankaŭ malaltaj knabinoj povas esti belaj.
   'Short girls, too, can be beautiful.'
4 Mia patro estas sana ĉar li ne trinkas vinon.
   'My father is healthy because he doesn't drink wine.'
5 La bonaj monaĥinoj volis preĝi en la preĝejo.
   'The good nuns wanted to pray in church.'
6 Lerni la esperantan lingvon estas facila.
   'It's easy to learn Esperanto.'
7 Mi vidis ŝian onklon en la trinkejo.
   'I saw her uncle in the bar.'

8 La beleco de la lingvo estas ĝia facileco.
  'The beauty of the language is its simplicity.'
9 Ĉu vi konas miajn onklojn?
  'Do you know my uncles?'

(i)   Did her aunt know my mother?
(ii)   His health deteriorated.
(iii) The boys can also learn difficult languages at school.
(iv)   The monks adorned the church.
(v)   Does your mother want to put the boys to sleep?

2

Basic Concepts and Pre-generative Approaches

Introduction

This book is intended neither as an exhaustive survey of the literature nor as a detailed history of the development of theories of morphology. Nonetheless, in order to understand many of the questions currently on the research agenda it is necessary to be aware of some of the classical problems and classical solutions to them (as well as the problems with those solutions).

In this chapter we begin with the ways linguists have classified languages according to their morphological systems, in other words, with morphological typology. In section two we take a critical look at three crucial notions in morphology, that of morpheme, word and lexicon. We discover that each of these concepts hides a vast, uncompleted research project in itself. The third section gives an overview of the principal issues that concerned the structuralist theories of morphology which preceded generative theories. First, we examine three structuralist (pre-generative) approaches to word structure, each of which has found reflection in more recent theories of morphology within generative grammar. Then, we look at the interface between morphology and phonology, otherwise known as morphophonemics, morpho(pho)nology, phonomorphology (as well as other terms). Here we note a number of problems with some of the earlier structuralist approaches, as well as setting out some of the basic phenomena which a generative theory would have to deal with.

2.1 Morphological typology

Linguists like to classify languages according to various criteria, and one of these is morphological structure. According to a traditional typology, morphological systems fall into four groups: **isolating, agglutinating, (in)flectional**, and **polysynthetic**. An isolating language is one with very little morphology (except compounding) in which separate grammatical concepts tend to be conveyed by separate words and not by morphological processes. Chinese is a familiar example, Vietnamese is the prototypical isolating language. In an agglutinating language we tend to find long, polymorphemic words in which each morpheme corresponds to a single lexical meaning or grammatical function. Languages such as Hungarian and Turkish are the paradigm examples. The Turkish word *evleriden* means 'from their house' and can be glossed 'house–PLURAL-POSSESSIVE-ABLATIVE'. Even the components '3rd person possessive' and 'plural', which are fused together in the English word *their*, are separated in the Turkish form. Inflectional languages are like agglutinating languages and unlike isolating languages in that words are typically polymorphemic. However, the formatives which make up the words often fuse together several different meanings or functions, especially in the inflectional paradigms (hence, the commonly used term **fusional**). Languages such as Latin or Russian provide examples of inflectional languages. We saw in chapter 1 that the *-omu* ending of the adjective *bol'šomu* 'large (masc./neut. dat. sg.)' codes gender, case and simultaneously (together with the fact that the word is an adjective). Finally, the polysynthetic languages are those which, like Chukchee, permit processes such as noun incorporation, so that a single word can encode a meaning which would require a fairly elaborate sentence in many other languages.

This typology, though sanctioned by tradition, has been criticized for being both incoherent and useless. It is useless because nothing of any interest follows from classifying languages in this way (cf. Anderson, 1985a). It is incoherent for several reasons. First, it is obvious when we look at varieties of languages that we are dealing with a continuum rather than four discrete types. For example, even the most agglutinative language will show elements of fusion. Worse, there are many languages for which the typology just doesn't seem relevant. Thus, English has very little inflection and therefore resembles the isolating languages with regards to inflectional categories, but it would probably be thought of as agglutinating with respect to derivational categories, while synthetic compounds such as *horseriding* in *Harriet spends her weekends horseriding* suggest a limited degree of polysynthesis!

Another problem is that the typology begs important questions about the relation between morphology and syntax. In particular, it says virtually nothing about the nature of compounding in languages or about the way this relates to syntactic processes. For instance, in some respects German and French are alike in being (moderately) inflectional languages. Yet the two languages have almost complementary systems of compounding. French compounds are almost exclusively reflections of syntactic, phrasal structures. For instance, we have a great many of the type *porte-parole* 'spokesman', literally 'carries word', consisting of a verb plus its object, and we also frequently find whole phrases becoming compounds, as in the example cited in chapter 1, *cessez-le-feu* 'cease fire'. This sort of thing is as marginal in German as it is in English. The 'typical' German compound is a Noun-Noun compound, and this type is rather rare in French. The fourth problem with the traditional typology concerns polysynthetic languages, which fit rather badly into the classical scheme. As a matter of fact, all the standard examples of polysynthetic languages would also be called agglutinating. Polysynthesis is actually a type of compounding, but compounding doesn't figure in the traditional typology. Thus, we have one language type which should probably be properly included in another. And again, if we take a poly-synthetic language like Chukchee we find that in many respects it has an agglutinating derivational system and to some extent an agglutinating inflectional system. However, we also find a good deal of fusion in the person/number inflections of verbs, so here we would have to call the language (partially) inflectional. The same is true of a number of other so-called polysynthetic languages.

If the traditional classification is so bad why mention it? The reasons are twofold: first, it is still often referred to in the descriptive (and some of the theoretical) litera-ture, so readers should at least be familiar with the terminology. More important, there is concealed in the typology the assumption that agglutination is the primary type of word formation and that other types are 'deviations' from this. Specifically, the distinction between agglutination and the fusional morphology typical of inflec-tional languages forms the core of the typology, and it lies at the heart of much theorizing about the nature of inflection and about morphological structure in gen-eral. Indeed, the very concept of the morpheme tends to presuppose that all mor-phology is agglutinative, at some level of abstraction. It is therefore worth examining the concepts of 'agglutinative system' vs. 'inflectional system' in more detail.

To begin with we should note that the distinction only makes any real sense if we distinguish inflection from derivation, and then it only applies with any force to inflectional morphology. This is partly for terminological reasons, partly for largely covert and seldom discussed theoretical reasons. A typical derivational morpheme, say, an affix, has the function of creating a word out of another word, as when the suffix *-ness* creates the noun *happiness* from the adjective *happy*. We tend to think of such affixes as conveying a single meaning or having a single function, though in a sense this is misleading. It is not uncommon for the derivational morphemes of a language to convey several aspects of meaning. For instance, *-ness* creates abstract nouns, not just any kind of noun. Some languages have causative affixes which convey different types of causation (for instance, compulsion as opposed to permis-sion). At the same time, we frequently find lots of different morphemes being used for essentially the same purpose. For instance, the process of nominalizing a verb in English can be effected by such suffixes as *-(at)ion*, *-ment*, *-al*, *-ance* as well as others.

Now, when a derivational morpheme conveys a compound meaning we don't speak of fusion. This is generally because we don't usually regard the set of meanings con-veyed by derivation as forming a paradigmatic system. The characteristic of inflec-tional paradigms is that we have a small number of independent categories (e.g. case, number and gender in Russian adjectives) and a large number of words for which these categories are conjointly relevant. In other words, the case/number/gender system forms a kind of cluster of categories which keeps recurring throughout the grammar of the language. Since the categories are nonetheless distinct we might expect them all to be conveyed in exactly the same way, that is, we might expect one morpheme for each category and each category to be realized by just one morpheme. This is the ideal agglutinating system from which inflectional systems are felt to be deviations.[1] Yet, in a sense, we would be equally justified in regarding the variety of English nominalizing suffixes as deviations from agglutination. This tends not to be done, because the real reason for the distinction itself lies in how inflectional paradigms are viewed, not in the theory of morphology as a whole.

2.2 Morphemes, words and the lexicon

2.2.1 Morphemes and allomorphy

The notion of the morpheme introduced in the first chapter is not without its difficulties. The problem posed by fusional inflecting morphology is particularly acute, since in such cases it seems as if one and the same morph has a multiplicity of functions or meanings, and classical morphemic doctrine demands that there be only one meaning per morpheme (excepting accidental cases of homonymy). This is something we'll discuss in more detail later in the chapter. There is another important manifestation of the form–function problem for the notion of the morpheme as the minimal unit of meaning. In a sense, it is the opposite of that posed by fusion.

A familiarly drastic example is provided by horticulture. In 2.1 we have a (non-exhaustive) list of compound nouns in English referring to types of berry:

2.1   blueberry   blackberry
         raspberry   strawberry
         loganberry   cranberry

At first sight the meanings of these compounds seem to be determined compositionally, that is, by simply adding together the meanings of the parts (e.g. *blue* + *berry*). This is not obviously true, however, of *strawberry* and clearly untrue of *raspberry*. The example *cranberry* poses particular difficulties. The *cran-* formative must contribute something to the meaning of the whole, since a cranberry is a specific type of berry (different from a loganberry, for example). But what does *cran-* mean? For the majority of English speakers there are no other words which make use of this 'morpheme', so it is important to give a principled answer.

A morpheme such as the *cran* of *cranberry* has neither meaning nor grammatical function, yet it is used to differentiate one word from another. In other words, it is an example of a form which lacks a meaning of its own, an ultimate example of a deviation from the one–one correspondence between form and function. One conclusion that can be drawn from this is that the notion of 'morpheme' should be defined in terms of the constituents of words and relationships between word forms, and not in terms of meanings (much in the way that syntacticians discusses the well-formedness of sentences without appeal to meaning). Morphemes such as *cran* are not actually a rarity (we'll see more examples from English in chapter 3). Their theoretical significance has earned them a technical name: **cranberry morpheme**.

Our next problem concerns the notion of 'allomorph' (though it is one which tends to get ignored in the literature). Recall that we discussed the phonologically conditioned allomorphy of the plural ending in English. Now, we could say that plural allomorphy was far more extensive than this. Consider the plural forms in 2.2:

2.2   oxen   teeth
         formulae   cherubim
         criteria   memoranda
         mafiosi   schemata
         indices   crises

The grammatical category signalled in these words is the same in each case, namely 'plural', but the means used is different. In *oxen* we have a rare vestigial *-en* affix; in *formulae*, *criteria* and *memoranda* we have a Greek or Latin plural ending replacing what might be thought of as a singular ending *-a*, *-on*, or *-um*. *Schemata* shows a more complex example of a Greek plural. I earlier analysed *indices* as *indice + s*, but, given the existence of these other latinate plurals, I could just as easily have given the more traditional analysis of *indic + es*, in which case we would no longer be dealing with the addition of *-s* to the stem but of a different formative, *-es*. Are all these allomorphs of a single morpheme? If so, what reasonable theory of allomorphy will allow us to say that the vowel ablaut of *teeth* and the *-im* of *cherubim* bear the same relation (of allomorphy) to each other as the different pronunciations of the -Z plural morpheme bear to each other?

The English plural case suggests that it might be better to talk of grammatical categories and their **exponents** (i.e. the linguistic material that expresses those categories) rather than of morphemes and their allomorphs. In chapter 10 we will discuss similar cases from derivational morphology in English, and in chapter 11 we consider specific proposals for separating off morphemes and their allomorphs from the meanings and grammatical functions they realize. We will explore further problems associated with the doctrine of the morpheme in further chapters. In a sense the question of what morphemes are is a key question in morphology, and different theoretical approaches are often most sharply contrasted in the way they tackle the problem.

2.2.2 *The nature of words*

The whole of chapter 1 was concerned with words, their formation and their inflections, yet we have not explained what a word is and how one is to be recognized. This is far from being a trivial question; indeed, it is one of the most difficult and important problems in morphological theory. This is not so much because theorists interested in morphology have contributed explicitly and self-consciously to the long-standing debate on the definition of wordhood, but rather because at every turn theoretical decisions tend to hang on what is understood by the notion 'word' and related concepts such as 'word formation', 'lexicon', and so on.

One way to try to define wordhood is in terms of other linguistic constructs, such as phonology, syntax or semantics. When such criteria are developed for individual languages they may be quite successful, though finding a set of criteria which will work universally, for all languages, is an entirely different matter.

There are very few semantic properties of words which will distinguish them from morphemes or phrases. However, in some cases a semantic criterion can be useful. Consider the meaning of *tea* in the examples 2.3:

2.3   a) a pound of tea
         b) a teapot

We might ask if these two expressions are single words. An important consideration would be how the component *tea* in each expression is interpreted. In 2.3a *tea* refers to a particular kind of stuff and the meaning of the whole expression contains the meaning *tea* in a fairly direct way (it is determined compositionally). This is not the case with 2.3b. There is no sense in which the *tea* in *teapot* actually makes reference to the stuff tea in determining the reference of the whole expression. For instance, if we found someone referring to a packet of coffee using expression 2.3a, we would say they had made a mistake: *tea* doesn't mean 'coffee'. But if someone tried to make coffee in a teapot we couldn't seriously accuse them of making a semantic error. Moreover, we can refer back to the tea in 2.3a using an anaphoric device such as a pronoun, as in *He took the pound of tea and put two spoonfuls of it into a teapot*. This is impossible in the case of *teapot*: we couldn't say *He took the teapot and poured it into the cup* meaning *He poured the tea into the cup*. We say that words tend to be **referentially opaque** in that it is impossible to 'see inside' them and refer to their parts. A related term is **anaphoric island**: we cannot refer to the *tea* of *teapot* using an anaphor because words tend to be anaphoric islands. Anaphoric islandhood is a special case of a more general property of words: **lexical integrity**. The general pattern is for *no* syntactic process to be allowed to refer exclusively to part of words.

In some languages, word boundaries are marked (or at least hinted at) by phonological phenomena such as the span of vowel harmony, the position of stress or **phonotactic constraints**[2] which make reference to word boundaries (such as a ban on word initial or word final clusters). These criteria define for us a notion of **phonological word** for the language. We effectively appealed to this notion when we assumed earlier that Chukchee incorporation forms words and not some sort of tightly bound syntactic unit, on the grounds that the incorporated material undergoes vowel harmony, and the span of vowel harmony is the word.

These criteria have to be applied with great care, however. The main problem is circularity. In Finnish, vowel harmony is bounded by the word (i.e. roots, plus derivational and inflectional suffixes). However, in compound words such as *pääkaupunki* 'capital (city)' we find that each component defines its own harmony span (the vowel *i* is neutral with respect to harmony, while *ä* belongs to a different harmony set from *a* and *u* and therefore shouldn't co-occur with them). Stress also serves to demarcate words in Finnish: it always falls on the first syllable of the word. In compounds we find a single main stress falling on the first syllable of the compound, suggesting that the compound is, after all, a single word. Which phonological criterion do we choose?

Another problem is illustrated by Czech. In this language stress always falls on the first syllable of a word. However, a monosyllabic preposition before an unmodified noun will usually attract stress to itself. In this way we obtain examples 2.4 (where stressed syllables are printed in bold):

2.4   a) ten **stůl**   'that table'
           b) na ten **stůl**   'onto that table'
           c) **na** stůl   'onto the/a-table

If the phonological criterion were considered overriding we would have a curious situation in which 2.4a were two words, 2.4b three words, but 2.4c only one word. This presumably would mean we are forced to say that *na* is a preposition in 2.4a, b, but a prefix (or at least part of a compound) in 2.4c. This would be unsatisfactory, for the only difference in behaviour is with regard to stress.

It is cases such as these that have led phonologists working on the problem of 'prosodic domains' to stress the mismatch between formal characterizations of wordhood and the notion of 'phonological word' (cf. Nespor and Vogel, 1986, for example). Thus, while phonological criteria for wordhood constitute a fascinating research question for the phonologist they generally provide at most one of a number of sometimes conflicting criteria for the morphologist.

Rules of syntax as generally conceived take words as their smallest unit and compose them into phrases and ultimately sentences. In most theories, such rules don't operate on parts of words. We implicitly appealed to this criterion when we denied word status to 2.4c on the grounds that Czech rules of phrase structure allow the determiner *ten* to intervene between the preposition and its complement. Related to this criterion is that of the **minimal free form**: a word is the smallest unit that can exist on its own.

There are two constructions which pose difficulty for syntactic criteria, and both compromise the criterion because they beg the question of what constitutes a syntactic process.

The first is compounding. When two words (as opposed to roots) are compounded each is a minimal free form by definition. But is the resulting compound a word? If we regard the compounding process as essentially syntactic (as we are at liberty to do), then the answer is presumably 'no'; if compounding is a morphological process the answer will be 'yes'.

The second problem is posed by clitics. These are not minimal free forms by definition, and they cannot therefore stand alone. The morphological entities they attach to are words. However, what is the status of the result? If we say that, for instance, the French expression *donnez-les-moi* is itself a word, then we are in effect claiming that cliticization is part of word formation and that clitics are really affixes. But if it isn't a word, what is it? This is a particularly hard question to answer given that nothing may intervene in the position of the dashes. A slightly different problem is posed by the Latin clitic conjunction *-que*, meaning 'and'. It appears to form a new word since, for instance, it attracts word stress to the preceding syllable. Sentences 2.5a and 2.5b are therefore synonymous:

2.5   a) Puéllae et   púerī cánunt.
            girls   and boys   sing
            'The girls and the boys are singing.'
        b) Puéllae puerīque cánunt

The problem is that, when *-que* is used to coordinate two sentences, any word of any syntactic category can be its host provided it is the second word of its clause. We can continue 2.5a, b with either of 2.6, for instance:

2.6   a) ...canuntque   fēminae.
               sing -que women
            'and the women are singing.'
        b) ...haecque   canunt   fēminae.
               these -que sing   women
            'and these women are singing.'

Even if we were to concede that French pronominal clitics are really affixes and that *donnez-les-moi* is an inflected verb form, we would have difficulty stating what kind of affix -*que* might be, given that there are absolutely no morphological constraints on its attachment, only a syntactic constraint.

A final criterion we might propose as a property of words relates to the first, semantic, criterion we discussed. I mentioned that the meaning of a phrase tends to be determined compositionally from the meaning of its component words. However, the meaning of words is not always determined compositionally. In some cases it is the word as a whole which bears the meaning, and the relationship between the meaning of the parts and the meaning of a whole word can be obscure. For instance, we may know the meanings of *broad* and *cast*, and may even be able to perceive an etymological relationship between these two words and the word *broadcast*, but that wouldn't help us understand the precise meanings that *broadcast* can take. The limiting case of this is found with words containing cranberry morphemes.

This doesn't give us a criterion for wordhood, however, since there are objects which look like phrases and which behave syntactically like phrases but whose meaning is not determined compositionally. These are the **idioms**, such as *take advantage of* or *kick the bucket* (in the sense of 'die'), as well as phrasal verbs (collocations of verbs plus particle). There is nothing in the meanings of *put*, *up*, and *with* which shows that *put up with* means *tolerate*. Nor does *slow up* mean the opposite of *slow down*. Such phrases have a lexicalized meaning, that is, their meaning has to be listed in the dictionary as an idiosyncratic fact about the whole expression, much as the meaning of *cat* has to be listed as an unpredictable fact about the sequence of phonemes /kat/.

Moreover, if we take lexicalized meaning as a criterion for wordhood it tends to contradict other criteria in a serious way. One result of this is a class of the so-called **bracketing paradoxes**. Consider 2.7a:

2.7   a) transformational grammarian

This expression is normally taken to mean 'someone who practices 2.7b':

2.7   b) transformational grammar

It could in principle mean 'a grammarian who is transformational' though this reading isn't the one that initially springs to mind (except to punsters). Now, if we think about the meaning of the affix -*ian* then the way the meaning of 2.7a is constructed can be represented as in 2.8a.:

2.8   a) [[transformational grammar]-ian]

The bracketing indicates that -*ian* meaning 'person who practices something' applies to (or 'takes within its semantic scope') the whole of the expression *transformational grammar*. But this semantic bracketing contradicts the bracketing implied by the conventional word divisions, namely that of 2.8b:

2.8   b) [[transformational]   [grammarian]]

In other words, we would like to say that syntactically 2.7a is composed of the words *transformational* and *grammarian* as in 2.8b, but semantically it is composed of *transformational grammar* and *-ian* as in 2.8a, hence the 'paradox'. I shall discuss bracketing paradoxes further at various points in the book and especially in chapter 10.

Not only are there considerable difficulties pinning down any universally applicable notion of 'word', it appears that even when we restrict ourselves to morphological criteria within a single language we find that the term itself covers a multitude of sins, which need to be carefully distinguished.

If we look back to the declension of the Russian adjective *bol'šoj* we find that the word appears in a variety of forms. Yet in a sense each of those forms is itself a word. We can call the latter **word forms** and use a special term such as **lexeme** for the more general sense. It is sometimes convenient to represent lexemes in upper case, so that we can say that *bol'šimi* is a form of the lexeme BOL'ŠOJ.

Our Russian lexeme provides an example of another ambiguity inherent in the term 'word'. Russian adjectives display **syncretism**, that is, a single inflected form may correspond to more than one morphosyntactic description. For example, the dat. and instr. case forms of the fem. sg. are always identical. This means that a word form such as *bol'šoj* requires more than one (in point of fact, six) separate morphosyntactic descriptions. But in this sense, the one word form (of a single lexeme) represents six different words. We might say that these are **morphosyntactic words**.

The notion of 'morphosyntactic word' is only coherent within a particular view of the organization of inflection. What about the plural forms of the adjective? Although nouns have different inflections in the plural depending on their gender, Russian adjectives never distinguish gender in the plural. Does that mean that each of the plural forms of BOL'ŠOJ is actually three homophonous morphosyntactic words? This seems counterintuitive. The reason is that for adjectives, at least, there is never an opposition between genders in the plural. We only want to discern homophony between word forms when there is some chance that another lexeme will have different word forms for those morphosyntactic categories. Since the gender distinction is neutralized in the plural for all adjectives, this situation can never come about.

In fact, the situation is more complex than this. Recall that the word form *bol'šoj* represents six different morphosyntactic categories. Now it happens that no Russian adjective distinguishes between the oblique case forms in the feminine singular. What this suggests is that there is only one morphosyntactic category of 'oblique case' for the feminine, with one marker, namely *-oj*. Therefore, there is only one morphosyntactic word corresponding to this category. It is still homophonous, however, with the masculine direct case forms. Moreover, this is not morphologically determined homophony (i.e. syncretism): the reason for the homophony is phonological. Russian adjectives which are stressed on the ending take the form *-oj* in the masculine direct cases, but if the stress falls on the stem they take the form *-ij*. The feminines still take *-oj* in oblique cases, however, even if it is unstressed. The relevant forms of the two adjectives are contrasted in 2.9, with stress indicated by an accent:

2.9   Masc. nom./acc.   Fem. oblique
      a) málen'kij   málen'koj
      b) bol'šój   bol'šój

Since the homophony of *bol'*šoj is conditioned phonologically (in terms of stress placement), it is accidental homophony as far as the morphology is concerned. We can therefore legitimately say that *bol'*šoj (though not, presumably, *malen'koj*) represents two (at least) separate morphosyntactic words.

This discussion would be little more than a terminological exercise were it not for the fact that it has repercussions for the definition of morphosyntactic categories. Traditionally, students of Russian have said that BOL'ŠOJ has the usual six case forms in the feminine singular but that four of them are identical. Why is it not customary to say that the adjective simply doesn't have separate genitive, dative, instrumental and prepositional forms? Apart from the fact that it would make it difficult to draw tables in textbooks of Russian, this would actually cause complications elsewhere in the grammar. Recall that the reason for having all these case forms in the first place is so that the adjective can agree with the noun it modifies. Feminine nouns have different forms for the oblique cases. When confronted with two NPs such as in 2.10 it seems easier to reflect the fact that the adjective agrees with the noun for gender and case by saying that *bol'šoj* is both the genitive and the dative form, just as we say it's the masculine nominative form in 2.11:

2.10   a) bol'š-oj   košk-   i
                  fem. gen   fem.   gen.
                  'of a large cat'
             b) bol'š-oj   košk-   e
                  fem. dat.   fem.   dat.
                  'to a large cat'

2.11   bol'š-oj   stol
                  masc. nom. masc. nom.
             'a large table'

It wouldn't be impossible to label the elements of 2.9 as in 2.12, however, and indicate that the genitive and dative cases are members of the larger set of oblique cases by means of a rule such as 2.13:

2.12   a bolš- oj   košk-i
                  fem. obl.   fem. gen.
             b) bolš- oj   košk-e
                  fem. obl.   fem. dat.

2.13 $\begin{bmatrix} \text{gen.} \\ \text{dat.} \\ \text{instr.} \\ \text{prep.} \end{bmatrix} \Rightarrow [\text{obl.}]$

This would just require a more sophisticated theory of morphosyntactic categories and of agreement than is usual in traditional grammar. Nonetheless, it illustrates how even an apparently innocuous notion like 'word' can have ramifications throughout the grammar.

The question of how best to represent inflectional morphosyntactic categories was an important issue in pregenerative theories of morphology, and it has recently been foregrounded in the generative research literature. I shall devote some discussion to it in chapter 6.

2.2.3   The lexicon

The term **lexicon** means simply 'dictionary', and a dictionary is a list of words together with their meanings and other useful bits of linguistic information. A dictionary such as the *Complete Oxford English Dictionary* will not only give the spelling of each of its entries, but will also provide information such as the first attested use of a word, its etymology (that is, historical derivation) and possibly other information. In linguistic theory, a dictionary, or lexicon, is a more modest affair. It is usually taken to represent information about (i) the pronunciation, (ii) the meaning, (iii) morphological properties and (iv) syntactic properties of its entries. Under the heading of morphological properties there might be included such facts as which morphological class a word belongs to, for example whether it is a 1st conjugation or a 2nd conjugation verb, masculine or feminine gender noun and so on. The syntactic information will include the syntactic class of the item and, for instance, whether it is a transitive verb or an intransitive verb. As a bare additional minimum the lexicon must contain any idiosyncratic information about its entries. For example, the plural form, *men*, of *man*, which cannot possibly be predicted from any of the properties of the word, must in some way or other be represented in the lexical entry.

All linguists are agreed about this much. However, beyond this matters become more complex. There are several questions connected with the nature of the linguistic lexicon which we will discuss in great detail throughout this book. In this section we will touch on one of those, namely, the question of what exactly is listed in the lexicon.

One approach is to say that the lexicon contains only the information that is completely idiosyncratic. This, for instance, is the approach taken by the American structuralists, following the lead of Bloomfield (1933). Any property of a word which can be predicted from, say, the phonology or the syntax, will therefore be excluded from the lexicon. As we will see, generative linguists typically assume that a grammar has to include a set of rules for constructing words out of morphemes, that is, a set of **word formation rules**. For many theorists, such rules are housed in their own independent component of the grammar, and work by selecting morphemes from the lexicon and combining them. On such an approach, then, all the lexicon need contain is a list of morphemes. In this type of theory the job of the morphologist is to extract as much redundant information as possible from the structure of words and write that information into the word formation rules.

Not all linguists are happy with this approach (for reasons which will be discussed in greater depth in chapter 3). The most obvious problem is that the meaning of a word isn't always predictable from the meaning of its morphemes. And in some cases the final pronunciation of a word can't be predicted from the phonological form of its component morphemes. Therefore, another approach is to say that the lexicon contains a list of complete words, rather like the *Oxford English Dictionary*.

The problem now is to decide what we mean by 'word'. Even restricting ourselves to the lexeme, it is easy to show that by adopting a fairly inclusive definition we obtain the result that for many, if not all, languages, the lexicon will be infinitely large.

This can be seen by considering the formation of compound nouns in English. If we say that a compound such as *film society* is itself a word (and not a phrase) then we will also have to say that expressions such as those in 2.14 are words:

2.14   a) student film society
            b) student film society committee
            c) student film society committee scandal
            d) student film society committee scandal inquiry
            e) etc.

Clearly there is no linguistically principled limit to the lengths to which we can go in producing such compounds (as readers of newspaper headlines will be aware). The reason is that a compound noun can be formed by adding a noun to another compound noun. This 'self-feeding' property of the compounding rule is known as **recursion**. As a result, compound nouns are, in principle, infinitely long, and there are, in principle, infinitely many of them. In other languages, word formation processes such as affixation are recursive, so for them we would not even have to adopt the possibly contentious assumption that compounds are words in order to reach this conclusion.

If we don't like the idea of an infinitely long dictionary containing infinitely long words then we can try drawing a distinction between *potential words* and *actual words*. An actual word could be defined as any word form that some speaker has been observed to use. This style of definition is fraught with technical difficulty, but let's suppose that such a distinction can be drawn. Then we would say that the linguistic lexicon is a list of actual words. Such a list is sometimes referred to as the **permanent lexicon**. We can contrast it with the (unbounded) list of potential words (which is often referred to as the **conditional lexicon** or **potential lexicon**). If we sharpen our characterization of 'actual word' to mean just those attested words with which most of the speech community is familiar, then we won't have to bother about the thousands of compound nouns that are used by newspaper subeditors and which never get used again.

One way of achieving this result is to restrict the permanent lexicon to a list of lexemes. In that way, we will not include (regular) compounds, because these can be regarded as just concatenations of lexemes formed by rule. Moreover, we also avoid a problem which is posed by languages with rich inflectional systems, in which a single lexeme may therefore correspond to a great many word forms (and morphosyntactic words). A drastic example of this problem is that presented by the language Archi, spoken in the Daghestan mountains in the USSR, and described in great detail by Kibrik et al. (1977). In their preface the authors point out that the morphological system of the language is such that a regular verb is capable of appearing in over a million different forms. Even accounting for the fact that some of these are analytical constructions involving auxiliary verbs, this still means that an average speaker might go through his life without hearing certain grammatically impeccable forms of certain words. Therefore, it seems advisable to regard regularly inflected word forms (including, say, regular plurals in English) as part of the potential lexicon, and not the actual lexicon. This might even be the best policy in the case of common-or-garden word forms such as *cats*, which are attested quite frequently.

The problem of determining what the permanent lexicon consists of (assuming this is a coherent notion) is related to another important concept in morphology, that of **productivity**. If we look at the word formation resources of most languages we find that some of these are regularly and actively used in the creation of totally new words, while others have fallen into desuetude with the passage of time, or have been borrowed from elsewhere and are only used in restricted circumstances. A familiar example of this in English is given by affixes which turn adjectives into nouns. The suffix *-ness* can be attached to pretty well any adjective even if there is a more conventionally acceptable alternative. Thus, we might hear people use a word form such as *sterileness* (instead of *sterility*), particularly when using the adjective in its more general sense, rather than in the specific sense of 'physiologically incapable of producing offspring'. We say that *-ness* is a productive affix. We can contrast it with the affix *-th* which performs the same role, but only for a handful of words, sometimes accompanied by other idiosyncratic changes: *warmth, strength, health* (related historically to *hale* and *whole*). The affix *-th* is unproductive: it is only ever found with a limited number of stems and cannot be used to create new words. If a new adjective enters the language the favoured abstract nominalization of it will almost always be with *-ness*, whereas *-th* will never be used for this purpose. We might even doubt that *-th* could be regarded as a genuine morpheme in contemporary English.

Another way of restricting what goes into the lexicon, then, is to say that the lexicon contains a list of morphemes, and also a list of words formed by unproductive morphological processes, but does not contain words produced by productive processes whose meanings can be determined solely from the meanings of their components. This would mean that regularly inflected word forms would not be listed, nor would regular nominalizations in *-ness*. As we will see in chapter 3 there remain interesting problems with the notion of productivity, so the question of what the lexicon contains can't be said to have been settled.[3]

2.3 Structuralist theories

2.3.1 *The three models*

As the concept of the morpheme was developed in structuralist theories of language, particularly in America, so word formation came to be viewed as the disposition of morphemes in a word. Morphology came to be dominated by the metaphor of word analysis rather than word formation as linguistic theory sought to provide techniques for decomposing words into their component morphemes. The resulting approach was dubbed by Hockett (1958a) the **Item-and-Arrangement** (IA) theory.

From our overview of morphological phenomena in Chapter One it will be evident that there are many morphological relationships which don't fit neatly into the IA scheme. Hockett discusses a simple case in some detail, namely the use of ablaut in the formation of strong past tenses in English verbs, as compared with the regular formation consisting of affixation of *-ed* to the basic form (as *bake ~ baked*). He points out that descriptive linguistics up to that time had a variety of means for describing the fact that *took* is the past tense form of *take*, and proceeds to compare them.

Hockett's list (1958a: 393) goes as follows:

(1) *took* is a single morpheme < ... >.

(2) *took* is a portmanteau representation of the two morpheme sequence *take* and /ed/.

(3) *took* is an allomorph of the morpheme which appears elsewhere as *take*, plus a zero allomorph of /ed/.

(4) *took* is a discontinuous allomorph /t ... k/ of *take*, and an infixed allomorph /u/ of /ed/.

(5) *took* is *take* plus a replacive morph /u/ ← /ey/ (read '/u/ replaces /ey/').

This citation is self-explanatory except for the term **portmanteau**, which in this context means type of fusion of two morphemes into one (see below).

Hockett objects to solution (5) because it appeals to the idea of a morpheme which consists of a process of replacement, and this is foreign to the IA approach by definition. On the other hand, the maximally simple solution (1) is unsatisfactory because, in effect, it fails to capture the fact that *took* is the past tense form of *take* just as *baked* is the past tense form of *bake*. The second solution is able to capture this but has the disadvantage that it fails to distinguish ablaut from total suppletion of the kind *go ~ went*. Solution (3) attempts to force the ablaut forms into an agglutinating straitjacket by equivocation over the notions of 'morpheme' and 'allomorph'. This solution, in effect, likens the *took ~ take* alternation to the stem allomorphy found in *electric ~ electricity*, except that the phonological alternation is caused by an allomorph which has no physical realization. Hockett therefore rejects this solution, too.

The option Hockett seems to prefer is that of (4), though he explicitly denies that this means that the form *take* is comprised of /t ... k/ plus an infix /ey/. However, this preference is relative to IA theory. As Hocket points out, in a different theoretical framework we would expect different solutions to be favoured. Hockett mentions one other approach in passing, the Word-and-Paradigm theory, and devotes much of his discussion to what he sees as the main alternative to IA, the **Item-and-Process** (IP) theory.

In an IP account we would distinguish between basic or underlying forms of a morpheme and forms derived after the application of certain processes. Thus, we would say that *bake* and *take* were underlying forms and that two distinct process applied to them in the formation of the past tense. In the first, the process is affixation of *-ed* (or perhaps of the allomorph /t/); in the second the process is phonological in that the vowel of *take* is replaced by, or changed into, /u/. This solution to the 'took' problem is reminiscent of the fifth of Hockett's IA analyses, which he rejected because of its processual underpinnings.

The IP approach historically precedes the IA approach described by Hockett (its most extended defence is probably given in Sapir, 1921). Hockett has a number of quibbles about what exactly is meant by 'process', but on the whole he seems to believe that both theories could handle these data and similar problems equally well.[4]

There remains a class of phenomena which neither IA or IP seem well equipped to handle and that is the fusional nature of inflectional systems. The problem is that both IA and IP are fundamentally agglutinating theories. In IA, in which there is no distinction between underlying forms and surface forms, all morphology is essentially agglutinative. Thus, even a form such as *took* consists of two morphemes whose allomorphs are /t ... k/ and /u/ and word formation consists of combining these. In IP word structure need not necessarily look agglutinative on the surface, but it is assumed to be agglutinative at the underlying level. Thus, *took* is formed from *take* plus the ablaut process, and this can be thought of as a base morpheme plus a past tense process, whose 'combination' results in the change in vowel quality. The difficulty becomes apparent when we ask how the IA or IP theories would handle the problem posed by Russian adjectival forms such as *bol'šomu* 'big (masc./neut. dat. sg. adjective)'. Here we have four morphemes all realized by a single portmanteau morph, as in 2.15, (an example of **multiple exponence**):

2.15

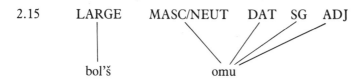

The problem is made more acute by the fact that Russian nouns and adjectives never distinguish masculine from neuter gender in oblique cases. It is quite unclear how even a version of Hockett's solution (4) could cope with this in a principled fashion within the IA framework. But it is equally implausible that we would find a set of processes operating over underlying forms to express the separate categories of masculine/neuter, dative, singular and adjective.

In a portmanteau morph, then, several categories are realized by one surface formative, an instance of a one–many correspondence between form and function. In addition, we often find situations in which a single category is realized in more than one way within a word, that is, when there is many–one correspondence between form and function. This has been referred to as **extended** or **overlapping exponence**. English strong verbs provide a simple example of this. Most such verbs end in *-en* in the past participle. However, many of them also show ablaut, and in certain cases the vowel of the stem is unique to the past participle form, for instance: *write, wrote* but *written*. The extended exponence of the past participle category can be diagrammed as in 2.16:

2.16

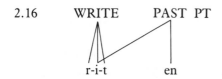

It might be open to the IA (or IP) theorist to say that we have a phonological process of vowel change triggered by the *-en* affix here. Other cases of multiple exponence are less easy to handle, however. Matthews (1972) discusses an example from Latin which is typical of the problems posed by inflecting languages. The 1st sg. ending of verbs in the active voice is *-o:* in the Imperfective Present and *-i:* in the Perfective. Thus, we have forms such as those in 2.17:

2.17   a) am-o: am-a:-w-i: 'love'
        b) mon-e:-o: mon-u-i: 'advise'
        c) reg-o: re:k-s-i: 'rule'
        d) aud-i:-o: aud-i:-w-i: 'hear'

In the (a, d) examples, the *-w-* element is a regular marker of the Perfective, and in

2.17b the -*u*- marker serves this purpose. In the form *re:ksi:* the -*s*- element marks the Perfective, but this category is also signalled in part by the vowel lengthening of the root and the g/k alternation. The latter would be regarded as an automatic phonological alternation, though the vowel lengthening is non-automatic and could plausibly be said to be a partial realization of the category of Perfective. This means that a mapping from the morphosyntactic categories to their surface realizations for *re:ksi:* would look like 2.18:

2.18   RULE   PERF   1ST SG

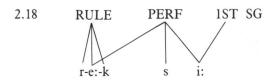

r-e:-k   s   i:

A simple response to this challenge is to bite the bullet and concede that the relation between morphological form and morphosyntactic function is, in the most general case, many–many and not one–one. This is the **Word-and-Paradigm** (WP) approach to inflectional morphology, first presented in an articulated form in Robins (1959), and defended meticulously within a generative framework by Matthews (1972; cf. also Matthews, 1974). Robins pointed out that there are certain generalizations which can only really be stated at the level of the whole word. Some of these have been mentioned in §2.2.2, and others will be discussed in later chapters. He also pointed out that the notion of 'inflectional paradigm' seems to play some role in grammatical organization. Again, we will see detailed exemplification of this later. His proposal was to revamp a much earlier tradition of word analysis derived from classical grammarians (some writing 2,500 years ago, such as Pāṇini and Aristotle) describing classical languages such as Latin, Greek and Sanskrit.[5]

The key to the WP approach is our notion of the morphosyntactic word. Each inflected form has (at least) one morphosyntactic description (for example 'past tense form' or 'dative singular of the masculine/neuter adjectival form') and the grammar then makes available paradigms that specify the formatives which correspond to these categories. In an agglutinating system the correspondence rules will be rather simple, amounting to one morphosyntactic category per formative and one formative per category. But there is no necessity for the categories and the morphological elements which express those categories to be in a one–one correspondence, as there is in the IA theory.

A result of this approach is that it is rather a simple matter to describe syncretism. For instance, the fact that all oblique cases have the same ending in the feminine singular (namely -*oj*) can be stated directly in the WP approach, in which the morphosyntactic description is separated from the morphological formatives as such.[6] At the same time the extended or overlapping exponence found in Latin poses no problems, since, again, we simply have to write our rules in such a way that a given morphosyntactic category for certain lexemes has to be signalled by root allomorphy as well as by affixation. A potential price for this descriptive luxury is that it would appear possible to describe any conceivable patterning of data this way, including hypothetical systems which never seem to occur in real life. This is the kind of property that tends to arouse the suspicions of generative linguists.

In chapters 3 and 6 we will see other potential advantages that follow from being able to make direct reference to the notion of 'inflectional paradigm'. On the other hand, in chapters 4 and 5 we will see how changes in assumptions concerning the relation between morphology and phonology have allowed some theoreticians to propose basically IP or IA models which can handle some of the problems posed by inflectional and other types of non-agglutinative morphology.

2.3.2 Morphophonemics

Although I have spoken at various times about the allomorphic realizations of morphemes, my discussion of theories of morphology has been oversimplified in that I haven't discussed yet the ways in which structuralists linked morphological structure to allomorphic variation. This connects morphological theory with phonological theory (what is known in structuralism as 'phonemics'), and for certain schools of structuralism the result was an intermediate *morphophonemic* level.

In chapter 1 I mentioned that morphemes may appear in different phonological shapes because of the effects of general phonological processes. The English regular plural suffix is an example of this. This involves a number of phonological complications, so to illustrate how structuralist theories approached phonologically conditioned variation in its simplest form I'll begin with a relatively unproblematic example from Russian. The word for 'foam' in the nom. sg. is pronounced [p'ɛnə], where the apostrophe represents palatalization of the consonant. In the dative the word is pronounced [p'en'ə], with palatalization of the [n] and a raising of the stem vowel from [ɛ] to [e]. In other words, [e] is an allophone, or variant, or the *e*-phoneme which occurs whenever that phoneme is both preceded and followed by a palatalized consonant. This is an example of an automatic alternation, governed solely by the phonological form of the words concerned, and applying to every word of the appropriate form in the language. Moreover, the e/ɛ distinction is never by itself contrastive in Russian, that is, there can be no pair of words which differ solely in that one has /e/ where the other has /ɛ/. In contemporary generative phonology a situation like this would be handled by taking the /ɛ/ allophone as basic and postulating a raising rule applying in the environment of palatalized consonants. In the tradition of structuralist phonemics we would say that the two allophones of the *e*-phoneme occur in complementary distribution: that is, there is one set of environments where /e/ occurs and another entirely distinct set of environments where /ɛ/ occurs.[7]

The situation is a little more complex in the case of our second example. In 2.19 we see the genitive singular form (ending -*a*) of three Russian masculine nouns:

2.19   a) luka   'onion-GEN'
        b) luka   'bow-GEN'
        c) luga   'meadow-GEN'

Notice that *luka* means both 'of an onion' and 'of a bow'. This means that we have a case of homonymy, rather like the homonymy we find in the English word *case* (as in *suitcase*, *court case*, or *genitive case*).

Matters get more interesting when we look at 2.20, the nominative/accusative forms of these three words:

2.20   a) luk 'onion'
         b) luk 'bow'
         c) luk 'meadow'

Now we seem to have three homonyms (just as with English *case*). However, the *luk* case is different from the *case* case. This is because the sudden appearance of a /k/ sound at the end of the word for 'meadow' is the automatic consequence of a general rule of Russian phonology. There are no voiced obstruents in word final position in Russian (which is why the English words *back* and *bag* sound alike when spoken with a Russian accent). The second sequence [lug] would therefore be an unpronounceable word in Russian (witness what I said about speaking English with a Russian accent), so where we might expect [lug] we actually hear [luk].

In contemporary (and also in European structuralist) parlance the g/k alternation illustrated here is a case of **neutralization** of a phonemic contrast. We again have an automatic alternation, since it applies to all words of the right phonological shape, but it destroys a contrast between the g/k phonemes (and between all the voiced/ voiceless pairs in Russian). Neutralizations pose problems for certain IA approaches to morphology. In the post-Bloomfieldian tradition represented by, for example, Hockett, statements about morphemes have to be kept distinct from statements about phonemes. The reasons for this are to do with controversial assumptions about the way linguistic analysis has to proceed and about the nature of phonological representations. In the American structuralist tradition it was thought that a full phonemic analysis had to precede a morphological analysis (which in turn had to precede a syntactic analysis). Why this should be so was never made clear but it had the effect of placing stringent conditions on the way that grammars could be written. It was also thought that the phonemic representation of a word should be deducible directly from its phonetic representation, the so-called **biuniqueness** requirement (sometimes encapsulated in a slogan, 'once a phoneme, always a phoneme').

In the case of [p'ɛnə/p'en'ə] there is no problem. Since [e] is a phonologically conditioned allophone of the /ɛ/ phoneme we can write the two forms in phonemic transcription as /p'ɛnə/ and /p'ɛn'ə/, on the understanding that purely phonological principles of allophony will tell us the precise pronunciation of each vowel. In the case of the [lug ~ luk] alternation we have a problem. The two variants consist of different phonemes and the type of entities that consist of different phonemes are morphs, for example, allomorphs of a single morpheme. Hence, as morphologists we must set up the two forms /luk/ and /lug/ of the stem for 'meadow' and note that the former occurs when there is no suffix, and the latter when there is. The big problem here is that the k/g alternation is just as automatic as the ɛ/e alternation and so it should really be handled by means of a phonological statement, not a morphological one. In other words, we have a case which is essentially allophony, but we're forced by theoretical assumptions to treat it as allomorphy.

A solution favoured by post-Bloomfieldian structuralists was to set up a further level intermediate between that of phonemes and morphemes. This was the **morphophonemic level** and its elements were **morphophonemes**. Some of these would bear a direct correspondence to phonemes, namely those which didn't ever alternate, or those which failed to alternate in a particular word. Others would have an indirect

*The problem is that the conditioning factors don't say how to correct the lexical [g] ⊆ [k] → //g// etc. [g̊]

relation to the phonemes which realized them, and these would represent the alternating sounds. The word 'meadow', ending in an alternating consonant, would be given representations along the lines of 2.21, in which the *G* represents the alternating morphophoneme:

2.21   luG 'meadow'

On the other hand, words such as *luk*, as well as words such as *gul* 'rumble' and *kul'* 'type of bag' containing *k/g* sounds which never alternate, would have representations such as 2.22, with *k* and *g* morphophonemes which are distinct from the *G* morphophoneme:

2.22   a) luk   'onion/bow'
         b) gul   'rumble'
         c) kul' 'type of bag'

Special rules would then state that *G* corresponds to the phoneme /g/ in some contexts and to /k/ in others.

In the Prague School tradition of structuralism, which followed the ideas of Trubetskoy and Jakobson, the *G* of 2.21 would have particular properties, in that it would be regarded as a bundle of distinctive features characterizing velar plosives, but not marked for the voicing feature. This feature would then be specified as a function of its position (whether word final or not). A partially specified phonological element of this sort is called an **archiphoneme**. It codes in a rather direct way the idea that an otherwise distinctive opposition is suspended or neutralized in certain circumstances.

The American concept of morphophonemics was somewhat different from this, however. The biuniqueness requirement meant that phonemes were not allowed to change into other phonemes. Hence, the concept of neutralization as such was not part of the theory. Consequently, the concept of neutralization could not be formalized by appeal to the archiphoneme, and the *G* element of representation 2.21 is not intended as a phonetic intermediary between /k/ and /g/—it can only be interpreted as an entirely separate entity.

This type of approach leads to a discrepancy between the generalizations which are stated about phonemes and those stated about forms of morphemes. This discrepancy becomes really serious when we note that there is a process of voicing assimilation in Russian which can take place either within words (e.g. across morpheme boundaries) or across words, if the words are, phonologically speaking, clitics. One such clitic is the conditional morpheme *by* (pronounced [bɨ]). This can attach to any word in the sentence, including a direct object:

2.23   a) lug by uvidel   '(he) would see the onion'
         b) lug by uvidel   '(he) would see the bow'
         c) lug by uvidel   '(he) would see the meadow'
         d) ludʒ' by uvidel   '(he) would see the ray'

As might be guessed from these data, only a voiced consonant may precede the voiced /b/ of *by*. Thus, a sequence such as /*lukby/ or /*lutʃ'by/ is unpronounceable in Russian. This too, is a general phonological fact about the language. In the case of the *luk - lug* alternations illustrated in 2.23a, b, this gives rise to a neutralization (in the opposite direction to the neutralization observed in the nom. sg. of the word for 'meadow'). However, there is no phoneme /dʒ/ in Russian. This sound is merely a voiced allophone of the sound /tʃ/ which ends the word *lutʃ'* (gen. sg. *lutʃ'a*) 'ray (of light)'.

It is obvious to anyone who knows the facts of Russian that the reason for the alternations in 2.23a, b, is the same as the reason for the alternations in 2.23d and the failure of the opposite alternation in 2.23c. However, the post-Bloomfieldian account cannot state this. The alternation between [tʃ'] and [dʒ'] is allophonic and must therefore be stated at the level of phonemes. The alternation between [k] and [g] is phonemic and therefore must be stated at the level of morphophonemes. The two levels cannot be 'mixed' because of the biuniqueness restriction. Therefore, the post-Bloomfieldian has to say that we are dealing with two formally distinct processes. In other words, the structuralist assumptions prevent us from stating the obvious truth about the language. This is a rehearsal of Halle's (1959) celebrated refutation of the structuralist approach.

If the IA insistence of biunique phonemics and static principles of 'arrangement' of morphemes prevented insightful solutions to problems such as voicing assimilation in Russian, how well do IP accounts fare? I have used the term 'American structuralism' effectively as a synonym of 'post-Bloomfieldian structuralism' hitherto, but in fact the type of structuralism practised by Bloomfield himself (and also by Sapir and originally by Nida) was more oriented towards IP analogies than the IA model. The type of analysis we find in Bloomfield's (1939) analysis of the Amerindian language Menomini illustrates this very well.

Keeping to our Russian example, the way the IP model might have handled this is as follows. We take one form of the alternating morpheme *lug-* 'meadow' and decide to regard one form as basic. This will be the form which appears in the most contexts, or the most general of the alternants. Then we assume a rule which changes the /g/ phoneme into a /k/ in specific contexts (such as at the end of a word), and another rule changing /k/ into /g/ in the voicing assimilation contexts. These two rules apply in the order of mention, not the other way round. We can also postulate a different rule which changes a /k/ into a /g/ in voicing assimilation contexts. The upshot is a series of derivations such as those in 2.24:

2.24	luk	luka	lug	luga	luk by	lug by	lutʃ' by	
	N/A	N/A	luk	N/A	N/A	luk by	N/A	Devoicing
	N/A	N/A	N/A	N/A	lug by	lug by	ludʒ' by	Voicing
	luk	luka	luk	luga	lug by	lug by	ludʒ' by	Output

Since we aren't hidebound by biuniqueness or the need to 'separate levels' we can account for the alternations observed in a maximally simple fashion, and still keep sight of the basic generalizations. The idea of a set of 'mutation' rules applying in a set order to a basic underlying form is, of course, central to generative phonology (see chapter 4).

The derivational format, then, allows us to capture allomorphic variation which is phonologically (or phonetically) motivated. In effect, we allow the phonological rules to 'interfere' with the phonological forms of morphemes. This type of grammatical organization allows us to dispense with interlevels such as the morphophonemic level, and the concept of the morphophoneme (though in generative phonology the concept of the archiphoneme plays an important role). This is one of the most important consequences of adopting the Bloomfieldian IP approach: there is no linguistic level of representation between the morphemic and the phonemic. Thus, morphemes are comprised of phonemes, and not morphophonemes.

2.4   Summary

This chapter has been concerned with the central concepts of the morpheme, the word and the lexicon. We saw that the simplest conception of the morpheme, that of a single form with a single function, encounters considerable difficulties when confronted with the facts. This means that the conceptually simplest type of morphological system, the purely agglutinating system, is an ideal which is seldom approached by real morphologies, so much so that one could question whether agglutination really does represent an ideal in any sense. Having surveyed a number of form–function problems for the morpheme concept, we also noted that the notion of 'word' is by no means clear-cut. We have to distinguish four distinct notions (the lexeme, the word form, the morphosyntactic word, and the phonological word), but even then there are no universal hard-and-fast criteria for determining wordhood. At the same time, we noted that the concept of a store of words, a lexicon, hides more complexity than first meets the eye. Finally, in the third section we saw the way that pre-generative theories attempted to solve the problems with definitions of the morpheme and related concepts. Having outlined the three models, IA, IP and WP, we contrasted the IA and IP approaches to certain notorious morphophonemic problems. We discovered that the IA approach, which attempts to retain at all costs the idea of a one–one correspondence between form and function, has great difficulty in providing a satisfactory solution to these problems.

EXERCISES

2.1   Hungarian allomorphy. Consider the data set below. Isolate all the morphemes with their allomorphs, and provide a gloss for each (i.e. a meaning or a grammatical function). Which of the allomorphy seems to be conditioned purely phonologically and which purely morphologically? [Hint: the 3rd sg. possessive form has two *lexically* conditioned allomorphs.] What is the rule for forming the possessed form of a plural noun? [sz = [s], ü = [y], ö = [œ], ő = [œ:], V́ = long vowel. All vowels are pronounced separately].

Paradigm 1: szoba 'room'

	Sg.		Pl.	
Nom.	szoba	'room'	szobák	'rooms'
Iness.	szobában	'in a room'	szobákban	'in rooms'
Acc.	szobát	'room'	szobákat	'rooms'

Possessed forms

Sg.	1	szobám	'my room'	szobáim	'my rooms'
	2	szobád	'thy room'	szobáid	'thy rooms'
	3	szobája	'his room'	szobái	'his rooms'
Pl.	1	szobánk	'our room'	szobáink	'our rooms'
	2	szobátok	'your room'	szobáitok	'your rooms'
	3	szobájuk	'their room'	szobáik	'their rooms'

Paradigm 2: nap 'day'   Paradigm 3: kép 'picture'

	Sg.	Pl.	Sg.	Pl.
Nom.	nap	napok	kép	képek
Iness.	napban	napokban	képben	képekben
Acc.	napot	napokat	képet	képeket

Possessed forms

Sg.	1	napom	napjaim	képem	képeim
	2	napod	napjaid	képed	képeid
	3	napja	napjai	képe	képei
Pl.	1	napunk	napjaink	képünk	képeink
	2	napotok	napjaitok	képetek	képeitek
	3	napjuk	napjaik	képük	képeik

Paradigm 4 fürdő 'bath'   Paradigm 5 film 'film'

	Sg.	Pl.	Sg.	Pl.
Nom.	fürdő	fürdők	film	filmek
Iness.	fürdőben	fürdőkben	filmben	filmekben
Acc.	fürdőt	fürdőket	filmet	filmeket

Possessed forms

Sg.	1	fürdőm	fürdőim	filmem	filmjeim
	2	fürdőd	fürdőid	filmed	filmjeid
	3	fürdője	fürdői	filmje	filmjei
Pl.	1	fürdőnk	fürdőink	filmünk	filmjeink
	2	fürdőtök	fürdőitek	filmetek	filmjeitek
	3	fürdőjük	fürdőik	filmjük	filmjeik

Additional data:
szobámban 'in my room', napjaidat 'thy days (Acc.)', képeben 'in his picture', fürdőinkben 'in our baths', filmjeiteket 'your films (Acc.)'

2.2   Below is a list of nineteen sentences in Czech, written in broad phonemic transcription, with English glosses. Word divisions are not indicated. Identify the Czech words and their meanings, and give as much information as you can about their inflectional forms. [č = [tʃ] , c = [ts] , š = [ʃ]]

(i)   nejsoudji:ʃki
        'They are not girls.'

(ii)   rixlepracovalixlapci.
'The boys worked quickly.'

(iii)   ʔirinajefʔolomouci
'Irina is in Olomouc.'

(iv)   ʔolomoucjestare:mnjestonamoravje
'Olomouc is an old town in Moravia.'

(v)   dji:fkimudalisklenkupiva
'The girls gave him a glass of beer.'

(vi)   mu:jʔotetspracovalfʔostravje
'My father worked in Ostrava.'

(vii)   šelrixlekʔivanovi
'He walked quickly towards Ivan.'

(viii) xlapciznalili:du
'The boys knew Lida.'

(ix)   tadijemu:jbratr
'Here's my brother.'

(x)   ʔonjinejsoufčeskoslovenskuʔaledji:fkisoutam
'*They* aren't in Czechoslovakia but the girls are there.'

(xi)   fsklencejepivo
'There's beer in the glass.'

(xii)   ʔevaznalatohoxlapcu
'Eva knew that boy.'

(xiii) dalixlapcovidobrouknjihu
'They gave a good book to the boy.'

(xiv)   jevbrnje
'He's in Brno.'

(xv)   ʔevama:českouknjihu
'Eva has a Czech book.'

(xvi)   česka:pivasouznamenjita:
'Czech beers are famous.'

(xvii) ʔostravaʔaʔolomoucsoučeska:mnjesta
'Ostrava and Olomouc are Czech towns.'

(xviii) šlimlade:dji:fkikʔostravje
'The young girls walked to Ostrava.'

(xix)   novousklenkurozbili
'They broke the new glass.'

2.3   Identify the word boundaries in the following fourteen sentences of Serbo-Croat. [č = [tʃ], š = [ʃ], ž = [ʒ], c = [ts], ć = [tɕ], h = [x]; otherwise, assume the orthography is IPA.]

(i)   devojkesumugadale
'The girls gave it to him.'

(ii)   videlismogajuče
'We saw him yesterday.'

(iii)   znaojedasamjojihdao
'He knew that I gave them to her.'

(iv)   knjigesmovamostavilinastolu
       'We left you the books on the table.'
(v)   predstaviosimuse
       'You (masc. sg.) introduced yourself to him.'
(vi)   ženesunamprodalecveće
       'The women sold us flowers.'
(vii) momcisujojotpevalipesmu
       'The boys sang her a song.'
(viii) bogdanimladensutisepredstaviliuuredu
       'Bodgan and Mladen introduced themselves to you (sg.) in the office.'
(ix)   nastolusuvideliknjige
       'On the table they saw the books.'
(x)   većsamimsepredstavio
       'I have already introduced myself to them.'
(xi)   bogdanjojjedaocveće
       'Bogdan gave her the flowers.'
(xii) cvećesteostaviliuuredu
       'You (masc. pl.) left the flowers in the office.'
(xiii) jučeimjeprodaoknjige
       'Yesterday he sold them the books.'
(xiv) ženesumiihpredstavile
       'The women introduced them to me.'

*2.4   Describe in detail the criteria you used for solving problems 2 and 3. What other information might have been useful? What practical difficulties are there in applying these criteria to the data of 2 and 3?

2.5   Analyse the words in sets (i-iii) into their component morphemes. What problems do these words present?

(i)   conceptual; criminal; managerial; professiorial; residual; tidal.
(ii)   anthropocentric; gastro-enteritis; Graeco-Roman; gynocologist; hypothetico-deductive; misanthropist; misogynist; politico-economic.
(iii) Congolese; Javanese; Mancunian; Panamanian; Peruvian.

2.6   Consider all the regular inflectional categories of English nouns and verbs. Isolate all the cases in which we regularly find syncretism, i.e. in which single word forms correspond to more than one morphosyntactic word. Likewise, consider a representative sample of irregular ('strong') verbs. Identify situations in which syncretism (i) occurs for a small class of verbs only; (ii) is found with all strong verbs.

2.7   Analyse the following verb forms from the paleosiberian language Itel'men (also known as Kamchadal), spoken on the Kamchatkan peninsula. Note that a transitive verb agrees both with its subject and its direct object in person and number.

What problems do these data pose for a morphemic analysis? What deviations from strict agglutination are there in these data? To what extent would these deviations encourage us to regard the system as 'fusional' or 'inflectional'? [Note there are no reflexive forms in the paradigm, e.g. corresponding to 'I brought me' or 'I brought us'.]

Stem: əntxla- 'bring'

	Subject (singular)		
Object	1	2	3
Sg. 1	_____	əntxlaxkmiŋ	əntxlaxkomnen
2	təntxlaxkin	_____	əntxlaxkin
3	təntxlaxkicen	əntxlacgin	əntxlaciŋnen
Pl. 1	_____	əntxlaxkmiʔŋ	əntxlaxlaxkomnaeʔn
2	təntxlakisxen	_____	əntxlakisxen
3	təntxlakiceʔn	əntxlacgiʔn	əntxlaciŋneʔn

	Subject (plural)		
Sg. 1	_____	əntxlaxkmiŋsx	nəntxlaxkomnen
2	nəntxlaxkin	_____	nəntxlaxkin
3	nəntxlakicen	əntxlasxik	nəntxlagenen
Pl. 1	_____	əntxlaxkmiʔŋsx	nəntxlaxkomneʔn
2	nəntxlakisxen	_____	nəntxlakisxen
3	nəntxlakiceʔn	əntxlaxkiʔn	nəntxlageneʔn

*2.8   Take the processes exemplified in chapter 1 (§1.4: stress, tone, reduplication, mutation and morphological conversion) and outline a description of them in IA terms. What are the major empirical and conceptual difficulties? How might a structuralist linguist attempt to describe such phenomena in terms of morpheme theory?

*2.9   The masculine prepositional singular form of Russian adjectives is invariably homophonous with the dative plural form. Can we draw the same conclusions from this that we drew when considering the feminine singular forms and the plural forms of Russian adjectives? What sort of criteria would bear on this question?

3

Early Generative Approaches

3.1 Phonology and syntax in the Standard Theory

3.1.1 The Standard Theory in outline

In the earliest models of generative grammar, morphology as such scarcely existed. Allomorphic variation was regarded as primarily the result of the operation of phonological rules, and other aspects of word formation (including compounding, derivation and inflection) were handled by rules of syntax. The model was crystallized in the form of Chomsky's *Aspects of the Theory of Syntax* (1965), subsequently known as the *Aspects* model, or more technically as the **Standard Theory**. In this theory sentence structures are generated in three stages. In the **base component** there is a set of **context free phrase structure rules**, which generate **initial phrase markers** (**IPM's** or **deep structures**). The IPMs are then modified by syntactic **transformations**. These rules differ from the phrase structure rules, which simply construct the basic phrase markers, in that they operate on ready-made structures and have the power to delete, move, substitute or add material. The first of the transformations is the set of **lexical insertion** transformations, which insert items from the lexicon under syntactically appropriate terminal nodes in the IPM. The result after all the transformations have applied is the syntactic **surface structure**. Both the IPMs (or deep structures) and the surface structures are represented in the linguistics literature by the (in)famous device of the tree diagram.

The meaning and pronunciation of sentences is determined by two interpretive components. The **semantic component** reads off the meaning of the sentence from its deep structure representation. The pronunciation, however, is specified from the surface structure. This forms the input to the **phonological component**, a set of transformational phonological rules. The general picture is schematized in figure 3.1

In many respects, the organization of phonology and the organization of syntax were very similar in the Standard Theory of Transformational Generative Grammar

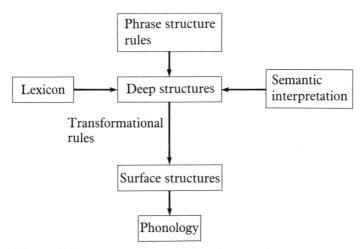

Figure 3.1 The 'classical' model of generative grammar

(TGG) as represented in *The Sound Pattern of English* (Chomsky and Halle, 1968, SPE) and *Aspects*. Both components included a battery of transformational rules applying to underlying structures to produce a surface form. Theorizing in generative syntax and phonology at this time was built around an important (though sometimes tacit) assumption concerning the nature of linguistically significant generalizations. Put somewhat crudely, whenever a relationship between two linguistic forms could be discerned, that relationship had to be captured by assuming a common basic form and deriving each alternation from that underlying form by means of a battery of transformational rules. In the general case, the underlying form might be fairly 'abstract' compared with its surface manifestations.

3.1.2 The SPE model of phonology

In the SPE model of phonology a derivation starts from an **underlying representation** (UR) which encodes all the information about the pronunciation of a word which cannot be predicted by rule. This undergoes phonological rules which substitute one segment for another, delete segments, insert segments or alter the order of segments. The result is a **surface representation** (SR).

In this model, the root of two words such as *divine* and *divinity* are identical, namely /divIn/, where the vowel /I/ represents a sound which is not actually heard in any of the variants of the root which surface, and which is never actually found in the pronunciation of any word of English. Such a segment is often called an **abstract** segment and it is invariably changed into something else by the phonological rules. This is a species of neutralization, and whenever we have an abstract segment such as this which *never* surfaces anywhere in the language we speak of **absolute neutralization**.

The SPE model of phonology didn't pay much attention to the problem of building up morphemes out of phonemes. Rather, the starting point for a phonological derivation is the string of segments constituting the UR. Now, generative phonologists

clearly recognized the fact that there are stable regularities governing the way phonemes are strung together (i.e. *phonotactic constraints*; see chapter 2, §2.2.2 and note
2). Moreover, it was also noted that there are regularities governing the structure of
morphemes (sometimes restricted to particular classes of morphemes), known as
morpheme structure conditions, or MSCs. Thus, there are no (native) morphemes
beginning with more than three consonants in English (an example of an MSC which
derives from a phonotactic constraint). In some Mayan languages, on the other hand,
all roots have to have the form CVC, in a number of Semitic languages there are constraints on what kind of phonemes may be combined to form a triliteral root, and,
in Yoruba, nouns (though not other parts of speech) have to be polysyllabic.

These sorts of relationships are captured by **lexical redundancy rules**. These are
rules which state that the grammar (or lexicon) of English is more 'highly valued' to
the extent that it eschews words or morphemes such as /mpklstrag/. They are not
generative rules, however. They don't create any structure (in the way that phrase
structure rules do in syntax), nor do they alter structure (unlike transformations or
certain phonological rules).

3.1.3 Morphosyntax in the Standard Theory

The nature of the *Aspects* model of syntax determined in large part what kind of
approach could be adopted towards morphosyntax. One important feature of the
model is the nature of lexical entries. In particular, the insertion of words into the
syntactic structures generated by the phrase structure rules is governed by the lexical
properties of certain words. For instance, a transitive verb has to be followed by a
direct object NP. This is formalized in *Aspects* by the concept of **subcategorization**.
We can say, for example, that transitive verbs form a subcategory of the category of
verbs, by virtue of the fact that they must be followed by an NP complement (that
is, their object) at the stage when lexical insertion takes place. In other words, it is
the presence of the object which gives rise to the subcategory of transitive verbs. We
can therefore say that the object *subcategorizes* the verb (or that the verb is *subcategorized* by its object). The way this is formalized in *Aspects* is to say that the lexical
entry for a transitive verb includes a special symbol (or feature) indicating that the
verb must be followed by an NP. This feature is called the verb's **subcategorization
frame**. An example, the entry for the transitive verb *hit*, is given in 3.1:

3.1   hit: [____NP]

The notion of subcategorization will prove very important in some theories of
morphology.

In syntax the assumption of a common underlying source for related structures
meant that an active sentence such as 3.2 had the same deep structure as 3.3a-c,
namely something like 3.4[1].

3.2   Tom gave a rose to Harriet.

3.3   a) Tom gave Harriet a rose.
           b) Harriet was given a rose (by Tom).
           c) A rose was given to Harriet (by Tom).

3.4

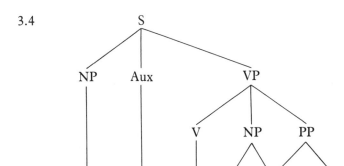

Transformational rules of various kinds would then rearrange the word order and delete a preposition (to give 3.3a), and add a preposition and auxiliary verb as well as putting the verb in the past participle form (to give 3.3c). This is a simple illustration of the way that an important piece of English morphology, namely the passive participle form of verbs, is the responsibility of a syntactic rule in the Standard Theory, since it has repercussions for the syntactic organization of the sentence as a whole.

One of the syntactic phenomena which the transformational component had to account for is that of agreement or concord. In 3.5 we must guarantee that *runs* agrees with its subject by appearing with the *-s* ending, and in 3.6 we must ensure that the same ending is *not* present:

3.5   The boy runs.

3.6   I/you/we/the boys run.

This is achieved by assuming that the grammatical person and number of the NPs *the boy* or *the boys* is marked in the tree by a set of **syntactic features**. These are comparable to the distinctive features of phonology. A singular 3rd person nominal such as *the boy* would bear the features [-plural] and (redundantly, since all nouns other than pronouns are 3rd person in English) [+3rd], while *the boys* would bear the feature [+plural]. Then we assume a transformation which copies the features for person and number from the subject NP onto the verb. This produces a tree of the form 3.7 for sentence 3.5:

3.7

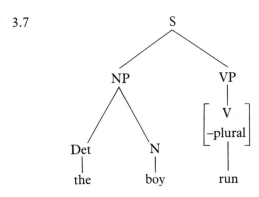

In chapter 6 we'll see that the use of syntactic features of this sort effectively allows us to formalize the notion of 'paradigm'. Chomsky himself explicitly argues for a paradigmatic account of agreement morphology over an Item-and-Arrangement approach (which he describes as 'clumsy').

So far we have generated a verb marked with a [-plural] feature specification, and not the word form *runs*. The final 'spelling-out' of the word form with appropriate morphology is the job of the phonological component. A tree such as 3.7 could be sent directly to the phonology since the rule for affixation of the 3rd sg. *-s* is perfectly regular. In some cases, however, the syntactic tree passed to the phonology requires tidying up. Thus, in examples such as that schematically represented in 3.8, in which we have irregular inflection, we need some way of deriving the correct phonological representation over and above the information provided by the syntax:

3.8   THE [GOOSE-PLURAL] [BE-PRES] [BE-PROG] [FEED-PAST PT]

This can be done by means of special rules which specify that the formative underlying the phonological form of GOOSE (/gu:s/) undergoes a special phonological rule to become /gi:s/, that BE-PRES-PLURAL, the form of *be* agreeing with *geese*, takes the suppletive form /a:/, and so on. Exactly what form such rules take varies from one analysis to another, depending on whether the linguist regards /gi:s/ as the result of a phonological rule, or as partial suppletion. Where partial suppletion is involved then one way of fixing up the syntactic representation so that the phonology can produce the right output is to modify the UR of the formatives introduced by lexical insertion by means of **readjustment rules**. In SPE these are rules which adjust the syntactic representation so that the phonological rules can operate correctly. One common form of readjustment rule is the kind which introduces irregularities into morphophonemic forms, allowing the phonological rules proper to be stated in a more general form. We will have occasion to speak about the types of readjustment rule which are of relevance to allomorphy in more detail later in this chapter and in chapter 4.

What is true of the passive voice morphology and of agreement morphology is also true of derivational morphology. One example of such morphology of some interest to grammarians was the nominalizations, such as the word *nominalization*, the abstract noun derived from the verb *nominalize* by affixation of *-ation*.

If in *Aspects* sentences with the same meaning were derived from a common underlying deep structure by means of transformations, then the same should be true of sentences and their nominalized forms. Consider the relationship between 3.9 and 3.10:

3.9   Tom gave a rose to Harriet.

3.10   a) Tom's gift (of a rose) (to Harriet)
        b) Tom's giving of a rose (to Harriet)

From what we have said so far we might expect 3.9 and 3.10 to share at least some elements of deep structure, even though 3.9 is a full sentence and 3.10a, b are merely NPs.

There are, of course, a good many differences between 3.10a and 3.10b. One startling difference is the fact that *gift* is idiosyncratic morphologically and phonologically, while *giving* is a gerund form, constructed according to perfectly regular inflectional processes. In addition, not all verbs in English form a nominal along the lines of *gift*. For example, the only nominalization we can create for verbs such as *hand, send, despatch*, are the gerunds. A minimal pair in this respect is *offer* (which has *offer* as its nominalization) and *proffer*, which has only the gerund.

Both the syntactic and the phonological half of TG had a theory of exceptions to call upon, however. It was not difficult, therefore, to ignore the differences between *gift* and *giving* and to concentrate on the similarities, particularly the syntactic similarities. In fact, the phonological component would have little difficulty factoring out the differences between /gift/ and /giv/ and concentrating on the phonological similarities. Thus, it seemed that derivational morphology could be handled both phonologically and syntactically by the machinery independently needed, namely, the theory of syntactic transformations, the theory of phonological transformations, and a theory of exceptionality in each domain.

3.2 Chomsky's 'Remarks on Nominalization': Lexicalist Grammar

3.2.1 *Generative Semantics and lexical transformations*

Generative grammar developed along two rather different paths from the Standard Theory established in *Aspects*. One path was to stress the importance of transformations and use this formal device to express as many relationships between linguistic forms as possible. This led to the appearance of Generative Semantics. The rationale for these developments, together with much interesting historical background and a critique of the theory, are presented in Newmeyer (1980), and I shall not discuss them here. The important points from our point of view are that, in this theory, the level of deep structure is abolished, or, more accurately, identified with semantic structure. In the more sophisticated variants of the theory (e.g. Bach, 1968; McCawley, 1968) the syntactic deep structures of *Aspects* are replaced by something resembling representations in logical calculus (formally, a kind of 2nd order predicate calculus).

The implications this had for morphology were not at first considerable. Inflectional morphology, as we have seen, was regarded as part of the phonological component which served to spell out the phonological realizations of syntactic features (which themselves were distributed by syntactic rules). Derivational morphology was the result of transformations operating over deep structures in which, for instance, a nominalization was represented as an underlying sentence. Lees (1960), working within a theory of generative grammar which predated the *Aspects* theory, already derived compounds transformationally from underlying sentences (see Scalise, 1984: 8ff for a review). Thus, the major phenomena of morphology seemed to come under the purview of syntactic and phonological transformations and the effects of Generative Semantics seemed to reinforce the trend towards making the major phenomena of morphology solely the responsibility of syntax and phonology.

In chapter 1 we saw examples of morphological causatives. Generative Semanticists noticed that a verb such as *kill* in English could be regarded as a kind of causative. Thus, it was argued (most famously by McCawley, 1973) that 3.11a is synonymous with 3.11b:

3.11   a) Tom killed Dick.
        b) Tom caused Dick to die.

If this is true, then we would expect them to share a common underlying structure. In fact, McCawley claimed that sentence 3.12 is three-ways ambiguous, having readings corresponding to 3.13:

3.12   Tom almost killed Dick.

3.13   a) Tom almost did something, the result of which would have been Dick's death.
        b) Tom did something which almost caused Dick's death.
        c) Tom did something to Dick, so injuring him that he almost died.

Therefore, he argued, the underlying form of 3.11a must look something like 3.14 (simplifying McCawley's original representations somewhat):

3.14

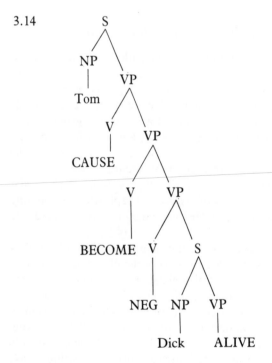

The adverb *almost* could then be placed so as to dominate the whole sentence, or just the VP headed by CAUSE or just the VP headed by BECOME, to obtain representations corresponding to each of 3.13.

To derive 3.11 from 3.14 a lexical transformation ('Predicate Raising') would take the predicate ALIVE and join it to NEG to produce NEG + ALIVE (= 'dead'). This combination would then itself be raised and joined to BECOME to produce 'die', which would further be raised and joined with CAUSE to become 'kill'. In other words, Generative Semantics treated even highly idiosyncratic lexical relationships such as the suppletion between *kill* and *die* as effectively underlain by a kind of 'agglutinative' syntax, in which each element of meaning is represented by an underlying element, such as CAUSE or NEG.

As a theory, Generative Semantics ultimately petered out, but it left its influence on a number of other approaches within generative grammar. In particular, the idea of splitting up a word into its semantic constituents, that is, the notion of **lexical decomposition**, is a continuing theme in studies of lexical semantics and morphology.[2] We will see that, in more recent treatments of derivational morphology, ways have been proposed of capturing the relationships noted by Generative Semanticists while remaining within a thoroughly syntactic framework (particularly the work of Baker discussed in Chapter 7).

3.2.2 *Lexicalism*

For a variety of reasons having more to do with syntax than morphology, the Generative Semantics program proved to be antithetical to the basic research programme which Chomsky inaugurated. The first of Chomsky's replies to Generative Semantics was 'Remarks on nominalization' (Chomsky, 1970). The primary importance of this paper for morphology was that it pointed to the need for a separate theory of derivational morphology, distinct from the theory of syntactic transformations.

Chomsky's 'Remarks' have been ably summarized in several places (including Hoekstra et al., 1980, Newmeyer, 1980; Scalise, 1984), so I will present just a brief résumé. Chomsky argued that transformations should capture regular correspondences between linguistic form, and that idiosyncratic information belonged in the lexicon. This is related to the familiar question of productivity. A syntactic transformation in the ideal case is supposed to capture productive and regular relationships between sentences. For instance, with a handful of systematic exceptions, all transitive verbs in English form a passive. Moreover, in this construction, the complement which is adjacent to the verb in active form always corresponds to the subject of the passive form. Morphologically, of course, passive participles differ from one another, but (nearly) all verbs have an identifiable passive participle and this is always identical in form to the past participle. Finally, the active and corresponding passive sentences have extremely close meanings.[3] Thus, there is something general and regular about the passive relation in English. It is therefore an appropriate candidate for a transformational treatment.

Chomsky contrasted this ideal with the situation found with English nominalizations of the sort illustrated earlier in 3.10a. He called these **derived nominalizations**, since they are traditionally regarded as the result of derivational morphology and therefore contrast with the gerundive nominalizations in *-ing*, which were regarded as the result of inflectional processes.[4] The essence of the argument is that derived nominalizations share many of the properties of words, including monomorphemic words, while the gerundive nominalizations behave more like syntactic collocations. Moreover, derived nominalizations are morphologically, syntactically and semantically idiosyncratic, while gerundive nominalizations are regular and transparent.

Chomsky capitalizes on these differences to argue that it would be wrong to lump the two kinds of phenomenon together by deriving both types from a common source and applying separate batteries of transformations. Only the gerundives can be derived transformationally. The derived nominalizations are not derived at all (!), they are listed in the lexicon. Let's now look at some of these differences in turn.

Syntactic differences: all sentences have a gerundive nominalization, but not all sentences have the expected derived nominalization. More generally, we can say that gerundives **inherit** the subcategorization properties of the verb, while this is not generally true of the derived nominalizations. Thus *amusement* can't have a direct object in 3.15c, unlike the gerundive in 3.15b:

3.15   a) Tom amused the children with his stories.
          b) Tom's amusing the children with his stories ...
          c) *Tom's amusement of the children with his stories ...

Gerundives are modified by adverbials, like verbs, while derived nominalizations are modified by adjectives, like nouns:

3.16   a) Dick sarcastically criticized the book.

          b) Dick's $\begin{Bmatrix} \text{sarcastically} \\ \text{*sarcastic} \end{Bmatrix}$ criticizing the book.

          c) Dick's $\begin{Bmatrix} \text{*sarcastically} \\ \text{sarcastic} \end{Bmatrix}$ criticism of the book.

Semantic differences: the meaning of the gerundive nominalization is always derivable compositionally from that of the underlying verb. In fact, it may be a little misleading to say that a gerundive has a meaning distinct from its verb in the first place; it is simply a nominal form of the verb, used to name the action, state or whatever (with perhaps additional aspectual nuances). Derived nominalizations always seem to add some component of meaning and this is generally unpredictable .[5] For instance, the meanings of *amusement* in 3.17 are something like 'the state resulting from being amused' and 'equipment designed to provide amusement in a fairground etc.'. In neither case is it a 'pure' nominalization of the verb:

3.17   a) Tom's stories provided endless amusement.
          b) The children spent all their pocket money on the amusements.

The gerundive is impermissible in these contexts, 3.18:

3.18   a) *Tom's stories provided endless amusing.
          b) *The children spent all their pocket money on the amusing(s).

Morphological differences: a gerundive can be formed from any verb whatever by adding -*ing*. Derived nominalizations are formed in all sorts of ways and often involve drastic allomorphy or suppletion, and in general the morphological means is unpredictable. Moreover, as we saw earlier, not all verbs have derived nominalizations.

While gerundive nominals are not identical to derived nominals, there are some important similarities. Some of these will become apparent in later sections. One morphological similarity is that derived nominalizations are usually derived from a base which is formally relatable to a corresponding verb. In some cases, it is by simple affixation to the verb, as with *amuse* ⇒ *amusement*. We therefore need a way of capturing these relations in the absence of transformations.

Another similarity is syntactic. In nominalizations such as those of 3.10 (repeated here as 3.20) the possessor expression, *Tom's*, corresponds to the subject of the corresponding sentence, 3.19:

3.19   Tom gave a book to Harriet.

3.20   a) Tom's giving a book (to Harriet).
            b) Tom's gift of a book (to Harriet).

A good many derived nominalizations permit a possessor of this sort to function as a kind of subject. How is this to be represented?

Chomsky's answer to the first problem was to suggest that a theory of the lexicon be constructed in which the relevant relationships could be captured by *lexical redundancy rules*. This was tantamount to a call for a new, generative, theory of morphology. Much of the work which will be described in later portions of this book can be seen as a response to this call.

Chomsky's reply to the second problem was to have far-reaching significance throughout the theory of grammar: he proposed a radical revision to the theory of phrase structure rules. Instead of rules such as 3.21 giving us partial trees such as those of 3.22, he argued for a general rule schema of the type 3.23, which generates a structure 3.24:

3.21   a) S   →   NP   VP
            b) VP   →   V   (NP) (PP)
            c) NP   →   (Det) N   (PP)
            d) Det →   NP

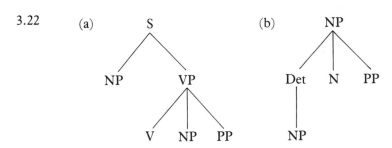

3.22   (a)   S   (b)   NP

                    NP   VP   Det   N   PP

                          V   NP   PP   NP

3.23   a) X″ → SpecX X′
            b) X′ → X (YP) (ZP)

3.24

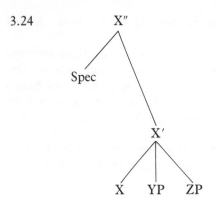

In 3.23, *X* is a variable standing for any major category (N, V, A, P), *X″* ('X-double bar') corresponds to XP (i.e. NP, VP, AP, PP, and also S). The X category is the **head** of the phrase (and, since it represents a word, that is, since it is a lexical category, we call this the lexical head of the phrase). The X′ and X″ nodes are called **projections** from this lexical head. In some varieties of the theory there are at maximum two bar levels, so that X″ represents the **maximal projection**. (In other versions of the theory, the maximal projection of certain categories might involve more bar levels.) The intermediate category *X′* ('X-bar') is an innovation, since no such category is systematically provided for in the theory of phrase structure grammar adumbrated in *Aspects* (though such a thing isn't ruled out either). It also provides the name for the new theory: **X-bar syntax**.

The intermediate X′ category is of great importance, for it allows us to draw a parallel between a verb heading a verb phrase and governing its complements on the one hand and a noun heading a noun phrase and governing its complements. Similarly, we can draw a parallel between the subject of a verb phrase and the determiner of a noun phrase, as in the examples 3.19, 3.20 above. In 3.19 *Tom* is the **Specifier** of the S category (which is assumed to be a special type of maximal projection) and in 3.20 *Tom's* is analysed as the Specifier of the NP category. This means that possessor NPs such as *Tom's*, as well as possessive pronouns such as *my*, *his*, etc., are regarded as a species of Determiner, similar to the definite and indefinite articles, and the demonstratives as in *that hat*. It is now a short step to identify the notion of 'Specifier' with the grammatical relation 'subject' (at least for nouns and verbs).

For syntax, there are many advantages to a theory of this sort and it has been more-or-less universally accepted as a formalization of phrase structure grammar. The theory is of importance to morphology because some have suggested that a phrase structure grammar is the best way to represent word structure, and that means that we would expect the X-bar schema to be applicable to morphology too. I shall discuss proposals of this sort in §6.2.

3.2.3 Concluding remarks on 'Remarks'

'Remarks on nominalization' can be thought of as 'Remarks on derivational morphology' since exactly the same arguments apply to most derivational processes. This is enshrined in a principle formulated by Jackendoff (1972), the **(Extended) Lexicalist Hypothesis**. The content of this is that transformations should only be permitted to operate on syntactic constituents and to insert or delete named items (like prepositions). This means that they can't be used to insert, delete, permute or substitute parts of words. This in turn means that they can't be used in derivational morphology. This principle was adhered to rigidly by the so-called lexicalists (which soon meant most generative grammarians). Moreover, the Lexicalist Hypothesis came to be extended by some to the domain of inflection, too (the **Strong Lexicalist Hypothesis**).

Another important extension followed, as some of the transformations of the Standard Theory were abandoned and replaced by non-transformational devices. For some syntacticians (e.g. Bresnan, 1978; Wasow, 1977) argued that even Passive should be regarded as a lexical relationship, that is, that it should be formalized as a lexical redundancy rule. There are many strong arguments for taking this step (particularly in the case of the 'adjectival' passive) though space doesn't permit me to rehearse them in this book. One of the consequences of this move was the development of a theory of syntax based in the lexicon, Lexical Functional Grammar (LFG).

Even in models which are not as heavily oriented towards the lexicon as LFG, a good many syntactic relationships formerly realized by transformations are treated as statements of lexical redundancy. Even where this trend is partial it threatens to lead to the mirror image of the conceptual problem which Chomsky identified in the Generative Semantics programme. For if everything were to be handled lexically, how could we distinguish between derived nominalizations and gerundives?

The saga of nominalizations illustrates vividly the way that changes in sets of assumptions in one component of grammar (e.g. syntax) will have repercussions for morphology, a point that will be a recurrent theme as we proceed. We will return to the questions raised here later in the book. For the remainder of this chapter we examine the way linguists met Chomsky's call for a theory of generative morphology.

3.3 Halle's 'Prolegomena'

I said in the previous section that Chomsky's 'Remarks' had opened the way to the development of a generative theory of morphology. However, generative grammarians were rather slow to respond to this initiative. One of the earliest, and in many respects most influential, essays in this field came from a linguist who had for a long time been Chomsky's collaborator in the development of generative phonology, Morris Halle.

Halle's (1973) programmatic statement begins by asking how grammatical theory is to answer the following three questions: how does the grammar encode:

(i)   the inventory of actually existing words in the language?
(ii) the order in which morphemes appear within words?
(iii) the idiosyncratic features of individual words?

Behind these questions there are a number of (largely) tacit assumptions. These assumptions will figure in developments to be discussed later and so it is worth teasing them out before we proceed.

The first question conceals the assumption that we are characterizing the knowledge of the ideal language user, not that of ordinary mortals, who, in general, will not actually know all the words in their language. However, there is room for confusion here. Generative grammar is concerned with the grammatical systems of human beings, as represented in the mind of the language user. In Chomsky's more recent terms (Chomsky, 1986b), it is concerned with **internalized language** (or **I-language**). It does not deal with the language itself, what Chomsky calls **externalized language** (or **E-Language**). What we would like to be able to say is that it doesn't matter what the (fixed) vocabulary of the language is and how many real language users know what proportion of it, provided we have some way of distinguishing between existing words and non-words. Nor should it matter to morphological theory that some speakers might have various archaisms, technical jargons, loan words and so on in their vocabulary which are missing from the lexicons of certain other speakers. Where the problem has theoretical significance is when we then try to draw the additional distinction between actual words and potential words (see chapter 2).

The second question seems uncontroversial, though in fact we could refine it a little. Halle observes that the ideal speaker of English knows that the word *transformational* has the morphemic composition *trans + form + at + ion + al*, and that the component morphemes come in the order given: any other sequence, say, **al + ion + at + form + trans*, is impossible. However, in many languages it is possible for morphemes to appear in different orders and for this to be associated with systematic differences in meaning. An example is given by Muysken (1981) in his discussion of word structure in Ecuadorian Quechua. This language has a causative suffix, *-chi*, meaning 'to cause' or 'to allow', and a reciprocal suffix *-naku*. They can occur in either order with respect to each other, with systematic differences in meaning:

3.25   maqa-naku-   ya- chi-   n
        beat REC   DUR CAUSE 3
        'He is causing them to beat each other.'

3.26   maqa-chi-   naku-rka-   n
        beat CAUSE   REC pl.   3
        'They let each other be beaten.'

This type of phenomenon is not especially uncommon in highly agglutinative languages. What it shows is that the grammar must record the significance of morpheme order, whether this means significance for the meaning of the word or significance for the well-formedness of the word itself.

Halle introduces the question of lexical idiosyncrasy by turning to derived nominalizations in English. Words can be idiosyncratic in a variety of ways: semantically (by having some unpredictable aspect to their meaning), phonologically (by being an exception to a phonological rule) and morphologically. Morphological idiosyncrasy is illustrated by the data in 3.27-9. Some of these derived nominals are formed from the suffix *-al*, some from the suffix *-(a)tion* (in some variant) and some from either.

3.27   a) arrival, refusal
        b) *arrivation, *refusation

3.28   a) derivation, description
          b) *derival, *describal

3.29   a) approval, recital, proposal
          b) approbation, recitation, proposition

Halle distinguishes derivational morphology from inflection in his 1973 paper, and he points out that it is not just derivational morphology which exhibits these types of idiosyncrasy. Inflectional morphology is no less wayward. Halle's nicest examples are all from Russian.

Russian nouns, it will be recalled, inflect for case. One of these is the Instrumental, whose basic meaning is 'using *noun* as an instrument'. For instance, the Instrumental form *molotkom* 'with a hammer' is found in *Vanja udaril Sašu molotkom* 'Vanja hit Sasha with-a-hammer'. One of the many other uses of the Instrumental occurs with a lexically restricted set of nouns, including names for seasons, and the words *nočʼ* 'night', and *denʼ* 'day'. Here the Instrumental can be used to mean 'during'. Thus, *leto* 'summer' gives us *letom* 'during the summer', while *denʼ* gives us *dnʼom* 'during the day'. However, a word like *god* 'year', or *maj* 'May', or *vtornik* 'Tuesday' cannot be used in the Instrumental with this meaning. This, then, is an instance of semantic idiosyncrasy in inflection.

Halle offers a somewhat involved example of phonological idiosyncrasy in the stress system of Russian nouns. I shall illustrate his point with a similar, but slightly simpler, example from Czech declension. Czech feminine nouns ending in -*a* in the nominative singular have the declension shown in 3.30a. However, some nouns with a long /a:/ in the root shorten this in oblique cases in the plural, as seen in 3.30b. A handful of nouns apply this shortening only in the genitive plural, 3.30c (length is represented by an acute accent in Czech orthography):

3.30	a) Sg.	Pl.	b) Sg.	Pl.	c) Sg.	Pl.
Nominative	správa	správy	vrána	vrány	jáma	jámy
Genitive	správy	správ	vrány	vran	jámu	jam
Dative	správě	správám	vráně	vranám	jámě	jámám
Accusative	správu	správy	vránu	vrány	jámu	jámy
Prepositional	správě	správách	vráně	vranách	jámě	jámách
Instrumental	správou	správami	vránou	vranami	jámou	jámami
		'repair'		'crow'		'pit'

This means that we have a phonological rule of vowel shortening whose application is governed partly by purely lexical factors. That is, words have to be specially marked in the grammar in some fashion if they are to undergo this rule. Of this subset of words, some will have to be marked only to undergo the rule in the genitive plural, and not in other oblique cases in the plural. Thus, a phonological rule has to have access to the structure of an inflectional paradigm.

Inflectional morphology is notorious for being morphologically idiosyncratic. It is very common to find words in a particular inflectional form taking the 'wrong ending'. The Russian humorist Zoshchenko once wrote a short story about the difficulties a nightwatchman had in ordering a batch of five pokers because he (like most Russians) didn't know the genitive plural form of the word for 'poker'. (Alas for students of Russian, nouns modified by numerals greater than 'four' have to go into the genitive plural.)

On Halle's model, the non-existence of words such as *arrivation or *derival is interpreted as something idiosyncratic. That is, such words are expected to exist and thus we need a special explanation for why they don't. This is to regard *arrivation (and millions of non-words like it) as an **accidental gap**. This is a conclusion some have found suspect, because an accidental gap is usually thought of as a 'hole' in a paradigm, and derivational morphology is not usually considered to operate over paradigms. In inflection, on the other hand, we encounter quite uncontroversial examples of accidental gaps. For instance, some Russian verbs lack a 1st pers. sg. form, even though there is no particularly strong grammatical reason (say, semantic or phonological) for not having such a form.

The model Halle proposes to answer his set of questions is based on the assumption that the lexicon consists of a list of morphemes and that these are concatenated by *word formation rules* (WFRs). However, these rules **overgenerate**. In order to account for the fact that only a subset of the possible morpheme strings are actual or possible words, Halle first postulates a *Dictionary* which lists all the occurring word forms. Idiosyncratic information about words is recorded in rather a brute force fashion by means of a *Filter*. This adds idiosyncratic semantic information, adds diacritic morphophonemic features to block phonological rules from applying, and marks accidental gaps with the feature [-lexical insertion]. This feature doesn't, apparently, prevent the item from entering the Dictionary, but it does prevent it from being inserted into syntactic trees by the lexical insertion transformations. This part of the model is shown in figure 3.2, which includes a box labelled 'Syntax'. This represents the route from Dictionary to deep structures which is realized by lexical insertion.

The *List of Morphemes* is little more than that, a list. However, its members contain a certain amount of useful information. For instance, a morpheme such as *take* will be marked with a morphosyntactic class membership feature such as [+EN] to indicate that it forms its past participle by adding *-en*.

A further task of the WFRs in Halle's model is to compose affixes with bound stems, and record the syntactic category of the output, as shown in examples 3.31:

3.31   [STEM+ant]_A: vac+ant, pregn+ant, mendic+ant, ambul+ant
         [STEM+ity]_N: pauc+ity, prob+ity, credul+ity, serendip+ity

They must also be able to compose affixes with words, taking into account the syntactic category membership of the input and that of the output, as in 3.32:

3.32   a) [VERB+al]_A: recital, appraisal, conferral
         b) [ADJ+ity]_N: serenity, fecundity, obesity

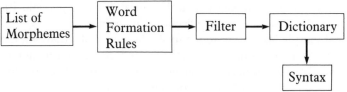

Figure 3.2   Halle's (1973) model (simplified)

In addition to indicating the syntactic category of the output word, some WFRs must add semantic information. For instance, the affix *-hood*, as in *boyhood*, changes a concrete ([-abstract]) noun into a [+abstract] noun. This is a general property of this affix, and not just an idiosyncrasy of certain of the words so derived. Therefore, this fact must be captured by the WFRs, and not in the Filter, for the Filter only adds unpredictable changes in meaning. Finally, some properties of a word are inherited when that word is affixed. For instance, the *-ing* gerundives of English form nominalizations which retain (some of) the subcategorization characteristics of the verb, as in *the giving of money to charity*. In some manner which is not clearly specified, the WFRs are supposed to effect such inheritance, provided it is a general property of the affix.

Halle's model is actually more articulated than would appear from figure 3.2. First, recall that WFRs may combine affixes with words as well as with stems. But the List of Morphemes doesn't contain any words; they reside in the Dictionary. This means there must be a loop linking the WFRs with the Dictionary, so that the WFRs can take words from the Dictionary and add affixes to them.

Halle raises another point which tends to be overlooked in phonological and morphological theorizing, the **phonological conditioning** of morphological rules. From this phenomenon he draws interesting conclusions about the nature of WFRs.

There are two ways in which phonological structure can influence word formation. First, a morpheme may be restricted to combining only with morphemes of a particular phonological form. Halle himself doesn't discuss this situation specifically, but a number of examples are given by Carstairs (1987). In Hungarian the 2nd pers. sg. affix for verbs in the indefinite form of the present tense has two allomorphs, *-ol* and *-(a)sz*. These allomorphs cannot be derived from a common UR by motivated phonological rules of Hungarian. They are thus like the past participle affix allomorphs *-en* and *-ed* (*spoken* vs *walked*) or the plural allomorphs *-z* and *-en* (*cows* vs *oxen*) in English. However, unlike that of the English examples, the distribution of the Hungarian affixes is predictable: *-ol* combines with a stem ending in a sibilant and *-(a)sz* appears elsewhere.

The second type of phonological conditioning occurs when the application of a WFR is determined by the phonological shape of the output of the rule. A familiar example of this is the inchoative affix *-en*, which attaches to adjectives to produce verbs meaning 'cause to be *Adj*' (e.g. *red*⇒*redden*). Now, this affix seems to be subject to phonological conditioning of the first type, since it only attaches to monosyllabic stems and, moreover, only if they end in an obstruent, optionally preceded by a sonorant. Thus we observe the data of 3.33:

3.33   a) quicken   b) *slowen
           redden   *greenen
           roughen   *apten
           shorten   *laxen

However, there are also examples such as 3.34 in which this restriction appears to have been violated, for *-en* has attached to a stem ending in two obstruents, /ft/ or /st/:

3.34   soften, moisten, fasten

The intriguing thing about these examples is that a subsequent phonological rule applies to delete the /t/. Then the *-en* is attached to a stem which respects the phonological condition, namely *sof-*, *mois-* or *fas-*. This means that the condition must be stated as follows: *-en* attaches to monosyllabic stems which will ultimately end in (sonorant plus) obstruent after the operation of phonological rules.

In the Standard Theory all phonological rules apply after all syntactic rules. But the word formation component introduced by Halle strictly precedes the syntax (see figure 3.2). Therefore, in order to state such phonologically defined constraints on surface forms it is necessary to allow the phonology to send words back again to the word formation component.

These two refinements to the model are illustrated in figure 3.3, in which loops from the Dictionary and from the phonological component to the WFR component have been added. This is the final form of Halle's model of word formation.

Halle makes a number of important theoretical observations about this model. First, he says that the WFRs and especially the Filter will have to perform operations which are unlike those performed by standard transformational rules or phonological rules. Second, the organization of the morphological component is different from that standardly assumed in the *Aspects* model, in which a derivation proceeds in a strictly sequential fashion from basic form, through intermediate derived forms, to the final output. In Halle's model, the grammar allows a form to loop back and resubject itself to processes which it has already had the opportunity to undergo. This permits certain grammatical processes a 'global' view of the derivation, since, in effect, they can be triggered or blocked depending on what their later consequences are going to be. Third, the examples of phonological conditioning on outputs suggest that the format of the WFRs has to be different from standard transformations. Although he doesn't formulate the rule in question, Halle says that the grammatical process within the WFR component which accounts for the 'soften' examples must have access to the form which is produced by the phonology. This means that some WFRs, at least, are not just adjoining one morpheme to another, but are a totally different sort of formal operation, namely, a **derivational constraint**. In other words, an affixation rule 'conspires' with the phonological component to ensure that the output of the derivation is constrained so as to comply with a certain canonical form.

The conclusions drawn from this are that WFRs might be grammatical processes of a very different type from those of syntax or phonology. This is seen as an advantage, because it locates all the formally unusual processes in the word formation component, leaving the rules of syntax and phonology in their standard format.

There are a great many questions left unclear in Halle's model, some of which will

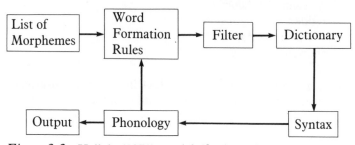

Figure 3.3   Halle's (1973) model (final version)

be broached later in the book. However, the purpose of Halle's paper was not to solve problems so much as to raise central questions in an area which till then had been largely neglected. The fact that all the questions which Halle raised are still the subject of intense debate gives an indication of how successful Halle was in this aim.

3.4   Siegel's level ordering hypothesis

An important feature of generative grammar since its inception has been the use of the mechanism by which rules can be stipulated to apply in a fixed order, that is the mechanism of **extrinsic rule ordering**. However, whenever rule ordering has been invoked it has prompted an adverse reaction in many linguists. One of the more telling arguments against extrinsic ordering is that it is difficult to see how a child can learn in which order the rules are supposed to apply. One way in which we can have our cake and eat it with respect to ordering is to split the grammar into well-defined and well-motivated **blocks**, **components** or **modules**, and establish an ordering between the blocks. This strategy will work perfectly whenever all the rules of the earlier block may or must precede all those of the later block. If the relative ordering of the blocks can be easily related to some other salient property of the grammar, then this type of ordering will presumably not pose a learnability problem.

Putting sets of rules or processes together in the same block might be expected to correlate with other sets of similarities between those processes. This idea was used by Dorothy Siegel (1979) to capture certain commonalities in the phonological and morphological behaviour of affixes in English. In SPE a distinction is drawn between two sorts of affix,[6] associated with different **boundaries**, + and #. Of these, the +(morpheme or 'plus') boundary affixes and the #(word or 'cross-hatch') boundary affixes are the most important for morphological theory. Siegel uses the terms **Class I** and **Class II** respectively to refer to these affixes. She shows that they can be distinguished in terms of their phonological properties and their morphological properties. Commonly cited examples of Class I and Class II affixes are:

Class I suffixes: +ion, +ity, +y, +al, +ic, +ate, +ous, +ive
Class I prefixes: re+, con+, de+, sub+, pre+, in+, en+, be+
Class II suffixes: #ness, #less, #hood, #ful, #ly, #y, #like
Class II prefixes: re#, sub#, un#, non#, de#, semi#, anti#

Phonology distinguishes the two classes of affixes in a variety of ways. The Class I (+ boundary) affixes trigger and undergo phonological processes while the Class II (# boundary) affixes are phonologically inert. Most importantly, Class I suffixes may cause stress shift in the base to which they attach. Class II suffixes never do this (they are **stress-neutral**).

3.35		Class I	Class II
	prodútive	productívity	prodútiveness
	frágile	fragílity	frágileness

Class I affixes may trigger other **non-automatic** phonological processes, that is, processes which depend on precisely which types of morpheme are involved, and are not simply triggered by all forms having a given phonological composition. Class II affixes may only trigger **automatic** processes, i.e. those which apply irrespective of the morphological structure of the word. For instance, the Class I -*ity* triggers a rule of Trisyllabic Laxing, one of whose effects is to turn [ai] into [i]; the Class I -*y* spirantizes /t/ to /s/. However, the Class II -*ness* and Class II -*y* (a homophone of Class I -*y*) don't condition any such changes:

3.36

	Class I	Class II
fatuous	fatuity	fatuousness
frag[ai]l	frag[i]lity	
democrat	democracy	
cat		catty

Class I affixes may undergo non-automatic phonological processes; Class II affixes never undergo phonological processes simply as a result of attaching to their base. An oft-cited example is that of nasal assimilation in prefixes, in which a final /n/ becomes labial (/m/) before a labial (/p b m/) and a liquid (/l r/) before a liquid:

3.37

	Class I	Class II
	inedible	uneatable
but	illegal, *inlegal	unlawful, *ullawful
	impossible *inpossible	unruly, *urruly
	contain	
but	complain *compliant	non-basic
	correct *conrect	non-racial
	(notice also: coincide *conincide)	

Some Class I prefixes attract the stress from the base word to themselves (at least in some words). This doesn't standardly happen with Class II prefixes:

3.38   a) fínite → ínfinite
         b) maríne → súbmarine

There are several ways in which the two types of affix differ morphologically. The class I affixes appear nearer to the root that the Class II affixes when there are members of both classes in a word. This is referred to by Selkirk (1982) as the **Affix Ordering Generalization**. It is this which rules out sequences of Class II + Class I suffixes, as in *hopefulity*, and prefixes, as in *irrefillable*. Class I affixes may attach to stems (i.e. bound morphemes). Class II affixes only ever attach to words:

3.39

Class I	Class II
re-fer	re-fur
flacc-id	child-like
in-ept	un-fair
tortu-ous	motion-less

Notice that the *re-* of *refer* is a different morpheme from the *re-* of *re-fur*. (The latter has a meaning, for one thing.)

These facts suggest that there are systematic differences between the two sorts of affix. Siegel shows how we can account for the stress-neutrality of Class II affixes by assuming that the two types of affixation take place in separate blocks, with Class I affixation occurring first, and assuming that the stress rules apply between the two blocks. This gives the model of 3.40:

3.40   Class I affixation
            Stress rules
            Class II affixation

For instance, to derive *productivity*, we first add together *pro, duct, ive* and *ity* (all Class I). Then we apply the stress rules which tell us that *-ity* attracts stress to the previous syllable to give *productívity*. On the other hand, to derive *productiveness*, we first concatentate *pro, duct* and *ive*, then we apply the stress rules, to give *prodúctive*, and only then do we have the chance to add the Class II suffix *-ness*, giving *prodúctiveness*. Since the affixation of *-ness* occurs 'downstream' of the stress rules, we correctly predict that *-ness* cannot alter the stress already assigned to *prodúctive*.

Following the terminology of Margaret Allen (1978), the boxes are more often referred to as **levels** (or, more recently, **strata**). The claim embodied in Siegel's dissertation is known as the **Level Ordering Hypothesis**.

Allen (1978) observed that when words are concatenated to form compound words, as in *houseboat*, the components of the compound behave rather like Class II affixes, in that they fail either to condition or to undergo non-automatic phonological rules. Moreover, such compounds don't seem to accept Class I or Class II affixes: *passion fruit*, but not **com + passion fruit* or **passion fruit # y*. However, compounds do accept regular inflections, e.g. [[house boat] s], [[over price] ing], [[emulsion paint] ed]. We can explain these facts if we assume that compounding (of words, at least) takes place after Class II affixation but before (regular) inflection. This model is known as the **Extended Level Ordering Hypothesis:**[7]

3.41   Level I (+ affixation)
            Stress rules
            Level II (# affixation)
            Level III (compounding)
            Level IV (regular inflection)

The (Extended) Level Ordering Hypothesis is of great importance in the development of Lexical Phonology (chapter 4). We will discuss the further fate of the hypothesis in chapter 6.

3.5 Aronoff's *Word Formation in Generative Grammar*

3.5.1 The model in outline

The model of word formation proposed by Mark Aronoff (1976) marks a watershed in the development of morphological theory within generative grammar. A good deal of the work done subsequently is an extension of, or reaction to, Aronoff's theory. The model shares certain characteristics with that of Halle, most obviously in assuming the existence of a separate component in the grammar which houses word formation rules. In addition, Aronoff assumes roughly the same model of syntax and phonology as Halle, namely the Standard Theory of *Aspects* as modified in Chomsky's 'Remarks' (1970). However, Aronoff differs from Halle on a number of fundamental points. I shall give a brief overview of Aronoff's model, against the background of Halle's, and then discuss the motivation behind the innovations.

The most important feature of Aronoff's theory is the assumption that word formation rules operate over words and not morphemes, that is, Aronoff adopts a theory of **word-based morphology**. As a consequence, the rules which add affixes to pure stems in Halle's model have no place in Aronoff's. A number of implications flow from this assumption and we will therefore be looking at it in some detail. A second feature is that Aronoff explicitly restricts himself to derivational morphology. This is because he regards all other aspects of morphology, including cliticization (or 'incorporation'[8]) and inflection, as syntactic. Curiously, no mention is ever made of compounding, though one presumes Aronoff would have regarded this as syntactic, too. Finally, Aronoff only considers what can properly be called 'productive' morphological processes. This, too, is an important and rather controversial aspect of his theory, and requires some closer examination.

The typical operation of a WFR, then, is to take an existing word and add an affix to it. However, it may turn out that other phonological changes will occur, in the base, sometimes of a fairly drastic kind. This results in allomorphy which is often lexically or morphologically governed (i.e. only certain words or morphemes undergo it) and which in some cases is substantially different from bona fide phonological alternations.

Aronoff proposes that such alternations be handled not in the phonology but in the word formation component, by means of special rules called **allomorphy rules**. One example discussed by Aronoff is the verb suffix *-fy* as in *electrify*. Words ending in this suffix (fairly) productively nominalize by taking the affix *-ation*. However, the *-fy* is then replaced by an allomorphic variant *-fic*. In SPE this alternation is handled by assuming that the /k/ of *-fic* is present in URs and that it is deleted before a word boundary.

3.42   # # elektri + fi:k # # ⇒ elektri + fi: (⇒ elektrifai)

However, Aronoff argues that this is an arbitrary solution. In effect, we are treating something totally idiosyncratic as though it were formally similar to a regular process (namely, a genuinely phonological alternation). He concludes that it is better to regard such cases as partial suppletion, by writing a rule stating that when *-ation* is added to the suffix *-fy*, the latter is replaced by the *-fic* allomorph.

If word formation is word-based how do we account for the formation of words such as *lubricant*? This word is apparently derived by means of a suffix *-ant*, which has a relatively transparent meaning (viz. 'someone/something that performs the action of VERB-ing'). But the verb in question is *lubricate*. Therefore, word-based morphology predicts that the form should be **lubricatant*. This is not an isolated example. Nearly all verbs ending in *-ate* which allow affixation by *-ant* behave similarly: *negociant*, *officiant*. Exceptions are words like *inflatant* and *dilatant*. However, interestingly, in these words the *-ate* is part of a morpheme (*-flate*, *-late*), whereas in the *lubricant* case it is a morpheme itself. On the basis of a number of examples like this from a variety of languages, Aronoff argues that there must be rules which selectively delete certain morphemes which are adjacent to other morphemes. Such a rule is called a **truncation rule**. It has the general form of 3.43:

3.43 $[[\text{root} + A]_X + B]_Y$
                    1   2   3 $\Rightarrow 1 \quad \emptyset \quad 3$

where X and Y are major lexical categories.

Allomorphy rules and truncation rules both have the function of patching up the phonological form of words which have been produced by WFRs. For this reason (echoing the terminology of SPE) they are collectively called **adjustment rules** (though the SPE term *readjustment rule* tends to be used more commonly). They mediate between the output of WFRs proper and the phonological component and perform some of the messier phonological operations which are handled by supposedly phonological rules in SPE.

Each type of readjustment rule performs drastic operations on words. However, truncation rules are constrained by the schema of 3.43 to delete named morphemes in the environment of other morphemes. Similarly, Aronoff restricts allomorphy rules (which in principle could perform any operation whatever). His characterization is (1976: 98): 'A rule which effects a phonological change, but which only applies to certain morphemes in the immediate environment of certain other morphemes ... ', and such rules 'cannot introduce segments which are not otherwise motivated as underlying phonological segments of the language.' This is a property which is later to appear (within the framework of Lexical Phonology) under the name of **structure preservation**. Under Aronoff's overall assumptions, structure preservation distinguishes allomorphy rules quite sharply from phonological rules proper.

Readjustment rules will be discussed in more depth in Part II, when we explore the implications of Aronoff's assumptions for phonological theory. Now we turn to a more detailed examination of the WFRs themselves, before finally asking what motivated Aronoff's initial assumptions.

3.5.2   *The form and function of WFRs*

I have said that Aronoff assumes a word-based morphology: WFRs are defined solely over words, and those words belong to major syntactic classes (roughly the 'open-ended' lexical classes). Scalise (1984: 40; slightly modified) spells out these assumptions as follows:

1 The bases of WFRs are words.
2 These words must be *existing* words. Thus, a possible but non-existent word cannot be the base of a WFR.
3 WFRs can take as a base only a single word, no more (e.g. phrases) and no less (e.g. bound forms).
4 Both the input and
5 the output of a WFR must be members of the categories N, V, A, P.

We will see later that most of these assumptions have been challenged.

A further important property of WFRs is that they only ever operate over a single type of syntactically or semantically defined base (the **Unitary Base Hypothesis** or UBH). Thus, an affix may attach to members of the category 'abstract noun', or 'transitive verb', but never to a class which can only be defined disjunctively, such as 'either noun or transitive verb'. There are some apparent exceptions to this, such as affixes which attach to either nouns or adjectives. However, within the theory of syntactic features which Aronoff is presupposing it is possible to refer to these as a natural class, that of 'nominals', defined as either of the two categories bearing the feature [+N]. In other cases where a disjunction appears to be necessary, Aronoff argues that we are dealing with two homophonous affixes, and that this can be seen in the difference in properties of the affixes, independently of the different bases to which they attach.

Not only must the base of a WFR be unique but so must the operation (e.g. the affixation) it performs. This means in particular that a WFR can't add a prefix and a suffix simultaneously. Nor could a WFR add one affix and delete another affix, or add an affix and at the same time change a vowel from front to back, or retract the position of stress.

It will be recalled that the WFRs in Halle's model not only defined the syntactic category of the output but also added other syntactic and semantic features such as [+abstract]. In addition they defined the meaning of the new word. The same is true of Aronoff's SFRs. Again, like (some of) Halle's rules, the WFRs will specify the type of boundary which separates the concatenated affix from its base, as well as retaining the internal bracketing. A hackneyed example of such a process is the WFR which attaches the suffix *-er* to verbs to produce an agentive noun with the meaning 'one who VERB-s'. This can be represented as 3.44 (cf Aronoff, 1976: 50)[9]:

3.44 $[[X]_V \# er]_N$ 'one who Xs habitually, professionally, ... '

In word-based morphology rules can't combine bound morphemes to each other, for only words can form the base of a WFR. However, it is clear that there are many words which, while not formed productively by means of WFRs, nonetheless have an articulated structure. English speakers know, for instance, that there is some morphological relationship between words such as *possible, legible, edible, tangible, probable*. Aronoff therefore argues that the WFRs can operate 'backwards' to analyse such words into components such as $[poss + ible]_A$. In this way we can account for the intuition that each word contains a component which contributes some sort of meaning ('such that X can be Y-ed' very roughly), and which determines the syntactic class of the final word. This component is the morpheme *-able*. Since the WFR acts to analyse an existing word and not produce a new one, there is no reason to expect it to identify a proper major class word base in addition to the suffix. All that we know about the stem is that it has the form *poss-*, and in the case of other such stems we may know a little about its meaning, if it has one, and its allomorphy properties.

Aronoff's WFRs, like Halle's, are 'once-only' rules: once a word has been formed, and registered in the dictionary, it can't be unformed. This distinguishes WFRs from syntactic rules (since there is no obvious sense in which sentences, once constructed, are stored). Therefore, WFRs are best regarded as lexical redundancy rules.[10]

3.5.3 *Justifying the model*

Aronoff departs from Halle's model in a number of respects and each of these departures requires some justification. The assumptions we will look at here are:

(i)   only derivational morphology is properly lexical
(ii)   word-based morphology
(iii) the organization of the Dictionary

The essence of Aronoff's model is that WFRs in their productive or synthetic function create new words by adding morphemes to old words. Moreover, in their function as redundancy rules they serve to analyse existing words into their component morphemes. This means that the morpheme has an important role to play, even in this theory. However, the notion 'morpheme' does not include the notion 'exponent of inflectional category', as it does for Halle. Inflectional morphology in Aronoff's theory is properly a part of syntax, and categories such as 'plural', 'genitive case' or 'subjunctive' are morphosyntactic categories and cannot be regarded as morphemes. This stance (which is effectively a return to the *Aspects* position) means that Aronoff is not troubled by problems which beset the structuralist tradition of morphology. We have seen that the Item-and-Arrangement approach to inflection has difficulty handling multiple exponence. This problem arises rather seldom in derivational morphology and so Aronoff can afford to ignore it. Furthermore, neither suppletive forms nor accidental gaps can occur in derivational morphology given Aronoff's assumptions (especially the hypothesis that morphology is word-based).

Aronoff offers several arguments for word-based morphology. The most direct justification is simply that productive processes of derivational morphology don't seem to operate over anything other than words. Other types of word formation, such as acronyms, clippings, blends and so on are not productive in any language according to Aronoff.

A second piece of evidence is theory internal. The operation of phonological rules is sometimes sensitive to the internal constituency of words. Aronoff illustrates this with the example of the contrasting pronunciations of the words *prohibition* and *Prohibition* (in American speech, at least). The former, the standard nominalization of the verb *prohibit*, is pronounced /prohibiʃn̩/, while the latter, referring to the period in American history when alcoholic drinks were illegal, is pronounced /proəbiʃn̩/. The former is the pronunciation expected if the UR is [[prohibit] + ion], while the latter is what is expected if there are no internal brackets. This is because the reduction process which turns the syllable *-hi-* into a schwa is blocked if that syllable bears any degree of stress. In the nominalized form we first apply phonological rules, including stress, to the innermost bracketing (the word *prohibit*), and then apply those rules to the whole word. This is an example of a **cyclic** derivation (see chapter 4). On this second pass through the rules the stress on the syllable *-hi-* therefore blocks the reduction. However, the lexicalized word 'Prohibition' is treated as a single unanalyzed word, so the stress rules never get an opportunity to assign any stress to the *-hi-* syllable and it duly gets reduced.

Backformations[11] provide more evidence for word-based morphology. If we consider a backformation such as *self-destruct* within Halle's model, we see it poses serious problems. The word is formed from the noun *self-destruction*. This noun will be formed from (the URs of) *self* and *destroy* in Halle's system. This means that **self-destroy* is generated as a potential word which is then filtered by receiving the mark [-lexical insertion]. But if **self-destroy* is generated by the WFRs, why does this form not surface when speakers decide to create the verb corresponding to *self-destruction*? In Aronoff's model there is no such problem. The form **self-destroy* never existed at any stage. Moreover, by a principle of least effort, plus the observation of extant word pairs such as *construct–construction*, we can understand that any reasonable strategy for backformation will lead us to *self-destruct* as the most transparent, while morphologically possible, source verb for the noun *self-destruction*.

Perhaps the most powerful support for word-based morphology comes from considerations of meaning. In traditional morphological theory the morpheme was the 'smallest unit of meaning' or, in a different terminological tradition, the 'minimal sign'. However, it seems clear that morphemes can't constitute the 'minimal sign' because sometimes, as in the case of cranberry morphemes, they don't have any meaning. Aronoff strengthens the argument from cranberry morphemes by pointing out that the phenomenon is fairly widespread for an important portion of the English lexicon. There are a great many words in English formed from latinate roots and affixes. Aronoff gives two lists, one for stems (3.45), one for prefixes (3.46):

3.45

X-fer	X-mit	X-sume	X-ceive	X-duce
refer	remit	resume	receive	reduce
defer	demit		deceive	deduce
prefer		presume		
infer				induce
confer	commit	consume	conceive	conduce
transfer	transmit			transduce
	submit	subsume		
	admit	assume		adduce
	permit		perceive	

3.46

re-X	con-X	in-X	de-X
repel	compel	impel	
remit	commit		demit
refer	confer	infer	defer
resume	consume		
receive	conceive		deceive
reduce	conduce	induce	deduce

The problem for a morpheme-as-minimal-sign theory is to find the meaning of each of the prefixes and each of the stems. In some cases it is impossible to relate the meaning of a stem of a word to the meaning of the stem in a different sense of the same word. For instance, what does *-ceive* mean in (either of) the two main senses of *conceive*? We could try to claim that elements like *-ceive* aren't 'real' morphemes in some sense, but this isn't borne out by closer examination. For instance, any verb formed on *-ceive* will have a nominalization in which the *-ceive* part is replaced by the component *-cept*. If *-ceive* is not a morpheme, then the completely systematic *-ceive/-cept* alternation cannot be allomorphy. But if it isn't allomorphy, what is it?

The problem is compounded by the fact that the same argument can be run on all of these stems. Thus, we must accept that -*ceive* and their kin are morphemes even though they don't mean anything.

However, the hypothesis that morphology is word-based hasn't gone uncriticized. Scalise (1984) provides a good summary of the issues.

In many languages it looks as though roots constitute the basis of word formation rather than words. This is particularly true of inflecting languages (Scalise suggests for this reason that we understand the term 'word' to mean 'completed word minus its inflections'). For instance, in Russian we can add an affix -*yv*- to a verb root to give an aspectual meaning of roughly 'to do regularly', as in *igr-yv-at'* from the verb *igrat'* 'to play'. But here we are adding the derivational suffix to a root (and not even a stem, which in this case would be *igra*-). There is no verbal word form with the shape *igr*. This type of morphology is typical of Russian. Of course, even if we do interpret 'word' to mean 'word minus inflections', this means we are committed to finding a principled distinction between derivational and inflectional morphology, a vexed topic. The incorporation process of Chukchee is likewise defined over roots (or occasionally stems) and not words, even though incorporation is essentially a form of compounding. Moreover, even in English, in which the basic form of a word is typically an uninflected root, we find cases such as *cannibalistic* which appears to have been derived from the non-existent word *cannibalist*. Such examples suggest that word formation can be defined over units smaller than the word (i.e. the word *cannibal*, plus the morphemes -*ist*, and -*ic*). On the other hand, if we take certain varieties of English compounding into account, it is clear that word formation processes can include phrases, as in *no waiting zone* or *American history teacher* (on the reading 'teacher of American history'). This will be discussed in more detail in chapters 8 and 10.

In Halle's model all potential words are generated from the List of Morphemes by the WFRs, and those that pass unscathed through the Filter are stored in the Dictionary. Aronoff dispenses with the List of Morphemes and the Filter, and lists only (attested) words. This means that words formed by entirely regular, productive processes are not listed. For instance, Aronoff notes that pretty well any adjective can form an adverb by adding the affix -*ly*. These adverbs are not listed specially, since their existence, their form and their meaning can be predicted from the WFR which creates them.

There is a further reason for rejecting Halle's model of lexical organization. Semantic idiosyncrasy is introduced by the Filter on Halle's model, which has the power to add extra clauses in the semantic characterization of a word. This is fine for cases such as *transformation*, which acquires added nuances of meaning in the terminology of generative linguistics, but this is not the only kind of semantic flux to which words are prone. A word left to its own devices will often acquire new usages which, over time, are likely to become more like new meanings. This is the traditional concept of polysemy, as exhibited by old favourites such as *mouth*. This word may refer (*inter alia*) to the opening of the buccal cavity or to the point where a river joins the sea. Sometimes, meanings drift inexorably apart to the point where all speakers (except etymologists) agree that there are two separate words which just happen to sound alike (homonymy). The two meanings of *bank* (river____ and savings____) used to be examples of polysemy (cognate with the modern word *bench*) but they are not nowadays perceived as semantically related.

The point of this is that Halle's Filter is ill-equipped to account for extreme polysemy or frank homonymy. This is going to cause problems precisely when the
semantic representation of a morphologically complex word bifurcates, so that one
of its meanings is (more-or-less) compositional while the other bears no relation to
the meanings of its component morphemes. Aronoff's example of this situation is the
word *transmission*. The regularly determined meaning is 'act of transmitting', but its
meaning in the technical vocabulary of motor-car engineering is to all intents and
purposes divorced from the source verb *transmit*. For Aronoff this is not a problem.
On its idiosyncratic readings the word *transmission* will be listed in the Dictionary.
Once there, it can drift as much as it likes, just as any other lexically listed word
might.

Lexical listing, then, means adding some sort of idiosyncrasy to a word.
Homonymy is an extreme consequence of lexical listing, in the semantic domain. The
very least that can happen when a morphologically complex word is listed is that
some aspect of the process which produced that word fails to be completely general.
This is to say that the rule ceases to be completely productive in some sense. The
notion of productivity is extremely slippery and Aronoff spends some time expli-
cating it. It would be insufficient, for instance, to say that a WFR W_1 is more productive than a WFR W_2 simply if it produces more words. This will not be helpful if
W_2 applies, say, to adjectives while W_1 applies to nouns and it just happens that there
are lots more nouns than adjectives in the language. More sensible is to adopt a
relativized notion of productivity under which we measure the ratio of the number
of bases which undergo the WFR to the number which in principle are permitted to
undergo it.

Aronoff sets up an experiment to investigate productivity. He compares two very
similar affixes, #*ness* and +*ity*, and the result of attaching them to a constant set of
bases, namely those ending in another affix, *-ous*. This produces four interesting
reflexes of lowered productivity among the +*ity* words, distinguishing them from the
#*ness* words.

The first reflex is phonological. No phonological idiosyncrasy is observed with
#*ness* words, whereas +*ity* induces two types of phonological peculiarity which
cannot be attributed to any more general rules of morphophonemics.[12] First, +*ity*
always attracts the stress to the previous syllable. Thus, we have *cúrious* but *curiósity*.
Second, +*ity* induces the wholesale loss of the *-ous* morpheme in some words (a case
of truncation): *various–variety*.

The first reflex also provides an example of the second reflex: lexical government.
Not all *-ous* words undergo truncation with +*ity*, and for most words there is no
way of telling which words do and which words don't truncate (compare *nebulous–
nebulosity* with *credulous–credulity*). Therefore, such words have to be marked
lexically to indicate whether they truncate or not.

A third reflex is semantic. All the words of the form *Xousness* mean each of the
following three things:

3.47   a) 'The fact that Y is Xous', e.g. 'His callousness surprised me'.
          b) 'The extent to which Y is Xous', e.g. (again) 'His callousness sur-
             prised me'.
          c) 'The quality or state of being Xous' e.g. 'Callousness is not a vir-
             tue'.

Thus, the meaning of the derivate is transparently a composition of the meaning of the stem and that of #*ness*. Aronoff calls this 'semantic coherence'. The *Xosity* words in some cases have, additionally, idiosyncratic meanings. Some of Aronoff's examples of idiosyncratic meaning are given in 3.48:

3.48   a) There are several *varieties* of fish in the pond.
        b) They admired his dress, but only as a *curiosity*.
        c) The *continuities* for next week's episode ...

Finally, let us return to the question of lexical government. We have seen that +*ity* affixation is less productive with -*ous* words than is #*ness* affixation, and this has been linked to the fact that +*ity* affixation affects phonological form, is not semantically 'coherent' and is lexically governed. Lexical government affects productivity very directly, for it entails that some -*ous* words simply fail to accept +*ity* for completely arbitrary reasons.

However, there is one set of cases in which failure to affix +*ity* is non-arbitrary and this is illustrated in 3.49:

3.49   glorious   *gloriosity   gloriousness
        furious   *furiosity   furiousness
        gracious   *graciosity   graciousness
        fallacious   *fallacity   fallaciousness
        acrimonious   *acrimoniosity   acrimoniousness

In each case +*ity* affixation is disallowed. But this can be linked to the fact that for each of the adjectives *glorious*, etc. there already exists a corresponding noun, namely those of 3.50:

3.50   glory, fury, grace, fallacy, acrimony

In fact, whenever a corresponding underived noun already exists, the +*ity* form is impossible. Aronoff assumes that the lexicon eschews complete synonymy between its entries as far as possible. In other words, there will only be one 'slot' in the Dictionary for the noun corresponding to, say, *glorious*. Since this slot is filled by *glory*, there is no room for *gloriosity*. This phenomenon is referred to as **blocking**.

Why, then, can *gloriousness* and its ilk be formed? This is because these words are generated by fully productive WFRs, unfettered by lexical government. Therefore, such words are not actually listed in the lexicon. Since they are not listed it is not possible for their places to have been usurped. Therefore, it is impossible to block *gloriousness*.[13]

Aronoff's main conclusions concerning productivity can be summarized simply (1976: 45):

(i)   [P]roductivity goes hand in hand with semantic coherence.
(ii) The listing of the output of a WFR in the lexicon leads to a loss in productivity.

These conclusions follow naturally from the assumptions Aronoff makes about the organization of the lexicon.

3.6   The 'classical' model of generative morphology: conclusions

To conclude Part 1 of the book I shall summarize the model Halle proposed as a point of departure for introducing the way morphological theorizing has developed subsequently. In summary form, the questions Halle raises, implicitly or explicitly, are the following:

(i)   How is the structure of a word represented in a grammar?
(ii)   If there is a separate grammatical component for morphology, how does it interact with other components (the lexicon, syntax, phonology, semantics)?
(iii)   What do WFRs apply to (morphemes? words? something else?)?
(iv)   What is the format of WFRs and what aspects of linguistic structure do they have access to?
(v)   How are idiosyncrasies in word structure to be accounted for?
(vi)   How is the existence of a word represented in the grammar? Is there a distinction between 'actual' word in a language and 'potential' word?
(vii)   Is there a role for the notion 'inflectional paradigm'?

Halle's answer to these questions were:

(i)   The structure of words is represented by WFRs.
(ii)   The word formation component is effectively a part of the lexicon. This means that it serves to feed the syntactic component, through the operation of lexical insertion. The syntactic component is interpreted itself by the semantics and the phonology. However, the phonology is allowed to feed back into the lexicon.
(iii)   WFRs apply both to words and to (bound) stems.
(iv)   WFRs have access to, and can alter, syntactic category information, semantic features, and internal constituent structure.
(v)   Idiosyncratic information about a morpheme such as its ascription to a morphological class is listed with the morpheme itself. Other idiosyncrasies are added by a Filter, placed between the WFRs and the Dictionary. Included in its operations is the function of marking accidental gaps, or non-existent forms which might otherwise be expected to occur (overgeneration).
(vi)   There is a distinction between 'potential' and 'actual' words. The morphology generates all the potential words, of which a large proportion may be discarded by the Filter. Words formed by WFRs and not so discarded are all listed in the Dictionary.
(vii)   Morphology must recognize the notion of 'inflectional paradigm'.

These answers have all been the subject of intense debate. As we have seen, claim (iii) has been rejected by Aronoff, though it is accepted by many other morphologists. Aronoff, in effect, rejects the claim that WFRs have privileged access to internal constituent structure, claiming that cyclicity effects are a consequence of word-based morphology. Aronoff also rejects the idea that all words which are well-formed are necessarily listed (point (vi)).

The very existence of a separate morphological component with WFRs ((i)) has been questioned, e.g. by Pesetsky (1985) and by Sproat (1985a). Of those who accept the claim for a separate component, some have maintained that word formation may also take place in the syntax (e.g. Baker, 1988a), and Anderson (1982) builds a model in which much inflectional morphology is constructed in the phonology component. Borer (1988) and Shibatani and Kageyama (1988) have also rejected the idea that the morphological component is restricted to the lexicon ((ii)).

Many different theories have been advanced concerning the types of information that WFRs have access to ((iv)). Of particular importance for phonology is the question of internal constituent structure and cyclicity. The theory of Cyclic Phonology (cf. Mascaró, 1976) and later Lexical Phonology (Kiparsky, 1982a) are based on these ideas (see chapter 4).

In many ways, the problem of idiosyncrasy ((v)) is one of the core issues in morphology. Different types of idiosyncrasy (purely morphological, morphophonological, morphosyntactic, semantic) have been handled in different ways within different theories, as we shall see. The idea of an all-powerful Filter has been fairly unanimously rejected. However, this doesn't mean complete rejection of the idea that components of a grammar might perform a filtering function of some sort. Finally, there are divided opinions about the notions of 'actual' and 'potential' words, and the related issues of 'productivity' ((vi)). These questions become particularly acute when the domain of morphology is no longer restricted, as in Aronoff's model, to derivation, but includes such phenomena as inflection, compounding, noun incorporation, and cliticization.

These are the questions that Halle addressed. Equally interesting, in some respects, are the questions he doesn't raise. Of the traditional concerns discussed in chapters 1 and 2 the most obvious omission is discussion of what constitutes a word in the first place. The notion is simply taken for granted, but it remains no less problematic, as Di Sciullo and Williams (1987) have stressed more recently. The problem of wordhood finds reflexes in another question Halle doesn't mention, namely the status of the distinction between inflection, derivation and compounding. Recall that many of the conundrums concerning the definition of wordhood centered around compounds, and they pose a big problem for Halle's model (cf. Booij, 1977). It should not be surprising that compounds have been the subject of intense research. Halle explicitly lumps inflection together with derivation and regards them as reflexes of the same phenomenon, namely affixation. This assumption was explicitly rejected by Aronoff and a number of morphologists have followed his suit, placing derivation and inflection in totally disjoint components of grammar. For instance, in Anderson's Extended Word-and-Paradigm theory (see chapter 6), derivation is lexical, but inflection is part of the phonological component, fed by the syntax. In those theories which incorporate Siegel's Level Ordering Hypothesis, less drastic ways are found of separating the two. Rather curiously, although Halle doesn't distinguish derivation and inflection, he does suggest (albeit tentatively) that there might be a role for the notion of 'paradigm' in generative grammar. This idea has been exploited in two subsequent approaches to inflection, that of Anderson (1982) and that of Carstairs (1987) (as well as proponents of 'Natural Morphology', such as Wurzel, 1984).

It is likely that one could raise all these questions about Halle's model, and debate them fiercely, even if everything else in grammatical theory were held constant and the Standard Theory of *Aspects* remained unchanged. However, every conceivable facet of syntax, phonology and semantics has been subjected to scrutiny during the period of development of generative morphology. Another glance at Halle's model will remind us that only slight changes in the organization of other grammatical components might cause us to completely rethink morphology. Indeed, one of the main reasons why morphology is a significant domain for contemporary theory construction is precisely because it is necessary to bear in mind the implications of changes elsewhere in the overall theory of grammar.

We have already seen one example of this interdependence in the implications for morphology of the theory of Generative Semantics (a theory which was ultimately rejected by most generative grammarians). However, other changes, or proposed changes, remain pregnant with meaning for morphology. For those readers who are familiar with the relevant concepts from other areas of linguistic theory, the changes include the following:

thematic roles (θ roles) have to be represented in the grammar (see chapter 6, §6.1.3, chapters 7, 8)
lexical insertion is performed at S-structure (see chapters 6, 9)
some or all of the traditional (cyclic) syntactic transformations are lexical rules, relating items listed in the lexicon (see chapters 6, 7)
a generalized movement rule ('Move-alpha') applies at all levels of syntactic structure, including, perhaps, the lexicon (see chapters 7, 8, 10, 11)
phonological processes applying to words as opposed to phrases take place in the lexicon (see chapters 4, 9)
phonological representations are 'multidimensional', and not linear as assumed in SPE (see chapter 5).

Not all these assumptions characterize any given approach to generative grammar, and some approaches may remain agnostic about some of these proposals. However, it turns out that each of them will have implications for the construction of a theory of morphology.

EXERCISES

3.1   Nominalizations in *-ing* may have idiosyncratic readings. Provide a listing of as many as possible and compare them with derived nominalizations. Do your findings affect Chomsky's argument in any way? If so, how?

3.2   Enumerate as many as you can of the morphological devices used to produce derived nominalizations. Which of these are most likely to show the same subcategorization properties as the source verbs (i.e. which take the same set of complements)?

3.3   Not all derived nominalizations have corresponding verbs. Think of some examples. How might the existence of such cases affect Chomsky's argument?

★3.4 The derivation of *kill* from underlying *cause to become not alive* is a *locus classicus* in the development of Generative Semantics. Take Chomsky's arguments against a syntactic (transformational) treatment of derived nominalizations and run them on causatives of adjectives. You will need first to provide a reasonably representative compilation of causatives derived from adjective roots. [You will find it helpful to consult Chomsky (1970) for the theory, and Marchand (1969) for the data].

3.5 Take a representative sample from the literature of Class I and Class II affixes (the ones I have cited will do for starters. A useful source of data is the affix index of SPE). Which of them follow all the criteria for membership of their class? Do any affixes give ambiguous results?

★3.6 Kiparsky claimed that irregular inflection takes place at Level I and that, given the Extended Level Ordering Hypothesis, we can therefore explain why we find irregular plurals inside compounds (the 'teeth marks' cases).

Test out the generality of Kiparsky's claim by (i) constructing a list of all the types of compound that can be formed from combinations of N, V, A; (ii) examining the behaviour of irregular inflections for these parts of speech with respect to compound formation.

★3.7 For the following expressions, indicate the constituent structure which is implied by their meaning. What implications do your analyses have for morphology and for the Level Ordering Hypothesis in particular?
transformational grammarian   forty-ninth
nuclear physicist   lieutenant-colonelcy
workman-like   square sectional
sub-postmaster   set theoretic
South American   re-air-condition

3.8 Aronoff notes that a handful of adjectives fail to form adverbs in -*ly*, e.g. *good*. He suggests that this is because of the existence of *well*. Explain why this explanation is at odds with Aronoff's other assumptions.

3.9 For each of the major lexical categories of English (N, V, A) find two productive WFRs which derive the same or another of the categories. (There are three input and three output categories so you should look for $2 \times 9 = 18$ different WFRs.)

3.10 Aronoff's list of latinate cranberry morphemes isn't complete. Complete it.

3.11 Aronoff adduces an argument very similar to the argument from -*ceive* morphemes using the example of the verb *stand*. This has at least two different syntactic subcategorizations (as in (1) and (2)) and at least two totally different meanings (cf. (1), (2) and (3)). Moreover, the same morpheme seems to turn up in yet more senses when prefixed ((4), (5)):

(1) We stood there for a while.
(2) We stood the chairs in a corner.
(3) I stood it as long as I could, and then I left.
(4) I understood the question
(5) My double-glazing withstood the blast.

However, we seem to be dealing with just one morpheme here, because in each case it shows the same allomorphy in inflection (*stand–stood–stood*).

Is this an isolated phenomenon? Investigate it by checking the different meanings (polysemy or homonymy) of the 200 or so English strong verbs. How could you check if for the other categories?

3.12 Think of other examples of 'transmission' words. What factors lead to this situation in language change?

*3.13 The only WFRs which can be used as redundancy rules are those which are also used as productive rules. Discuss this assumption with reference to the words in the following two lists:

(i) enlarge, embolden, enrich, embitter
(ii) encumber, enthrall, enchant, encompass, endure, enforce

Is there a WFR at work here? If so, is it productive in any sense? Does it apply in both sets of words? How do your answers to these questions relate to Aronoff's theory?

*3.14 Carefully examine Aronoff's arguments in favour of word-based morphology. Which of them provide additional arguments against Halle's Filter.

3.15 Word formation from stems: how are the words in list (a) formed? Is the process in any sense productive? To what extent and in what ways do these data resemble the 'mit' morpheme cases (as in 'commit')? When people (usually scientists) coin words of this type, what governs their choice? Are the constructions of list (b) actual words? Are they morphologically well-formed? Could they mean anything, and if so what? Do your answers to these questions support or undermine word-based morphology? [You may find it interesting to compare the list (a) examples with N-N compounds of the kind 'sound image', 'blood cell', 'eye probe', 'light meter', 'fingerprint' and the list (b) examples with the nonce formations: 'cell print', 'measure science', 'eye cell', 'blood meter'.]

List (a):
morpheme, lexeme, phoneme, phonaestheme, toneme, chroneme, grapheme
photograph, telegraph, sonograph, micrograph
telegram, sonogram
photometry, telemetry, micrometry, ophthalmometry
telescope, microscope, ophthalmoscope, hydroscope
cytology, haematology
haemocyte, leucocyte, melanocyte, phagocyte
cytophage, bacteriophage
cytolysis, electrolysis, hydrolysis

List (b):
cytograph, metrology, ophthalmocyte, haemometer

*3.16   N-N compounding and productivity; NV conversion:

(a) Two nouns can be compounded more or less without restriction to form a compound noun whose precise meaning will usually depend on pragmatic factors. At the same time, there are many idiosyncratically formed N-N compounds whose meaning may be very different from that of their components (e.g. *housewife*, *ladybird*), or which may exhibit phonological idiosyncrasy (e.g. the vowel reduction and cluster simplification in *postman*). Furthermore, some discussions of lexical semantics have hinged on the synonymy of expressions such as *optician* and *eye doctor*.

(b) A morphologically simple noun can be used as a verb more or less without restriction, the precise meaning usually depending on pragmatic factors. At the same time there are instances of verbs derived by N to V conversion (one of) whose meaning(s) may not be readily derived from that of the base (e.g. *to table*, *to chair*, *to carpet*), and some which exhibit phonological changes (e.g. *to house*). Moreover, some of these words seem to be synonymous in all their uses with pre-existing words (e.g. *to house–accommodate*).

Do either of the sets of observations in (a) or (b) pose problems for Aronoff's conception of lexical organization? If not, how are they explained? If so, how might you modify Aronoff's theory to accommodate (or house?) them?

*3.17   The Unitary Base Hypothesis is an empirical hypothesis which is falsifiable by finding a single affix which concatenates with two types of base which can only be characterized disjunctively. At the same time, every WFR yields a unique category of word, whose meaning is a compositional function of the meaning of the base. Assess the empirical import of the UBH by listing a reasonably large collection of syntactic categories and subcategories and then constructing suitable pseudo-WFRs with feasible semantics for disjunctions defined over your list. On the basis of your experiment, to what extent can you derive the UBH from other principles?

PART II

The Morphology–Phonology Interface

4

Approaches to Allomorphy

Introduction

Our discussion of the morphology–phonology interface opens with the 'classical' position adopted in SPE. The rest of the chapter charts reactions to various aspects of the SPE system. The theory of Natural Generative Phonology, which we touch upon in §4.2, argued for much less 'abstract' and more 'concrete' analyses, playing down the notions of 'underlying representation' and 'phonological derivation'. In §4.3 we trace the development of the highly influential theory of Lexical Phonology, from its precursors in the early work of Kiparsky, via the notion of Cyclic Phonology. The next section reviews a different approach to morphophonemics, which emphasizes the morphological function of allomorphic variation and questions the assumption that morphophonemically determined allomorphy should be handled in a purely derivational fashion. In §4.5 we briefly survey the views of Dressler, the most influential of the Natural Morphologists, who argues for a separation of role types to reflect function with respect to allomorphy. In the final section we consider the proposals advanced by Zwicky to account for allomorph selection outside the lexicon, in the syntax.

4.1 The SPE model

We have seen that in the Standard Theory (figure 3.1, chapter 3) the generation of a sentence starts with a syntactic deep structure. From this a surface structure is generated by means of transformational rules. This surface structure consists of morphemes in their underlying phonological form. These forms are then subject to phonological rules which ultimately specify the pronunciation of those morphemes. In this model morphology as such plays no role: the order of morphemes is determined by syntactic rules and the different shapes assumed by morphemes are accounted for solely by the phonological rules. Only the most drastic types of allomorphy (i.e. partial or total suppletion) are handled by means of readjustment rules. In chapter 3 I pointed out that Aronoff (1976) proposed that some of the allomorphy which was derived by means of highly idiosyncratic phonological rules in SPE should be handled by means of readjustment rules (especially allomorphy rules) but the general picture remains the same even on Aronoff's model.

The phonologically based approach is ideally suited to handling automatic alternations, that is, alternations which can be defined purely in terms of the phonological context. We saw an example of this in §2.3.2, when we compared IA and IP approaches to neutralization. The famous case of German final obstruent devoicing is another example worth looking at briefly.

By assuming a general rule which devoices a voiced obstruent word finally, we can easily account for the alternations of 4.1 by assuming the underlying representations (URs) of 4.2, since the devoicing rule can only apply to /bund/, not to /bund + es/:

4.1   a) bunt 'colourful'   buntes 'idem. gen. sg. masc.'
       b) bunt 'union'   bundes 'idem. gen. sg.'

4.2   a) /bunt/   /bunt + es/
       b) /bund/   /bund + es/

Languages frequently show allomorphic variation which is non-automatic, but rather is **morpholexically conditioned** (i.e. triggered only by specific morphemes, morphological classes or specific words). This means that it is limited to a particular class of items or limited to particular morphological contexts. A commonly cited case is German **umlaut**. This refers to a phonological process in which back vowels or diphthongs are fronted. It is represented orthographically by placing a diaeresis over the vowel or diphthong umlauted. There are several ways of forming plurals of nouns in German, some of them dependent on the phonological shape of the stem, some dependent on the morphological class which the noun belongs to (for instance, whether it is masculine, feminine or neuter in gender). Many nouns undergo umlaut in the plural (sometimes in addition to receiving an affix such as -e or -er). However, in general it is not predictable which nouns are umlauted and which not. Thus, *Lauch* 'leek' has plural without umlaut, *Lauche*, while in the word *Bauch* 'belly' we see umlaut in the plural, *Bäuche*. The umlauting alternation is conditioned by the grammatical category of plural, and not by the -e affix, since we observe exactly the same thing in words which do not have an affix in the plural, e.g. *Onkel* 'uncle', plural *Onkel* without umlaut, as opposed to *Apfel* 'apple', with umlaut in the plural, *Äpfel*. Moreover, a variety of other inflectional and derivational contexts condition umlaut in this way, again with exceptions for particular lexical items.

It is possible to write a phonological rule which relates back vowels to umlauted front vowels. Therefore, since the alternation can be described phonologically in the classical approach we would write a rule of umlaut in the phonology and make sure it was triggered by particular contexts. In some cases, we could say that a particular affix triggered umlaut. For instance, it is generally the case that the adjectival affix -*lich* and the feminine affix -*in* umlaut a back vowel stem. Thus, from *Bauer* 'farmer' we obtain *bäuerlich* 'rural', and *Bäuerin* 'farmer's wife'. However, this is not always the case, since, for example, *Bau* 'building' gives us *baulich* 'architectural' and not *★bäulich*.

Since generative phonologists and morphologists never reached a consensus about how to handle inflectional morphology there was no widely agreed way to handle such alternations. However, one way would have been to say that certain affixes, including the plural endings *-e* and *-er* and the derivational affixes *-lich* and *-in*, were marked by means of a feature which triggered the phonological umlaut rule, say, [+U]. The underlying forms of words like *Onkel* and *Apfel* in the plural would be marked with an unpronounced feature [+plural] by syntactic inflectional rules, and this feature could also be associated with the [+U] feature. Words which failed to undergo umlaut in these contexts would then have to be marked with an exception feature, which would override the [+U] umlaut trigger. Notice that on this analysis it is the failure to undergo umlaut which is regarded as exceptional. Although umlaut is not an automatic phonological rule, it would be regarded as the regular case on this analysis. We can call this general approach to non-automatic allomorphy the 'rule feature' approach.

In the German umlaut case there are grounds for saying, then, that umlaut is the regular condition. In other cases, it is only a minority of items which undergo a particular rule. In English, for instance, we observe a vestige of earlier Germanic umlaut in plural formation in words such as *feet, teeth, geese*. We can describe this alternation phonologically as the fronting of a high back vowel to a front vowel. However, it only applies to these three items:[1] **yeeth* isn't the plural of *youth*, nor is **meese* the plural of *moose*. In this case, then, it is the roots themselves which have to be marked with a diacritic feature to trigger 'umlaut' in the plural. A rule of this sort, which is only undergone by a smaller number of items, is called a **minor rule** (cf. Lightner, 1968), and the feature which triggers it is a minor rule feature. In the framework of Aronoff, it is possible to reanalyse many minor rule alternations not as phonological rules but as allomorphy rules. However, the general tendency has been to write a phonological rule wherever possible. Moreover, there aren't any hard-and-fast criteria for distinguishing allomorphy rules from minor rules, so the choice has often been decided by determining which solution provides the neatest grammar overall (with the assumption that one should fall back on allomorphy rules only as a last resort). Furthermore, the difference between the 'rule feature' approach illustrated by German umlaut, and the 'minor rule feature' approach is somewhat arbitrary, since there are situations in which the forms which fail to undergo the rule are roughly as numerous as those which do undergo it. It then makes no sense to ask which is the regular case and which the irregular (cf. Kenstowicz and Kisseberth, 1979, for an example of this sort from Russian stress in verbs).

Classically, generative phonologists have tried to use rule features as sparingly as possible. The usual tactic when confronted with two forms which look identical on the surface but which differ in their phonological behaviour is to assume that they have distinct underlying forms. This phonological difference in UR can then be used to trigger particular phonological rules in certain environments, say, when the morpheme is next to certain morphemes but not others. In this way, what appears superficially to be morphological or lexical conditioning of a phonological rule is actually treated as phonologically conditioned allomorphy, of the kind illustrated by the German *bunt ~ bund* case above. Frequently, such an analysis bears a close resemblance to the presumed historical development.

This solution is available when a given morpheme is regularly associated with some process, either by triggering it or by undergoing it. Let's look at an example which was influential in establishing the SPE approach over its competitors. The Slavonic languages exhibit complex patterns of alternations in which a vowel seems to disappear. Examples of such vowel–zero alternations are provided in 4.3, 4.4 for different case forms of Czech nouns:

| 4.3 | a) les | lesa | 'nom. sg. ~ gen. sg., forest' |
| | b) pes | psa | 'nom. sg. ~ gen. sg., dog' |

| 4.4 | a) konzerva | konzerv | 'nom. sg. ~ gen. pl., tin can' |
| | b) barva | barev | 'nom. sg. ~ gen. pl., colour' |

In contexts where vowel–zero alternations are found we often find palatalizations of particular sorts, too. For instance, the diminutive affix *-ek* has an alternating vowel, and it also conditions a palatalization of velars, e.g. turning /k/ to /č/:[2]

4.5	a) pták	'bird'
	b) ptáček	'(diminutive)'
	c) ptáčka	'(diminutive, gen. sg)'

Some nouns seem to licence a double diminutive formed from *-ek* + *-ek*. In this case the first affix, ending in a velar, is palatalized so that the affixes together take the form *-eček*:

4.6	chvíle	'moment'
	chvilka chvilek	'nom. sg. ~ gen. pl.'
	chvilečka chvileček	'nom. sg. ~ gen. pl.'

Interestingly, the first *e* of the compound *-eček* affix never alternates, even though the *e* of a single *-ek* and the second *e* of *-eček* do alternate. This on the surface is a bewildering patterning of data: why do we have some *e*'s which never alternate (as in *les*), some which always alternate (as in *pes*) and others which only alternate when final in the world (as in *-ek*)?

The traditional generative solution is a phonological one (reflecting the history of the process).[3] We assume that the vowel which underlies the alternating *e*'s (but not the non-alternating *e*'s) is a vowel which only ever appears in URs, never in surface forms. In fact, Slavicists generally assume there are two such vowels, called 'jers' (or 'yers'). These are high vowels like /i ɨ u/ but differ from them in having a lax articulation. In the formalism of SPE distinctive feature theory we would say that they bear the features [+high, -tense]. One of the jers is a front vowel (/ĭ/) and this triggers certain palatalizations. The other is a back vowel (/ɨ/).

A jer is either lowered to [e] or deleted depending on the environment. The basic generalization is that if two jers occur in adjacent syllables, then the one on the left is lowered. In all other cases, the jer is deleted. The rule is shown informally in 4.7:

$$4.7 \qquad \begin{bmatrix} +\text{high} \\ -\text{tense} \end{bmatrix} \Rightarrow \begin{cases} e & / \underline{\hspace{1em}} C_0 \begin{bmatrix} +\text{high} \\ -\text{tense} \end{bmatrix} C_0 \\ \emptyset & / \text{ elsewhere} \end{cases}$$

Thus, in the gen. sg. of *pes*, i.e. *psa*, we have a UR /pĭsa/, and in the nom. sg. of *barva* we have the UR /barɨva/. These contain only one jer, which is by definition last of its sequence, so it deletes. Why then doesn't the same jer delete in the nom. sg. *pes* or the gen. pl. *barev*? We just need to assume that the masc. nom. sg. and the fem. gen. pl. endings are themselves jers (in fact, back jers). Then the URs for *pes* and *barev* will be /pĭsɨ/ and /barɨvɨ/ respectively. The first jer in each word meets the structural description of the lowering part of rule 4.7 and hence it will surface as [e] just as we require.

There are several important aspects to this approach to vowel–zero alternations. First, it relies on two 'abstract' underlying segments, the jers (recall that these undergo absolute neutralization; see §3.1.2 for these terms). In this case we can justify the abstraction because it allows us to account for palatalizations in a unified way as well as the vowel-zero alternations (Gussman, 1980, argues this point at some length). Second, the masc. nom. sg. and fem. gen. pl. 'affixes' are represented by phonological forms which never surface, because they are never followed by a morpheme containing a jer. It is as though the entire affix has undergone absolute neutralization. That is, an abstract phonological element is being used to represent a morphological category (i.e. a gender/case/number category).

This latter observation reflects two things: first, the tendency to code morphological idiosyncrasy in phonological terms where possible; second, the tendency for generative phonological analyses to maintain agglutinative morphology in URs wherever possible. In other words, at the level of underlying form, the SPE approach to allomorphy presupposes an Item-and-Arrangement theory of morphology. The second point to observe is that, whatever the means used to code allomorphy, whether allomorphy rules, minor rules, diacritically triggered rules, rules triggered by morphological categories, or abstract phonological rules such as Jer Lowering and Deletion, the phonological operations are invariably applied *after* the morphological operations (i.e. the operations of affixation).

We will see later that some affixation processes seem to be sensitive to the phonological form of the stems to which the affixes are attached. The SPE organization will only permit this if the phonological sensitivity can be stated at the level of UR. There is no way for an affix to be restricted to stem allomorphs which have undergone a phonological rule. Putting this another way, phonologically sensitive affixation cannot be sensitive to derived allomorphy. We will return to the significance of this implication later in the chapter.

4.2 Natural generative phonology

For many linguists the basic premises of the generative approach with respect to morphology and allomorphy remained unchanged for the ten years following the publication of SPE. In particular, the assumption that morphology precedes all phonology was never challenged. However, two proposals were made by separate groups of researchers for modifying the highly abstract approach of SPE, and these explicitly dealt with questions of allomorphy. The first of these modifications was part of a much wider challenge to the edifice of SPE, namely **Natural Generative Phonology** (NGP).

In Natural Generative Phonology (Hooper, 1976), a strong claim is made about allomorphy, namely that all alternants of a morpheme must be possible surface forms. This means amongst other things that absolutely neutralized underlying segments such as jers are excluded. NGP also excluded the possibility of ordering rules extrinsically with respect to each other. This too had implications for the type of rule systems which could be written to describe morphophonemics. In practice it meant much greater morphological conditioning of phonological rules, and this was seen as a disadvantage by generativists in precisely those cases in which an abstract analysis seemed to account neatly for a whole range of phonological phenomena.

As far as allomorphy is concerned, NGP returned to a position which was essentially that of structural linguistics, for certain types of allomorphy at least. Consider a favourite example, the English umlauted plurals such as *goose* - *geese*, and *man* - *men*. A generative phonological account of these alternations would take one form as basic and derive the other by a minor rule. Alternatively, it might postulate some third form as UR (possibly with an 'abstract', non-occurring underlying vowel) and derive both singular and plural forms by means of special rules. Hudson (1974), however, suggested, on the basis of an analysis of the Semitic language Amharic, that the best way to represent the allomorphy is to set up lexical representations such as 4.8:

$$4.8 \qquad \text{a)} \; g \begin{Bmatrix} \text{u:} \\ \text{i:} \end{Bmatrix} s \qquad \text{b)} \; m \begin{Bmatrix} \text{a} \\ \text{e} \end{Bmatrix} n$$

In this theory there is no phonological rule deriving the allomorphy, rather the alternation is stated directly in lexical entries.

This type of approach would fail to distinguish quasi-phonological alternations such as 4.8 from total suppletion. The problem is that there is still some discernible phonological relationship between the two alternants. The way such relationships are stated in NGP is through the **via-rule** (Venneman, 1972). This is a lexical redundancy rule which states that a given derived alternant (say, *geese*) is related to its basic alternant, *goose*, 'via' a relationship such as that shown in 4.9:

$$4.9 \qquad \text{u:} \rightarrow \text{i:}$$
$$\text{a} \rightarrow \text{e}$$
$$\text{au} \rightarrow \text{ai}$$

Strictly speaking, we shouldn't speak about a *derived* alternant: the two forms, *gu:s* and *gi:s* are listed in the lexicon and their relationship is stated by rule 4.9, but there is no sense in which *gi:s* is actually derived from *gu:s*. Via-rules therefore have exactly the same function as the lexical redundancy rules proposed by Jackendoff (1975). Indeed, Jackendoff himself suggests that the alternations in English known as the Great Vowel Shift should be handled by such redundancy rules.

The general philosophy of NGP did not enjoy a wide resonance. Phonologists argued at great length about whether abstract phonemes were permissible, and whether rules could be extrinsically ordered or not, often without really settling the issue. Hudson's original proposals went largely without comment, though his approach to allomorphy, under the heading of the 'morpheme alternant' theory, was severely (if rather obliquely) criticized by Kenstowicz and Kisseberth in their textbook of 1979. Their principal arguments were that (i) abstract analyses are sometimes necessary; (ii) it is often necessary to distinguish between a basic alternant and derived alternants, in other words it is necessary to postulate an underlying form from which other allomorphs can be derived; and (iii) the morpheme alternant theory presupposes that the alternations are idiosyncratic and so cannot handle cases in which the alternations are the regular case. We will return to these criticisms later.

Natural Generative Phonology didn't attract many followers and the approach petered out by the end of the 1970s (though some of the principles of the theory, such as the importance of syllable structure, are now part and parcel of contemporary phonological theory). There were perhaps two main intellectual reasons for this: first, a great deal of effort was being expended on the new 'non-linear' approaches to phonology from 1976 onwards and, second, the relationship between phonology and morphology was being redefined by Kiparsky and his collaborators.

4.3   Lexical phonology

4.3.1   Kiparsky's Alternation Condition

Historically, the first challenge to the view of allomorphy contained in SPE came from Paul Kiparsky in a number of papers (some of which form part of the volume Kiparsky, 1982a, some of which were published as Kiparsky, 1973a). Kiparsky was originally concerned with highly abstract analyses which made extensive appeal to absolute neutralization. He argued that in many cases appeal to abstraction was merely an unilluminating way of coding exceptionality in the guise of regularity by using phonetic features to do the job of exception features. In an earlier paper (1968; reprinted in Kiparsky, 1973a, and 1982a) he discussed the now notorious case of the English velar fricative. In SPE a rule of Trisyllabic Laxing (Shortening) or TSL is defended. TSL is the rule mentioned in §3.3, which laxes (or shortens) a tense (long) vowel when it is followed by two short syllables. It is this rule which accounts in part for alternations such as *sane ~ sanity, divine ~ divinity, verbose ~ verbosity, obscene ~ obscenity.* In SPE, Chomsky and Halle note that it fails to apply in the case of *right ~ righteous.* The *-eous* affix is analysed as disyllabic in underlying form. Given SPE assumptions we must suppose that the stem is the same in both words. So why doesn't the laxing rule apply to give a form [ritjəs]? Chomsky and Halle offer an ingenious solution. Suppose that the stem vowel is actually short and that there is some sort of consonant following it which is ultimately deleted but which serves to lengthen the preceding vowel after the application of TSL. On the grounds of the economy of the underlying phoneme system, they conclude that the consonant must be a voiceless velar fricative /x/ (which historically was true, of course, as is reflected in the current spelling). We therefore have in simplified form derivations such as 4.10:

4.10	a)	b)	c)	d)	
	sæ:n	sæ:n + iti	rixt	rixt + eu:s	
	———	æ	———	———	TSL
	———	———	i:	i:	Pre-x L.
	———	———	Ø	Ø	x-Deletion
	ei	———	ai	ai	Vowel Shift
	———	———	———		jəs	Other rules
	[sein]	[sæniti]	[rait]	[raitjəs]	Output

Notice that this sort of solution crucially appeals to extrinsic rule ordering: 'Pre-x lengthening' must not be permitted to feed TSL.

Kiparsky, however, argued that such an analysis is unwarranted because there is no other justification for positing the underlying /x/ than to account for the exceptional behaviour of *righteous* with respect to TSL. In other words, we are guilty of using phonetic elements purely as exception features. He pointed out that in general there are no ways of identifying the precise nature of such underlying segments if only one rule applies to them. For instance, how can we be sure that the consonant in question is not a laryngeal fricative, or even an underlying click? Such analyses pose intractible learnability problems when there is absolutely no way open to the child for figuring out the underlying form. He proposed the **Alternation Condition** to constrain derivations. The wording of this condition went through a number of metamorphoses, some weaker than others. The 'strong' version is given in 4.11 (cf. Kiparsky, 1982b, 148):

4.11   Obligatory neutralization rules cannot apply to all occurrences of a morpheme.

Neutralization rules are those which effect a phonological neutralization, i.e. replace one phoneme with another, as opposed to allophonic rules, which merely specify in further detail the pronunciation of a phoneme. The Alternation Condition, then, ensures that, where a morpheme is subject to a neutralization rule, there will be some allomorph somewhere in the language to which that neutralization hasn't applied. This has important consequences for the learnability of morphophonemic rules. Absolute neutralization induces **opacity** of a particularly strong kind. This is Kiparsky's technical term describing a situation in which it is impossible to tell exactly what the UR of a word is from mere inspection of its surface phonological form. Thus, the language learner confronted with cases of absolute neutralization is in the same position as the linguist, in that he must analyse the language in some detail before he can work out the underlying phoneme inventory and hence the URs of his language.

Given this perspective, one way of viewing the problem with the English velar fricative in *righteous* is as follows. On the surface we have a diphthong, /ai/, the underlying form of which we would normally expect to be a tense vowel. However, if there was a tense vowel in this position it should have undergone TSL and surfaced as lax /i/. The solution sketched in 4.10d creates a tense vowel from an underlying lax vowel in a fashion which crucially relies on the existence of our abstract velar fricative. The only reason for postulating the offending segment is to allow the derivation to bypass the effects of TSL (thus inducing opacity in the form of an apparent exception to TSL). In other words, there is no phonetic motivation for the occurrence of /x/, it merely serves as a rather complicated and misleading alternative to the statement that *righteous* is an exception to TSL.

One way of preventing the use of abstract phonetic elements as exception features in this way and at the same time ensure that the Alternation Condition is respected is to permit neutralization rules only if they are triggered by a morphological process. Then what will happen is that there will be two allomorphs of the morpheme containing the neutralized segment: the base allomorph (in which the segment surfaces) and the morphologically derived allomorph (in which the segment is turned into something else by the neutralization process). In other words, we impose a ban on absolute neutralizations that also apply to monomorphemic roots. In this case we will be unable to postulate an /x/ segment in the UR of *right* because there is /x/ in the surface form of the base allomorph.

This reasoning leads us to the **Revised Alternation Condition** (cf. Kiparsky, 1982: 152):

4.12   Revised Alternation Condition
        Obligatory neutralization rules apply only in derived environments.

The definition of **derived environment** is given in 4.13 (Kiparsky, 1982b: 152):

4.13   Environment E is derived with respect to rule R if E satisfies the structural description of R crucially by the combination of morphemes or by application of a rule.

What 4.13 says is that a neutralization rule is possible if it is fed by affixation (just as TSL is fed by affixation of *-ity* in derivation 4.10b). The rider about phonological rules themselves creating derived environments is necessary because, in keeping with generative tradition, many processes have to be broken into separate stages in order to state them as maximally general phonological operations, and it's essential that these stages be allowed to feed one another in a derivation. As an example, consider the rule of Jer Lowering discussed in §4.1. A fully accurate generative grammar might well split this up into two parts where it applies to the back jer /ɨ/, by first lowering /ɨ/ to a back mid unrounded vowel /ɤ/ and then fronting this to /e/ (as Rubach, 1984, proposes for the same process in Polish). Now, the fronting of /ɤ/ to /e/ would be considered an absolute neutralization, but it is possible in Kiparsky's terms because it would be fed by the jer lowering rule. We may think of this as indirect triggering of a rule by affixation.

The Revised Alternation Condition is an important stage in the development of ideas about allomorphy in generative phonology, because it is the first explicit statement of the role of morphology in phonological derivations.

4.3.2   Cyclic phonology and lexical phonology

In 1976, Joan Mascaró, working primarily on his native Catalan, proposed an approach to the question of alternations which made crucial use of the notion of **cyclic rule**. What he proposed was that rules which effect obligatory neutralizations should apply in a cyclic fashion, as determined by morphological structure. This means that the rules which apply only in a derived environment are precisely the rules which apply cyclically.

The fundamental idea behind theories of cyclic rule application is to permit one and the same rule to apply more than once in a derivation. Having applied a set of cyclic rules, we then expand the string over which the rules apply (for instance, by adding another affix), and then apply the whole rule set to the new string. Each application of the rule set constitutes a single **cycle**, and the given string to which the rules apply is a **cyclic domain**. However, it turns out to be necessary to ensure that a rule which applies cyclically can only apply on its own cycle, and cannot return to an earlier cycle to reapply. In other words, a cyclic rule can't apply to a subdomain which is contained within its current domain. In this way we can prevent a rule from continually reapplying to the same small substring. The principle that prevents this is the **Strict Cycle Condition** (SCC), often known as *Strict Cyclicity* or the *Strict Cyclicity Condition*.

A simple example of the operation of the SCC operating in phonology is provided by Catalan (Mascaró, 1983: 64–5). In 4.14 we see the derivation of the word *ruin-osissim*, 'very much in ruins', whose morphological structure is [[[ruin] oz] isim] . Each morpheme has underlying stress, which according to Mascaró, is deleted in certain cases, by a rule of Deaccentuation. An unstressed high vowel following another vowel is subject to Glide Formation. These rules apply in the order mentioned. Derivation 4.14a shows what happens without the SCC – an incorrect pronunciation [*ruynuzisim] is generated. The correct derivation is shown in 4.14b. Here the SCC blocks the second application of Glide Formation and the correct form is ultimately given:

4.14   a)   b)

          Cycle 1
          ruin + oz   ruin + oz

                                                        Glide Formation
          ————   ————
             ǐ   ǐ   Deaccentuation
          Cycle 2
          ruinoz + isim   ruinoz + isim
             y   BLOCKED   Glide Formation
             ǒ   ǒ   Deaccentuation
             u   u   Other rules
          Output:
          [*ruynuzisim]   [ruinuzisim]

In the theory of Cyclic Phonology developed by Mascaró the SCC is incorporated by means of a reformulation of the Revised Alternation Condition, given in 4.15:

4.15   a) Cyclic rules apply only to derived representations.
          b) A representation is derived with respect to rule R in cycle j if it results from the combination of morphemes in j or the operation of a phonological rule in j.

One of the consequences of this view of phonological rules is that cyclic rules are unable to apply to monomorphemic items. This means that Velar Softening in English will automatically be prevented from applying to a word such as *king* since there is no derived environment in which it could apply. In the case of *king* there is only one morpheme and hence only one cycle. No rule feeds Velar Softening on this cycle, and no morphological rule applies. Therefore, the environment is non-derived. Therefore, assuming that Velar Softening is a cyclic rule, it cannot apply to *king*.[4]

As the reader can verify, there is exactly one other circumstance when the SCC comes into play. This is when two rules are ordered in a **counterfeeding** relationship. Suppose we have two rules, A and B. Suppose now that application of A creates a derived form of the kind that B can apply to. Then, if A precedes B we say the rules are in a **feeding order**. If the two rules are ordered B < A then B will already have applied before A and hence A will no longer be able to feed B. This is known as a *counterfeeding order.*[5] Given two rules in a counterfeeding order, cyclic application without the SCC would allow rule B a second bite at the cherry. This is because even if A counterfeeds B on cycle n, B can apply on cycle n + 1 to the output of rule A on the previous cycle. The SCC simply blocks this second application of B. This is exactly the situation illustrated in the Catalan example above, where Glide Formation corresponds to rule B and Deaccentuation corresponds to rule A.

The Kiparsky–Mascaró theory of Cyclic Phonology has considerable implications for the theory of allomorphy. What it implies is that an identifiable class of phonological rules, namely the cyclic rules, are responsible for morphologically conditioned allomorphic variation. In this way the old distinction between non-automatic alternation (of the *electric ~ electricity* kind) and allophony which is conditioned purely phonologically can easily be drawn, but without special stipulation. Rather, the distinction is a consequence of the organization of the grammar.

Kiparsky (1982b) considerably extended the compass of Cyclic Phonology in a remarkable paper which proposed a radically different perspective on the relation between phonology and morphology. We have been assuming so far that cyclicity is a stipulated property of rules and that cyclic application is a mode of application which has to be written into the grammar specially. In an unpublished paper written in 1979, Pesetsky argued that the effects of cyclicity could be obtained if we assumed that the battery of cyclic phonological rules applied every time a morphological operation applied. In other words, he proposed that the process of affixation itself should be the trigger for the application of rules of phonology. In this way, we would mimic cyclic application of phonological rules but this would follow from the organization of the morphology. This insight is the germ from which grew the theory of Lexical Phonology.

What Kiparsky actually proposed was to obtain the effects of cyclicity by introducing a version of Siegel's Level Ordering into the theory of phonology. Siegel had appealed to Level Ordering to account for the stress neutrality of Class II affixes. Kiparsky argued that this model was the key to understanding the operation of all cyclic phonological rules. His model is presented in figure 4.1. (Kiparsky, 1982b: 132).

In Kiparsky's own words (1982b: 131–2):

> Each level is associated with a set of phonological rules for which it defines the domain of application. ... [T]he output of each word-formation process is submitted within the lexicon itself to the phonological rules of its level. This establishes a basic division among phonological rules into those which are assigned to one or more levels in the lexicon, and those which operate after words have been combined into sentences in the syntax. The former, the rules of *lexical phonology*, are intrinsically cyclic because they reapply after each step of word-formation at their morphological level. The latter, the rules of *postlexical phonology*, are intrinsically noncyclic [emphasis original].

A number of consequences flow from this model, together with certain other assumptions. Kiparsky (1973b) introduced the **Elsewhere Condition** as a principle

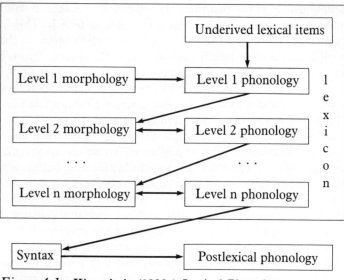

Figure 4.1   Kiparsky's (1982a) Lexical Phonology

governing (in part) the application of rules. It is an important notion, which recurs throughout morphological theory. Kiparsky's (1982b: 136–7) statement of it is given in 4.16:

4.16   Rules A, B in the same component apply disjunctively to a form Φ if and only if
(i) The structural description of A (the special rule) properly includes the structural description of B (the general rule).
(ii) The result of applying A to Φ is distinct from the result of applying B to Φ.[6]
In that case, A is applied first, and, if it takes effect, then B is not applied.

The crucial notion here is that of **disjunctive ordering**: either one rule applies, or the other, but not both. Thus, the Elsewhere Condition guarantees that the more specific rule will pre-empt the more general.

The Elsewhere Condition makes it possible to write rules in such a way as to account for all the least general cases first and then simply state the most general case in the form 'otherwise, such-and-such'. Another way of putting this is to say that the condition allows us to capture the notion of **default case**. For example, suppose we wish to account for regular plural allomorphy in English. We could state the rule as 'add /z/ and then (i) insert an epenthetic schwa after a sibilant stem; (ii) devoice /z/ to /s/ after a voiceless stem'. The two parts of the rule have to apply in the order mentioned, because if the rules applied in the opposite order the /z/ would be incorrectly devoiced after voiceless sibilants and we would obtain [*diʃəs] for 'dishes'. Given the Elsewhere Condition we don't need to state this ordering. The set of environments in which the epenthesis rule applies is completely contained in the set of environments in which the devoicing rule applies. Therefore, the epenthesis rule is the more specific. Therefore, it will have priority over the devoicing rule and will pre-empt it. Hence, voiceless sibilant stems will end up with a plural allomorph which has undergone epenthesis but not devoicing, as required. All we have to state is: 'epenthesize after a sibilant; otherwise, devoice after a voiceless consonant'.[7]

Kiparsky next introduces an ingenious idea concerning the notion 'lexical entry'. He suggests that a lexical entry such as *king* or *trousers* should be regarded as a kind of degenerate rule (in effect an identity rule) of the form *king* → *king*. If this step is adopted, then a lexical entry will be the most specific kind of rule there is since, by definition, it only applies to one lexical item. Therefore, it will always be ordered before any other rule by the Elsewhere Condition. Consider words such as *guide* or *cook*. These words can be either verbs or agentive nouns. However, the usual way of forming an agentive noun from a verb is to add an affix such as *-er* to the verb. We must prevent this since **guider* and *cooker* are either non-existent or have a different meaning. However, let's say that the two nouns are lexical entries in their own right, and that a lexical entry is a rule applying to one item. Now, this 'lexical entry' rule is as specific as it can possibly be, since by definition it only applies to one item. Hence, a more general rule such as affixation of *-er* will be prevented from applying to such items by the Elsewhere Condition. In effect, the affixation rule will be pre-empted by the lexical entry itself. Thus, the theory of Lexical Phonology (with the Elsewhere Condition) can neatly account for blocking phenomena. Moreover, if we assume that the result of irregular affixation such as the plural *oxen* or the past tense *brought* is also 'recycled' into the lexicon to form a separate lexical entry, then we can account for their blocking of regular affixation and the non-existence of **oxens* and **broughted*.

The model so far leaves certain questions unanswered. Of particular importance are these: (i) Why do certain cyclic rules appear to apply in non-derived environments? (ii) Why do cyclic rules appear to mimic the effects of morpheme structure conditions (MSCs)? Kiparsky makes particular mention of the English Stress Rule of Hayes (1982) in connection with the first question. He accepts arguments that this rule is cyclic, but the obvious problem is that it applies to monomorphemic words in violation of the Strict Cycle Condition. Question (ii) is simply the persistent question of the **Duplication Problem**, which was never satisfactorily resolved in generative phonology (cf. Kenstowicz and Kisseberth, 1979).

Kiparsky's solution to both these problems relies on a reformulation of the SCC and the introduction of a notion of **underspecification**.[8] He assumes that English words whose stress can be computed by rule are represented in the lexicon without any stress marks. In the model of stress that he is adopting (that of Metrical Phonology), stress rules build metrical tree structures which represent patterns of strong and weak syllables.[9] The details of stress assignment are not important to us here. What is important is the observation that the stress rules build up a portion of the phonological representation from scratch, but they don't change a pre-existing representation of stress into another representation. That is, the stress assignment rules are **structure-building** and not **structure-changing** rules. This means that we can regard a word which has not yet been assigned stress as unspecified (or 'underspecified') for stress. In technical terms, this means that a representation of the word *parent* in 4.17a without stress is non-distinct (see note 6) from a representation such as 4.17b in which stress is marked:

4.17 a) parent
    b)

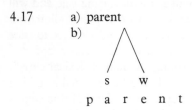

To return to the problem of stress rules applying in non-derived environments: the SCC as formulated so far prevents this, and so it prevents the derivation of 4.17b from 4.17a.

However, Kiparsky has argued that a lexical entry is itself a rule. Since it is a rule it will be subject to the Elsewhere Condition, and this is how we have accounted for cases of blocking. How does the lexical entry 'rule' interact with phonological rules? Consider a word such as *nightingale*. This word is problematic for SPE because it is an exception to Trisyllabic Laxing. However, given the assumptions of Cyclic Phonology, Strict Cyclicity prevents TSL applying to it, since it is a monomorphemic and hence underived item. If both the word *nightingale* and the rule TSL are actually rules, then they too will be ordered disjunctively with respect to each other given the Elsewhere Condition. The *nightingale* rule is obviously the more specific and hence will apply first. Part of the rule will be the specification of the first vowel of the word as tense. This will therefore pre-empt TSL. Thus, we predict that TSL will fail to apply to *nightingale* even without the SCC. Kiparsky uses this observation to argue that the SCC is actually a consequence of the Elsewhere Condition and the assumption that each lexical entry is a rule.

There is, however, a crucial difference between the two ways of deriving strict cyclicity effects. For the Elsewhere Condition only imposes disjunctive ordering between rules if the output of the rules is distinct. Now consider the lexical rule introducing the item *parent* and the stress rule. We have seen that, in the technical sense, the outputs of these two rules (i.e. 4.17a, b, respectively) are *non*-distinct. Therefore, the SCC, reformulated as the Elsewhere Condition, doesn't apply to them. Thus, Kiparsky ingeniously derives the result that a rule such as stress assignment can apply to non-derived environments without violating the SCC.

The same type of argumentation can be applied to the problem of morpheme structure conditions. Kiparsky contrasts the case of *nightingale*, which does not undergo TSL, with the case of *sycamore*, which, at the very least, is compatible with TSL. His way of representing this distinction is to say that TSL can function as an MSC, providing the tenseness (or length) of the first syllable of *sycamore* is not specified in underlying representation. This means that approximate URs for the two words will be as in 4.18:

4.18 a) niːtingæːl
    b) sIkVmoː

The *I* of 4.18b represents a high front vowel which is unspecified for tenseness. Hence, representation 4.18b is non-distinct from either of 4.19:

4.19 a) sikVmoː b) siːkVmoː

We may assume that the feature [tense] in the first syllable of 4.18b is given the value [0tense] (as opposed to [+tense] or [-tense]). By the technical definition of distinctness the feature specification [0tense] is distinct neither from [+tense] nor from [-tense]. The rule of TSL is now assumed to be able to switch the value [0tense] to [-tense] in the right phonological environment. In this case it is acting just like the stress rule in that it does not create a representation which is distinct from the UR. In other words, form 4.19a is non-distinct from 4.18b, thus the lexical rule introducing 4.18b and the rule of TSL will not be disjunctively ordered by the Elsewhere Condition.

This situation contrasts with the case of *nightingale*, to which we can now return in more detail. The tenseness of the initial vowel is assumed to be specified underlyingly. Therefore, if TSL were to apply to 4.18a it would produce a representation which is distinct from that of 4.18a, since 4.18a has a specification [+tense] and TSL would turn this feature marking into [-tense]. Therefore, the Elsewhere Condition would come into play, and the *nightingale* rule would be ordered disjunctively before TSL, effectively blocking the application of the latter.

We have reviewed in some detail the phonological side of the morphology–phonology interface in Lexical Phonology. There remain two assumptions concerning word structure which are of importance.

In SPE phonology there were several different classes of affixes, most notably the '+' and the '#' boundary affix. The phonology could refer specifically to these boundary symbols, and this allowed SPE to make use of morphological information in phonological rules, albeit in a somewhat indirect fashion. However, in SPE, boundaries are treated formally as the same kind of animal as genuinely phonetic segments, and many phonologists were unhappy with this idea, particularly once the functions of boundary symbols were taken over by prosodic categories in Prosodic Phonology (see Booij, 1985a). In Lexical Phonology the boundary symbols are replaced by a direct representation of constituent structure, a **(labelled) bracketing**. The degree to which words have a constituent structure, and the exact manner in which it is represented, is still a matter of controversy, which we'll touch on several times in part III (particularly §6.1.2). For the present we just note that an SPE-type form such as 4.20a would be simply represented as 4.20b in Lexical Phonology:

4.20   a) [[un#[fastidi+ous]]#ness]
        b) [[un[[fastidi]ous]]ness]

The phonological differences between the two classes of affix are then accounted for, as we have seen, by level ordering.

At the end of each level words become phonologically 'inert', in the sense that they can no longer be affected by cyclic phonological rules. In this regard they are treated as though they were monomorphemic lexical items. This inertness extends to morphological processes in the lexicon according to Kiparksy. Thus, both phonology and morphology are blind to the internal structure of words exiting a level. This is captured by modifying the SPE convention of **bracket erasure**. Kiparsky (1982b: 140) adopts the following **Bracket Erasure Convention**:

4.21   BEC (Kiparsky)
        Internal brackets are erased at the end of a level.

The phenomenon of morphological conversion (or zero-affixation) provides a good illustration of this. It has often been noted that verbs derived from nouns such as *to ring (a bird)* are never 'strong', so that they never show the ablaut-type allomorphy typical, say, of verbs ending in *-ing*. Thus, we get contrasts such as *rang the bell* and *ringed the pigeon*. This even happens when the noun is itself derived from a strong verb, as in the case of *to grandstand*, whose past tense is regular (*they grandstanded the stadium*, not **grandstood*). Moreover, the form does not need to be a compound. The noun *hide*, meaning 'a specially constructed concealed location for the observation of wildlife', is derived from the verb *hide* (by conversion). Now, if we wished to use the derived noun as a verb (by double conversion) to mean something like 'fit out a locality with hides', we would say *the ecologists hided the forest*, not *the ecologists hid the forest*.

A regular past tense such as *grandstanded* contrasts with the strong past tense of the prefixed form *withstood*. Kiparsky (1982b) explained this contrast in terms of level ordering. He assumed that irregular inflection takes place at Level 1, and that so does verb-to-noun conversion. Noun-to-verb conversion, however, is a Level 2 process, as is compounding. Finally, regular inflection is at Level 3. The derivations of *grandstanded* and *withstood* are then given in Figure 4.2 (Kiparsky assumes that *withstand* is a compound.

In this way Kiparsky can use the machinery of level ordering in Lexical Phonology to render opaque the irregularity of the strong verb *stand* in the compounded (and converted) form.

Adopting Siegel's Level Ordering Hypothesis (in whatever variant) imposes strong constraints on word formation processes, as we have seen. Unfortunately, in many respects these constraints are too strong. We'll be discussing a number of problems with level ordering in some detail at the beginning of chapter 6. One problem noted from the outset in Lexical Phonology concerns the prediction level ordering makes about the order of morphemes in complex words. For instance, as we have just seen, Kiparsky (1982b) assumes that regular inflection takes place after compounding.

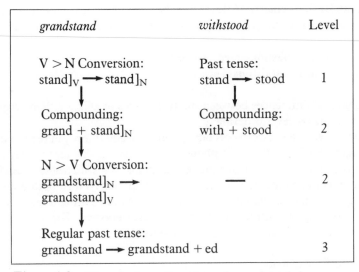

Figure 4.2   Kiparsky's explanation of *grandstanded*

This means that we shouldn't ever find regular plurals inside a compound. However, we do find precisely such cases, as in *parks commissioner* and *systems analyst*. Kiparsky argues that we can simply say that the plural is a special form (with specialized meaning) and therefore listed in the lexicon. This means that it can be subject to compounding just like any other lexical item. However, other lexical phonologists (notably Mohanan, 1986) argue that, in general, languages will have to be able to break free of the stringent restrictions imposed by level ordering and allow words formed in one stratum or level to **loop** back to the previous stratum, to undergo further word formation. Not surprisingly, many linguists regard this as an admission that level ordering is not the right way to approach the problem of morpheme ordering.

The commonest cases necessitating a loop involve compounding, and Mohanan himself discusses the two main types of Malayalam compounding process at some length in this regard. Compounding poses its own special problems for morphological theory and chapter 8 is devoted to this topic. Here we'll just note that the level ordering subtheory of Lexical Phonology is at its least clear when compound formation is concerned.

A number of different models of Lexical Phonology have been proposed, making slightly different assumptions about the nature of phonological rules and representations or morphological processes or the interaction between the two. Pulleyblank (1986) discusses tone systems (particularly that of Yoruba), Harris (1983) is a lexical analysis of Spanish stress and syllabification, and Rubach (1984) is devoted to the segmental phonology of Polish, with detailed discussion of the role of allomorphy rules, while Mohanan (1986) develops a general theoretical approach with generous illustration from Malayalam.

An aspect of the theory which is particularly prone to variation is level ordering. Kiparsky himself has presented a number of different versions of level ordering for English. A fairly drastic revision is proposed by Halle and Mohanan (1985) in their model of the segmental phonology of English. They expand the number of levels, or strata, to a total of four. More significantly, they claim that, of these, only Strata 1 and 3 contain cyclic phonological rules. Strata 2 and 4 contain rules which therefore do not observe Strict Cyclicity. In addition, they assume that certain 'clean-up' rules (that is, rules whose sole justification is to readjust the values of certain features after the rules capturing the main morphophonemic alternations) apply postlexically. Since the bulk of the rules they postulate fall into Strata 2 and 4 or are postlexical, this means that most of the rules of English phonology are non-cyclic, bringing Halle and Mohanan's theory very close to that of SPE.

In an Appendix, Halle and Mohanan provide an account of (nearly) all the strong verbs in English. This requires them to add a number of diacritically conditioned phonological rules to their grammar, specific to the strong verb system. Their analysis represents one extreme of generative approaches to allomorphy, since they claim that the alternations found in the strong verbs are essentially phonological (albeit triggered in many instances by morpholexical diacritic features). This even applies to alternations such as *think ~ thought* and *bring ~ brought* (which apply only to these two words).

Halle has now abandoned this analysis of strong verbs (Halle and Vergnaud, 1987: 77). He has also abandoned the assumption that morphology and phonology are connected in a single system, the Lexical Phonology. Rather, he argues that morphology and phonology are separate (though phonology still comprises cyclic and non-cyclic strata). This separation of phonology and morphology (introduced under the influence of Sproat's, 1985a, critique of Lexical Phonology) will be discussed in more detail in chapters 10 and 11.

Kiparsky, too, has revised his attitude to Lexical Phonology (Kiparsky, 1985). In this later paper, he argues for a different formulation of Strict Cyclicity (one which doesn't suffer from certain technical flaws marring the original version), and for a new principle, that of *structure preservation*. According to this a lexical phonological rule can't refer to features which aren't distinctive.[10] What this means is that all lexical phonological rules have to be defined over sets of (underlying) phonemes and the output must consist of sets of phonemes.

An example adduced by Kiparsky to illustrate the value of this principle is Finnish vowel harmony. In Finnish, a root with back vowels, /a o u/ selects suffixes with back vowels and a root with front vowels /æ ø y/ selects suffixes with front vowels. However, the front vowels /i e/ are 'neutral': they co-occur with either front or back vowels. Kiparsky argues that the neutrality of these vowels is connected with the fact that they lack [+back] congeners: the vowels /ɨ ɣ/ don't exist in Finnish. Therefore, the feature [back] is redundant for these two phonemes. Being redundant (i.e. non-distinctive), it can't be referred to by the vowel harmony rule. Therefore, vowel harmony is unable to create the two missing back congeners even as allophonic variants (on the assumption that harmony is a lexical process in Finnish).

On the face of it, structure preservation is a desirable principle of Universal Grammar, since it limits the types of grammars a child might have to learn. If it can be defended, the principle will be of importance for our view of allomorphy. For it would mean that lexical (or at least, cyclic) phonological rules would be defined purely in terms of lists of phonemes, just like Aronoff's allomorphy rules (§3.5.1). It must be said that not all Lexical Phonologists accept the idea of structure preservation, mainly because there are a few cases in which the neatest phonological analysis seems to demand the use of non-distinctive features at a cyclic level of the lexicon (see note 10). But such arguments can be rather difficult to adjudicate, since, to construct a firm counterexample to the principle of structure preservation, we would need a fully analysed and motivated underlying phoneme inventory. In practice this generally means that we would need an analysis of most of the phonology of the language.

A somewhat different model of Lexical Phonology has been proposed by Geert Booij and Jerzy Rubach (1984, 1987) (amplifying, in certain respects, on suggestions made in Kiparsky, 1985). They do not devote much discussion to the problem of level (or stratal) ordering (though in the earlier paper, Booij and Rubach, 1984: note 14, they explicitly distance themselves from the level ordering approach and propose to handle affixation in terms of stratal selectional features). Instead, they concentrate on the organization of phonological rules of different types in the lexicon. They distinguish between two types of non-cyclic rule: the *postlexical rule*, which applies after the syntax to whole phrases, and the *postcyclic lexical rule*, which applies in the lexicon (like the cyclic rules) but is not cyclic. In this respect, their proposal is reminiscent of Halle and Mohanan's theory, in that in both models some lexical rules are non-cyclic. However, they explicitly state that the cyclic rules precede the postcyclic rules in the lexicon and in this respect they differ from Halle and Mohanan. Their model is diagrammed in figure 4.3 (Booij and Rubach, 1987: 3).

Perhaps the simplest example of a postlexical rule would be that of stress rules in

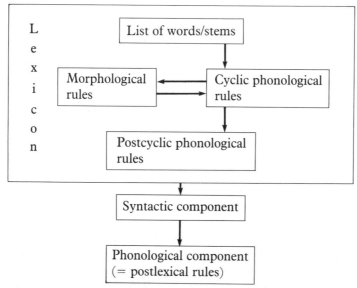

Figure 4.3 Booij and Rubach's (1987) model

fixed stress languages. For instance, in Czech or Hungarian, the stress always falls on the first syllable of the word, irrespective of its morphological structure. The easiest way of accounting for such a situation is to say that the stress rule, while lexical (since it only applies to the domain of the word), applies after all other phonological rules (including any which might insert or delete vowels).

Polish provides stronger evidence for this conception of fixed stress rules. The stress falls regularly on the penultimate syllable, whether in monomorphemic words or in suffixed versions of those words (stressed syllables are italicized):

4.22   a) in*te*res   'interest (nom. sg.)'
          b) inte*re*su   (gen. sg.)
          c) intere*sa*mi   (intr. pl.)
          d) intere*so*wać   'to interest'
          e) interesu*ją*cy   'interesting (masc. nom. sg.)'
          f) interesują*ce*go   (masc. gen. sg.)

However, in certain word forms the stress falls, exceptionally, on the antepenult. These exceptions can't be defined phonologically and so have to be marked lexically. When such an exceptional word is suffixed, either the stress remains on the antepenult or it shifts to its regular position on the penult. The basic generalization is that, in exceptional items, stress is marked to fall on a particular syllable irrespective of affixation, but that this is overridden if the stress would end up more than three syllables from the right edge of the word (cf. Hammond, 1989). Two sets of cases are shown in 4.23 and 4.24:

4.23   a) gra*ma*tyka   'grammar (nom. sg.)'
          b) gra*ma*tyki   (gen. sg.)
          c) gra*ma*tyk   (gen. pl.)
          d) gramaty*ka*mi   (instr. pl.)

4.24   a) uni*w*ersytet   'university (nom. sg.)'
         b) uniwersy*t*etu   (gen. sg.)
         c) uniwersyte*t*ami   (instr. pl.)

In *gramatyka* we can assume that stress is lexically marked on the syllable *ma*, where it surfaces in all forms except 4.23d. Here, it is impossible because it would be four syllables from the end of the word and so the regular stress rule takes precedence. Likewise, we can assume lexical stress marking on the *w*er syllable of *uniwersytet*.

It is not important exactly how these rules are written. The point is that the regular rule must wait until the end of all affixation processes before applying. In addition, it applies after the vowel-zero alternations similar to those described earlier in the chapter for Czech. Therefore, it can't sensibly be regarded as a cyclic rule. However, the fact that the stress rule is defined over the domain of the word, and that it is subject to lexical exceptionality, shows that it must be a lexical rule. Hence, we have a lexical rule which must apply (non-cyclically) after the cyclic rules.

Since postcyclic rules aren't cyclic, we don't expect them to obey Strict Cyclicity, and so they can apply to monomorphemic (underived) items even if they effect a change in structure. Apparently, postcyclic rules are not intended to respect structure preservation either. This means that a postcyclic rule can give rise to segments or syllable structures which aren't underlyingly contrastive, for example, by creating a reduced vowel which doesn't appear in the underlying phoneme inventory of the language.

If the notion of postcyclic lexical rules is substantiated, it would be tempting to regard them as the first stage in the lexicalization of genuinely phonological (automatic) rules of the phrase phonology. This should have interesting implications for theories of historical phonological change.

4.3.3 *Lexical phonology: summary*

Let's now summarize the leading ideas behind Lexical Phonology so as to judge the importance of its contribution to our understanding of morphology. In structuralist approaches to morphophonemics it's common to find the notion that a morphophonemic alternation serves, in part, as a signal of a morphological relationship. For instance, in /hauzəz/, the plural of 'house', the category of plurality is expressed partly by the ending and partly by the voicing of the stem final /s/. Lexical Phonology has as one of its aims the formalization of this notation. For in Lexical Phonology phonological rules are triggered by morphological processes (particularly affixation). Thus, allomorphy is directly coded as a kind of biproduct of affixation. This is achieved by the interleaving of the morphological rules with the phonological rules.

A further important consequence of this interleaving is that it permits certain morphological rules to be sensitive to the derived phonological shape of morphemes. We saw a number of cases of this in chapter 3. Provided the morphological rule applies after (that is, in a later stratum than) the phonological rule which gave rise to the derived allomorphy, there is no difficulty in writing affixation processes which are sensitive to the derived allomorphy. (Some of the implications of this observation will be expanded upon, however, in §4.4.)

Lexical phonology permits a precise characterization of what counts as a morphophonemic rule. Such rules are lexical redundancy rules, defined over items in the lexicon. They are thus different in kind from the postlexical rules which apply after the syntax. The resulting model, especially when it incorporates the notion of structure preservation, bears a certain resemblance to the structuralist morphophonemic theories discussed in chapter 2 (cf. Kiparsky, 1985: 114). Although certain phonologists working within the SPE tradition had suggested at times that the output of the phonology might need to be able to feed morphological processes (Gussman, 1980, makes just such a claim for certain facts about Polish word formation), Kiparsky's is the first generative model to incorporate the idea as an essential component.

The theory is still a species of generative phonology. The key ideas of SPE are largely retained, though in greatly modified form where so-called non-linear approaches, discussed in chapter 5, are introduced into the model. Thus, a phonological component has underlying forms mapped onto surface forms by extrinsically ordered rules defined over natural classes of distinctive features using the SPE notational conventions. Where two allomorphs of a morpheme bear a phonologically definable resemblance to each other, it is (often tacitly) assumed, with SPE, that there is a common underlying form from which both allomorphs are derived by means of phonological rules.

Although the Level Ordering Hypothesis has played a large role in the development of Lexical Phonology, it doesn't seem to be an essential component of the theory. The model proposed by Booij and Rubach (1984, 1987), for instance, is able to dispense with the notion completely. What is essential to Lexical Phonology is the interaction between phonology and morphology and the distinction between lexical processes and postlexical processes. In the rest of this chapter we'll look at other attempts to cover the same ground by formalizing the morphology–phonology interaction in different ways.

4.4   Morpholexical phonology

Having morphological rules intermixed with the phonology as in Lexical Phonology permits interactions which would otherwise be impossible. In particular, it is possible for certain phonological rules to feed morphological rules. However, simply allowing phonological rules to apply before affixation processes still doesn't of itself account for all the ways in which morphology can restrict phonology. It is still the case that some lexical phonology rules apply only to certain classes of morpheme, for instance, only to verb forms, or only to specially marked lexical items such as those etymologically identified as foreign borrowings. This includes cases in which only a minority of items in a given class actually undergo the rule, the so-called minor rules. In some cases minor rules apply not only in a minority of the phonological environments meeting their structural description but also in a minority of the potential morphological environments. In this case the rules have to be governed by morphological features, such as [+strong verb], [+3rd declension], [-indicative] and so on.

A rule may be 'minor' either because only a limited number of morphemes undergo the rule, or because only a limited number trigger it.[11] As an example of the former type, we might suppose that there was a rule shortening /ai, i:/ to /i, e/ in the past tense of certain monosyllabic verbs ending in *t*/*d*, as in *bite ~ bit, hide ~ hid, bleed ~ bled, feed ~ fed*. However, this 'regularity', though it can be stated in phonological terms (in many brands of generative phonology), only applies to a small minority of verbs. Even strong verbs of the right shape don't necessarily undergo it (quite apart from those like *cite* or *cede* which have completely regular past tense forms), witness: *fight, ride, smite, stride, write*. As an example of a minor rule triggered by a minority of items, consider the stress attraction induced by affixes such as *-ic* and *-ity* in *system ~ systemic* and *luminous ~ luminosity*. The majority of affixes in English don't have this effect on stress.

Although Kiparsky doesn't discuss the question in any detail in his later writings it seems that he would accept that certain phenomena handled by phonological rules in SPE are better treated as readjustment rules, i.e. truncation rules or allomorphy rules of the kind Aronoff (1976) describes. Rubach (1984) in his description of Polish within a Lexical Phonology framework explicitly includes such readjustment rules. Readjustment rules resemble phonological rules in that they may only apply after at least one morphological process. In certain cases the morphemes which undergo them or trigger them will have to be marked with special diacritic symbols in their lexical entries. This is because phonologically similar morphemes sometimes fail to condition the alternations. In this respect the readjustment rules are very similar to minor rules.

However, there is still one essential feature of the phonology–morphology interface which Kiparsky's model retains from SPE: the first rule of the cyclic segmental phonology which applies on the first cycle follows at least one rule of morphology. One consequence of this for morphophonemics is that Lexical Phonology adheres to the principle that, where there is allomorphic variation, it is only the basic alternant that appears in underlying form. The other variants are derived allomorphs and are derived either by readjustment rules, or by (cyclic) phonological rules. What is excluded is the possibility that two allomorphs of a morpheme may be housed in the lexicon before any morphological or phonological processes are applied. For instance, confronted with the /haus ~ hauz/ allomorphy of the word *house*, a Lexical Phonologist would be obliged to set up an underlying form (presumably /haus/ since this is the form found in the morphosyntactically basic variant) and derive one or both allomorphs from that form. There is no sense in which we could say that both allomorphs were underlying.

This assumption is directly challenged by Rochelle Lieber (1980, 1982). We will discuss her overall model of morphology in much greater detail in chapter 6. For the present we will look at her theory of allomorphy. Lieber argues that there are cases in which word formation rules need to have access to derived allomorphs before the phonology has had chance to derive those allomorphs. This means that the derived allomorph, as well as its basic form, must be available in the lexicon before the phonology applies. Hence, it cannot be the case that the allomorphy is the consequence of a phonological rule. Lieber claims that in such cases the allomorphs are listed in the lexicon and associated by means of a lexical redundancy rule which she refers to as a **morpholexical rule**. [12]

Listing derived forms of allomorphs in the lexicon, so that they are available before any morphological processes apply, is a break with the traditions of SPE phonology, and likewise with the assumptions made by Aronoff, or by Kiparsky. In order for the proposal to be workable, it is necessary that a theory of allomorph selection be provided. We saw in chapter 3 that in Halle's 1973 model of morphology all morphemes were listed and some special provision had to be made in order to ensure that we derive words such as *conception, retrieval* and *bereavement*, from *conceive, retrieve* and *bereave* and not nonsense such as **conceivement, *retreption* or **bereaval*. One straightforward way of doing this is to mark roots with features corresponding to the affixal morphemes they take, and ensure that the affixes are so marked as to select just those roots marked with the appropriate feature. Lieber's model of morphology introduces just such a type of selection (which she calls **morphological subcategorization**, by analogy with the subcategorization of verbs in terms of the complements they take).

One intriguing possibility is that an affix might be given a lexical marking which specifies that it selects not a root marked with a particular diacritic feature, but rather any root of a particular phonological shape. We have already encountered sporadic examples of phonologically governed allomorph selection of this kind. The inchoative -en affix, discussed in §3.3, which derives verbs from adjectives, bears a selection feature ensuring that it attaches only to monosyllabic roots ending in (Sonorant) Obstruent. If the root doesn't fit this description then the affix won't attach to it. Carstairs (1987) has discussed a number of cases in which the choice of suppletive allomorphic variants is determined by phonology. An instance which recurs throughout the Turkic family of languages is the allomorphy of the Passive morpheme. This takes the form -*Il* after all consonants except /l/ and -*In* after /l/ and -*n* after vowels (where 'I' represents the vowel harmony variants / ɨ i u y/). In 4.25 we see some examples from Turkish (Lewis, 1967: 149):

4.25   a) Root   Passive
            yap- 'make'   yapɨl
            sev- 'love'   sevil
            tut- 'hold'   tutul
            gör- 'see'   görül
        b) al- 'take'   alɨn
            oku- 'read'   okun

Cases in which suppletive allomorphs are selected phonologically can be handled within the SPE framework because the two allomorphs, being suppletive, by definition can't share a common underlying form. Therefore, both forms must be listed in the lexicon before any affixation takes place. What would be very difficult for such theories would be a case of non-suppletive allomorphy, in which independent phonological rules relate the two allomorphs, and in which the derived allomorph is selected or itself selects on phonological criteria. The reason this is problematic for the SPE model is that all morphology precedes all phonology. Therefore, at the stage when phonologically conditioned selection of a derived allomorph is supposed to be taking place, the derived allomorph still hasn't been created. Lieber argues that just such cases exist and that the SPE approach to non-suppletive allomorphy can't be correct.

Lieber (1982) discusses such a case from the Australian language Warlpiri (see Nash, 1980). Warlpiri verbs have five conjugation classes, each taking a different set of allomorphs of tense affixes. This is shown in 4.26:

4.26   Warlpiri tense markers

	Nonpast	Past	Imper.	Imm. Fut.	Pres.
1	(mi)	ja	ya (-ka)	ju	nya
3	nyi	ngu	ngka	ngku	nganya
2	rni, ni	rnu	ka	ku	rninya
4		nja	lku		
5	ni	nu	nta	nku	nanya

Warlpiri has a rule of reduplication (which Lieber assumes is a morphological rule
– see chapter 5 for a detailed discussion of reduplication processes). This rule is
stated informally in 4.27 and exemplified in 4.28:

4.27   Warlpiri reduplication
          'Copy the first two syllables (or the first syllable if it has a long vowel) of
          a verb to the left.'

4.28   pu-ngka 'hit it (Imper.)' pungka-pungka 'hit it quickly'

Now, several of the forms in the columns of 4.26 are phonologically similar to each
other and it would be tempting in an SPE framework to derive some of them at least
from a common underlying form, subject to minor rules triggered by conjugation
class features. However, the phonological conditioning on the reduplication rule prevents this. In order to work properly reduplication must 'know' the number of syllables in the affix. Therefore, it is not possible to select an abstract underlying
representation of, say, the 3rd conjugation form of the present tense, apply reduplication in the morphology, and then apply the phonological rule spelling out the precise
shape of the affix. The reduplication rule must already 'know' whether the suffix is
a monosyllable or a disyllable when affixed to a stem such as *pu*. For in the former
case the whole of the suffix will get reduplicated and in the latter case only its first
syllable will be reduplicated. Marantz (1982) presented a number of similar cases,
again from the interaction of phonological rules with reduplication, to argue the same
point.

Lieber's arguments show that the SPE model is inadequate. However, they don't
necessarily affect Kiparsky's Lexical Phonology. For the morphology–phonology
interaction is the whole point of this model. Cases in which phonology feeds morphology are therefore precisely the sort of evidence we would look for in order to
substantiate this model. It is partly for this reason that the Lieber/Marantz arguments were largely ignored. However, there is one situation which Lexical Phonology
still rules out, namely, phonologically governed selection of a derived allomorph on
the very first cycle. This is because in Lexical Phonology the first (cyclic) phonological rule has to be fed by a morphological process of some sort in order to satisfy
strict cyclicity. If we can find such a case this would argue in favour of the
morpholexical rules approach (which we may call **Morpholexical Phonology**).

In Spencer (1988a) I claim that Czech illustrates a case of the sort we need. Czech
has a rich inflectional system and a complex morphophonemic patterning. Czech

nouns have three genders, two numbers, and seven case forms. Many affixes have two
sets of allomorphs which, following tradition, we can call 'hard' and 'soft'. The soft
affixes tend to begin with front vowels and are found with stems ending in a pala-
tal(ized) consonant. Other sorts of stem take the hard affixes. The hard/soft distinction isn't purely phonetic: due to historical change an earlier plain vs. palatalized
distinction has been lost for the consonants /s z l/ and the labials, but stems ending
in these consonants are still morphophonemically either soft or hard (or both in the
case of some stems). In table 4.1 I give the declension of the nouns *úhel* 'corner', a
hard stem and *uhel* 'coal', a soft stem. You can see from these paradigms that some
of the endings (though not all) alternate, for instance, the genitive singular has the
form *-u* for the hard stem and *-e* for the soft stem.

Let's concentrate on the prepositional plural (also called the locative). This has a
hard allomorph *-ech* and a soft allomorph *-ích*. Throughout the language, despite the
wealth of exceptions to virtually every rule in Czech, we find that all soft stem allomorphs co-occur with the soft *-ích* affix allomorph and all hard stem allomorphs co-
occur with the hard *-ech* affix allomorphs.[13] There is a minor rule of Czech, called
traditionally 'Second Velar Palatalization' (which I shall shorten to 2VP). This has
the effects shown in 4.29, where /c/ is IPA [ts] /h is [ɦ] and /š/ is /ʃ/. Orthographic
ch represents IPA [x], so *-ích* is [iːx]:

4.29   k → c
            g → z
            h → z
            x → š

This set of alternations in languages like Czech is generally regarded as the result of
a phonological rule in generative studies of Slav morphophonemics. For instance, its
equivalent in Polish is a cyclic rule in Rubach's (1984) lexical phonology of that language. One reason for assuming this is that although its occurrence is morphologically restricted to a small set of affixes, it applies with great regularity even to recent
loans. One of the affixes which triggers it is the prep. pl. desinence *-ích*. Thus, we

Table 4.1 Czech 'hard' and 'soft' declensions

| | úhel 'corner' | | uhel 'coal' | |
	Sg.	Pl.	Sg.	Pl.
Nom.	úhel	úhly	uhel	uhle
Gen.	úhlu	úhlů	uhle	uhlů
Dat.	úhlu	úhlům	uhli	uhlům
Acc.	úhel	úhly	uhel	uhle
Voc.	úhle!	úhly!	uhli!	uhle!
Prep.	úhlu	úhlech	uhli	uhlích
Instr.	úhlem	úhly	uhlem	uhli

The accents ´ and ˚ indicate long vowels; the orthographic distinction between 'y' and 'i' has no effect on pronunciation in
these forms, it simply reflects the lost palatalization present in
earlier stages of the language.

find the data of 4.30:

4.30   zvuk   'sound'   zvucích
        filolog 'philologist'   filolozích
        prah   'threshold'   prazích
        hrax   'pea'   hraších

The standard assumption would be, then, that a form like *zvucích* is derived as in 4.31:

4.31   /zvuk/ + /ích/
        /zvuk + ích/

           c   2VP
        [zvucích]   Output

Now, the phonemes which result from 2VP, namely, /c z š/ are all 'soft'. Thus, it is to be expected that they co-occur with the soft allomorph of the prep. pl., *-ích*. However, there is a serious problem with the derivation in 4.31. For here we find that *zvuk* has selected a soft affix allomorph, *-ích*. But the velar consonants are all morphophonemically hard, and so would be expected to select hard allomorphs (as they do elsewhere in the paradigm). We have an inescapable degree of irregularity here. We would expect to see **zvukech*, but such a form is completely excluded. However, the derivational approach illustrated in 4.31 poses us a serious additional problem. For the form /zvuk/, being a hard stem, has no right selecting a soft suffix allomorph. This problem is compounded when we realize that the rule of 2VP has the function of rectifying the fault: it guarantees that our exceptionless surface generalization will be maintained, despite its having been broken at the level of URs.

If we assume that 2VP is a derivational rule operating after affixation, and hence after allomorph selection, the generalization about the selectional restrictions on hard and soft allomorphs becomes a complete accident. However, if we assume that 2VP is a morpholexical rule, that is, a redundancy rule defined over lexical entries, there is no such problem. All we have to say is that velar stems (regularly) use the palatalized allomorph for the prep. pl. This will automatically mean that the *-ích* affix allomorph will be selected. In effect, we are saying that hard, velar stems shift into the soft stem category for this one inflectional form (not an uncommon phenomenon in inflectional systems).

How can we tell when we have a morpholexical rule which looks like a cyclic rule, and a genuine cyclic rule? The most parsimonious assumption to make is that all cyclic rules are actually morpholexical relationships. The solution will only be attractive to the extent that it can capture all the generalizations which a derivational, rule-based approach can capture. For segmental phonology it isn't difficult to see that the basic properties of the generative, derivational model are straightforwardly translatable into the morpholexical, representational approach. In effect, we just split up the generative rewriting rule into two parts, the change induced by the rule (i.e. the *structural change*) and the context of application (i.e. the *structural description*). The structural change (the context free portion), is then the morpholexical rule, while the context is recorded in terms of selection features defined over the allomorphs created by the context-free rule. What is impossible in such a system is extrinsic ordering of rules. However, this is one of the most controversial aspects of phonological rule systems. Notice that effects reminiscent of rule ordering can be achieved if we assume a distinction between lexical and postlexical phonology. Thus, we can have a lexical rule counterfeeding, or bleeding a postlexical rule. The opportunity for such apparent ordering interactions increases if we adopt the Booij/Rubach model discussed in the previous section. For non-segmental morphophonemics the picture is more complicated, though in Spencer (1988b) I suggest how to treat morphologized reduplication in Latin in a purely representational version of non-linear phonology (a static version of one of the approaches discussed in chapter 5).

The morpholexical approach to cyclic phonological rules also has the advantage that it already entails both structure preservation and (one part of) strict cyclicity without any stipulation. Morpholexical rules are defined before the phonology, at the level at which lexical entries are listed. Therefore, they are automatically restricted to phonemes. Hence, structure preservation is an automatic consequence of the organization of the grammar. Strict cyclicity as it applies to monomorphemic items states that a cyclic phonological rule will not apply to a form in an environment which doesn't trigger an alternation. Morpholexical rules create allomorphs for selection by morphological processes. Without such selection there is no derived allomorph and hence we will always observe the effect of the rule only when we see allomorphy induced by the morphology. But this is strict cyclicity (as it applies to underived items). In other words, this aspect of strict cyclicity is simply a consequence of the fact that we are dealing with allomorphy.

It is fair to say that phonologists are generally unwilling to abandon the full descriptive power of derivational theories of morphophonemics, and especially the luxury of extrinsic rule ordering, even though such rule ordering, together with highly abstract underlying forms, would appear to make phonologies unlearnable (cf. Spencer, 1986). As a consequence, it is unclear whether the morpholexical approach to phonologically governed allomorphy will ever become popular. However, the fact that such an idea can be entertained at all within a generative theory gives an indication of the impact that morphology has made on phonology in recent years.

4.5 Allomorphy in natural morphology

Natural morphology is the term given to an approach to morphology developed by Dressler, Wurzel, Mayerthaler and their colleagues, which seeks to provide a theory of what constitutes a 'natural' morphological system, and what laws govern deviations from that natural (or 'unmarked') state. It mustn't be confused with Natural Generative Phonology, discussed earlier in the chapter (though there are certain points of similarity). The historical starting point for Natural Morphology is the theory of Natural Phonology developed by Stampe (1979). We will hear about the Natural Morphologists' approach to inflection in chapter 6. Here I will briefly sketch the approach to morphophonemics (or morphonology) developed by Dressler (1985a, 1985b).

The essence of Natural Morphology is that the most natural type of morphology is fully 'transparent', in the sense that every morpheme has one form and one meaning, and every meaning (or grammatical category) corresponds to exactly one form. This relationship is called **biuniqueness**. One example of a derivation from biuniqueness is allomorphy. Dressler argues that there are three ways in which morphemes may end up with variant pronunciations. In one case the variation may be simply due to automatic Phonological Rules (PRs). For instance, Dressler argues that the alternation in the English plural suffix between /z s əz/ is the result of exceptionless ('low-level') phonological rules of epenthesis and voicing assimilation. Another very familiar example would be the rule in English aspirating isolated voiceless plosives at the beginning of a stressed syllable. The second type of variation is caused by Morphonological Rules (MPRs). These, too, are phonological rules, in the sense that they can be written in a phonological formalism (Dressler uses a modified version of the standard formalism of SPE). However, unlike PRs, MPRs are rules which are lexically or morphologically governed. An example would be English Velar Softening, which always has the effect of relating allomorphs ending in /k g/ to allomorphs ending in /s ʤ/, as in *electri*[k] – *electri*[s]*ity* and *analo*[g] – *analo*[ʤ]*y*. Since there are exceptions to this alternation it cannot be an automatic PR: *monar*[k] – *monar*[k]*y* and *do*[g] – *do*[g]*y*. The third type of alternation is brought about by Allomorphy Rules (AMRs). The alternations in English referred to collectively as the Great Vowel Shift are said to come under this heading. Thus, the rule of Trisyllabic Laxing (responsible for alternations of the type *sane* – *sanity* mentioned in §4.3.1) would be an AMR.

Dressler's distinctions are valuable as rule of thumb characterizations of different sorts of process which give rise to allomorphic variation. However, he is careful to point out that he doesn't intend his typology to define watertight distinctions, so that the boundaries between the types of rule are fuzzy. Dressler provides a summary of the general properties of MPRs (1985a: 146ff). In addition to being non-automatic and morpholexically conditioned, they have the property that they can neutralize phonological contrasts. For instance, the contrast between /k/ and /s/ is neutralized by Velar Softening. MPRs have phonemes as their input and their output. In other words, MPRs cannot be used to induce purely allophonic variation. This property is similar to Kiparsky's notion of structure preservation. Like PRs, but unlike AMRs, the MPRs may be applied in word games, and may be ignored in alphabetic writing systems. Thus, the /k ~ s/ alternation induced by Velar Softening is not recorded in English orthography, so that the writing system treats this alternation like a predictable phonological rule. (Some MPRs in English are, however, reflected in the orthography, for example the voicing alternations in plurals such as *wife* – *wives*.) Like AMRs, but unlike genuine PRs, the MPRs tend not to be applied to neologisms or to nonsense items in psycholinguistic experiments. Genuine PRs, however, reflect what is pronounceable in a language and so these rules are applied in such cases. [14]

For Dressler, then, MPRs represent a half-way stage between AMRs, the fully morphologized alternations, which are effectively a type of suppletion, and properly phonological rules. As has often been observed, the MPRs reflect a stage in historical development of phonological rules which are becoming morphologized or lexicalized, but which still retain a certain degree of generality. Dressler claims that MPRs don't get generalized in historical change, though this can happen in both PRs (as phonological processes are generalized) and to AMRs (as morphological rules are generalized).

Compared with the classical model of generative phonology represented by SPE, the typology offered by Dressler (like that of Natural Generative Phonology) is closer to the traditional structuralist typology. However, there is an important difference between both these approaches on the one hand, and post-Bloomfieldian structuralism as represented by, say, Hockett, on the other. This is the lack of a separate 'morphophonemic level' which characterizes the later forms of American structuralism. Thus, although for Dressler MPRs mediate in a certain sense between morphology and phonology, this doesn't mean that the units in which morphophonemic alternations are defined are different entities from phonemes.

Dressler's survey of MPRs is a useful compendium of information, though it has to be admitted that Dressler's aim is to provide a theory of languages rather than a theory of grammars. In this respect, the theory should perhaps be thought of as a theory of what Chomsky (1986b) has called 'E-language', rather than 'I-language' (cf. §3.3). It is for this reason that he is not too concerned to provide hard-and-fast criteria for distinguishing the different sorts of rule. As such his approach is very different in motivation from those deriving from the SPE tradition of generative grammar, such as Kiparsky's Lexical Phonology, or the theory of Morpholexical Phonology. The distinction isn't always apparent since the notational conventions Dressler and his colleagues use are generally those of generative phonology. Moreover, they make considerable appeal to 'external evidence' in the form of child language data, psycholinguistic experiments and data from language pathology, suggesting the search for a 'psychologically real' characterization of the morphological system. However, the kind of psychological reality which is at stake is very different from that which is central to the philosophy of generative grammar.

4.6 Zwicky's shape conditions

In a number of papers Arnold Zwicky has been developing an approach to morphology which pays particular regard to the interfaces between morphology and phonology and between morphology and syntax. In this section I shall outline his views on allomorphy, with particular reference to a set of problems which we have hardly touched on before. Zwicky (1986) distinguishes between Allomorphy Rules, Morphonological Rules and Phonological Rules, rather as Dressler has done. He suggests that the best way to formalize MPRs and PRs is as generative rules operating over a base form (UR), as in standard versions of generative phonology. However, for the AMRs he suggests that derived allomorphs (which are listed in the lexicon) will then be particular forms, marked to be chosen in particular contexts. The basic allomorphs are then chosen by default, an instantiation of the Elsewhere Condition. AMRs will precede MPRs which will precede PRs. In short, the general overall picture is broadly that of Lexical Phonology, Morpholexical Phonology and Natural Morphology (though, of course, with important differences of detail).

Zwicky points out, however, that it isn't just morphemes undergoing word-internal morphological processes which exhibit allomorphy. One type of allomorphy which tends to get overlooked is that shown by words such as the English indefinite article *a/an*. This word has two allomorphs whose choice is governed by the phonological environment: *an* appears before a vowel-initial word and *a* appears elsewhere. However, unlike the situations we have seen hitherto in which allomorph selection has been governed by phonology, here the allomorph selection has to take place after syntactic rules have applied. In other words, we are gradually straying from the domain of morphology proper. The indefinite article allomorphy is a rather troublesome alternation if we wish to maintain that lexically or morphologically conditioned alternations are limited to the lexicon, for this alternation is certainly lexically conditioned (it only happens to one word!), yet it seems to take place in the syntax.

We could at least write a phonological rule to describe the *a* ~ *an* alternation. For instance, we might simply say that there was a lexically governed postlexical rule deleting the /n/ of *an* before a non-vowel. Indeed, recently there has been an upsurge in interest in phonological rules which apply to phrasal or syntactic domains (e.g. Kaisse, 1985, Nespor and Vogel, 1986), so perhaps as morphologists we could carry on ignoring the problem and leave it to our phonologist colleagues. Nonetheless, the phonological solution would still be rather upsetting to theories in which all postlexical rules have to be automatic, 'allophonic' rules. However, not all alternations of this kind even admit of a phonological description. Take the case of the alternation found in French with adjectives such as *beau* ([bo]) 'beautiful'. This word has an irregular feminine stem allomorph, *belle* ([bel]). However, the same allomorph (but spelled *bel*) is also found modifying masculine nouns if the following word begins with a vowel, *un bel homme*, [ɛ̃ bel om], 'a handsome man', not **un beau homme*. We even see the same happening to an adverbial form of the same word in the idiom *bel et bien* 'well and truly'. Similar allomorphic variation is shown by the possessive pronouns, *mon* ~ *ma*, 'my', *ton* ~ *ta*, 'thy', and so forth. Thus, we have *mon père* 'my father', *ma femme* 'my wife', *mon ami* 'my friend (masc.)', *mon amie* 'my friend (fem.)' (with the same pronunciation as the previous example), but *ma petite-amie* 'my girlfriend'. What we have here is a case of partial suppletion in which allomorph choice isn't determined until the syntax.[15]

Another type of allomorphy determined in the syntax is represented by the initial consonant mutation of Nivkh (Gilyak) (among other languages) discussed in chapter 1. Recall that in Nivkh the initial consonants of words undergo specific phonological processes such as voicing and spirantization when those words are in specific grammatical contexts (e.g. the direct object of a verb). Again, allomorph selection can only be decided here after the syntax.

Finally, a very common source of such allomorphy is clitics. (Some would say that the indefinite article allomorphy came under this heading.) The whole of chapter 9 is devoted to the problem of clitics so I'll defer discussion till then.

Zwicky proposes to lump these types of 'external' allomorphy together with other types of allomorphy in a separate component of grammar called the **Shape Component**. This component contains the lexicon itself, together with separate sets of rules for inflectional morphology and derivational morphology (Zwicky explicitly distinguishes these notions). In addition, this component houses **Shape Conditions**, those conditions governing the selection of different allomorphs (or morpheme 'shapes') postlexically, that is, in the syntax. Hence, it is here that rules governing the distribution of the *a*/*an* allomorphs is stated, as well as the form of French adjectives, the different mutated forms of Nivkh words, and so on.

Relatively little attention has been devoted to these types of problems by morphologists, though they offer some of the most intriguing puzzles in the discipline. These questions exemplify particularly well the thesis that morphology is essentially the discipline of interfaces, since it is in this area that morphology, phonology and syntax all meet and interact. Given the complexity of the resulting problems it would be too sanguine to expect widely accepted solutions to appear overnight, but it does make this one of the more interesting of present-day research areas.

4.7   Summary

The theme of this chapter has been the interface between morphology and phonology. We have seen how the notion of allomorphy has altered since the publication of SPE. As morphology has become increasingly important for linguistic theory in general and phonological theory in particular, so the theoretical devices used to describe allomorphic variation and alternations have become more diverse. This is in keeping with a general trend towards the 'modularization' of grammatical theory. Rather than attempting to cover as many disparate phenomena as possible with a single apparatus (as was proposed in SPE), linguists are constructing separate subtheories with their own sets of rules, representations and principles, and examining the way these subtheories interact. Thus, in Lexical Phonology we see first a distinction drawn between lexical phonology and phrase phonology, and an explicit theory of the close interaction between the lexical phonology and the theory of morphology. The recent work of Zwicky illustrates the theme of the modular interaction of independent (sub)components particularly well.

A number of ideas have been resuscitated from pre-generative theories and given a generative gloss. The notion of allomorphy itself has been reintroduced, as a concept distinct from phonology. The notion of phonemic contrast has been emphasized in Kiparsky's principle of structure preservation. However, despite the modular nature of contemporary theories there seems to be one distinction familiar from pre-generative structuralism which has not re-emerged, namely, the idea of an independent morphophonemic level. Morphemes consist of phonemes (or other phonological entities like tones, stress patterns, and so on). There is no intermediate level between phonology and morphology. In this respect contemporary theories of morphophonemics remain true to a Prague School conception rather than the post-Bloomfieldian conception of the subject.

Finally, the early preoccupation with the purely lexical aspects of allomorphy is gradually being redressed with the rekindling of interest in the problem of allomorphy at the syntactic level.

However, considerable though the changes in the conception of allomorphy in generative grammar have been, we have so far told only a small part of the story. For we have restricted ourselves primarily to allomorphy which takes the form of alternations in the particular segments within a morpheme. However, we know from chapter 1 that there are rather more drastic types of alternation found in languages, some of which stretch the very notions of 'morpheme' and 'allomorphy' to their conceptual limits. It is to these types of allomorphy that we turn in the next chapter when we trace the development of 'non-concatenative' morphology.

EXERCISES

4.1 Give the UR for *chvileček* and *chvilečka* and show how to generate the surface forms using rule 7. What assumptions do you have to make about the application of the rule to get the derivation to work?

4.2 The Strict Cycle Condition: Rubach (1984) argues that the Polish phonological system includes the rules 1–6. Rules 1–5 are cyclic and rule 6 is postcyclic. (Rubach, 1984, only distinguishes cyclic and postcyclic, i.e. postlexical, rules.)

Cyclic

1) Adjective Strident Palatalization
   š, ž⇒ś, ź /_____ i] Adj.
2) First Velar Palatalization
   k, g, x⇒č, ž, š /_____ i, e, j
3) Gliding
   i⇒j /_____ V
4) Nominal Strident Palatalization
   š⇒ś /_____ i] Dim./Aug.
5) Glide Deletion
   j⇒Ø/ {ś, ź, š, ž} _____

Postcyclic

6) Retraction
   i⇒y/ {š, ž, č} _____

The cyclic rules are applied in a specific extrinsically determined order. On the basis of data sets A, B (given in broad Slavicist transcription), determine what this order is. Data set A consists of neuter augmentatives formed from noun stems of any gender. Data set B consists of the nominative fem. sg. of denominal adjectives. Assume that the UR of the neuter ending is /o/, the feminine ending, /a/ and the Denominal Adjective suffix, /i/. Rubach assumes that each morpheme triggers a new cycle. Given this assumption, and given your proposed rule order, how does data set A provide an argument for the Strict Cycle Condition?

Set A: neuter augmentatives

kapeluš	'hat'	kapeluśiško
noga	'leg'	nožyško
xwopak	'boy'	xwopačyško
gmax	'building'	gmašyško

Set B: Denominal adjectives

byk	'bull'	byča
myš	'mouse'	myśa
papuga	'parrot'	papuźa
mnix	'monk'	mniśa

4.3 What would the explanation be, given the model of Kiparsky (1982b), for the following contrasts? Give complete derivations.

(i) a) The policemen $\left\{ \begin{array}{l} \text{rang} \\ *\text{ringed} \end{array} \right\}$ the doorbells.
   b)

(ii) a) The policemen $\left\{ \begin{array}{l} *\text{rang} \\ \text{ringed} \end{array} \right\}$ the demonstrators.
   b)

4.4 'Elsewhere' in morphology: Write a set of informal rules (i.e. in prose) to account for the following Czech paradigms, making crucial use of the Elsewhere Condition.

		Class A 'to do'	Class B 'to suffer'	Class C 'to take'	Class D 'to be'
Sg.	1	dělám	trpím	beru	sem
	2	děláš	trpíš	bereš	seš
	3	dělá	trpí	bere	je
Pl.	1	děláme	trpíme	bereme	sme
	2	děláte	trpíte	berete	ste
	3	dělají	trpějí	berou	sou

(Classes A, B are regular classes, Class C is a minor, irregular class, Class D is a unique irregular verb.)

4.5 Allomorphy in Palan Koryak (Žukova, 1980): Identify the component morphemes in the following paradigm from the Palan dialect of Koryak (a paleosiberian language spoken in Kamchatka and NE Siberia). What phonological constraints govern the allomorphy? Write a set of phonological rules to account for these forms.

ŋəvok 'to begin'

		Present	Past	Future
Sg.	1	təŋvotkən	təŋvok	tətaŋvoŋ
	2	ŋəvotkən	ŋəvojja	taŋvoŋə
	3	ŋəvotkən	ŋəvojja	taŋvoŋə
Pl.	1	mətəŋvolatkən	mətəŋvolamək	məttaŋvolamək
	2	ŋəvolatkənetək	ŋəvolatək	taŋvolatək
	3	ŋəvolatkən	ŋəvolat	taŋvolaŋ

4.6 Possessed nouns in Welsh. Determine the possessive morphemes and list the noun root allomorphs shown in the data. Determine what pattern the root allomorphy follows, and use this to predict a full set of allomorphs for each noun root. What is the base form of each root? How might you define the root allomorph classes in phonological terms? In this allomorphy conditioned purely phonologically, purely morphologically, or by a mixture of these? [Note: n^h, ŋ^h, m^h indicate aspirated nasals, otherwise the transcription is IPA.]

ajxdevajdxi	'your sheep'	ajxkawsxi	'your cheese'
ajavre	'his goat'	ajblentine	'his child'
ajbarnhi	'her opinion'	əŋavri	'my goat'
əŋ:mi	'my game'	ajdevajdhi	'her sheep'
ajxti:xi	'your house'	ajflentinhi	'her child'
ajaxawshi	'her cheese'	əmarni	'my opinion'
ajgavrxi	'your goat'	ənevajdi	'my sheep'
əm^{h}arseli	'my parcel'	ajvajke	'his bicycle'
ajge:mhi	'her game'	ənusteri	'my duster'
ajvarne	'his opinion'	əmajki	'my bicycle'
ajdre:ne	'his train'	əŋ^{h}awsi	'my cheese'
əŋ^{h}ofii	'my coffee'	ajxbarnxi	'your opinion'
ajfarselhi	'her parcel'	ən^{h}re:ni	'my train'
ajθi:hi	'her house'	aje:me	'his game'
ajgawse	'his cheese'	ajgavrhi	'her goat'
ajgofie	'his coffee'	ən^{h}ʻi:i	'my house'
ajðustere	'his duster'	ajxplentinxi	'your child'

5

Nonlinear Approaches to Morphology

Introduction

Morphophonological theory, as we have seen in the previous chapter, has undergone profound changes since the publication of *The Sound Pattern of English*. However, in chapter 4 we saw only part of the story. The development of phonological theory since the mid-1970s has ushered in even more fundamental changes in morphophonology and morphology in general. The most important development from our point of view was the theory of Autosegmental Phonology, proposed by John Goldsmith in his doctoral dissertation in 1976 (for his most recent statement see Goldsmith, 1990). This was essentially a theory of tone languages (particularly African tone languages) in which the tonal properties of a word are factored out and treated separately from the segmental properties. Goldsmith proposed a two-tiered representation in which tones are associated to tone-bearing segments (usually vowels, sometimes sonorant consonants) according to certain universal conventions. The key idea here is that a phonological representation is more than just a sequence of segments, each with its properties. Rather, it consists of a string of segments, together with a string of other elements, called **autosegments**, and a specified mapping between them. In other words, we have, for example, a sequence of consonant and vowel phonemes, and simultaneously a sequence of tones, together with an indication of which tones are linked to which vowels. Since we have more than one 'line' of phonological elements, such a representation is often called **nonlinear** (though the alternative **multilinear** is rather more accurate).

In the first section we'll see how the principles of Autosegmental Phonology were applied by John McCarthy (1979) to the problem of Semitic root-and-pattern morphology to produce what is often called a theory of **nonconcatenative morphology**, that is, a 'non-agglutinative' theory. As we saw in chapter 1, root-and-pattern systems pose serious problems for traditional theories based on the linear, agglutinative approach to morphology. It's hard to overestimate the importance of McCarthy's proposals. Every aspect of the theory of morphology and morphophonology has had to be reappraised in one way or another in the wake of his analysis of Semitic and other languages. This section overviews McCarthy's original theory, giving the basic facts in justification of it, and the essentials of the theoretical machinery McCarthy introduces. In addition, it looks briefly at latter developments in the theory in relation to Lexical Phonology.

The second section deals entirely with one type of morphophonological phenomenon: reduplication. This has excited considerable interest over the past decade, perhaps mainly because the multilinear approach has opened up possibilities of analysis which are so much more insightful than the earlier transformational approaches. As a result, rather arcane facts from 'exotic' languages, which had been little more than descriptive curios, have assumed a major significance in deciding between competing, though often rather similar, theoretical models. This explosion of interest in just a single type of phenomenon is a good example of the way scientific discovery and the appraisal of empirical facts depends in large part on the theoretical apparatus at the disposal of the scientific community.

Section three surveys other types of morphological processes in which we need to separate one aspect of phonological structure from others. We first look at processes involving the quality of the phonemes in the representation themselves, starting with morphologically motivated harmony systems (**prosodies**). Then we see how nonconcatenative approaches can shed light on a phenomenon known as 'echo-words', on English strong verbs, and on language games. Next we look at analyses in which the pattern of consonants and vowels, irrespective of which particular consonants and vowels they are, can be manipulated by rules of morphology or allomorphy. The examples we examine are from Yokuts and Czech.

In the fourth section we return to the tonal origins of autosegmental theory and look at a recent influential account of how to handle tones which seem to function as morphemes.

The last section looks forward to future developments. We see an example of how McCarthy's original treatment of Arabic plurals has been modified to gain a more satisfactory coverage of the data, and touch on a particularly interesting example of nonconcatenative morphology, that of Sign Language.

5.1   The autosegmental approach to morphology

5.1.1   McCarthy's theory

For many morphologists the prototypical word formation processes have been (linear) affixation, of the kind found in agglutinating languages. However, we saw in chapter 1 that many processes (including some found in Indo-European languages) do not conform to this Item-and-Arrangement ideal. Quite frequently it appears as though it is a phonological alternation which is expressing the morphological category, and not a morpheme proper. We have seen this for tone, stress, vowel length and other prosodic characteristics, as well as processes affecting the phonological makeup of a root such as the initial consonant mutations of Nivkh, or apophony (ablaut), found in English forms such as *sing ~ sang ~ sung ~ song*, in which the vowel of a root changes. All these types of process pose problems for a simple-minded version of IA.

The Semitic languages offer a particularly strong challenge to so-called linear models of word formation. The difficulty which a linear IA theory has with such languages was used by proponents of the generative form of the Item-and-Process approach as an argument against IA. However, the classical generative approach is still at heart an approach based on linear representations, in that URs are still assumed to take the form of linearly concatenated strings of morphemes. This assumption has been seriously questioned by a highly influential theory of Semitic morphology, developed by John McCarthy in his 1979 doctoral dissertation (published as McCarthy, 1982a).

Recall that, in Arabic, words are commonly formed on the basis of a triliteral root, a set of three consonants between which are inserted (or 'intercalated') sets of vowels. In some cases the sequence of vowels itself signifies a grammatical category such as 'perfective active'. Thus, if we take the root *ktb* 'write', and the vowel sequences of 5.1, we obtain the verb stems in 5.2:

5.1   a) a a
       b) u i
       c) a u
       d) u a

5.2   a) katab   perfective active
       b) kutib   perfective passive
       c) aktub   imperfective active
       d) uktab   imperfective passive

If we say (as I suggested in chapter 1) that the morphological realization (morph) corresponding, say, to 'perfective passive' is the vowel sequence 5.1b itself, then we will have a discontinuous root morph *k-t-b* and a set of discontinuous infixes (and prefixes) as shown in 5.3:

5.3   a) perf. act.   b) perf. pass.

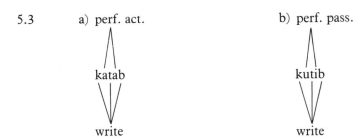

The problem, then, is how to ensure that the vowels and consonants appear in the right order.

A further dimension to this problem is revealed when we look at, say, the perfective active in more detail. A complete table of verb patterns corresponding to that given in 1.23, chapter 1, would take the form of 5.4, bearing in mind that in general a verb would not appear with all of these patterns (this table is based on McCarthy,

1982a: 134; cf. also the discussion of these phenomena in Goldsmith, 1990, especially p. 97):

5.4

I	katab	IX	ktabab
II	kattab	X	staktab
III	kaatab	XI	ktaabab
IV	?aktab	XII	ktawbab
V	takattab	XIII	ktawwab
VI	takaatab	XIV	ktanbab
VII	nkatab	XV	ktanbay
VIII	ktatab		

In some cases these have more than the three consonants of the original root. Inspection of similar forms for different roots would reveal, for instance, that the initial ?-, t- and n- of IV, V, VI, VII are prefixes and the first t of VIII is an infix, as is the n of XIV. Inspection of other verbal categories with different vocalism reveals that the shifts in vowel length, as seen in III, VI, IX, are independent of the selection of vowels. In other words, vowel length itself is part of the binyan, and thus is an exponent of the morphological categories illustrated in 5.4. The same is true of the consonant gemination seen in II and V, and of the repetition of the /b/ at the end of IX, XII, XIV.

How does McCarthy apply the ideas of autosegmental phonology to these data?[1] The first plank in his theory is the notion of a **prosodic template** (or **CV tier** or **CV skeleton**). This is a representation of a morpheme or word simply in terms of the string of consonants and vowels which make it up but without any indication of the precise identity of those consonants and vowels. Phonologists informally use the same idea when they speak, say, about a closed syllable as a 'CVC syllable'. McCarthy claims that a specification of CV templates is part of the grammar of Arabic. The language specifies eight distinct patterns of CV sequences and these define the basic (skeletonic) structure of the fifteen binyanim. The eight templates needed to generate all the forms of 5.4 are given in 5.5 (following McCarthy, I show only the commoner of the binyanim and ignore the marginal patterns):

5.5

C V C V C	I
C V C C V C	II, IV
C V V C V C	III
C V C V C C V C	V
C V C V V C V C	VI
C C V C V C	VII, VIII
C C V V C V C	XI
C C V C C V C	XIV

Crucial to McCarthy's theory is the idea that separate identifiable exponents of a morphological category, such as the triliteral root or the vowel sequence, are represented on separate planes or dimensions of the representation. These planes are usually called **tiers**. The CV template is the basic tier of the representation of an Arabic word. For verbs this tier also conveys morphological information, by indicating which binyan the word belongs to. The other two tiers consist of ordinary phonemic segments, the sequence of root consonants and the vowel sequences. These segments are called **melody** elements. They have to be associated to the C and V slots of the CV template, and this is where the principles of autosegmental phonology make their appearance.

Ignoring the binyanim with affixes, let us consider patterns I, III, XIV, concentrating for the moment on the consonant tier. We'll get the correct forms if we can associate the melody elements to the C slots in the manner shown in 5.6a–c:

5.6

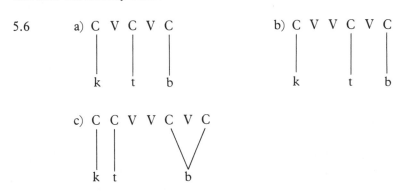

The representations of 5.6 can be built up from those of 5.7 by means of a simple set of principles governing the association of melody elements to CV slots:

5.7   a) C V C V C   b) C V V C V C

               k t b   k t b

           c) C C V V C V C

               k t b

A given melody element on a given tier is attached to a C slot in a one-to-one fashion from left to right, respecting the **Well-Formedness Condition**, 5.8 (which I present here in a simplified form):

5.8   a) Every CV skeletal slot must be associated with at least one melody element and every melody element must be associated with at least one appropriate C or V slot.
           b) Association lines must not cross.

'Appropriate' in 5.8a means that a consonant melody element links to a C slot and a vowel element links to a V slot. Application of this procedure to 5.7 will yield 5.9:

5.9

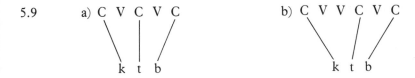

Since there are as many C slots in 5.9a, b as there are melody elements, nothing further needs to be done with these examples, but the final C slot of 5.9c remains unlinked. Therefore, we invoke a process of automatic **spreading** (again from left to right) to complete the derivation. Thus, we obtain 5.10:

5.10

Finally, we need to attach vowel melody elements to the V slots. The simplest case is a vocalic melody consisting of just a single element such as the /a/ of the perfect active. Again, the vowels occupy their own separate tier, which we can show by writing them above the CV template. Assuming we have already associated consonants to C slots, all we need do is take a single *a* element and associate it to all the V slots, as shown in 5.11:

5.11
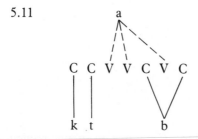

(The use of dotted lines in such representations is meant to convey the idea of association in progress, as opposed to association which has already been effected. This notational ploy has no theoretical status, though.)

When the vocalic melody consists of two elements, the association process is very similar to that found with consonants. For instance, to generate the perfective passive, *kutib*, we need to associate the melody /u i/ as in 5.12:

5.12
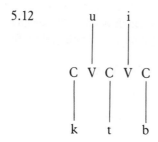

Matters are complicated slightly by the fact that a sequence of two adjacent vowels, written as VV in the prosodic template, represents a single syllabic nucleus in the form of a long vowel. Thus, a skeleton such as CVVCVC with a vowel melody /u i/ will give *kuutib* in which the /u/ links to the first VV sequence, and not **kuitib* (which would be unpronounceable in Arabic).

Notice that it is very important that the vowel and consonant melody tiers be separated and that the association of consonants and vowels to the prosodic template be independent. Otherwise, we would end up with crossing association lines as in 5.13, corresponding to 5.6a, c. This would be true in the case of 5.13c even if we assumed that there were two separate *a* vowels:

5.13

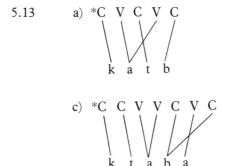

Now let us consider the forms with affixes. McCarthy identifies three prefixes ʔ- 'causative', *t*- 'reflexive' and *n*- with no fixed function. We have seen that the consonant and vowel melodies have been separated and set on different tiers. This reflects an important assumption of McCarthy's, namely that *every morpheme* making up a word is assigned to a separate tier. This assumption is known as the **Morphemic Tier Hypothesis**, and it is crucial to much current work in phonology and morphology.[2] This means that a word with an affix will consist of four tiers: the prosodic template, the root consonants, the vowels and the affix itself. (It quickly becomes impossible to notate such representations accurately on two-dimensional paper.) Using the Greek letter μ to represent a morpheme and hence to define a morphemic tier, we can represent the final structure of binyanim IV–VII from 5.4 as 5.14:

5.14

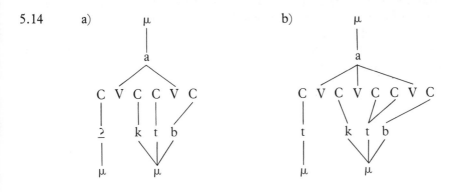

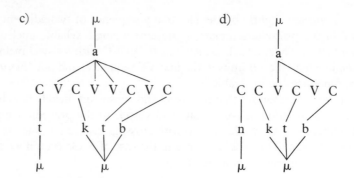

Similarly, binyan XIV, with infix -*n*-, can be represented as in 5.15 (ignoring vowels):

5.15

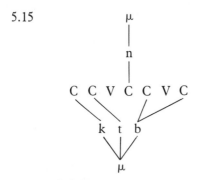

These representations result from the association principles already discussed given the additional proviso that the affix material is associated before the root melody (otherwise, the first consonant of the triliteral root would always associate to the first C slot of the template, and there would be no prefixes in the language).

There remain a few troublesome cases. One of these is representation 5.14b, corresponding to binyan V. Given the principle that association is left-to-right and one-to-one, we would expect this to take the form *takatbab* (rather like the binyan IX form, *ktabab*), and yet 5.14b has a geminated *t*. The same applies to binyan II. The second problem is that the reflexive affix *t* appears as an infix in binyan VIII not as a prefix.

McCarthy deals with these hiccups by means of two phonological rules. These illustrate quite neatly the way the phonology and morphology interact in non-linear approaches to morphophonemics. The second case is the simplest. McCarthy assumes a rule of *Eighth Binyan Flop* which dissociates the *t* prefix and moves it one position to the right on the skeleton:

5.16   Eighth Binyan Flop

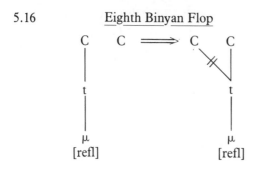

This is by now a standard nonlinear formulation of a rule of **metathesis** (i.e. a process in which adjacent elements are interchanged).

The first case is dealt with by a rule erasing one of the association lines (**delinking**) in the binyan II and V forms. We may represent this as in 5.17:

5.17   Second, Fifth Binyan Erasure

$$C \ V \ C]^{II,V}$$

[ ]

μ

[root]

By convention, delinking is followed by respreading from the left. The derivation of *kattab* is shown in 5.18:

5.18

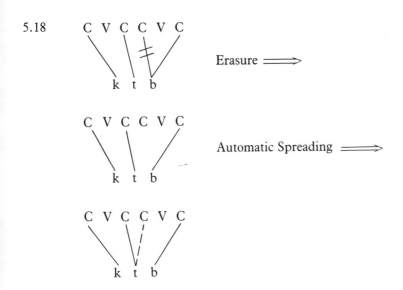

C V C C V C

k   t   b   Erasure ⟹

C V C C V C

k   t   b   Automatic Spreading ⟹

C V C C V C

k   t   b

A great many analyses in phonology nowadays appeal to this type of compound rule consisting of dissociation followed by automatic reassociation.

Before we briefly consider other aspects of Arabic root-and-pattern morphology let's take stock of what has been achieved. We have adopted the assumption that Arabic word structure separates out consonant and vowel melodies, and a CV skeleton or prosodic template. Each of these three is regarded as (the exponent of) a single morpheme or morphological category (such as 'binyan') and each of these exists on its own tier. Given these assumptions, together with the two special rules 5.16, 5.17, many of the more recalcitrant features of the morphology of the Arabic verb system have now the automatic consequence of completely general principles of phonological and morphological organization.

Nouns in Arabic, like verbs, exhibit complex patterns of root-and-pattern morphology, which is most obvious when we look at plural formation. Arabic nouns form their plurals in one of two ways: either addition of a suffix (the 'sound plural') or by a change in the CV skeleton and change in the vocalism (the 'broken plural'). The sound plurals are simply examples of concatenative affixation of a familiar kind. It is the broken plurals which are of interest to us.

McCarthy provides 5.19 amongst his examples of broken plurals. (The symbol /9/ represents a voiced pharyngeal continuant, and /H/ its voiceless congener):

5.19   a) quadriliteral roots
              maktab   makaatib   'office'
              miftaaH   mafaatiiH   'key'
          b) quinqueliteral roots
              9ankabuut   9anaakib   'spider'
              9andaliib   9anaadil   'nightingale'
          c) triliteral roots: CVVCV(V)C
              jaamuus   jawaamiis   'buffalo'
              xaatam   xawaatim   'signet'

These plural forms all have a template of the form CVCVVCVC or CVCVVCVVC, the length of the final vowel being the same as that of the final vowel of the singular form. In all the plurals the final vowel is *i* and the preceding vowels are always *a*. In the (b) forms the final consonant of the singular fails to appear in the plural, while in the (c) forms an extra consonant *w* appears in the middle of the word.

These observations can be accounted for if we assume that the broken plural for this class of nouns is defined by the template 5.20a and the vocalic melody 5.20b:

5.20   a) CVCVVCV(V)C   b) a   i

                                               [plural]

We then assume that the derivation begins by associating the *i* of 5.20b with the rightmost vowel position. The rest of the vowel and melody and the consonant melody are then associated left-to-right as usual:

5.21   a)   a   i   b)   a   i

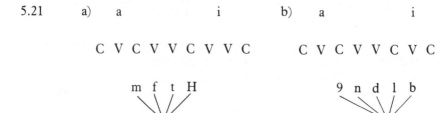

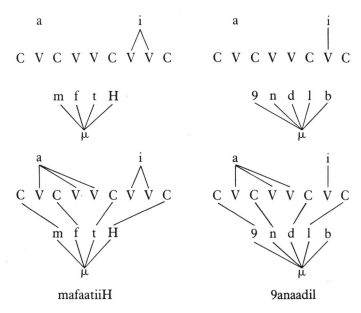

mafaatiiH   9anaadil

Notice that the prosodic template has only four C slots. Therefore, there are insufficient slots for all the five consonants of the quinqueliteral roots. Since the consonants associate in one-to-one fashion from left to right, this means that the final consonant remains unassociated. By general (universal) convention, any melody element which fails to associate by the end of the derivation is deleted (**Stray Deletion/Erasure**).

McCarthy accounts for the insertion of a *w* in the (c) examples by means of a special rule which associates *w* with the second C slot of the template. This rule applies after root consonants have been associated to the template. In autosegmental theory it is assumed that it is universally impossible for a slot to be associated with two melody elements from different morphemic tiers. Therefore, when the *w* is inserted it automatically causes the association between its slot and the root consonants to be severed (by automatic delinking). McCarthy assumes that this process is taken further and that all the consonants to the right of the *w* are reassociated. The derivation of *xawaatim* is shown in 5.21c, ignoring the vocalism:

5.21   c)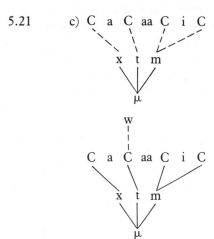

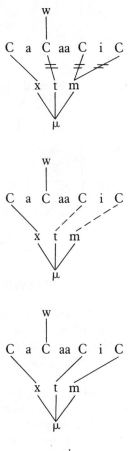

xawaatim

5.1.2 Some theoretical consequences of McCarthy's approach

McCarthy's adoption of the theory of Autosegmental Phonology has allowed him to formalize the notion of a discontinuous morpheme such as the triconsonantal roots of Semitic. This effectively means that he can provide an IA analysis of root-and-pattern, nonconcatenative morphology, but one on which the items are arranged in a multidimensional space and not a linear string. This is a big advance over earlier generative theories of such phenomena, which were obliged to appeal to complex transformational rules to modify the phonological structures of words and which therefore had great difficulty extracting what was similar about the various patterns observed. However, the main disadvantage to the transformational treatments was that they made use of descriptive devices which were extremely powerful. The formalisms that were capable of handling Arabic verb patterns would have been equally capable of describing all manner of alternations which are totally unattested in the world's languages and which most linguists would regard as somehow universally impossible.

Let's illustrate this conceptual point with a hypothetical example (modifying

McCarthy's own discussion of this matter somewhat). Consider the way we might formalize broken plural formation for the quadriliteral and quinqueliteral roots discussed in the previous subsection. We need to write a rule which will derive the plurals shown in 5.22 from corresponding singular forms:

5.22   a) miftaaH$\Rightarrow$mafaatiiH
        b) 9ankabuut$\Rightarrow$9anaakib

Recall that the CV sequence of the broken plural is *CaCaaCi(i)C* irrespective of the vowels of the singular. The consonants are determined by the root itself. A simple transformation to handle this is given in 5.23 (ignoring the length alternation in the final vowel in the plural):

5.23 $C_1 \ V_1 \ C_2 \ C_3 \ V_2 \ C_4 \ (V_3 \ C_5) \Rightarrow C_1 \ a \ C_2 \ aa \ C_3 \ i \ C_4$

Actually, this is a shorthand version of something which would be rather more complex in a properly formalized grammar. This rule correctly captures the vocalism of the plural and also the fact that the final consonant is omitted from the plural in the case of quinqueliteral roots. It also correctly reflects the fact that the consonants themselves remain in the same order as the singular, even though their position relative to the vowels might change.

There are problems with this formalism, however. First, it doesn't adequately capture the fact that the consonant sequence of the plural remains identical to that of the singular form. Strictly speaking, a rule such as 5.23 would have the same status as a rule such as 5.24, in which the consonants are reordered in a random fashion:

5.24 $C_1 \ V_1 \ C_2 \ C_3 \ V_2 \ C_4 \ (V_3 \ C_5) \Rightarrow C_5 \ a \ C_1 \ aa \ C_4 \ i \ C_2$

Yet rules such as 5.24 are unheard of in phonological systems (though similar things do occur in word games and other extralinguistic phenomena).

What we need is some way of extracting out the root consonant sequence in both singular and plural form and ensuring that this sequence isn't specifically mentioned in the rule. This is because the sequence itself doesn't change and therefore serves as part of the context for the structural change of the transformation. However, this would mean taking a representation something like 5.25, in which the consonants and vowels are separated, and adding a further rule to slot the vowels into the right positions with respect to the consonants in both singular and plural form (as in 5.25a, b respectively):[3]

5.25   a) $C_1 \ C_2 \ C_3 \ C_4 \ (C_5) + V_1 \ V_2 \ (V_3) \Rightarrow C_1 \ V_1 \ C_2 \ C_3 \ V_2 \ C_4 \ V_3 \ C_5$
        b) $C_1 \ C_2 \ C_3 \ C_4 \ (C_5) + a \ aa \ i \Rightarrow C_1 \ a \ C_2 \ aa \ C_3 \ i \ C_4$

However, we again have the problem that the transformational rule is a very powerful formal device. If we are permitted to write a rule which can position vowels in some order with respect to a string of consonants, there is still going to be nothing to stop us writing a rule such as 5.24. Indeed, if anything, such a rule would appear to be simpler. Moreover, we haven't really solved the problem of representing the invariance of the consonantal root with rules like 5.25.

Another example of this type of formal, conceptual problem is illustrated by the verb binyanim. Recall that binyan XI has the form CCVVCVC, so that we get the word form *ktaabab* from the root *ktb*. Again, this could be represented by a rule such as 5.26:

5.26 $C_1 V_1 C_2 V_2 C_3 \Rightarrow C_1 C_2 V_1 V_1 C_3 V_2 C_3$

This rule has an interesting deficiency. It correctly states that the last two consonants are identical to the last consonant of the root. However, this is treated as a formal accident. It could just as easily have been the first two consonants. Worse, we could just as readily have written rules such as 5.27 using this formalism (or its more sophisticated variant along the lines of 5.24):

5.27   a) $C_1 V_1 C_2 V_2 C_3 \Rightarrow C_1 C_3 V_1 V_1 C_2 V_2 C_3$
         b) $C_1 V_1 C_2 V_2 C_3 \Rightarrow C_1 C_2 V_1 V_1 C_1 V_2 C_1$

By checking through these rules you will find that they produce forms such as *kbaatab* and *ktaakak* from *katab*. Now, forms, such as this would be impossible to derive using the machinery of autosegmental phonology. This is because the only way to achieve such a result is by allowing crossing association lines. For instance, the representations implied by 5.27 would be 5.28 (ignoring vowels):

5.28   a) C C aa C a C   b) C C aa C a C

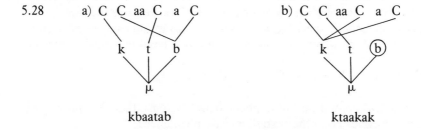

kbaatab   ktaakak

In addition, 5.28 would violate the principle that all melody elements get associated if there is an appropriate slot available. The fact that the /b/ of the root is repeated in *ktaabab* is an automatic consequence of the universal principles of (left-to-right) association in McCarthy's analysis. Therefore, this is the form we would expect from three root consonants and four C slots. Anything else would be highly marked and would require a good deal of justification on the part of the analyst. However, on the transformational account, such a result is no more or less expected than a host of alternatives which simply aren't attested in the world's languages.

What this means is that the autosegmental formalism allows us to build elements of a theory of *markedness* (or 'naturalness') into the theory by constraining the types of structures that can be generated by the formalism. Research over the past ten years suggests that the structures permitted by the theory are more or less those and only those which tend to recur throughout the languages of the world.

The device that makes transformational theories of morphology too powerful is, of course, the transformation. With the limited exception of phonological rules of metathesis (which seems to require some sort of transformational treatment in virtually everybody's theory), McCarthy makes no appeal whatever to transformational rules. Consequently, he is able to take the step of banning transformations altogether from morphology proper by formulating principle 5.29 (which formally limits morphological rules to at most context-sensitive rewriting rules[4]:

5.29   Morphological Transformation Prohibition (MTP)
        All morphological rules are of the form A → B/X, where A, B and X are (possibly null) strings of elements. (McCarthy, 1982a: 201)

The next set of theoretical points McCarthy makes concerns the relationship between morphology and the lexicon. McCarthy accepts Halle's contention that the lexicon contains all word forms including inflected words. Morphological rules, then, function as redundancy rules to **parse** (that is, analyse) existing lexical entries, though they can also be used generatively to construct neologisms. He pictures the lexicon as a set of tree structures with each tree representing a single root from which other stems or word forms are derived. A typical structured lexical entry for Arabic then looks (in part) like 5.30 for our familiar triliteral root *k-t-b*:

5.30

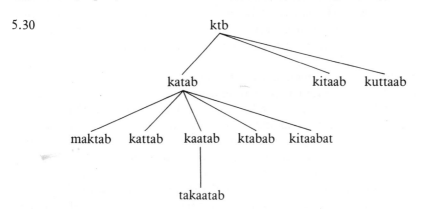

Unpredictable aspects of morphology or morphophonemics (such as idiosyncratic meanings for certain forms, or special allomorphy) are notated by diacritics on the root node. If a derived form exhibits its own special behaviour then it is furnished with its own set of diacritics, in which case it becomes the root node of another lexical entry tree. Notice that in general the nodes of the lexical entry tree represent roots and stems, not necessarily whole words. In this respect, McCarthy doesn't adhere to Aronoff's word-based morphology.

In his original dissertation, McCarthy pointed out that nonconcatenative systems such as Arabic seem to pose serious problems for models such as Lexical Phonology. This is because Lexical Phonology is built on the idea that morphologically complex words are formed by affixation from simpler words or roots, but, once word formation processes have applied in a given stratum or level, the resulting word form is treated as an unanalysed word. This, recall, is the consequence of bracket erasure. The question now arises of what corresponds to bracket erasure in a nonconcatenative theory. The key problem here is that in nonconcatenative morphology there is no obvious sense in which a derived form can be said to 'contain' its source.

Therefore, it is difficult to give an interpretation to the notion of cyclic word formation and hence the cyclic operation of lexical phonological rules.

McCarthy illustrates this with the root *d-r-s* 'study'. This gives rise to the following derivatives (amongst many others):

5.31   Binyan I
          daras   'to study'   gerund: dars
                                    occupation: darraas 'student'
          Binyan II
          darras   'to teach'   gerund: tadriis

While we might consider the gerund of *daras* to be derived from the basic verb form by deletion of the second vowel (conditioned, say, by a zero gerund affix), there is no way that *tadriis* can be said to contain *darras* as a proper subpart. Similarly, it is difficult to see how the form *darraas* 'student', can be analysed as 'daras + something'. This is because *darraas* is related to *daras* by two processes of gemination. In the autosegmental theory this is handled by assigning to *darraas* an appropriate CV template. This is much more reminiscent of treating a morpheme as a rule than as an object. The conclusion McCarthy draws is that lexical relatedness is a much more complicated matter than would appear from the inspection of concatenative morphologies.[5]

McCarthy (1986) offers a programmatic, but intuitively very plausible, answer to the question of how nonconcatenative morphology is to be reconciled with Lexical Phonology. Recall that in Semitic-type languages such as Arabic and Hebrew, phonological representations corresponding to individual morphemes reside on separate tiers. However, when a word in one of these languages is actually uttered, it is pronounced as a linear string of segments. Therefore, by the time a multitiered phonological representation is phonetically interpreted it must have been linearized. McCarthy refers to this process as **Tier Conflation**. A simple graphical representation of the process is shown for a Classical Arabic word such as *yaktubna* 'they (fem.) are writing'. This has the underlying form 5.32a, in which each morpheme, *y-* 'imperfect prefix', *-na* '3pl. suffix', *a u* 'imperfect active vocalism' and *ktb* (root), sit on distinct tiers (I've illustrated the suffix *-na* with consonant and vowel melody elements on the same tier, since there's no evidence for separation of C and V elements in suffixes as opposed to roots):

5.32   a)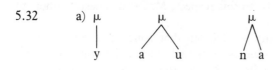

              C + V C C V C + C V

To derive the surface form, we associate the consonants and vowels to the CV skeleton in the familiar way and then we 'fold together' the consonant and vowel melodies onto a single tier, as in 5.32b:

5.32   b)

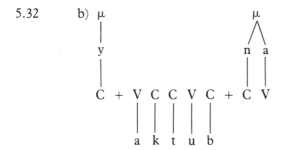

Then we perform the same operation with the remaining, morphologically determined, tiers containing the affixes. This gives us the final form, 5.32c:

5.32   c) C V C C V C C V
           | | | | | | | |
           y a k t u b n a

Although McCarthy isn't very explicit about how exactly tier conflation operates, he unambiguously claims that tier conflation is the same process as bracket erasure. Remember that he assumes that, in any language, distinct morphemes reside on distinct tiers in underlying representation. Therefore, even in concatenative morphological systems which make use solely of conventional affixation and compounding, we will need the tier conflation operation. Therefore, Semitic languages are seen to be just like other types of languages except that for them consonant and vowel sequences can constitute morphemes, and therefore, these, too, will be subject to tier conflation.

This perspective solves most of the problems of accommodating nonconcatenative morphologies to Lexical Phonology. It also makes some interesting predictions. For, in Lexical Phonology, bracket erasure takes place at the end of each level or stratum. Therefore, there are phonological rules which precede it and others which follow it on the next level, and still others, namely the postlexical rules, which always follow bracket erasure. McCarthy argues that there are phonological rules in languages such as Semitic which must be sensitive to the pre-conflation structure, and other types of rules which must be insensitive to this structure, and which therefore follow the tier conflation operation. Moreover, the pre-conflation rules have the properties of cyclic lexical rules, while the post-conflation rules have the properties of postlexical rules (and, perhaps, postcyclic rules, on the model of Booij and Rubach, 1987). It would take us too far into phonological theory to discuss McCarthy's reasoning in detail. Suffice it to say that the phonological arguments give good grounds for saying that bracket erasure and tier conflation are one and the same.[6]

5.2 Reduplication

In chapter 1 we saw examples of reduplication from the Philippine language Tagalog. Here they are again:

5.33	sulat	'write'	su-sulat, mag-sulat-sulat
	magpasulat	'make someone write'	magpa-pa-sulat
	basa	'read'	mam-ba-basa

We can see that one reduplication process reduplicates the first CV of the root, while another reduplicates the whole root. In *magpapasulat* it appears that part of the prefix has been reduplicated (to the right).

If we look at reduplication throughout the world's languages we encounter what at first seems to be a great variety of types. The reduplication can take place to the left of the root, as a prefix, to the right, as a suffix, or inside the root, as an infix. The material reduplicated can be a whole word, a whole morpheme, a syllable or sequence of syllables, or simply a string of consonants and vowels which doesn't form any particular prosodic constituent (i.e. syllable, foot, morpheme, etc.). Other variations on reduplication patterns will be mentioned as we proceed. Some characteristic examples of these reduplication types are given in 5.34–5.42:

5.34   Agta (Marantz, 1982: 439)
- a) bari 'body'   barbari-k kid-in 'my whole body'
- b) mag-saddu 'leak (vb)'   mag-sadsaddu 'leak in many places'
- c) ma-wakay 'lost'   ma-wakwakay 'many things lost'
- d) takki 'leg'   taktakki 'legs'
- e) ulu 'head'   ululu 'heads'

5.35   Madurese (Marantz, 1982: 451)
- a) búwáq-án 'fruit'   wáq-búwáqán' 'fruits'

5.36   Dakota (Broselow and McCarthy, 1983: 29)
- a) ksa   ksaksa 'to cut'
- b) hạska   hạskaska 'to be tall'
- c) xap-a   xap-xap-a 'to rustle'

5.37   Palan Koryak (Žukova 1980: 42–3)
- a) liŋ   liŋ-liŋ 'heart'
- b) wiru   wiru-wir 'seal'
- c) jiŋe   jiŋe-jiŋ 'mist'
- d) mətq   mətq-mət 'fat'
- e) tərg   tərg-tər 'meat'

5.38   Classical Greek (Goodwin, 1894)
- a) ly:o: 'I release'   lelyka 'I have released'
- b) thy:o: 'I sacrifice'   tethyka 'I have sacrificed'
- c) grapho: 'I write'   gegrapha 'I have written'

5.39   Yoruba (Marantz, 1982: 449)
   a) lọ 'to go'   lílọ '(nominalization)'
   b) dùn 'to be tasty, sweet' dídùn '(nominalization)'

5.40   Yidin^y (Marantz, 1982: 453)
   a) ḍimurU 'house'   ḍimuḍimurU 'houses'
   b) gindalba 'lizard'   gindalgindalba 'lizards'

5.41   Samoan (Broselow and McCarthy, 1983: 30)
    sg.   pl.
   a) taa   ta-taa   'strike'
   b) nofo   no-nofo 'sit'
   c) moe   mo-moe 'sleep'
   d) alofa   a-lo-lofa 'love'
   e) maliu ma-li-liu 'die'

5.42   Temiar (Broselow and McCarthy, 1983: 39)
   a) kɔ̄w 'to call'   kwkɔ̄w 'simulfactive)'
   b) slɔg 'to lie down, marry' sglɔg '(simulfactive)'

Reduplication has excited a good deal of interest from generative phonologists and morphologists in recent years (following in large part from the impetus given to the subject by Wilbur's (1973) dissertation). This is because reduplication appears to be fundamentally nonconcatenative and hence it has important implications for autosegmental theories of phonology and morphology. A further interest is in the interaction between reduplication and other rules of morphology and phonology. Reduplication processes are of peculiar interest to morphophonology because reduplication itself has a morphological and a phonological aspect. Teasing these apart is a significant challenge to current theories.

McCarthy (1982a) discussed reduplication in Semitic and other languages in some detail. We begin, however, with the theory of Marantz (1982), which itself is based on McCarthy's proposals, and which has had a considerable impact on subsequent research into reduplication.

Within a linear phonological framework, reduplications of the kind cited above would have been handled by means of (a set of) transformational rules which would have had the effect of copying a string from the root to the left, to the right, or in the middle of the root. This is the analysis adopted, for instance, for Tagalog by Carrier (1979), and, following her, Lieber (1980). It is also the type of analysis adopted by Aronoff (1976; 73ff). We saw in the previous section that McCarthy's thesis contains arguments that such transformational ways of handling nonconcatenative morphology would appeal to rules having the formal power to perform any conceivable rearrangement of the segments of a root. Now, we have seen a fair variety of types of reduplication, but this variety is nothing like what would be expected on a transformational theory. Marantz therefore proposes that reduplication is essentially affixation but that what is affixed is a CV skeleton, or prosodic template. The phonemic content of the reduplicative affix is then obtained by copying the complete phoneme melody of the root and linking it to the affixal CV template respecting the principles of association familiar from autosegmental phonology. Taking the first set of examples above from Agta, Marantz proposes the derivation in 5.43:

5.43   Agta reduplication *taktakki* 'legs' (Marantz, 1984)

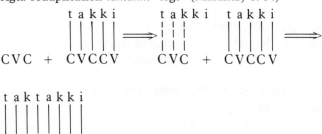

Marantz imposes four conditions on the linking of melody tier to prosodic template. These are paraphrased in 5.44:

5.44

Condition A: Melody consonants link to C slots and melody vowels link to V slots.

Condition B: Linking is strictly one-to-one; no multiple links are allowed.

Condition C: CV slots may be prelinked to specific phonemes. Prelinking takes precedence over autosegmental linking from the root melody.

Condition D: (i) directionality of linking: either the leftmost melody phoneme links with the leftmost appropriate CV slot and linking proceeds from left-to-right; or, the rightmost melody phoneme links with the rightmost appropriate CV slot and linking proceeds right-to-left. In the unmarked case, linking proceeds towards the root, i.e. left-to-right for prefixes, right-to-left for suffixes.

(ii) Linking is 'melody driven' in the sense that the association algorithm starts with a melody phoneme and then tries to find an appropriate CV slot, not the other way around.

In accordance with autosegmental principles, any melody elements or prosodic template slots left unassociated at the end of the derivation are deleted by convention, as in the case of the melody phonemes *-ki* in derivation 5.43.

Condition A is illustrated in the derivation of example 5.34e, shown in 5.45a:

5.45   Agta *ululu* 'heads'

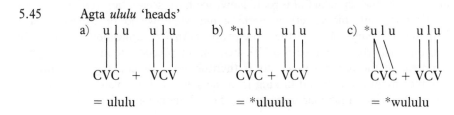

If melody elements could associate to the wrong type of slot then we would expect derivations such as 5.45b. If a single melody element were allowed to link to two distinct slots in violation of Condition B, we might expect a derivation such as 5.45c (assuming that the vocalic element linked to a C slot is here interpreted as the corresponding glide, /w/, as is common in the autosegmental literature).

These Agta examples also illustrate Condition D(ii). If association were template-driven then we would expect a derivation such as 5.45d:

5.45   d) *u l u   u l u
                 || ||| = *luulu
                CVC   +   VCV

Finally, even respecting Condition D(ii), if association were from right-to-left we would expect derivation 5.45e:

5.45   e) *u l u   u l u
                 || ||| = *luulu
                CVC   +   VCV

The Greek and Yoruba examples illustrate Condition C, which permits melody elements to be **prelinked** or **preassociated** in lexical representations, before the operation of the usual association procedures. Marantz's analysis of Yoruba *lílọ* is shown in 5.46:

5.46   l ọ   l ọ   l ọ   l ọ   l ọ
            || || | ||
           CV ⟹ CV + CV ⟹ CV + CV ⟹lílọ
                          | |
                          í   í

The vowel of the phoneme melody is unable to associate to the V slot of the reduplicative affix because that slot is already preassociated to the /i/ vowel. Marantz also mentions cases where a V slot is associated not with a completely specified phoneme but with a distinctive feature, which modifies the character of the vocalic melody element which is associated to that slot by reduplication. (This analysis presupposes some form of underspecification for melody elements, though Marantz isn't explicit about this.)

The Agta examples show that the reduplicative prefix template is simply a sequence CVC irrespective of the syllable structure of the root. The Yidin^y data show that it is possible for a sequence of syllables to be reduplicated irrespective of the CV structure of the syllables. Notice that the syllable divisions (indicated by a period) of examples 5.40 are those of 5.47:

5.47   a) ḍi.mu.rU
           b) gin.dal.ba

In each case it is the first two syllables, *ɖi.mu* and *gin.dal*, that are reduplicated, even though the CV templates would be CVCV and CVCCVC respectively. Marantz assumes that affixation of a particular CV template is the norm and that syllable reduplication is a rarity. However, Levin (1983) argues that there are many cases which are ambiguous between syllable affixation and CV affixation and that we should regard such cases as instances of syllable reduplication. This point of view seems more consonant with the current received wisdom amongst phonologists on syllable structure.

The Marantz model has been extended by Broselow and McCarthy (1983), with certain changes, to accommodate cases where the reduplicative affix is an infix. (Such cases were dealt with only cursorily by Marantz.) The basic idea behind their treatment of infixing reduplication is the same as that which underlies prefixing and suffixing reduplication: a CV template is infixed into the root, the root melody is copied, and then its elements are mapped right-to-left or left-to-right depending on the language. For example, in the Temiar examples in 5.42 we assume that association is right-to-left as in derivation 5.48 for *sglɔg*:

5.48

$$
\begin{array}{ccccccccc}
s & l & ɔ & g & & s & & l & ɔ & g \\
| & | & | & | & & | & & | & | & | \\
C & C & V & C & \Longrightarrow & C & + \begin{array}{c} C \\ | \\ | \\ | \\ slɔg \end{array} + & C & V & C & \Longrightarrow \text{sglɔg}
\end{array}
$$

Since an infix is neither a prefix nor a suffix, directionality must be stipulated separately for each language. Note that Broselow and McCarthy differ slightly from Marantz in that they assume that the reduplicative affix is a separate morpheme and hence, according to the Morphemic Tier Hypothesis, that it has its own tier.

One of the claims Broselow and McCarthy make is that in some cases only a portion of the root melody is copied, namely that which forms a **metrical foot** constituent. A foot is a sequence of syllables beginning with a stressed syllable and followed by zero or more unstressed syllables, up to, but not including, the next stress. In Samoan, stress falls on the penultimate syllable. Thus, the foot in Samoan will consist of the last two syllables of the word. The derivation they assume for *alolofa* is given in 5.49, where 'F' stands for 'foot':

5.49

Broselow and McCarthy argue that their solution to the problem is superior to that implied in Marantz's account. First, they have a principled reason for copying just the *lofa* part of the phoneme melody (namely, because that is the foot). If the whole phoneme melody were copied we would get the wrong result, viz. *aalofa. Second, they claim that Samoan infixation is really a kind of prefixation, namely prefixation to a foot. From this it follows that the unmarked direction of association will be left-to-right, and, indeed, this is the direction of association.

There have been a number of amendments and refinements to the proposals of Marantz and of Broselow and McCarthy. Ter Mors (1983) argues that the Marantz account can be generalized and simplified by assuming that the CV template affixation rule takes the form 'Affix to X', where X is a variable which can stand for either side of the root, or either side of a prosodic constituent such as a foot, or either side of any other element, such as 'the first consonant in the root'. What is then copied is just that portion of the phoneme melody corresponding to the X portion. The derivation for the Samoan cases is essentially that of Broselow and McCarthy, but that for Temiar is slightly different, namely 5.50:

5.50   Temiar: prefix C to medial consonant position.

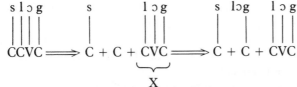

Here the portion of the melody copied is *lɔg* because this is the 'X' of the affixation rule. The direction of association is the marked direction, since the infix is effectively a prefix yet linking is right-to-left. (Broselow and McCarthy make no predictions concerning the markedness of direction in cases such as Temiar.)

Ter Mors's analysis provides a neat way around difficulties which are encountered in Broselow and McCarthy's approach. For instance, consider the following data from the Austroasiatic language Nakanai:

5.51   a) haro   hararo   'days'
         b) velo   velelo   'bubbling forth'
         c) baharu   bahararu   'widows'

Again, stress is penultimate in this language and we have another case of prefixation to a foot, this time of a VC affix. However, if we adopted the same analysis as that for Samoan we would derive entirely the wrong results, as shown in 5.52:

5.52   *baharu* 'widows'

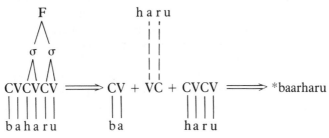

The problem, of course, is that the infixed -*ar*- is on the wrong side of the /h/ or *bah*-. The derivation needed by Broselow and McCarthy is 5.53, in which the foot is broken up by the infix:

5.53

```
                                    F                        a r u
                                   / \                        | |
                         σ      σ      σ                      | |
                         /\     /\     /\                     | |
          CVCVCV ==> CVC + VC + VCV ==> CVC  +  VC  +  VCV    | |
          ||||||        |||    |||        |||        |||
          b a h a r u   b a h  a r u      b a h      a r u
```

Broselow and McCarthy justify this analysis by pointing out that the phonotactics of the language don't permit consonant clusters. Therefore, infixing VC before CVCV is impermissible and it has to be infixed after *bah*-, as shown. However, Broselow and McCarthy are not now able to analyse this case as an example of prefixation to a prosodic constituent. Rather, we have a case of infixation *within* a prosodic constituent. In addition, the derivation only works if the phonemic copy is restricted to the -*aru* sequence. Again, we would get the wrong result if the melody of the whole foot were copied and associated left-to-right.

Ter Mors argues that we need simply stipulate affixation of VC to the sequence -VCV #. Then, all the Cs and Vs end up in the right place, and we automatically predict that only the last three phonemes of the melody will be copied, i.e. -*aru*, for this is the 'X' of the 'Affix-to-X' rule.[7]

5.3   Further applications of nonconcatenative morphology

5.3.1   *Alternations affecting melody elements*

In principle any morphological operation which appeals to discontinuous morphemes, or to morphophonemic processes which can be analysed as the spreading or delinking of autosegments, is susceptible to an analysis akin to that seen in §§5.1 and 5.2. In addition, the concept of a root template has proved valuable in a number of languages other than those of the Semitic family. In this section we will look at some of the phenomena that have been discussed in the more recent literature, so as to give some flavour of the wide applicability of the nonconcatenative mode of analysis.

The classic cases in which a discontinuous stretch of material serves to signal a grammatical or lexical contrast are harmony systems. The commonest of these are probably vowel harmony systems and nasal harmonies. In Terena, an Arawakan language of Brazil (Bendor-Samuel, 1966), we find examples of both types. In general, the language uses only oral vowels /i e o a u/ and its only nasal consonants are /m n/. However, in words referring to the first person we find that in those without obstruents all the vowels are nasalized, while in those which contain obstruents all the vowels from the left are nasalized up to the first obstruent, which itself becomes a prenasalized stop (i.e. a type of *complex segment* notated as ᵐb ⁿd, ᵑg, in which the stop element is preceded by a homorganic nasal element:

5.54   a) emoʔu   'his word'
        b) ẽmõʔũ   'my word'

5.55   a) owoku   'his house'
        b) õw̃ñ ᵑgu   'my house'

5.56   a) piho   'he went'
        b) ᵐbiho   'I went'

In an autosegmental treatment this can be formalized by assuming a feature [+nasal] as an autosegment representing the 1st person morpheme. Vowels are not specified for this feature (there are no nasalized vowels underlyingly, so nasalization is not lexically contrastive). A word in the 1st person form, such as 5.54b, is represented as a combination of the base form (essentially identical to 5.54a) and the [+nasal] autosegment. This is a **floating autosegment**, that is, it is not associated with any particular segment slot in underlying representation. We can therefore represent this UR as 5.57a. Association proceeds from left to right in the customary manner, and the autosegment links to any vowel and skips any sonorant consonant. In the case of 5.54b this means that all the vowels of the word are nasalized, as shown in 5.57b:

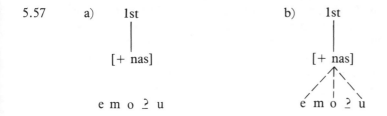

When the [+nasal] autosegment encounters an obstruent, however, its progress is blocked and the autosegment 'coalesces' with the stop to form a complex segment, the prenasalized stop. Complex segments of this sort are usually analysed as single skeletal slots which are doubly linked to opposite values of a single feature, in this case [nasal]. The derivation of 5.55b will therefore be as in 5.58 (where I have indicated the double linking on the prenasalized stop /ᵑg/, for clarity):

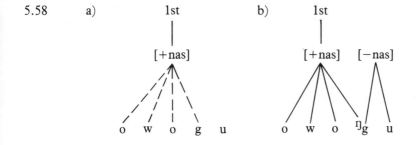

Finally, in 5.56b, the autosegment doesn't get past the first segment, so none of the vowels are affected, and the only reflex of the 1st person morpheme is the initial prenasalized stop.

Terena also illustrates a very interesting morphological use of umlaut.[8] While in Germanic languages umlaut is usually a morphophonemic concomitant of affixation or compounding, in Terena it has the character of a morpheme, much like the nasalization just discussed, in that it signals the 2nd person category. Simplifying somewhat, we may say that in words beginning with one of the four vowels other than /i/, the 2nd person form begins with /j/ (which is written as 'y' in these transcriptions). In words beginning with a consonant, the first vowel in the word other than /i/ is replaced with a 'palatal', umlauted congener, so that /a o/ are replaced by /e/, while /e u/ are replaced by /i/. This is illustrated in 5.59–5.61:

5.59	a) otopiko	'he cut down'
	b) yotopiko	'you cut down'

5.60	a) kurikena	'his peanut'
	b) kirikena	'your peanut'

5.61	a) piho	'he went'
	b) pihe	'you went'

Phonologically, the process is rather more complicated than nasalization, but our brief description shows that the principle is essentially the same.

An intriguing example of nonconcatenative morphology in which consonants and vowels seem to behave as independent morphemes has been the subject of analysis by McCarthy (1982b). He describes the formation of echo-words in Gtaʔ, a South Munda language of India. In this language, different vowel patterns are productively associated with modifications of the meaning of a given root. For instance, from the words *kiton*, 'god', and *kesu*, 'wrapper worn against the cold', we can form the echo-words of 5.62 and 5.63:

5.62	katan	'being with powers equal to kiton'
	kitin	'being smaller, weaker than kiton'
	kitan/katon	'being inferior in status to kiton'
	kutan	'being other than kiton (e.g. spirits, ghosts etc.)'

5.63	kasa	'cloth equivalent to kesu in size and texture'
	kisi	'small or thin piece of cloth'
	kesa/kasu	'large piece of thick cloth, torn or worn out, serving as a kesu'
	kusa	'any other material usable against cold'

Finally, a little nearer home, I have suggested (Spencer, 1988b) that ablaut alternations in so-called strong verbs in Germanic languages such as English should be analysed in multilinear terms. For instance, the base form of a verb such as *sing* would be represented as 5.64a, with an underspecified vowel slot:

5.64   a)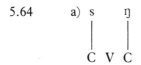

A lexical redundancy rule defined over verbs marked in the lexicon as belonging to a particular 'strong' class would then tell us that the preterite was signalled by /a/, the past participle by /u/ and the base (default) vowel was /i/. This means that structure-building redundancy rules would create for us a complex, multidimensional lexical representation of the form 5.64b (in which I have conflated the consonant melody elements and skeletal slots for typographical convenience):

5.64   b)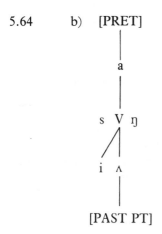

When a form of the verb *sing* is selected for lexical insertion, this complex entry is accessed from the lexicon, and the correct morphological form (base form, preterite or past participle) is then constructed by the process of tier conflation. Thus, if we wish to select the past participle form, we collapse representation 5.64b into 5.64c:

5.64   c)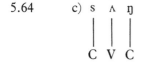

In effect, we are assuming that English exhibits a very limited version of the Semitic root-and-pattern morphology.

The last example in this subsection is an example of extralinguistic evidence which bears on the nature of morphophonemic representation, namely, certain types of language game. McCarthy (1982b), Yip (1982) and a number of others have investigated word games from the point of view of nonconcatenative morphology, and shown that in many cases they can best be regarded as operations over multidimensional representations, even in languages which do not usually make much reference to such representions in the morphology proper.

McCarthy (1982b) argues that a language game in Hanunóo, a language of the Philippines which is not usually associated with root-and-pattern morphology, appeals to the notions 'root melody' and 'root template'. Some examples of the game are given in 5.65:

5.65   a) rignuk   nugrik   'tame'
        b) bi:ŋaw   ŋa:biw   'nick'
        c) katagbuʔ   kabugtaʔ   (no gloss given)

The game is played by swapping the first and last consonant + vowel melody elements of the root. Since the prosodic template is not affected this means that vowel length is not affected by this transposition. Thus, the first vowel of *bi:ŋaw* remains long in *ŋa:biw*. The *ka-* or *katagbuʔ* is a prefix and this is why it fails to participate in the transposition. This is explicable on McCarthy's theory since the prefix and the root sit on different tiers, and it is only the root melody that is transposed in the game.

5.3.2 Alternations affecting the CV skeleton

In most of the analyses just discussed we have seen cases in which a morphological or lexical category is signalled by a particular type of melody, akin to the triliteral consonantal root in Semitic. However, the independence of the CV prosodic template has also been used to explain morphological alternations outside of Semitic.[9]

In the Yawelmani dialect of the Yokuts language of California (Archangeli, 1983) we find that the CV template of a verb root depends in certain cases on the affix that is attached to the root. There are six templates for regular verbs, show in 5.66:

5.66   a1) CVC   a2) CVCC
        b1) CVVC   b2) CVVCC
        c1) CVCVV   c2) CVCVVC

Certain affixes ('Class 1 affixes') don't affect the shape of the verb root, while others ('Class 2 affixes') select one of the templates in 5.66. In regular cases the underlying templates for a verb root are taken from the list in 5.66, too.

Consider the examples in 5.67 (modified from Archangeli, 1983: 386, abstracting away from other morphophonemic processes):

5.67   luk'l- 'bury'   huluus 'sit'
        luk'l-t 'was buried'   huluus-hn 'sat'
        luk'uul-wsiil 'cemetery'   huluus-wsiil 'place for sitting'
        luk'l-iixok' 'remain buried!' huls-iixok' 'remain seated!'

Archangeli argues that the affixes *-t* and *-hn* are Class 1. Any root which receives these affixes appears in its basic form. In the case of 'bury' this is the 5.66a2 form, CVCC, in the case of 'sit' it is the 5.66c2 form. On the other hand, the affixes *-wsiil* and *-iixoo* (the form *-iixok'* is a further affixed form of this) are Class 2 affixes selecting templates 5.66c and 5.66a respectively. In the case of the root *huluus-* the fact that affixation by *-wsiil* induces selection of the (c) template is obscured by the fact that the (c) template is in any case the basic or default template for this verb root. However, the root *luk'l* has an (a) type basic template, and therefore has to change its template to a (c) type when affixed by *-wsiil*. Contrariwise, *-iixoo* selects the 5.66a template. This has no effect on the (a) type root *luk'l-*, but forces the reselection of the template in the case of the (c) type root *huluus-*.

Notice that there is a significant difference between the Yokuts case and the Semitic root-and-pattern morphology. In Semitic, a particular CV template signals a morpholexical category such as 'binyan VIII' or 'plural'. In Yokuts this is true to a much more limited extent, in that a template is associated with the base form of each verb. But when a non-basic template is selected by a Class 2 affix, then the new template does not signal the new morphological category in and of itself, it is simply a morphophonemic concomitant of the affixation process. In this respect it is a template allomorph. In a sense, therefore, the CV skeleton is part of the lexical entry for each verb root. We might draw an analogy with a typical vowel harmony language such as Hungarian, Turkish or Chukchee. In Hungarian, affixes have two forms, one with back vowels, the other with front vowels. Roots with back vowels select the back vowel allomorph and roots with front vowels select the front vowel allomorph. However, while most current analyses of vowel harmony try to account for this alternation by means of a phonological rule (for example, autosegmental spreading of a feature [+back] or [-back]), there is no way that the different templates can be derived from a single source. Rather, the morphology of the language has to make each template available for a given verb.

The idea of root template selection has not been pursued as much as the other aspects of nonconcatenative morphology, though it would seem to be a promising way of analysing phenomena which involve segment deletion or insertion, particularly when this is morphologically or lexically governed and can't be ascribed to general phonological rules or phonotactic constraints.

Consider, for instance, the vowel-zero alternations in Slavic exemplified in §4.1. The traditional generative approach has been to assume 'abstract' underlying high lax vowels, called 'jers' (which we can represent by the symbol #), which either get vocalized to /e/, /o/ or /a/ (depending on the language) or are deleted. In the basic pattern, when we encounter an unbroken string of syllables containing jers (i.e. with no full vowel intervening), we lower all but the rightmost jer to the appropriate mid or low vowel. The remaining jer then deletes. Thus, in Polish, from an underlying form /cuk#r#č#k#/ (simplifying somewhat) with a string of four consecutive jers we obtain [cukereček].[10]

A particular problem is posed by vowel-zero alternations in prefixes in these languages. In the case of Polish we find the following situation. Prefixes ending in a consonant (such as *pod-* or *roz-*) end in /e/ when prefixed to one of thirty or so verb roots. Thus, in Polish, from *roz-*, 'apart', and *br*, 'take' we obtain the form *rozebrać* 'to take apart'. This can be analysed by assuming that the consonant final prefixes actually end in a jer (i.e. /roz#/) and that the verb root contains a jer (/b#r/). The underlying form of the prefixed verb therefore contains a succession of jers (/roz#b#r ać/). Given our rule it is not surprising that the prefixal jer vocalizes and the jer of /b#r/ deletes, and so we end up with *rozebrać*, as predicted. In finite forms, a full vowelled allomorph of the verb root is selected, *bior*, so that the UR for the 1sg. form is /roz# bior ę/. Since it is solitary, the prefix jer now deletes to give us *rozbiorę*. Corresponding forms in Russian behave in a similar fashion.

In many cases the facts concerning prefixes are rather more complex than this, which has led to a number of ingenious phonological solutions being proposed (e.g. by Rubach, 1984). However, in Czech, the morphemes concerned are rather less

well-behaved than in Polish. Here, we find that analogical levelling and other historical processes have occurred to obfuscate the original phonological conditioning
so that the choice of prefix allomorph (with or without vowel) is largely determined
lexically, or is subject to free variation. However, there is a residuum of phonological regularity here, since when vowel-zero alternations do occur, it is always the
standard jer vowel, found elsewhere in the language, which shows up. Some
examples are given in 5.68–5.70. (Similar examples could be cited from Slovak,
Sorbian and Serbo-Croat.) In Slovene, Macedonian and Bulgarian, the alternations
in prefixes have been lost entirely, so consonant final prefixes never have vowel final
allomorphs):

5.68   a)   roze-brat   'to take apart (inf.)'
        b)   roze-beru   '1sg.'

5.69   a)   roze-slat   'to send away (perfective, inf.)'
        b)   roze-sílat   'ibid. (imperfective, inf.)'
        (cf. roz-stříkat 'to spray')

5.70   a)   roze-psát   'to write out (perfective, inf.)'
        b)   roz-písat   'ibid. (imperfective, inf.)'
     or   roze-písat

The example *rozstříkat* shows that we are not dealing with a phonologically determined form of epenthesis here, since we don't find the *roze-* allomorph of the prefix
preceding the *stř-* cluster, even though we do find *roze-* appearing before a singleton
/s/ in *rozesílat*. What has happened is that the originally phonological vowel-zero
alternations have gradually become lexicalized.

We could, of course, simply list each prefixed form separately as an unanalysed
word in the lexicon of Czech, and deny that there was any redundancy to capture.
Ultimately, this may be how such forms are stored in the mind of the Czech speaker,
and only careful linguistic and psycholinguistic research would settle that question.
However, assuming that there is a linguistic regularity to be captured here, and
bearing in mind the fact that the quality of the vowel, when it appears, is phonologically predictable, we can describe this situation by saying that particular verb root
allomorphs select particular prefix allomorphs. The basic redundancy statement is
that root allomorphs which themselves alternate will (almost invariably) select the
vowelled prefix alternant. In other cases, it will depend on the individual words. The
vowelless alternant can be represented as the melody /roz/ and the template /CVC/
(i.e. the default representation). However, the vowelled prefix alternant can be given
the melody /roz/ but this time the template /CVCV/. When this template is selected,
the spare vowel is spelled out according to the default rules of the language (in the
case of Czech /e/, in the case of Serbo-Croat, /a/, in the case of Slovak as /e/ or /o/
depending on the previous consonant, and so on).

If this analysis of vowel-zero alternations is correct, we have a case of a template
allomorph being selected not by a particular morpheme, but by a particular allomorph of a morpheme. This is slightly different from the situation with Yokuts
described by Archangeli. It will be interesting to see, therefore, the extent to which
such phenomena can successfully be analysed in terms of prosodic template selection.

5.4 Tones as morphemes

In chapter 1 we saw examples in which a tone or tone pattern appeared to function as a morpheme, signalling a morphosyntactic category such as tense. In this section we look at recent proposals for handling such phenomena within the theory of auto-segmental morphophonemics. [11] The examples are all taken from Pulleyblank (1986), a very influential theory of the phonology and morphophonology of tone in African languages. To some extent this brings Part II of the book full circle, since Pulley-blank's monograph is a detailed investigation of the morphophonology of tone within the framework of Lexical Phonology.

In Tiv, a member of the Benue-Congo group of languages, there are two tones, High, á, and Low, à (which are conventionally abbreviated to H, L respectively). Verb stems in the language may be mono-, di-, or tri-syllabic, and may be marked lexically as inherently High or inherently Low toned. In addition, the language exhibits a phenomenon of no little interest to tonologists, **downstep**. This is a slight lowering of a H tone when preceded by an L tone under certain circumstances. It is conventionally notated by an exclamation mark, !.

In 5.71 we see the paradigm for six representative verbs in the Recent Past (this tense form also induces ablaut of certain types of stem, so that the underlying segmental representations of 'came', 'went' and 'heard' are *va*, *dza*, and *ungwa* respectively):

5.71   *Recent Past*

high tone stem		low tone stem	
vé	H	dzé	H
'came'		'went'	
óngó	HH	vèndé	LH
'heard'		'refused'	
yévésè	HHL	ngòhórò	LHL
'fled'		'accepted'	

At first sight it may not seem as though there is much pattern to these data. However, we can discern that the high tone stems all begin with a H tone, while the low tone stems begin with a L provided they have more than one syllable. Moreover, it is apparent that the second syllable of the word form is always H toned.

Pulleyblank analyses these data by making the following assumptions (for which he provides independent motivation in most cases). First, we assume that the lexical representation for a verb stem contains a single tone autosegment, H or L, but that it is not associated with a specific vowel. In other words, we assume that the tone is a *floating autosegment*, much like the [nasal] and [palatal] autosegments of Terena discussed in §5.3.1. Thus, for *yévésè* and *ngòhórò* we have the URs shown in 5.72:

5.72   a) $\begin{bmatrix} \text{yevese} \\ \text{H} \end{bmatrix}$ b) $\begin{bmatrix} \text{ngohoro} \\ \text{L} \end{bmatrix}$

Next, we assume that the Recent Past morpheme is represented as a floating H in the form of a suffix. Thus, the URs of the tense forms corresponding to lexical entries

5.72 will be 5.73:

5.73   a) $\left[\begin{bmatrix}H \\ \text{yevese}\end{bmatrix} H\right]$ b) $\left[\begin{bmatrix}\text{ngohoro} \\ L\end{bmatrix} H\right]$

Pulleyblank claims that initial assignment of lexical tone is a lexical, indeed cyclic, process. However, he argues for a different association convention from that assumed in the earlier literature on autosegmental phonology (including that dealing with tones). In his original analysis of root-and-pattern morphology in Semitic, McCarthy followed Goldsmith's original model of tone and assumed that a melody element would automatically spread to the right to associate to unoccupied skeletal slots, in the absence of any language particular constraint against this. Pulleyblank, however, denies that spreading is an automatic (i.e. universal) process. Instead, he claims that in the general case a tone element only links to a *single* unassociated slot. Hence, spreading will only occur in certain languages, where it must be specially stipulated.

Given the representations in 5.73 we can almost derive the correct forms. A partial derivation for each is shown in 5.74:

5.74

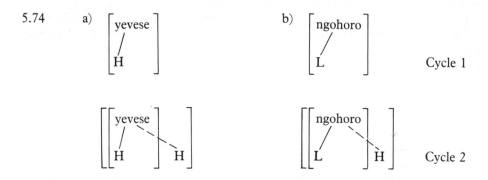

In each case, the final vowel is left without a tone. In general in this language, it turns out that when there is no way of specifying a tone value as a lexical property or the result of a morphophonological rule, that value is L. In other words, we can assume a default tone assignment rule, which assigns L to any untoned syllable at the end of a derivation. Since there are no more morpholexically determined tones to assign, and since every syllable in Tiv has to bear some tone, the final syllables in each of our two cases must receive the default value, L. Thus, corresponding to the forms shown in 5.71, we end up with the representations in 5.75:

5.75

You should be able to check that these assumptions give the correct results for the disyllabic stems, too. To derive the monosyllabic stems we need to make one further assumption (which, in fact, we've already seen in our discussion of Arabic broken plurals). This is that an unassociated melody (here, tonal) autosegment gets erased at the end of the derivation ('Stray Erasure' or 'Stray Deletion'). This, together with the fact that only one tone may associate to a given vowel in Tiv, accounts for the monosyllabic forms.

5.76 shows the paradigm for the General Past tense for our six verb stems:

5.76   *General Past*

high tone stem		low tone stem	
!vá	!H	dzà	L
'came'		'went'	
!úngwà	!HL	vèndè	LL
'heard'		'refused'	
!yévèsè	!HLL	ngòhòrò	LLL
'fled'		'accepted'	

Here we see a slightly simpler situation. The low tone stems just have L tones throughout, while the high tone stems all begin with a downstepped H, and any other syllables are L. Pulleyblank argues that downstep is the result of a floating L auto-segment preceding the downstepped H. Accordingly, we just need to posit a floating L autosegmental prefix as the General Past morpheme. Thus, the URs for *!yévèsè* and *ngòhòrò* will be 5.77:

5.77   a) $\left[\text{}_{L}\left[\text{}_{H}\text{yevese}\right]\right]$ b) $\left[\text{}_{L}\left[\text{}_{L}\text{ngohoro}\right]\right]$

The derivation proceeds very straightforwardly: on the first cycle we have association of the lexical tone, then we have (in any order) downstep, and Default Low Tone Assignment. (Check the derivations for each of the six verb forms in 5.74.)

Finally, let's look at the Past Habitual tense forms, where we will see the interaction of the cyclically applied association conventions with a morphotonemic rule. The paradigm is given in 5.78:

5.78   *Past Habitual*

high tone stem		low tone stem	
!vááǹ	!HHL	!dzááǹ	!HHL
'used to come'		'used to go'	
!úngwáǹ	!HHL	vèndáǹ	LHL
'used to hear'		'used to refuse'	
!yévéséǹ	!HHHL	ngòhóróǹ	LHHL
'used to flee'		'used to accept'	

The first point to notice is that this tense form is signalled by a suffix *-n*, and not solely by tone alternations. Moreover, this suffix always bears L. The second point is that all the forms beginning with a H have this H downstepped. This suggests that the Past Habitual is signalled by two morphemes, one a floating L prefix (as in the General Past), and the other a L *-n* suffix. However, matters are rather more complex than in the previous two paradigms, since we must also assume that there is a floating

H suffix between the stem and the -n suffix. (We'll ignore the vowel length alternations in the monosyllabic stems.)

However, this still doesn't account for some of these forms. How do we explain the sequence of two Hs in the middle of the polysyllabic forms? The key to this mystery is a general lexical rule of Tiv, called H Spread. This rule spreads a H tone to the right if the next vowel is associated to a L tone (provided this L toned vowel is not the final vowel in the word). It is formulated in 5.79:

5.79   *H Spread*

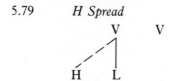

Since there are no lexical contour tones in Tiv (i.e. no vowels can be associated with more than one tone in the lexical phonology), association to the H tone automatically means delinking from the L tone, which is then left floating.

We can see how this all works if we look at the derivations of *!yévéséǹ* and *ngòhóróǹ* shown in 5.80 (URs) and 5.81 (cyclic derivations):

5.80   a) $\left[_L \left[\left[_H^{yevese} \right]_H \right]_L \right]$ b) $\left[_L \left[\left[_L^{ngohoro} \right]_H \right]_L \right]$

5.81

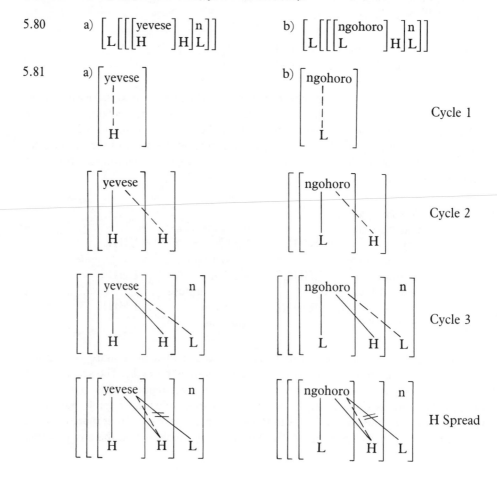

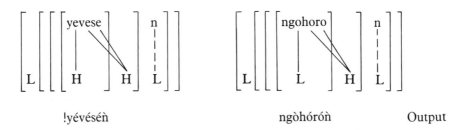

!yévésèn   ngòhórón   Output

The case of Tiv tense forms provides a striking illustration of the way in which the autosegmental approach to morphophonemics permits us to fractionate out those aspects of complex alternations which are constant and thereby capture the generalizations underlying the patterns of data. Like the analyses of Semitic discussed earlier in the chapter, Pulleyblank's treatment of tone offers a way of dealing with what appears to be a complex set of morphophonemic processes realizing a morphosyntactic category, and represent this as the realization of an underlying set of morphemes. In the case of the tonal alternations discussed here we end up with an analysis in which the morphological structure of underlying forms is actually closer to the common-or-garden concatenative, affixal kind.

An important feature of these analyses, and one which has been partly responsible for the enormous interest shown in autosegmental morphophonemics in recent years, is the fact that very simple conventions seem to govern such apparently disparate phenomena as root-and-pattern morphology in Semitic and morphosyntactic tonal alternations in African languages. This is very important because it suggests that there are deep, universal properties of phonological and morphological representations which can be stated at a relatively abstract level of description. Given the generality and abstractness of these properties, they can't be directly linked to purely phonetic (acoustic or physiological) aspects of the speech system but must presumably be mental attributes, in other words, properties of the language faculty.

5.5   Prospect

This chapter has been concerned with the basic ideas behind so-called nonlinear approaches to morphology and morphophonemics. Of necessity we've had to limit our discussion and concentrate on those aspects of most significance for understanding morphological theories. Development of ideas in this area is proceeding hand in hand with developments in phonology, and keeping track of these is beyond the scope of the book. In this concluding section I shall just mention one or two current growth points which have implications for morphology.

An interesting question at present hotly debated is the nature of the CV skeleton. It is widely assumed nowadays that the skeleton consists just of positions, or timing slots, unmarked for features which would distinguish consonants from vowels (e.g. Kaye and Lowenstamm, 1981, Levin, 1983, Lowenstamm and Kaye, 1986). These are often referred to as **X slots**, **timing slots** or **points**. In this respect the skeleton or template indicates simply the number of segments, and perhaps the position of rhyme heads (syllable nuclei). One of the principal motivations for this move is that it permits a process of association to associate vowels to consonant positions and consonants to vowel positions. We may associate a vowel element to an unspecified slot which later rules will specify as a consonant position. The result will then be a glide, such as /j/ or /w/. On the other hand, a vowel may spread to a neighbouring slot which is already occupied by a consonant, which subsequently dissociates. The result would be a lengthening of the vowel (because it is attached to two slots), a phenomenon known as **compensatory lengthening** (see the papers in Wetzels and Sezer, 1986, for a survey). More recent variants of these ideas take syllable structure into account and attempt to make use of universal or language specific redundancies to predict properties of the skeleton (as, for instance, in widely disseminated but as yet unpublished work by McCarthy and Prince, as well as the rather different Government approach associated with Kaye, Lowenstamm, Vergnaud, and others).

The theories of reduplication proposed by Marantz, Broselow and McCarthy, Ter Mors and a number of other linguists remain controversial, and a great many issues are far from settled. In part, this is because approaches to reduplication rely heavily on certain assumptions governing phonological representations, and so changes in phonological theory are likely to have important consequences for accounts of reduplication. The replacement of the CV skeleton with a sequence of X slots is a good example of this. This idea was first explored systematically in the context of reduplication in an unpublished, but widely cited paper by Juliette Levin (1983). [12]

A question which is likely to have important repercussions for morphophonological structure is the extent to which it is possible to account for reduplication and root-and-pattern type morphology in terms of manipulation of the melody separately from the skeleton. For instance, Clements (cited by Hammond, 1988) argues that it is not possible. He claims that we must analyse reduplication by associating the reduplicative CV affix template to the CV template of the stem, not to just its (reduplicated) melody. In other words, we transfer the melody of the stem to the CV template of the affix, through the CV template of the stem itself. This allows us, amongst other things, to transfer information about vowel and consonant length if we wish. Using this 'transfer' approach we would derive the Agta example 5.43 cited earlier in discussion of Marantz's theory in the manner of 5.82:

5.82   a) stem

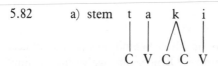

b) stem plus 'parafix' (corresponding to reduplicative prefix)

t   a   k   i
| | /\ |
C   V   C   C   V

C   V   C

c) derivation: association of parafix to stem skeleton (not melody)

d) linearization of parafix (into prefix)

The virtue of this approach is that it allows a given melody element, for example, a set of vowel features, to be copied by the reduplication rule irrespective of its association in the stem form. Mtenje (1988) has argued that this approach is necessary to account for tonal patterns in reduplication in Bantu.

Hammond (1988) argues that it is the best way of accounting for certain details in the formation of Arabic broken plurals, which we have seen earlier in this chapter. Consider the examples in 5.83:

5.83   a) šuʔbuub   šaʔaabiib   'shower of rain'
           b) nuwwaar   nawaawiir   'white flowers'
           c) maktab   makaatib   'office'
           d) miftaaH   mafaatiiH   'key'

The problems here are that the length of the final vowel in the plural is the same as that of the final vowel in the singular, and the consonant that spreads in the plural in 5.83a, b is the same consonant that has spread in the singular. What this suggests is that the plural formation rule 'knows' more than just the consonantal melody pattern of the singular (as suggested in our earlier discussion). It must also know something about the pattern of association of melody to skeleton in the singular and copy certain aspects of that. Otherwise, how would we prevent the generation of incorrect forms such as *šaʔaaʔiib, *nawaariir, *šaʔaabib, *makaatiib and so on?

The derivations Hammond proposes are illustrated in 5.84–5.87. First, we assume a plural template consisting of a CV skeleton and the characteristic plural melody [a i], 5.84 (notice that this template has a long final vowel, represented by two V slots):

5.84   C V C V V C V V C

           a   i

We then associate this template by transfer to the skeleton of the singular. The derivation for *šaʔaabiib* is shown in 5.85:

5.85

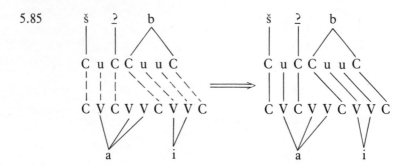

For this to work, Hammond assumes a special rule for the plural which pre-links the /i/ element to the final two vowel slots. I have written the vowels on the CV tier to make the autonomy of the consonant melody more clear. We now assume that the melody association of the plural overrides that of the singular. This gives us 5.86 as our final representation:

5.86

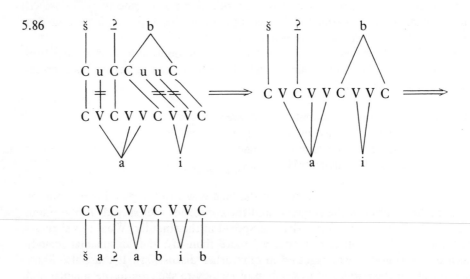

Similarly, to derive *makaatib* from *maktab* we have derivation 5.87:

5.87

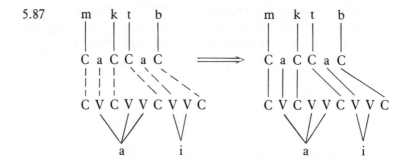

The last vowel slot is associated to the /i/ melody of the plural template, but Hammond's idea is that it is not 'licensed', so to speak, by the template of the singular. This is because the singular template only has one vowel slot in this position. Therefore, we have to do something about the final V slot which is unlinked to the singular template, and Hammond proposes a rule deleting it. In this way, we can account for the fact that the final vowel of the plural is the same length as that of the singular (though it must be admitted that this is only one technical solution to the problem, and it doesn't preclude other, more satisfactory solutions within the same overall framework). The result is the desired representation, 5.88:

5.88

This 'transfer' approach has not passed uncriticized. Aronoff (1988a) has argued that such a device is unnecessary and undesirable in the case of reduplication (though his alternative relies on a theoretical device which itself doesn't enjoy universal favour).

We conclude this prospect with a brief mention of research that promises to throw light on the structure of languages which might appear rather different from those we have discussed hitherto, namely the sign languages. By 'sign languages' I mean the languages which have evolved amongst communities of the deaf and which are learnt naturalistically by children brought up in signing environments.[13]

In sign languages we have a number of 'phonological' dimensions which can be manipulated to create morphological structures. The principal ones are: the handshape, the place where the sign is made, and the movements involved (if any). In addition, signs may be made with one or two hands, and in a few cases the orientation of the hand (e.g. palm up or palm down) is distinctive. The point for students of nonconcatenative morphology is that the nature of signing permits these phonological elements to be combined simultaneously and not just sequentially. A well-known instance of this concerns inflection. Certain types of verb show a form of agreement with a direct object. The verb 'give' or 'hand to', for instance, will have a different handshape depending on the thing given. In BSL 'give a glass' has a handshape similar to that of a hand grasping a glass (technically a C hand), while in 'give a book' the handshape resembles that of a hand grasping a book (technically an angled C hand). The iconicity of these examples is a little misleading, for we are not dealing with mime in any sense here, but rather something that is linguistically defined. The resulting system is akin to the predicate classifier systems of the Athapaskan languages (such as Navajo; see McDonald, 1983), in which a transitive verb stem takes different forms depending on whether the direct object is flat, or round, or long and rigid and so on.

There has been a certain amount of interest amongst students of sign languages in formalizing descriptions of their phonology and morphology. An intriguing set of suggestions for using a nonconcatenative approach comes from Liddell and Johnson (1986). It must be admitted that this line of research is in its infancy. For one thing, it is difficult to apply the methodology of analysis of spoken languages to signing because it isn't clear what constitutes a phoneme, a syllable, a segment, a morpheme and so on in these languages. (A number of Liddell and Johnson's assumptions are criticized by Padden and Perlmutter, 1987, for example.) However, as we have seen, in many respects this merely puts sign languages at the edge of a continuum of descriptive complexity, since in many cases some of these traditional linguistic notions are very difficult to apply to spoken languages, too.

Quite apart from the immense intrinsic interest that sign languages present to linguists, there will be very important implications if it turns out that the universal principles of grammar postulated for spoken languages are equally valid for sign languages, but not, say, for other, *artificially* constructed, communication systems. This is because we would then have evidence for linguistic principles of organization which are independent of the medium of expression. This would make those principles even more general and abstract, and even less dependent on phonetic form than suggested at the end of the previous subsection. Thus, the comparative study of sign language morphophonology and spoken language morphophonology could in principle provide some of the strongest evidence for an autonomous language faculty in the sense of Chomsky.

5.6   Summary

In this chapter we have seen how McCarthy's application of autosegmental theory to problems of root and pattern morphology in Semitic have led to an upsurge of interest in 'nonlinear' or 'multilinear' phenomena in morphology. This has had interesting, in some respects ironic, consequences. On the one hand, morphology is no longer the detailed study of 'well-behaved' agglutinating languages plus attempts to fit other, 'deviant', language types into the agglutinating strait-jacket. On the other hand, McCarthy's nonlinear techniques have allowed morphologists to take phenomena which used to be uncontroversially processual and analyse them in terms of often rather abstractly represented morphemes sitting on separate tiers and combined in an essentially IA fashion. In particular, many cases which might have earlier been cited as good instances of morphemes taking the form of rules or processes can be reanalysed in this representational format. This is true of Semitic ablaut, reduplication and tone morphophonemics. But whether that means that all morphological processes can be reanalysed as things remains to be seen. Furthermore, many linguists are still suspicious about some of the technical devices that have to be appealed to in nonconcatenative analyses, and it is often asked whether such analyses, while seemingly representational, aren't really sneaking in processes by the back door.

If these questions are ever settled it will not be in the near future.

EXERCISES

5.1   Below is a list of numbers in Modern Standard Arabic along with the words for the corresponding fractions. To what extent is there a regular relationship between the two forms? How might the cardinals and corresponding fractions be related to each other in a theory of nonconcatenative morphology such as that of McCarthy?

2	ʔiθnaan	1/2	niSf
3	θalaaθa	1/3	θulθ
4	ʔarba9a	1/4	rub9
5	xamsa	1/5	xums
6	sitta	1/6	suds
7	sab9a	1/7	sub9
8	θamaaniya	1/8	θumn
9	tis9a	1/9	tus9
10	9asra	1/10	9usr

5.2   Provide a derivation for the Palan Koryak data in 5.37. How do these data relate to Marantz's Conditions?

5.3   Below are data from a child Rosey (Grunwell, 1987, Spencer, 1984). Write a set of rules to account for her productions, on the assumption that she hears the adult form accurately, and that her own pronunciations are the result of a set of rules applying to the adult surface form, treated as an underlying representation. (You will need to assume rules that serve to remove structure from the underlying form, in addition to rules of a more conventional nature.) Use the model of reduplication proposed by Marantz (1982).

1	bobo	'bottle'	8	buʎi:	'budgie'
2	fefe	'feather'	9	doʎi:	'dolly'
3	fifi	'finger'	10	muʎi:	'monkey'
4	lele	'letter'	11	biʎi:	'pinney'
5	lili	'little'	12	deʎi:	'telly'
6	mimi	'middle'			
7	bebe	'paper'			

13	ʎeʎi	'elephant'	14	ʎiʎi	'indian'

5.4   Pulleyblank doesn't explain how to derive the monosyllabic low stem Past Habitual form *!dzáàǹ*. What additional assumption does he need to generate this form? (Continue to ignore the vowel length alternation.)

⋆5.5   Given the data from §5.4, is it necessary for Pulleyblank to assume that each tone belongs lexically to an affix? In other words, is there a nonconcatenative analysis of Pulleyblank's Tiv data in which the entire tone pattern of the verb could be represented as a separate morpheme? How would this relate to McCarthy's claim that tier conflation is a generalization of bracket erasure?

PART III

The Morphology–Syntax Interface

6

Later Generative Theories

Introduction

In this chapter we look at some of the theoretical proposals which have followed the groundwork laid by linguists such as Halle, Siegel, Aronoff and Kiparsky, and we also examine in more detail some of the issues introduced earlier, especially in part I.

The first section opens with a number of questions about the validity of level (or stratal) ordering. Despite its considerable influence, and despite the key role it has played in the development of Lexical Phonology, the various versions of the Level Ordering Hypothesis have encountered scepticism from a number of quarters (including some Lexical Phonologists). Next, we look at alternative ways of viewing word structure and constraints on affixation, introducing the notion that words have their own constituent structure and their own head-dependency relations. Finally, we briefly survey some of the basic issues surrounding the question of inflectional morphology (as a prelude to the discussion culminating in §6.5).

Section two is a survey of two highly influential approaches to word structure based on constituent structure, and incorporating the generative device of a phrase structure grammar. Much of the technical apparatus presented in this section has been presupposed by other researchers, and without a solid understanding of the principles of these theories it will be difficult to understand much of what is currently being written on morphological theory.

In section three we briefly make the acquaintance of the notion of syntactic affixation, itself not new in generative grammar, but an idea which is being exploited increasingly by researchers interested in the morphology–syntax interface.

The fourth section looks at something of a morphological cinderella: the idea that certain complex morphological systems can best be described in terms of 'position classes'. This is of interest for three reasons. First, it is a set of descriptive problems which morphological theory has tended to ignore but which will eventually have to be rediscovered if justice is to be done to the facts of language. Second, very similar descriptive problems are encountered in clitic systems, which we'll discuss in chapter

9. And third, some of the theoretical problems posed by position class morphologies are also encountered with inflectional systems.

This then leads us into section five, in which we look at a number of works which have tried to take seriously the notion of 'inflectional paradigm'. Since a number of the authors reviewed earlier in the chapter deny the role of such a notion in linguistic theory, it is of no little interest to see how different species of generative grammar attempt to handle the problem.

We will continually meet with a number of general questions during the course of this chapter. One of the more important issues is: where in the grammar do morphological processes take place, or morphological well-formedness constraints apply? In particular, is morphology essentially a property of the lexicon (as in the theories of Williams and Lieber, as well as Lexical Phonology) or is morphology split across different components (as one might expect in latter-day 'modular' theories of grammar)? According to the Strong Lexicalist Hypothesis, morphology is a thoroughly lexical phenomenon, and word structure, while perhaps similar in some respects to sentence structure, obeys different principles. Such morphologists, then, have to account for the fact that certain aspects of word structure are nonetheless accessible to syntactic rules, for example, rules of agreement. In other words, such linguists have to explain how the morphology interfaces with the syntax.

Many (though not all) linguists agree that some regular morphological processes, specifically derivational processes, are performed in the lexicon, where they can interact in particular ways with listed lexical items. However, many believe that conditions on inflectional morphology have to be stated at a different level of representation, after the syntax. Such linguists, then, subscribe to the Weak Lexicalist Hypothesis. The accessibility of word structure to syntactic rules such as agreement is easily explained, for such rules turn out to have been part of the syntax all the time, and not essentially morphological. The problem for such theoreticians is to account for the commonalities and interactions between the syntactic aspects of word structure and the morphological and lexical aspects. In other words, they have to explain how the syntax interfaces with the morphology.

Related to the nature of lexicalism and the extent to which morphological theory is the theory of the lexicon or of something else is the question of basic distinctions such as derivation and inflection. For some, especially those who espouse Weak Lexicalism, it is important that this distinction be drawn. For others, notably the Strong Lexicalists, it is equally important to show that the distinction is spurious. This, in turn, has important implications for the notion of 'paradigm'. Those that appeal to a derivation–inflection distinction (the so-called **split-morphology hypothesis**) tend to incorporate some notion of paradigm into their models. Those that do not accept the distinction equally deny the status of the paradigm. This issue is not restricted to the nature of inflection, however. In part IV we will see that paradigmatic aspects of lexical organization have recently been (re)applied to derivational morphology and other aspects of lexical relatedness.

Cross-cutting these discussions will be the extent to which word structure resembles sentence structure. Ironic though it might seem, the proponents of Strong Lexicalism have tended to analyse words as comprised of discrete morphemes concatenated to form constituents, just as words form phrases in syntax. Moreover, the notion of headedness, which is very important in X-bar theories of syntax, has been incorporated into such theories of word structure. This has meant that such theorists have been committed to an essentially Item-and-Arrangement view of morphology (if we abstract away from morphophonological processes), and it is for this reason that they stress the syntagmatic ('horizontal') aspects of word structure at the expense of the paradigmatic ('vertical') aspects.

6.1 Basic issues

6.1.1 Problems with level ordering

Despite the impact which Siegel's level ordering thesis had on the development of morphology and especially on Lexical Phonology, not all linguists were convinced of its correctness. Almost as soon as it was proposed a series of difficulties were exposed, which have ultimately caused many morphologists and even certain Lexical Phonologists to reject the idea. A convenient summary of some of the more important objections has been provided by Aronoff and Sridhar (1983, 1987).

The central theme of level ordering is that Class I affixation takes place before Class II affixation, and that Class II affixes are therefore external to Class I affixes (the *Affix Order Generalization*, or AOG). We have seen (§4.3.2) that the extended version of this thesis, that enshrined in the Extended Level Ordering Hypothesis, encounters problematical instances in which regular plural inflection seems to occur both before and after compounding (as in a form such as *systems analyst*). This had to be handled by means of a 'loop' in Lexical Phonology. To this we could add cases in which an entire phrase is compounded. This happens fairly regularly in West Germanic languages, such as German, Dutch and Afrikaans and also to some extent in English (*car-of-the-month competition*). Here we need to loop the syntactic component of the grammar into the lexicon, an even more drastic violation of the assumptions of level ordered morphology.[1]

A perhaps more serious difficulty is that there is a host of exceptions even to the unextended version of the AOG. In other words, there are cases in which Class I affixes occur external to Class II affixes. There are four theoretical possibilities, shown schematically in 6.1–6.4:

6.1   root–II–I

6.2   I–II–root

6.3   [II–root] –I

6.4   I–[root–II]

Of these, we encounter types 6.1 and 6.3. The other cases don't seem to be attested (possibly because there are so few Class I prefixes which have a meaning and can therefore be used extensively in word formation).

Aronoff (1976) was the first to record exceptions of the first sort. In a word such as *organization* we have a Class II suffix *-ize* inside a Class I suffix *-ation*. Other examples (Aronoff and Sridhar, 1983, 1987) are words ending in *-ability* and *-istic*.

One worrying aspect of these counterexamples is their productivity: the 'illicit' Class I affix *-ation* is the commonest way of nominalizing a derived verb ending in *-ize*. Likewise, the *-ity* is the standard way of nominalizing adjectives in *-able*.

An interesting example of this problem is provided by West Greenlandic (Jenkins, 1984). For example, suffixes regularly induce consonant assimilation when attached to consonant final stems, as shown in 6.5a:

6.5   a) qanik-li-voq   ⇒ qanillivoq
            approach-become-more-3sg   'gets closer'

We would regard these as class II affixes. However, there are some suffixes, such as *-ler*, which induce consonant deletion instead, as seen in 6.5b:

6.5   b) qanik-ler-poq   ⇒ qanilerpoq
            approach-begin-3sg   'begins to approach'

These would presumably be regarded as Class I affixes. Unfortunately, it is possible for the deleting ('class I') affix to appear outside the more regular ('class II') affix if the meaning dictates, as in 6.6:

6.6   qanik-li-ler-poq   ⇒ qanillilerpoq
           'begins to get closer'

The 6.3 type of exception has spawned a large literature, and it is readily illustrated by a celebrated example, *ungrammaticality*. This word contains a Class I suffix, *-ity*, and a Class II prefix *un-*. Therefore, on level ordering grounds we would expect the word to have the structure of 6.7:

6.7

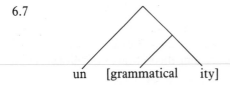

un   [grammatical   ity]

However, there is a problem, because the result of affixing *-ity* to *grammatical* produces a derived noun, *grammaticality*, yet the prefix *un-* only ever attaches to adjectives, never nouns (with the whimsical exception of Orwell's *unperson*, which is in any case a word of the language Newspeak, not of English). Therefore, on syntactic selection grounds we would assign the word the structure of 6.8:

6.8   N

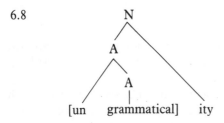

[un   grammatical]   ity

For reasons which will be obvious, problematic constructions such as these are known as *bracketing paradoxes* (cf. §1.2.3; chapter 10).

The next set of problems with level ordering centres not so much around counterexemplification, but around the limited explanatory range of the hypothesis. While it accounts for the basic relative ordering of stress-neutral and stress-sensitive affixes, it fails to account for restrictions between affixes within one class or the other. Thus, one of Halle's (1973) most important seminal questions remains largely unaddressed by the Level Ordering Hypothesis. The fact that level ordering has nothing to say about this means that the hypothesis is in danger of being undermined by a principled account of such data which doesn't need to invoke level ordering. The problem has been discussed from precisely this point of view by Fabb (1988a). He points out that there are severe restrictions on affix ordering in English which have nothing to do with levels. His argument is disarmingly simple. Taking 43 commonly occurring English suffixes, he points out that there is a theoretical maximum of 1849 possible pairings. Some of these will be impossible because affixes select only certain syntactic categories and yet they themselves belong to certain categories. Thus, an affix which takes an adjective stem such as *-able* won't appear after a noun affix such as *-ness* or *-ity*. Add to this some of the phonological restrictions mentioned in chapter 4 and the theoretical maximum is reduced to 614. By dividing the original 43 suffixes into class I and II Fabb computes that level ordering further restricts the number of combinations to 459. However, the number of attested combinations is about 50. Therefore, there must be other restrictions operative.

What Fabb found is that there are four groups of suffixes. One group attaches to any word of any form of the right category. These are the genuinely productive, free suffixes and they are *-ness*, *-able* and deverbal *-er* (as in *driver*).

Members of the second group fail to attach to a word which is already suffixed. This is quite a large group, 29 of the 43, and it includes class I affixes, such as *-ous* and *-ify* as well as class II such as *-hood* and *-ish*.

Group 3 consists of six suffixes which attach either to a bare unsuffixed stem or to just one other particular suffix. These are listed in 6.9:

6.9   -ion-ary   revolutionary (noun and adjective)
      -ion-er   vacationer
      -ist-ic   modernistic
      -ific-atory modificatory
      -enc-y   residency

Now, an affix pair such as *-ionary* has the same selection restrictions as *-ion*. Moreover, whenever a word can be formed with *-ion* there is one we can form with *-ionary*. Finally, the meaning of the doubly affixed word is derived from the meaning of *-ary* plus that of *-ion*. Therefore, we want to be able to say that *-ary* is productively affixed to *-ion*, not that we are dealing with some kind of idiosyncratic compound affix.[2]

Fabb argues that we can account for these cases by assuming that the outer suffix is permitted to attach not only to words but also (exceptionally) to another suffix. This means that the morphological structure of such a word is [modern [ist ic]], even though the semantic structure is [[modern ist] ic]. In other words we have a semantically induced bracketing paradox.

The final group is rather interesting because it consists of (mainly latinate) suffixes which attach to stems ending in some, but not all, suffixes of the right category. For instance, *-ity* combines with *-ive, -ic, -al, -an, -ous, -able*, as in *sensitivity, publicity, grammaticality* and so on. There are a number of ways of capturing these restrictions, though the small number of combinations involved make it seem easier just to list those combinations which are permitted.

Finally, there are more subtle problems with level ordering, and particularly Kiparsky's interpretation of the Extended Level Ordering Hypothesis, centring around some of the theoretical claims to which it commits the morphologist. Booij (1987) argues that Kiparsky is committed to the view that it is only morphemes that are listed in the lexicon. In other words, Kiparsky is obliged to reject Aronoff's word-based model. This entails that Kiparsky is unable to distinguish actual from potential words by appeal to the grammar. For the grammar, which represents the ideal language user's competence, or knowledge of the language, will generate all the complex words that WFRs are capable of generating in theory, and which of these turn out to be actual words will be a matter for performance. This means that Kiparsky will have no way of accounting for the effects described by Aronoff, which seem to demand that complex words can themselves be the base of a word formation process. Booij enumerates a number of more-or-less serious problems that this approach brings with it, of which I shall mention just some of the more important.

On a morpheme-based view of the lexicon it is difficult to avoid treating non-productive processes as though they were productive and this gives rise to some very counterintuitive analyses. Booij cites a Dutch case. A corresponding English example would be this: in English we can add affixes such as *-(u)al*, and *-ive* to latinate stems to form adjectives from verbs. A root such as *-ceive* in *perceive* will take both of these suffixes (with slight, though unpredictable, difference in meaning): *perceptive, perceptual*. However, other words based on *-ceive* may only take one or the other suffix: *conceive, conceptual, *conceptive* (despite the existence of *contraceptive*!) vs. *receive, receptive, *receptual*. Kiparsky's position would commit him to the view that the absence of *conceptive* and *receptual* is merely a matter of performance, since he is unable to mark the whole word *receive, conceive* or *perceive* for the suffix(es) it accepts.

Booij also discusses a number of problems related to historical change in one way or another, and all confirm the general picture, which is a commonplace in diachronic studies of phonology and morphology, that lexicalization plays an important role in the course of change. Some of these will be mentioned later in the chapter when we discuss inflectional paradigms.

A rather more interesting set of cases which bring to prominence the role of the word in word formation concerns so-called paradigmatic word formation, where the term 'paradigmatic' is applied to derivation rather than inflection. The idea that derivational morphology might be defined in terms of paradigms, while in a sense traditional, is not something which is generally accepted by contemporary morphologists, and I shall be reviewing some of the evidence in favour of such a position in part IV. An example of what is meant will suffice to explain why such a phenomenon crucially relies on the notion of 'existing word'. The word meaning 'sailor who serves in a submarine' is *submariner*. This is correctly pronounced (i.e. by submariners themselves) with antepenultimate stress, *submáriner*, to rhyme with *mariner* (though dictionaries permit the pronunciation *sùbmaríner*, rhyming with *marina*, presumably a landlubber's spelling pronunciation). Now, *submariner* cannot be the result of any regular word formation process. It is a result of the systematic connection that links the (existing, actual, permanently stored) words *marine*, *mariner* and *submarine*. In chapter 10 we'll see that in fact it's just a very specific example of an extremely general process.

6.1.2   *Constituent structure in morphology*

Some of the misgivings about level ordering have motivated the development of alternative views of word structure. In this section we look at a number of leading ideas that have played a prominent role in theory construction.

One assumption that has been prevalent, particularly as far as compounds and derivational morphology is concerned, is that complex words have a hierarchical constituent structure which can be represented by tree-diagrams of a familiar sort. For instance, a word such as *indecipherability* might be associated with the tree structure in 6.10a or equivalently the labelled bracketing in 6.10b:

6.10   a)

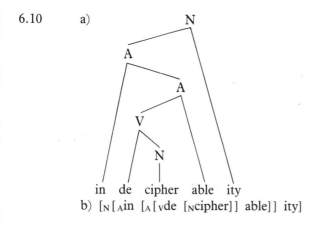

b) [N [A in [A [V de [N cipher]] able]] ity]

This type of diagram or labelled bracketing is a representation of the derivational history of the word. We begin with the noun *cipher* from which we create the verb *decipher* by prefixation of *de-*, which in turn produces the adjective *decipherable* and so on. As we will see, the most popular theories of morphology would all assign just such a structure to the word.

However, there is something misleading about this picture. For, in general, the internal make-up of a word is opaque to morphological processes, or, in other words, word formation processes tend to be blind to the derivational history of the base on which they are operating. For instance, we tend not to find morphological rules along the lines 'add affix X to an adjective only if it is derived from a noun'. Another way of thinking of this is to say that affixation is sensitive only to the properties of the node immediately adjacent to the affix. In other words, an affix may be sensitive to the properties of the X node in 6.11 but not to any of the internal nodes, Y, Z etc:

6.11

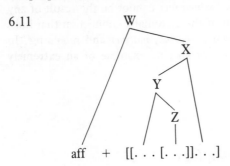

The phenomenon of morphological conversion (or zero-affixation) provides a good illustration of this. We saw in §4.3.2 that verbs derived from nouns by conversion never conjugate as strong verbs. This was illustrated with a hypothetical example in which we took the verb *hide*, converted it to a noun (as in *the ecologists observed the bird from a hide*) and then reconverted that noun to a verb (*to hide a forest*). If we do this, the new verb behaves like a regular verb (*the ecologists hided the forest*). It is as though the past tense formation rule were oblivious to the fact that the base *hide* is 'really' strong verb. This contrasts with the behaviour of prefixed strong verbs such as *withstand*, which continue to conjugate like their simplex base verbs (*withstood*).

Lexical Phonology has a number of ways of capturing such behaviour. Recall that Kiparsky accounted for the conversion facts by appealing to level ordering. Strong past tenses are formed at Level 1, noun-to-verb conversion takes place at Level 2 and regular past tense formation occurs at Level 3. Therefore, by the time the converted noun *hide* is formed from the verb (in Level 2) it is too late for the strong past tense rule to apply. In other instances, a phonological or morphological rule may fail to apply (or fail to be blocked) because bracket erasure has applied, thus rendering the complex word indistinguishable from a simplex word.

An alternative approach is possible, however, which retains the complete structure of the complex word. Returning to our conversion example, suppose we say that the vowel alternations in *hide ~ hid*, *stand ~ stood* are governed by a readjustment rule triggered when an abstract affix PAST is attached to a verb root marked with a feature (say, [+ablaut]), as shown in derivations 6.12:

6.12   a)

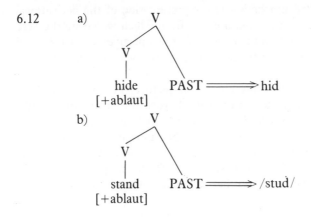

Suppose we also assume that conversion is achieved by the addition of a phonetically null affix, i.e. that conversion is really zero-affixation (see §1.5.)[3] We can now contrast 6.12 with the regularly formed past tense form *grandstanded*. The derivation is shown in 6.13:

6.13

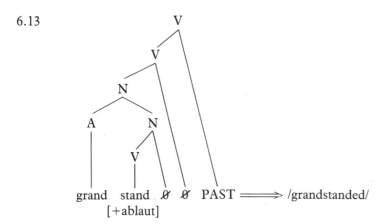

In the derivations 6.12 the PAST morpheme is attached directly to a V node which exhaustively dominates the strong verb root. In a labelled bracketing there would be only one bracket between the two morphemes. In 6.13, however, the PAST morpheme is attached to a V node which is separated from the strong verb root by other affixes (namely, the two tokens of the zero affix). Thus, the PAST morpheme is not attached directly to the strong verb but to something which properly contains the strong verb. The same is true of the *hided* example, 6.14:

6.14

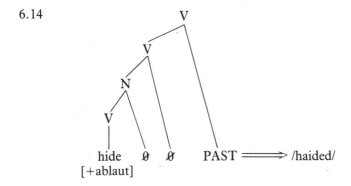

What we can say, then, is that the ablaut rule fails to apply when the triggering morpheme, PAST, is not adjacent to the strong root itself but to some other category. In other terms, we can say that the ablaut rule is unable to apply across more than one bracket. This is essentially the idea behind the **Adjacency Condition**, due originally to Siegel (1977) and taken up by Allen (1978) (see Scalise, 1984, chapter 8 for detailed discussion). What it says is that an affixation process can be made sensitive to the content of an internal morpheme only if that morpheme is the one most recently attached by a morphological rule. Intuitively, it prevents a morphological process from looking into the internal structure, or the derivational history, or morphologically complex words.

By assuming that affixation induces constituent structure and by imposing the Adjacency Condition, we can account for why the past tense of doubly converted *hide* comes out as *hided*, or why the past of *to grandstand* is *grandstanded*. However, we still have to deal with violations of Adjacency, such as *withstood*. In Kiparsky's analysis this word arises from prefixation of *stood* by *with*, so there is no problem. But if we are to take constituent structure seriously, then this leads to an incorrect analysis: semantically speaking, *withstood* is the past tense of *withstand*. In fact, *withstood* has nothing at all to do with *stood* if we take meaning into consideration. This implies that the constituent structure of *withstood* should be 6.15:

6.15

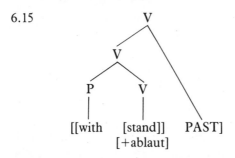

But in that case the PAST morpheme must be able to see inside the complex word *withstand* in order to condition the allomorphy on *stand*, in violation of the Adjacency Condition. Given that there are a great many such prefixed strong verbs, this is not just an isolated phenomenon.

Williams (1981a) provided a somewhat different solution to the adjacency problem. He noted that the counterexamples to the Adjacency Condition have in common the fact that the offending affixation operation fails to change the syntactic category. In a sense, then, the prefix in *withstand* is rather like a modifying element rather than a genuine derivational morpheme. Williams proposed, for this and other reasons, that a crucial concept needed to explain these structures is that of a *head*. He argued that we should regard the verb root, *stand*, as the head of *withstand*, where 'head' means more-or-less what it means in syntax. One of the syntactic properties of heads is that any feature marked on the head of a construction will **percolate** up to the dominating node, in other words, that properties of heads are inherited by the constructions of which they are the head. This means in effect, that a complex verb such as *withstand* will be treated as a strong verb just like its head, i.e. *stand*. This is pictured in 6.16, once in tree form, once in labelled bracket form (with [+A] being the [+ablaut] feature).

6.16   a)

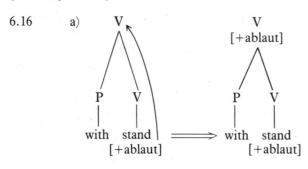

b) [with [stand] $_{[+A]}$] $\Rightarrow$ [with stand] $_{[+A]}$

When we attach the PAST morpheme to *withstand* it can trigger the ablaut process because it is now adjacent to the percolated [+ablaut] feature.

Williams further argued that all words are headed, and that the head is the right-most morpheme of the construction (the **Righthand Head Rule**, or RHR). This has a number of immediate consequences. First, in a word such as *cats* the plural affix is the head of the word. Second, by virtue of the RHR all suffixes are heads and no prefixes (or, presumably, infixes) are heads. Third, morphemes which can be heads (i.e. roots and suffixes) must be assigned to a syntactic category. This is because the head of a construction determines its syntactic category, and so must itself belong to a syntactic category. This means that the structure of the word *cats* will be that of 6.17:

6.17

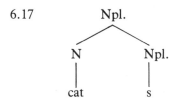

The concept of head easily carries over into compounds, where the RHR explains two salient facts about most compounds. First, the syntactic category of a compound is determined by its rightmost member; second, the meaning of a compound is contained in the meaning of its rightmost member. To appreciate the first point note that, in examples such as 6.18, the compound is respectively a noun, adjective and verb, irrespective of the category of its first member:

6.18   a) houseboat; blackbird; undercurrent; swearword
            b) breastfeed; underplay
            c) canary yellow; dark blue; overripe

To appreciate the second point, notice that a houseboat is a kind of boat (and not, for instance, a kind of house), to breastfeed is to feed (in a particular fashion), 'over-ripe' means 'ripe (to an excessive degree)'. Allen (1978), borrowing earlier psycholin-guistic terminology, described this by saying that a compound such as *houseboat* stands in an **ISA** relation to *boat* (in that a houseboat 'isa' boat).

With the concept of head we can reinterpret the Adjacency Condition. Williams, in fact, replaces the condition altogether with his **Atom Condition**. This states (1981a: 253; 'af^x' means 'affix'):

6.19   Atom Condition
            'A restriction on the attachment of af^x to Y can only refer to features realized on Y.'

This amounts to the restriction that an affixation process can be sensitive only to features borne by the head of the base. This is a slightly different condition from the Adjacency Condition, which says, in effect, that affixation may be sensitive only to the 'most recently attached' morpheme (cf. Williams, 1981a: 254).

The operation of the Atom Condition is illustrated further by another set of systematic exceptions to the Adjacency Condition. We have seen that English has a large class of 'latinate' suffixes, which are derived historically from Latin (or Greek) and which only co-occur with Latin or Greek roots. For instance, the nominalizing suffix *-ion* cannot be used with native (Germanic) verb roots (**breaktion*), only Latinate ones (*deduction*). Assuming that *deduce* is formed by prefixing *de-* to *duct*, we predict by the Adjacency Condition that further suffixation will not be sensitive to idiosyncratic features of the root morpheme *duce ~ duct*. However, it can be argued that the choice of nominalizing suffix is indeed determined by *duct*. For example, other prefixed forms of this root behave in exactly the same way: *reduction, production, introduction* (or, even worse, *reintroduction*). We could also add Williams's own example *conduct ~ conduction* (with a different root allomorph in the verb form). Likewise, when such prefixes are attached to a different root, that root may select a different suffix or suffix allomorph. For example, the root *pose* forms (some of) its nominalizations in *-ition*, giving us pairs such as *depose ~ deposition, propose ~ proposition, compose ~ composition*. All these facts show incontrovertibly that it is the root which selects the suffix, even after prefixation.

Let's assume that the latinate roots bear morpholexical features such as [+ion] indicating which nominalizing suffixes they take. For a morphologically complex word such as *deduction*, this implies the derivation 6.20:

6.20

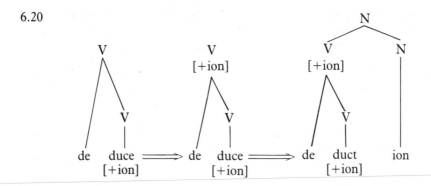

Notice, too, that the root allomorphy of *duce*, which is comparable to that of *stand* in *withstood*, can be understood in the same way, as the percolation of an allomorphy feature to the top of the entire verb. In effect, we could say that the prefixed verb *deduce* inherits the allomorphy of its head, the root.

The concept of head is not unproblematic. The Righthand Head Rule itself embodies an extremely strong universal claim about word structure, which on the face of it is simply wrong. A main effect is to prevent prefixes from being heads, yet in de-adjectival or denominal verbs such as *ennoble* or *decipher* we have just such a prefixal head. Moreover, Williams's theory predicts that all inflectional affixes will be heads (because they determine the category of the complete word). Therefore, the RHR predicts there will be no languages in which inflections are prefixes. However, there are a great many languages in which inflections can be prefixes (not to mention other non-suffixes such as infixes, ablaut process, tone shifts, accent rules or initial consonant mutations).

Not all words are headed in Williams's theory. Thus, while compounds in English are generally right-headed, the word *pickpocket* is an unheaded compound, or an exocentric compound (note that it doesn't refer to a kind of pocket). Another headless construction for Williams is morphological conversion. Williams rejects a zero-affixation analysis and instead argues for a rule which simply relabels a noun as a verb or whatever. All such relabellings are then said to give rise to headless constructions.

Later, we will see a number of difficulties with the head concept in morphology. Despite these problem areas, the idea that words are headed remains extremely influential.

The idea that words have their own constituent structure has been predominant, to the extent of being taken for granted in some circles. However, it is not a necessary assumption, and in §§6.4–5 we will see approaches in which constituent structure plays a less prominent role or no role whatever. An important point to bear in mind is that the concept of constituent structure only makes sense if we assume that word formation is essentially the linear agglutination of morphemes. This means that constituent structure is a problematic notion if we take into serious account such things as nonconcatenative morphology and phonological processes serving as morphemes.

There are also internal problems with a thorough-going application of constituent structure analysis even to agglutinating morphologies. When we consider the nature of constituenthood in syntax, we find that there are various properties of word sequences which can be explained if we assume those sequences have the familiar hierarchical structure of phrases (though even for languages like English not all linguists are absolutely convinced by the need for constituents). However, many of these properties involve phenomena such as movement or deletion. Now, in morphology we simply don't find constituents moving or deleting in the same sort of way. If we enumerate all the arguments for assigning a constituent structure to most complex words formed by affixation (as opposed to compounding) we find that there is remarkably little positive evidence in favour of constituenthood. In fact, given the existence of things such as bracketing paradoxes (see chapter 10), we often encounter strong evidence against it. So if we take a complex word such as Turkish *çalıştırılma-malıymış* 'they say that he ought not to be made to work', do we really want to say that it has the hierarchical structure of 6.21 rather than a flat structure such as 6.22?

6.21

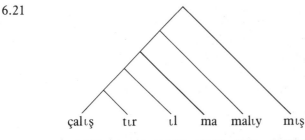

çalış   tır   ıl   ma   malıy   mış
WORK CAUS PASS NEG OBL INFER

6.22   a)

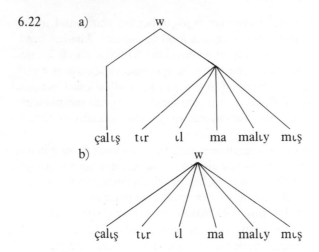

çalış   tır   ıl   ma   malıy   mış

b)

çalış   tır   ıl   ma   malıy   mış

Those familiar with recent debate in metrical phonology will know that exactly this sort of question has been asked about metrical accounts of stress systems which imply constituent structure for which there is no motivation. Halle and Vergnaud (1987) have argued for a general theory of stress which includes only the bare minimum of information about constituent structure, by bracketing two adjacent syllables into a binary constituent, one of whose members is the head. Perhaps a compromise of this sort will ultimately be needed for morphological theory.

6.1.3 Argument structure

One of the most important questions in syntax and morphology concerns the **valency** of verbs, that is, what kinds of complements a verb takes. In the *Aspects* model of syntax, valency is represented by subcategorization frames (see §3.1.3). However, it became clear as syntactic theory developed that the more semantic aspects of valency were also important for syntax. In this fashion the theory of **thematic roles** was developed (also called **theta roles** or **θ roles**, and also frequently referred to as **semantic roles**). The tally of theta roles assumed in grammar differs from one theory to the next. However, most theories assume the following:

Agent (Ag) – the (usually animate) instigator of an action.
Instrument (Instr) – (self-explanatory).
Patient (Pat) – entity undergoing an action.
Goal (Go) – end point of motion in concrete or abstract sense.
Source (So) – starting point of motion in concrete or abstract sense.
Location (Loc) – (self-explanatory).
Benefactive (Ben) – person on behalf of whom action is carried out.
Experiencer (Exp) – (passive) recipient of a sensation or mental experience.
Theme (Th) – entity undergoing motion or in a certain state.

Many authors conflate Patient and Theme roles, making this something of a default semantic role. I shall use the term Theme for both roles. Not all linguists distinguish between Goal and Benefactive roles.

In many cases the particular semantic role of a NP will be marked by a preposition, case ending or other device. However, this is not always the case, and we frequently find differing roles assigned to subjects. This is illustrated in 6.23, where the subject has the role of Agent (6.23a), Theme (6.23b, c) and Instrument (6.23d):

6.23   a) Tom opened Harriet's door (with his key).
        b) Harriet's door opened.
        c) Harriet's door was opened (by Tom/by Tom's key).
        d) Tom's key opened Harriet's door.

The sentences of 6.23 could all be describing the same event, even though the subject of each is different. By referring to theta roles we can abstract away from the syntactic differences and capture the semantic similarity by saying that in each case there is an event which we can represent schematically as in 6.24:

6.24   OPEN   (Tom,   door,   key)

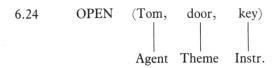

                Agent   Theme   Instr.

We will refer to *Tom*, *door* and *key* as **arguments** of the verb (or predicate) *open*, and 6.24 will be called a representation of the **argument structure** of that predicate. For many linguists, labels such as 'Theme' or 'Goal' are at best convenient general purpose mnemonics, whose implied semantic classification shouldn't be taken too seriously. Most generative grammarians would agree that what is most important about semantic roles is that they should be associated with the argument structure of the verb.

A more abstract representation of argument structure would simply list variables in a particular order to serve as slots for NPs such as *Tom* or *key*, as shown in 6.25a (the angled brackets mean that the list x, y, z is ordered). Where we also name the theta roles associated with each argument, as in 6.25b, we call the representation a **theta grid** (in practice, the terms 'argument structure' and 'theta grid' are often used interchangeably):

6.25   a) OPEN ⟨x, y, z⟩
        b) OPEN ⟨Ag, Th, Instr⟩

Williams (1981b) was the first to propose that argument structure played an important role in morphology. He drew an important distinction between two types of argument, the **external argument** and **internal arguments**. A predicate (in English this means a verb or adjective) may have at most one external argument, and any number of internal arguments, but not all predicates have an external argument. When it is present in the argument structure the external argument always appears as the subject. Moreover, if there is an Agent, then, with certain important exceptions, it will always be the external argument (and hence always surface as the subject). Williams indicates the external argument by underlining it. Thus, a notationally more accurate version of 6.25b would be 6.25c:

6.25   c) OPEN ⟨<u>Ag</u>, Th, Instr⟩

Williams argued that many alternations in the syntactic valency of a verb are the result of rules affecting the argument structure of the verb. For instance, in 6.23b, no Agent is implied or stated. As a result, the Theme becomes the subject. In 6.23c we have a passive form of the verb in which the Agent role is implied (and can be realized by means of a *by*-phrase), but this role doesn't become the subject, a position which is again taken by the Theme. Finally, in 6.23d we see that the Instrument has usurped the position of subject and, again, no Agent is implied.

Alternations such as these will be the subject of the whole of chapter 7 and much of chapter 8, so we shan't dwell on them here. Instead, we'll look at other morphological processes which seem to appeal to argument structure. Consider the examples of 6.26–6.30:

6.26   a) Tom read a book to the children.
        b) This book is readable.
        c) ⋆Tom is readable.
        d) ⋆The children are readable.

6.27   a) These books can fit on this shelf.
        b) ⋆These books are fittable (on this shelf).

6.28   a) Tom knows how to swim.
        b) ⋆Tom is swimmable.

6.29   a) employ someone
        b) employee

6.30   a) The factory is modern.
        b) They modernized the factory.

The examples of 6.26–6.28 show that *-able* affixes to transitive verbs to give an adjective which is predicated of the Theme argument of the original verb. It cannot be predicated of the Agent (6.26c, 6.28b) nor can it be predicated of the Theme of an intransitive verb (6.27b) or a non-Theme argument of a transitive verb, such as a Goal (6.26d). Similarly, in 6.29 the affix *-ee*[4] has taken a transitive verb and created a noun referring to the Theme argument.

The example of *-ize* affixation is slightly more complex. Here we see a predicate, the adjective, which has a single (external) Theme argument, as shown in 6.31a. The affix creates a (causative) verb which has a new external argument, an Agent, and an internal Theme argument corresponding to the verb's original argument, as shown in 6.31b:

6.31   a) MODERN ⟨Th⟩
        b) MODERNIZE ⟨Ag, Th⟩

Williams (1981b) argues that the two processes represented by *-able/ee* and *-ize* affixation basically exhaust the morphological rules which operate on argument structure. (Rules such as passive pose some problems here, but we'll leave discussion of these until the next chapter.) He analyses these rules as (i) **externalization** of an internal argument, and (ii) **internalization** of an external argument. Thus, *-able* affix-ation has the effect shown in 6.32 (what exactly happens to the Agent argument is a matter of some controversy, as we'll see in chapter 8):

6.32   read $\langle \underline{Ag}, Th \rangle \rightarrow$ readable $\langle Ag, \underline{Th} \rangle$

Internalization has two stages. It is probably easiest to think of these as, first, addition of a new external argument, and then demotion of the old external argument to internal position. General theoretical considerations (deriving from Williams's (1980) theory of predication) prevent a predicate from having two external arguments, so in a sense we are talking about the addition of an argument here, rather than simply internalization. The process is represented schematically in 6.33:

6.33   modern $\langle \underline{Th} \rangle \rightarrow$ modernize $\langle \underline{Ag}, Th = \underline{Th} \rangle \rightarrow$ modernize $\langle \underline{Ag}, Th = Th \rangle$

The notation 'Th = Th' indicates that the new Theme is identical to the old Theme, and hence captures the semantic relationship between 6.30a and 6.30b.

6.1.4 *The nature of inflection*

The nature of inflectional morphology is one of the most problematic areas of mor-phological theory and one on which there is perhaps more disagreement than any other aspect. We have seen that inflection is traditionally regarded as change in the grammatical or morphosyntactic form of a word (or lexeme) as opposed to derivation, which is the formation of a new lexeme from another lexeme. Derivation, therefore, typically changes the syntactic class membership of the word, say, adjective to noun; inflection is not supposed to change class membership. Inflection creates forms of words which have a syntactic function in, say, agreement or government. Inflectional affixes are attached more peripherally to the stem than are derivational affixes. Inflectional morphology often organizes itself into paradigms, while this is not so obviously true of derivation.

The difficulty for a general theory of morphology is that pretty well every claim in the previous paragraph has been questioned. For instance, the creation of participles, gerunds and infinitival forms of verbs seems to involve a change of category, and yet the traditional, and in many respects most motivated, view is to regard them as part of the inflectional paradigm of the verb, not as a species of derivational morphology. Even if we were to relax the category membership clause, we can't always recognize inflection by its significance for syntactic rules of agreement and government. This is because in many cases morphology which looks inflectional realizes gram-matical categories which aren't reflected in rules of agreement and government. One obvious example of this occurs when inflectional processes realize arbitrary, purely morphological categories such as conjugation class.

Assuming that we can identify inflectional morphology in a given language we will usually find that inflectional affixes are external to derivational ones. This is logical since we have to have our lexeme (by derivational processes) before we can have a set of inflectional forms of it. Bybee (1985) argues that this follows from a more general principle under which affixes which are more 'relevant' for the meaning of a given stem, for instance, causatives on verbs, appear nearest to the stem, while affixes which are least relevant, such as person/number affixes, appear furthest from the stem. This seems to be the case as a rule of thumb, but even this generalization is problematic. Nonconcatenative morphology makes the notion 'external to' rather difficult to interpret, and even in some linear morphological systems there are occasional reports of derivational affixation appearing externally to syntactically relevant inflectional affixation (e.g. Rice, 1985).

Although inflection is typically associated with paradigmatic organization, there is a good deal of debate over the nature of paradigms, and in many respects the notion itself is no less obscure than that of 'inflection'. One symptom of this is that a number of morphologists are exploring the idea that derivational morphology can best be thought of in terms of paradigmatic organization.

Some of these problems are illustrated by Spanish conjugation. Spanish verbs fall into three conjugations, each with its characteristic 'theme' vowel, which appears immediately after the root. Consider the imperfect tense paradigm for the verb *hablar* 'to speak' in 6.34:

6.34   Sg.   Pl.

     1   habl-a-ba   habl-á-ba-mos
     2   habl-a-ba-s   habl-a-ba-is
     3   habl-a-ba   habl-a-ba-n

We could analyse this by saying that the 1st conjugation theme vowel, -*a*-, is followed by the 1st conjugation imperfect marker -*ba*-, following by person and number desinences. It is only the person/number endings that are relevant for syntax (in agreement processes). This might suggest that we should analyse the theme vowel and the -*ba*- formative as non-inflectional affixes, i.e. as derivational. This is the traditional assumption for the theme vowel (though it could be questioned). However, the imperfect is a morphosyntactic category (one of tense) and not a lexical category (like abstract noun), so this is a counterintuitive solution for this affix.

There is one characteristic property of inflectional paradigms which might appear to distinguish them from systems of derivational morphology. Recall in §2.2.2, we discussed syncretism in Russian adjective forms. A dramatic example of this is found in the plural, where the three-way gender system of the singular is completely neutralized. This can be described in a number of ways. Zwicky (1985a), for example, argues for **rules of referral**, which effectively allow us to say 'the masc., fem. and neut. forms in the plural of adjectives are identical'. Similar rules could be written for the syncretism of oblique case forms in the fem. sg. of adjectives. Any theory of inflection (or of morphology as a whole) which failed to make allowance for such phenomena would be sadly deficient.[5]

The most frequently cited cases of syncretism are, of course, from inflectional affix systems. But it's important to realize that the phenomenon isn't restricted to this. For instance, stems can undergo syncretism, too. Thus, in Spanish the stem form of a verb in the present subjunctive form is identical to the stem form used for the 1sg. present indicative form (with four highly irregular suppletive exceptions; Spencer, 1988a). And in Russian, you can form the present participle of any verb by deleting the -*t* ending of the 3pl. (imperfective) present and adding -*šč*-. The Spanish case can be handled by a rule of referral, provided it can refer to stem allomorphs marked with features such as [1sg. pres. indic.]. The Russian participle case is somewhat bizarre, since it involves forming an inflectional (or derivational?) form from a stem plus half an affix. It's not clear (to me at least) how linguistic theory ought to handle such a case (provided there's no way of analysing the decapitated 3pl. form as a bona fide stem).

Lastly, one might argue that syncretism (like suppletion) is found in derivation, only not as often and not so obviously. A possible example is provided by English stative adjectives, such as *broken* in *a broken promise*. These are invariably formed from the past participle of the verb (see chapter 7 for further discussion). (Of course, this participle is itself invariably homophonous with the past participle used to form the perfect.) Stem syncretism in derivation is actually very common, though it isn't described in such terms. It occurs whenever the stem allomorph for a given WFR is systematically identical to the stem allomorph for another WFR. A simple example of this is found in the formation of Russian agentive or instrumental nouns from verb stems by the suffixation of *-tel'*, as in *pisatel'* 'writer' from *pisat'* 'to write', and *nositel'* 'bearer' from *nosit'* 'to carry'. Notice that, although such observations might tend to undermine the distinction between inflection and derivation, what they tend to support is the idea that the organization of both types of morphology is to some degree paradigmatic.

Russian provides another example of the fuzziness of the inflection–derivation distinction. One of the long-standing problems of Slavic linguistics is how to treat the aspectual distinction in verbs. In a languages such as Russian nearly all verbs come in aspectual pairs. One form expresses the perfective aspect (indicating completed or single action) and the other expresses the imperfective aspect (indicating incomplete, continuous or repeated action). For simple verbs it is usually the case that the perfective is derived morphologically from the imperfective, by prefixation (6.35) or by change of the theme extension added to the stem (6.36). (The *-t'* ending is that of the infinitive):

6.35		Imperfective	Perfective	
	a)	delat'	s-delat'	'do'
	b)	pisat'	na-pisat'	'write'
	c)	prosit'	po-prosit'	'ask'
	d)	pit'	vy-pit'	'drink'
	e)	bastovat'	za-bastovat'	'go on strike'

6.36				
	a)	rešat'	rešit'	'solve'
	b)	kivat'	kiv-nut'	'nod'

Occasionally, the imperfective is derived from the perfective, usually by addition of a suffix:

6.37		da-va-t'	dat'	'give'

A few aspectual pairs are formed suppletively:

6.38				
	a)	brat'	vzjat'	'take'
	b)	klast'	položit'	'place'
	c)	govorit'	skazat'	'say'

It is undoubtedly the case that aspect is grammaticalized in Russian. The question arises as to whether it is an inflectional category or a derivational one. Since (pretty well) all verbs form aspectual pairs we might be inclined to say that the distinction is inflectional. The fact that some pairs are suppletive, a characteristic of inflection, supports this. Another indication that aspect is an inflectional category comes from syntax. Both aspectual forms conjugate for person and number. Thus, from example 6.35a we derive *delaju* and *sdelaju* '1st sg.'. The imperfective form *delaju* means 'I am doing, do (in general)', that is, it has a present tense interpretation. However, the perfective form *sdelaju* has future tense meaning, 'I shall do (once)'. Now, we can form a future from the imperfective, using the auxiliary verb *byt'* 'to be' and the infinitive to get *budu delat'* 'I shall be doing'. It is impossible to use this auxiliary with the perfective aspect (**budu sdelat'*) showing that the aspectual category is important for syntax. Following, say, Anderson's (1982) characterization of inflection as morphology which is relevant to syntax, this would make aspect inflectional.

The problem is that several of the morphological means for expressing pure perfectivity are also used with other verbs to express what are often called **Aktionsarten** (the plural of 'Aktionsart', or mode of action. See Comrie, 1976: 6, note 4, for discussion of this term). Thus, verbs frequently take prefixes to modify their meaning (often corresponding to English prepositions). In 6.39 we see some of the verbs derived from *pisat'* 'to write':

6.39	a) po-pisat'	'do a bit of writing'	
	b) s-pisat'	'copy'	
	c) vy-pisat'	'write out, excerpt'	
	d) za-pisat'	'note down, record'	

There are several reasons why we would want to regard this type of word formation as derivational. First, the meaning of the derived word is different from that of the stem. In some cases the meaning of the whole is derived more-or-less compositionally from the stem and the prefix (for instance, *vypisat'* from *vy-* which means 'out'). However, in other cases the meaning is partly or fully lexicalized, as in *zapisat'*. Moreover, we can use the prefixed verb as the base for further derivation. For instance, from *zapisat'* we derive *zapis'* 'a recording', *zapiska* 'a note' and so on. Nonetheless, as we have seen in 6.35, each of these prefixes can be used with 'pure' perfective meaning.

Since prefixation creates a new verb we expect this verb to form an aspectual pair. In fact, each of 6.39 is perfective and forms its imperfective by means of a suffix *-yv-*: *popisyvat'*, *spisyvat'*, and so on. This is where the descriptive problem begins. For the type of prefixation shown in 6.39 almost invariably causes the verb to become perfective. The verb can then be rendered imperfective by suffixation or by changing the stem extension, as in *ugovorit'*, 'to persuade (perfective)', *ugovorjat'*, 'to try to persuade (imperfective)', derived from the verb *govorit'*, 'to say'. An imperfective so formed is called a Derived or Secondary Imperfective. But if the perfective/imperfective distinction is inflectional, this means that we have a derivational process which is simultaneously inflectional, a contradiction in terms.

The upshot of the discussion is this. Aspect is grammaticalized (and not just lexicalized) in Russian and it is expressed by affixation (and other morphological processes). Moreover, aspect can be said to have relevance for the syntax. But if we regard this as implying that aspect is inflectional then we seem forced to say that Aktionsart prefixation is also inflectional, though by other criteria it would clearly be derivational.[6] For the moment we will simply note this as typical of the sort of conceptual problem raised by the inflection/derivation distinction.

Russian aspect provides an example of what appears at first sight to be inflectional morphology behaving like derivational morphology. Likewise, we can have instances of what is apparently derivational morphology behaving like inflectional morphology. One notorious such case which is frequently discussed in the theoretical literature is that of the diminutive. Many languages have productive and wide-spread diminutive formation processes, often involving a whole set of affixes. In Spanish one of these affixes is -*it*-. This is usually attached to a noun, to produce a noun, so the diminutive induces no category change. Indeed, in most cases the diminutive is even 'transparent' to the gender of the noun to which it attaches. A masculine noun appears with the ending -*ito* while a feminine noun appears with the ending -*ita*. So the diminutive doesn't even affect the morpholexical class of the word.

Russian provides an especially intriguing version of the same problem. One of the innumerable diminutive endings of some productivity in Russian is -*ša*. One way of forming a diminutive with this suffix is to add it to the stressed syllable of a name minus its coda. Thus, from *Pavel* (Paul) we derive *Paša* and from *Maria*, *Maša*, and from *Aleksandr* (masculine) and *Aleksandra* (feminine) we derive *Saša*. The -*a* ending is typical of feminine nouns, and a diminutive so formed always takes the case endings typical of a feminine noun. However, when the noun enters into agreement processes it behaves the way its source would have behaved. So *Paša* takes masculine agreements, while *Maša* takes feminine agreements, and the agreements of *Saša* depend on whether it is the name of a boy or a girl. This poses enormous problems for a definition of inflection because we have an affix which is irrelevant for syntax, since it is the base which determines agreement and not the affix, but which never changes the syntactic category of the base, though it does determine its morphological class membership (i.e. which declensional class the noun will join). It thus seems to fall exactly midway between inflection and derivation.

Faced with these and other kinds of conundrums, many linguists have chosen to abandon the distinction between inflection and derivation.[7] A more positive reason for this choice is the fact that there never seems to be a principled morphological distinction between the two types of morphological process, in the sense that the morphological devices of affixation, phonological processes and so on are just as likely to be used for derivation as for inflection. Nonetheless, a number of attempts have been made in recent theories to motivate and define the distinction, and in some theories it is very important that the distinction be drawn.

6.2   The constituent structure of words

In §6.1.2 I said that constituent structure and headedness have come to play an important role in models of word formation. The proposal that words have internal constituent structure implies that there must be the equivalent of a constituent structure or phrase structure grammar (psg) to generate those structures. In this section we look in some detail at two, closely related proposals.

6.2.1 Psg approaches

Edwin Williams and Lisa Selkirk independently proposed that word structure be accounted for by a context free phrase structure grammar. The most detailed set of proposals has been given by Selkirk (1982) so I shall base this subsection on her exposition. A leading idea is that the grammar needs to be able to represent general features of word structure in a language. For instance, Selkirk claims that it is necessary to have a direct representation in the grammar of the fact that a language is, say, exclusively suffixing. For this to be possible it is necessary to be able to identify a category of suffix (or at least 'affix which follows its stem'). This means that the grammar will contain a rule such as $N \rightarrow N + aff$ where the 'affix' slot can be filled by items such as *-dom* or *-less*. This differs from the theory of Aronoff in which such affixes are all introduced by their own WFR.

The psg approach in the form proposed by Selkirk is designed solely for strictly concatenative morphology, i.e. suffixing, prefixing and compounding (it can also handle conversion). Without extra assumptions, it cannot account for infixation or reduplication, or for Semitic 'root-and-pattern' type morphology. Nor can it cope directly with any morphology which takes the form of a phonological process, such as tone shifts or mutation.

The type of psg Selkirk assumes is a variant of X-bar syntax (see §3.3.2). This defines the structures of **W(ord)-syntax**. The 'maximal projection' is identical to the zero level projection in S(entence)-syntax, i.e. the lexical category, or *Word*. Selkirk argues that the only other categories needed are *Root* and *Affix*, though only the category of Root falls within the X-bar hierarchy proper. W-syntax differs from S-syntax in that the R(oot) level category can't dominate the W level category. This means we can't have structures comparable, say, to V′ dominating NP in syntax. It also prevents syntactic phrases from appearing inside words. Like syntactic expressions, elements of W-syntax belong to syntactic categories (N, V, A, P).

The rules of W-syntax are housed in the lexicon. This comprises a *Dictionary* of free morphemes together with a list of bound morphemes. These two lists constitute the *Extended Dictionary*. The Extended Dictionary and the word formation rules make up the word structure component or the morphological base. No distinction of principle is drawn between inflection and derivation. Moreover, compounding is regarded as a morphological (i.e. lexical) rather than syntactic phenomenon. Thus, the overall conception of morphology is more Hallean than Aronovian. However, there is no place for inflectional paradigms in Selkirk's system.[8] As usual, the WFRs are regarded as essentially redundancy rules defined over the permanent lexicon, but which can also be used to create novel words.

Commitment to an X-bar model means that in the typical case a morphologically complex word will have a head, which will have the same syntactic category as its mother. Other features (morphological features, diacritics of various sorts and so on) may percolate up the word tree. In this section I concentrate mainly on Selkirk's treatment of affixation, saving compounding for chapter 8. Selkirk's X-bar schema is given in 6.40:

6.40   a) $X^n \rightarrow \cdots \ Y^m \ X^{af} \ \cdots$
            b) $\quad\qquad Y^{af} \ X^m$
            c) $\quad\qquad X^m \ Y^{af}$
            d) $\quad\qquad X^{af} \ Y^m$

where X, Y are syntactic categories, $0 > n > m$

Rules a, c refer to suffixes, and b, d refer to prefixes. In the a and d cases the affix is the head, in the b, c cases the base is the head. In English the value of n, m are Word and Root.

A concrete instantiation of this schema for English affixation is given in 6.41:

6.41   a) Suffixation:
                $X^n \rightarrow Y^n \ X^{af}$
        b) Prefixation:
                $X^n \rightarrow Y^{af} \ X^n$
        where n stands for Word or Root.

The nonexistence of suffixes forming adjectives from adjective roots, or forming verbs from verb roots, is assumed to be accidental. For the small class of (idiosyncratically) category-changing prefixes in English (e.g. *en*-rage, *de*-bug) Selkirk assumes the rules of 6.42:

6.42   a) $A^r \rightarrow A^{af} \ V^r$
        b) $V^r \rightarrow V^{af} \ \{N^r, A^r\}$
        c) $V \ \rightarrow V^{af} \ \{N, A\}$

Those affixes which attach to Words are identified with Class II ('neutral') affixes, while those concatenating with Roots are essentially the Class I ('non-neutral') affixes. Which affix belongs to which set is accounted for by assuming that affixes have subcategorization frames which state the category type to which they affix (i.e. W or R) and the category itself (i.e. N, V, A). The category membership of the whole word is that of the affix. This fact is derived from the principle of headedness together with a percolation convention: the affix is the head and its syntactic feature set percolates to the top of the word tree.

Selkirk disputes the claim of the Affix Ordering Generalization, on which level ordered morphology is based. The aspect which she accepts, however, is the generalization that Class I affixes may not appear outside compounds, the **Compound Affix Ordering Generalization** (CAOG). This is a consequence of the fact that Roots are always generated 'inside' the Word level, while (native) compounding is defined over Words. Thus, no affix subcategorized for a Root could ever appear outside a compound.

A final point to make about Selkirk's system is that it represents a Strong Lexicalist model, in that it categorically excludes word formation by means of syntactic transformation, an issue which will become important in later chapters. This is enshrined in 6.43, the **Word Structure Autonomy Condition** (1982: 70):

6.43   No deletion or movement transformation may involve categories of both W-structure and S-structure.

This rules out, amongst other things, any syntactic analysis of inflection, such as the Affix Hopping analysis of English verb inflection (see §6.3 below), or the head movement analysis (e.g. Pollock, 1989), as well as being completely incompatible with the head movement (incorporation) analysis of valency changing operations such as causatives and passives proposed by Baker (1988a) (see §7.4). The condition can also be related to Selkirk's assumption that inflectional affixes are not different from derivational affixes, and that the inflection/derivation distinction has no theoretical status.

Although inflectional affixes in this theory can't be distinguished in terms of their form from derivational affixes, they do behave somewhat differently according to Selkirk. She points out that the convention governing percolation assumed by Williams, namely, that features percolate from heads, will not account satisfactorily for certain types of inflectional system. Consider a language in which, say, person and number are signalled by two different suffixes. It doesn't matter for the sake of the argument whether we assume the constituent structure of the inflected word to be 'layered', as in 6.44a, or 'flat' as in 6.44b:

6.44   a)   b)

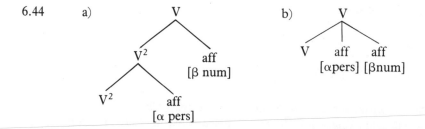

In either case the ordinary assumptions about percolation and headedness fail to account for how both sets of features can percolate. In 6.44b we would have to assume that one of the affixes was the head, say, the number affix. Its features would percolate, but then how would the person feature percolate, given that percolation comes only from heads? Adopting structure 6.44a is to no avail; although the person feature can percolate to the level of V^2, after that its rise is blocked, since again the number affix is now the head and only *its* feature will be permitted to percolate to the top of the tree.

Selkirk's solution (also adopted by Di Sciullo and Williams as the notion **relativized head**) is to modify the percolation conventions, by effectively introducing the idea of underspecification into morphological feature theory. She distinguishes between those nodes which bear a mark for a morphosyntactic feature, F, that is, those which bear the specification [+F] or [−F], and those left unmarked for that feature. The revised Percolation Convention is given as in 6.45 (1982: 76), where [uF] means 'not marked for feature F':

6.45   a) If a head has a feature specification $[\alpha F_i]$, $\alpha \neq u$, its mother node must be specified $[\alpha F_i]$, and vice versa.

   b) If a non-head has a feature specification $[\beta F_j]$, and the head has the feature specification $[u F_j]$, then the mother node must have the feature specification $[\beta F_j]$.

What this means is simply that feature specifications can percolate from non-heads provided there is no marking for that feature elsewhere. (The revision resembles Lieber's Feature Percolation Convention III discussed below.) Given this, the base can be a head and an inflection a non-head. Though Selkirk fails to make this observation, it also means that no inflectional affix need be assigned a syntactic category. Since inflections don't change category, an affix unmarked for any category will permit the category features of the base to percolate to the top node.

One advantage Selkirk claims for her system is that it codes in a direct form the notion of 'position class' for inflectional affixes (see §6.4). Thus, the structure of the Spanish imperfect forms discussed in §6.1.4, such as *hablábamos* 'we were speaking', could be generated by a rule such as 6.46, stating that the tense suffix precedes person/number suffixes:

6.46   V → Vr Vaf   Vaf
          [tense] [p/n]

This rule captures directly the inflectional structure of these Spanish verb forms (though it would have to be made more sophisticated to cope with all verb forms in the language). In other frameworks, including that of Lieber, this is only achieved indirectly.

A good many of Selkirk's ideas are retained in other psg-based frameworks. Zwicky's (1985a) model, for instance, captures position class information in roughly the same manner as 6.46. At the same time, changes in the theory of phrase structure grammar have led to an enrichment of Selkirk's model in various ways, particularly those associated with the theory of Generalized Phrase Structure Grammar (GPSG) and its descendants (see Gazdar, Klein, Pullum and Sag, 1985). The highly articulated feature system (under which features can take other features as values) is potentially of considerable importance in capturing the notion of morphological subclasses. For instance, if we wish to identify those strong verbs in English which have the vowel /a/ in the past tense we could set up two features, say, [STRONG] and [A-PAST], and capture the fact that all the [A-PAST] verbs are also strong verbs by stipulating in a redundancy rule that [A-PAST] is a value of [STRONG]. Hence (ignoring the redundancy statement), a verb such as *sing* would receive the feature marking [STRONG [A-PAST]] (cf. Spencer, 1988b: 629).

Another important innovation in psg theories is the separation of information about linear order from information about constituency, or immediate domination. This is potentially of considerable significance for morphology, given that linear adjacency is very important in morphological systems, while solid evidence for constituenthood is hard to come by. A number of morphologists are therefore working with models which do not require specification of the kind of hierarchical organization captured by a psg. In practice this often means using finite state grammars, which have the mathematical property of generating a smaller class of languages than the phrase structure grammars. An enormous effort is being devoted to such work in the field of computational linguistics, where choice of formalism has engineering consequences of some moment.

6.2.2 Lieber's 'Organization of the Lexicon'

The second major lexical approach which embodies a constituent structure grammar for words is that of Rochelle Lieber (1980). Now, in Government-Binding theory, phrase structure rules as such are all but superfluous. The fact that a transitive verb is followed by an NP is already reflected in the fact that the verb is subcategorized to take an NP. Therefore, in GB theory we allow verbs to be freely followed by NPs, and if the verb takes such a complement then the subcategorization restriction is met, and if not there will be a violation of the subcategorization frame (technically, violation of the Projection Principle; see chapter 7). Lieber's theory of morphology developed the same sort of idea independently of its application to syntactic theory. In her system, all morphemes, bound or free, are listed in the lexicon with information such as their syntactic category membership. Affixes are additionally provided with a subcategorization frame which states what other categories they must attach to. For instance, the English morpheme -*hood* will have the subcategorization frame of 6.47:

6.47   hood: [{ [A], [N] } _____] [N, +abstract]

This states that the affix attaches to an adjective or a noun and that the result is an abstract noun. Similarly, the plural affix -*z* has the frame 6.48:

6.48   z: [[N] _____]; [N, +plural]

The effects of the Adjacency or the Atom Conditions are achieved by permitting subcategorization frames to relate morphemes only to sisters, thus making subcategorization frames strictly local. This means that frames such as those of 6.49 will be ill-formed:

6.49   a) X: [[[... Y] Z] _____]
                or [[[... Y]] _____]
          b) X: [_____ [Z [Y ...]]]
                or [_____ [[Y ...]]]

It should be obvious that the subcategorization frames replace the WFRs of Aronoff's theory. Instead of a rule introducing the affix *hood* we simply concatenate *hood* with another morpheme or concatenation of morphemes and filter out the result if it violates the subcategorization frame. In syntax the old phrase structure rules are reflected in the principles of X-bar syntax. In Lieber's morphology the phrase structure rules of Selkirk and Williams maintain a ghostly presence in the form of a minimal phrase structure grammar, which generates unlabelled trees corresponding to possible word structures. These trees have nodes with at most two branches. Lexical entries, the stems and affixes, are inserted under the terminal nodes of these trees and they determine the labelling of the whole tree by percolating their morphosyntactic features upwards. This is accomplished by means of four **Feature Percolation Conventions**. These are of some importance because similar conventions have been adopted by a number of subsequent theorists.

The first two conventions are:

FPC I: The features of a stem are passed to the first dominating non-branching node.

FPC II: The features of an affix are passed to the first dominating node which branches.

A stem is defined as a morpheme which lacks a subcategorization frame, and an affix is a morpheme with a subcategorization frame.

In 6.50 we see how these conventions can account for a word such as *falsehoods*:

6.50

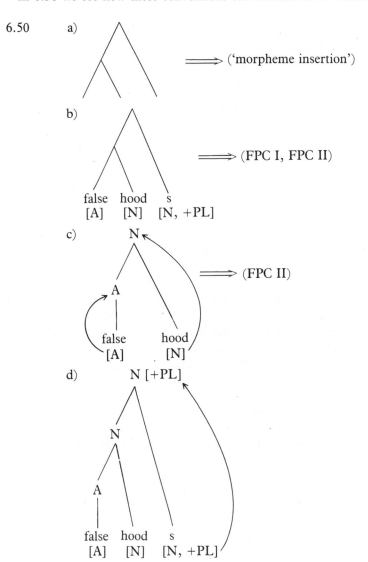

The effects of these two FPCs, then, are to create structures such that (i) affixes 'know' whether they are attaching to a stem of the right category; (ii) the most recently attached affix will be the head of the word.

Two more FPCs are needed. FPC IV will be discussed in connection with compounding in chapter 8. FPC III accounts for the situation in which a formative has no features of its own to assign. This occurs with affixes such as *counter* and with diminutives (see §6.1.4). The syntactic category of a word formed with *counter* is precisely the category of the word it attaches to. Thus, we have examples such as *counter-sign* (verb), *counter-example* (noun), *counter-intuitive* (adjective). The lexical entry for *counter* will include a subcategorization frame allowing it to attach to any verb, noun or adjective but will not specify its own syntactic class membership. The third FPC then allows such a structure to be labelled by taking the label of the word to which *counter* has attached:

FPC III: If a branching node receives no features by FPC II then it is labelled by the next lowest labelled node.

The derivation for *counter-sign* is therefore as in 6.51:

6.51

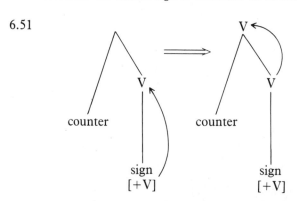

It will be obvious from examples such as 6.47–6.48 that inflectional affixes and derivational affixes are treated exactly the same. Lieber accepts the arguments that there are no purely morphological differences between the two sorts of affix. She stresses, for example, that inflectional and derivational affixes admit the same sort of allomorphy. Moreover, stems to which affixes attach don't distinguish between inflectional and derivational affixation. English provides examples of this. The noun *house* has an irregular plural stem allomorph with a final voiced fricative, /hauz/. However, this stem allomorph is also used as the verb stem allomorph, *to house*. The differences which are observed in the behaviour of derivational and inflectional formatives arise from the interaction of fully formed words and the syntax. One consequence of this perspective is that there is no room for the notion 'inflectional paradigm' in Lieber's system.

Another feature of Lieber's system is that she claims to have a way of representing the notion of 'lexical class', for example, '3rd conjugation' or '5th declension', without resort to diacritic markers (such as [+3rd conjugation]), at least when there is overt marking of class members, say, by means of a theme vowel. Suppose we consider the members of the Latin 1st conjugation, whose stems end in -*a*. These stems with themes will all be related to those without by a morpholexical rule along the lines of 6.52 (see §4.4, for the notion of 'morpholexical rule' in this sense):

6.52 $C_0 \, V \, C_0 \sim C_0 \, V \, C_0 \, a$

In Lieber's system the mere fact that stem allomorphs are so related is sufficient to define their class membership. What this means is that, if a rule of grammar or the subcategorization frame of an affix selects 1st conjugation stems with a theme vowel, then instead of selecting a stem marked [+1st conjugation] it will look for a stem allomorph ending in the phoneme /a/. In this way, reference to the arbitrary diacritic feature is replaced by reference to phonological form. If this were true of all languages there would never be any need for such morpholexical diacritics.

Unfortunately, the argument isn't quite as strong as it looks. There are obvious cases when a diacritic is still necessary, namely, when there is no phonological marker of class membership. Thus, French nouns still have to be marked [±masc.] in the lexicon. But even for the Latin cases Lieber discusses, it turns out that the subcategorization frames of certain inflectional affixes have to refer to entities labelled [±Theme Vowel] in order to prevent the affixes from attaching in the wrong order. Moreover, in the most general case this can't be specified in purely phonological terms. In the verb system of Spanish, where there is a very similar pattern of roots and theme vowels, the /a/ theme vowel has to be marked as such to ensure that a-conjugation inflectional suffixes attach only to genuine a-stems and not to a verb root from another conjugation which just happens to end in the vowel /a/ (such as caer 'to fall'). Again, in Czech much allomorphy is determined by whether or not the stem belongs to a palatalized or a non-palatalized set (see the discussion in chapter 4). This is largely definable in phonological terms, but there are three consonants which formed palatalized and non-palatalized pairs in the medieval language, but for which the phonological distinction has now been lost, /s z l/. Roots ending in one of these consonants may belong to either of the two allomorphy classes (and some vacillate between both) (cf. Spencer, 1988a). This situation cannot be described in purely phonological terms (unless resort is had to unmotivated phonological abstraction). This case is especially telling because much of the allomorphy is definable in phonological terms. It is therefore not like the French gender case, which Lieber could safely ignore on the grounds that it doesn't affect allomorphy.

Lieber's claims about allomorphy have had less impact than her model of word structure and lexical organization. Nonetheless, she raises important questions about allomorphy (some of them reviewed in chapter 4) which remain largely unresolved.

6.3   Syntactic affixation

The models of morphology we've discussed so far in this chapter have all fallen within the lexicalist camp. However, since the earliest days of generative grammar it has been usual to assume that inflectional morphology is an aspect of syntax. Recall that Aronoff's monograph paid almost no attention to inflection, regarding this as outside the domain of morphology proper. For many generativists, inflection remains in the syntax.

When we investigate inflectional morphology, as with many aspects of morphological structure, we have to ask ourselves two separate questions: (i) in what way are
inflectional systems organized? and (ii) how does inflectional morphology interact
with other aspects of grammar (particularly phonology and syntax)?

We'll be looking at the first question, that of the internal organization of inflectional systems, in §6.5 when we discuss the notion of the inflectional paradigm. The
second, 'interface', question poses particularly acute problems for contemporary
theories of morphology. First, inflectional morphology is tightly enmeshed with
phonology. It is not uncommon for inflectional processes to take the form (superficially at least) of phonological operations, and, even when we have relatively
agglutinating affixation, it is very common to find inflections inducing and undergoing a bewildering variety of allomorphic and morphophonemic processes. We have
seen a good many examples of this in part II of the book, so I shan't provide further
illustration here.

The second interface, with syntax, brings problems of a different kind. When
linguists discuss such syntactic phenomena as subject–verb agreement or the government of certain cases by prepositions, they frequently speak of inflection in an
ambiguous fashion. To take a concrete example, consider the celebrated rule of Affix
Hopping found in Chomsky (1957), and still regarded by many generative linguists
as the basis on which to explain the tense/aspect morphology of English. A generic
version of this rule is illustrated in 6.53 (the technical details of the process differ in
a great many ways from author to author):

6.53   a) Tom ED + (HAVE + EN) + (BE + ING) + see Harriet ⇒
         b) Tom (HAVE + ED) + (BE + EN) + (see + ING) Harriet
            'Tom had been seeing Harriet.'

Here, the past participle affix, -EN, and the present participle affix, -ING, are generated in underlying structure together with their corresponding auxiliary verbs,
HAVE and BE. In order to formalize the fact that the perfect auxiliary is followed
by the past participle form of the next verb, and the progressive auxiliary is followed
by the present participle form of the next verb, we 'hop' these affixes onto the immediately following verb form. The same process applies to the tense marker, —ED.

The problem comes when we interpret this movement metaphor as referring to
'actual' morphemes. No harm is done if we take the morpheme transcribable as /iŋ/
and attach it to the morpheme /siŋ/ to produce /siŋiŋ/. However, we obviously
encounter serious difficulties taking a morpheme /d/ (or /ən/) and attaching it to
/hav/, /siŋ/, or /breik/. The drastic allomorphy which afflicts the strong verbs of
English, all the way down to suppletion, means that we must separate the purely syntactic properties of these affixes from their morphophonological properties. The
interface problem here, then, amounts to the problem of ensuring that the phonological forms provided by rules of allomorphy and phonology are matched up with
morphosyntactic categories (like tense and aspect) so that a phonological form such
as /had/, /sʌŋ/, or /broukən/ can correspond to a morphosyntactic representation
such as HAVE + EN, SING + EN, or BREAK + EN.

In a lexicalist theory agreement and government phenomena of this kind are
handled by some sort of feature matching process. The syntax includes rules which
distribute morphosyntactic features such as [past participle] throughout the syntactic

representation. At the same time the lexical representation of inflected word forms includes an indication of their featural properties. Thus, the form /sʌŋ/ will bear a feature characterizing it as the past participle of 'sing'. At lexical insertion, the features borne by the inflected word form then have to match the feature content of the syntactic node into which the word form is inserted. The interface between the morphology and syntax is thus represented as the shared vocabulary of morphosyntactic features. An explicit theory of agreement along such lines is found in Lapointe (1981).

In a syntactic approach to inflection the need for two sets of features is obviated, since the features which govern word structure are those provided by syntactic rules. However, this would not in itself be sufficient reason for rejecting a lexicalist approach. In fact, if this were all that were at stake it would be difficult to distinguish the two types of model. The reason many grammarians reject Strong Lexicalism is because they believe that inflectional morphology (and some derivational morphology) gives rise to word structures which reflect specifically syntactic principles. We can't discuss such principles in great detail in this chapter; the next two chapters will provide illustrations of the sort of claims I have in mind.

For the present it is sufficient to appreciate that in GB syntax the well-formedness of sentences is governed by sets of constraints whose effects are to rule out ungrammatical sentences. In other words, the older approach, under which a set of rules generates all and only the grammatical sentences, has been drastically modified. In current theory, the rule system is very simple and very free and generates a good many structures which are not part of the language. However, most of these structures violate one or other of the constraints and so they are 'filtered out'. Put in other words, current syntactic theory is 'overgenerating'.

One of the key assumptions of this approach is that the rules and constraints can operate over several different levels of syntactic organization. GB theory distinguishes D-structure and S-structure, and two interpretive representations, *Logical Form* (LF), and *Phonological Form* (PF). Syntactic principles such as government operate over the first three of these. Some linguists believe that certain such principles hold at the level of PF, too (e.g. Kaisse, 1985, Aoun, Hornstein, Lightfoot and Weinberg, 1987). This is a key feature of Government Phonology, in which syntactic notions, such as government and the licensing of empty elements, pervade the theory (Kaye and Lowenstamm 1981, Kaye, Lowenstamm and Vergnaud, 1985, Charette, 1989).

Given these trends, it is legitimate to ask if the syntactic principles operate over parts of individual words. Such a move has certain desirable effects, as we shall see, for there are intra-word relationships which very much resemble the syntactic relationships between phrases, and if this resemblance is not accidental then we must ensure that the same set of syntactic principles account for both.

The aspects of word structure which are generally cited as the result of syntactic rules rather than lexical rules are regular inflections. This has given rise to the *split-morphology* hypothesis. One of the earliest and staunchest proponents of this approach is S. R. Anderson, whose theory is discussed in §6.5. Other writings in defence of the hypothesis include Scalise (1984, 1988) and Perlmutter (1988). Recently, Badecker and Caramazza (1989) have added psycholinguistic evidence (from an Italian aphasic patient) to the arguments in favour of splitting inflection and derivation.[9]

Scalise (1988) has provided a convenient summary of the arguments for distinguishing derivational morphology from inflection. More generally, Fabb (1984: 38–9), in a thesis which explicitly argues for syntactic affixation, summarizes the difference between syntactically governed morphology and lexical morphology in the following terms (paraphrased somewhat): a syntactic word-formation process is (i) productive; (ii) its output is predictable in all its properties; (iii) it takes syntactic constituents as its input; (iv) the parts of the word formed by the process bear some kind of syntactic relation and respect syntactic well-formedness principles.[10] Most linguists would say that conditions (i) and (ii) are necessary conditions for syntactic affixation; it would appear that Fabb and other GB syntacticians regard (iii) and (iv) as sufficient conditions. Less explicitly, Fabb characterizes a lexical word-formation process as one whose output must be listed, or whose output undergoes lexical processes.

One rather interesting aspect of the syntactic affixation hypothesis is that it doesn't apply just to inflection, and is therefore wider than the split-morphology hypothesis. Fabb argues that some derivational affixes may be syntactic, and this is a suggestion that Roeper (1987, 1988) and Sproat (1985a) have made. More spectacularly, Baker (1988a) has claimed that a whole host of morphological processes which affect grammatical functions (such as subject and object) are the result of syntactic processes. These claims will be discussed in the next chapter. In a sense, the claim that morphological processes are the consequence of the syntax is the most direct way of accounting for the morphology–syntax interface, and this is no doubt one of the reasons for its appeal amongst theoreticians. One of the threads which will be running through the third part of this book will be the extent to which the concept of syntactic affixation is valid.

6.4   Template morphology

The view that complex words have a constituent structure, at least in the case of concatenative morphologies, has been very influential. However, there are many languages with rich morphological systems for which there is little evidence for this degree of structure. Typically, in such languages we find that the verb consists of a stem together with a set of obligatory affixes and a variety of optional ones. What is striking about such languages is that it is difficult or impossible to analyse the formation of such complex words as the addition of affixes one by one to a stem. Rather, we seem to find that each affix has its position in the string and optional affixes are slotted into this string, at the appropriate point in the sequence, as required. Many languages of the Americas seem to be of this character, and in the American structuralist tradition descriptions often made use of *position classes* to define the order in which the affixes appear.

Navajo, an Athapaskan language of New Mexico, is typical of this kind. Navajo morphology is almost exclusively prefixing, and following tradition the position of the stem on the far right is labelled X and the positions of the prefixes are labelled in descending order from right to left from IX to I. The precise meaning of the grammatical terminology used for labelling the prefixes is irrelevant for our present concerns (and in any case it is fairly arbitrary).[11] In examples 6.54–6.56 we see some

Navajo verbs, together with an analysis into separate morphemes at a more abstract level of structural analysis and an indication of the position of each morpheme:

6.54   náánáoshtééł
        'that I might bring him again'
        nááná-Ø -o -sh -ł -tééł
        I   IV VII VIII IX X
        SEMELITERATIVE + DO + OPT + 1sg. + CL + STEM

6.55   náádeíníilteeh
        'we (3+) are again carrying him along'
        náá-da-Ø -yí-ní-ii -ł -teeh
        I   III IV VII VIII IX STEM
        SEMELIT. + DIST + DO + PROG (compound pref.)
                                    + 1duopl. + CL + STEM

6.56   biih dínééshniił
        'I will stick my head into it'
        (biih)   di -ni -yi -sh -Ø -niił
        (into-it) VIb VIc VId VIII IX X
                 FUT + CL + PROG + 1sg. + CL + STEM (Prog)

Young and Morgan's (1980) description of the Navajo verb includes ten basic positions or **orders**, shown in 6.57:

6.57   I   II   III   IV V   VI VII   VIII IX X
        TH ITER DIST DO SUBJ TH MODE/ASP SUBJ CL STEM

(The abbreviations mean *theme, iterative, distributive, direct object, subject, mode/aspect, classifier*.) Positions I and VI are split up into sub-positions. For instance, we have seen three separate position VI prefixes in example 6.56.

Positions which are obligatory are X, the stem, IX, the classifier, VIII, for the subject agreement marker, and VII the mode prefix. In a transitive verb, Position IV, the object prefix position, must be filled. Any of these positions except the stem position can be occupied by a null morpheme. For instance, the 3sg. direct object prefix in Position IV of examples 6.54–6.55 is expressed as zero. If all the prefixes are null and the verb form is thus monosyllabic, then a meaningless prefix *yi-* is added to make sure the verb is disyllabic.

The cover term *thematic prefix* covers a variety of adverbial, aspectual and 'Aktionsart' prefixes (indicating the manner in which an action is carried out). Position V is occupied by the *obviative* subject pronoun, which may refer to people in general, or to 'someone'. The Position VIII subject is a subject agreement marker of any person or number. The classifier is an element which sometimes has a purely idiosyncratic, lexical function and at other times affects the transitivity of the verb stem.

In practice it can be rather difficult to analyse a Navajo verb because, in addition to zero morphs, we have to contend with phonological rules which assimilate or completely delete certain formatives in certain phonological environments. In addition, just to make the whole thing a little more interesting, there is a variety of metathesis rules which reverse the relative order of pairs of prefixes under certain well-defined conditions.

Another complicating factor, typical of this kind of system, is that there may be non-local dependencies holding between pairs of positions. What this means is that a particular prefix in one position may require a certain type of prefix in another position (or a particular stem allomorph) to which it is not strictly adjacent. In other words, we may find **discontinuous dependencies**, analogous to the dependency between the components of a circumfix, or that between a verb and particle in phrasal verbs such as *look the answer up*. A number of thematic prefixes from Positions I and VI form discontinuous compound prefixes, for instance. Many thematic prefixes from both these positions co-occur only with certain of the aspectual prefixes of Position VII. In addition, some of the thematic prefixes select certain sorts of verb stem (and vice versa).

Example 6.55, repeated here as 6.58, illustrates two cases of such discontinuous dependencies:

6.58   náádeíníílteeh
       'we (3+) are again carrying him along'
       náá-da -Ø -yí-ní-ii -ł -teeh
       I   III IV VII VIII IX STEM
       SEMELIT. + DIST + DO + PROG (compound pref.) + 1dpl.
                                      + CL + STEM

The first is seen between the compound Progressive prefix *yí-ní* in position VII, and the Distributive prefix *-da-*, position III. The Distributive prefix specifically selects the *yí-ní-* prefix. The second is a case of stem allomorph selection. A given verb stem in Navajo comes in a variety of shapes which are used for different aspects. In 6.55–6.58 we see that the usual stem allomorph for the verb 'carry', namely *téél*, seen in 6.54, is replaced by the Momentaneous Imperfective stem *teeh*. Again, it is the Distributive prefix *da-* which is responsible for this selection.

In example 6.56, repeated here as 6.59, the VIc prefix *-ni-* is a generic classifier meaning 'roundish object' (here referring more specifically to the speaker's head):

6.59   biih dínééshniił
       'I will stick my head into it'
       (biih)   di -ni -yi -sh -Ø -niił
       (into-it) VIb VIc VId VIII IX X
                 FUT + CL + PROG + 1sg. + CL + STEM (Prog)

It comes between the compound prefix *di-yi* which is a compound of an inceptive prefix *-di-* and the Progressive Mode prefix *-yi-*. The stem *-niił* is the Progressive allomorph of a stem meaning 'to initiate the free movement of a solid roundish object'.

All the examples cited so far illustrate some of the complex morphophonemic alternations which take place when morphemes are concatenated, as you can see by comparing the segmented 'underlying forms' of the affix strings with the surface forms. We haven't yet seen a case of metathesis, however. This is illustrated in example

6.60:

6.60   badi'ní'ą
        'I loaned it (a solid roundish object) to him'
        ba-'a -di -ni -Ø -'ą⇒
        I   IV VIa VII IX X
        ba-di -' -ni -Ø -'ą

The -'a- position IV prefix, which means 'something', is placed unexpectedly between VIa and VII position prefixes. It then undergoes regular phonological reduction to /ʔ/ after a vowel and before /n/. Of course, one could think of this as simply putting an affix in a position not defined by the template order. However, there are two reasons for regarding this as morphological metathesis. First, this happens under specific (apparently morphological) conditions. Second, the affix placed in the 'wrong' order is displaced only by one position. The -'a- suffix in 6.60 would never be found, say, between positions VII and IX, since this would involve skipping over two filled positions. It seems better then to think of this process as involving the interchange of two affixes, -'a- and -di-. (Metathesis in general in phonology and morphology seems always to involve the interchange of two strictly adjacent elements.)

Navajo exhibits a second type of discontinuous dependency, which makes it a little reminiscent of non-concatenative systems. Example 6.61 illustrates this phenomenon, sometimes called 'interrupted synthesis':

6.61   yáshti'
        'I talk'
        yá-sh -Ø -ti'
        I   VIII IX X

Here the Position I Theme (Adverbial) element yá- means 'to do with talking', and it only co-occurs with verb stems which mean something to do with speech. On the other hand, the stem -ti' only appears in company with the prefix yá-. Thus, we have a kind of discontinuous verb stem. The effect is a kind of morphological idiom, the morphological equivalent of an expression such as *wreak havoc*. Since the Position I prefix and the stem are as far apart as they can be, we could in principle find the components of this idiom separated by a good many affixes. Such formations obviously pose problems for a concatenative approach to Navajo morphology in which affixes are just added from right to left, because we then need some additional mechanism to guarantee that Position I is occupied by yá- just in case the stem is that of a verb like *say*.

Finally, Navajo abundantly illustrates a phenomenon which is very familiar in inflectional paradigms of the more familiar kind but which tends to be ignored by those who adopt a 'morphemes as things' approach. This is the phenomenon of affix homophony. There are two kinds which are commonly found.

In the first we have a single formative which conveys slightly different meanings depending on its position. Obvious examples of this, familiar from a good many languages, concern pronoun affixes. In Navajo, a pronominal affix such as *shi*- will refer to an indirect object, direct object or subject depending whether it appears in position I, IV or VIII. A more subtle example concerns a collection of *ni-* prefixes, all having a terminative or completive aspectual meaning, but with different nuances and usages, and which appear in positions I, VI and VIII depending on their function. This type of homophony may best be thought of as a kind of polysemy, or (in the case of the pronominal affixes) as instances in which position contributes some well-defined component of meaning, much as word order in English syntax can contribute to meaning.

The second type of homophony occurs when we have a single morph with several unrelated meanings, in other words when we have genuine affixal homonymy. Again, this is amply illustrated in Navajo, particularly as a result of phonological attrition of affixes which were originally distinct. Amongst the functions of the ubiquitous *yi-* prefix are 3rd person object, Progressive Mode marker, a Semelfactive marker (indicating 'to do something once'), and a thematic element relating to the passage of night. This type of homonymy is reminiscent of the affixal homonymy found in classical inflectional paradigms of the sort we surveyed in chapter 1.

A problem which is sometimes posed by languages of this type (though not, as far as I know, by Navajo itself) is that the relative order of certain affixes may not be immutably fixed but may depend on the presence of surrounding affixes. This gives rise to what Grimes (1983: 6–7) calls 'cycles' of affixes. He gives an interesting example from a Colombian language, Tucano. In 6.62–6.64 we see schematic cases of verb suffixation in this language:

6.62   ROOT-si'n   -ti   -TENSE
          -want to-NEG-

6.63   ROOT-ti   -ca'   -IMPER
          -NEG-EMPH-

6.64   ROOT-ca'   -si'n   -mi   -TENSE
          -EMPH-want to-3MASC

Assuming that the morpheme order isn't determined by semantic scope (as was the case, for instance, with the Quechua examples 3.25–3.26 from chapter 3), we have here an instance of morpheme order being influenced by very specific morphological environments. This kind of thing, if found to be more widespread, would cause serious problems for any theory of affixation based solely on a phrase structure grammar approach. It would also make it more difficult to analyse template morphology as a strictly linear phenomenon.

The problem of template morphology has not been widely discussed in the generative literature. One of the few contributions to debate the problem is Simpson and Withgott (1986).[12] They distinguish template morphology from morphology which implies a constituent structure (which they call *layered morphology*). Some of the criteria they use to distinguish template morphology from layered morphology are given below.

(i)   Zero morphemes are prevalent in template morphology but not in layered morphology.

(ii) Layered morphology gives rise to headed structures, template morphology doesn't.
(iii) Layered morphology is constrained by some principle of Adjacency, template morphology isn't.
(iv) Layered morphology doesn't permit an 'inner' morpheme to be chosen on the basis of what an 'outer' morpheme will be; template morphology permits this kind of 'lookahead'.[13]

We have seen most of these illustrated in the Navajo examples. Point (i) simply reiterates the fact that in order to make the template analysis work it is necessary to analyse absence of an overt marker in a given slot as a zero morph. We'll discuss this point in a little more detail in the next section when we talk about inflectional paradigms. Point (ii) reflects the fact that the whole template contributes equally, so to speak, to the structure of the word. There is no sense in which the morphosyntactic category of the word is determined by the last affix to be added. Points (iii) and (iv) encapsulate the cases of discontinuous dependency and 'interrupted synthesis' which languages like Navajo illustrate.

Simpson and Withgott argue that, typologically speaking, the differences between template morphologies and layered morphologies are sufficient to warrant distinguishing between the two types in morphological theory. Very interestingly, they point out that very similar templatic properties are found in clitic systems in a variety of languages. This will be the subject of chapter 9, so I shall simply mention here that ever since Perlmutter's (1970) study of clitic order in Spanish, Serbo-Croat, Warlpiri and other languages, the question of how to account for the order of clitics, as well as other aspects of cliticization, has been a largely unsolved problem for generative grammar.

From our point of view the main interest of the possibility of template morphologies is twofold. First, it is necessary to distinguish a separate type of system with its own set of principles? Second, if the first question is answered positively, how does this separate type relate to other types?

Not all linguists are happy about adding a new morphological type to the universal inventory if this means adding a new set of grammatical devices to handle it. Speas (1984) for example, argues that Navajo prefixation can be handled by means of standard machinery in GB theory. Unfortunately, a key set of assumptions she makes (borrowed from the proposals of Pesetsky, 1985) have been largely abandoned by morphologists (see chapter 10; also Sproat, 1984), and in any case it is far from obvious how her approach would work for the clitic cases which I shall describe in chapter 9. Moreover, as we have seen, the introduction of constituent structure into morphology, which is assumed by alternatives to template morphology, is not without its own problems. So it looks as though template morphology may be with us to stay.[14]

A very interesting aspect of template morphologies is that they introduce an element of paradigmaticity into the morphological system. When we look at the layered, Item-and-Arrangement theories of Williams, Selkirk, Lieber and others, we find that morphological relationships are defined syntagmatically. That is, any change in the structure of a word is defined in terms of the addition of an affix (at some level of abstraction), and co-occurrence restrictions on combinations of affixes are determined in 'horizontal' terms, for example, by guaranteeing that one type of affix is subcategorized to follow only certain types of stem. In particular, there is no direct way to represent the fact that one affix excludes another affix in this kind of approach. To take an obvious example, in a language which has different person/number endings on verbs, there is no direct statement of the fact that selection of the 1sg. affix precludes selection of the 2sg., 3sg. and so on.

In a paradigmatic approach to word structure we would find a way of stating directly that the person/number affixes enjoy a paradigmatic, or 'vertical', relationship to each other. In order words, a formal theory which appealed to the notion of paradigmatic relationship would have a way of stating that there are (say) six person/number endings and that a given verb chooses exactly one of them. This paradigmatic aspect is built into the template model. Although in principle it would be possible to find a language in which every slot in a template could be filled by one and only one affix, this does not seem to happen. In practice, we always find that the slots are really columns, representing paradigmatic choices of affixes. For instance, if we home in on a partial version of our Navajo template we see the following picture (for those interested in minute detail, the whole template is given in Young and Morgan, 1980: 107):

6.65

IV	VII	VIII	XI	STEM
shi	i	shi	Ø	
ni	yi	ni	ł	
bi	ni	Ø	d	
yi	si	ii	l	
ha/ho	o	o		
'a				
nihi				

The prefixes in columns IV and VIII represent pronominal affixes marking various person/number categories. The markers in position VII are the Modal and Aspectual markers, again mutually exclusive. Finally, the position IX markers are classifiers which in part determine transitivity and other grammatical and lexical aspects of the verb stem. The important point is that in each column one affix will exclude each of the others.

To summarize briefly, then, the template approach gives a direct solution to two problems. It provides us with an entire string of formatives over which to state the long-distance dependencies characteristic of languages like Navajo, and it allows us to capture paradigmatic relationships very naturally. On the other hand, introducing the template concept into generative grammar leaves us with the question of how to formalize the notion, and how to accommodate it into a principled universal theory of word structure.

6.5   Approaches to inflection

6.5.1   Basic issues

In this section we look at the basic problems we face in attempting to describe an inflectional system. A very good account of what needs to be done is given by Zwicky

Table 6.1   Fragment of paradigm for *parlare* 'to speak'

Infinitive: *parl-a-re* 'to speak'

	present indicative		present subjunctive			imperfect indicative	
	Sg.	Pl.	Sg.	Pl.		Sg.	Pl.
1	parl-o	parl-iamo	parl-i	parl-iamo	1	parl-a-v-o	parl-a-va-mo
2	parl-i	parl-a-te	parl-i	parl-i-ate	2	parl-a-v-i	parl-a-va-te
3	parl-a	parl-a-no	parl-i	parl-i-no	3	parl-a-v-a	parl-a-va-no

(1985a), discussing German inflection. I shall summarize some of the basic points he raises using a fragment of Italian verbal morphology, since this illustrates some, though by no means all, of the commoner problems. The data are given in table 6.1 and represent the commonest and most productive of the conjugational paradigms.

This fragment of morphology isn't fully agglutinating, and, in fact, shows a number of the characteristics of inflectional systems discussed in chapters 1 and 2. Nonetheless, there are certain regularities that are immediately apparent. For example, the 1pl. ending consistently ends in *-mo*, and the imperfect indicative is marked by *-v(a)*. Moreover, the distinction between persons is neutralized in the singular forms of the present subjunctive. At the same time, there are certain deviations from strict agglutination. For instance, we find a theme vowel *-a-* in the imperfect and half of the present indicative forms, much as in the Spanish example from §1.4. However, this vowel is lacking in the 1sg., 1pl. and 2sg. forms. It looks as though the verb uses a different theme vowel, *-i-*, in the subjunctive, but this vowel also appears before the *-amo* of the 1pl. present indicative form. (In fact, the 1pl. ending turns out to be *-iamo* for both the present tense forms, indicative and subjunctive, in all three conjugations.)

In addition to these deviations from agglutination there are further intriguing descriptive problems. For instance, how do we relate the recurrent 1pl. formative *-iamo* to its truncated cousin *-mo* in the imperfect? Is the subjunctive form *parliate* to be segmented as *parl-i-a-te* or *parl-i-ate* or something else, given that we have *parlino* and not *parliano*? Far from being the exception, these sorts of puzzle are typical of inflectional systems.

Once we have decided on how to segment inflected words, the parsimonious way to describe much of the system will be to present all the exceptional cases first and then say that 'elsewhere', such-and-such happens. For instance, the *-a-* theme occurs through much of the paradigm (including a good many forms not given), while the *-i-* formative is characteristic of the subjunctive in this class, so one possibility would be to say that the theme vowel for the subjunctive is *-i-* and it is *-a-* in other forms (i.e. elsewhere). A number of theoretical approaches have made use of this notion of the 'elsewhere case', familiar from phonology (after Kiparsky, see chapter 4). Van Marle (1985) claims that use of elsewhere statements should be regarded as a hallmark of paradigm systems.

It is also noticeable from these data that formatives corresponding to particular morphosyntactic categories tend to occur in a particular form. For example, the imperfect marker precedes the person/number (P/N) markers (just as in our cognate Spanish example in §6.1.4). Again, there are different ways of capturing this. In the psg approaches discussed in §6.2 the ordering would either be the result of linear ordering statements in the phrase structure rules, or would be handled by the wording of subcategorization statements. Similarly, in the position class or template models discussed in §6.4, the formative order would be directly stipulated. However, other possibilities are open.

In the rest of this section we will examine some of the more influential answers to these and other questions, and we'll take a more detailed look at the properties of inflectional paradigms. For the purposes of the section, then, it will be necessary to abandon the scepticism of authors such as Lieber and accept the idea of a paradigm as an object of description. To the extent that this perspective allows us to throw additional light on the nature of inflectional morphology, this will provide us with evidence that the notion of 'paradigm' isn't superfluous.

6.5.2 Anderson's 'Extended Word-and-Paradigm' theory

Stephen Anderson (1977, 1982, 1984a, 1986, 1988b; see also the papers in Thomas-Flinders, 1981) has developed an approach to inflection which takes as its point of departure the Word-and-Paradigm model of Robins, Matthews and others described in chapter 2. He regards the problems of multiple exponence which we saw in that chapter as evidence against the morpheme concept in inflectional morphology. He proposes to incorporate paradigms into a generative grammar by generating them by means of a specially constructed set of rules (in effect, extending earlier proposals of Matthews, 1972). These rules, called **morpholexical rules** by Anderson (and not to be confused with Lieber's polysemous term) specify how a given morphosyntactic category, such as 'dative plural' or '3sg. imperfect subjunctive' is to be spelled out in phonological form. The resulting system is known as the **Extended Word-and-Paradigm** model (EWP).

Anderson's specific analyses use binary morphosyntactic features. The feature specifications [+me] and [+you] indicate 1st and 2nd person forms, while 3rd person forms are [−me, −you]. For familiar Indo-European pronoun systems a redundancy rule would specify that [+me] entails [−you] and [+you] entails [−me], so when one of these features bears a positive value the other needn't be specified. A concrete example would be the feature sets for the Italian verb forms *parlo* 'I speak' and *parlavano* 'they were speaking', shown in 6.66 (where the specification [+indic] in 6.66b reflects the fact that there is also an imperfect subjunctive form which we haven't discussed):

6.66   a) $\begin{bmatrix} +\text{me} \\ -\text{pl} \\ +\text{indic} \\ +\text{pres} \end{bmatrix}$ b) $\begin{bmatrix} -\text{me} \\ -\text{you} \\ +\text{pl} \\ +\text{indic} \\ +\text{imperf} \end{bmatrix}$

The morpholexical rules will take the representations in 6.66 and provide all the desinences, viz. -*o*, and -*no*. The stem will be provided by the lexicon, by other morpholexical rules, or by the output of phonological rules applying to an earlier stage in the derivation.

Let's think of our simple Italian example in terms of a morphological template, or

sequence of position classes, such as described in §6.4. Disregarding certain difficulties with the 1/2 sg., we would say that there is a root position, a theme vowel,
an optional imperfect formative and the P/N endings, in that order. We have also
seen that the exact form of the 1pl. ending depends on the tense form. This is shown
in 6.67:

6.67   root +1   +2   +3
                 a   va   o
                 i   ∅   i
                                     ∅
                                     mo, iamo
                                     te
                                     no

At this point we must make our first theory-internal choice, by deciding which of
these formatives are to be regarded as inflections proper. Clearly, the P/N
desinences in order +3 are inflectional. The -va- formative poses the problems
mentioned in the introduction to this section, so let's suppose it is an inflectional
morpheme. The theme elements are often regarded as derivational, stem-forming
suffixes, which would suggest that their presence should be accounted for by other
rules (namely, derivational rules in the lexicon). However, in a certain sense these
theme vowels are part of the paradigm and interact with other, genuinely inflectional,
suffixes in complex ways. Therefore, we shall assume that it is our morpholexical
rules which introduce the theme vowels. (Platt, 1981, makes the same assumption for
another Romance language, Medieval Provençal.)

We now need a grammar which will put these affixes in the right order, linking
each word form with the right morphosyntactic characterization. In 6.68–6.70 we see
a short grammar fragment sufficient to generate the forms indicated in 6.67, using
our morphosyntactic feature system, and ignoring other forms not mentioned in our
fragment in table 6.1:

6.68   i)   [+subj]
                $|X| \to |X+i|$
           ii) $|X| \to |X+a|$

6.69   [+imperf.]
                $|X| \to |X+va|$

6.70   i) $\begin{bmatrix} +\text{you} \\ +\text{pl.} \\ +\text{subj.} \end{bmatrix}$ v) $\begin{bmatrix} +\text{you} \\ +\text{pl.} \end{bmatrix}$

                $|X| \to |X+ate|$ $|X| \to |X+te|$

           ii) $\begin{bmatrix} +\text{me} \\ +\text{pl.} \\ -\text{imperf.} \end{bmatrix}$ vi) [+pl.]

                $|X| \to |X+iamo|$ $|X| \to |X+no|$

iii) $\begin{bmatrix} \text{-pl.} \\ \text{+subj.} \end{bmatrix}$

/X/ → /X/

iv) $\begin{bmatrix} \text{+me} \\ \text{+pl.} \end{bmatrix}$

/X/ → /X + mo/

vii) [+me]

/X/ → /X + o/

viii) [+you]

/X/ → /X + i/

The rules are to be interpreted as stating that a morphosyntactic feature set is realized as a particular morphophonological operation. In the present case the operation happens always to be the addition of a set of segments to the right of the morphophonological form generated so far (represented by 'X'). This is therefore the format for representing suffixation.

These rules are applied in two conjunctively ordered blocks. In other words, the rules in 6.68 apply to roots taken from the lexicon. Thus, if we are forming *parlavano*, we will start with X = *parl* and then add -*a* to it by rule 6.68ii. This stem, *parla*, then becomes input to the rules in 6.69 (giving *parlava-*) and finally the rules of 6.70 apply to the output of 6.69 to add the 3pl. desinence, giving *parlavano*. This ordering of blocks has the effect of reconstructing the three position classes in 6.66.

Within a block the individual rules are disjunctively ordered. Hence, when one rule in a block has applied we skip all the others and move on to the next block of rules. The rules within the block are all written on the assumption that Kiparsky's Elsewhere Condition holds. That is, if several rules 'compete' for application, it is the most specific which wins out, just as in our prose descriptions at the beginning of this section. This disjunctive organization captures the paradigmatic nature of the system, with disjunctive ordering capturing the notion of mutually exclusive affixation. This means that there is no need to specify an ordering for rules extrinsically, in this example, at least. However, Anderson makes it plain that, in other cases, he believes that extrinsic rule ordering might be necessary.

If you compute the full feature representation of all the forms of table 6.1 and follow through the derivations of each form, a number of important points will become apparent. First, there is no explicit mention of 3rd person in 6.70vi. This is the default person specification: if the form is neither 1st nor 2nd person, it can only be 3rd person, therefore there is no need to state this explicitly in the rule. This is a simple illustration of the way rules can be parsimoniously written to take advantage of the 'elsewhere' principle.

On the other hand, there is no rule at all realizing the 3rd singular forms. In many inflectional systems, 3rd person singular is the default P/N specification. In Italian, as in many other languages, it receives no special marker. In other words, it is represented by a zero morph. Given the rules as written, nothing will happen when a 3sg. specification is encountered, so the final form will be that of the stem which has been generated by rules 6.68–6.69. This is one of a number of ways of capturing the idea of a zero morph.

The singular forms of the subjunctive also illustrate a zero morph, this time for all three persons. This type is generated rather differently, however. The singular of the subjunctive is not a default case, rather it is a set of specifications whose realization has to be explicitly stated. This is done in our fragment by stating that the inflected form is identical to the stem form. In other words, we make explicit what is implicit in the previous case of a zero morph.

An obvious point about these rules (and the tabulation in 6.67) is that they generate incorrect forms. Specifically, the 1/2 sg. forms appear as *parlao, *parlai, *parlavao, *parlavai. Likewise, we generate the forms *parlaiamo, *parliiamo for the 1pl. present indicative and subjunctive. There are several ways permitted by the theory for handling this. Anderson's most popular solution seems to be to assume a phonological rule wherever feasible. In the present case, this would delete a (theme) vowel before any 'block 3' desinence beginning with a vowel. This is the third way of representing a zero morph (here the zero theme vowel): we generate it and then get rid of it. Notice that none of the three ways of generating zero morphs makes any reference to zero forms as such.

My analysis of the Italian fragment is not meant to be definitive (it would have to take into account the entire Italian conjugation system to be that); rather it illustrates the way a theorist might go about describing an inflectional system in the EWP framework. Approaches which are in many respects similar (such as, say, Zwicky's) would in certain cases adopt different solutions. For instance, with a different feature system, we might be able to write a rule of referral for the singular of the subjunctive stating directly that the person distinction is neutralized, forming a single morphosyntactic category of 'subjunctive singular', thereby treating this as a case of 'systematic inflectional homonymy', or syncretism.

The EWP model was developed to handle much more complex types of inflection than Indo–European conjugation. In table 6.2 we see a small portion of the conjugation system of Georgian.[15] Transitive verbs agree with both the subject and the direct object. In the glosses in table 6.2 the subject P/N is shown first, then that of the object. Thus, v-xedav-t means 'I/we see him/them'. Note that 'you' stands for

Table 6.2 Transitive conjugation in Georgian

Verb root *xedav* 'see'

Subject Object	1sg. 'I'	1pl. 'we'	2sg. 'thee'	2pl. 'you'
me	———	———	m-xedav	m-xedav-t
thee	g-xedav	g-xedav-t	———	———
him	v-xedav	v-xedav-t	xedav	xedav-t
us	———	———	gv-xedav	gv-xedav-t
you	g-xedav-t	g-xedav-t	———	———
them	v-xedav-t	v-xedav-t	xedav	xedav-t

Subject Object	3sg. 'he'	3pl. 'they'
me	m-xedav-s	m-xedav-en
thee	g-xedav-s	g-xedav-en
him	xedav-s	xedav-en
us	gv-xedav-s	gv-xedav-en
you	g-xedav-t	g-xedav-en
them	g-xedav-t	xedav-en

2pl. and 'thee' for 2sg. The gaps in the conjugation system are systematic: they arise wherever the subject would have the same person as the object (i.e. a reflexive form).

These forms show characteristics which are typical of conjugational systems of this kind. Although there are correspondences between form and function, these are not straightforward. For instance, the marker of 3pl. subject is always *-en*; the usual marker of 3sg. subject is the suffix *-s*; in most cases, whenever there is a 2pl. form as subject or object, the suffix *-t* appears. However, the *-t* desinence overrides the *-s* desinence in the 3sg.–2pl. form *g-xedav-t* and the *-en* desinence overrides the *-t* desinence in the 3pl.-2pl. form *gv-xedav-en*. Moreover, the prefix *v-* appears to systematically represent the 3rd person object, but only when the subject is 1st person. Thus, our paradigm exhibits a variety of deviations from strict agglutinative organization and shows complex dependencies between one morphosyntactic category and another. However, in one respect the system seems similar to the simple Italian case described earlier: there appears to be at most one prefix slot and one suffix slot for the subject/object markers. This again suggests columns of mutually exclusive affixes, which in the EWP model suggests blocks of disjunctively ordered rules.

At the level of morphosyntactic features there is an obvious descriptive problem in distinguishing subject agreement from object agreement. The most direct way is to have features such as [+subject], [+object] in the morphosyntactic representations. Anderson eschews this, however, because he is presupposing a Government-Binding approach to syntax on which grammatical relations such as 'subject' and 'object' are derived notions and not primitive. A subject is defined as the NP daughter of S and a direct object as the NP daughter of VP (or V′). He therefore incorporates this structural definition into his morphosyntactic feature representations, by a notational device of 'layering'. This means that one set of features can appear inside another set of features.[16] The representation for 'he sees me' is shown in 6.71:

6.71
$$\begin{bmatrix} -\text{me} & \begin{bmatrix} +\text{me} \\ -\text{you} \\ -\text{pl.} \end{bmatrix} \\ -\text{you} \\ -\text{pl.} \end{bmatrix}$$

The morpholexical rules which spell out these features are made sensitive to this layering. Thus, the rules accounting for the data of table 6.2 appear as in 6.72–6.73 with the 'X' inside feature sets being a variable over sets of morphosyntactic features:

6.72 a) [X [1st sg.]]
      $/X/ \rightarrow /m + X/$
   b) [X [1st]]
      $/X/ \rightarrow /gv + X/$
   c) [X [2nd]]
      $/X/ \rightarrow /g + X/$
   d) [1st]
      $/X/ \rightarrow /v + X/$

6.73 a) [1st sg. [2nd pl.]]
      $/X/ \rightarrow /X + t/$
   b) [3rd pl.]
      $/X/ \rightarrow /X + en/$
   c) [(X) [2nd pl.]]
      $/X/ \rightarrow /X + t/$
   d) [pl.]
      $/X/ \rightarrow /X + t/$
   e) [3rd]
      $/X/ \rightarrow /X + s/$

Rule system 6.72 provides the prefixes and system 6.73 provides the suffixes. The two blocks of rules are unordered with respect to each other.[17] (For ease of deciphering I have resorted to features such as [1st sg.] rather than [+me, −pl].) The fact that the variable over subject features is in parentheses in 6.73c means that we may omit the subject feature layer, in which case the features for [2nd pl.] will be the only layer of features and will hence itself refer to subject features. Hence, the -*t* suffix may signal [2nd pl.] not only for objects but also for subjects. [18]

Having witnessed the mechanics of the EWP model we are in a position to examine its theoretical underpinnings.

For Word-and-Paradigm theorists the most important feature of inflectional systems is their tendency towards non-agglutination, manifested as overlapping exponence and fusion. Anderson therefore argues that these problems indicate a fundamental flaw in the whole of the Item-and-Arrangement approach to inflection. He rejects the view that inflectional formatives are 'morphemes' in the sense of affixal objects attached to stems. Although his morpholexical rules look rather like affixation rules (similar to the WFRs of Aronoff) they are in fact intended as essentially phonological rules and they are ordered amongst phonological rules proper in the PF component. In other words, Anderson presses the view that inflectional morphemes are processes and not things. This means that there is no principled difficulty in assimilating the 'morphemes as rules' data of chapter 1 into his system. Anderson's system is thus diametrically opposed to the psg models of Selkirk, Williams or Lieber, in which morphemes are objects, stored in the lexicon and concatenated by rules.

On the other hand, Anderson regards derivational morphology in much the same way that Item-and-Arrangement lexicalist theorists view it. That is, derivational processes take place in the lexicon and are basically affixational. [19] This means that Anderson accepts the split-morphology thesis. He therefore rejects the Strong Lexicalist Hypothesis and regards the morphosyntactic aspects of inflection as essentially syntactic in nature. Indeed, he explicitly defines inflectional morphology as 'what is relevant to syntax' (Anderson, 1982: 587; cf. 1988b). In other words, rules of syntax distribute morphosyntactic features, such as those for agreement or government, onto words. The inflectional rule system therefore has to apply after the syntax, in the PF component. This position resembles that of Lexical Phonology, which also permits phonological rules to be interspersed among morphological rules. However, there is a significant difference, in that, for Anderson, *all* morphophonemic processes affecting inflection must occur after the syntax (i.e. postlexically), whereas, in Lexical Phonology, inflectional processes will be handled in the lexicon if they belong to a lexical stratum. (Admittedly, there is some vagueness in EWP here, since clearly lexical conditioning of inflectional forms, such as suppletion, will still have to be handled in the lexicon.) Lest we should fall into the trap of oversimplifying this issue, Anderson (1988b) makes it clear, however, that the real question is not 'where does inflection happen?' but rather 'where is morphophonological well-formedness defined for inflection and where is morphosyntactic well-formedness defined?' In common with a growing number of theorists, he adopts the view that the answers to each of the latter two questions will be different.

In somewhat simplified form the overall organization of grammar envisaged by EWP is that of figure 6.1 (the full model is given in Anderson, 1982: 594).

Despite the upsurge of interest in inflectional morphology and the morphology–syntax interface generally, Anderson's model has not met with whole-hearted approval amongst generative linguists. Jensen and Stong-Jensen (1984) argue that all

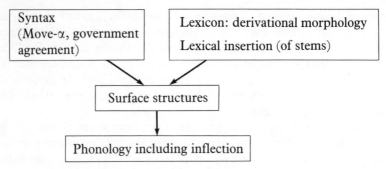

Figure 6.1   Anderson's model of grammar

of Anderson's examples can be reanalysed on a morphemic basis within the overall framework of Lieber's theory. To give a brief example, let's consider how they generate Georgian verb forms. They employ a similar feature system to Anderson, and appropriate his idea of the layered features to express subject and object relations. However, instead of rewriting certain feature values as formatives, they associate each formative (i.e. each affix) with an underspecified feature set. By using the Feature Percolation Conventions (plus certain other plausible assumptions) they claim they can reanalyse the entire system reported by Anderson.

To see how their reanalysis works we consider how the form *gxedavt* 'I see you (pl.)' is generated. The affixes have the lexical entries of 6.74 (using Anderson's notational conventions to ease comparison):

6.74   a) g- :   [[+you]]
          b) -t2:   [+me [+pl]]

These code the fact that *g*- signals a 2nd person object (of either number) while -*t2* signals 1st person subject acting on plural object. (There is a homophonous morpheme, -*t1*, with a different feature characterization in Jensen and Stong-Jensen's analysis.) When affixed to a verb root each of these affixes percolates its own features to the dominating node. This is shown in 6.75:

6.75

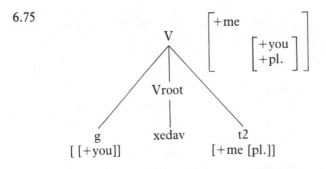

Default rules specify the remaining unmarked features with the negative value to give 6.76:

6.76

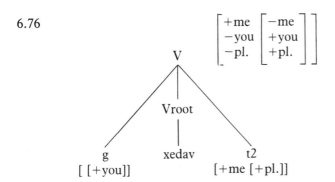

$$V \begin{bmatrix} +\text{me} & \begin{bmatrix} -\text{me} \\ +\text{you} \\ +\text{pl.} \end{bmatrix} \\ -\text{you} \\ -\text{pl.} \end{bmatrix}$$

Vroot

g   xedav   t2

[[+you]]   [+me [+pl.]]

What we see here is an analysis which is very similar to that of Anderson, except that the feature percolation is bottom-up in the case of Jensen and Stong-Jensen's analysis, while it is top-down in Anderson's case. As a result, it is not entirely clear where the difference really lies, at least for those aspects of inflection which retain an agglutinating character. For Anderson, formatives such as *g-* and *-t* are not morphemes, they are merely exponents of morphosyntactic feature sets. For lexicalists, on the other hand, these affixes will be morphemes but their 'meaning' will be a collection of morphosyntactic features. The key here seems to be the systematic use of features to capture the function of morphological material, rather than other aspects of the overall architecture of the theories under comparison. The most important potential difference between the two approaches would be in their handling of deviations from agglutination. Here, Jensen and Stong-Jensen argue that we are often dealing with allomorphy statements, and that different allomorphs of roots and affixes would be listed together with a featural characterization of what categories they (partially) realize (see, for instance, their discussion of Old English inflection for further details of this).

The principal difference between the two approaches can't really be decided on just a handful of competing analyses, because it concerns fundamental assumptions about the nature of the language faculty. Anderson's model retains the assumptions of the Standard Theory that regularity should be captured by isolating common underlying forms of morphemes and applying a battery of rules to account for the variation those morphemes show in various contexts. For Jensen and Stong-Jensen (in keeping with by far the dominant tendency in generative phonology and syntax), rules are replaced by a combination of general principles of grammatical organization (the principles of Universal Grammar) and specific information encoded in more complex sets of underlying representations. In other words, the specific and idiosyncratic components of a rule are extracted and written into the representations themselves.

Anderson, however, retains the notion of rule as an important part of UG, along with principles of rule organization, particularly rule ordering and other types of interaction. Anderson's emphasis on rule systems is very clear in his review of the history of phonology (Anderson, 1985c), in which the development of phonology is taken as the development of a theory of phonological rules from an earlier theory of phonological representations. A number of generative phonologists seem to regard phonology as essentially processual, or rule based, while syntax is essentially representational (for instance, Bromberger and Halle, 1989, endorsed, it would seem, by Chomsky, MS). For those that regard phonology as essentially representational, the question is whether morphology is distinct from phonology and syntax in being processual. For those who regard phonology as processual the question is whether morphology is more like phonology or like syntax. Given that morphology has an interface with both domains and also may well have it own principles of organization, there can be no a priori answer to any of these questions.

Where does this leave the paradigm? If the lexicalist stance is taken then the paradigm will remain an epiphenomenon of the morphosyntactic feature system, and therefore of no intrinsic interest. But this presupposes that lexicalists can answer the various criticisms that have been levelled against the Item-and-Arrangement approach to morphology (including some that we'll discuss in chapter 11). On the other hand, to have a firm argument in favour of the existence of paradigms, what we really need is evidence that linguistic processes make appeal to a level of representation which includes paradigms. Simply providing a mechanism for generating paradigms doesn't of itself prove the need for them. In the next two subsections we'll look at some attempts to justify the paradigm as a representational entity.

6.5.3 *Paradigms as systems*

In several places I have suggested that morphologists tend to regard the 'ideal' morphological system as one which is completely agglutinative, whose affixation processes are associated with a completely compositional semantics, which lacks homonymy in its affixes, which doesn't have allomorphy other than that dictated by automatic phonological processes, and which doesn't divide up its lexicon into arbitrary, morphologically defined inflectional classes.

This 'state of nature' of the archetypical morphological system has been elevated to the status of a theoretical construct in the theory of Natural Morphology proposed by Mayerthaler (1981) and developed in various ways by Dressler, Wurzel and their colleagues (see §4.5). Deviations are regarded as 'unnatural', so that there will tend to be a pressure towards regression to the primeval state, for instance, in historical change, in child development, in speech errors and language disorders. This is to say that Natural Morphologists assume something like Jakobson's (1968) approach to universals of language, in which the most natural, or least 'marked', phenomena are the most universal (and will tend to be the most widespread in languages of the world).

Natural Morphologists also follow Jakobson in assuming that certain morphosyntactic categories are 'simpler' than, or prior to, others. For example, 'singular' is a basic category, while 'plural' is in some sense derived. Hence, the natural way of signalling the plural is to take a form which conveys the singular and do something extra to it. For instance, we might add an affix, or mutate the first consonant. Such a process is **iconic** (because 'more' semantically is represented by 'more' morphologically). Affixation is more iconic than consonant mutation because affixation actually makes the plural form longer than the singular. (Presumably, the most iconic would be full reduplication.) Some morphological processes are non-iconic. The plural *sheep* of *sheep* is a case in point. This will also be true of suppletion. On the other hand, if the more complex category is represented by a simpler form, then we have a counter-ionic process. Subtractive morphology is an example of this. A frequently cited example is the genitive plural of feminine and neuter nouns in -*a*/-*o* in Russian, which are formed without any affixation at all: *kniga* 'book', *knig*, and *mesto* 'place', *mest*. The principle that semantically more implies morphologically more is called **constructional iconicity**. Natural Morphologists claim that historical changes will occur in the direction of less iconic to more iconic.[20]

The object of study in Natural Morphology is languages and not grammars, so that a detailed examination of the claims of its adherents would take us beyond our brief, namely, morphology in generative grammar. However, many of the issues addressed by Natural Morphologists are of importance to generative linguists. In addition to posing problems for generativists, inflectional paradigms, on the face of it, violate most naive naturalness conditions. In this subsection we shall therefore look briefly at a carefully constructed theory of inflection proposed by Wolfgang Wurzel, a linguist who has been highly influential, both in generative linguistics and within the Natural Morphology school, specifically his 1984 monograph.

Wurzel accepts the broad validity of the Natural Morphology perspective but points out that it oversimplifies the situation with inflection. This is because the universal tendencies summarized by the principle of constructional iconicity can be overridden by language particular factors. Wurzel observes that in a language with any degree of morphological complexity there will be stable, productive inflectional classes, alongside semi-productive ones, alongside moribund, 'irregular' classes, generally historical relics. For instance, in English, regular plurals are formed by affixation of *-z*. Certain types of Latin or Greek derived words form their plurals in *-i*, *-ae*, *-a* and so on. One word, *ox*, now forms its plural by adding *-en* (though this used to be the productive form at an earlier stage of the language). The stable systems are the productive ones, in the sense that, other things being equal, loan words and newly coined words will enter those systems, and words in non-productive classes will tend to migrate towards the productive ones, but not vice-versa.

Inflectional paradigms in a given language obey their own sets of principles, what Wurzel calls **system-defining structural properties** (SDSP). Sometimes these are determined by non-morphological factors such as phonology or meaning. Wurzel lists six properties that make up the SDSPs of an inflectional system:

(i) the set of morphosyntactic categories;
(ii) whether inflection is defined over the base form of a word or over a bound stem;
(iii) whether several categories are fused into one marker or whether the system is strictly agglutinating;
(iv) whether there is syncretism;
(v) what type of morphological markers are used (prefixes, suffixes, infixes, ablaut, consonant mutation etc.);
(vi) whether there are morphological classes (for example, arbitrary gender classes, conjugations, declensions).

The extent to which the forms in a paradigm conform to the SDSPs of that inflectional class determines the degree of system congruity. The assumption is that there is a pressure on inflectional systems to be **congruent** (i.e. 'regular').

A simple example of an SDSP in Russian is this: masculine nouns tend to end in a consonant, feminines in *-a* and neuters in *-o*. Here we have a partly semantic, partly grammatical criterion linked to morphology. Wurzel provides a nice example of our Russian SDSP at work in explaining the shape of certain loans from German. The feminine nouns *Büchse* ([byxsə]) 'beech', and *Hülse* (hylzə]) 'shell' were borrowed as *buksa* and *gil'za*. Here, the gender of the originals influenced which inflectional class the words should enter. Since the productive feminine class ends in *-a* the two loans were furnished with this suffix and entered the most stable of the feminine noun classes.

In addition, inflectional systems often respect **paradigm structure conditions** (PSC). These are implicative regularities of the kind 'if a member of the paradigm has affix x in the genitive then it has affix y in the dative'. A simple example of a PSC from English is this; if a strong verb has an irregular past participle then it has an irregular past tense. Where a language has a lot of inflectional classes or subclasses the PSCs will often play an important role in identifying those classes. For instance, in Czech there is a subclass of neuter nouns with 'soft' stems which take an extension *-et-* in oblique cases in the singular and *-at-* in all cases in the plural. Thus, beside the normal case *moře* 'sea', *moře* 'gen. sg.', *moře* 'nom. pl.', we have *kuře* 'chicken', *kuřete* 'gen. sg.', *kuřata* 'nom. pl.'. The biconditional, that the *-et-* extension in the singular implies the *-at-* extension in the plural, and vice versa, is one of the PSCs of Czech nouns.

Sometimes a language will have competing PSCs for a paradigm. In English (as in German, Wurzel's example), 'latinate' plural formation, for example, *addenda*, *phenomena*, *formulae*, *concerti*, conflicts with the general rule for English plural formation, so that a number of borrowed words have purely native plural forms (for instance, *electron*, *spatula*, *mulatto*). This can be interpreted as the influence of a dominant PSC for plural formation, which sometimes supersedes the non-dominant PSCs, and which often attracts members of the non-dominant subclass (as in *formulas* and *concertos*). Wurzel defines a notion of inflectional class stability in terms of adherence to the dominant PSCs. A class which is system congruent and also stable in this technical sense will be productive, for example, it will attract new words, loans and often, members of non-productive classes.

A central assumption guiding this approach is that stable morphological systems don't change of their own accord. Change comes from essentially three sources: unstable morphological classes change (into more stable ones); phonological changes affect the shape of morphological markers, thereby indirectly changing otherwise stable systems; and large influences of loan words (especially from closely related languages) may upset the morphological balance of a system. Since historical morphological change goes beyond our brief, we won't discuss these phenomena in any detail. However, it should be borne in mind that such questions are not irrelevant to generative grammar.

This picture of inflectional morphology is very useful for providing us with an overview of the type of paradigmatic systems encountered. Has it helped us in our quest for the paradigm? This depends on how paradigms behave in historical change, language acquisition, and other aspects of language use. Wurzel's typology of inflectional systems has made it clear that the traditional notion of paradigm is a conflation of SDSPs and PSCs (perhaps amongst other factors). It may ultimately turn out that these different factors tend to respond in a concerted fashion to shifts in the structure of the language. In that case, there will appear to be a 'conspiracy' between disparate factors to maintain the paradigm. This would give us evidence for the autonomous existence of paradigms. We might then wish to build a theory in which they are represented as structured lists of items in the mind. On the other hand, it might turn out that there is no such evidence of concerted action, and that individual rules and properties change of their own accord, perhaps in accordance with distinct principles. In that case, the paradigm concept would be no more than an epiphenomenon after all, and would not enjoy an autonomous existence. At the current state of play, the evidence Wurzel presents, while suggestive, doesn't adjudicate between the two possibilities. In the final subsection we'll look at a further attempt at individuating the paradigm.

6.5.4 Paradigm economy

The final contribution to the study of inflection we'll discuss doesn't form part of a global theory of grammar. Rather, it is a set of observations on the nature of inflectional paradigms which is compatible with a number of different theoretical models. Our starting point will be a question about allomorphy. We know that it is typical for inflecting languages to have arbitrary morphological categories, such as conjugational or declensional classes. These are defined in terms of the affixes which they employ to signal the different morphosyntactic categories. Recall our discussion of Russian conjugation in chapter 1. There, we saw that there are basically two ways of conjugating a Russian verb, in other words, we can say there are two distinct verb paradigms. Two questions arise out of this. The first is: 'How do we determine the number of paradigms?' The second is: 'What limits are there on the number of paradigms a language is likely to have?'

These and related questions concerning the allomorphy of inflectional affixes have been addressed by Andrew Carstairs in a number of publications, an overview and synthesis being Carstairs (1987). In addressing these questions Carstairs appeals to the notion of inflectional paradigm in a crucial fashion. To answer our two specific questions we'll follow him in considering Hungarian verb inflections. A sample of relevant cases is shown in table 6.3 (slightly modified from Carstairs's own account). If we collect together all the different endings which signal the six person/number categories we end up with the list in 6.77:

6.77   Sg. 1 ok, ök, em
            2 ol, el, sz, esz, asz
            3 Ø, ik
        Pl. 1 unk, ünk
            2 tok, tök, tek, etek, otok
            3 nak, nek, enek, anak

As things stand, we have 21 different affixes for our six person/number categories. The maximum number of distinct combinations we could produce, and hence the maximum number of conjugation classes in Hungarian (given these data), would be $3 \times 5 \times 2 \times 2 \times 5 \times 4 = 1200$. However, it turns out that there are only two different conjugation classes represented here. How do we restrict the number of possible paradigms?

A knowledge of the morphophonemics of Hungarian helps us to understand most of this variation. First, we have vowel harmony. Verb stems with back vowels (*olvas*, *mond*) select back vowel suffixes such as *-ok*, *-unk* and *-nak*, while (most) verbs stems with front vowels select front vowel suffixes, such as *-ök*, *-ünk* and *-nek*. Second, consonant clusters of three members are split up by an epenthetic vowel (whose identity

Table 6.3   Hungarian conjugation ('Present Indefinite')

Stem		olvas- 'read'	ül- 'sit'	esz- 'eat'	ért- 'understand'	mond- 'say'
Sg.	1	olvas-ok	ül-ök	esz-em	ért-em	mond-ok
	2	olvas-ol	ül-sz	esz-el	ért-esz	mond-asz
	3	olvas	ül	esz-ik	ért	mond
Pl.	1	olvas-unk	ül-ünk	esz-ünk	ért-ünk	mond-unk
	2	olvas-tok	ül-tök	esz-tek	ért-etek	mond-otok
	3	olvas-nak	ül-nek	esz-nek	ért-enek	mond-anak

['s' = [ʃ], 'sz' = [s], 'ü' = [y], 'ö' = [œ], V̂ = long vowel].

depends in part on morphosyntactic factors rather than purely phonetic factors). Thus, we have *ülsz* but *mondasz*, *esznek* but *értenek*. Third, in the 2sg. form a stem ending in a sibilant takes *-ol* (back vowel stem) or *-el* (front vowel stem). However, any other stem takes *-sz*, *-esz* or *-asz* (where the vowel is added to split up clusters and the exact choice of vowel is determined by vowel harmony).

Given these phonological constraints, we can see that there are severe limits on the distribution of the affixes. The combinations are shown in 6.78 (where I've represented vowel harmonic variants as just the back vowel variant):

6.78

		non-ik	ik
Sg.	1	ok	om
	2	ol/ (a)sz	ol
	3	Ø	ik
Pl.	1	unk	unk
	2	(o)tok	(o)tok
	3	(a)nak	(a)nak

It is clear that there are only two conjugations (called in traditional Hungarian grammar the 'ik' and the 'ikless', or 'non-ik' conjugations). The differences are in the singular only, where the 1st person of the *ik*-conjugation has *-om* (in more formal styles, at least), the 2nd person only has the *-ol* form, and the 3rd person ends in *-ik*.

Carstairs uses this sort of procedure to determine what constitutes a paradigm, given all the allomorphs of the morphemes which signal the categories of the paradigm. One contentious question here is whether we should lump together verbs such as *mond-* and *olvas-* even though they differ in several of their forms. In one sense, we might want to say that they represent distinct paradigms even though the differences are phonologically predictable. In another sense, they are examples of 'the same thing', and so we might want to say they belong to the same paradigm. To overcome this definitional problem, Carstairs reserves the option of applying the narrow characterization of 'paradigm', under which these two verbs would represent different paradigms, and introduces the notion of **macroparadigm**. This is a collection of paradigms which are distinct in phonologically, morphosyntactically or semantically predictable ways (like the four non-*ik* verbs, *olvas-*, *ül-*, *ért-* and *mond-*) or any paradigm which can't be conflated in such a manner with another paradigm. Since the distinction between the *ik*-verbs and the non-*ik* verbs is purely morphological and can't be predicted on any other basis, this means that these two sets of verbs belong to different macroparadigms (and hence, a fortiori, to two different paradigms).

We have, then, situations in which stems in principle have a free choice as to which affix to take for a given morphosyntactic category (in the sense of combination of morphosyntactic features such as '3pl. preterite'). It is this which permits the formation of distinct paradigms. However, we have yet to answer a question. Ignoring the 2sg. forms, we noted that both the 1sg. and 3sg. forms have a choice of desinence. Would it then be possible to find a language (or a dialect of Hungarian) with a similar set of affixes, but in which we had more than one distinct paradigm? For instance, could we find the pattern illustrated hypothetically in 6.79?

6.79

	A	B	C	D
1	ok	ok	om	om
3	Ø	ik	Ø	ik

In this case we have four paradigms, making full use of the combinatoric possibilities opened up by the alternative affixes.

Carstairs argues that such a system would not be tolerated in a natural language, in that it would violate a universal principle, the **Paradigm Economy Principle**. Consider a situation in which there are several distinct affixes for a set of morphosyntactic feature combinations. For instance, some combinations might have just one affix, others three; still others might have six distinct affixes. Clearly, there will be some combination or set of combinations of features which will have the largest degree of variation. Suppose for simplicity's sake that there is exactly one. Carstairs argues that the number of (macro)paradigms found in the language won't exceed the number of different affixes for the feature combination with the greatest variety of affixes. In our Hungarian example there are two combinations with maximal variation, the 1sg. and 3sg. forms, and these have two distinct affixes each. Hence, there can be only two different paradigms.

The Paradigm Economy Principle brings into sharp relief an important fact about inflectional systems, namely, that they are far more constrained than would be expected without such a principle. To be sure there are apparent counter-examples (a number of which Carstairs reanalyses at some length). As far as I'm aware no one has tried to provide an explanation for the phenomenon in generative terms. It's possible, of course, that there is no properly linguistic explanation. It might simply be, given processing constraints on children acquiring language, that morphological systems always tend to shift towards a situation consonant with the Paradigm Economy Principle, without the principle itself being an inherent feature of the language faculty. Certainly, if the principle is valid, most generativists would want it to follow from some deeper properties of Universal Grammar.

Perhaps the most interesting implication of work such as this is that, if it captures a linguistic universal, and if it can be shown that that universal must form part of the human language faculty, then it is difficult to see how linguistic theory will be able to do without the notion of 'paradigm' (in one form or another). Carstairs's work therefore presents a challenge to those who would maintain that the paradigm is a mere epiphenomenon, with no autonomous role in Universal Grammar.

6.6 Summary

We shall close this chapter with a brief summary of the most important ideas that have emerged in the theories we've been reviewing. Perhaps the most important shift is the greater emphasis on syntax as a model for morphology. In chapter 4 we saw the introduction of labelled bracketing to replace segment-like boundary symbols. This manoeuvre naturally leads to the idea that words have their own constituent structure. From this it is a short (though not unproblematic) step to assume that one of the constituents is the head and that the whole structure obeys something like the principles of X-bar syntax. Add to this a thorough-going featural analysis of morpho-syntactic properties and we have a view of word formation very different from that of Halle or Aronoff.

Syntax also plays an important role in the approaches based on syntactic affixation, in which the interface between the morphology and syntax is represented as the operation of essentially syntactic, rather than morphological, rules. This viewpoint is controversial. Strong Lexicalism of roughly the kind Halle espoused is still a defensible position. On the other hand, a good many morphologists have adopted a Weak Lexicalist position, or 'split-morphology' approach, by distinguishing (syntactic) inflection from (lexical) derivation. We will see that some linguists have argued that syntax is even implicated in derivational processes.

This set of questions has relevance for the autonomy of morphology. Here we have seen essentially two positions, differing with respect to attitudes to the morphology–syntax interface. On the one hand we can argue that there is a separate morphology component (possibly a subcomponent of the lexicon itself). The interaction between morphology and syntax is then described in terms of a common vocabulary expressing an overlap in the two domains. This is the position adopted by Strong Lexicalists. On the other hand, we can argue that apparent redundancy or duplication of information between morphology and syntax should be excised. Since we need syntax anyway, the autonomy of morphology must suffer, so that the interface between morphology and syntax is here expressed by an encroachment of syntax into morphology. This is the basic tenet of syntactic affixation and approaches labelled Weak Lexicalism, or the split-morphology hypothesis. On this view, morphology will be autonomous only as a set of (lexical) redundancies, and we shall see later that some theoreticians have argued that morphology has *no* autonomy and that the lexicon is simply a list of idiosyncratic forms.

Finally, there remain a host of unresolved questions which don't relate to the key issues I've just identified. One of these is the status of inflectional paradigms. Lexicalist models such as those of Halle (1973) and Williams (1981a) claim to be able to accommodate the notion of paradigm. However, for other lexicalists, such as Lieber (1980), the paradigm is a mere side-effect with no theoretical status. At the same time Weak Lexicalism permits the paradigm to play a role (Anderson, 1982) but doesn't demand this.

Another issue which is resolved in different ways by different authors is the question of whether morphological relationships are to be handled as agglutinative affixation or whether we should accept that some morphemes are, after all, processes and not things. This question depends crucially on other aspects of representation, notably as regards morphosyntactic and morphophonemic features and as regards the reliance we put on nonconcatenative approaches to morphology. The strong pressure towards representational models in generative linguistics gives stronger impetus to advocates of the 'morphemes as things' and Item-and-Arrangement. But there remain unresolved problems here, in the form of recalcitrant pockets of processual morphology which make it difficult to accept a purely representational theory.

Many of these issues and related questions will be taken up in the subsequent chapters and I shall attempt an informed overview of current theoretical trends in the final chapter in part IV.

EXERCISES

6.1   Explain the non-existence of *grandstood*, *rang the pigeons* and so on, given the Atom Condition and the assumption that conversion produces headless constructions.

6.2   Analyse the following Swahili words (taken from Ashton, 1944) into component morphemes. Provide a gloss for each morpheme. What governs the linear ordering of the morphemes? What assumptions would you have to make in order to explain this ordering in terms of level ordered morphology?

wamewaona	'they have seen them'
wametuona	'they have seen us'
mwaniona	'you see me'
aliniona	'he saw me'
nilimwona	'I saw him'
atatuona	'he will see us'
tutamwona	'we will see him'

★6.3   For Lieber the paradigm is a derivative notion which plays no role in linguistic theory. Assuming that the claims of Carstairs's Paradigm Economy Principle are true, how might we try to accommodate this within Lieber's framework? Begin by determining what the equivalent of a paradigm would be for Lieber, and then rewrite the Principle as a constraint on the form of lexical entries for affixes. Does your solution compromise Lieber's basic assumptions and claims in any way? (You may find it useful to take the Latin data of exercise 6.15 as a starting point.)

6.4   Assume that there is a principle of word structure stating that all nouns must be marked for number in English. Use this, together with Lieber's Percolation Conventions and her subcategorization frames, to write a different derivation for *falsehoods* from that suggested in §6.2.2, making crucial use of FPC III. Supposing this alternative to Lieber's derivation is viable, what might this tell us about the lexical entries for inflectional affixes?

*6.5   Discuss Feature Percolation Conventions I, II, with respect to English words such as *cytoplasm* and *phenomenal*. What are the lexical entries for each component? Are there any difficulties with Lieber's original set of assumptions? If so, how might they be overcome within her theory?

6.6   Provide a 'position class' analysis of the data from Exercise 2.1 (chapter 2). Be careful to state all dependencies.

*6.7   Provide an analysis of the data from Exercise 2.1 (chapter 2) in Lieber's framework, by identifying all the affixal morphemes and providing them with subcategorization frames. Ensure your analysis accounts for all the dependencies.

6.8   Itel'men verb forms. Volodin (1976) distinguishes a transitive and an intransitive conjugation. Some verb stems follow either conjugation, for instance, *gilkes* 'to drink (intr.)', *giles* 'to drink something (tr.)'. The antipassive is a special intransitivized form of the verb (see §1.4; chapter 7). A number of morphophonemic processes are evident from these data, the most important being: insertion of a glide /w/ between two vowels; truncation of a morpheme final vowel (usually before a vowel); epenthesis of a vowel (usually before a cluster); assimilation of voicing (e.g. /s/ → /z/).
    Identify all the morphemes in the following data and provide a position class analysis. [c = [tʃ]

> ampəlsxenaʔl'kes 'to bite all the time (antipassive)'
> anan'cpaʔl'kes 'to teach (antipassive)'
> an'cpalas 'to teach someone a little'
> an'cpatal 'to go and teach someone'
> gilatakes 'to go and have a drink'
> ilwsal'qzomiŋsx 'you wanted to listen to me'
> kopsxenkes 'to stumble repeatedly'
> nowalakes 'to eat a little, snack (intr.)'
> nowalatakes 'to go and have a snack'
> omtsxenalas 'to lengthen something (e.g. rope) slightly by tying onto it'
> omtsxenes 'to tie something up continually'
> tgilal'qzokicen 'I wanted to drink something'
> t'ilwsal'qzocen 'I wanted to listen to him'
> əmpχalas 'to nick something'
> əmpχasxenes 'to cut something several times'

*6.9   Write a phrase structure grammar fragment after Selkirk (1982) to generate the data of the previous exercise. What additional descriptive devices, if any, do you need to capture all the facts?

★6.10   What devices does generative grammar make available for describing the case of 'cycles' discussed by Grimes (illustrated in 6.41–6.43) within the framework of Lieber's theory of affixation? What are the advantages and disadvantages of these methods?

6.11   Possessive affixation in Moksha Mordvin (Feoktistov, 1966). Below is a selection of the case forms of the basic and possessed forms of the word *alaša*, 'horse', in Moksha Mordvin, a Uralic language spoken in Western Siberia. Analyse these data into component morphemes. Give an informal, prose description of the structure of these paradigms. Comment on the problems these data might pose for the various approaches to inflection outlined in this chapter ([š = [ʃ], c = [ts], n' = [ɲ]]).

	'horse'		'horses'
Nom.	alaša		alašat
Gen.		alašan'	
Dat.		alašandi	
Abl.		alašada	
Iness.		alašasa	
El.		alašasta	
Ill.		alašas	

	'my horse'		'my horses'
Nom.	alašaze		alašane
Gen.	alašazen'		alašanen'
Dat.	alašazendi		alašanendi
Abl.		alašadon	
Iness.		alašason	
El.		alašaston	
Ill.		alašazon	

	'thy horse'		'thy horses'
Nom.	alašace		alašatne
Gen.	alašacen'		alašatnen'
Dat.	alašacendi		alašatnendi
Abl.		alašadot	
Iness.		alašasot	
El.		alašastot	
Ill.		alašazot	

	'his horse'		'his horses'
Nom.	alašac		alašanza
Gen.	alašanc		alašanzon
Dat.	alašancɨ		alašanzondɨ
Abl.		alašadonza	
Iness.		alašasonza	
El.		alašastonza	
Ill.		alašazonza	

	'our horse/s'	'your horse/s'	'their horse/s'
Nom.	alašan'ke	alašante	alašasna
Gen.	alašan'kon'	alašanten'	alašasnon
Dat.	alašan'kondi	alašantendi	alašasnondɨ
Abl.	alašadonk	alašadont	alašadost
Iness.	alašasonk	alašasont	alašasost
El.	alašastonk	alašastont	alašastost
Ill.	alašazonk	alašazont	alašazost

6.12 Fähnrich (1987), in a descriptive grammar of Georgian, suggests that the transitive verb morphology is essentially agglutinating, with the following analysis:

(i)

		Subject markers	Object markers	
Sg. 1		v-	m-	
2		_____	g-	
3		-s	_____	
Pl. 1		v- -t	gv-	
2		-t	g-	-t
3		-en	_____	

He implies that -*t* is a plural marker, and further states that, when a non-null object and subject affix are adjacent, the subject affix truncates. Can this analysis provide the basis for a grammar generating the fragment of conjugation in (i)?

In (ii) we see the conjugation pattern for intransitive verbs and transitive verbs when they don't explicitly reference an object. Is this what would be predicted on Fähnrich's analysis? Is this what is predicted by the analysis of Anderson and of Jensen and Stong-Jensen?

(ii)

	Sg.	Pl.
1	v-	v- -t
2	_____	-t
3	-s	-en

★6.13 Take the six system defining structural properties identified by Wurzel and take one of the following theories of morphology: Di Sciullo and Williams (1987), Selkirk (1982), Lieber (1980) or Anderson (1982). Which of the SDSPs finds direct reflection in that theory? Which of them finds indirect reflection, and how? Which of them is ignored? How does the theory of your choice capture Paradigm Structure Conditions (if at all)?

6.14 Chukchee verbal inflection. Identify the roots and affixes in the following verb paradigms from Chukchee. To what extent do the paradigms exhibit agglutination and to what extent are they fusional? Write a set of realization rules within Anderson's EWP framework to generate these paradigms.

Paradigm I (intransitive)

təkətgəntatgʔak	I ran	mətkətgəntatmək	we ran
kətgəntatgʔe	thou rannest	kətgəntattək	you ran
kətgəntatgʔe	he ran	kətgəntatgʔat	they ran

Paradigm II (transitive)

I left somebody	thou left ...	he left ...	Subject
			Object
_____	enapelagʔe	enapelagʔe	... me
təpelagət	_____	napelagət	... thee
təpelagʔan	pelagʔan	pelanen	... him
_____	petlakogʔe	napelamək	... us
təpelatək	_____	napelatək	... you
təpelanat	pelanat	pelanenat	... them

we left ...	you left ...	they left ...	
_____	enapelatək	napelagəm	... me
mətpelagət	_____	napelagət	... thee
mətpelagʔan	pelatkə	napelagʔan	... him
_____	pelatkotək	napelamək	... us
mətpelatək	_____	napelatək	... you
mətpelanat	pelatkə	napelanat	... them

⋆6.15   Despite its name, the Extended Word-and-Paradigm theory makes very little crucial reference to the notion of paradigm itself. How would the concept of paradigm be incorporated in EWP explicitly as a primitive notion, and why would this be necessary? Illustrate your answer by providing an EWP-type analysis for the following (highly selective) Latin data (based on Greenhough *et al.*, 1983), showing noun declension. [Note x = [ks], the macron over a vowel indicates length.]

	amīca '(girl) friend'		amīcus '(boy) friend'	
	Sg.	Pl.	Sg.	Pl.
Nom.	amīca	amīcae	amīcus	amīcī
Voc.	amīca	amīcae	amīce	amīcī
Acc.	amīcam	amīcās	amīcum	amīcōs
Gen.	amīcae	amīcārum	amīcī	amīcōrum
Dat.	amīcae	amīcīs	amīcō	amīcīs
Abl.	amīcā	amīcīs	amīco	amīcīs

	dux 'leader'		lacus 'lake'		diēs 'day	
	Sg.	Pl.	Sg.	Pl.	Sg.	Pl.
Nom.	dux	ducēs	lacus	lacūs	diēs	diēs
Voc.	dux	ducēs	lacus	lacūs	diēs	diēs
Acc.	ducem	ducēs	lacum	lacūs	diem	diēs
Gen.	ducis	ducum	lacūs	lacuum	diēī	diērum
Dat.	ducī	ducibus	lacuī	lacibus	diēī	diēbus
Abl.	duce	ducibus	lacū	lacibus	diē	diēbus

7

Grammatical Relations

Introduction

Our first view of the morphology–syntax interface will be the morphological expression of valency. In the survey of functions of morphology in chapter 1 I mentioned the phenomenon of voice, in which the argument structure of a predicate (such as a verb or adjective) is altered by affixation. This chapter begins with a much more detailed overview of such phenomena. We start with constructions in which valency is (or can be) reduced. We look at the great variety of passive constructions found in the world's languages, and constructions which are often genetically related to the passive, such as the middle voice, and reflexives, as well as a comparable construction found primarily in ergative languages, the antipassive. Then we survey valency increasing constructions, such as causatives, applicatives and possessor raising.

After this fairly detailed tour of the data we turn in §7.2 to theoretical accounts of valency changing. The theoretical apparatus we'll look at comes primarily from Government Binding theory and includes subcategorization, theta marking and Case assignment. We then summarize briefly the transformational theory of syntactic passives, which remains highly influential, though by no means universally accepted, within GB theory. Finally, we review a concept which is of great importance for several theoretical approaches to theories of valency changing, the Unaccusative Hypothesis.

In the next three sections we look at three specific models of valency changing. In these sections we again see both a complex interplay and a tension between lexical and syntactic approaches. In §7.3 I present the essentials of an intricate theory of valency changing which combines something of each approach, that of Marantz (1984). This theory helps set the theoretical scene for the next two approaches. §7.4 outlines Baker's syntactic theory, in which regular and productive valency changing processes are seen as the result of a rule of lexical incorporation, a generalization of the noun incorporation process we met in languages such as Chukchee in chapter 1.

This is contrasted with the approach of Williams (as summarized most recently in Di Sciullo and Williams, 1987), with a heavy lexicalist bias.

7.1   Overview of the phenomena

We have already seen examples of morphological processes which make reference to the argument structure of a predicate. The affixation of -*able* in English turns a transitive verb into an adjective with the meaning (roughly) 'such that can be verb-ed'. For instance, the two place predicate *read* ('x reads y') becomes a one place predicate *readable* ('y is readable'). Conversely, it is possible to take an adjective (i.e. a one place predicate) such as *red*, and turn it into a verb (which can be used transitively, as a causative, or intransitively, as an inchoative) i.e. *redden*.

Cases such as these are regarded as indubitably derivational morphology because words from one syntactic class are created from words of another. However, in many languages we find a number of morphological processes which affect the argument structure of predicates (chiefly verbs) but which turn a verb of one valency type into a verb with another. These are the traditional voice alternations, the most famous of which is the Passive. By adding the passive morpheme[1] to a transitive verb we obtain a verb with one argument less. Thus, the transitive verb *break* in 7.1 becomes the intransitive, passive form *broken* in 7.2:

7.1   Dick broke the vases.

7.2   The vases were broken (by Dick).

These sentences illustrate what we might call the 'canonical' passive construction: the active subject, *Dick*, is **demoted** and becomes an optional oblique phrase or adjunct (the *by*-phrase); the active object is **promoted** to become the subject with all the usual properties of subjects (such as subject-predicate agreement, in English); the verb appears in a special morphological form. It is common to find the NP *the vases* and *Dick* in both 7.1 and 7.2 referred to as the 'logical object' and 'logical subject' respectively, while *Dick* and *the vases* are the 'grammatical subjects' of 7.1, 2 and *the vases* is the 'grammatical object' of 7.1. Sentence 7.2, being passive and hence intransitive, has no grammatical object.

In languages with morphological case, the new subject is usually marked with the case characteristic of subjects (e.g. the nominative), while the adjunct often appears in an oblique case. Thus, in Russian we see alternations such as 7.3–7.4:

7.3   Kolxoznik   ubil   utjonka.
           farmer-NOM killed duckling-ACC
           'The farmer killed the duckling.'

7.4   Utjonok   byl ubit (kolxoznikom).
           duckling-NOM was killed (farmer-INSTR)
           'The duckling was killed (by the farmer).'

The English passive is an **analytic** or **periphrastic** construction, in that it requires an auxiliary verb *be* (or *get*) for its formation. The participal form itself is not unique to the passive. With a different auxiliary, *have*, it forms the perfect tense/aspect form, and used on its own it is a stative or resultative adjective (*A broken vase, The vase is completely broken*). In many languages, however, the passive is formed purely **synthetically**, by some morphological process such as affixation, not requiring any kind of auxiliary. Not infrequently, such types of passive enter into a paradigmatic opposition with other voice forms. Even within one family such as Indo-European we find a great variety of forms.

Latin had two ways of forming the passive, a synthetic form for the imperfective aspect and an analytic form for the perfective. In chapter 1 (example 1.44) we saw the active and passive conjugations of a typical Latin verb. In 1.45, repeated here as 7.5, we see an example of the synthetic passive. This can be contrasted with the analytic construction shown in 7.6:

7.5   Puella   ā mīlitibus amātur.
        girl-NOMsg. by soldiers   love-3sg.PASS
        'The girl is loved by the soldiers.'

7.6   Puella   ā mīlitibus amāta   est.
        girl-NOMsg. by soldiers   love-PAST PART/FEM/NOMsg. be-3sg.
        'The girl was/has been loved by the soldiers.'

As can be seen from 7.5 and 1.44 the synthetic passive form seems to involve a formant in -*(u)r* though the passive paradigm is essentially fusional, and cannot be said to derive through simple addition of a passive affix. In a more strongly 'agglutinating' language it is often easier to isolate a specifically passive morpheme. The Altaic languages are characteristically agglutinating. In Yakuts, for instance, a Turkic language spoken in Eastern Siberia, the passive can be formed by adding the suffix -*ilin* (whose vowels undergo vowel harmony depending on the vowels of the stem). Examples are given in 7.7–7.9 (abstracting away from morphophonemic changes), taken from Xaritonov (1963):

7.7   Saala muostata köbüörünen sab-ilin-i-bit.
        hall   floor   carpets   cover-PASS-PERF-3sg.
        'The hall floor has been covered with carpets.'

7.8   Biir taabirin taaj-ilin-t-ta.
        one riddle   solve-PASS-PAST-3sg.
        'One riddle was solved.'

7.9   Ehigi sarsiarda   čitaRa   ataar-ilin-a-Rit.
        you/pl. in-the-morning to-Chitu send-PASS-PRES-2pl.
        'You are being sent to Chitu in the morning.'

Notice that in Latin the passive morpheme -*(u)r* (where it is identifiable as such and isn't fused) occurs outside the other verb endings (tense/aspect and person/number), while in Yakuts the passive morpheme is closer to the verb root than the inflectional endings proper. This makes the Yakuts passive element look more like a derivational affix than an inflectional one.

The passive in English is capable of reducing the valency of ditransitive verbs, making them appear (mono)transitive. In other words it can take a verb with two objects, direct and indirect, and produce a verb with only one object, as in 7.10:

7.10   a) Tom gave Harriet a rose.
        b) Harriet was given a rose (by Tom).

Not all languages allow arguments other than direct objects to be passivized. However, some allow other types of participant, including even adjuncts, to be promoted. A number of the languages of the Malayo-Polynesian group illustrate this. In Malagasy (Keenan, 1976), a language of Madagascar, there is a complex voice system in which the verb appears in one of three different 'passive' forms depending on whether an active direct object, indirect object, or adverbial is being promoted. (Similar facts have been described for Philippine languages such as Tagalog, Ilokano, Cebuano and a good many others.) Note that in Malagasy the usual order of constituents is V(ADV)OS:

7.11   a) Manasa lamba amin ity savony ity Rasoa
           wash   clothes with this soap   this Rasoa
           'Rasoa is washing clothes with this soap.'
        b) Anasan   dRasoa   lamba ity savony ity
           wash-PASS by-Rasoa clothes this soap   this
           'This soap is being used to wash the clothes by Rasoa.'
        Lit.: 'This soap is being washed the clothes with by Rasoa.'

7.12   a) Mitoetra amin ity trano ity izahay
           live   in   this house this we(ex.)
           'We live in this house.'
        b) Itoerana   nay ity trano ity
           live-PASS we   this house this
           'This house is lived in by us.'

In each case so far the valency of the verb has been reduced by one, from 3 to 2 or from 2 to 1. In some languages intransitive verbs can also be passivized, with the result that valency is diminished from 1 to 0. In this case we find suppression of the subject, but no promotion of the complement because there isn't one. The resulting construction is often called an **impersonal passive**. Examples 7.13–7.15 are respectively German, Polish and Latin:

7.13   Es wurde getanzt.
        It became dance-PASS
        'People danced/were dancing.'

7.14   Było chodzeno.
        was-NEUTER-sg. walk-PASS-NEUTER-sg.
        'People were walking about.'

7.15   Curritur.
            run—PASS/3sg.
            'People run.'

Note that 7.13 typically has the gloss given, in which *es* is nonreferential. This means it cannot refer back to a previously mentioned lexical noun such as 'tango' to mean 'the tango was danced' (which would be an example of a canonical passive). The subject, *es*, is an 'expletive' (similar to the *it* of *It seems that Tom has left*). German (like English and French) is not a **null subject language**, and so the subject position must be filled by a meaningless pronominal, or 'dummy', element. In 7.14 we see that the passive participle and the auxiliary agree and take the neuter singular form (typical for languages with gender and number distinctions). Polish and Latin are null subject languages, so that they do not require an overt subject.

In all the examples of the passive so far we have seen that a verb promotes one of its complements (if it has any) to the subject position, after the subject is suppressed. However, even when the subject is suppressed with a transitive verb, it is not always the case that the complement is promoted. In some languages a complement can remain in place and be case marked as a direct object, even though the verb is now in the passive form and not the active. The Ukrainian examples in 7.16 are from Sobin (1985):

7.16   a) Zbudovali cerkvu v 1640 roc'i.
               they-built church-ACC in 1640 year
               'They built the church in 1640.'
            b) Cerkvu   bulo   zbudovano   v 1640 roc'i.
               church-ACC was-NEUT/sg. built-PASS/NEUT/sg. in 1640 year
               'The church was built in 1640.'

This **transitive passive** is optional and a passive similar to the Russian or Latin periphrastic passive is also found, as in 7.16c:

7.16   c) Cerkva   bula   zbudovana   v 1640 roc'i
               church-NOM/FEM/sg. was-FEM/sg. built-FEM/sg. in 1640 year
               'The church was built in 1640.'

In example 7.16b the verb has retained its ability to assign accusative case to the object after passivization, just as if it were active (cf. 7.16a). In languages with rich case morphology it isn't uncommon to find verbs which assign a case distinct from that normally assigned to direct objects. For instance, the Latin verb *inuideo*, 'I envy', assigns dative rather than the customary accusative case. Normally, when a language has verbs assigning a specific case of this sort ('Inherent Case'; see §7.2 below) the verb doesn't form a passive. However, Latin is an exception to this, and so we find passives such as 7.17 (from Keenan and Timberlake, 1985), in which the direct object of the active form retains its inherent dative case markings. Notice that the passive verb fails to agree in person and number with the object, indicating that no promotion to subject has taken place:

7.17   Mihi inuēditur.
          I-DAT envy-PASS/3sg.
          'I am envied.'

In the examples of passives seen so far, the morphosyntactic process which signals passivization has been affixation of the verb. However, many languages have constructions which resemble passives in many respects except that the verb is in its active form and the passive meaning is conveyed by the addition of a clitic pronoun which otherwise functions as a reflexive, with the same meaning as the *-self* pronouns in English.[2] The Romance languages provide well-known examples of this, and it is often referred to by its traditional French term of **se-moyen construction**:

7.18   Cette racine se   mange.
          this   root   REFL eats
          'This root is edible.' (French)

7.19   I dolci al cioccolato si mangiano in questa pasticceria.
          the sweets to chocolate REFL eat in this confectioners
          'Chocolates are eaten in this store.' (Italian)

Similar examples can be found in German and in Slavic:

7.20   Solche Sachen sagen sich nicht oft.
          such things say REFL not often
          'Such things are not often said.' (German)

7.21   Etot zavod stroit-sja kollektivom inostrannyx rabočix.
          this factory build-REFL collective of-foreign workers
          'This factory is being built by a foreign workforce.' (Russian)

7.22   To se nedělá.
          that REFL not-do-3sg.
          'That isn't done.' (Czech)

7.23   Często się słyszy o wypadkach.
          often REFL hear-3sg. about accidents
          'One often hears about accidents.' (Polish)

7.24   Tŭk se prodava xljab.
          here REFL sells bread
          'Bread is sold here.' (Bulgarian)

Just as morphological passives may have language particular idiosyncrasies, the same is true of reflexive passives. Many languages disallow an agent phrase with reflexive passives. This is true in Romance, and is largely true of most of the Slav languages. However, this does not distinguish the two sorts of passive, because there are some languages in which morphological passives cannot take agent phrases (e.g.

Latvian, Urdu, Seri; cf. Comrie, 1977) and, as is evident from the Russian example 7.21, there are languages in which a reflexive passive can co-occur with an agent.

We also saw that in some languages passive morphology doesn't preclude marking the underlying direct object with the accusative case characteristic of objects of active verbs. In Polish, for instance, the same is true of the reflexive passive:

7.25   Otwiera się kasę o ośmiej.
        opens REFL ticket office-ACC at eight
        'The ticket office opens at eight.'

Finally, we have seen that a morphological passive can be used impersonally, for example with intransitive verbs. Exactly the same is true of reflexive passives in some languages. Thus, alongside examples such as German 7.12 we have 7.26 (Perlmutter and Postal, 1984):

7.26   Es tanzt sich   gut hier.
        it dances REFL good here
        'There is good dancing here.'

Examples 7.27–7.29 come from Polish, Czech and Serbo-Croat respectively (Ružička, 1986):

7.27   Zostało się mężatka.
        became REFL married-woman
        'One became a married woman.'

7.28   Tancovalo se až do rána.
        danced REFL up until morning
        'People were dancing until the morning.'

7.29   U klubu se pevalo i igralo.
        at club REFL sang and played
        'There was singing and playing at the club.'

There is an interesting construction in English which might appear to exemplify the passive of an intransitive verb. This is the **pseudo-passive**, formed from prepositional verbs. A prepositional verb is an intransitive verb followed by a prepositional phrase which permits Preposition Stranding. This means that the passive construction can treat the NP complement of the preposition as a kind of direct object and promote it to subject, leaving the preposition behind, as in examples 7.30–7.32:

7.30   a) Someone has slept in my bed.
        b) My bed has been slept in (by someone).

7.31   a) Someone is pointing at me.
        b) I don't like being pointed at (by anyone).

7.32   a) The competitors skied under the bridge.
        b) The bridge was skied under (by the competitors).

Not all verbs allow this. In particular, the unaccusative verbs[3] (see §7.2.3) never form pseudo-passives. This can be illustrated with the contrast between 7.30–7.32 and 7.33–7.35:

7.33   a) Many people are sleeping in London.
        b) ⋆London is being slept in (by many people).

7.34   a) The signpost points towards a hill.
        b) ⋆A hill is being pointed towards (by the signpost).

7.35   a) Trolls existed under the bridge.
        b) ⋆The bridge was existed under by trolls.

Other types of intransitive verb which cannot be passivized in English (or the majority of languages) include Raising-to-Subject verbs (7.36) and passives themselves (7.37). This is generally true even in languages, such as Polish and German, which permit impersonal passives:

7.36   a) It seemed that he was a hero.
        b) ⋆It was seemed by him to be a hero.

7.37   a) Harriet was kissed by Dick.
        b) ⋆There was been kissed by Harriet (by Dick).

A number of theoretical analyses of passive have been proposed which would have the effect of excluding such constructions as 7.36, 7.37 universally (see §7.2.2 on the 1-AEX). It is therefore interesting that there are languages in which such constructions are possible. Timberlake (1982) and Keenan and Timberlake (1985) (see also Baker, 1988a) report a number of examples from Lithuanian of exactly this sort (I omit tone and length markings in these examples):

7.38   Kur mus gimta, kur augta?
        where we-GEN bear-PASS/Nsg. where grow-PASS/Nsg.
        'Where were we born, where did we grow up?'
        (Lit. = 'Where was there being born by us, where being grown?')

7.39   Jo pasirodyta esant didvyrio.
        he-GEN/Msg. seem-PASS/Nsg. being hero
        'He seemed to be a hero.'
        (Lit. = 'By him it was seemed to be a hero.')

7.40   To lapelio buta vejo nupusto.
        that leaf-GEN/M/sg. be-PASS/N/NOMsg. wind-GEN
        blow-PASS/M/GENsg.
        'The leaf was getting blown down by the wind.'
        (Lit. = 'By the leaf there was getting blown down by the wind.')

Finally, it should be pointed out that there are some languages which have constructions which have been analysed as passives but which involve neither a PASS verbal affix, nor a reflexive, nor any other type of morphological device except for a marker of the agent phrase. This has been argued for Achenese (or better Acehnese) by Lawler (1977) and Perlmutter and Postal (1977) for example, where the verb agrees with the underlying subject even if it surfaces in an agent phrase (though see Durie, 1988, Lawler, 1988, for more recent discussion of this particular case).

7.41   a) Gopnyan ka gi-com lon.
           she PERF AGR-kiss me
           'She kissed me.'
        b) Lon ka gi-com le-gopnyan.
           I PERF AGR-kiss by-her
           'I was kissed by her.'

Perlmutter and Postal (1977) also cite examples 7.42 illustrating the fact that in Mandarin Chinese the only overt signal of passive is the 'preposition' (or coverb) *bei* marking the agent:

7.42a)   Zhù laŏshī píyè- le wŏ-de kăoshì.
          Zhu Prof. mark-ASP my test
          'Prof. Zhu marked my test.'
      b) Wŏ-de kăoshì bei Zhù laŏshì píyè-le.
          My test by Zhu Prof. mark-ASP
          'My test was marked by Prof. Zhu.'

Given that the passive has played such an important part in theorizing about morphosyntax, it is interesting to speculate why languages should have such a construction. One important functional motivation comes from syntax. In many languages syntactic constructions such as relative clauses or control of PRO are permitted only with reference to subjects and not other grammatical functions. In such cases a language will need a device for promoting objects to subject position to increase the domain over which such rules operate. Another important functional motivation concerns **topic-comment articulation** ('functional sentence perspective'). In English, for example, one of the functions of the passive is to take a direct object out of a relatively focal position into the position of a topic, i.e. subject position. Much of the Prague School literature on topic-comment structure took the English passive as a paradigm example of this phenomenon. The relative frequency of passive in English compared to its scarcity in Slav languages was linked to the fact that Slav languages have free word order and therefore don't need a syntactic ordering device like passive to put objects in topicalized position.

An interesting and influential viewpoint on the functional motivation of passive universally has been presented by Shibatani (1985). He points out that passive constructions are often associated with a good many other effects. In some languages the passive construction acquires a 'potential' meaning, of the kind *Force may be used to open this door.* We often observe passives used to convey a spontaneous event (*The tree fell down*), but in addition we find (for instance, in Japanese) the passive being used as part of the honorific system (as when in English a waiter will say *Are you being served?* rather than *Is anybody serving you?*). He also points out that it is unlikely that object topicalization is the primary universal function of prototypical passive constructions, since in the Philippine languages we have focusing constructions (which topicalize non-subjects) and also a passive construction.

Shibatani therefore suggests that the principal function of passive is to defocus the Agent. This will prototypically also have the effect of reducing the valency (since the Agent is no longer explicitly mentioned), and since surface subjects are usually obligatory syntactically (even if represented by a null pronoun), this will generally mean that the Patient will be promoted to subject.

Finding functional motivation for a set of constructions is only half the story, of course. We must also construct a theory which will explain precisely why the structural patterns we observe come about, rather than other conceivable patterns compatible with the functional motivation we have discerned. Structurally, the 'canonical' passive voice is an alternation affecting transitive verbs, which is usually signalled by special morphology, and in which the active subject is demoted to an adjunct, while the object is promoted to subject. There are deviations, however, from all of these characteristics in constructions which linguists would generally call 'passive'. The central structural facts to be accounted for are summarized below:

(i)   the suppression of the subject ('agent defocusing')
(ii) the promotion of a complement or adverbial
(iii) the implicit realization of the subject theta role (e.g. by an agent phrase)
(iv) case marking of complements
(v)   the relation between personal and impersonal, and morphological and reflexive passives.

There are two constructions which are closely related to the passive, both of which are called the **middle voice** in many descriptive sources. One of these types of middle voice is illustrated for English in example 7.43:

7.43   a) Bureaucrats bribe easily.
        b) These clothes wash readily.
        c) The book reads fluently.
        d) The car steers badly.

(In English it is difficult to obtain a middle reading without the adverbial.) The important property of the middle is that the grammatical subject is a notional or logical object, just as in the passive. In other words, it is not the bureaucrats who are doing the bribing, rather it is some unspecified agent acting on the bureaucrats.

Apart from the fact that middle verbs have active and not passive morphology, there is an important difference between English middles and passives. Although in both constructions there is an 'understood' notional subject, or **implicit argument**, it is only in the passive that this agent can be expressed (as in 7.44) or can control the PRO subject of an infinitival purposive clause (as in 7.45; cf. Manzini, 1983):

7.44   a) *Bureaucrats bribe easily by managers.
        b) Bureaucrats are often bribed by managers.

7.45   a) *Bureaucrats bribe easily [PRO to secure government contracts].
        b) Bureaucrats are often bribed [PRO to secure government contracts].

A construction similar to the middle is illustrated in 7.46–7.47:

7.46   a) Dick broke the vase.
           b) The vase broke.
           c) The vase was broken (by Dick).

7.47   a) Harriet hung the clothes on the line.
           b) The clothes hung on the line.
           c) The clothes were hung on the line (by Harriet).

Examples 7.46b–7.47b are sometimes called **anticausatives** because the transitive form has roughly the meaning 'cause X to V', where V is the intransitive form. Examples such as 7.46b are sometimes linked to **inchoatives**, that is, a verb derived from an adjective meaning 'to become Adj.' or 'to begin to be Adj.', cf. 7.48:

7.48   a) The sky brightened (became bright(er)).
           b) Harriet's face reddened.

Actually, it might be more consistent to relate 7.46a, b to 7.46d, and call the adjectival use of the passive participle in 7.46d an 'anti-inchoative':

7.46   d) The vase is broken.

Example 7.47b would often be regarded as a **stative** because it refers to a state and not an event like 7.46b. Both types of alternation in 7.46–7.47 can be thought of as **resultatives**. That is, 7.46b can be conceived of as a result of 7.46a, while we can think of 7.47b as the result of 7.47a. However, some linguists would draw a distinction between a resultative proper (e.g. 7.46) and a stative such as 7.47. Matters are complicated somewhat by the fact that, although we have explicitly mentioned agents responsible for breaking or hanging in 7.46a, 47a, an agent is not necessary. Thus, we can say things such as 7.49–7.50. We certainly don't want to say that 7.50 presupposes that someone (even God!) actually hung the cherries on the branches, and in 7.49 we explicitly deny that any agent was involved:

7.49   The vase just broke of its own accord.

7.50   Cherries hung from the branches.

I referred earlier to Romance passive constructions involving a reflexive element (*se/si*). In different Romance languages these reflexive constructions have different properties. Since a number of linguists have drawn explicit comparisons recently between uncontroversially morpholexical processes affecting argument structure and the reflexive constructions of Romance, it will be useful to summarize the salient facts. I give here a brief overview of data from Italian, which has a rich set of such constructions, basing my account on Manzini (1986).

We have a straightforward reflexive/reciprocal construction, illustrated in 7.51. Here *i bambini* is the subject and *si* is the direct object:

7.51   a) I bambini si lavano.
         The children *si* wash-3pl.
         'The children wash themselves.'
      b) I bambini si parlano.
         The children *si* talk-3pl.
         'The children talk to each other.'

In 7.52 we see again the middle/passive use of *si*. In this (homophonous) construction the children are not the ones doing the washing (though they still get washed):

7.52   I bambini si lavano (volentieri).
        The children *si* wash (willingly)
        'The children wash willingly.'

Example 7.53 illustrates the impersonal *si*, generally translated by something like 'one'. In 7.53a the children are the direct object, but this time it is the *si* which functions as the subject, and the verb agrees with it in number. Examples 7.53b, c, d illustrate this use of *si* with an unaccusative verb, the copula, and with a passive. (The copular verb *è* in 7.53c, d shows singular agreement, while the predicative adjective *nervosi* and passive participle *invitati* show plural agreement. These are default agreement markers, used in impersonal constructions. Italian is odd in using singular number as its default assignment for verbs, and plural as its default for adjectives):

7.53   a) Si lava volentieri i bambini.
           Si wash-3sg. willingly the children
           'One willingly washes the children.'
        b) Si va volentieri.
           Si go-3sg. willingly
           'One willingly goes.'
        c) Si è facilmente nervosi.
           Si be-3sg. easily nervous
           'One is easily nervous.'
        d) Si è invitati volentieri.
           Si be-3sg. invited willingly
           'One is invited willingly.'

Finally, in 7.54 we see an interesting use of *si* cliticized to the passive participle:

7.54   gli unici bambini lavatisi.
        the only children washed-*si*
        'the only children who washed themselves'

The curious thing about this construction is that the use of a restrictive modifier of this kind is limited to passive participles and unaccusative past (perfect) participles. Thus, *lavati* in 7.54 cannot be a transitive perfect participle but has to be a passive form. In this construction, then, we seem to have a reflexive element which remains as the object of a passive participle.

The English middle shares many features with the passive, particularly in that the logical object appears as the grammatical subject. The reflexive passive discussed earlier can often be translated either by English passives or by middles, so it is not surprising that linguists often lump together the two constructions as more-or-less equivalent. The second type of construction which is traditionally called the middle has somewhat different properties. This is exemplified by Ancient Greek, which distinguished active, middle and passive voices (though the middle and passive were only distinguishable in a couple of tense forms). The basic meaning of the middle seems to have been that of a subject acting in his own interests. Goodwin (1894) illustrates the difference with sentences 7.55, pointing out what 7.55b would properly be said of the law-maker himself:

7.55   a) Ho de:mos tithetai   nomous.
             The people make-MID-PRES laws-ACC
             'The people make laws for themselves.'
          b) Tithe:si   nomous.
             he-makes-ACT laws-ACC
             'He makes laws.'

The middle voice is also widely used in Greek as a reflexive or reciprocal. Thus, we have contrasts such as 7.56 (Barber, 1975):

7.56   a) Louo: ta imatia.
             I-wash-ACT the clothes-ACC.
             'I wash the clothes.'
          b) Louometha.
             We-wash-MID
             (i) 'We wash ourselves.' (ii) 'We wash each other.'

Barber's very interesting discussion of the Greek middle suggests a basic (and chronologically prior) distinction between the active voice on the one hand and the medio-passive voice on the other. The medio-passive, then, can be thought of as the set of forms in which the subject is acted upon in some way, whether by himself (reflexive), by the object he himself is acting on (reciprocal), some possibly unspecified agent (passive), or in a more indirect way by benefiting specifically from his own actions (middle).

We have seen that many languages use constructions with reflexive pronouns or clitics to express alternations corresponding to the passive voice. In many languages reflexives and reciprocals form a separate voice category of their own. The Altaic languages present well-known examples of this. Let's return to Yakuts for examples.

A transitive verb in Yakuts can be made reflexive by affixation of -n to vowel stems or -in (with vowel harmony variants) to consonant stems:

7.57   Min timnii uunan suu-n-a-bin.
          I cold water-INSTR wash-REFL-PRES-1sg.
          'I wash myself with cold water.'

In this usage the verb is intransitive since the direct object is effectively the -n suffix, just as the reflexive pronoun in Romance and Slavic languages functions as the object.

However, there is a commoner use of the reflexive which makes it look rather like the Ancient Greek middle voice:

7.58   a) Ot tiej-e-bin.
            hay carry-PRES-1sg.
            'I am carting hay.'
        b) Ot tie-n-e-bin.
            hay carry-REFL-PRES-1sg.
            'I am carting hay for myself.'

In 7.58b the verb remains transitive since the object, *hay*, is retained. The reflexive affix has a 'middle of interest' function. This function is also found amongst reflexive clitics in a number of languages. Thus, we would translate 7.58b into Czech as 7.59:

7.59   Vozím si seno.
        I-cart REFl hay

Although the reflexive suffix can assume the full role of direct object, in specially emphatic contexts it can also co-occur with an explicit reflexive pronoun direct object (comparable in many respects to 'clitic doubling' constructions. See chapter 9):

7.60   Kini bejetin xajRa-n-a-r
        he self-ACC praise-REFL-PRES-3sg.
        'He praises himself.'

7.61   Op-pun tie-n-e-bin.
        hay-SELF/1sg. cart-REFL-PRES-1sg.
        'I am carting my own hay.'

7.62   Ot-un bejete tie-n-e-r.
        hay-SELF/3sg. SELF cart-REFL-PRES-3sg.
        'He is carting his own hay.'

A further similarity between the reflexive voice and reflexive clitic systems is revealed when we look more carefully at the passive voice in Yakuts. As is usual in Turkic languages, the passive -*il in* formative is only found with consonant final stems. With vowel final stems (and certain others) we find the suffix -*n*. This means that verb stems ending in a vowel have homophonous forms for the reflexive and the passive.

In the Romance and Slavic clitic systems, as well as the Greek middle voice, the reflexive form is often homophonous with the reciprocal form. In Yakuts these two functions are kept separate, for like other Turkic languages it has a distinct *reciprocal-cooperative* voice. This is expressed by the suffix -*s*, for vowel final stems, and -*Is* (where /I/ represents vowel harmony variants -*i*, -*ɨ*, -*u*, -*ü*) for consonant final stems. The basic meanings are 'to do to each other' (reciprocal) and 'to do together with someone' or 'to help someone to do' (cooperative). In some cases the suffix is doubled to become -*sIs*. There is a tendency for this pleonastic suffix to be interpreted as the reciprocal rather than the cooperative voice. The cooperative isn't possible with passivized, stative or unaccusative verbs.

In 7.63–7.66 we see examples of the reciprocal voice, and in 7.67–7.69 the co-operative voice. Note in 7.66 that the reciprocal refers to an indirect object rather than a direct object:

7.63   Kör-üs-tü-ler.
          see-RECIP-PAST-3pl.
          'They saw each other.'

7.64   Bil-is-ti-ler.
          know-RECIP-PAST-3pl.
          'They recognized each other.'

7.65   Suruj-s-a-llar.
          write-RECIP-PRES-3pl.
          'They correspond.'

7.66   Ies ber-s-e-ller.
          loan give-RECIP-PRES-3pl.
          'They give each other loans.'

7.67   Kini miexe ot tiej-is-te.
          he me/DAT hay cart-COOP-PAST/3sg.
          'He helped me to cart the hay.'

7.68   Kiniler miexe   ot tiej-is-ti-ler.
          they   me/DAT hay cart-COOP-PAST-3pl.
          'They helped me to cart the hay.'

7.69   ORolor bari ita-s-ti-lar.
          children all cry-COOP-PAST-3pl.
          'The children all burst out crying (at once).'

Like the reflexive, we find the object 'doubled' in some cases, with both cooper-ative and reciprocal uses. (In 7.71 the cooperative suffix is realized as -h-, which is the usual morphophonemic variant of /s/ intervocalically):

7.70   Bari xardarita sonunu bil-ler-s-e-ller.
          all reciprocally news know-CAUSE-RECIP-PRES-3pl.
          'They all tell each other the news.'

7.71   Biirge ulele-h-e-r.
          together work-COOP-PRES-3sg.
          'He works together (with someone).'

The various reciprocal pronouns and adverbials found in these constructions can also be used on their own, with a verb in the active voice, as in 7.72–7.73:

7.72   Biirge bültüü-bün.
        together hunt-1sg.
        'I hunt together (with someone).'

7.73   Beje-bejelerin xolunnara-llar.
        each-other ball out-3pl.
        'They ball each other out.'

So far we have seen cases in which a verb loses its subject and in which the object
is promoted to subject position. In this way a transitive verb becomes (more like) an
intransitive verb. A large number of ergative languages can detransitivize verbs by
suppressing the direct object role. This type of process, which we were introduced
to in chapter 1, §1.4, is usually referred to as the 'antipassive' construction. In some
languages (for instance, Dyirbal and Chukchee) this construction is found to the
exclusion of passive. Just as many languages permit the suppressed subject in a
passive construction to be optionally expressed by an adjunct, so in many languages
the suppressed direct object surfaces as an oblique case marked NP. However, not
all languages have antipassives which permit this. For example, in the Mayan
language Tzotzil, the object is implicit in the meaning of the construction but can't
be overtly expressed (Aissen, 1987). The antipassive construction is shown schematically in 7.74, where -AP refers to a notional antipassive affix:

7.74   a) NP1   V   NP2
           Erg.   Abs.
           SUBJ   OBJ
        b) NP2   V-AP   (NP1)
           Abs.   Obl.
           SUBJ   ADJUNCT

Chukchee is interesting in that it has two distinct antipassive morphemes, a prefix
ine- and a suffix *-tku*, with subtly different semantic effects (Skorik, 1977).

7.75   a) Gəmnan tə-tejkə-rkən orwoor.
           I-ERG 1sg.SUBJ-make-ASP/3sg.OBJ sledge-ABS
        b) Gəm t-ine-tejkə-rkən (orw-etə).
           I-ABS 1sg.SUBJ-INE-make-ASP sledge-DAT
           'I am making a sledge.'

7.76   a) Gəmnan tə-retə-rkən tekičg-ən.
           I-ERG 1sg.SUBJ-carry-3sg.OBJ meat-ABS
        b) Gəm tə-retə-tku-rkən (tekičg-e).
           I-ABS 1sg.SUBJ-carry-TKU-ASP meat-INSTR
           'I am carrying the meat.'

In each case we see that the demoted object can be expressed optionally by a NP in
an oblique case: Instrumental, Locative or Dative. The choice of surface case in
which the optional object (or the 'chômeur' of Relational Grammar) appears is a
lexical property of individual verb stems.

We have concentrated so far on operations which eliminate or otherwise neutralize one of the arguments of a predicate. There are also operations which increase the valency of a verb. The most researched of these is the causative construction. We will also look briefly at applicative (or applied verb) constructions, and possessor raising.

It is not difficult to think of English verbs derived from adjectives or nouns which seem to have a causative component in their meaning.[4] For instance, we might be tempted to interpret a sentence such as *Tom bottled the beer* as 'Tom caused the beer to be in bottles'. Likewise, *Tom cleaned the bottles* seems to mean 'Tom caused the bottles to be clean'. Interesting though such constructions are, most research effort has been devoted to accounting for the morphology and syntax of causative verbs formed from other verbs. There are two types of construction to examine. The first is the derivation of a transitive causative from an intransitive verb (i.e. a monadic predicate). This is most similar to the causatives derived from, say, adjectives. Schematically, such a causative relates sentences of the form 7.78a to sentences of the form 7.78b, where V' represents the causative form of the verb V. In languages which distinguish surface subjects from surface objects, NP_1 will be a subject in 7.78a and an object in 7.78b:

7.78   a) NP_1 V $\Rightarrow$
       b) NP_0 V' NP_1

We have seen constructions superficially similar to 7.78b in the anticausatives such as 'break'. However, English also has genuine causatives of this type formed by conversion from unergative and unaccusative verbs. A selection is illustrated in examples 7.79–7.81:

7.79   a) Fido walked.
       b) Harriet walked Fido in the park.

7.80   a) The tree fell.
       b) Dick felled the tree.

7.81   a) The boat sank.
       b) Tom sank the boat.

More interesting is what happens when we form a causative from a transitive verb. Let's assume for simplicity that we have a language with surface case marking which distinguishes Nominative for subjects, Accusative for objects and Oblique for other NPs. We find that there are essentially three varieties of causative construction in those languages which can retain all the participants of the original verb. These are illustrated schematically in 7.82–7.84:

$$
\begin{array}{llll}
NP_1 & V & NP_2 & \Rightarrow \\
\text{Nom.} & & \text{Acc.} &
\end{array}
$$

7.82 NP_0 V' NP_1 NP_2
       Nom.   Acc. Obl.

7.83   NP$_0$ V'   NP$_1$ NP$_2$
      Nom.   Acc. Acc.

7.84   NP$_0$ V'   NP$_2$ (NP$_1$)
      Nom.   Acc. Obl.

Type 7.83 is rather uncommon, though it has been reported in, for instance, a number of Bantu languages. Type 7.82, in which the underlying subject becomes the direct object of the causative, is more common, but the most frequently encountered construction is probably that represented in 7.84, in which the old object remains the object and the old subject becomes an optional adjunct.

    Examples of these types of construction are given below:

7.85   Ha na'-taitai häm[i ma'estru] [ni esti na lebblu].
        3sg.SUBJ CAUSE-read us-OBJ the teacher OBL this PTCL book
        'The teacher made us read this book.' (Chamorro)

7.86   Maria a-li-m-lip-isha Johni pesa kwa watoto.
        Mary she-PAST-him-pay-CAUSE John money to children
        'Mary made John pay the money to the children.' (Swahili)

7.87   Dişçi mektub-u müdür-e imzala-t-tɨ.
        dentist letter-ACC director-DAT sign-CAUSE-PAST
        'The dentist made the director sign the letter.' (Turkish)

    Another type of valency-affecting process which increases the number of arguments of the verb is **applicative** formation or the **applied verb** construction, originally best known from Bantu languages but now recognized in a variety of languages throughout the world. In this construction an oblique argument (such as a Benefactive) becomes a direct object. In some languages this is a very regular process. Although the usual target for promotion to direct object status is a Benefactive (or Malefactive), there are languages in which the process can affect other types of argument or adjunct such as Locatives or Instrumentals. Example 7.88 is Bahasa Indonesian, taken from Chung (1976); examples 7.89–94 are Ainu, from Shibatani (1990). (I use the gloss APPL throughout in these examples to refer to the applied affix):

7.88   a) Saja mem-bawa surat itu kepada Ali.
          I TRANS-bring letter the to Ali
          'I brought the letter to Ali.'
       b) Saja mem-bawa-kan Ali surat itu.
          I TRANS-bring-APPL Ali letter the
          'I brought Ali the letter.'

7.89   a) Huci matkaci orun upackuma.
          grandmother girl to tell/old/stories
       b) Huci matkaci ko-paskuma.
          grandmother girl APPL-tell/old/stories
          'Grandmother told old stories to the girl.'

7.90   a) Poro cise ta horari.
        big house in live
        b) Poro cise e-horari.
        big house APPl-live
        'He lives in a big house.'

7.91   a) A-kor kotan ta sirepa-an.
        1sg.-have village to arrive
        b) A-kor kotan a-e-sirepa.
        1sg.-have village 1sg.-APPL-arrive
        'I arrived at my village.'

7.92   a) Newa anpe orowa tumi-ne.
        that thing from war-become
        b) Newa anpe o-tumi-ne.
        that thing APPL-war-become
        'From that thing, the war began.'

7.93   a) tek ari kar-pe
        hand with make-thing
        'things made with the hands'
        b) tek-e-kar-pe
        hand-APPL-make-thing
        'hand-made goods'

7.94   a) pone tura kuykuy
        bone with bite
        b) pone ko-kuykuy
        bone APPL-bite
        'bite (something) together with a bone'

Next I consider the phenomenon of **possessor raising**. There are a number of languages in which a process represented schematically as 7.95 is regularly observed:

7.95   a) Dick stole Harriet's sandwich. ⇒
           NOM   GEN   ACC
        b) Dick stole Harriet the sandwich.
           NOM   ACC   ACC

Here a possessor NP inside an object NP has been 'raised' so as to become the direct object. The original direct object becomes a secondary object.

A live example is given in 7.96 from Chicheŵa (Baker, 1988a). Notice that in this example the applied affix is implicated:

7.96   a) Fisi a-na-dy-a nsomba za kalulu.
        hyena SP-PAST-eat-ASP fish of hare
        b) Fisi a-na-dy-er-a kalulu nsomba.
        hyena SP-PAST-eat-APPL-ASP hare fish
        'The hyena ate the hare's fish.'

Finally, it will be recalled from chapter 1 that many languages have a process (usually called 'incorporation') in which an argument such as a direct object can be fused with the verb to form a single morphological complex. In a number of such languages the resulting compound verb is intransitive (as can be seen from the verbal morphology itself or from surface case assignment). Thus, in Chukchee, when a verb incorporates its object, the subject is assigned Absolutive, not Ergative, case and the verb receives intransitive agreement affixes, as shown in 7.97 (note that the verb root (and future prefix) in 7.97b have undergone vowel harmony as a result of incorporating the root *wala-*):

7.97   a) Morgənan mət-re-mne-ŋənet walat.
            we-ERG 1pl.SUBJ-FUT-sharpen-3pl.OBJ knives
            'We will sharpen our knives.'
         b) Muri mət-ra-wala-nma-gʔa.
            We-ABS 1pl.SUBJ-FUT-knive-sharpen-1pl.SUBJ
            'We will do some knife-sharpening.'

In this case we might want to regard incorporation as a kind of valency reduction (and we will see later in the chapter that this idea has been taken up in a rather different guise).

In several languages it has been reported that noun incorporation of this kind can 'feed' possessor raising. There is limited evidence of this happening in Chukchee. Thus, examples such as 7.98–7.99 have been attested (Skorik, 1948):

7.98   T-re-wilu-cwitku-gət.
         1st.SUBJ-FUT-ear-cut-2sg.OBJ
         'I'll cut your ears off.'

7.99   Nə-pilgə-cwi-qin peneelʔən.
         3pl.SUBJ-throat-slit-3sg.OBJ corpse-ABS
         'They slit the corpse's throat.'

The verb in both these examples is inflected transitively, in 7.98 agreeing with the (understood) 2nd sg. possessor of the ears, and in 7.99 agreeing with the raised possessor 'corpse', which duly appears in the Absolutive. (Had it remained a genuine possessor it would have received a special possessive affix.)

A number of syntactic relationships have been reported which I have not included in this list, most obviously, *inversion*, in which a subject becomes an indirect object. This has received a certain amount of discussion in terms of grammatical function changing in the Relational Grammar literature (e.g. Harris, 1984), and Belletti and Rizzi (1988) discuss a related phenomenon from a GB standpoint. However, in general, GB students of grammatical functions would seem to agree with Baker (1988a: chapter 8, note 5), who argues that inversion should not be regarded as typologically related to the valency changing operations we have discussed hitherto. Recall, too, that Anderson (1982, 1984a) proposed a purely morphological analysis of Georgian inversion (see chapter 6, Note 18).

7.2   Theoretical preliminaries

7.2.1   *Representing grammatical relations*

There have been several proposals for coding grammatical relations such as 'subject' or 'indirect object' in a grammar, and each of these has found reflection in theories of morphology. The simplest and most direct way is to make explicit reference to the relations themselves. This is the position adopted in Lexical Functional Grammar and also in Relational Grammar. This way of approaching the problem is relatively recent in generative grammar, however, and it is rejected by linguists working within the Government-Binding framework.

The traditional generative approach was to define grammatical relations in structural terms, as properties of phrase markers. Thus, a subject is defined as that NP which is the immediate constituent of the sentence (notated [NP, S]) and a direct object is the NP immediate constituent of VP. It was to capture the idea that certain verbs require complements of certain types that Chomsky (1965) introduced the notion of strict subcategorization.

In current GB theory, strict subcategorization is replaced by appeal to the argument structure of the verb (cf. §6.1.3). This makes sense, for instance, when we consider a verb such as *put*. In the *Aspects* model, this verb would be subcategorized by the frame in 7.100:

7.100   put: [_____ NP PP]

However, this fails to indicate that the PP which is selected by the verb has to be a locative PP. Thus, the sentences in 7.101 represent violations of the argument structure of *put* even though they respect the subcategorization frame in 7.100:

7.101   a) ⋆Tom put the eggs for Harriet.
           b) ⋆Tom put the eggs inside five minutes.

Moreover, 7.100 fails to explain why *put* can be followed by a pro-form or even an adverb in certain circumstances, provided they refer to locations, as in 7.102:

7.102   a) Tom put the eggs there.
           b) Tom put the eggs inside.

A solution to this problem is to say that *put* selects arguments which bear a particular theta role, namely a theme and a location. The lexical entry for a verb then includes not a subcategorization frame but a theta grid, of the form ⟨Agent, Theme, Location⟩. Note that I have included the theta role of the subject here (but see below for more on this).

The last way of representing grammatical relations is through the notation of Case marking. We know from chapter 1 that verbs in some languages mark their arguments with particular cases. Typically, we find one of two situations, defining so-called nominative/accusative languages and ergative languages. These are summarized in 7.103:

7.103   a) Nominative-Accusative marking:
                Intransitive subject: Nominative Case
                Transitive subject: Nominative Case
                Direct Object: Accusative Case
       b) Ergative marking:
                Transitive Subject: Ergative Case
                Intransitive Subject: Absolutive Case
                Direct Object: Absolute Case

Many languages with nominal case marking also mark other complements and adjuncts with special cases, functioning much as prepositions in languages such as English. Commonly, a language will have a special case (Dative) for the Indirect Object, and also common is a special case for means, manner or agent (Instrumental case).

The nominative/accusative system tends to be regarded as the 'canonical' case system in generative grammar (a fact which is perhaps not unconnected with the fact that none of the languages in which linguistics is commonly written is an ergative language!). It therefore forms the basis for a theory of **Abstract Case**, which plays an important role in Government-Binding Syntax. Chomsky (1981, 1986b) argues that all NPs must be assigned an Abstract Case by a Case assigner (essentially a verb or a preposition). Any overt (i.e. non-empty) NP which fails to receive such a Case violates a **Case Filter**, which renders the sentence ungrammatical. It would take us too far afield to discuss all the intricacies of Case theory (or the Case module) in GB theory. I summarize here some of the more important facts.

Nominative (or subjective) Case is assigned by a tense element in **Infl** (Infl means roughly the position of auxiliary verbs in languages such as English). This means that a non-tensed clause such as an infinitival is unable to assign a Nominative Case to its subject. Therefore, an infinitival can surface with an overt subject NP only if there is some other way for that NP to receive Case. In some instances this will be from the matrix verb, provided that verb belongs to a special class of **Exceptional Case Marking** verbs, capable of assigning Accusative Case to the embedded subject. Hence, we have a contrast between 7.104a in which we find *expect*, an ECM verb, and 7.105a, with *try*, which doesn't have this exceptional property. As the (b) examples show, both verbs permit a non-overt (empty) subject NP (PRO):

7.104   a) Tom expected [Harriet to stay]
       b) Tom expected [PRO to stay]

7.105   a) *Tom tried [Harriet to stay]
       b) Tom tried [PRO to stay]

In other instances the infinitival complement is introduced by a prepositional complementizer *for*, which is able to assign (presumably Oblique) Case to the infinitival subject, as in 7.106:

7.106   Tom arranged [for [Harriet to stay]]

Chomsky (1986b) argues that there are two different ways of assigning Case. Nominative and Accusative Case is typically assigned as a function of surface configurations, and therefore different NPs can receive these Cases depending on the operation of movement rules. This is **Structural Case** assignment and it is a property of S-structure. However, in some situations it appears that a given verb assigns a particular Case as a lexical property. In many languages, for instance, it is observed that certain verbs assign Dative and not Accusative to their direct objects. An oft-cited example here is German *helfen*, 'to help'. Similarly, in Russian the verb *želat'*, 'wish', assigns Genitive Case, the verb *pomoč'*, 'help', assigns Dative and *upravljat'*, 'control', assigns Instrumental Case (cf. chapter 1, §1.4). This is **Inherent Case** assignment, a property of D-structure which cannot be altered by any type of syntactic rule.

We can see, then, that there are four distinct ways of saying that *hit* is a transitive verb. We can say it takes a DIRECT OBJECT argument, that it is subcategorized by an NP, that it selects a Theme complement and that it assigns Accusative Case. In GB theory only the last two of these options is available, since direct reference to grammatical relations is excluded, and since subcategorization is derived from principles of semantic selection (essentially Theta theory). Nonetheless, this leaves the GB syntactician with three choices in describing changes in transitivity in terms of general grammatical properties. They can be represented as changes of theta marking properties, or of Case marking properties, or a combination of these two.

7.2.2 *Transformational theories of Passive*

Having seen how grammarians have represented argument structure, we now turn to the ways in which changes in argument structure have been represented. In the *Aspects* model, a frequently discussed transitivity alternation was the English Passive. This alternation was the result of a special, complex transformation. It operated over a D-structure which corresponds to the active form of the sentence, except that it was furnished with a triggering feature attached to a Manner Adverbial Phrase. This feature triggered the transformation, as illustrated in simplified form in 7.107. It was assumed that the transformation also added the appropriate auxiliary verb and put the lexical verb into the passive participle form. Notice that here the morphological change undergone by the verb in receiving the passive participle affix is viewed as something akin to inflection.

7.107   a)

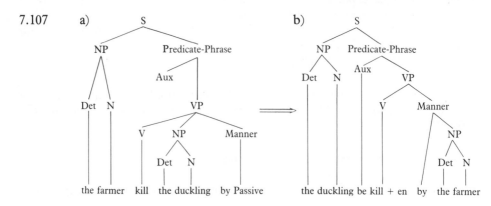

With the advent of Chomsky's (1970) 'Remarks on nominalization' (§3.2), relationships that had to be handled transformationally in the Standard Theory could now be handled by means of a lexical redundancy rule. Applied to passive alternations, this would mean that an active sentence and a corresponding passive sentence would not be related syntactically, although the corresponding verb forms would be related morphologically. This sort of lexical approach to valency changing operations is characteristic of a number of theories of syntax (most notably Lexical Functional Grammar). The passive construction and its associated morphology is effectively regarded as a species of derivation on such an approach.

The syntactic (transformational) approach and the lexical approach needn't be in opposition. A theory which permits both lexical and transformational rules leaves open the possibility that one language may have a lexical passive (with all the hallmarks of lexical rules: exceptionality, non-productivity, semantic and morphological idiosyncrasy and so on) while another has a fully syntactic passive. Indeed, it is not inconsistent to argue that one and the same language could have the two sorts of passive, and this is exactly what is claimed by Wasow (1977). For instance, a sentence such as 7.108 is ambiguous. Either we interpret it as a syntactic (or verbal) passive, as in 7.109a, or we interpret it as an adjectival passive, with stative or resultative meaning as in 7.109b:

7.108   The vase was broken.

7.109   a) Someone broke the vase.
         b) The vase was in a broken state.

As transformational grammar developed, rules such as Passive illustrated in 7.107 were split into their components, until ultimately there remained only one transformational rule, Move-Alpha. For transformational grammar the important aspect of the Passive rule was the promotion of the object by raising it to the position of the subject. The subsequent demotion of the subject was regarded as a spin-off of object promotion. In later formulations of Passive, a 'short' passive (lacking an adjunct *by*-phrase) was generated from a D-structure with an empty subject position into which the object moves. Later, even the 'long' passives (i.e. those which have a *by*-phrase) were generated this way, with the *by*-phrase generated in D-structure, just like any other adverbial phrase. Thus, the more recent syntactic accounts of Passive have retained the idea that object promotion to subject position is the core of the alternation.

Chomsky's (1981) GB analysis of English passive uses Theta theory and Case theory to motivate the promotion of the object. The argument structure (theta grid) of a typical transitive verb such as *kick* will have two positions, ⟨Agent, Theme⟩. The Theme role is that of an internal argument, assigned to the direct object by the verb itself. The Agent role is that of the external argument, assigned from the whole VP to the subject. In addition, the verb will license the assignment of two structural Cases, Nominative (through Infl) to the subject, and Accusative to the object.

Chomsky assumes that the addition of passive morphology to a transitive verb (the *-en* affix) has two related effects: it 'absorbs' the external theta role, which can therefore no longer be assigned to any NP, and at the same time it 'absorbs' the Accusative Case associated with the verb. There is a general tendency for verbs which do not assign an external theta role to fail to assign Accusative Case. This observation is known as **Burzio's Generalization**. A good deal of research effort has been devoted to investigating and trying to explain this generalization.

An obvious question is how well the other cases of valency changing can be fitted into any of these theoretical schemas. This will be the subject of much of the rest of this chapter. Before we look at this research, there is another phenomenon of theoretical importance which must be discussed, the 'Unaccusative Hypothesis'.

7.2.3 *The Unaccusative Hypothesis*

The **Unaccusative Hypothesis** was first advanced within the theory of Relational Grammar (see Perlmutter and Postal, 1984, and, for historical commentary, Pullum, 1988). This hypothesis states that there are two types of intransitive verb. The first has a subject perceived as actively initiating or actively responsible for the action of the verb, such as *run, talk, resign*. These are known as **unergative verbs**. It is usually assumed that subjects are assigned an external argument by such verbs, namely the thematic role of Agent. The second type has subjects which lack this active participation, and they include verbs such as *arrive, die, fall*. These verbs are the **unaccusative**[5] verbs and in many languages they are distinguished from unergative verbs syntactically or morphologically. For example, in some languages (including Italian and Danish) unergative verbs form their perfect tense with the verb *to have* while the unaccusative verbs use *to be*. At the theoretical level it is generally assumed that unergatives have an underlying subject but no object, while unaccusatives have an underlying object (which becomes a surface subject later in the derivation of the sentence) but no underlying subject. In GB theory the D-structures for *Tom ran* and *Tom arrived* would thus be 7.110 and 7.111 respectively:

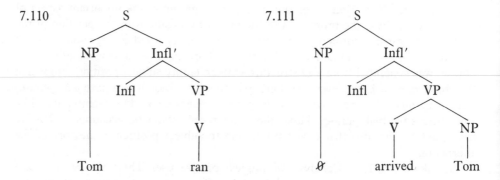

Theories which accept the Unaccusative Hypothesis therefore have to have some mechanism for guaranteeing that *Tom* in 7.111 becomes the subject. The standard assumption in GB theory is that unaccusative verbs, and in general any verbs which fail to assign an external theta role, also fail to assign Accusative case to an object position. This is another instantiation of Burzio's Generalization. Therefore, in 7.111, *Tom* will fail to be assigned Case unless it moves to the subject position (where it will, of course, receive Nominative from the Infl position).

An important observation (first discussed in detail by Perlmutter and Postal, 1984) is that unaccusative verbs cannot generally be passivized. In the framework of

Relational Grammar this follows from the **1-Advancement Exclusiveness Law** (1-AEX), which states that no more than one argument can be advanced to subject position in the course of a derivation. Amongst other things this law prevents the formation in English of pseudo-passives (i.e. passives derived from prepositional verbs such as those exemplified in 7.30–7.32) from unaccusatives. Thus, alongside the grammatical 7.32b we have the ungrammatical 7.35b (repeated here as 7.112–7.113):

7.112   The bridge was skied under by the competitors.

7.113   ⋆The bridge was existed under by trolls.

This contrast is accounted for in Relational Grammar in the following way. The passive form 7.112 is generated by a rule which promotes the object to subject, and demotes the old subject to an adjunct (a 'chômeur'). This means that the passive transformation of *Aspects* is largely retained. Thus, the underlying structure for 7.112 is something like 7.114:

7.114

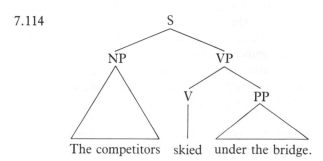

The competitors   skied   under the bridge.

Since the preposition is associated with the verb (in some manner), the NP *the bridge* is treated like an object for the purpose of passive and is therefore promoted to obtain 7.112.

Example 7.113, however, is ruled out by the 1-AEX for the following reasons. By the Unaccusative Hypothesis the underlying structure must be something like 7.115 (very schematically):

7.115

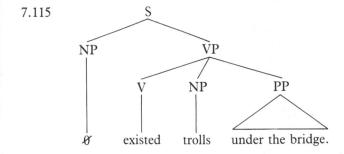

ø   existed   trolls   under the bridge.

To form a passive it is necessary to promote an object and thereby demote a subject. This means that *trolls* must be raised to subject position before passive can apply. However, in that case we will have had two distinct NPs, *trolls* and *the bridge*, raised to subject position in the course of one derivation, in violation of the 1-AEX. Hence, 7.113 is underivable.

GB theory has different ways of excluding such derivations. We will see some of these later in the chapter, especially in §7.4.

7.3 Marantz's theory

7.3.1 Introduction

Theories such as Relational Grammar and Lexical Functional Grammar made great headway in revealing patterns in the way that languages manipulate grammatical relations, but the topic wasn't seriously broached within a Chomskyan framework until Alec Marantz's thesis in 1981 (later revised and published as Marantz, 1984). Marantz adopts a model of syntax which owes considerably to Government-Binding theory but which departs from it in a number of important details. In addition, Marantz's overall framework is highly elaborated, so a small change in one part of the theory would have repercussions throughout. This makes it difficult to compare his system with other approaches. I shall therefore give a basic outline of Marantz's theory, concentrating on the implications for morphological theory and hence omitting a good deal of very interesting syntactic theorizing.

In Marantz's model there are three main levels of syntactic representation, **logico-semantic structure (1-s structure)**, **syntactic structure (s structure)** and surface structure, together with a lexicon of roots and affixes, whose lexical entries contain information about argument structure, transitivity, the semantic roles assigned and so on. The levels are constructed independently and related to each other for a given sentence by means of a **mapping principle** which guarantees that crucial aspects of structure, specifically those relating to grammatical relations, are automatically preserved from one level to the next. This means that the theory is not derivational: we don't start with a D-structure and then transform it into an S-structure. Instead, the grammar provides lists of structures at the three levels and the mapping principles determine which set of structures correspond to each other.

We can visualize the three levels of representation very roughly by taking an example like *Tom gave Fido a bone* (ignoring irrelevancies like tense). The 1-s, s and surface structures would be something like 7.116a–c:

7.116   a) [Tom-Agent [GIVE (Fido-Goal, bone-Patient)]]
        b) [Tom [give Fido bone]]
           SUBJ   I.O. D.O.
        c)

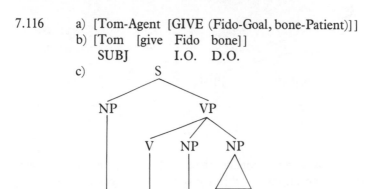

These are misleading representations in that it is only at surface structure that elements receive a linear ordering; the 1-s and s structure representations are defined purely in terms of constituency (immediate dominance). Marantz actually writes 1-s and s structures as trees, so that 7.116a, b would both be very similar to 7.116c.

The level of 1-s structure corresponds more-or-less to GB's level of theta structure; surface structure is GB's PF ('Phonological Form'). An important feature of 1-s structure is that every element with an argument structure has a separate representation at 1-s structure, even if it ultimately gets represented by a bound morpheme in surface structure. In the case of some constructions, this gives the appearance of 'lexical decomposition', superficially reminiscent of the proposals of Generative Semantics (§3.2.1). However, in GB theory there is no counterpart to Marantz's s structure. The 1-s and s levels, at which semantic relations and syntactic relations are defined, are universal. Languages differ in how they represent the abstract s level grammatical relations (i.e. whether by word order, case marking, agreement or whatever).

The most important mapping in Marantz's theory is that between 1-s structure and s structure. This is achieved by **principle M** (for 'Mapping'), a deceptively simple principle, which nonetheless has far-reaching implications. Essentially what it states is that, where 1-s constituents bear a logico-semantic relation to each other, then corresponding s constituents bear a syntactic relation to each other. In concrete terms, *Fido* in 7.116a bears a logico-semantic relation to *give*, namely being its first (internal) argument. Therefore, the s structure counterpart to *Fido* will bear some syntactic relation to the s structure counterpart of *give*, namely that of an object. (In traditional grammar it is called the indirect object, though Marantz would regard it as a direct object, for reasons which will become clear presently.) In the case of *Tom*, we have a NP which is the logical subject of the verb at 1-s structure, but it doesn't bear any syntactic relation to the verb at s structure. This is because we assume that a syntactic (s structure) subject is the subject of a VP, not of a verb. Therefore, the principle M is so written as to allow a syntactic relation between the NP *Tom* and the phrase headed by the verb, i.e. the VP. The upshot of principle M is that every element in 1-s structure will get represented somehow in s structure (and ultimately in surface structure by virtue of language particular 'mapping rules'). Moreover, the canonical mappings between elements at these different levels is determined by a single universal principle, not by a specific set of rules.

Marantz is careful to distinguish two notions which tend to be conflated in other varieties of grammatical theory, namely, that of predicate-argument structure and that of semantic (theta) role assignment. For instance, the verb *give* takes two internal arguments corresponding to the traditional direct and indirect object. This is true of both 7.117a and 7.117b:

7.117   a) Tom gave a bone to Fido.
        b) Tom gave Fido a bone.

In 7.117a *a bone* is a direct argument and receives the theta role of Patient directly from the verb. *Fido* gets its theta role indirectly from the preposition. In 7.117b, however, *Fido* now corresponds to a direct argument of the verb and therefore behaves like a direct object, receiving its theta role from the verb. However, *a bone* receives its theta role indirectly by virtue of a special structural position (that of the 'second object'. Notice that the tradition of description by which *Fido* would be an 'indirect object' in both sentences isn't applicable here).

This means that the lexical representation of the verb in these two cases is slightly different. That for 7.117a is 7.118a, in which the direct argument (italicized) is the Patient; that for 7.117b is 7.118b, in which the direct argument is the Goal:

7.118   a) give (*Patient*, Goal)
          b) give (Patient, *Goal*)

At the syntactic level a transitive verb, say, is an argument taker, which takes syntactic arguments (e.g. a direct object NP) to form a VP (corresponding to the predicate phrase at 1-s structure). However, such an NP can only serve as the syntactic argument of a verb if it receives a syntactic role, for example from the verb itself. A verb which assigns a syntactic role is marked with a feature value [+transitive]. Since this feature is part of the s structure representation and independent of 1-s structure it is in principle possible for an NP to be an internal argument to a [−transitive] verb and hence not to receive a syntactic role from that verb. This corresponds to a situation in which, in GB terms, a lexical item takes a complement but does not assign that complement Abstract Case. This, of course, is just what we find with unaccusative verbs. Similarly, a transitive verb may assign a syntactic role to an NP (assign Abstract Case) without taking that NP as a syntactic argument. This is exemplified by Exceptional Case Marking constructions such as *Tom believes Dick to be a liar*. Here *Dick* is the object of *believe* (in a certain sense) but isn't an argument of that verb, and there is therefore no entailment that Tom believes Dick. Finally, not all predicates form a predicate phrase at 1-s structure capable of taking a subject (or assigning an external argument). Those that do are lexically marked [+log sub], and those that don't are marked [−log sub]. An unaccusative verb is therefore not only [−transitive] but also [−log sub], while an unergative verb is [−transitive, +log sub]. By Burzio's generalization [−log sub] verbs (verbs which fail to assign an external argument) are also [−transitive] in the unmarked situation.

7.3.2 *Affix-mediated alternations*

To exemplify Marantz's approach in detail we turn first to his analysis of the regular (syntactic) passive alternation. Marantz assumes that regular processes of this sort must be mediated by regular morphology (which we describe by the cover term 'affixation'). An affixation process can't change the arguments of the verb root itself, but it can add arguments of its own, or alter the way the verb's arguments are expressed. This entails that affixation can't reduce the number of arguments (though it can prevent an argument from surfacing). In the passive alternant the logical object becomes the syntactic subject, while the logical subject, if expressed, is realized as a syntactic modifier phrase (the *by*-adjunct).

The key to Marantz's analysis is the observation that a passive participle is basically like an unaccusative verb. Unaccusative verbs bear a feature matrix indicating that they (a) cannot take an object ([-transitive]) and (b) do not assign a semantic role to an external argument ([-log sub]). Therefore, we may assume that the passive affix, *-en*, simply has the effect of imposing these feature values on the active verb stem. By principle M, this will mean that the only way for the logical object to be expressed is as a syntactic subject, while the logical subject can't be directly expressed as a syntactic argument.

Marantz follows Lieber (1980; cf. §6.2.2) in assuming that affixes are lexical items which have subcategorization frames indicating the category to which they attach, as well as other inherent features. We therefore give *-en* the lexical entry 7.119:

7.119   -en:]v _____, [-log sub] [-transitive]

This affix may only be attached to stems bearing the features [+log sub] [+transitive], that is, to transitive verbs. This is a consequence of a general principle, the **No Vacuous Application Principle** (NVAP), which states that an affix marked with a given feature value cannot attach to a stem marked with the same value. Amongst other things this will automatically prevent *-en* from attaching to unaccusative verbs or to passive participles.

We still have to ensure that the passive participle bears the features of the affix and not those of the root. The affix is the head, so, by Lieber's conventions, its features will percolate to the top node. If they conflict with those of the root they will therefore override the root features. In 7.120 we see the results of attaching *-en* to the verb *give*:

7.120

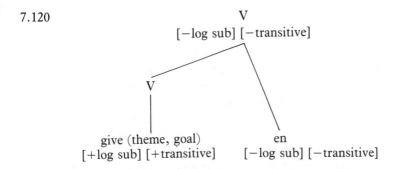

Suppose that we take the form of *give* in which the theme is the direct argument. Then this argument will correspond to the logical object at 1-s structure. Since the verb has received the *-en* affix, the derived verb is marked [-log sub] and hence it cannot co-occur with a logical subject. Thus, we are able to insert the participle *given* into an 1-s structure such as 7.121:

7.121

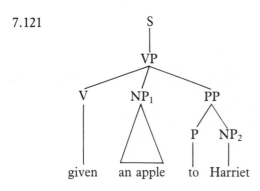

In 7.121 the verb has NP₁ as its logical object. By principle M, in the s structure to which 7.121 corresponds, NP₁ must bear a syntactic relation to the verb or the VP. From 7.120 we know that *given* is intransitive and so the s structure representation cannot contain a logical object. On the other hand, since the verb is [-log sub], there is no syntactic subject to correspond to a logical subject. Thus, in an s structure representation, the position of the subject is free to be occupied by something else. Since English makes no provision for an alternative way of relating 7.121 to an s structure, this means that the logical object has to correspond to a syntactic subject in order to be expressed at all and in order to bear a relation to the verb or the VP. Thus, the only s structure representation possible for 7.121 is 7.122:

7.122

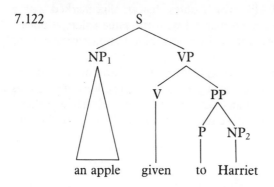

How can we account for the impersonal passives found in Dutch, German, Polish, Czech and a variety of other languages? Recall that these are passives of unergative verbs (i.e. intransitive verbs which assign an external theta role), with glosses such as *it was danced (by the girls)*. If the passive morpheme had the same feature characterization as *-en* in 7.119 then the NVAP would prevent it from attaching to a verb which was already [-transitive]. Marantz therefore suggests that in languages such as Dutch the passive morpheme just has the [-log sub] value. Since it is unmarked for the feature [transitive] this permits the affix to be attached to an intransitive stem. If nothing else were said, this would mean that the passive of a transitive verb would lack a logical subject (external theta role) but would remain transitive, predicting the occurrence of sentences such as *(it) was built a church-ACC (by the workmen)*. In Dutch this is impossible, so Marantz assumes the operation of a redundancy rule 7.123 (which effectively states Burzio's generalization):

7.123   [-log sub] ⇒ [-transitive]

(Presumably, this rule is lacking in a language like Ukrainian, which permits logical objects of passives to surface with objective case marking.)

Marantz discusses at some length the phenomenon of lexical reflexivization, which we saw illustrated by Yakuts in examples 7.58ff. Here, a transitive verb alternates by regular morphological process with a verb form of reflexive meaning. Marantz argues that the reflexive morpheme is essentially identical to the English *-en* morpheme, in that it bears the features [-log sub] [-transitive], and that it bears an additional feature stipulating that the object is coreferential with the subject.

A third morpheme which lacks its own argument structure but which modulates the realization of a verb's arguments is the antipassive affix. The antipassive construction is repeated notionally in 7.124 (assuming ergative surface case marking, where OBL stands for Oblique Case):

7.124   a) Tom-ERG killed the bear-ABS.
          b) Tom-ABS killed-AP (the bear-OBL).

What happens here is that the derived verb retains its ability to license a logical subject (*Tom*), but it becomes intransitive, so that the logical object can only be licensed in the manner of an indirect argument (e.g. by oblique case marking). This is easily accounted for by assuming that the antipassive affix bears the feature value [−transitive]. Such an affix can only attach to [+transitive] verbs (by the NVAP), and in practice this means it only attaches to [+log sub] verbs (assuming Burzio's generalization).

7.3.3 *Morphological merger: causatives*

In 7.125 we see the canonical form for a causative construction.

7.125

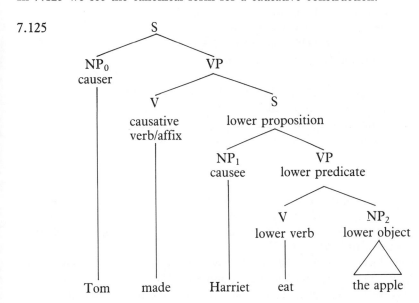

This is the surface form of the causative in many languages, of course (e.g. English). However, in many others the causative elements appears as a regular morphological operation, so that in those languages we are dealing with an affix-mediated operation. In that case we obtain a surface form looking like 7.126:

7.126   Tom eat-CAUS Harriet the apple
          NP_0 NP_1 NP_2

We saw in examples 7.82–7.84 that the surface marking of the arguments varies from language to language. In addition to this variation, it is now widely accepted that there are basically two types of causative construction, which I shall call (for reasons which will become apparent) **monoclausal** and **biclausal**. The principal differences between the two types are visible only when transitive verbs are causativized. We then find that the monoclausal type of causative can be characterized schematically in the following fashion:

(i)   The causee (NP_1) appears as an oblique or indirect object, not as the direct object of the verb. If the language has verb-object agreement, the derived verb will agree with NP_2, not NP_1.

(ii) If the lower object (NP_2) is a reflexive it may only take the matrix subject, NP_0, as antecedent, not the underlying lower subject, NP_1.

(iii) If the causative is passivized, NP_2, and not NP_1, is promoted to become the matrix subject.

Remaining schematic, we can represent these facts in pseudo-sentences 7.127–7.129:

7.127   Tom eat-CAUSE the apple to-Harriet.

7.128   a) Tom watch-CAUSE himself to-Harriet.
            'Tom made Harriet watch him.'
         b) ⋆Tom watch-CAUSE herself to-Harriet.
            'Tom made Harriet watch herself.'

7.129   a) The apple eat-CAUSE-PASS to-Harriet (by-Tom).
            'The apple was made to be eaten by Harriet (by Tom).'
         b) ⋆Harriet eat-CAUSE-PASS the apple (by Tom).
            'Harriet was made to eat the apple (by Tom).'

In the biclausal causatives we find the following properties:

(i)   The causee (NP_1) appears as the direct object of the derived matrix verb; the lower object, NP_2, appears either as a 'frozen' 2nd direct object or receives an oblique case marking. If the language has verb-object agreement the derived verb will agree with NP_1, not NP_2.

(ii) If the lower object (NP_2) is a reflexive it may only take the causee, or lower subject, NP_1, as antecedent, not the matrix subject, NP_0.

(iii) If the causative is passivized, the causee, NP_1, and not the lower object, NP_2, is promoted to become the matrix subject.

Again, we can represent this type of construction using the schematic examples 7.130–7.132:

7.130   Tom eat-CAUSE Harriet (of) the apple.

7.131   a) Tom watch-CAUSE Harriet (of) herself.
            'Tom made Harriet watch herself.'
         b) ⋆Tom watch-CAUSE Harriet (of) himself.
            'Tom made Harriet watch himself.'

7.132   a) Harriet eat-CAUSE-PASS (of) the apple (by Tom).
          'Harriet was made to eat the apple (by Tom).'
         b) ⋆The apple eat-CAUSE-PASS Harriet (by Tom).
          'The apple was made to be eaten (by) Harriet (by Tom).'

As can be seen from the English glosses to the hypothetical examples in 7.127–7.132 the English analytic causative with *make* patterns like a biclausal causative. Syntactically, such analytic causatives are usually analysed as having a biclausal structure even at surface structure, as in 7.125. However, the lower subject behaves in many respects like the direct object of *make*. For example, it passivizes and appears in the object case form if it is a pronoun (*Tom made her/⋆she eat the apple*). In other words, *make* is an Exceptional Case Marking verb. It is a hallmark of syntactic approaches to causatives (such as Marantz's, or Baker's) that the causative morpheme is regarded as an ECM predicate.

We now need to know two things: how to represent morphological causatives of each type, and how to distinguish the two types.

To answer the first question we must relate the 1-s structure in 7.125 to a morphological structure in which the causative verb is represented as an affix. In Marantz's theory this is achieved through a process of **merger**, to give a representation such as 7.133:

7.133

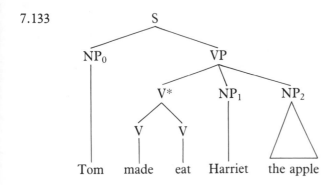

The matrix (causative) verb has been combined with the lower verb to form a derived causative, V⋆. This has two objects and its argument structure is that of 7.134. Recall that *make* represents an affix in 7.134, and that it is therefore the head of the stem as a whole. Since the causative affix will transitivize an intransitive verb, it must be furnished with the features of a transitive verb, as shown in 7.134:

7.134   make-eat
                   (make (X eat (Patient))
                   [+log sub, +transitive]

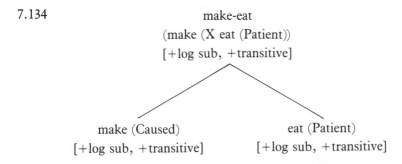

         make (Caused)   eat (Patient)
     [+log sub, +transitive]   [+log sub, +transitive]

The *make* predicate takes a proposition as its argument, notated in 7.134 as 'Caused'. This argument structure is combined with that of the non-head, *eat*, where 'X' is a variable standing for the subject of *eat*.

To answer the second question we look at two cases discussed in some detail by Marantz, Malayalam and Chi-Mwi:ni.

Malayalam, a Dravidian language of Southern India, represents the monoclausal type of causative. The causative affix is *-ik'k'-/-ičč-* and an example of its use is given in 7.135:

7.135   a) Kutti annaye nulli.
              child-NOM elephant-ACC pinched
              'The child pinched the elephant.'
          b) Amma kuttiyekkonta aanaye nulličču.
              mother-NOM child-INST elephant-ACC pinch-CAUSE-PAST.
              'Mother made the child pinch the elephant.'

Notice that the causee appears in an oblique case while the lower object remains in the accusative. The l-s representation for this sentence is given in 7.136, where for ease of deciphering I have imitated the word order of English (recall the linear order is in any case irrelevant at l-s structure):

7.136

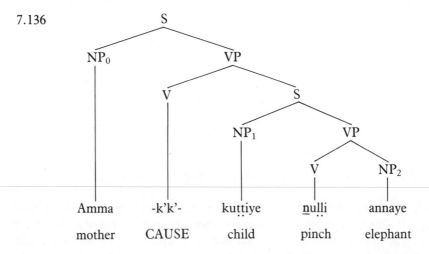

The derived causative verb stem, *nullik'k'-*, will have a lexical structure given in 7.137:

7.137

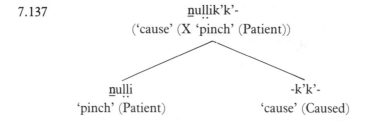

The crucial assumption is that merger takes place at the l-s level with monoclausal causatives. Intuitively, we might say that this makes the monoclausal causative closer to an ordinary transitive verb, and hence it shows fewer remnants of its biclausal past. The post-merger l-s representation corresponding to 7.136 is given in 7.138. This will presumably be essentially the s structure, too, so that, syntactically, the causative in Malayalam behaves as though it were a single clause.

7.138

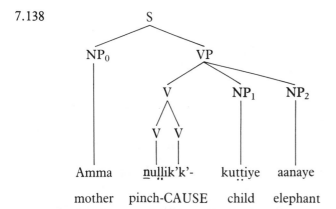

An example of a biclausal causative construction is presented by the Bantu language, Chi-Mwi:ni. An illustration is given in 7.139:

7.139   Mwa:limu wa-ándik-ish-ize wa:na xati.
         teacher OBJ-write-CAUSE-T/A children letter
         'The teacher made the children write a letter.'

Marantz assumes that merger does not take place until s structure in Chi-Mwi:ni. Therefore, the l-s structure will remain essentially that of 7.125. Marantz represents the ECM construction as a kind of notational Raising-to-Object, in which the lower subject is represented simultaneously as the object of the matrix verb while remaining represented as the subject of the embedded verb. This means that the s-structure of 7.139 will be 7.140. (Since the English verb *make* is an ECM verb in its causative use, 7.140 will also correspond to the s-structure of the English sentence *The teacher made the children write a letter*):

7.140

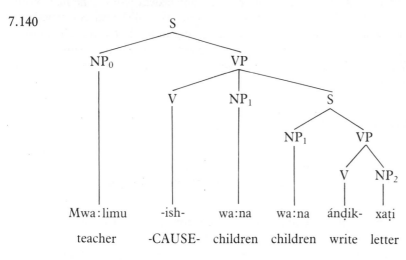

Merger takes place at s-structure, mapping representation 7.140 into 7.141, superficially similar to the l-s level post-merger structure of the Malayalam causative:

7.141

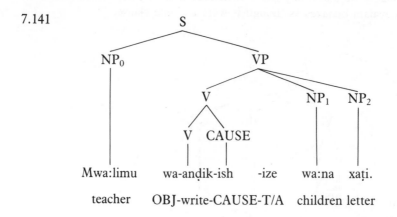

We have yet to see how these two types of derivation explain the differences between the two causatives. Let's consider biclausal causatives first. For this we need to refer back to diagram 7.140. The causative predicate takes a direct object (because it is a Raising-to-Object, or ECM predicate). The lower verb, too, takes a direct object. After merger, then, we might expect there to be two direct objects. However, the syntactic properties of the affix take precedence over those of the root in Marantz's theory, so that the object of the derived verb is the object of the causative at pre-merger s-structure. By contrast, in the case of the monoclausal construction, the causative predicate doesn't take an object, so the object of the derived verb will be that of the root. In this way we obtain the contrasting constructions illustrated in 7.130 and 7.127.

On the assumption that the Binding Theory applies at s-structure, we have an explanation for the reflexives contrast. A reflexive will be coreferential with the nearest appropriate antecedent in subject position. In the case of biclausal causatives, the nearest such antecedent for a reflexive NP$_2$ is the lower subject, NP$_1$. Hence, the data of 7.131. However, since merger has already taken place by s-structure in the case of monoclausal causatives, the only possible antecedent will be the matrix subject, as in 7.128. Finally, if the causative predicate in a biclausal construction is passivized, this will turn that predicate into a Raising-to-Subject verb. Therefore, it is the lower subject which is passivized, not the lower object. In other words, we find the data of 7.132 for the same reason that we have example 7.143a and not 7.143b, corresponding to 7.142:

7.142   Tom expected Harriet to eat the apple.

7.143   a) Harriet was expected (by Tom) to eat the apple.
         b) ⋆The apple was expected (by Tom) Harriet to eat.

On the other hand, in the case of the monoclausal construction it is the object of the lower verb, NP$_2$, which becomes the object of the derived verb, and hence it is this argument which passivizes, as we saw in 7.129.

7.3.4 *Morphological merger: applied verbs*

There is one further valency changing operation for which Marantz provides an explicit account, namely the applied verb construction (the theory has little to say about Possessor Raising or Noun Incorporation). This is similar to the causative construction in that it increases surface valency. I shall not discuss Marantz's account in great detail because the basic principles are very similar to those required for understanding causatives.

In an applied verb construction we have an affix on the verb which fulfils the same role as a preposition in an analytic construction. This means that the affix and the preposition have the same argument structure. The applied affix can then start life at l-s structure as a kind of underlying preposition, and merge with the verb, just as the causative affix merges with the verb.

Chi-Mwi:ni again provides us with an illustration. In 7.144 we find a verb with two surface objects:

7.144   Hamadi Ø-wa-pik-il-ile wa:na cha:kuja.
         Hamadi SUBJ-OBJ-cook-APPL-T/A children food
         'Hamadi cooked food for the children.'

The prefixes on the verb root -*pik*- coreference the subject *Hamadi* and one of the objects, *wa:na*, respectively. The suffix -*ile* is a tense/aspect marker, and -*il*- is the applied affix. The l-s representation of 7.144 will be 7.145:

7.145

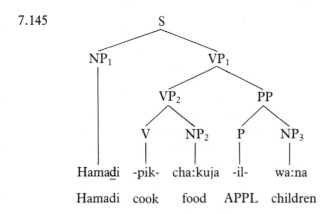

Merger in the case of applied verbs takes place only at l-s structure, so the s structure representation will be 7.146:

7.146

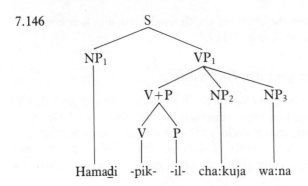

Like the causative affix, the applied affix can transitivize intransitive verb roots, so the lexical representation of the affix will be that of 7.147. Combined with a transitive verb such as 'cook' this will give us 7.148:

7.147   -il-:   ]$_V$ _____ 'for' (Benefactive), [+transitive]

7.148   -pik-il-

                              ('cook' (Patient) 'for' (Benefactive))

                                   [+log sub] [+transitive]

      -pik-   -il- APPL
'cook' (Patient)   'for' (Benefactive)
[+log sub] [+transitive]   [+transitive]

The applied affix is the head in this lexical structure, so the [+transitive] feature which percolates will be that corresponding to the element which assigns the Benefactive semantic role. Hence, it is the Benefactive which becomes the derived direct object proper of the new verb. The Patient argument then becomes some kind of indirect argument. What this means is that it is the derived Benefactive argument which behaves like a true direct object: for instance, only the Benefactive can become the subject if the derived verb is passivized, the object prefix refers to the Benefactive not the Patient and so on. This is exactly the situation, of course, with the English gloss, in the form *Hamadi cooked the children some food*. In the English sentence it is *the children*, not *the food* which behaves like the direct object. In both languages the indirect argument, *some food*, receives its syntactic role (or Abstract Case marking) from its structural position as daughter of VP.

Descriptively, we often refer to the alternations represented by these English sentences (and already illustrated above in 7.117) as the result of **Dative Shift**. The name is taken from the terminology of earlier models of transformational grammar in which *Tom gave Fido a bone* would be derived by the transformation of 'Dative Shift' (or 'Dative Movement') from a structure underlying *Tom gave a bone to Fido*. The Dative Shift alternation is very reminiscent of the Chi-Mwi:ni applied verb construction. There is an important difference, however, on Marantz's theory. As we saw in the introduction to this section, Marantz provides Dative Shift verbs such as *give* with two distinct argument structures, linked by redundancy rule. Hence, the alternation is represented solely in lexical entries, not by a general (syntactic) process of merger as in the case of Chi-Mwi:ni applied verbs. It might be asked whether it is possible to treat Dative Shift as a kind of applied verb construction. As we will see, this is explicitly argued for by some.

7.4 Baker's incorporation theory

7.4.1 The basic principles

Of the theories of grammatical relations which stress syntactic explanation over morphological explanation, perhaps the most radical is that proposed by Mark Baker in his 1985 PhD dissertation (published as Baker, 1988a). Baker's starting point is unusual: an analysis of noun incorporation (NI)[6] in terms of syntactic movement (Move-Alpha) operating over lexical categories rather than maximal syntactic projections. He argues that regular NI submits to the same principles that other movements in syntax obey. (For this purpose 'syntax' means the theory of movement proposed by Chomsky, 1986a, the so-called *Barriers* model.)

Baker considers passives, antipassives, causatives, applied verb constructions (applicatives) and possessor ascension (or possessor raising). He succeeds in constructing an elaborate but tightly argued theory around the startling, but extremely simple, idea that all of these phenomena are instances of incorporation of lexical categories by a lexical head. In most cases the incorporating element is the main verb. In all cases the incorporated element is itself the head of its phrase.

I shall illustrate Baker's approach to NI first, showing how it accounts for possessor ascension in NI languages. In 7.149 we have a schematic sentence in which the direct object has been incorporated, stranding its possessor for good measure. The possessor then becomes the derived direct object of the compound verb *spear-steal*. The D-structure source for 7.149 is shown in 7.150 and in 7.151 we have the representation of 7.149 after incorporation has taken place. Notice that there is a trace (e_i) of the moved noun in the position formerly occupied by that noun. It is a general assumption in GB theory that Move-Alpha leaves such a trace, and that it must be coindexed with the moved element it corresponds to. The possessor NP, *Tom*, being stranded, has assumed the position of derived object.

7.149   a) Dick stole Tom's spear. ⇒
          b) Dick spear-stole Tom.

7.150

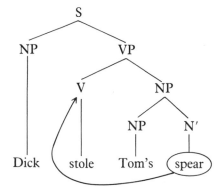

7.151

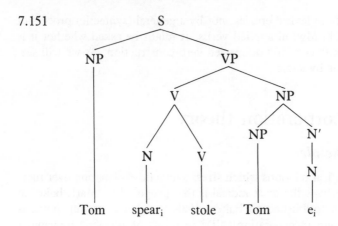

Now let's turn to causatives. In a morphological causative construction such as that schematized in 7.152, the causative affix, CAUSE, is represented in D-structure as a verb taking a clausal complement, 7.153. The lexical verb, *fall*, in this complement clause is then incorporated by the matrix causative predicate, as in 7.154:

7.152   Harriet fall-CAUSE the vase.
         'Harriet dropped the vase.'

7.153

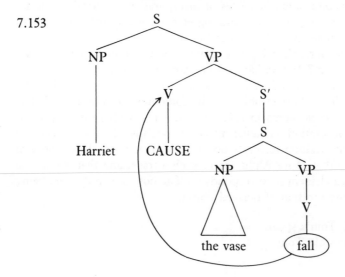

7.154

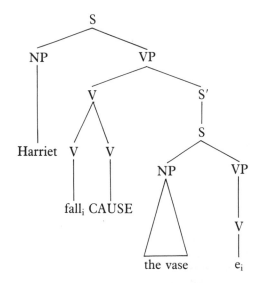

Applicatives are the result of **Preposition Incorporation**. A notional applied verb as in 7.155 is derived from D-structure 7.156, as shown in 7.157:

7.155   Harriet danced-APPL Tom.
         'Harriet danced for Tom.'

7.156

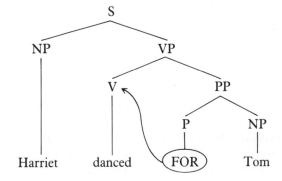

7.157

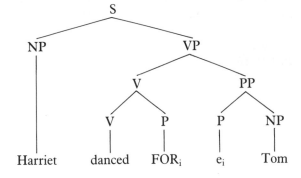

The antipassive construction results when the object position is occupied by an NP which happens to be morphologically a bound affix. In order to form a morphologically acceptable string the affix must incorporate onto the verb (stem). In other respects, it behaves like a normal NP argument. Hence, the antipassive is just a special case of NI.

7.158   Tom killed-AP.
         'Tom killed (something).'

7.159

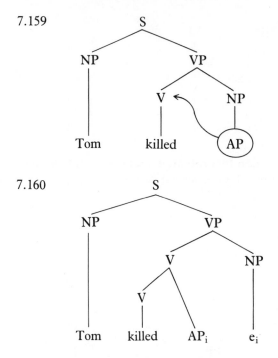

7.160

Perhaps the most ingenious implementation of the incorporation thesis is the analysis of passives. Baker assumes that the passive morpheme, *-EN*, is a nominal, just like the antipassive morpheme, but that it is generated in the position of Infl (I), as though it were an auxiliary verb. In the *Barriers* model, verbs receive tense/aspect and agreement morphology as the result of being raised into the I node. In the passive voice, this node contains, in addition to normal inflectional elements, the *-EN* morpheme. This incorporates the verb, but at the same time receives the subject theta role that the verb would normally assign. This is illustrated in 7.161–7.163:

7.161   The vase broke-EN.
         'The vase got broken.'

7.162

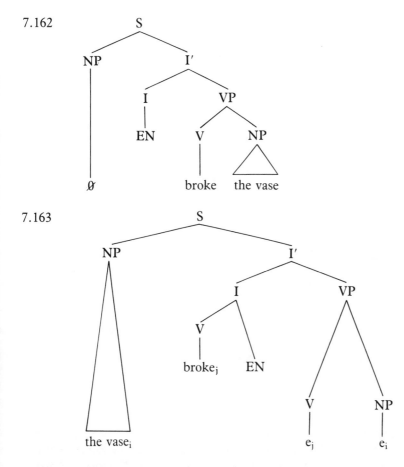

7.163

Finally, Baker argues that NI can take place without overt syntactic movement. In this case the noun undergoes Abstract Incorporation, so that it is linked to the verb as though incorporation had taken place (a process also called Reanalysis). Syntactically, the results are exactly those of genuine incorporation. In particular, the reanalysed noun can no longer function as the head of its phrase, and this role can be taken over by, say, a possessor NP, just as in 7.149. The result is the phenomenon of possessor ascension again, this time without overt NI. In 7.166 I have notated Reanalysis using an asterisk:

7.164   a) Dick stole Tom's spear. ⇒
         b) Dick stole Tom the spear.

7.165

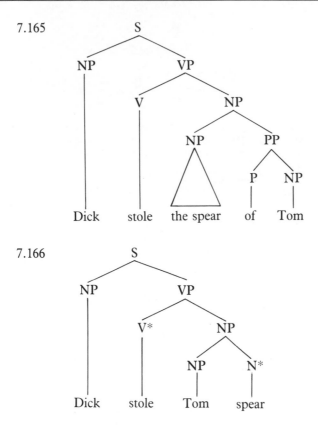

7.166

Baker argues that all the other types of incorporation we have just reviewed may too be realized in the form of Reanalysis.[7] Thus, he claims that the Romance causative construction is an example of Abstract Verb Incorporation. The idea of Abstract Preposition Incorporation is used to account for pseudopassives in English (see examples 7.30–7.32). Baker argues that, in a sentence such as *This bed has been slept in (by someone)*, the preposition has been reanalysed as part of the verb, without actually being incorporated in the way the true applied affix is. This means that the complement of the preposition, *this bed*, becomes a derived object which can subsequently undergo passivization.

In what sense do these structures conform to syntactic principles? The first point to note is that incorporation respects the **Head Movement Constraint** (HMC). This constraint (originally formulated by Lisa Travis), states that a lexical item such as a verb may only incorporate those words which it properly governs. For our purposes, **proper government** is the relation between a theta role assigner such as V or P and the position to which it assigns a theta role (for instance, its NP complement).[8]

This is straightforward for NI, antipassive, passive and applicatives, though for causatives we will need to add to our account to show how they respect the HMC. The HMC rules out a great many types of incorporation which are not attested. The most important types of incorporation which are prohibited by the HMC are incorporation of subjects by verbs and incorporation from adverbials, that is, non-theta marked adjuncts. Subjects can't be incorporated because a verb only governs a position if it c-commands that position, and it is the subject which (asymmetrically) c-commands the verb. It is impossible to incorporate from adverbials because an adverbial is not theta marked and non-theta marked positions constitute a 'barrier' to government in Chomsky's (1986a) *Barriers* model. Hence, the adverbial's phrasal node (AdvP, PP, NP etc.) would be a barrier and would prevent the verb complex from governing the trace of the incorporated lexical item.

Baker also argues that when, say, a verb incorporates a preposition, then the complex derived verb governs anything which was governed by the incorporated element before it became incorporated. Thus, in 7.157 the verb complex *dance-for* governs *Tom* because *for* governs *Tom* in 7.156. This principle is the **Government Transparency Corollary**. (Baker actually derives this from other assumptions.)

Given these assumptions, all the traces in the incorporation structures we have seen will be (properly) governed. On the other hand, in a good many unattested types of incorporation we would have traces which would fail to be (properly) governed. This failure constitutes a violation of a very general principle, the **Empty Category Principle** (ECP). Baker's theory therefore links the impossibility of certain types of incorporation with other, apparently unrelated, syntactic phenomena, which lends considerable theoretical interest to his proposals.

This is the core of Baker's theory. In the next sections we will examine each of these analyses in some more detail to see how he deals with the complexities of some of these constructions.

7.4.2 *PF identification*

We have seen how Baker relates morphologically complex constructions to underlying representations in which affixes figure as fully fledged lexical heads. A key idea here is that constructions, or parts of constructions, which show the same theta role (predicate-argument) relations should have the same underlying representation. For instance, consider a language in which the verb *drop* has the structure of a regularly formed causative, as in our notional sentence *Harriet CAUSE-fall the vase*. Baker argues that we must represent in underlying structure the fact that *the vase* bears the same semantic role to the complex verb *CAUSE-fall* that it bears to the simple verb *fall*. Moreover, this underlying structure must represent the fact that Harriet caused a situation to come about, described by the proposition *the vase fell*. Baker therefore follows Marantz in adopting a type of lexical decomposition analysis. For this purpose he proposes a principle which he calls the **Uniformity of Theta Assignment Hypothesis**, or UTAH. This states that whenever a theta role assigner, say, the verb *fall*, assigns a particular theta role, such as Theme, but in a variety of different surface structures, as in the intransitive and causative forms above, then the D-structure representation corresponding to those surface structures has to remain the same. In other words, the D-structure for *CAUSE-fall* has to include a representation in which *fall* assigns a Theme role. In effect, the principle helps us to determine the D-structure of a sentence by inspecting its meaning.

If D-structures for different constructions are to be similar, how do we represent differences in grammatical relations? GB theory doesn't permit direct reference to grammatical relations. The UTAH implies that we can't capture valency changes by rules which alter the theta grids (argument structure) of verbs. Strict subcategorization is all but replaced in GB theory by theta role assignment, so this leaves us with

Case Theory coupled with incorporation to account for alternations in valency. For this reason Baker develops an elaborated theory of Case.

One rather obvious observation is that languages have a number of different ways of realizing Abstract Case. These include word order (as in English), morphological case marking, and verb agreement. Baker suggests that in talking about Case assignment we should abstract away from these differences and proposes a more general term, **PF Identification** (PF for 'Phonological Form').

A number of constructions involving NI point to the conclusion that a noun which is incorporated doesn't necessarily have to receive the abstract Accusative Case feature which it would have received had it not been incorporated. The most obvious of these constructions are possessor raising constructions in, for instance, the Iroquoian languages. Mohawk verbs don't assign morphological case to their arguments, but they do agree with them for number and gender. In 7.167 the verb bears a suffix cross-referencing the subject (which at D-structure would be an unaccusative direct object). (The possessed noun *house* also agrees with its possessor, *Sawatis*):

7.167   Ka-rakv ne Sawatis hrao-nuhs-aʔ.
          3NEUT-white POSS John 3MASC-house-SUFF
          'John's house is white.'

After NI, however, the predicate *rakv* no longer agrees with the neuter noun *nuhs*, 'house', but with the masculine noun *Sawatis*, 'John', as in 7.168:

7.168   Hrao-nuhs-rakv ne Sawatis.
          3MASC-house-white POSS John
          'John's house is white.'

Recall that *Sawatis* in 7.168 is the derived argument of the verb, following possessor raising. Therefore, it has been Case marked by the verb (in the form of agreement shown by the *hrao-* prefix). The verb no longer agrees with its former argument, 'house'. This would seem to suggest that *rakv* is without Case, in violation of the Case Filter (Visibility). How can this come about?

Baker argues that this means that incorporation is itself a variety of Case marking, or, more generally, of PF Identification. When a verb which would normally assign Case to ('identify') an argument incorporates that argument, it may have a Case feature 'left over', so to speak, which can then be assigned to another NP, such as a stranded possessor. A similar phenomenon is shown in 7.169, this time with a transitive verb, the language being the closely related Oneida:

7.169   Wa-hi-nuhs-ahni:nu: John.
          AOR-1sg.S/3MASC-house-buy John
          'I bought John's house.' (lit: 'I house-bought John.')

Incorporation is itself, then, a form of PF Identification, and an incorporated noun need not receive further identification (say, from verb agreement). There is variation between languages, here, however. In Iroquoian (and in Ainu (Shibatani, 1990)) a transitive verb which incorporates its object remains transitive (for example, by still agreeing with its incorporated object). In the Eskimo languages, NI obligatorily makes a transitive verb intransitive. Baker interprets this by saying that in Eskimo the incorporated object still requires the Abstract Case feature. Since the objective Case is 'absorbed' by the incorporated noun it can't be assigned outside the verb, hence the verb behaves as though it were intransitive. Baker ingeniously relates this to the failure of Eskimo to incorporate subjects of unaccusative verbs: unaccusatives don't assign Case, yet the incorporated noun must receive Case. In addition, Eskimo verbs can't Case mark stranded possessors. Unfortunately, this picture is muddied by the existence of languages such as Niuean and Chukchee, in which incorporation renders the verb intransitive, but where it is possible to incorporate from unaccusatives (and marginally in Chukchee to Case mark stranded NPs). Here, Baker says that the incorporated noun prefers to receive Case but is prepared to waive this privilege if there is none available or if another noun has greater need of it.

Another point about PF Identification is that a Case assigning item, such as a verb or a preposition, doesn't seem able to mark more than one NP in one and the same way. Thus, we don't usually find verbs assigning two Nominative Cases and it is very rare for a language to allow transitive verbs to mark two objects with the same Case. Baker argues that since incorporation is a form of PF Identification we wouldn't therefore expect a verb to be able to incorporate more than one of its arguments. This seems to be generally true.

The next consequence is of some importance when we look at applied verb constructions. Baker claims that incorporation doesn't increase the ability of an item to assign Case, over and above the maximum allowed for that category in the language. Hence, a verb which incorporates a preposition or another verb will not be expected to assign more than one structural Case to its complement, because, in general, this is the maximum allowed in languages. Putting it another way, if basic transitive verbs in a language only have one genuine direct object (as is generally the case), then Preposition Incorporation won't be able to create a verb which takes two genuine direct objects. Baker refers to this stipulation as the **Case Frame Preservation Principle** (CFPP).

7.4.3 *Causatives*

Given the UTAH, wherever a language relates a verb of valency n to a causative of valency $n + 1$ by means of some regular morphological process, we must assume an analysis in which the causative predicate incorporates the lower verb, V, to produce a complex predicate, 'cause to V'. Baker adopts essentially Marantz's typology of causative constructions. Now, Marantz explained the difference in behaviour between monoclausal and biclausal causatives in terms of the level at which merger takes place. How then does Baker reconstruct this distinction? To answer this we must look in slightly more detail at the structure of the clause in the 'Barriers' framework assumed by Baker.

One of the innovations introduce by Chomsky (1986a) is to assume that both the Infl (I) and the Comp (C) elements head maximal projections. This gives us a basic structure 7.170:

7.170

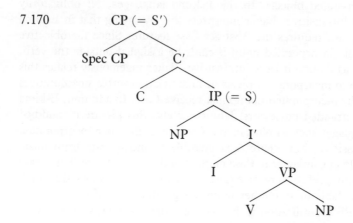

The C position is for complementizers such as *that* or *for* in English, while the Spec CP position is for *wh*-phrases. Assuming that causative predicates take non-finite clausal (CP) complements (as opposed to IP or VP), this means that the general form of a causative construction at D-structure will be something like 7.171:

7.171

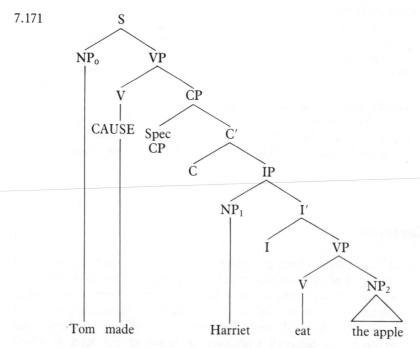

In morphological causatives the matrix CAUSE predicate surfaces as an affix which has incorporated the lower V. There are two main ways of achieving this, depending on whether we have a monoclausal or a biclausal type of causative.

In monoclausal causatives we saw that the lower object, NP_2, becomes the true direct object of the causative verb, while the causee (lower subject), NP_1, is treated as an adjunct or obliquely marked secondary object. This result is obtained by raising the whole of the lower VP to the position Spec CP, as in 7.172. From that position, the verbal head of the lower VP can incorporate into the CAUSE predicate, as in 7.173.

7.172

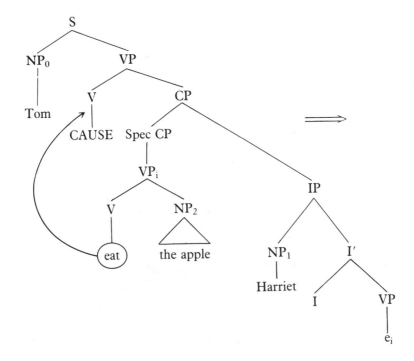

7.173

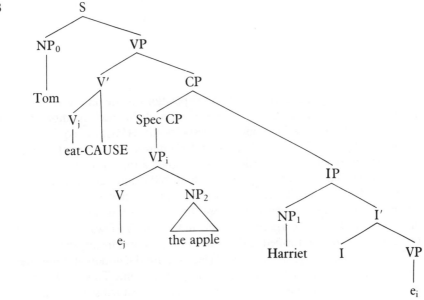

The VP is able to govern its trace in the embedded sentence under the assumptions of GB theory. Likewise, the derived causative verb governs into the VP inside the

Spec CP position. Therefore, this incorporation respects the HMC and is permitted by syntactic principles.

Turning now to biclausal causatives, the lower subject, NP_1, becomes the true object of the derived causative verb, rather as in ECM constructions with verbs like *believe*. What we can assume here is that just the lower V (not the whole VP) is raised and incorporates into the matrix causative verb. This leaves the lower object, NP_2, stranded in the lower VP, while the lower subject can be Case marked and thus becomes the new direct object. The V movement takes place in several stages, via the positions of I and C in the embedded clause as illustrated in 7.174:

7.174

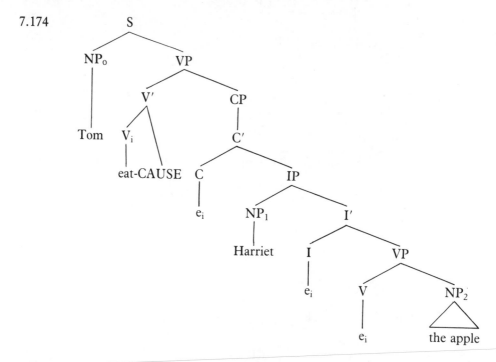

Moving the verb successively into I and C positions is the only way in which such a causative can be generated. The traces form a chain, each member of which is governed. Therefore, this incorporation respects the HMC, as required.

The lower object, NP_2, in 7.174 presents an interesting problem for which Baker finds an ingenious solution. In order to be assigned a theta role it must be PF identified ('made visible') in some way. Yet such an NP is too 'far away' from a suitable verb to get identified in the usual ways. Baker argues that this NP must therefore be rendered visible in some fashion before the lower verb is raised. One form of PF Identification is Noun Incorporation, and, indeed, in S. Tiwa a biclausal causative of this kind can only be formed if the lower object is first incorporated by the lower verb. We have also seen that some languages exercise the option of Noun Reanalysis, a kind of abstract Noun Incorporation without movement. This is what gives rise to some types of possessor raising constructions. In the next subsection we will see that Noun Reanalysis is implicated in the Dative Shift alternation, in that languages permitting Noun Reanalysis are precisely those which permit Dative Shift. Baker argues that the second object of biclausal causatives is made visible in the same way, by

Reanalysis with the verb. His claims are bolstered by the observation that it is only languages which have a Dative Shift construction which permit biclausal causatives. He argues that Chicheŵa provides a 'minimal pair' with respect to this claim: one dialect of the language has no Dative Shift and therefore has no Reanalysis, and therefore permits only monoclausal causatives. Another dialect does have Dative Shift and hence has the biclausal type of causative.

7.4.4 *Applicatives (applied verbs)*

Recall that in an applicative or applied verb construction, an argument, such as a Goal, a Benefactive, a Malefactive or an Instrumental, which is marked with an oblique case, a preposition or a postposition, becomes a derived direct object. The old direct object then becomes 'frozen' and ceases to behave like a genuine object. Baker refers to this patterning as 'Marantz's Generalization'. Again, by manipulating assumptions about Case Theory (PF Identification) we can provide an account for these surface transitivity alternations.

We have seen a schematic example of an applicative in 7.156–7.157, in which an intransitive verb becomes transitive. Let's consider a real example, this time with a basic transitive verb. In 7.175 we see two sentences from Chicheŵa (tones omitted):

7.175   a) Mbidzi zi-na-perek-a msampha kwa nkhandwe.
             zebras SUBJ-PAST-hand-ASP trap to fox
             'The zebras handed the trap to the fox.'
    b) Mbidzi zi-na-perek-er-a nkhandwe msampha.
             zebras SUBJ-PAST-hand-APPL-ASP fox trap.
             'The zebras handed the fox the trap.'

The basic structure of 7.175b is 7.176:

7.176

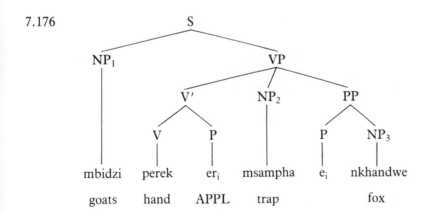

By Marantz's Generalization we have the curious fact that NP$_3$ has become the true object, displacing NP$_2$. We must explain first how NP$_3$ becomes the object, and second, how NP$_2$ can be PF identified.

Recall from §7.4.1 that the verb complex V' in 7.176 governs NP$_3$ because the incorporated preposition governed NP₃ before incorporating (Government Trans-parency Corollary). Therefore, V' is able to assign its objective Case to NP₃, and, in fact, V' is the only source of Case marking for this NP. What about NP₂? This can no longer get the verb's Case, because that has to be assigned to NP₃. The solution is to assume that NP₂ has undergone prior Abstract Incorporation, or Reanalysis, as in the case of possessor raising. Then, we predict that NP₂ will not behave like a genuine direct object, but rather will be 'frozen', as is the case.

Baker argues that it is not necessary for the P Incorporation process to be repre-sented formally by affixation of the verb. He claims that the Dative Shift alternation found in, say, English is the consequence of P Incorporation in which the base form of the verb and its applied form are homophonous. This means that English has a zero applied affix, and abstract Noun Incorporation. Hence the structure of a sentence such as 7.177 is 7.178 (recall that the asterisk represents reanalysis):

7.177   Tom gave Harriet a rose.

7.178

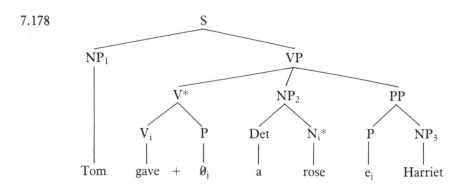

Interestingly, in some languages Dative Shift alternations are only permitted where genuine Noun Incorporation has taken place. Chukchee is an example (Nedjalkov, 1976):

7.179   a) ətləg-e akka-gtə qora-ŋə təmnen.
         father-ERG son-DAT reindeer-ABS killed-3sg.S/3sg.O
         'The father killed a reindeer for the son.'
         b) ətləg-ən akka-gtə qaa-nm-at-gʔe.
         father-ABS son-DAT deer-killed-SUFF-3sg.S
         'Ibid.'
         c) əltəg-e ekək qaa-nmə-nen.
         father-ERG son-ABS deer-killed-3sg.S/3sg.O
         'The father killed the son a reindeer.'
         d) ⋆ətləg-e ekək ŋaaka-gtə qaa-nmə-nen.
         father-ERG son-ABS daughter-DAT deer-killed-3sg.S/3sg.O
         'The father killed the son a reindeer for the daughter.'

Nedjalkov (1976: 199) reports that 7.179d is uninterpretable because it has, in effect, two benefactives. Note that Chukchee has no overt affixal applicative construction. The Dative Shift construction in Chukchee is therefore just like that in English, except that we have genuine NI instead of the abstract variety.

7.4.5 Passives and antipassives

The incorporation theory of antipassives is relatively straightforward. Consider the Chukchee example in 7.180. We assume a D-structure for this in the form of 7.181:

7.180   Gəm t-ine-tejk-ərkən orw-etə.
          I-ABS 1S-AP-make-ASP sledge-DAT
          'I am making a sledge.'

7.181

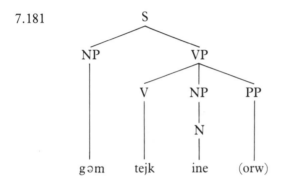

The oblique argument (corresponding to the active direct object) is optional, appearing here in the Dative case. Since *ine-* is morphologically an affix, incorporation is obligatory. The trace it leaves is properly governed by the verb, as required.[9] This analysis explains, *inter alia*, why it is that the antipassive construction only applies to direct objects. If a non-theta marked adjunct or a subject were so incorporated there would be an ECP violation. It appears that antipassive constructions are always intransitive. This means that the antipassive morpheme must always be assigned the verb's structural Case. In this (as in a number of other respects), antipassive differs from pure NI.

If the antipassive morpheme is generated as a nominal in object position and subsequently incorporated into the verb, it is tempting to adopt a similar approach to passives. However, the argument position which appears to be lost in the passive is that of the active subject, and this causes a problem for an incorporation analysis. Recall that (genuine) subjects can't undergo NI. This is because the verb doesn't govern the subject position, so such an incorporation would leave an ungoverned trace. So we can't assume that the passive morpheme is simply the antipassive morpheme in subject position.

Baker's solution to this problem is to assume that the passive argument is a nominal affix, but that, unlike the antipassive, it belongs to a special part of speech making it somewhat similar to an auxiliary verb. The effect of this is to ensure that the passive morpheme has the syntactic category of Infl, so that it can only be generated in that position. In a language such as Chicheŵa, in which the passive morpheme simply appears on the verb stem, we can assume that the verb then moves into the Infl position where it gets associated with the passive affix (as well as various tense, aspect and agreement markers). This type of V-to-I movement is precisely what is assumed by many specialists in Germanic syntax, and it has given rise to a rich literature on the so-called V2 phenomenon.

Verb movement to Infl presumably doesn't literally occur in English, which lacks the V2 properties of other Germanic languages. Therefore, we may assume Reanalysis takes place, followed by a special 'Affix Hopping' process (which somehow is not subject to the ECP). This is diagrammed in 7.182 for the structure underlying *The duckling was killed by the farmer*:

7.182

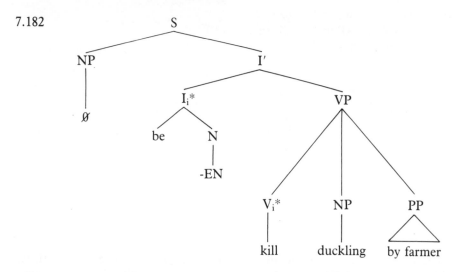

The verb has to assign a theta role to the -EN morpheme. Since that morpheme is external to the VP, it must be the external argument role which is assigned. As we know, some verbs don't have an external argument role, for instance, the unaccusative verbs and Raising-to-Subject verbs. On Baker's analysis this would mean that such verbs would be unable to form a passive.[10] But this is precisely what is stated in the 1-Advancement Exclusiveness Law (1-AEX) discussed earlier in the chapter.

We noted that the 1-AEX has exceptions in certain languages, such as the double passive of Lithuanian. Baker handles these cases by assuming that in such languages the passive morpheme differs from the passive of, say, English, in that it isn't categorically a member of Infl. Rather, it is a genuine nominal and thus can be generated in any NP position, provided it appears under Infl (or affixed to a verb) by surface structure. The derivation for the Lithuanian example (repeated here as 7.183, and schematically as 7.184) is then shown in 7.185:

7.183   To lapelio buta vejo nupusto.
the leaf-GEN/M/sg. be-PASS/NOM/N/sg. wind-GEN
blow-PASS/GEN/M/sg.
(Lit.) 'By that leaf there was getting blown down by the wind.'

7.184   Be-PASS₁ blow-PASS₂ (by wind) (by leaf)

7.185   a)

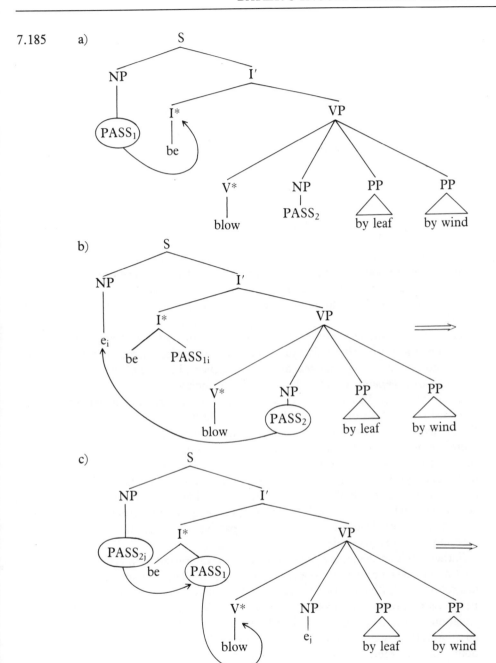

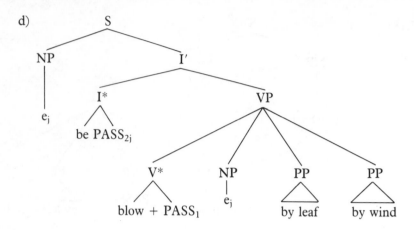

In 7.185 the asterisk on I and V indicates abstract V-to-I movement (Reanalysis). The passive argument in subject position (PASS$_1$) then incorporates into Infl, and the passive argument in object position fills the vacated subject slot. Next, the PASS$_1$ element moves, by Affix Hopping, onto the lexical verb, while PASS$_2$ moves into the I node.

The rather baroque analysis illustrates one of the several strengths of Baker's approach. From very slight alterations in a representation (here, the category of the PASS morpheme), we get far-reaching consequences, because of the way this change interacts with general, universally applicable principles.

Before we leave Baker's theory, we turn to Case assignment in passives. In the standard GB analysis of passives, the verb's underlying complement has to move to the subject position, because the passive participle doesn't assign a Case, and it is therefore only in the subject position that the complement can receive Case. Since the external argument role of the verb necessarily has to be assigned to the passive morpheme in the passive construction, and can't be assigned to a 'genuine' argument, we can think of passive participles as falling under Burzio's generalization, according to which verbs which fail to assign an external theta role also fail to assign an internal Case. However, we've seen passive constructions which constitute exceptions to this generalization.

Earlier, we identified three ways in which Case interacted with NI: (i) the incorporated noun never needs Case (e.g. Mohawk); (ii) the noun usually receives Case, but can relinquish it if another NP needs it in the syntax (Niuean); (iii) the noun always needs Case (Greenlandic Eskimo). In Baker, Johnson and Roberts (1989) a fourth situation is described, that of Nahuatl (the language of the Aztecs). Here, an unaccusative verb may incorporate its (D-structure) object, showing that the incorporated noun does not require Case. However, unlike the situation in Mohawk or Niuean, a transitive verb cannot relinquish its unneeded Case when it incorporates its object.

The simplest hypothesis is that a similar situation holds with passives. Thus, for each of the four variants of NI we would expect to find a passive type. Baker et al. (1989) argue that this is roughly true. (We'll assume that a passive morpheme may only receive Case from the verb.)

In type (iii) passives, the passive morpheme must receive Case. This will be possible providing the verb has an internal Case, and providing the verb has undergone V-to-I movement. The stipulation that the passive element requires (the verb's) Case thus derives Burzio's generalization as it applies to passives. In languages with such a passive (e.g. English), there will be no impersonal passives and no transitive passives. English is thus the equivalent of Eskimo.

In a type (iv) passive we would find that an intransitive (Caseless) verb could be passivized, because the passive morpheme doesn't absolutely require Case from a verb. However, a transitive verb, which does have Case, would be forced to assign it to the passive morpheme, and couldn't, say, assign it to a direct object. Therefore, type (iv) defines a language in which there are impersonal passives but no transitive passives. This is exemplified by German, which is thus the analogue to Nahuatl.

In a type (ii) passive we would expect the same situation as in type (iv) just described, and in addition the possibility of assigning the Case of a transitive verb to a direct object NP if it needed it. In §7.1 we saw examples of Ukrainian and Polish 'transitive passives'. In these constructions the agent takes the form of neuter agreements with arbitrary reference, while the object remains in situ, still marked with accusative case. We may assume that the passive morpheme receives the external theta role from the verb but not its Accusative Case, which is instead assigned to the object. The identification of the passive morpheme is then expressed by the default neuter singular form (which also serves to express the arbitrary reference). Since these languages also permit ordinary passives of transitive verbs, Ukrainian and Polish can be considered equivalent to Niuean.

7.4.6 Conclusions

Baker's theory of valency changing operations represents a radical approach to morphology. A great many of the regular aspects of morphology are regarded as the consequence of principles of syntax, and not as morphological phenomena at all. This is a property which Baker's theory shares with that of Marantz. As we will be seeing later, some have argued that there is little of general interest in morphology as such, and that all regularities in word structure are essentially the result of principles of phonology and syntax. (Baker himself doesn't adopt such an ultra-radical stance.)

Elegant and comprehensive though Baker's theory is, it doesn't solve all the problems. A closer examination of Baker's analyses would reveal that there are many areas of uncertainty. Moreover, it is not at all clear what implications Baker's theoretical apparatus for valency changing has for the other examples of morphology–syntax interaction we'll be discussing, namely compounds and clitics. However, the work both of Baker and Marantz has shown how extremely fruitful it is to look at the morphology–syntax interface from the perspective of the latter.

While Marantz's theory makes explicit reference to the lexical structure of words and morphemes, and explicitly adopts a version of Lieber's (1980) framework, Baker is relatively silent about the purely morphological aspects of the processes he discusses. In a sense that is a pity, because many of the valency changing processes he talks about, including NI, get lexicalized in many languages and lose their syntactic generality. It would therefore be of great interest to know exactly how genuinely morphological phenomena are handled in such a theory (Baker, 1988b, offers some very interesting commentary on this question). We'll be taking up these questions again in Part IV.

One very specific claim is, however, to be found in Baker (1985a). Here, Baker

advances the **Mirror Principle**, which states that the order of morphological operations, as revealed by the order of affixation, is always identical to that of syntactic
operations. We've already seen a reflex of this in the examples from Quechua shown
in chapter 3, examples 3.25–3.26. There, we saw that the order in which reflexive
and causative affixes are attached mirrors the order of reflexivization and causativization. Baker argues that productive morphological processes always reflect syntax in
this fashion and attributes this to the essentially syntactic nature of the morphological
processes themselves. The significance of Baker's observations and their implications
have not gone unquestioned, however (Grimshaw, 1986).

   As we will discover in the next two chapters, a number of the problems posed by
NI recur in other, more familiar types of compounding, and in pronominal cliticization. In chapter 9 we'll find that opinion is divided as to whether to regard, say,
French cliticization as effectively the incorporation of a pronoun into the verb,
leaving a trace, or whether to regard the process as essentially one of affixation. On
the second theory, the clitic/affix would then identify an empty pronoun (referred to
as 'small *pro*' in the generative literature), an empty category with all the properties
of a real pronoun except that it is phonetically null. In other words, we have a choice
between analysing the French sentence in 7.186 as 7.187a or b:

7.186   Je le vois.
          I him see
          'I see him.'

7.187   a) Je le$_i$ vois t_i.
          b) Je le$_i$ vois *pro*$_i$.

   Not surprisingly, a similar analysis of NI can be justified which appeals to the *pro*
empty category and not to the trace of head movement. Rosen (1989) claims that the
morphological compounding process of incorporation is always lexical but that there
are two types of syntactic construction in which it participates. In the first, lexical
compounding of a verb's direct argument fails to satisfy the argument structure of
the verb in the lexicon itself. Hence, a transitive verb remains transitive and takes
a syntactic direct object at all levels of syntactic representation. The identity of the
object is already indicated in the incorporation complex, so for semantic reasons we
would usually only expect an empty category to appear as direct object, that is, *pro*.
This means that a notional sentence such as *Tom deer-hunts* would be represented as
in 7.188a:

7.188   a)

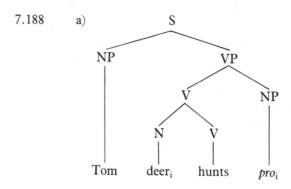

Rosen argues that this is the structure found in languages such as Mohawk, in which the verb remains transitive after incorporation. If we assume that the *pro* can be of category N or N', then we can also permit it to be modified by adjectives, determiners or relative clauses. This then permits modifier stranding and possessor raising.

On the other hand, Rosen claims, we might also find NI languages in which the verb's internal argument position is satisfied in the lexicon by the lexical compounding process. In that case, the compounded verb would become lexically intransitive and would fail to project a direct object position in syntactic representation. In such a language, incorporation structures should behave just like any other intransitive verb and should not permit modifier stranding.[11] Hence, our notional sentence would receive a structure such as 7.118b:

7.188   b)

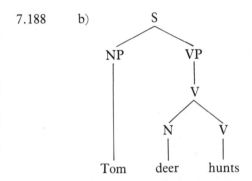

Rosen's analysis is particularly attractive for Chukchee. NI in this language gives intransitive verbs, and, except for a handful of marginal cases of possessor raising (which arguably should be analysed as something else anyway), it doesn't permit modifier stranding. Hence, we'd expect it to pattern along the lines illustrated in 7.188b. This would solve a serious descriptive problem which arises if we adopt a syntactic movement analysis. For in Chukchee the verb can freely incorporate non-theta marked adjuncts, in violation of the *Barriers* analysis of the ECP. This, for instance, is illustrated in a sentence cited in chapter 1 (example 1.20), repeated as 7.189 below (Skorik, 1961: 102), where the verb has incorporated what may well be an indirect instrumental argument ('gun') together with uncontroversial adverbials:

7.189   Tə-jaa   -racwəŋ -melgar-maraw-ərkən.
          I -distant-compete-gun   -fight -PRES
          'I am fighting a duel.'
          (Lit: 'I fight with a gun competing at a distance.')

Another example is 7.190, with its analytic counterpart, 7.191 (Skorik, 1977: 241):

7.190   Mən   -nəki -ure -qepl-uwicwen-mək.
          1pl.IMPER-night-long-ball -play   -1pl.
          'Let's play ball for a long time at night.'

7.191   Nəki-te   n   -ur -ʔew mən   -uwicwen-mək qepl-e.
          night-OBL ADV-long-ADV 1pl.IMPER-play   -1pl. ball -OBL

Examples such as this can be multiplied *ad libitum* from Chukchee. The same sort of behaviour is typical of Chukchee's close relative, Koryak, and it has also been recorded in the Australian language Tiwi (Osborne, 1974). If incorporation is purely lexical this is precisely the pattern of data we'd expect. Interestingly, incorporation in Chukchee (particularly in the texts collected at the turn of the century, before the wholesale russification of the language) seems to have been very free and productive, whilst it is claimed that in Mohawk, where incorporation is supposedly syntactic, it is rather restricted and lexically governed (Mithun, 1984, 1986).

7.5   Lexical approaches to valency alternations

7.5.1   Valency alternations in the lexicon

Although Baker's syntactic theory of grammatical function changing covers a good deal of ground, there are a number of alternations he doesn't treat. Morphologically mediated reflexivization is one obvious example, a case which Marantz's theory does, however, handle. There are several examples in the literature of morphological processes which affect valency which don't obviously yield to a syntactic analysis (at least not in terms of incorporation).

In §6.1.3, we saw examples of category-changing affixation (e.g. *-able, -ee, -ize*) which referred to argument structure. In addition to these processes, there are morphological operations creating verbs from verbs which affect valency in ways which can't obviously be accommodated in terms of incorporation or head-to-head movement. There are several cases in the literature of prefixation altering the valency of a verb. A well-known example of this is the prefix *out-*, which attaches productively to intransitive verbs (e.g. *snore*) and creates a transitive verb (e.g. *Dick out-snored Tom*). Presumably, this type of alternation must be handled in the morphology and not by syntactic rules.

A more general observation is due to Carlson and Roeper (1980). They point out that prefixation in general alters the subcategorization (selection) properties of verbs. In particular, there is a strong tendency for a prefixed verb to admit only NP direct objects, even if the unprefixed verb selects PPs, sentential complements, adverbial complements and so on. (This also seems true of verbs formed by suffixation from nouns and adjectives.) Some examples of this are shown in 7.192–7.195:

7.192   a) Tom calculated   ⎰our time of arrival.⎱
          b)   ⎱when we would arrive.⎰
          c) Tom miscalculated   ⎰our time of arrival.⎱
          d)   ⎱*when we would arrive.⎰

7.193   a) Dick managed   ⎰his finances prudently.⎱
          b)   ⎱to make ends meet.⎰
          c) Dick mismanaged   ⎰his finances.⎱
          d)   ⎱*to make ends meet.⎰

7.194   a) Harriet believes { Dick.

b)   { Dick to be a liar. }

c) Harriet disbelieves { Dick.

d)   { *Dick to be a liar. }

7.195   a) Tom printed { several posters for Harriet.

b)   { Harriet several posters. }

c) Tom reprinted { several posters for Harriet.

d)   { *Harriet several posters. }

Carlson and Roeper's suggested explanation for this behaviour is the *Case Complement Restriction*: all verbs created by a general lexical process assign objective Case, and thus take a single NP complement (i.e. they are simple transitive verbs). Only listed verbs can have different subcategorization or selection properties. To the extent that reflexives, causatives, applied verbs and so on fail to respect this generalization, we could say that those operations are cases of syntactic word formation rather than lexical, purely affixational word formation.

Earlier in the chapter was saw two ways in which a transitive verb can have an intransitive alternant. In 7.43 we saw examples of 'middles', and in 7.46, examples of 'anticausatives'. In 7.196–7.197 I give a further example of each:

7.196   These jeans wash easily.

7.197   The boat sank.

It has been argued by Keyser and Roeper (1984) that the distinction between two types of intransitive verb can be explained if the middles are derived syntactically (rather like passives), while the anticausatives (which they refer to as 'ergatives') are derived lexically. They note that there is a whole host of ways in which these superficially similar constructions differ. One of the most interesting differences is that the middle (like a syntactic passive) bears with it an implicit agent, at least as far as meaning is concerned. Thus, 7.196 implies that someone is washing the jeans. However, there is no agent implied in 7.197: the boat could have just sunk of its own accord, without actually being sunk *by* anyone.

Keyser and Roeper suggest that the middles are formed by a syntactic rule, in much the same way that syntactic passives are assumed to be formed in the syntax. The anticausatives, however, are said to be formed by means of a set of lexical transformations operating over the subcategorization frame of the verb (where 'subcategorization frame' has to be understood rather loosely, as it includes the subject NP position). The transformations map 7.198a into 7.198b:

7.198   a) sink: [NP [VP _____ [NP]]]

b)   [NP$_i$ [VP _____ [t_i]]]

The object NP in 7.198a is moved to the subject position, displacing that NP, and leaving behind a coindexed trace, to indicate where it came from.

Not everyone agrees, of course, that anticausatives should be handled by the lexical equivalents of noun incorporation.[12] More recently, Fagan (1988) has argued that not even middles are formed by a movement rule. Rather, she claims that middles result from two processes. One of these assigns the interpretation 'arbitrary entity' to the external argument. This accounts for why 7.196 has the meaning *People in general can wash these jeans easily*. It is usually assumed that when an argument position is given a particular interpretation in this fashion by a lexical rule, then that position can't appear in syntactic structure. This accounts for the loss of the original external argument. The second process is the externalization of the internal theta role, explaining why the Theme in 7.196 is the subject. This means that middle formation is rather similar to its effects to *-able* affixation (as in *These jeans are washable*). To distinguish the middles from the anticausatives such as 7.197, Fagan assumes that ergative formation is a lexical rule which simply deletes the external argument of a verb marked [+causative]. (Alternatively, one might want to say that the transitive alternant was derived from the intransitive by a causative rule taking the form of conversion, much as we would have to say for *Tom walked the dog*.)

7.5.2 Williams's theory

In the two syntactically based approaches to valency changing reviewed in §§7.3, 4 we were implicitly assuming that the argument structure or theta grid of the base verb remained constant during the syntactic derivation. Increases in surface valency were the consequence of incorporation or merger with other theta role assigners (verbs or prepositions) and decreases in valency were due to changes in Case assignment or to incorporation of arguments by predicates. In other words, the theories of Baker and Marantz adhere to Chomsky's **Projection Principle**. This states that the argument structure of a predicate is projected through the syntactic derivation and remains unaltered at all syntactic levels of representation. By the Projection Principle it is impossible for a verb which is intransitive in the lexicon and at D-structure to acquire a theta marked direct object of its own accord in the course of the derivation. If this appears to happen then there must be another theta role assigner at D-structure.

The Projection Principle plays an important role in GB theory and distinguishes it from a number of other conceivable syntactic theories. However, there is one way in which it can appear to be subverted, and that is by altering the argument structure of a verb in the lexicon, before the start of the syntactic derivation. Indeed, this is exactly the way that Marantz has handled the Dative Shift alternation. He assumes that Dative Shift verbs are given two argument structures (related to each other by a lexical redundancy rule). Therefore, the fact that the Dative Shifted alternant appears to have acquired an extra object is due to the difference in its argument structure compared with that of its unshifted homophone.

If we assume that regular and productive alternations, such as English Passive, can also be represented by lexical redundancy relations, then we are permitted an entirely different approach to the problem. In §6.1.3, I introduced Williams's lexical approach to valency affecting operations. In this theory, rules such as passive and causative are the result of altering the argument structure of the verb at the level of the lexicon. Let's begin by recalling a simple example. In a case such as *breakable*, affixation of a transitive verb creates an adjective whose external argument corresponds to the verb's internal argument (a case of *internalization*). This is illustrated in 7.199 (cf. chapter 6, example 6.32; recall that underlining indicates the external argument):

7.199   break $\langle \underline{Ag}, Th \rangle \rightarrow$ breakable $\langle Ag, \underline{Th} \rangle$

We can compare this with another deverbal adjective, the adjectival (or stative) passive form, *broken*, as in *The vase was completely broken.* We can assume that affixation (of *-EN*) has roughly the same effect:

7.200   break $\langle \underline{Ag}, Th \rangle \rightarrow$ broken $\langle Ag, \underline{Th} \rangle$

This account is adequate for the adjectival passive form, but is insufficient for the verbal or syntactic passive, in which the passive participle remains categorically a verb form and not an adjective. Williams (1981b) accepts Chomsky's viewpoint that the passive participle in this case fails to assign an external theta role. The external argument remains 'implicit', only capable of surfacing as a *by*-phrase adjunct. In this early account the argument structure of the syntactic passive participle is then exactly that of the basic transitive verb except that it lacks an external argument, indicated by erasure of the underlying, as in 7.201:

7.201   break $\langle \underline{Ag}, Th \rangle \rightarrow$ broken $\langle Ag, Th \rangle$

This analysis correctly represents the passive participle as a type of unaccusative verb. However, merely providing a representational notation doesn't make it clear exactly how the two different sorts of passive participle formation process are to be distinguished.

Di Sciullo and Williams (1987) adopt a slightly different approach to the verbal passive. They introduce a notion of control of an argument by an affix (not to be confused with the GB notion of Control, in which PRO is controlled by a matrix NP). This notion bears some similarity to the idea of Baker et al. (1989) who claim that the passive affix is the element to which the verb assigns its external theta role. The idea is that an affix may be specially linked to a position in the verb's argument structure, thereby preventing that argument from being realized as an external NP. For instance, in the word *employer*, the *-er* affix controls the Agent argument of the verb *employ*. In this way we can state that an employer is an Agent, and that the activity he engages in is that expressed by the verb. Moreover, we account for the fact that no other noun within the NP can express that argument. Thus, *Tom*, in *Tom's employer* or *employer of Tom*, cannot be the Agent. In like fashion, we can say that, in *employee*, the *-ee* affix controls the Theme argument (so that, in *Tom's employee*, *Tom* is the Agent not the Theme).

To account for the syntactic passive participle, what we now have to say is that the *-EN* morpheme controls the external argument. However, this argument can be expressed, namely, with a *by*-phrase. Therefore, we must assume that the affix is somehow linked to that *by*-phrase (where it occurs) and that the external argument theta role can be transferred to it. The way Di Sciullo and Williams achieve this is to assume that the *-EN* morpheme itself has an argument structure consisting of one argument, notated as $\langle X \rangle$. This is linked to a *by*-phrase if one is present, otherwise the connection is implicit. Next, we assume that affixation produces a composite argument structure, which is a combination of the argument structures of the verb and of the *-EN* affix. Hence, the argument structure of the participle *broken* will be something like $\langle X_i \langle Ag_i, Th \rangle \rangle$, where the indexing represents control. Notice that this lacks an external argument.

To implement this idea, Di Sciullo and Williams borrow a simple algebraic notion (used quite widely in categorial grammar approaches), namely that of **functional composition**. First, we regard an argument structure as a **functor**. A functor (also often called a *function*) is a way of expressing relationships between entities. For instance, if we wished to notate the idea that y is the father of x, we could express the property 'is the father of' using a functor, F, and write '$y = F(x)$'. We can illustrate functional composition by extending our family: let's notate 'y is the mother of x' as '$y = M(x)$' using another functor, M. Let's say we can also write 'z is the paternal grandmother of x' as '$z = M(F(x))$'. This is possible because $F(x)$ denotes an individual (say, y) and so our equation is equivalent to '$z = M(y)$'. Now, we can notate this new composite function more simply by adopting functional composition. We create a new function, G, defined as the result of applying M to F (generally notated $M \star F$). The new functor, G, is the composition of the two functors, M, F. Now, we can simply say '$z = G(x)$'.

After this digression all we need say now is that argument structures are functors, and that they can therefore be composed with each other. At the same time we stipulate that the *-EN* argument position controls the verb's external argument. This means that in a full ('long') passive the *by*-phrase will correspond to the active subject. Moreover, this will be true irrespective of the actual theta role which the verb assigns to the subject. In 7.202–7.203 I show examples of the passive participles of *kill* and *know* (as in *The wasp was killed by Tom* and *The answer was known by Dick*):

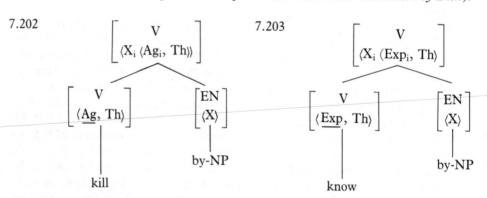

Di Sciullo and Williams claim that a number of affixes should be regarded semantically as functors, just like the *-EN* affix (they mention antipassives, applicatives and causatives in this regard, as well as nominalizations such as *completeness* and *destruction*).

To summarize this approach to passive:

(i)   In neither the early nor the later version of Williams's theory does the verb actually assign its external theta role to the passive morpheme, in the way proposed by Baker and others.

(ii) In the more recent version, the operation of control 'neutralizes' the external argument which becomes an implicit argument (specifiable with a *by*-phrase).

(iii) Since the verb's original external argument is controlled, and since the -*EN* affix has no external argument, the passive form as a whole lacks an external argument. As a result, there is no longer any specific rule of 'external argument erasure'.

Compared with the approaches of Marantz or Baker, the proposals which Williams has advanced are somewhat sketchy and programmatic. However, it seems clear that in principle a lexicalist account of valency changing can be envisaged even within a GB-style theory of syntax. I have obviously glossed over a number of important points, here, particularly as regards syntax. As far as morphology is concerned, the important point to note is that it is possible to construct a theory in which regular and productive valency alternations are coded by systematically altering argument structure in lexical representation. Such a theory involves a weakening of the importance of the Projection Principle, in the sense that the empirical coverage of that principle is narrower. In chapter 11 we'll look at further implications in Williams's approach for the organization of morphology.

7.5.3 *Excursus on adjectival passives (Levin and Rappaport)*

We conclude this look at a lexical analysis of valency changing with an account of the adjectival passive proposed by Levin and Rappaport (1986). This seeks to derive nearly all the features of the adjectival passive from general principles of grammar, and serves as a good illustration of the way that a variety of differences between constructions can be reduced to general considerations once we hit on the right formulation of the process and provided we make the right assumptions about basic lexical structure.

There are two particularly important features which distinguish the adjectival from the verbal passive: the adjectival passive form is categorically an adjective, not a verb, and the adjectival passive, unlike the verbal passive, assigns an external theta role. In other respects the two forms are similar. Levin and Rappaport make the interesting claim that the second difference is a consequence of the first, and that *Adjectival Passive Formation* (APF) is simply a question of relabelling the passive participle as an adjective.

An earlier approach (Wasow, 1977) had claimed that APF had as one of its components a subrule which specifically took the Theme of the verb argument structure and externalized it. This accounts for the fact that it is only direct and not indirect objects that can be subjects of adjectival passives. For instance, although we can promote the indirect object *Tom* of 7.204 to subject position in the verbal passive 7.205a, this is not possible if the participle is used adjectivally, as in 7.205b; only the direct object can become the subject (7.205c):

7.204   Dick sold Tom the car.

7.205   a) Tom was sold the car (by Dick).
          b) ⋆Tom remained unsold (the car).
          c) The car remained unsold.

There are problems with this proposal, however, because verbs like *teach*, *pay* and *serve* do allow both direct and indirect objects to become subjects after APF. For instance, we can speak either of unpaid money or unpaid creditors. Levin and Rappaport argue that the real generalization is that the argument which can be externalized is one which may stand as the sole complement of the verb (their *Sole Complement Generalization*). Thus, the reason for the failure of 7.205b is the non-existence of 7.206, compared with the possibility of 7.207:

7.206   *Dick sold Tom. (=Dick sold something to Tom).

7.207   a) Dick paid the money.
          b) Dick paid the creditors.

Evidence in favour of this comes from the well-known **spray/load verbs**. These are verbs which have two complements, one an affected Theme, the other a Locative, either of which can appear as the direct object, as in 7.208–7.209:

7.208   a) Tom loaded hay onto the wagon.
          b) Tom loaded the wagon with hay.

7.209   a) Harriet stuffed the feathers into the pillow.
          b) Harriet stuffed the pillow with feathers.

In the case of *load*, either the Theme or the Locative may surface as the sole complement (as in 7.210) but in the case of *stuff* it is only the Locative that can appear on its own (7.211):

7.210   a) Tom loaded the $\left\{ \begin{array}{l} \text{hay} \\ \text{wagon} \end{array} \right\}$.
          b)

7.211   a) Harriet stuffed the $\left\{ \begin{array}{l} \text{pillow} \\ \text{*feathers} \end{array} \right\}$.
          b)

Sure enough, this correlates with the type of subject with which the adjectival passive can co-occur (7.212–7.213):

7.212   a) the recently loaded $\left\{ \begin{array}{l} \text{hay} \\ \text{wagon} \end{array} \right\}$
          b)

7.213   a) the recently stuffed $\left\{ \begin{array}{l} \text{pillow} \\ \text{*feathers} \end{array} \right\}$
          b)

Levin and Rappaport account for this with a modification of the notion of lexical theta marking. They adopt Marantz's distinction between directly and indirectly theta marked complements. Each polyvalent verb has just one directly marked complement, the indirectly marked component being typically marked by a preposition, a case marker or some other means. For instance, the verb *put* has a direct complement, the Theme, and an indirect (but still obligatory) Locative complement. Some verbs alternate, such as the dative shift verb *sell*. This therefore has two theta grids, illustrated in 7.214, in which the italicized theta role is the direct role, and a role in parentheses is interpreted as optional:

7.214   a) sell: (*Theme*, (Goal))   ('sell a car (to Dick)')
         b) sell: (Theme, *Goal*)   ('sell Dick a car')

We could now rewrite the core of the APF rule as 'externalize the direct argument'. However, Levin and Rappaport argue that this is not necessary. They enumerate the six salient properties of adjectival passives in 7.215:

7.215   a) Affix -en.
         b) Change V → Adj.
         c) Suppress external role of verb stem.
         d) Externalize an internal role.
         e) Absorb objective Case.
         f) Eliminate direct object position.

Now, suppose we acknowledge that adjectival passives are derived from verbal passive participles by a rule corresponding to 7.215b. The fact that the source of the adjective is a passive participle at once gives us 7.215a, c. It is generally acknowledged that all adjectives must assign an external role. Given 7.215c this means that an external role must be provided, so part of 7.215d is accounted for. However, we must explain how it is that certain internal roles and not others get externalized. If a verb has two internal arguments and if the syntax permits expression of the role which is not externalized, then either internal role can be externalized. Thus, we find 7.216:

7.216   a) The pillow remained stuffed with feathers.
         b) The feathers remained stuffed into the pillow.

If, however, there is no way for an obligatory internal role to surface, then no grammatical structure can result.[13] Property 7.215e is a straightforward application of Burzio's Generalization, while 7.215f is a consequence of the Projection Principle: since the internal argument has now been externalized it can't surface as a direct object. Thus, all the properties of 7.215 can be regarded as an automatic result of 7.215b, given certain general principles. Moreover, these also derive the Sole Complement Generalization. That is, then, a good example of the way that current theory attempts to derive even facts about derivational morphology from independent principles, without appeal to construction-specific rules.[14]

7.6 Conclusions: syntactic and lexical approaches

The problem of valency alternations has sparked off one of the most interesting of the specific debates relating to the question 'where's morphology?'. Whatever we say about this debate we must ensure that we do justice to the 'interface problem': we must be able to reflect the fact that valency changing operations have syntactic repercussions, while respecting the close links between these operations and purely morphological or lexical aspects of the phenomena. This means that all approaches are in a sense a compromise between two competing extremes, the syntactic and the lexical.

Those who favour a more syntactic approach (especially Baker, and to a large extent Marantz) put a fair amount of emphasis on a parsimony criterion. If much of the phenomenology of valency changing can be related to general syntactic principles then there is no need for anything other than pre-existing theories of syntax. And when we look at distinctions such as that between monoclausal and biclausal causatives the question arises of how this could possibly be accounted for except by appeal to syntactic principles.

Those who adopt a more lexicalist stance can point to the fact that apparently syntactic constructions frequently become highly lexicalized as languages develop. At some point, then, these syntactic processes have to enter the lexicon, so why not assume that all such processes, where mediated morphologically, are given a single level at which they are represented, namely the morphological component, or the lexicon? A related argument, which is not explicitly discussed much in the literature, concerns semantic drifting in morphosyntactic constructions such as the passive. We saw in our brief discussion of Shibatani's (1985) account of the core meaning of passives that the construction often acquires a variety of distinct, if related, meanings. This process is very reminiscent of the polysemy which affects individual lexical items. Now, if the construction itself is somehow represented at a single, lexical, level, it is easier to see why it behaves like a single word with respect to semantic drift. If the effects of the construction are distributed amongst various levels of linguistic representation it is harder to see how this might come about.

A different point (which is explicitly raised, for intance, by Di Sciullo and Williams, 1987: 63) concerns alternations in argument structure which do not seem to be the result of syntactic principles. For example, must we say that nominalizations are syntactic? Is the *-able* affix added in the syntax? A more subtle question can be asked of causativization. In many languages which distinguish adjectives from verbs syntactically, it is nonetheless possible to form a causative verb from an adjective root using the same morphology as that used to derive causative verbs from (intransitive or transitive) verb roots. Indeed, this is true to a limited extent in English (e.g. *redden*). We may even causativize nouns in some languages. Does this mean that such causatives are formed syntactically as a species of verb incorporation, or morphological merger?

One answer to some of these lexicalist objections is to bite the bullet and claim that nominalization and *-able* affixation are examples of syntactic affixation after all (as argued for instance by Fabb, 1984, Roeper, 1987, and in part Sproat, 1985a). This means a return to the kind of thinking which dominated linguistics before Chomsky's 'Remarks on nominalization'. These suggestions will be discussed in greater detail in later chapters. Likewise, one way of solving the interface problem in a lexicalist approach is to cram increasingly more syntactic relationships and dependencies into lexical representations. Williams (1985, 1987) represents a step in this direction.

On the other hand we might seek a compromise by revising some of our assumptions about the architecture of linguistic theory and thereby trying to have our cake and eat it. That is, we might develop theories of syntax and morphology which are relatively autonomous and which can thus separately explain phenomena proper to the separate domains, but which are permitted to interact in well-defined and appropriately restricted ways to give just the degree of typological variety in morphosyntactic systems that we observe in the world's languages. To a certain extent this is adumbrated in Baker's approach (especially his 1988b paper), and it is certainly implicit to some degree in Marantz's model. In chapter 11 I shall be reviewing more specific proposals from other authors along these lines.

EXERCISES

7.1   Russian reflexives. Morphologically reflexive verbs end in *-sja/s'*. In the sentences below are a variety of such verbs, together with a non-reflexive congener, where it exists. Using the translations provided, classify the morphological reflexives as far as possible using the categories of §7.1. [Hint: with some verbs the reflexive element is determined purely lexically, and not grammatically.]

celovat':
: Služanka celovala detej.
  servant kissed children
  'The servant kissed the children.'

celovat'sja:
: Deti celovalis'.
  'The children kissed (each other).'

gret':
: Služanka greet sup.
  Servant heats soup
  'The servant is heating up the soup.'

gret'sja:
: Sup greetsja služankoj.
  soup heat by-servant
  'The soup is being heated up by the servant.'
  Služanka greetsja na sol'nce.
  servant heat on sun
  'The servant is basking in the sunshine.'

imet':
: Ivan imeet mašinu.
  Ivan has   car
  'Ivan has a car.'

imet'sja:
: V mašine imeetsja radio.
  In car there-is radio
  'In the car there is a radio.'

kusat':
: Sobaka kusaet rebënka.
  dog   bite   child
  'The dog is biting the child.'

kusat'sja:
: Eti   sobaki kusajutsja.
  these dogs   bite
  'These dogs bite', or 'These dogs are biting each other.'

	Ostorožno! Eta sobaka kusaetsja.
	'Look out! This dog bites.'
myt':	Služanka moet detej.
	servant washes children
	'The servant is washing the children.'
myt'sja:	Deti mojutsja mylom.
	children wash by-soap
	'The children are being washed with soap.'
	Deti mojutsja.
	'The children are washing.'
naxmurit':	Ivan naxmuril brovi.
	Ivan knit brows
	'Ivan knitted his brows.'
naxmurit'sja:	Ivan naxmurilsja.
	'Ivan frowned.'
ostanavlivat':	Voditel' ostanavlivaet mašinu.
	driver stops car
	'The driver is stopping the car.'
ostanavlivat'sja:	Mašina ostanavlivaetsja.
	'The car is stopping.'
	Mašina ostanavlivaetsja milicionerom.
	car stop by-policeman
	'The car is being stopped by a policeman.'
otkryvat':	Ivan otkryvaet dver'.
	Ivan open door
	'Ivan is opening the door.'
otkryt'sja:	Dver' otkryvaetsja.
	door open
	'The door is opening.'
	Dver' otkryvaetsja milicionerom.
	door open by-policeman
	'The door is being opened by a policeman.'
potupit':	Služanka potupila golovu.
	servant lowered head
	'The servant lowered her head.'
potupit'sja:	Služanka potupilas'.
	'The servant lowered her head, looked down.'
pričёsyvat':	Služanka pričёsyvaet rebёnka.
	servant comb child
	'The servant is combing the child's hair.'
pričesyvat'sja:	Služanka pričёsyvaetsja.
	'The servant is combing her (own) hair.'
prodolžat':	Ivan prodolžal lekciju.
	Ivan continued lecture
	'Ivan continued the lecture.'
prodolžat'sja:	Lekcija prodolžalas'.
	'The lecture continued.'

prosnut'sja:	Ivan prosnulsja.
	'Ivan awoke.'
spat':	Ivan spit.
	Ivan sleeps
	'Ivan is asleep.'
spat'sja:	Ivanu ne spitsja.
	to-Ivan not sleeps
	'Ivan can't get to sleep.'
xotet':	Ivan xotel est'.
	Ivan wanted eat
	'Ivan wanted to eat.'
xotet'sja:	Ivanu xotelos' est'
	to-Ivan wanted eat
	'Ivan felt like eating.'
videt':	Oni redko vidjat Ivana.
	they seldom see Ivan
	'They seldom see Ivan.'
videt'sja:	Oni redko vidjatsja.
	'They seldom see each other.'
vraščat':	Inženery vraščali kolesa.
	engineers rotated wheels
	'The engineers rotated the wheels.'
vraščat'sja:	Kolesa vrasščalis' inženerami.
	wheels rotated by-engineers
	'The wheels were rotated by the engineers.'
	Kolesa vraščalis'.
	'The wheels rotated.'
vstrečat':	Služanka vstrečala Ivana v gorode.
	servant met Ivan in town
	'The servant used to bump into Ivan in town.'
vstrečat'sja:	Služanka vstrečalas' s Ivanom v gorode.
	servant met with Ivan in town
	'The servant used to meet up with Ivan in town.'
zadumyvat':	Ivan zadumyvaet poexat' na jug.
	Ivan think travel to south
	'Ivan is thinking of going south.'
zadumyvat'sja:	Ivan zadumyvaetsja o buduščem.
	Ivan think about future
	'Ivan is thinking about the future.'

7.2   Marantz does not report cases of applied constructions in which merger applies at s structure. What would such a construction look like schematically? How would such a construction differ from that of Chi-Mwi:ni?

7.3   Take Baker's analysis of causatives and explain exactly how it accounts for the differences between monoclausal and biclausal causatives discussed in §7.3. Does the analysis explain all the differences?

7.4   Explain exactly what a type (i) passive would look like (§7.4.5).

★**7.5**   Baker (1988a: 78) claims that synthetic compounds (see chapter 8, §8.3) are formed lexically and not syntactically. What additional assumptions would Baker have to make in order to provide an incorporation-based account of synthetic compounds from (i) actor nominalizations (ii) process nominalizations (iii) passive participles?

8

Compounds

Introduction

In this chapter we will be looking at proposals that have been offered to acccount for the phenomenon of compounding. We'll begin §8.1 by briefly overviewing the more familiar types of compounding processes which tend to be most discussed in the literature. This will lead us to an in-depth survey of Turkish compounding.

Much of the theoretical work concerning compound formation has been based on English, and so this is where most of the rest of our data will come from. While this gives an often misleading bias, it has the virtue of allowing us to concentrate on a descriptively well understood area. There are two sorts of compounding which have been the subject of recent debate. The first of these, primary or root compounding, is the subject of §8.2, while the second, synthetic or verbal compounding, is discussed in §8.3.

In many respects compounding represents the interface between morphology and syntax *par excellence*. This is particularly true of **synthetic compounds**. These are compounds whose head is derived by affixation from a verb, such as *truck driver*, in which *truck* appears to be an argument of the (stem) verb *drive*. Such constructions raise a number of questions concerning the morphology–syntax interface, similar to those we've already seen from our investigation of grammatical relations.

Syntax can be thought of as the concatenation of words to form phrases. Compounding, however, is prototypically the concatenation of words to form other words. However, we have often no satisfactory, unequivocal way of distinguishing between a compound word and a phrase. This means that when compounding is a freely generative process (as it usually is) we are hard put to know whether we are looking at morphology or syntax or both (or, perhaps, something else). Another way of expressing this is to say that in looking at compounding processes we are looking albeit perhaps obliquely, at the problem of how to define the notion of 'word'. For, as I mentioned in chapter 2, the existence of compound words regularly poses difficulties even when we wish merely to provide a language-particular definition of wordhood. This question will lie in the background to much of our discussion and will reappear (in a slightly different guise) in chapter 11.

8.1 Overview of compound types

8.1.1 Basic concepts

In this introductory survey, we'll see that compounds have two sets of characteristic properties. The first set makes compounding resemble syntax, the second set brings compounding closer to word formation.

Compounding resembles syntactic processes in that it is typically recursive. This was illustrated for English in chapter 2 (§2.2.2) with example 2.44 (repeated here as 8.1):

8.1   a) student film society
         b) student film society committee
         c) student film society committee scandal
         d) student film society committee scandal inquiry ...

The second point is that compounds have a constituent structure, which in general is dependent on the way the compound is built up. For instance, we can interpret 8.1a as 8.2a or as 8.2b according to whether we assign it the bracketing of 8.3a or 8.3b:

8.2   a) film society for students
         b) society for student films

8.3   a) [student [film society]]
         b) [[student film] society]

Again, many would claim that affixation has this property, too, but as we saw in §6.1.3, this claim is controversial, and there is little independent evidence for assigning anything other than 'flat', non-hierarchical structures to affixed words. Note that the bracketings in 8.3 are assigned on the basis of meaning. This is possible because the semantic interpretation of each reading is compositional. This is typical of sentences, but not so typical of words, as we've seen in the various 'deviations' from strict agglutination already encountered.

A third aspect of compounding reminiscent of syntax is that the elements of a compound may have relations to each other which resemble the relations holding between the constituents of a sentence. The three important relations are head-modifier, predicate-argument, and apposition.

In **endocentric** compounds one element functions as the head. This is true of 8.1, in which *society* is the head on both interpretations. (A (student) film society is a type of society). Most English compounds are of this type. The modifier element of a compound has the function of attributing a property to the head, much like the function of an attributive adjective. For this reason many linguistic novices confronted with such compounds mistakenly label the first member as an adjective, even though formally it is a noun.

Not all compounds are endocentric. A compound which lacks a head is called **exocentric**. Such compounds are sometimes called **bahuvrihi** compounds, a term used by Sanskrit grammarians, which literally means '(having) much rice'. Examples in English are not common; many of those that do exist are (predominantly) pejorative terms referring to people, such as *pickpocket, lazybones, cut-throat*. In these compounds we can isolate a predicate-type element (*pick, lazy, cut*) and an argument-type element (*pocket, bones, throat*). However, neither element can be called the head of the construction.

Predicate-argument relations can be observed in endocentric compounds, too. The most important case is that of synthetic compounds, which we'll be discussing in great detail. Thus, a *truck driver* is someone who drives a truck, so *driver* is the head of the compound, which is therefore endocentric. However, the non-head, *truck*, functions as a kind of direct object to *driver* (or *drive*).

Finally, it is possible for a compound to be a simple conjunction of two elements, without any further dependency holding between them. The Sanskrit term **dvandva** (literally 'two-and-two', meaning 'pair') is used to describe these. Examples in English are *Austria-Hungary, mother–child* (as in 'mother–child relationship') and, perhaps, *learner-driver* (though some would regard this latter as a member of a further subclass of **appositional compounds**). We can liken such compounds to syntactic phrases of the type *Mr Bun, the baker*.

In different languages we find differences in the types of categories that can be compounded. Some languages (e.g. English) permit a great variety of noun-headed compounds but also allow compounds headed by adjectives or (to some extent) verbs. Other languages may only allow, say, noun-noun compounds, while yet others permit a greater range than English. We have already seen in chapter 7 how compounds can be headed by finite verbs in incorporating languages. When a verb incorporates its object or particular types of adverbial modifier we get the equivalent of a tensed synthetic compound.

In a number of languages (particularly those of the Far East) we encounter very rich systems of compound in which there appear to be a variety of endocentric, exocentric and appositional compound types. Vietnamese provides especially good examples (Thompson, 1965, is a standard source for this language). In 8.4 we see compound verbs formed from a verb and its complement, akin to a synthetic compound:

8.4   a) lấy vợ   'marry' (> 'take + wife')
           b) làm việc   'work' (> 'do + work')

In 8.5 we see examples of agentives with the formative *nhà* (meaning roughly 'person' in this context):

8.5   a) nhà địa lý   'geographer'
           b) nhà lịch sử   'historian'
           c) nhà khoa học   'scholar'

In 8.5 *địa lý* and *lịch sử* are themselves compounds meaning 'geography' and 'history', while *khoa học* is a compound of 'subject + teacher'. Both these types of compound appear to be left headed. Anderson (1985a) describes a very similar situation in Mandarin Chinese. Left-headed compounds violate Williams's Righthand Head Rule (§6.1.2). Interestingly, however, the Vietnamese compounds all seem to have the structure of syntactic phrases. The question therefore arises as to whether these represent the same kind of morphological process as that of English compounding. Arguably, what we have here is lexicalization of phrases (akin to English *Jack-in-a-box* or *forget-me-not*) rather than true compounding.

Interesting light is thrown on this question by the Romance languages. The French 'compounding' system, for instance, seems to be in near-complementary distribution with the compounding system of English. There are two main types of construction. One is formed from syntactic phrases (complete with function words, and inflected lexical items) such as *les hors d'oeuvre* 'hors d'oeuvre', *le cessez-le-feu* 'ceasefire' ('cease-the-fire'), *la mise-au-point* 'focus' ('putting-in-focus'). The second type consists of a verb followed by its object: *le porte-parole* 'spokesman' ('carries-word'), *le pince-nez* 'pince-nez' ('pinches-nose'). Both these types are highly marginal in English. On the other hand, the only type of Noun-Noun compound which occurs in French with any frequency is the appositional type, e.g. *homme-grenouille* 'frogman' ('man-frog'). The appositional nature of this type is evident from the fact that the plural is *hommes-grenouilles* ('men-frogs'), with both parts inflected. Again, we have a system which looks more like the lexicalization of syntax than a specific, morphological, compounding process. This has been argued for explicitly by Di Sciullo and Williams (1987) (see §11.1).

The head-modifier, predicate-argument and appositional relations together with constituent structure all tend to align compounding with syntax. However, compounds also have a number of features which make them resemble words, as we saw in chapter 2. First, compounds are often lexicalized. They are then often subject to semantic drift of a kind associated with stored words, which means that their meaning becomes non-compositional or even totally idiosyncratic. For instance, the term *penknife* no longer has any real link to pens though originally it meant the knife used for cutting quills. This type of drift is characteristic of all types of compounding, including Noun Incorporation. In a related fashion there are often lexical restrictions on which compounds are permitted, resulting in 'paradigmatic gaps' which resemble those found in derivational or inflectional affixation. For instance, in English we can speak of *rainfall* and *snowfall*. However, we can't say *hailfall* or *sleetfall*.

A further property which links compounds with the words is that of non-referentiality. If we look at the non-heads of the compounds illustrated so far, we find that they never refer to specific objects. For instance, neither *student* nor *film* in *student film society* serve to pick out any specific student or film. This is why these non-heads can be used attributively. In this respect, constituents of compounds differ from constituents of sentences. Related to this is the fact that non-heads of compounds typically fail to be inflected. Thus, neither an ex-pickpocket nor any of his earlier victims could be called a *pickedpocket*. In this respect, (true) compounds differ from true syntactic phrases. To be sure, there do exist cases in which compounds are internally inflected in English, such as *teethmarks* and *systems analyst*. However, these inflections can't generally be used to signal syntactic relationships such as subject–verb agreement outside the compound, and even inflected elements cease to be referential inside compounds. Kiparsky (1982a) used this to argue that *systems analyst* doesn't constitute a violation of level ordering, in that the plural form is in some sense lexical. .

One property of words which distinguishes them from phrases is morphological integrity: their elements can't be split up by other words or phrases, for example, by parentheticals. This is generally true of the constituents of compounds.

It is not uncommon for elements of compounds to become so frequently used and for the compounds they form to become so lexicalized that the element loses its status as an independent word and becomes a clitic or an affix. For instance, nominal case endings often start life as postpositions. Likewise, it is the frequent fate of adverbial or prepositional modifiers to get attached to the beginning of nouns or verbs, and develop into prefixes. For instance, in Russian it is not uncommon for a verb of motion to have a prefix which is homophonous with the preposition accompanying its locative complement, as seen in example 8.6:

8.6   ložit' 'to put'
       Ja založil ruki za spinu.
       I put arms behind back
       'I folded my arms behind my back.'

These prefixes have also acquired completely idiosyncratic meaning far removed from their original prepositional sources, as a result of becoming verbal prefixes. For instance, *za* as a preposition has a variety of meanings, including 'behind, beyond', 'after', 'because of', 'on behalf of'. As a prefix it has the meaning of 'behind' with some verbs (as seen in 8.6) but also conveys the meaning of inception, preparatory activity, wrapping up, and doing to excess, and it can also be used to mark the purely grammatical category of perfective aspect. None of these uses has any clear relation to the prepositional meanings.

Finally, there are often phonological processes that apply to compounds but not to phrases. A well-known example of this comes from English, where we have the Nuclear Stress Rule (of SPE) which places main stress on the rightmost constituent of a syntactic phrase, and the Compound Stress Rule which stresses the left member of a compound (see below, §8.2). In other languages there are often sets of sandhi rules which apply to compounds and to no other type of word formation or syntactic construction. Mohanan (1986) discusses such phenomena in Malayalam.

8.1.2 Compounding in Turkish

Turkish[1] has a particularly rich and informative system of compounding. My description follows that of Lewis (1967) (with additional data from Lewis, 1953).

First, we consider simple concatenations of words. These tend to be lexicalized. As we will see there is a somewhat different construction corresponding to English free compounding. The following types of compound are found: N N, A N, N A, N V, V V. I have written each element separately to facilitate analysis, though most of these would be written as one word in the official orthography.

Noun + Noun:
8.7   baş bakan   'head', 'minister' = 'Prime Minister'

| 8.8 | orta okul | 'middle school' |

Adjective + Noun:

| 8.9 | büyük anne | 'great', 'mother' = 'grandmother' |

| 8.10 | kırk ayak | 'forty', 'foot' = 'centipede' |

Noun + Adjective:

| 8.11 | süt beyaz | 'milk white' |

| 8.12 | el-i açık | 'his-hand', 'open' = 'generous' |

Noun + Verb (including participles):

| 8.13 | dal bastı | 'branch', 'it pressed' = 'fine and large (of cherries)' |

| 8.14 | yurt sever | 'land', 'loving' = 'patriot' |

Onomatopoeic word + Verb:

| 8.15 | şıp sevdi | 'plop!', 'he-has-fallen-in-love' = 'impressionable' |

Verb + Verb:

| 8.16 | vurdum duymaz | 'I hit', 'it-doesn't-feel' = 'thick-skinned' |

Phonologically, these compounds behave like single words, in that they have a single stress (though they violate vowel harmony, as is common with Ural-Altaic compounding). Other indications that these are lexical formations are that they often have non-compositional, sometimes idiosyncratic, meanings, and their components are non-referential. This type of compounding doesn't seem to be productive in Turkish.

A much more characteristic construction, the **izafet** construction, is found in Turkish, which more closely corresponds to English compounding. In Turkish, at least, the izafet is signalled by possessive affixes. Recall from chapter 1 (examples 1.42–1.43) that Turkish has two ways of realizing possession. In the first the possessor is put into the genitive case (cf. *Tom's brother* or *the brother of Tom*), while in the second the possessum (i.e. 'thing possessed') takes possessive agreement markers coreferencing the possessor for person and number (i.e. 'Tom his-hat'). The genitive suffix is *-In* (after consonants) or *-nIn* (after vowels), and the 3rd sg. possessive suffix is *-I* (after consonants) or *-sI* (after vowels).

There are two types of izafet, the *indefinite* and the *definite*. The indefinite takes the form Noun + Noun-poss ('Tom his-hat'). It frequently corresponds to an English compound (as in 8.17a–d). (The possessive affix is separated by a hyphen for clarity):

8.17	a) yatak oda-sı
	bed its-room
	'bedroom'

b) kılıç balığ-ı
   sword its-fish
   'swordfish'
c) 2000 sene-si
   2000 its-year
   'the year 2000'
d) İngiliz tarih-i
   Englishman his-history
   'English history'

Despite the literal glosses in these examples, it's obvious that the relation between the elements of these constructions can't sensibly be called that of 'possession'. Rather, the possessive affix simply marks some sort of attributive relation between the head and the modifying noun, a relation which is signalled by simple concatenation in English.

The definite izafet takes the form Noun-gen. + Noun-poss. ('of-Tom his-hat'). This construction generally corresponds to the English 'Noun's Noun' or 'Noun of the Noun', as in 8.18:

8.18   a) uzman-ın rapor-u
             of-expert his-report
             'the expert's report'
          b) otomobil-in tekerlekler-i
             of-car its-wheels
             'the wheels of the car'
          c) hafta-nın günler-i
             of-week its-days
             'the days of the week'

The attribute-head structure of the indefinite izafet can be seen particularly clearly from the following set of minimal pairs.

8.19   a) Orhan ism-i
             Orhan its-name
             'the name "Orhan"'
          b) Orhan-ın ism-i
             of-Orhan his-name
             'Orhan's name'

8.20   a) Atatürk Bulvar-ı
             Ataturk his-boulevard
             'Ataturk Boulevard'
          b) Atatürk-ün ev-i
             of-Ataturk his-house
             'Ataturk's house'

8.21　　a) çoban kız-ı
　　　　　shepherd his-girl/daughter
　　　　　'the shepherd girl'
　　　　b) çoban-ın kız-ı
　　　　　of-shepherd his-daughter
　　　　　'the sheperd's daughter'

8.22　　a) ordu subaylar-ı
　　　　　army its-officers
　　　　　'army officers'
　　　　b) ordu-nun subaylar-ı
　　　　　of-army its-officers
　　　　　'the officers of the army'

It's clear that the first element in the (b) examples is being used referentially, while in the (a) examples it's being used non-referentially.

There are several respects in which the indefinite izafet resembles an English compound while the definite izafet resembles a genitive NP construction. First, a number of indefinite izafets have become lexicalized ('frozen'):

8.23　　a) binbaşı　　(>bin baş)
　　　　　(army) major (lit. 'thousand its-head')
　　　　b) denizaltı　　(>deniz alt)
　　　　　submarine (lit. 'sea its-underside')
　　　　c) hanımeli　　(>hanım el)
　　　　　honeysuckle (lit. 'lady her-hand')

One of the reasons we know these are lexicalized is because the possessive affix no longer behaves like a proper affix. For example, it can be followed by the plural *-lEr*, which normally precedes the possessive affixes, as in *binbaşılar* 'majors'. Moreover, unlike a genuine izafet (definite or indefinite) the word for 'major' can take an extra possessive in the expression for 'his major', *binbaşı-sı*.

Second, the head of an indefinite izafet can't be modified syntactically. If the head does get modified, say by an adjective, then the non-head noun must go into the genitive and form a definite izafet:

8.24　　a) İstanbul camiler-i
　　　　　Istanbul its-mosques
　　　　　'Istanbul mosques'
　　　　b) İstanbul-un tarihi camiler-i
　　　　　of-Istanbul historic its-mosques
　　　　　'Istanbul's historic mosques'
　　　　　(cf. English *Istanbul historic mosques*)

However, we can form an indefinite izafet if the head is a compound noun:

8.25　　Türkiye Büyükelçisi
　　　　Turkey its-great-envoy
　　　　'the Turkish ambassador'

What these types of case show is that the head of an indefinite izafet has to be a word level, not a phrase level, category. This distinguishes the indefinite izafet from, say, an adjectival phrase or determiner in English, which typically modify (X'-level) phrases.

The third similarity with English compounding is recursion. The indefinite izafet exhibits two sorts of recursion. In the first, we have a right-branching structure in which the noun on the left modifies the constituent to its right, giving a structure of the form [N [N... [N N-poss] ...]]. Only the rightmost noun appears in the possessive in this type of structure. This is seen in examples 8.26–8.27:

8.26   Cumhuriyet Halk Parti-si
        republic people its-party
        'Republican People's Party'

8.27   Türk Dil Kurum-u
        Turk Language its-Society
        'Turkish Language Society' (Lit.: 'Language Society of the Turk')

Unlike their English counterparts, 8.26–8.27 aren't even in principle ambiguous. They can only be interpreted as [Republican [People's Party]] and [Turkish [Language Society]], not as the Party for Republican People or the Society for the Turkish Language.

Left branching is found in the second type of recursive indefinite izafet. In this construction we have an izafet serving as the non-head of another izafet, to give a schematic structure [... [[N N-poss] N-poss] ... N-poss]. This is illustrated by 8.28, which can be contrasted with 8.27, and by a slightly more complex example, 8.29:

8.28   Türk Dil-i Dergi-si
        Turk his-language its-journal
        'Turkish Language Journal'

8.29   İstanbul Üniversite-si Edebiyat Fakülte-si Türk Edebiyat-ı Profesör-ü
        'Professor of Turkish Literature of the Faculty of Letters of the
        University of Istanbul'

The difference in constituent structure between 8.27 and 8.28 is shown in 8.30:

8.30   a)   b)

        [Türk [Dil Kurum-u]]   [[Türk Dil-i] Dergi-si]

        Turk language its-Society   Turk his-language its-journal

In effect, the possessive affix of the izafet construction is a morphological marker of a right bracket in the constituent structure.

The definite izafet exhibits recursion, to the left:

8.31   Ford-un aile-si-nin araba-sı
          of-Ford of-its-family its-car
          'Ford's family's car' or 'the car of the family of Ford'

We can also have indefinite izafets inside the definite ones. For instance, in 8.32, the indefinite izafet *aile araba-sı* 'family car' (lit. 'family its-car') has been treated as a single (compound) head noun which is possessed by the noun *Ford*:

8.32   Ford-un aile araba-sı
          of-Ford family its-car
          'the family car of Ford'

A more interesting example is found in 8.33:

8.33   Ford aile-si-nin araba-sı
          Ford of-its-family its-car
          'the car of the Ford family' or 'the Ford family's car'

An illustration of most of these facts is provided by example 8.34:

8.34   Bohemya Kırallar-ı saray-ı-nın yeni sakin-i
          Bohemia its-kings of-its-palace new its-inhabitant
          'the new inhabitant of the palace of the Kings of Bohemia'

Given that the izafet is based on a possessive construction reminiscent of the English 'Tom's hat' or 'the hat of Tom', we might expect it to behave essentially like a syntactically formed phrasal construction. However, it is apparent that this is true only of the definite izafet. The indefinite izafet is much closer to a Germanic-type rightbranching compound. The non-head loses its referentiality and becomes simply a modifier of the head, losing at the same time many of its syntactic properties. Moreover, the non-head may only be a word or another indefinite izafet, suggesting that the indefinite izafet itself is a word level category. The fact that the non-head of an indefinite izafet may only modify a lexical noun, and not a phrase consisting of adjective phrase and noun, as shown by 8.24, follows then from the fact that we can't have phrases inside words (including compound words).

The definite izafet, on the other hand, looks much more like a phrase, with the possessor NP behaving essentially like the NP possessive determiner marked by 's in English. These facts are summarized in 8.35, which shows schematically the structure of 8.24, examples of indefinite and definite izafet respectively.

8.35   a)   b)

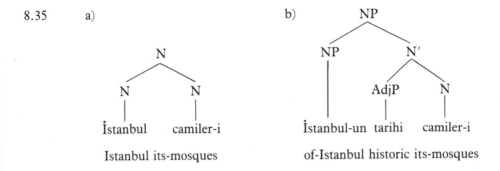

8.2 Root compounds

The bulk of theoretical discussion of compounding has taken English compounding
as its empirical basis. In 8.36 I list a selection of basic claims and assumptions about
English compounding that have influenced research. Not all researchers have
accepted these, and some of them are oversimplifications (or straightforwardly false):

8.36   a) Compounds are formed from concatenated words, e.g. *houseboat*.
        b) Compounds are formed from concatenated (bound) stems, e.g. *erythro-
           cyte*.
        c) (Endocentric) compounds are always rightheaded.
        d) Compounds do not include phrases, e.g. *black-as-coal bird*, *slightly-
           used-car salesman*.
        e) Only irregular inflection is found within compounds, e.g. *teeth-marks*
           but *nails-marks*.
        f) Minor categories (function words) are not compounded.
        g) All major categories participate in compounding though prepositions
           do not head compounds.
        h) Compounds may be either primary (root) or synthetic (verbal).
           Primary compounds are simply concatenated words (e.g. *houseboat*),
           synthetic compounds are formed from deverbal heads and the non-
           head fulfils the function of the argument of the verb from which the
           head is derived (e.g. *truck driver* 'one who drives a truck').

   In this subsection I shall only consider claims 8.36a–g, restricting the discussion
to root or primary compounds. These are, in one sense, easy to account for, since
all we need is a grammatical device which concatenates words (and possibly roots).
Linguists seem agreed that such compounds are directly generated in the base and
not constructed out of structurally distinct underlying forms by means of syntactic
rules. However, despite this apparent straightforwardness, primary compounding
conceals a number of interesting problems.
   A major difficulty is in distinguishing compounds from other concatenations, i.e.
from syntactic phrases. The standard assumption is that a true compound of two
elements is stressed on the first constituent (cf. SPE's Compound Stress Rule, CSR)
while a phrase is stressed on the last (major) constituent. Hence, we have *bláckbird*,
but *bláck bírd*. In more complex compounds of the form [A [B C]] we find that the

second constituent is stressed and that the stress falls on B. Hence, we have 8.37 in contrast with 8.38:

8.37   [student [fílm committee]]

8.38   [[fílm committee] chairman] .

Thus, stress will indicate constituent structure and can even disambiguate potentially ambiguous strings. For instance, given the above rule, a structure such as 8.39a will be stressed as in 8.39b, while a structure such as 8.40a will be stressed as in 8.40b:

8.39   a)

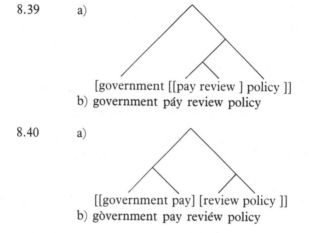

[government [[pay review] policy]]
b) government páy review policy

8.40   a)

[[government pay] [review policy]]
b) gòvernment pay revíew policy

Sure enough, 8.39b means 'government policy for reviewing pay', while 8.40b means 'policy for reviewing government pay'.

   This characterization encounters a number of unsolved problems (some of which are reviewed by Bauer, 1983). For instance, some expressions take compound stress while others, apparently identical in structure, take phrasal stress. The most notorious of these are street names: compounds with *Street* have compound stress while those with any other name (*Avenue, Road, ...*) take phrasal stress (*Fòrty-Sécond Street* vs. *Fifth Ávenue, Òld Kent Róad, Hỳde Park Córner*). This is not restricted to public thoroughfares: we have *tráde wars, Ópium wars* and the *séx war*, but the *Hùndred Years Wár* and the *Sècond World Wár*.

   Claim 8.36a is uncontroversial. However, not all accept claim 8.36b, concerning what are often called **neo-classical compounds** (or *non-native compounds*). In particular, free compounding of bound stems seems incompatible with the more obvious interpretations of world based morphology. Scalise (1984: 72ff) discusses this point in some detail.

   In the psg theories of Selkirk and of Williams there is a category below that of Word in the grammar which corresponds to these bound roots/stems. In the system of Di Sciullo and Williams (1987) we can generate a compound of the form [Word Word], with each Word node rewritten as Stem, as shown in 8.41a. Selkirk (1982: 98ff) chooses (tentatively) to designate the stem, which she calls Root, as a recursive category, the introduces a ps rule, Root → Root Root to account for *erythrocyte*, giving us 8.41b:

8.41

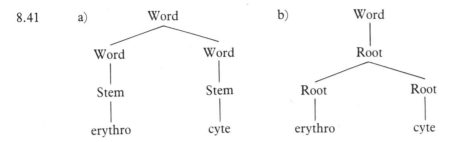

Claim 8.34c is Williams's Righthand Head Rule for compounds. This appears to be valid for English, though whether it is universally true depends largely on how we analyse compounds which mimic syntactic structure, such as the Vietnamese and French constructions discussed above. It's worth considering the possibility that all regular left-headed compounding is in reality the lexicalization of syntactic structures, and not a morphological process at all.

Claim 8.34d has been widely accepted as true for English, though it is not difficult to think of counterexamples. The famously ambiguous *American history teacher* is a case in point. Lieber (1988) draws far-reaching conclusions on the basis of examples such as *car-of-the-month competition* and *why-does-it-always-have-to-happen-to-me air*. In languages such as Dutch, compounding with phrases seems to be perfectly productive (see Botha, 1983, on Afrikaans). Botha dubbed the restriction the 'No Phrase Constraint'. Hoeksema (1986) points out that this expression violates the constraint it names!

Claim 8.34e is counterexemplified by cases such as *systems analyst*. These have motivated the introduction of a 'loop' in Lexical Phonology (§4.3.2). The psg approaches aren't troubled by such facts, which are only problematic for theories which accept the Extended Level Ordering Hypothesis.

The facts of English relating to points 8.36f, g are conveniently summarized in Selkirk (1982: 14ff). First, it is evident that only the major lexical categories, N(oun), V(erb), A(djective) and P(reposition), are productively involved in word formation. (Adverbs can be regarded as lexically equivalent to Adjectives.) Second, not all possible configurations of these categories are attested. I shall give examples both of clearly lexicalized compounds ((a) examples) and also of more-or-less compositionally formed compounds ((b) examples) where possible.

Nouns are the most productive class of possible heads, compounding with N, A, P and, rather unwillingly, with V.[2]

8.42   N N
a) housewife, penknife, dressing gown
b) salad dressing, party frock, shopping list
A N
a) blackbird, bighead, well-wisher, happy hour
b) postal order, nervous system, medical officer
P N
a) overcoat, outhouse, inroad
b) down trend, underpass
V N
swearwood, rattlesnake

Adjectives also head compounds with N, A, P, but not with V. It is particularly difficult to think of A A compounds with compound (initial) stress:

8.43   N A
a) trigger-happy, world-weary, bird-brained, earth-shattering
b) water soluble, girl crazy, class conscious
A A
a) rough-cut, well-formed, good-looking, worldly-wise
b) icy cold, bright pink, dark blue
P A
a) off-white, ongoing, inborn
b) over-explicit, underripe

8.44   P V
a) offload, overlook, up-stage
b) overfeed, underexploit, overcook

In considering this list we must be careful to distinguish genuine compounds, formed by concatenating two words, from apparent compounds such as *babysit*, *air-condition*, and *bartend*. These are backformations, and this represents a rather different source of word formation from regular concatenation. Selkirk argues, quite reasonably, that the very productive class of Verb + Particle nouns of the form *push up*, *turn off*, *blow out*, *come on* are derived by zero-formation or morphological conversion.

There are a number of purely empirical difficulties even at this stage of analysis. Since many words appear in homophonous noun-verb pairs it is not always possible to be sure which category a word belongs to. Thus, although *swearword* seems to be a V N compound, what about *password*: is *pass* an N or V? Also, it can be difficult to know whether we are dealing with a compound or a phrase when the structure of both is similar, as is the case with A N compounds.

A further problem concerns the generality of the patterns observed. For instance, although there are quite a few P V compound verbs, and although it is fairly obvious that some of these formations are productive (especially the *over-* and *under-* compounds), how do we account for the fact that only a small number of prepositions form compounds, and that some (e.g. *from*, *at*, *of*) never do? In general, the problem of productivity (in its various senses) is not raised in the theoretical discussions of root compounds, though it would appear to have a bearing on whether compounding patterns should be accounted for simply by a psg or by some other device (e.g. subcategorization frames for those words or roots which enter into compounds, or some kind of lexical redundancy rule approach for cases of non-productive lexicalized compounds).

It remains for us to see how the patterns of root compound given in 8.42–8.44 can be generated on the theories discussed in chapter 6. There are two approaches which have received particular attention in the theoretical literature, the psg approach exemplified by Williams and Selkirk (which I shall conflate here in favour of Selkirk's exposition), and the feature percolation theory of Lieber. We start with Selkirk's theory.

Selkirk (1982: 16) proposes the psg given in 8.45:

8.45   a) N → {N, A, V, P} N
        b) A → {N, A, P} A
        c) V → P V

This generates the desired structures directly. There are still some puzzles, for instance, 'bracketing paradoxes' such as *bird-brained*. This is a problem in that it seems to be derived by idiosyncratic affixation to the N N compound *bird brain*. (There is no verb *to brain* meaning 'to possess a brain' from which the past participle could be derived.) Selkirk adverts to Williams's (1981a) theory of lexical relatedness to account for such cases. (I provide my own solution in chapter 10.) The fact that compounds emerge as right-headed is a stipulated property of the rule system as Selkirk presents it (though in principle she could appeal to a general principle like Williams's Righthand Head Rule).

Lieber's three Percolation Conventions, discussed in §6.2.2, are insufficient to label the trees of compounds. For this reason she introduces a fourth convention:

8.46   Feature Percolation Convention IV
        In compound words in English features from the righthand stem are percolated up to the branching node dominating the stems.

We can label the trees associated with a compound such as *blackbird* in the following way. FPC I labels the non-branching nodes, as in 8.47a. Then, FPC IV labels the whole compound, guaranteeing its right-headedness, 8.47b:

8.47   a)   b)

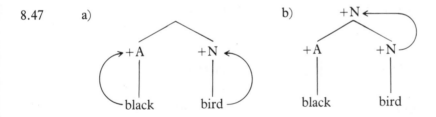

Lieber argues that it is necessary to adopt a language-particular formation on the grounds that there are languages which have left-headed compounds.[3] Thus, FPC IV differs from the first three, which are universal, and it differs from Williams's Righthand Head Rule, which is also intended to be universal. A question not addressed by Lieber is how the grammar knows it is dealing with a compound. One way would be to say that FPC IV has access to the subcategorization information of the components, so that, if free morphemes are concatenated, FPC IV comes into play.

What are the lessons to be drawn from this survey? The first observation is that the descriptive machinery used to account for the facts of 8.36a–g is generally speaking just that, namely descriptive. There has been little attempt in recent generative literature, for example, to explain why prepositions can't head compounds, or why function words aren't compounded.

One particularly interesting, but largely unexplored, question is what governs the differences in root compounding between languages. For example, in Slavic languages compounding is relatively poorly developed. Thus, we don't find expressions such as *London taxi driver* translated into Russian as compounds. Instead, we would have either 8.48 or 8.49, depending on the meaning:

8.48   voditel' taksi iz Londona
         driver of-taxi from London

8.49   voditel' londonskogo taksi
         driver of-london (adj.) taxi

On the other hand, Slav languages are rich in relational adjectives, such as *london-sk-ij* in Russian, which are poorly represented in English (see §11.2). Even when we have a relational adjective we tend not to use it, often preferring a compound instead. Thus, we would talk about the *Manchester telephone system* rather than the *Mancunian telephonic system*. Given the current emphasis on language variation (or 'parametrization') in generative studies, it's surprising that the topic of variation in compounding strategies hasn't been taken up in any detail.

There have been attempts at explaining such observations as 8.36c or e. However, there is still disagreement as to whether inflection really is found inside compounds. One of the reasons for this disagreement is the lack of agreement either that there is a principled distinction between inflection and derivation, or, if there is such a distinction, how exactly it is to be drawn.

Finally, not all the root compound types found in English can properly be said to be productive. The question of what governs productivity and whether it's necessary to distinguish productive from non-productive compounding types has not been discussed extensively in the theoretical literature.

8.3   English synthetic compounds

Introduction

According to claim 8.34h, there is a significant difference between the root compounds we've just reviewed and synthetic compounds. However, there remains the difficulty of deciding what constitutes a synthetic compound. All commentators agree that expressions like *truck driver* have an interpretation as a synthetic compound, namely 'one who (regularly or habitually) drives a truck'. For some observers this is the only reading.[4] Likewise, everyone seems to concur that gerunds and participles in *-ing* form synthetic compounds (*truck driving*). Some writers (e.g. Selkirk, 1982, Sproat, 1985a) claim that other forms of nominalization represent synthetic compounds, too (e.g. *slum clearance*), though this is disputed by others (for instance, Fabb, 1984) and yet others simply ignore the question. Most observers include compounds formed on passive participles as types of synthetic compound (*hand-made*, *moth-eaten*). A minority of theorists (notably Selkirk, 1982, Roeper, 1987) would include compounds based on adjectives (*machine-readable*).

There are a number of properties shared by synthetic compounds which must be explained. If we take 8.50 as our prototypical synthetic compounds, we must explain why the verb's (direct) internal argument is satisfied by the non-head. In other words, we must explain the relationship between 8.50 and 8.51:

8.50   a) truck driver   b) truck driving

8.51   drive a truck

Likewise, for those linguists who also relate the (a) examples in 8.52–8.54, in which the non-head represents an adjunct, to the (b) examples, we must explain how a synthetic compound can take such an adjunct as non-head:

8.52   a) fast-acting   b) act fast

8.53   a) pan-fried   b) fry in a pan

8.54   a) moth-eaten   b) eaten by moths

What has to be explained here is that the non-head must be a word which could appear immediately after the verb in the corresponding verb phrase. Thus, although we can say *quick-fried* (from *fry quickly*) we can't say *quick-driver* (from *drive a truck quickly*).

Explanation of these facts must also account for the second property, namely, that it is impossible for the non-head to function as the subject of the verb: *child driver* (on the reading 'child who drives'), *girl-swimming, *weather-changing.

The third property is that the heads of such compounds (i.e. *driver, acting, fried*) **inherit** the argument structure of the verb itself. These arguments can then be expressed by PPs within the NP, as an alternative to synthetic compounding. For example, corresponding to 8.50, we can have *a driver of trucks* and *the driving of trucks*.

Finally, it is generally the case that the range of structural types of synthetic compound in a language is no different from the range of root compounds. Since many linguists believe root compounds are generated lexically this might suggest that synthetic compounding is a lexical process. On the other hand, one could argue that both synthetic and root compounding are syntactic processes (as Lieber, 1988, now does). Or we can propose that certain aspects of synthetic compound formation are lexical, while other aspects are the result of syntactic processes.

Restricting ourselves to 'core' cases of synthetic compounding, there are a number of ways to go about accounting for the first three properties. One dimension along which accounts have differed is how they define 'complement of a transitive verb'. The possibilities have included appeal to strict subcategorization frames, direct references to grammatical relations, and appeal to operations on argument structure, or θ grids (§6.1.3).

Orthogonal to this is the question of whether synthetic compounding is essentially lexical or essentially syntactic. This brings us back to the topic of the last chapter: valency and morphological structure. In a syntactic theory, the fact that the non-head serves as an argument of the verb can be accounted for by pre-existing syntactic principles (provided we ensure that the verb stem can govern its complement in the compound). All we then need do is explain how the argument structure of the verb stem can be satisfied outside the deverbal nominal in phrases like *driver of trucks*. In a lexicalist theory, in which *truck driver* is simply the concatenation of *truck* and *driver*, we have to account for argument inheritance by *driver* in the case of the compound, as well as in the case of *driver of trucks*.

8.3.1 Roeper and Siegel (1978)

The first serious attempt to account for synthetic compounds in the grammatical framework which led from Chomsky's 'Remarks on nominalization' was that of Roeper and Siegel (1978), whose article formed the basis for much subsequent debate. Their idea was that the syntactic parallel between the compound and the corresponding verb phrase should be represented directly by incorporating aspects of the syntactic structure into the lexical representation of the compound. The parallelism noted in examples 8.50–8.54 forms the basis of Roeper and Siegel's central generalization, their **First Sister Principle**:

8.55   First Sister Principle:
         All verbal compounds are formed by incorporation of a word in first sister position of the verb.

Roeper and Siegel proposed deriving 8.50 and the (a) forms of 8.52–8.54 from an underlying lexical representation which resembles the (b) forms. This can be achieved by means of a transformational rule. However, for Roeper and Siegel the synthetic compounding rule applies in the lexicon. Therefore, they needed to propose a new device, the **lexical transformation**.

The technical details of Roeper and Siegel's proposal are fairly involved. I shall simplify matters by showing the essential steps in the derivation of a compound such as *pan-fried*. There are three main operations (plus two other tidying up processes which I shall ignore). First, we affix *-en* to the verb, by a special *Affix Rule*, simultaneously creating a slot to the left of the verb which the non-head will ultimately occupy. The verb is represented as followed by a PP complement in lexical representation, even though this PP is an adjunct:

8.56   fry $[\dots [\dots]_{NP}]_{PP} \Rightarrow$
         $[[\dots] + \text{fry} + \text{-en}]\ [\dots [\dots]_{NP}]_{PP}$

The next step is *Subcategorization Insertion*, in which a word is inserted into the subcategorization slot, PP:

8.57 $[[\dots] + \text{fry} + \text{-en}]\ [\dots [\dots]_{NP}]_{PP} \Rightarrow$
         $[[\dots] + \text{fry} + \text{-en}]\ [\dots [\text{pan}]_{N}]$

Finally we need a rule to move *pan* into the compound non-head position, by the *Compound Rule*, 8.58:

8.58 $[[\dots] + \text{fry} + \text{-ed}]\ [\text{pan}]_{N} \Rightarrow$
         $[[\text{pan}]_{N} + \text{fry} + \text{-ed}]$

Almost every aspect of Roeper and Siegel's formulation was criticized (a convenient summary of some of these criticisms is found in Botha's, 1983, review). Most observers have expressed misgivings about the nature of the lexical transformations, which are a unique and powerful addition to grammatical theory, and therefore suspicious. At the empirical level, for instance, this transformational device raises the question why it is that certain compounds are not found. Thus, despite the existence of Adv V and Adj V combinations of the type *fast-acting*, *good-looking*, and *stupid-sounding*, this type of compound isn't formed productively with all verbs. That is, we don't observe *beautifully dancing*, nor can we have *good-looked* or *stupid-sounded*. Furthermore, if we can derive *pan-fried* from something resembling *fried-in-a-pan*, why can't we derive *bird-sounding* from an underlying structure similar to *sounding-like-a-bird*?

In a sense, the details of these criticisms are no longer important. The key point is that Roeper and Siegel highlighted the First Sister generalization, and also the dual nature of synthetic compounds, as partly lexical and partly syntactic.

8.3.2 Selkirk (1982)

From the lexicalist standpoint it is suspicious that Roeper and Siegel should need a battery of lexical transformations in order to construct N N or N A structures which have to be directly generated anyway for root compounds. In a theory such as Selkirk's, in which morphological structure is accounted for solely by phrase structure rules, we can account automatically for the identity of structure between synthetic and root compounds because the structures for both types are generated directly by the same set of rules. This also permits Selkirk to widen the database by including examples such as 8.59, formed from suffixes other than the three discussed by Roeper and Siegel:

8.59	Nouns	Adjectives
	slum clearance	water-repellent
	self-deception	self-destructive
	troop deployment	machine-readable
	trash removal	disease-inhibitory

In Selkirk's theory, it is only when the non-head of the compound satisfies the head's argument structure that we have a case of synthetic compounding. Roeper and Siegel's example of *pan-fried* would therefore not be considered a synthetic compound by Selkirk, given that *pan* serves as an adjunct. Moreover, provided the verb stem of the head is not obligatorily transitive, for instance, *eat*, then a compound formed from it (for instance, *tree eater*) will be ambiguous between the synthetic compound reading and a root compound reading (cf. note 4). Thus, Selkirk's nonce form, *tree eater*, can mean 'one who eats trees' where *eat* is understood transitively and gives rise to a synthetic compound. However, it can also be interpreted as a root compound, with a meaning such as, say, 'one who eats in trees' (where *eat* has to be understood intransitively).

Grammatical functions, such as subject and object, are primitive (i.e. undefined) terms in Selkirk's theory, and so they can be referred to directly. The facts of synthetic compounding can therefore be captured by rule 8.60 (1982: 32):

8.60   *Grammatical Functions in Compounds*
        Optionally, in compounds, (i) a non-head noun may be assigned any of
        the grammatical functions assigned to nominal constituents in syntactic
        structure, and (ii) a non-head adjective may be assigned any of the gram-
        matical functions assigned to adjectival constituents in syntactic structure.

To rule out compounding of subjects (*girl-swimming*), Selkirk resorts to brute force
(1982: 34) by means of 8.61 (which I shall call the *Subject Restriction*):

8.61   The SUBJ argument of a lexical item may not be satisfied in compound
        structure.

Now let's turn to the inheritance problem. Given a phrase such as 8.62, and given
that a compound like *tree eater* is (we'll suppose) ambiguous, we would expect 8.63
to be a possible compound, with a meaning such as 'one who eats pasta in trees' (the
whimsical choice of these examples is Selkirk's):

8.62   eater of pasta in trees

8.63   *tree eater of pasta

The ungrammaticality of 8.63 is a corollary of the First Sister Principle, but that
principle has no explanation for why 8.64 is also poor:

8.64   *pasta eater in trees

The generalization seems to be that, given a choice, the verb's argument will always
be satisfied inside rather than outside the compound. Since a compound is allowed
only one non-head, this means that it is impossible to form compounds on heads
derived from verbs with more than one obligatory argument, as 8.65 indicates
(though not all linguists regard 8.65a as grammatical):

8.65   a) the putting of cats in the well
        b) *cat putting (in the well)
        c) *well putting (of cats)

Selkirk's alternative to the First Sister Principle as an explanation of these facts is
her **First Order Projection Condition** (FOPC, 1982: 37):

8.66   All non-SUBJ arguments of a lexical category X_i must be satisfied within
        the first order projection of X_i.

The first order projection of a category is simply the category that immediately
dominates it, whether in word structure or in syntactic structure proper. In example
8.67 we have a violation of the FOPC:

8.67

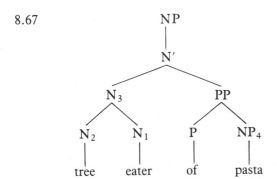

In 8.67, N_1, *eater*, has a non-SUBJ argument, which is represented by NP_4, *pasta*. However, the first order projection of N_1 is N_3 and the only other element inside this projection is N_2, *tree*, which is not the argument of *eater*. Hence, the representation is ill-formed. By contrast, in 8.68 the first order projection of N_1 is N':

8.68

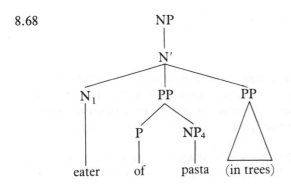

Within this projection we do indeed find the non-SUBJ argument of the deverbal noun, ('pasta'), so the construction is permitted.

8.3.3 *Lieber (1983)*

If we don't code the valency of deverbal heads in terms of subcategorization frames or by direct reference to grammatical functions, the principal alternative is to refer to the argument structure or theta grid of the verb. This is at the heart of Lieber's (1983) approach to synthetic compounding.

In 8.69 we see the constituent structure of *truck driver* analysed as a root compound. This has essentially the same structure as *village postman*:

8.69

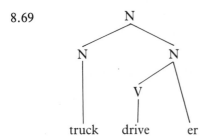

However, according to Lieber, this can't be the structure of the synthetic compound. Lieber assumes that a verb's argument structure is a kind of feature, subject to percolation. She also assumes that percolation is not possible to a dominating node of a different syntactic category. Therefore, the argument structure of the verb is unable to percolate to the N node of *driver*. Therefore, there is no way in which *truck* can receive the Theme role from *drive*: this role is 'trapped' inside the deverbal head.

In Lieber's theory, concatenation of morphological elements is constrained only by subcategorization requirements on morphemes. The *-er* suffix needs to attach to a V node, and words are freely compoundable. This means that a structure such as 8.70 will be legitimate, even though there is no source verb **to truck drive*:

8.70

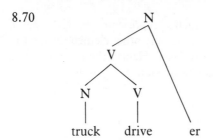

In 8.70, *drive* governs and hence assigns a theta role to its complement, so this represents the structure of the synthetic compound. Notice that this structure is an example of a bracketing paradox, because the morphophonological constituent structure is [[truck] [driver]] while the morphosyntactic constituent structure is [[truck drive] er].

In the synthetic compound, 8.70, the non-head *truck* has to be interpreted as the object of *drive*. In Lieber's theory this follows from a stipulation which she calls the **Argument Linking Principle**. This has two parts, the first of which says that, when a verb appears in a structure as sister to a potential complement, it must be able to assign ('link') all its internal arguments.

Since the distinction between root and synthetic compounds is simply due to the difference in constituent structure, the structure associated with a synthetic compound should be available to any compound formed by adding a suffix to a verb. This means that we must also find structures such as 8.71–8.72 corresponding to *strange-sounding* and *hand-woven*:

8.71   a)   b)

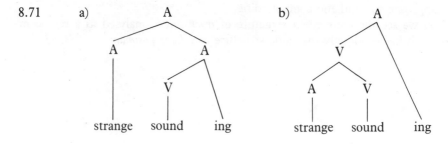

8.72   a)   b)

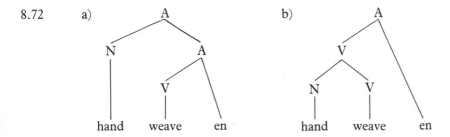

The (b) cases are synthetic compounds corresponding to the First Sister examples in which the first sister is an adjunct. In particular, *hand-woven* is exactly comparable to *pan-fried*. Lieber calls such adjuncts *semantic arguments* and accounts for them with the second part of the Argument Linking Principle. This states that in the (b) configurations of 8.71–8.72, the non-head must be a semantic argument (i.e. interpretable as Locative, Manner, Agentive, Instrumental, or Benefactive).

The putative source for *handwoven*, namely, the verb *handweave*, does, in fact, exist (it is a backformation, like *babysit*). In the active voice it is transitive, and must therefore be able to link its internal argument. Lieber says that this is possible because the compound verb will always form the head of a VP in the syntax. Hence, the argument structure of the verb will be able to percolate as far as the VP node and the internal argument will therefore be linked to the syntactic direct object of that VP, just as with any other transitive verb. The internal argument needn't therefore be satisfied within the compound itself. This is illustrated in 8.73:

8.73

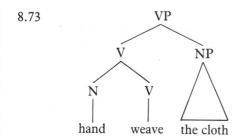

The two parts of the Argument Linking Principle capture some of the content of the First Sister Principle, in that an internal argument will be the first sister of a verb, and an adjunct with the force of a 'semantic argument' will frequently correspond to a first sister. The restriction to internal arguments has the effect of ruling out compounding of subjects (if we ignore unaccusative verbs).

However, a number of criticisms have been raised against Lieber's approach. Perhaps the most serious objection is levelled by Botha (1983) and Sproat (1985a) concerning the inheritance problem. Recall that Lieber's distinction between root and synthetic compounding hinges on the claim that percolation of argument structure is blocked by a change in category. But if this is the case, how can the argument structure percolate beyond the N node of *driver* or *eating* in expressions such as *a driver of trucks* or *the eating of pasta*? This sort of flaw makes it very difficult to accept Lieber's proposals as they stand. However, this doesn't oblige us to abandon the idea of implicating argument structure in our theory of synthetic compounding.

8.3.4 Di Sciullo and Williams (1987)

The lexicalist theory developed by Williams appeals to operations on argument structure to account for all the valency properties of verbs. Recall that Selkirk effectively split the First Sister Principle into her FOPC and the Subject Restriction. To account for FOPC violations such as *tree eating of pasta*, Di Sciullo and Williams (1987) stipulate that internal argument structure cannot pass beyond the first projection. This is effectively a restatement of Selkirk's FOPC.

The Subject Restriction is argued to be a property of predication theory as it applies to external arguments. The external argument role has to be assigned by a maximal projection, usually a VP, the typical recipient being the subject of the sentence. But maximal projections are not permitted inside compounds, so the external argument cannot be assigned there. It therefore has to be satisfied outside the compound, as when we say *Tom is a truck driver*. Here the external argument of *drive* is ultimately assigned to *Tom* (having percolated in the VP node).

Di Sciullo and Williams locate responsibility for the inheritance problem with the affixes which form synthetic compounds, namely, *-er*, *-ing*, *-en*, and presumably *-ion*, *-ance* and so on. They contrast the members of the minimal pair in 8.74:

8.74   a) baker of bread
            b) *bake-man of bread

They claim that this contrast shows that it must be some property of the suffix *-er* which permits the argument structure of *bake* to be satisfied externally to the noun by the PP *of bread*.

Technically, there are a number of ways of making the PP complement *of bread* accessible to the argument structure of *bake* in 8.74a, while denying such access in 8.74b. Among the possibilities are these: (i) the *-er* suffix is in some sense 'transparent' to the verb's internal argument and allows it to pass through; (ii) the internal role is somehow given to the suffix which then passes it on to the complement; (iii) the combination of verb stem and suffix has a composite argument structure including the internal argument of *bake* (even though *baker* is a noun and not a verb) and the Theme component of this composite can therefore be assigned to *bread* in 8.74.

The solution adopted by Di Sciullo and Williams is the third of these. First, they claim that affixes such as *-er* have their own grid, representing a 'referential' role, notated by R. Certain affixes, namely those which yield synthetic compounds, are semantically *functors*. This means that their own theta grid can act as a function taking the verb stem theta grid as a value. The result is a composite theta grid, which is a property of the whole word. A simplified representation of 8.74a will be 8.75:

8.75

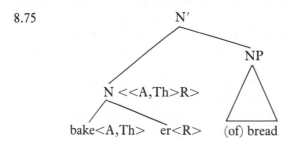

The composite theta grid for the N *baker*, $\langle\langle A, Th\rangle R\rangle$ shows that $\langle A, Th\rangle$ has become the 'value' of the theta grid $\langle R\rangle$.

A noteworthy feature of this solution to the thematic inheritance problem is that it is not, strictly speaking, the verb's argument structure which is satisfied, either in the synthetic compound or in the NP with PP complement. Rather, it is the (derived) argument structure of the deverbal nominalization *baker*. This means that the structure of the synthetic compound *bread baker* will be 8.76, in which the constituent structure implied by the phonology, viz. [bread [baker]], is also that implied by the syntax and semantics:

8.76

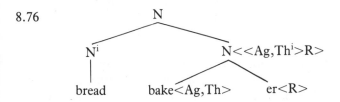

Thus, there are no bracketing paradoxes to explain and no account is owed of the non-existence of compound verbs such as *to bread-bake.

With this machinery Di Sciullo and Williams are able to maintain a strongly lexicalist approach to an apparently syntactic phenomenon, and without incurring the disadvantages of Selkirk's or Lieber's proposals. A number of aspects of their account have been criticized (e.g. by Baker, 1988c). One problem is worth noting here, since the issue will recur. Di Sciullo and Williams's arguments from examples 8.74 are intended to locate the special argument structure inheritance properties with specific morphemes. Di Sciullo and Williams only cite a single example of an ungrammatical formation, namely 8.74b. Unfortunately, this is formed from *-man* which doesn't generally attach to verbs, especially transitive ones. Hence, *bake-man* is ungrammatical with or without a complement, and so the example is irrelevant. If we look at non-agentive nominalizations we find that, as long as we have a process nominalization and not a result nominalization, then the deverbal noun always inherits its stem's argument structure, irrespective of the way the nominal is formed. In the expressions *the theft of cars* and *car theft* we see that this is true even of suppletive derivation: *theft* is the nominalization of the verb *steal*. Thus, perhaps what Di Sciullo and Williams would have to say is that it is the nominalization process itself that is associated with inheritance. If that is the case, we can't claim that inheritance is the property of an affix as such, and this may mean that the device of functional composition has to be modified.

8.3.5 Syntactic approaches

8.3.5.1 Fabb (1984)

We noted in §8.3.3 that Lieber stipulated an Argument Linking Principle which guarantees that a verb's argument structure will be satisfied inside a synthetic compound. In fact, this principle is very close in content to a principle of GB syntax, the **Theta Criterion**. For our purposes, the important part of this criterion is that if a verb has obligatory theta roles in its theta grid, then they must be assigned to an argument position. For instance, the verb *hit* is obligatorily transitive. English (unlike some languages, such as Chukchee) lacks an empty category, pro, which could appear in direct object position and receive the verb's theta role. Therefore, in a non-sentence such as *★Tom hits* we would have a verb with an obligatory (internal) theta role, but no argument position in the syntactic representation to which it could assign that theta role. This would then constitute a violation of the Theta Criterion.

In theory it would be possible to circumvent the Theta Criterion if we had syntactic rules which could change the argument structure of a verb during the derivation. However, there is another principle of GB syntax which prevents this, the Projection Principle (briefly introduced in §7.5.2). According to this principle, the theta grid of a verb is 'projected' to all syntactic levels: D-structure, S-structure and LF. Therefore, the Theta Criterion holds at these levels, too. As mentioned in chapter 7, it is widely agreed that the Projection Principle doesn't hold in the lexicon. Hence, a rule which appeared to violate the Theta Criterion would have to be lexical.

Given that the Projection Principle and Theta Criterion have essentially the same effect as Lieber's Argument Linking Principle, it is little surprise that linguists have suggested that synthetic compounds are formed in the syntax, where they will be subject to such syntactic principles. The first serious analysis along these lines was presented in Nigel Fabb's 1984 dissertation. Fabb argues that GB theory permits us to regard affixes as lexical elements on a part with stems and whole words, having their own syntactic properties. This means we can regard affixes as belonging to the X^0 level in the X-bar hierarchy as it applies to the internal syntax of words. In this he departs from Selkirk's assumption that affixes constitute their own category. Such affixes are attached by syntactic rules, and this is what we referred to in §6.3 as *syntactic affixation*. Under these assumptions, then, the claim that synthetic compounding is syntactic amounts to the claim that the affixes which regularly license synthetic compounds (e.g. *-er*, *-ing* and *-en*) are syntactic affixes.

In simplified terms Fabb claims that, in *driving of trucks* and *truck driving*, the verb stem *drive* can and must assign its internal theta role of Theme to the noun *truck(s)* in order to satisfy the Theta Criterion. Now, in order to assign a theta role to an element, a verb must *govern* that element. This essentially means that it must be a sister to the element in syntactic structure. Fabb therefore assumes structure 8.77 for the synthetic compound, i.e. the same constituent structure which Lieber proposes:

8.77

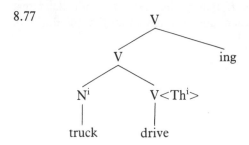

The symbol $\langle \text{Th} \rangle$ represents the verb's internal argument, which has been coindexed with the non-head of the compound, shown by the superscript.

For *driving of trucks* Fabb assumes structure 8.78:

8.78

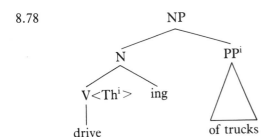

Here, the verb has to assign its theta role to a PP which is not its syntactic sister. Fabb therefore assumes that government is so defined as to permit theta role assignment in such a circumstance, provided it is within the NP. In this way, we can admit 8.78 while still ruling out, say, *Tom's driving was of trucks*.

8.3.5.2 Sproat (1985a)

Similar in its basic conception is the analysis which Richard Sproat proposed in his 1985 thesis. Restricting ourselves to the synthetic compounds for the present, he agrees that the verb is sister to the non-head noun and that we should permit the verb to associate its internal theta role to that noun. However, he assumes that it is only maximal projections, i.e. NPs, to which theta roles can genuinely be assigned. This means that the association between *truck* and *drive* in 8.77 must be something other than theta role assignment proper.

Sproat adopts Higginbotham's (1985) theory of theta roles, which I shall summarize in extremely brief outline. The first assumption is that all words, including nouns, have a theta grid. Second, verbs have not only the theta roles associated with the external and internal arguments, but also an Event theta role. Third, theta roles have to be associated with (or 'discharged to') their arguments, as in other theories, but there are three distinct ways of doing this. Two of these are of interest to us, viz.: **theta marking** and **theta identification**.

Theta marking refers to the assignment of a theta role to an argument. For example, in the VP *drives trucks* the verb assigns the Theme role to its direct object. For our purposes this is all we need say about it.

Theta identification is a way of capturing the idea that a phrase modifies the head of another phrase. A simple example would be modification of the noun *dog* by the adjective in the phrase *black dog*. Higginbotham argued that a common noun such as *dog* will have a theta role, which I shall represent simply as $\langle R \rangle$, borrowing the notation of Di Sciullo and Williams. This will be interpreted as roughly 'any member of the set of dogs' without actually referring to any such member. If we want to specify some particular dog or dogs, then we need a specifier (Spec) or determiner, such as *the* or *every*. This produces an NP which can actually refer to a particular dog or set of dogs. (Technically this is achieved by the third of Higginbotham's types of theta discharge, *theta binding*.) Adjectives, too, have a theta role. Unlike a verb, however, the adjective doesn't theta mark a complement or an external argument. The semantic interpretation of a (specifierless) phrase such as *black dog* is (roughly) 'any member both of the set of black entities and also the set of dogs'. We achieve this process of semantic modification by saying that the theta role of *black* is *identified* with that of *dog*.

The way we capture the broad semantic structure of *driving* (as in *truck driving*) is shown in 8.79–8.81:

8.79   a) DRIVE: $\langle Ag, Th, Ev \rangle$
         b) $\exists x \; \exists y \; \exists e \; drive \, (x, y, e)$

8.80   Event(z)

8.81 $z = e$ (i.e. drive(x, y, z))

Formula 8.79a is the lexical entry for the verb *drive*, where *Ev* stands for the Event role. This corresponds to the quasi-logical formula 8.79b, read as 'there is an entity x and an entity y such that there is an event e of x driving y'. The lexical entry for *-ing* is associated with the formula 8.80, representing the theta role of the affix. (In a similar fashion, the agentive affix *-er* of *driver* would have its own theta role, namely Agent(x).) Theta identification identifies the argument of 8.79 with the $\langle Ev \rangle$ argument in 8.79a to produce 8.81. We can interpret this to mean something like 'the event of x driving y'. Semantically, therefore, the nominalization refers to the actual event while the verb predicates a driving event of a driver and a thing driven.

Sproat assumes the same basic structure for synthetic compounds as Lieber and Fabb, namely 8.77. Like Fabb, but unlike Lieber, he assumes that this configuration is constructed in the syntax, not in the lexicon.[5] It must therefore submit to syntactic well-formedness principles. Taking the transitive reading of *drive*, this means that the verb must discharge its internal theta role to *truck*. If we wish to maintain a close parallelism with syntactic theta role discharge we can't say, with Fabb, that *truck* is simply assigned the verb's Theme role by theta marking. This is because syntactic theta marking is a relation between the head of a level 1 category (i.e. V') and an argument in the form of a maximal projection. A synthetic compound involves neither V' phrases nor maximal projections. However, we have an alternative form of theta discharge, namely, theta identification.

We therefore assume that the theta relation between the head *drive* and its argument *truck* is mediated by identification. This means that the sole theta role, $\langle R \rangle$, of *truck* will be identified with the $\langle Th \rangle$ role of *drive*. This makes the direct object rather like a modifier of the verb. By virtue of this identification, we then suppose that the verb's internal role can actually be discharged to the non-head noun, which therefore functions as the verb's object. This means that the Theta Criterion is satisfied, as required. The structure which results from this is shown in 8.82 (where identification is notated by $\star$ and $+$):

8.82

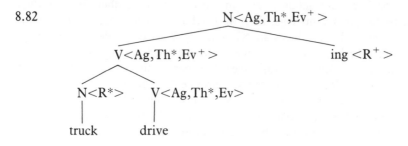

We must now turn to *the driving of trucks*, to see how Sproat deals with the inheritance problem. Under Fabb's analysis this is straightforward theta role assignment from the verb, on the assumption that the *-ing* affix can't interfere with government by the verb and hence doesn't affect the theta marking of the PP complement. Sproat, however, maintains (along with Lieber) that syntactic theta role discharge can't take place across a new syntactic category node, so that a verb stem which is part of a nominalization can't directly theta mark its complement. This means that the inheritance phenomenon isn't simply a consequence of constituent structure and independent syntactic principles.

Sproat's way of deriving inheritance is a principle called the *Cross-Categorial Theta-Grid Percolation Convention*. According to this, the theta grid of a verb is required to percolate to the next higher node when the theta grid of the verbal affix and the theta grid of the verb stem are associated by some regular process of theta discharge. In other words, when a verb stem undergoes syntactic affixation (e.g. by *-er*, *-ing* or *-en*) the theta grids of the affix and verb are identified (as in 8.81). As a consequence the derived nominal or adjective must receive the theta grid of the verb stem. So on this analysis inheritance is induced precisely by syntactic affixation.[6]

Being syntactic affixation, it must take place in the syntax. Now, it is possible to find cases in which, say, *-ing* is affixed in the lexicon. In these cases inheritance isn't observed. Thus, in a sentence such as *Harriet's cooking is tasty*, the noun *cooking* has an idiosyncratic meaning referring to the concrete results of cooking, not the fact of a cooking event. In this it differs from the eventive use in an example such as *The cooking of the lasagne took 30 minutes*. For this reason, we don't find the argument structure of *cook* projected in the first reading: **Harriet's cooking of lasagne is tasty*. Nor can we say **Harriet's lasagne cooking is tasty*, because *cooking* in this sense is formed in the lexicon by adding *-ing* to *cook*, whereas in a synthetic compound we add *-ing* to [*lasagne cook*].

Both Fabb and Sproat have succeeded in reducing part (a) of Lieber's Argument Linking Principle to the Projection Principle and the Theta Criterion (together with a revised theory of theta role discharge and feature percolation in Sproat's case). The FOPC effects are due to the fact that theta marking can only take place between sisters (or near-sisters in Fabb's theory), a universal syntactic principle. Sproat's assumptions lead him to posit a form of argument inheritance, in which the verb's argument structure percolates to the dominating N node of a nominalization, provided it is the result of regular (i.e. syntactic) affixation. In Sproat's theory the effects of compounding and syntactic affixation on argument structure are more akin to those of a modifier or attribute than to the effects of bona fide arguments.

Finally, we turn to an interesting aspect of Sproat's theory which, while not strictly central to questions of compounding and argument inheritance, has bearing on the nature of syntactic affixation.

Sproat restricts a syntactic affixation analysis to nominalizations which have a process or event reading, as opposed to, say, a resultative reading. Fabb restricted such affixation to the *-ing* suffix. However, Sproat observes that we can form event nominalizations by means of such suffixes as *-(a)tion*, *-ance*, *-ment*, or even conversion and suppletion. These nominalizations, provided they are given an eventive reading, permit the formation of synthetic compounds, despite fairly radical allomorphy. In other words, Sproat accepts Selkirk's claim that examples such as *slum clearance* or *bomb disposal* are genuine synthetic compounds (something which Fabb, for instance, explicitly denies).

If nothing else were said, we would have to postulate a long list of lexical entries, all with the same meaning, all syntactic affixes, but with different phonological forms and phonological properties. Sproat therefore assumes the existence of a single abstract nominalizing morpheme for events, NOM, whose phonological form will be a function of the lexical properties of individual stems, but whose syntax will be quite regular. He explicitly likens this situation to that of an inflectional paradigm. It is interesting that this proposal is essentially what I suggested would be needed by Di Sciullo and Williams, to get their lexicalist theory to work adequately.

Sample representations for *slum clearance*, *damage control* and *car theft* are given in 8.83:

8.83

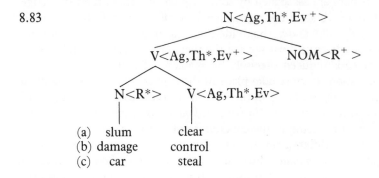

(a)	slum	clear
(b)	damage	control
(c)	car	steal

Representations such as these exacerbate the paradoxical nature of the bracketing, in that, for instance, *steal* and NOM, which have to be spelt out as *theft* by some kind of allomorphic readjustment rule, don't form a constituent.[7] This is an example of the type of problem we'll be discussing in chapter 10.

8.3.5.3   Roeper (1988)

In this subsection we have been exemplifying synthetic compounding using gerunds or *-ing* nominalizations. However, in a sense these are rather unusual constructions. As is well known, gerunds straddle the boundary between NPs and VPs, having properties of each. In 8.84, for instance, the *-ing* form of the verb combines with a possessive subject, an adjective modifier and a complement marked by *of*, all of which are characteristic of NPs. However, in 8.85, the same verb form combines with a non-possessive subject, an adverb and a complement with no special marking, just as though it were a finite verb form:

8.84   Tom's careful driving of the truck surprised us.

8.85   Tom driving the truck carefully was a welcome surprise.

Roeper (1988) argues that the gerunds which form synthetic compounds are of the verbal type. One interesting reason for this is that these compounds appear to include an empty subject position (PRO) which can be controlled by a higher NP. For instance, corresponding to 8.86 and 8.87 we can have 8.88, in which the implicit or 'understood' subject of *driving* (PRO$_i$) is interpreted as coreferential to Tom:

8.86   a) Tom likes to drive trucks.
        b) Tom$_i$ likes [PRO$_i$ to drive trucks]

8.87   a) Tom likes driving trucks.
        b) Tom$_i$ likes [PRO$_i$ driving trucks]

8.88   a) Tom likes truck driving.
        b) Tom$_i$ likes [PRO$_i$ truck driving]

One way to capture these facts is to assume that the gerunds are verb forms at D-structure and that in the syntactic derivation they undergo a rule changing them to NPs. Baker (1985b) proposed just such an analysis, arguing that the *-ing* affix is of the class N, that it is subcategorized to attach to a verb stem, and that it is generated in a non-finite Infl position. He then argued that the affix 'hopped' onto the verb stem, turning the verb into a noun. This is another example of syntactic affixation.

Baker (1985b) doesn't discuss synthetic compounding, but (in Baker, 1988a) he suggests that such compounds are formed lexically. However, Roeper proposes that Baker's analysis of Noun Incorporation should be applied to synthetic compounds (of gerunds, at least). In other words he argues that the synthetic compounds are the result of syntactic NI, moving the verb's direct object and leaving a trace which must be properly governed.[8] One of his reasons is Baker's UTAH (§7.4.2), which states that if two expressions have the same theta relationships then they are expressed by means of the same structural relationships at D-structure. Put crudely, Roeper seems to be interpreting the UTAH to mean that, since *drive trucks, the driving of trucks,* and *truck driving* all involve the same theta marking of *trucks*, they must all have the same underlying form.

The claim is, then, that the D-structure for *truck driving* is a sentence, 8.89, and that the *-ing* morpheme in Infl position is lowered onto the verb by a transformation, while the head of the object NP is incorporated by the verb, to derive 8.90:

8.89

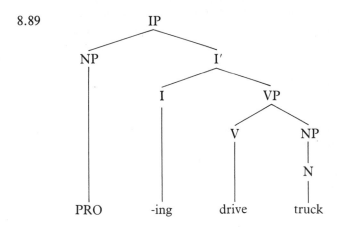

8.90

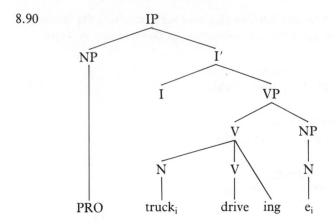

There then follows a rather drastic change, by which the VP in 8.90 is transformed into a NP, as shown in 8.91:

8.91

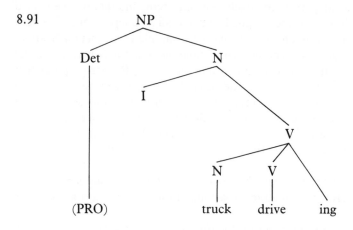

This change accounts, amongst other things, for the fact that English lacks genuine NI, and hence that we can't say *Tom truck drives for a living*. This type of category changing is essentially what is argued for by Levin and Rappaport (1986) in their analysis of adjectival passives (§7.5.3). However, for them, the change occurs in the lexicon, while Roeper argues that it can also be a syntactic phenomenon.

8.3.6 Postscript on inheritance

8.3.6.1 Roeper (1987)

Inheritance of argument structure has become an important issue in explaining the properties of synthetic compounds. We've seen various approaches to this problem, including functional composition of theta grids, and conditions for guaranteeing the percolation of argument structure. In this section I briefly discuss approaches to this question in more detail. The issue is somewhat controversial, so we will not be reaching any firm conclusions.

Roeper (1987) proposes a technical device for handling inheritance, thereby linking it with another phenomenon which has aroused a fair degree of interest, the licensing of implicit arguments. When we form a syntactic or verbal passive, we suppress the external argument of the verb. However, we don't abolish that argument entirely, for it can show up as an *implicit argument*. As we know from §7.1, such an argument can be detected in two independent ways: either it can be made explicit by means of a prepositional phrase, as in 8.92a, or it can control the null (PRO) subject of a purposive or rationale clause, as in 8.92b. Equally, of course, it can do both (8.92c):

8.92   a) The boat was sunk by its owners.
       b) The boat was sunk [PRO to collect the insurance].
       c) The boat was sunk by its owners [PRO to collect the insurance].

It is not just the passive participle which behaves in this way. Roeper argues that affixes such as *-ing*, *-er* and *-able* are also capable of licensing implicit arguments.

Many affixes are selective about what kinds of stems they attach to. The agentive *-er* creates a noun referring to an agent and only attaches to verbs which themselves bear the Agent theta role. Hence, it will attach to an unergative intransitive verb such as *swim* to give *swimmer*, but it fails to attach to an unaccusative verb such as *arrive* (*arriver). The suffix *-able* is able to take transitive verbs bearing the Agent and Theme roles and create adjectives predicated of the Theme. This sort of behaviour demands an explanation.

As with all the other accounts of inheritance we have seen, the central task is to distinguish between affixes which 'trap' the theta grid of their verb stem and prevent the verb's argument structure from being realized, and affixes which are transparent to that argument structure. Roeper distinguishes three sorts of deverbal affixation. The third type is represented solely by *-ing*, and we'll return to it in due course. The first type blocks percolation of the verb's argument structure and prevents it from assigning an internal theta role. This is illustrated by the affix *-ive* in 8.93:[9]

8.93   a) The grammar generates compounds.
       b) The grammar is generative.
       c) ⋆The grammar is generative of compounds.
       d) ⋆A compound generative grammar.

The second type of affix is that exemplified by *-er*, by nominalizations and by *-able*. Examples of the first two cases are already well known to us: *driver of trucks*, *destruction of the city*. In the case of *-able*. Roeper claims that an Agent role can be assigned to a PP to realize an implicit argument, much as in the case of passive participles (though some speakers, myself included, find the result rather strained). Thus, we might compare 8.94 with 8.95:

8.94   The game is playable by children.

8.95   The game is played by children.

How can we tie together these properties? Roeper argues that such affixes bear their own theta grid and that this grid must *match* the theta grid of the stem to which it attaches. For instance, *-er* will bear the grid ⟨Ag⟩, while *-able* will bear the grid ⟨Ag, Th⟩. By virtue of the matching requirement, *-er* will only attach to agentive verbs, and *-able* will only be affixed to transitive verbs. The affix is the head of the word and so its theta grid is free to percolate to the next node. Thus, Roeper accounts for the inheritance phenomena indirectly, by ensuring that the verb's argument structure is copied on the affixal head. From the dominating node, a theta role can be assigned to a PP complement. This is illustrated in 8.96–8.97 in which *-able* affixation is contrasted with affixation of *-ive*:

8.96

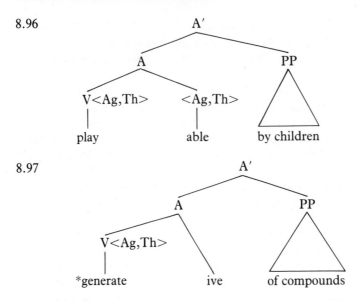

8.97

Roeper claims that percolation from the theta grid of the affix itself is the only way in which thematic inheritance ever occurs. In this way he accounts for failure of inheritance in Di Sciullo and Williams's example *bakeman of bread, though without having to appeal to a special formal mechanism such as functional composition. (Recall, however, that this case can be excluded on independent grounds.)

The third sort of affix is represented solely by the process nominalizer *-ing*. This affix has no theta grid of its own, and is thus able to affix to any verb stem, yet it inherits that of the verb to which it attaches. Thus we find *the sleeping of the dogs*, *the falling of the leaves*, *the driving of the trucks*, *the putting of books on shelves* and all the other examples with which we are now familiar. The *-ing* affix is hence the only genuine example of a 'transparent' affix. In this respect, of course, it is exactly like an inflectional affix, as in *drives/drove trucks*.

8.3.6.2   Semantically based accounts of inheritance

A number of authors have recently proposed that inheritance phenomena are the result of semantic aspects of word formation. Perhaps the proposal that comes closest to those we have seen so far is that of Booij and van Haaften (1988). (I shall follow the exposition of Booij, MS, here.) Booij distinguishes between the **Predicate-Argument Structure** (PAS) of a verb and its **Lexico-Conceptual Structure** (LCS). The PAS is essentially the verb's theta grid and as such is part of the syntactic structure of the verb. The LCS is closer to a representation of the actual meaning of the verb. A simple example will help clarify this. In 8.98–8.99 we see the LCS ((a) representations) and PAS ((b) representations) of the verb *break* in its anti-causative (intransitive) and causative (transitive) readings respectively:

8.98   a) [x BREAK]   8.99   a) [y CAUSE [x BREAK]]
        b) break: ⟨Th⟩   b) break: ⟨Ag, Th⟩

In the (b) representations we see the theta grid, with the external argument underlined, following Williams's (1981b) notation. In the (a) representations we see a variable corresponding to each of the argument positions, with the meaning of the transitive verb decomposed into a causative predicate and the basic predicate. To a certain extent the PAS representations are redundant because, knowing the LCS, we can generally predict the argument structure of the verb. For instance, all causatives have an Agent external argument. To a large extent, then, we can regard the PAS as a projection of the LCS.

According to Booij, there are no morphological operations defined over theta roles as such. At most we find rules which refer to external or internal arguments. Many of the rules which are alleged to refer to theta roles are actually rules affecting the LCS. An example is agentive *-er* affixation in English (and Dutch). Recall that one of the things we have to account for is how *-er* nominalizations such as *driver* are interpreted as Agents. For some, (e.g. Roeper, 1987, and also Sproat, 1985a) this is because the *-er* affix actually bears an Agent theta role. On Booij's analysis this is a consequence of the semantic operation induced by *-er* affixation. He claims that it has the effect of binding the subject position in the LCS. I represent this schematically in 8.100:

8.100   er: the x such that [*LCS of verb*]

For instance, the LCS of *driver* will be 8.101:

8.101   driver: the x such that [x DRIVE y]

When an argument in the LCS is bound in this way it fails to show up in the PAS. Thus, the only remaining theta role for *driver* is that of Theme.

Assuming that some affixes have the inheritance property, we can now see how most of the facts of inheritance come about. The Agent role of *drive* fails to be inherited by *driver* because that role has been bound, a semantic effect of *-er* affixation. Therefore, the only other role which can be inherited is the Theme role, as required.

Finally, where affixation has no semantic effect on the LCS of a verb, as is the case with inflections and with *-ing* nominalizations, we get inheritance of the entire LCS. Hence, we have *Tom's driving of trucks* or *the driving of trucks by Tom*, with both Agent and Theme roles expressed.

The various accounts we've reviewed in this chapter of thematic inheritance by no means exhaust all the possibilities. Nor can we be said to have come to a definitive solution. [10] In view of its importance for the nature of syntactic valency, and the all-pervading influence it has on basic word formation processes operating on verbs, we can expect this to remain an important topic of debate.

8.4   Summary and conclusions

In this chapter we've examined a variety of approaches to the phenomenon of compounding. Of great importance in recent theoretical debate has been the distinction between root compounds and synthetic compounds. Both types can be said to illustrate ways in which syntax and morphology interact. In root compounding we find the best evidence favouring constituent structure in morphology. In addition, if we agree that the result of compounding is itself a word, we have some evidence of certain types of phrases being compounded. An interesting, if rather neglected, topic is the way that modifier-head relationships are established in compounds and how these relate to modification in syntax. The data from Turkish are sufficient to show that there is much to be said about this question.

However, by far the greatest interest has been aroused by the problem of synthetic compounding and related questions of the satisfaction of argument structure in compounds and nominalizations. This currently seems to be revolving around the extent to which the behaviour of compounds is derivable from purely syntactic principles. Even within GB theory, radically different positions can be adopted. The lexicalist camp claims that compounding is a type of word formation process and hence a matter of lexical organization. The syntactic effects noted are the result of essentially morphological rules or principles permitting argument structure to be accessible outside the domain of the word itself, a limited 'leak' in the Strong Lexicalist Hypothesis. This is the tradition represented, for example, by Selkirk (1982), Lieber (1983), Di Sciullo and Williams (1987), and Booij and van Haaften (1988). At the other extreme are those who would have compound formation taking place largely or solely in the syntax, such as Fabb (1984), Roeper (1988), Sproat (1985a) and Lieber (1988). Some advocates of the syntactic approach have explicitly questioned whether there is any organization to the lexicon, beyond its function as a list of idiosyncrasies (especially Pesetsky, 1985, whose claims are examined in chapter 10, and also Sproat, 1985a). However, not all those who advocate a strongly syntactic approach to valency changing operations in general, and the kind of compounding exhibited in noun incorporation in particular, would accept this degree of radicalism (Baker, 1988a). In other words, the central 'interface' questions remain wide open and several of them will be taken up again in chapter 11.

EXERCISES

8.1   On a psg approach it is theoretically possible to generate such forms as *erythrocell*, and *cellplasm*, i.e. a mixture of words and bound stems, as well as compounds of affixed stem plus stem, such as *erythroidcyte*. Is there any evidence that this facility is required in English? If not, how could it be prevented?

8.2   In addition to *-er* affixation, agentive (actor) nominalizations can be formed in a variety of other ways in English. Using descriptive grammars or other handbooks such as those of Jespersen, Marchand or Bauer, enumerate the morphological devices found in English. Then list all the constructions in which deverbal nominalizations may satisfy their verb's argument structure. Then examine each of the agentive nominalizing devices to see to what extent they permit satisfaction of argument structure, either regularly and productively, or idiosyncratically, for certain choices of verbs.

8.3   Welsh compounds. In some compounds one or other member exhibits some kind of allomorphy involving consonants, in others there is no allomorphic change. Describe the consonantal allomorphic changes in phonological terms. What aspects of the compound govern whether or not allomorphy will be found? [ch = [x], dd = [ð], f = [v], ff = [f], ll = [ɬ], th = [θ], y = [i] or [ə], gw = [gw], otherwise, w = [w] before vowel, [u] before consonant.]

A)
gweithdy	'work house'	hirben	'shrewd'
cadeirfardd	'chaired bard'	llyfrbryf	'bookworm'
ôl-ddyddio	'to post-date'	pengam	'perverse'
llyfrwerthwr	'bookseller'	camgred	'heresy'
wyneb-ddalen	'title-page'	llawfer	'shorthand'
penwyn	'white-headed'	llawddryll	'pistol'
dyddlyfr	'diary'	penboeth	'fanatical'
aralleiriad	'paraphrase'	llawfeddig	'surgeon'
gwellwell	'better and better'	suddlong	'submarine'
hendref	'winter dwelling'	hinfynegydd	'barometer'

B)
wynepryd	'countenance'	popty	'oven'
croglofft	'garret, roodloft'	crocbren	'gallows'
gwritgoch	'rosy-cheeked'	picfforch	'pitchfork'
bracty	'malt house'	lletchwith	'awkward'
crocbont	'suspension bridge'		

C)
penteulu	'head of the family'	cae pori	'grazing field'
tŷ pridd	'earth house'	tŷ cornel	'corner house'
ceffyl gwedd	'team horse'	esgidiau dawnsio	'ballet shoes'

Additional vocabulary:
abad 'abott'; arall 'other'; ber 'short'; brag 'malt'; bryd 'mind'; cadeirio 'to chair'; coch 'red'; cred 'belief'; crog 'cross, hanging'; chwith 'left, wrong, strange'; dalen 'leaf'; dawnsio 'to dance'; dryll 'gun'; esgid 'shoe'; fforch 'fork'; geiriad 'wording'; gwaith 'work'; gwedd 'yoke, team'; gwerthu 'to sell'; gwrid 'blush'; gwyn 'white'; hen 'old, old-fashioned'; hin 'weather'; hir 'long'; lled 'partly, rather'; llofft 'loft'; llong 'boat'; meddyg 'doctor'; mynegi 'to tell'; ôl 'back (adj.)'; pig 'point'; pobi 'to bake'; poeth 'hot'; pont 'bridge'; pori 'to graze'; pren 'tree, wood'; pryf 'worm'; tref 'home, town'; wyneb 'face, front'.

8.4   Russian 'stub' compounds. Below is a set of Russian compounds (mostly taken from the *Glossary of Russian Abbreviations and Acronyms*, 1967), together with a gloss indicating the full form or title or the source and a more-or-less idiomatic rendering of the whole into English. What regularities, if any, seem to govern these constructions (including morphological and phonological regularities)? To what extent do these examples represent compounding and word-formation proper as opposed to non-standard forms of word creation? (In some case you will need to pay attention to the orthography of the original.)

> *zarplata*–zarabotnaja plata (<za 'for' rabota 'work' -n- adjectival suffix) 'for-work payment', i.e. 'salary'.
> *ispolkom*–ispolnitel'nyj komitet 'executive committee'.
> *profsojuz*–professional'nyj sojuz 'professional (i.e. trades) union'
> *sovxoz*–sovetskoe xozjajstvo 'soviet farm'
> *BaltNIRO*
> > Baltijskij naučno-issledovatel'skij institut morskogo
> > Baltic scientifico-research (adj.) institute of-sea (adj).
> > rybnogo xozjajstva i okeanografii
> > fish (adj.) economy and oceanography
> 'Baltic Research Institute for Sea Fisheries and Oceanography'
> *Glavprimorrybprom*
> > Glavnoe upravlenie rybnoj promyšlennosti Primorja
> > main administration of-fish (adj.) industry of-Primorye
> 'Central Administration of the Primorye Fishing Industry'
> *GlavPURKKA*
> > Glavnoe političeskoe upravlenie Raboče-Krestjanskoj
> > main political directorate of-worker-peasant (adj.)
> > Krasnoj Armii
> > red army
> 'Central Political Directorate of the Workers' and Peasants' Red Army'
> *Glavsevuralstroj*
> > Glavnoe upravlenie strojitel'stva predprijatij v rajonax
> > main administration of-construction of-enterprises in regions
> > Severnogo Urala
> > of-northern Urals
> 'North Urals Central Administration for Factory Construction'
> *Giprocvetmetobrabotka*
> Gosudarstvennyj naučno-issledovatel'skij i proektnyj institut
> state (adj.) scientific-research (adj.) and planning institute
> splavov i obrabotki cvetnyx metalov
> of-alloys and of-processing of-nonferrous metals
> 'State Research and Planning Institute for Alloys and Nonferrous Metals'
> *Giprošaxtostrojmaš*
> > Gosudarstvennyj proektno-konstruktorskij i
> > state (adj) planning-design (adj.) and

naučno-issledovatel'skij institut po sozdaniju novyx
scientifico-research (adj.) institute for creation of-new
mašin i mexanizmov gorno-proxodčeskix rabot
machines and of-mechanisms of-mine-sinking works
[NB šaxta 'mine']
'State Planning, Research and Design Institute for Shaft Sinking
Technology'

Gossortsemfond
Gosudarstvennyj fond sortovyx semjon
state (adj.) collection of-specialist seeds
'State Specialist Seeds Collection'

Lenoblsovprof
Leningradskij Oblastnoj Sovet Professional'nyx Sojuzov
Leningrad (adj.) regional council of-trades unions
'Leningrad Regional Trades Union Council'

Lensovnarxoz
Sovet narodnogo xozjajstva Leningradskogo ekonomičeskogo
council of-national economy of-Leningrad (adj.) economic
rajona
region
'Leningrad Region National Economic Council'

Lenximtexizdat
Leningradskoe Otdelenie Gosudarstvennogo ximiko-texničeskogo
Leningrad (adj.) branch of-state chemico-technological
izdatel'stva
publishing-house
'Leningrad Branch of the State Chemical Engineering Publishing
House'

Mosobžilupravlenie
Moskovskoe oblastnoe upravlenie žiliščnogo xozjajstva
Moscow (adj.) regional administration of-residential economy
'Moscow Regional Housing Administration'

Mosobispolkom
Ispolnitel'nyj Komitet Moskovskogo Oblastnogo Soveta
executive committee of-Moscow (adj.) regional council
Deputatov Trudjaščixsja
of-deputies of workers
'Moscow Regional Executive Committee'

Mostextorgsnab
Kontora material'no-texničeskogo snabženija glavnogo
bureau of-material-technological supply of-main
upravlenija torgovli ispolkoma Moskovskogo
administration of trade of-executive-committee of-Moscow (adj.)
gorodskogo soveta deputatov trudjaščixsja
municipal council of-deputies of-workers
'Moscow Technological Trade Supplies Bureau'

NIINAvtosel'xozmaš
Naučno-Issledovatel'skij Institut Informacii po
scientifico-research institute of-information on
Avtotraktornomu i Sel'skoxozjajstvennomu mašinostrojeniju
tractor and farming machine-construction
'Research and Information Institute for Tractor and Farm Machinery
Construction'

8.5   Provide a tree diagram for examples 8.31–8.34 (Turkish izafet). Which of the two English glosses does 8.33 more closely resemble and why?

8.6   According to Clark, Hecht and Mulford (1986) children from an early age make characteristic mistakes with compounds. Explain what might give rise to errors such as the following (all interpreted as 'wagon puller'):

pull wagon man
pull wagon
puller wagon
pull wagoner

8.7   Compounds such as *man-dying, *weather-changing and *train-arriving are ungrammatical. Use this fact to show that the Unaccusative Hypothesis is incompatible with obvious interpretations of the approaches to synthetic compounding proposed by Roeper and Siegel, and by Lieber.

8.8   Explain, giving as much relevant detail as possible, why expressions such as *a driver of trucks* or *the eating of pasta* pose problems for Lieber's (1983) theory.

8.9
a) How could Sproat derive *backseat driver*?
b) If *shelf book putter (with the meaning 'putter of books on shelves') is ungrammatical, why is it possible to say *motorway truck driver* (meaning 'driver of trucks on motorways') in Sproat's system?

8.10   Jacaltec (Day, 1973; Craig, 1977; Robertson, 1980), a Mayan language, is an ergative VSO language in which subjects and objects are cross-referenced by prefixes to the verb. State informally the relationship between compounding and theta role satisfaction in Jacaltec. In what way might these data be problematic for the theories we have reviewed? [T/A = tense/aspect]

1) ch   -co   lo [ixim wah]
   PRES -Erg1stpl. eat CLASS tortillas
   'we eat tortillas'
2) ch-hach'   il-w-i   'anma
   T/A-Abs2nd see-INTR-affix people
   'you watch people'
3) ch -hach   'il-wa-yi
   T/A-Abs2nd see-AP-affix
   'you see'
4a) potx'-om txitam   'pig killer'
 b) potx'-b'al txitam   'time, place or instrument for killing pigs'
 c) potx'-o' txitam   'pig killing'

Examples 5 are derived nominals from verb stems:

5a) 'il-wa-hom   'watcher'
 b) mak'-b'anil   'hitting instrument'
 c) 'il-wa-l   'watching'

Compare 5 with 6:

6a) 'il-om 'anma   'people watcher'
 b) ★'il-om   'watcher
 c) txahl-om   'one who prays'

Vocabulary:
-om/hom 'agentive', *-b'al* 'instrumental', *-b'anil* 'instrumental (antipassive form)',
-o'/l 'gerund', *wa* 'antipassive'.

★8.11   Roeper (1987) argues that adjectives in *-able* can project the stem verb's
argument structure in phrasal constructions in a regular fashion, as in *learnable by
a child*. Test the robustness of this claim by constructing a list of *-able* adjectives with
as wide a variety of verb stems as possible. What type of complements do these verbs
permit? Are there any restrictions on the kinds of synthetic compounds that can be
formed? Then repeat the exercise for other adjectival suffixes that have been claimed
to license synthetic compounds (see Selkirk, 1982).

★8.12   Compare and contrast the notions of 'percolation' and of 'head' as used by
Lieber (1983), Di Sciullo and Williams (1987) and Roeper (1987). To what extent are
these the same notions for these sets of authors? To what extent are these the notions
appealed to in syntactic theory? (You may find it useful to consult Zwicky, 1985a,
on the subject of heads.)

9

Clitics

Introduction

In this chapter we will be concerned with a topic which, strictly speaking, goes beyond the brief of part III of this book, the morphology–syntax interface. For we will be looking at a set of phenomena which represent the meeting point of morphology, syntax *and* phonology, namely the phenomena collectively known as cliticization.[1]

Clitics are elements which share certain properties of fully fledged words, but which lack the independence usually associated with words. In particular, they can't stand alone, but have to be attached phonologically to a *host*. This makes them look a little like affixes, in particular, inflectional affixes. Typically, clitics are function words, such as modal participles (e.g. interrogative participles), conjunctions, pronominals or auxiliary verbs. Historically, they generally develop from fully fledged words and frequently develop into inflectional affixes.

There are several practical and theoretical difficulties in isolating clitics. They are generally assumed to be incapable of bearing stress or accent (though, as Klavans, 1982, points out in some detail, strictly speaking, this is not always the case). In some cases, phonological processes which affect clitics are different from those which affect genuine affixes (as we will see in the discussion of Macedonian and Polish, below), but again this is not always the case. In general, cliticization is freer and less restricted lexically than affixation, in the sense that clitics will typically attach themselves to any old word provided it is in the right position in the sentence, while affixes usually only attach to specific classes of words or stems. However, there are plenty of exceptions to this rule of thumb, too. These difficulties of characterization have led some linguists to abandon the notion altogether as a theoretical primitive and regard the notion of clitic as simply a descriptive cover term. Other linguists, however, regard clitics as a separately identifiable morphosyntactic category.

There are several reasons why morphologists need to understand the nature of clitics. First, it will be impossible to construct an adequate theory of inflectional morphology if inflection is confused with cliticization, or if important types of inflectional system are mislabelled as clitic systems. I shan't discuss this aspect in further detail, since the point should be fairly obvious from our discussion of inflection in chapter 6, and from some of the examples of clitic systems we shall be examining. Second, the question of cliticization is crucial for our understanding of the nature of wordhood. Cliticization raises many of the most complex questions concerning the relationship between syntactic, morphological and phonological characterizations of this notion. Third, much debate in the syntax literature has concerned the nature of pronominal clitic systems in languages such as French, Italian or Hebrew. Some argue that clitics must be regarded as degenerate types of pronoun and that their behaviour must therefore be viewed from a primarily syntactic perspective. Others have argued that, morphologically, these clitic pronouns are rather like affixes, so that an adequate account of their syntactic properties will have to take cognizance of the morphology–syntax interface.

The chapter begins with an examination of a collection of clitic systems from the Slavic languages Serbo-Croat, Macedonian and Polish, and the Romance language Portuguese. These languages together illustrate a good many of the phenomena that are most often discussed under the heading of clitics (though these particular languages haven't been discussed in great detail in the theoretical literature). In the second section we examine recent attempts at classifying clitic systems, and specifically at attempts to provide a unified theory of cliticization. The third section deals with the relationship between pronominal clitic systems and syntax, and broaches the question of whether such clitics are really agreement morphemes.

9.1   Four case studies

9.1.1   Serbo-Croat

The clitic system of Serbo-Croat, a Slavonic language and the principal language of Yugoslavia, embraces auxiliary verbs and pronouns, as well as a question particle. It has been described in an *Aspects*-based transformational framework by Browne (1974). Any handbook of the language will provide information about the clitic systems and useful descriptive summaries can be found in De Bray (1980b) and Corbett (1988).[2]

Two verbs are used as auxiliaries, the verb *to be* in the formation of the past tense and the conditional and the verb *to want* in the formation of the future. The auxiliary clitics, like other verbs, inflect for person (1st, 2nd, 3rd) and number (singular and plural). The past is formed from the present of *be* with the past participle; the conditional is formed from the aorist of *be* with the past participle. The past participle agrees in number and gender (masculine, feminine and neuter) with the subject. The future is formed from the present of *want* with either the infinitive or a finite subordinate clause introduced by the complementizer *da* 'that'.

Clitic forms are contrasted with full (stressed) forms in table 9.1. The only difference between full form and clitic in the past tense is stress: the clitic forms are inherently unstressed (and therefore can never bear a tone). The full forms have short vowels and bear a falling tone.

Table 9.1 Auxiliary clitics (Serbo-Croat)

Be		(present tense)		(past)	
		full form	clitic	full form	clitic
Sg.	1	jèsam	sam	bȉh	bih
	2	jèsi	si	bî	bi
	3	jèst(e)	je	bî	bi
Pl.	1	jèsmo	smo	bȉsmo	bismo
	2	jèste	ste	bȉste	biste
	3	jèsu	su	bȉše	bi
Want					
		full form	clitic		
Sg.	1	hòću	ću		
	2	hòćeš	ćeš		
	3	hòće	će		
Pl.	1	hòćemo	ćemo		
	2	hòćete	ćete		
	3	hòće	će		

The past participle is formed by adding *-l* to the verb stem. The /l/ alternates with /o/ in syllable final (coda) position. To the past participle are added the agreement desinences, as shown in example 9.1, using the verb *stati* 'to stand', stem, *sta-*:

9.1

	sg.	pl.
masc.	stao	stali
fem.	stala	stale
neut.	stalo	stala

Examples of the past, conditional and future are given in 9.2–9.4:

9.2

a) Pisao sam pismo.
wrote AUX letter
'I (masc.) wrote a letter.'

b) Pisala sam pismo.
'I (fem.) wrote a letter'

c) Juče   ste   čitali knjigu.
Yesterday AUX read book
'Yesterday, you (masc. pl.) read a book.'

d) Ovu knjigu smo već   čitali.
this book   AUX already read
'We have already read this book.'

e) Devojke su   čitale ovu knjigu.
girls   AUX read this book
'The girls were reading this book.'

9.3   a) Ja bih   čitao ovu knjigu.
        I AUX read this book
        'I would read this book.'
    b) Momci bi   čitali ovu knjigu, kad bi   bila zanimljiva.
        boys   AUX read this book   if   AUX be   interesting
        'The boys would read this book if it were interesting.'

9.4   a) Bogdan će   pisati pismo.
        Bogdan AUX write letter
    b) Bogdan će   da piše   pismo.
        Bogdan AUX that he-writes letter
        'Bogdan will write a letter.'

The Dative and Accusative forms of the personal pronouns are given in table 9.2. These appear after (most of) the auxiliaries in the order Dative Accusative. This is illustrated in examples 9.5–9.9:

9.5   a) Ja mu   ga   dajem svaki dan.
        I 3sg.M-DAT 3sg.-ACC give   every day
    b) Svaki dan mu ga dajem.
    c) Dajem mu ga svaki dan.
        'I give it to him every day.'

9.6   a) Juče   sam   joj   ih   dao.
        Yesterday AUX-1sg. 3sg.F-DAT 3pl.-ACC gave
        'Yesterday, I gave them to her.'
    b) Ja sam joj ih juče dao.
    c) Dao sam joj ih juče.
        'I gave them to her yesterday.'

Table 9.2 Pronominal clitics (Serbo-Croat)

	1st sg. full	clitic	2nd sg. full	clitic	1st pl. full	clitic	2nd pl. full	clitic
Dat.	mèni	mi	tèbi	ti	nàma	nam	vàma	vam
Acc.	mène	me	tèbe	te	nâs	nas	vâs	vas

	3rd sg. masc./neut. full	clitic	fem. full	clitic	3rd pl. full	clitic
Dat.	njèmu	mu	njôj	joj	njìma	im
Acc.	njèga	ga	njû	je/ju	njîh	ih

Reflexive: Dat. (full only) sèbi
        Acc. full – sèbe, clitic – se.

9.7   a) U sali smo   im   se   predstavili.
        In hall AUX-1pl. 3pl.-DAT REFL-ACC introduced
        'In the hall we introduced ourselves to them.'
        b) Predstavili smo im se.
        'We introduced ourselves to them.'

9.8   a) On će   ti   ga   pokazati sutra.
        He AUX-1sg. 2sg.-DAT 3sg.N-ACC show   tomorrow
        b) Sutra će ti ga pokazati.
        'He will show it to you tomorrow.'

9.9   a) Vi biste   joj   se   predstavili u sali.
        I AUX-2pl. 3sg.F-DAT REFL-ACC introduced in hall
        b) U sali biste joj se predstavili.
        'You (pl.) would introduce yourselves to her in the hall.'

The exception is the auxiliary *je* which always comes last in a sequence of clitics, as in examples 9.10–9.11:[3]

9.10   a) Jovan mi   ih   je   dao.
        Jovan 1sg.-DAT 3pl.-ACC AUX-3sg. gave.
        'Jovan gave them to me.'
        b) Dao mi ih je.
        'He gave them to me.'

9.11   U sali nam   se   je   predstavio.
        In hall 1pl.-DAT REFL-ACC AUX-3sg. introduced
        'In the hall he introduced himself to us.'

The only other enclitic is the question word *li*. This appears first in a string of clitics. A sentence initial auxiliary verb then has to appear in the full form (as in 9.13–9.14):

9.12   Dolazite   li često ovamo?
        you-come Q often here
        'Do you come here often?'

9.13   Hoćeš   li doći?
        AUX-2sg. Q to-come
        'Will you come?'

9.14   Jeste   li joj   se   predstavili u sali?
        AUX-2pl. Q 3sg.F-DAT REFL-ACC introduced in hall
        'Did you introduce yourselves to her in the hall?'

An alternative construction is to begin the clause with the complementizer *da*, to form a kind of compound interrogative marker, *da li*. The rest of the clitics then follow this marker in their customary order, as shown, in 9.15–9.16:

9.15   Da li će   ti   ga   sutra   pokazati?
        DA Q AUX 2sg.-DAT 3sg.-ACC tomorrow to-show
        'Will he show it to you tomorrow?'

9.16   Da li mi   ih   je   dao Jovan?
        DA Q 1sg.-DAT 3pl.-ACC AUX-3sg. give Jovan
        'Did Jovan give them to me?'

Sentential complements are introduced by complementizers such as *da* (corresponding to English 'that'). The clitics always follow these complementizers:

9.17   Želim da mu   ga   dam.
        I-want that 3sg.-DAT 3sg.-ACC I-give
        'I-want to give it to him.'

9.18   Znam da me   je   Jovan video.
        I-know that 1sg.-ACC AUX-3sg. Jovan saw
        'I know that Jovan saw me.'

After this wealth of descriptive detail, let's summarize the position and draw some conclusions.

The first two points to notice concern word order. First, notice that although the clitics generally come immediately before the lexical verb of the clause, this is not invariable. It is common to find an adverbial or the subject intervening, as in 9.6b, 9.18. What is important is that the clitic string appears as the second 'constituent' of the clause. Since Serbo-Croat is a language with free word order the first constituent may be more-or-less anything: subject, verb, complement, adverbial. This clause-second position (P2) is often known as the **Wackernagel position**, after the nineteenth-century philologist who gave the first detailed description of the phenomenon in Indo-European, and the clause-second positioning of clitics is often referred to as **Wackernagel's Law**. Clitics which obey this law, 'Wackernagel' or 'P2' clitics, are found in a great variety of typologically and genetically diverse languages. For instance, in addition to Serbo-Croat (Slavic, Indo-European) we find Wackernagel clitics in Luiseño (Uto-Aztecan) and Warlpiri (Australian).

Unlike many languages with a Wackernagel system, Serbo-Croat allows itself some leeway in its definition of 'P2': it is the position after the first accented constituent (e.g. NP) or after the first accented word (where we have to regard subordinating conjunctions such as *da* as honorary accented elements). This means that clitics can break up a subject, clause-initial NP if it contains, say, an adjective or determiner. This is shown in 9.19:

9.19   a) [Taj pesnik]NP mi   je   napisao knjigu.
            That poet   1st.DAT AUX wrote book
        b) [Taj mi je pesnik]NP napisao knjigu.
            'That poet wrote me a book.'

Cases such as Serbo-Croat illustrate rather clearly that clitic placement is (or was originally) dependent on sentence accent or similar prosodic factors. For in 9.19b the clitic is attached to a prosodic element rather than a syntactically defined element. This gives rise to a constituent structure which is grossly at variance with what would be expected on syntactic grounds.

The second point is that the order of clitics itself is fixed, giving rise to a characteristic type of **clitic cluster**. In the case of Serbo-Croat the ordering is as given in 9.20:[4]

9.20   Serbo-Croat clitic order:
         li–Aux–Dat.–Acc.–Refl.–*je*

(Recall that the *je* in final position is the 3sg. present form of the verb 'to be', not the fem. sg. pronominal. 'Aux' must, of course, be taken to mean all the auxiliaries except *je*.)

This again is typical of languages with clitic systems. If we think of clitics essentially as words, then the order of clitics should be handled by rules determining word order, i.e. syntactic rules. But it was noted some time ago that clitic order tends to be rather different from word or constituent order in the syntax proper. This led Perlmutter (1971) to propose a special grammatical device to describe clitic order, a surface syntactic filter or template. The problem is well illustrated by Serbo-Croat. First, word order proper is very free in this language, whereas the clitic order is fixed. This makes clitics look more like bound morphemes than words. Second, the clitics must occupy second position in the clause. Apart from conjunctions and determiners (which arguably share a number of properties with clitics) this kind of ordering restriction simply isn't found elsewhere in the syntax of the language. Thus, if clitics really are words, then they are rather idiosyncratic words.

Another property of the Serbo-Croat system worth noting concerns an interesting alternation with the 3sg. feminine Acc. clitic, *je*. It is perfectly possible for this form to appear next to its homonym, the 3sg. auxiliary. When this happens the pronominal clitic form is substituted by its allomorph *ju*, as in 9.21:

9.21   Milan ju   je   video.
         Milan 3sg.F-ACC AUX saw
         'Milan saw her.'

We also find phonologically conditioned suppletive, or at least non-automatic, allomorphy determined across word or constituent boundaries. For instance, the choice of indefinite article allomorph *a/an* in English is governed by whether the following word (of whatever class) begins with a vowel or not. French adjectives such as *beau/bel* 'beautiful' and *vieux/viel* 'old' display similar allomorphy. As we saw in §4.6, such phenomena, though not uncommon, pose intriguing problems for theories of the phonology-syntax interface. The fact that such allomorphy is found in clitic systems compounds these difficulties.

Serbo-Croat provides another example of clitic allomorphy, which is interesting when we come to compare this language with the Romance language Portuguese. The future auxiliary will appear adjacent to the verb when there is no question particle and when the verb itself is the first accented element of the clause. Under these circumstances, the verb will be in the infinitive form and, with the exception of verbs whose infinitives end in *-ći*, such as *ići* 'to go', the clitic 'fuses' with the infinitive form, causing the *-i* ending of the latter to truncate. This can be seen from 9.22:

9.22   a) Knjigu ću   čitati
          book   1sg.-AUX read-INF
          'It's the book I'll read.'
    b) Čitaću   knjigu.
          read-1sg.-AUX book
          'I'll read the book.'

This fusion gives rise to allomorphic changes typical of the lexical (rather than phrase) phonology of the language. For instance, the verb *rasti* 'to grow' gives *rašču*, *rašćeš*, …, Here, the *-st* cluster has undergone Iotation, a form of palatalization one of whose effects is to turn /st/ into /šč/. This makes the auxiliary, at least, look very much more like a future tense affix than an auxiliary verb.

In summary, then, Serbo-Croat clitics are unstressed and hence unable to bear sentence accent and they exhibit allomorphy. This is uncharacteristic of real words. Moreover, they show ordering restrictions which are not true of the rest of the syntax. A specific example is the idiosyncratic behaviour of the auxiliary *je*. More generally, syntactic systems don't seem to include rules positioning a complete string of elements in a particular place in the sentence. To be sure, it isn't uncommon to find, say, that a particular lexical category has to be given a set position in the sentence. (This is essentially the 'V2' phenomenon in Germanic, in which a main verb has to occur as the second constituent.) But to find this type of restriction applying to a heterogeneous collection of elements such as the Serbo-Croat clitic cluster is unheard of outside clitic systems. Further, the structure of the clitic cluster itself is flat or linear, and doesn't show the sort of hierarchical organization we expect from syntactic constituents. (Recall my remarks about template morphology in §6.4.) From these observations we seem to be led to the conclusion that we are actually dealing with an unusual form of free-floating affixation, and that, as far as the syntax is concerned, clitics aren't words at all. Later we will see other properties of clitics in other languages which tend to reinforce this conclusion.

On the other hand, there are two important respects in which clitics don't behave like affixes (i.e. bound morphemes) in Serbo-Croat. Perhaps the most important of these is one which has already been amply illustrated: unlike affixes, clitics are completely unrestricted in what kinds of elements they attach to. The only constraint is that their host must be the first (accented) syntactic element of the clause. Yet we have seen that it is characteristic of affixation that it is governed by systematic selection restrictions (e.g. certain affixes only attach, say, to nouns) or by totally idiosyncratic restrictions. Totally unrestricted affixation would therefore be an anomaly. Freedom of association is, however, characteristic of words and syntactic elements in general.

The other property which makes the clitics look like words is the phenomenon of **clitic climbing**. In a number of languages (most famously in the syntax literature, Italian and Spanish), clitic pronouns which are objects to a verb in an infinitival subordinate clause can 'climb' out of their own clause and appear in the matrix clause. In Serbo-Croat, a verb such as *želiti* 'to want' can take either a finite or infinitival complement clause. In the former case the clitics remain in the subordinate clause; in the latter they appear after the first accented constituent of the matrix clause, even if this separates them from their own verb. Thus, in addition to example 9.17 with a finite complement, we can have example 9.26:

9.23   a) Želim mu   ga   dati.
             I-want 3sg.M-DAT 3sg.N-ACC give-INF
             'I want to give it to him.'
        b) Ja mu   ga   želim dati.
             I 3sg.M-DAT 3sg.N-ACC I-want give-INF
             'It's me that wants to give it to him.'

This kind of freedom of movement is not normally associated with affixes.[5]

Serbo-Croat, then, illustrates rather well not only a very typical clitic system, but also many of the descriptive problems facing the linguist wishing to make sense of clitic systems. In our other case studies we will see yet more evidence of schizophrenia on the part of clitics, behaving now as fully-fledged words, now as bound morphemes.

9.1.2 Macedonian

Macedonian is another of the languages of Yugoslavia and, like Serbo-Croat, is a member of the South Slav group. Indeed, it is so close to Serbo-Croat that the two languages are to a large extent mutually intelligible. Not surprisingly it has a similar clitic system. However, they diverge in very interesting ways, and some of the differences are of some import for current syntactic theory.

The first difference is that the future auxiliary, derived from the (extant) verb *hteti* in Serbo-Croat, has withered into an invariable modal particle in Macedonian, *će*. Similarly, the conditional is expressed by a particle *bi*, cognate with the 3sg. aorist form of the verb 'to be' in Serbo-Croat. This development represents the frequent fate of function words derived originally from content words which have become clitics. It illustrates that to a certain extent the precursors of the modern Serbo-Croat clitics and the Macedonian particles had properties of words, for it is very rare for affixes to become particles of this sort.

The verb 'to be' forms an auxiliary combining with a participle in *-l* to form a set of past tense forms, as in Serbo-Croat. Pronominal clitics occur in Dative and Accusative forms. The ordering within the clitic cluster is as in Serbo-Croat. Interestingly, the nominal case system of Macedonian has been lost so that it is only in the pronoun system that a morphological distinction between Nominative, Dative and Accusative is preserved. This is a very common phenomenon – much the same happened in English, for instance.

There are three striking differences between Serbo-Croat and Macedonian pronominal clitics. The first two relate to syntactic phenomena, word order and agreement. The third relates to the stress system and the notion 'phonological word'.

Macedonian clitics don't respect Wackernagel's Law. Instead, clitics tend to congregate around their verb. Their absolute position with respect to the verb depends, moreover, on the morphosyntactic form of the verb: the clitics follow verbs in the imperative or gerund forms, but precede verbs in other forms (which means the finite forms, since the infinitive has been lost in Macedonian). Hence, clitic clusters can (and frequently do) appear as proclitics in absolute sentence-initial position, as in

9.24–9.26 (example 9.24 also illustrates the use of an enclitic pronominal as a possessive):

9.24   Mi najde brat   mi.
        me found brother me-DAT/my
        'My brother found me.'

9.25   Mi   reče Nikola oti će   dojde.
        me-DAT said Nikola that FUT come
        'Nikola told me that he would come.'

9.26   Se   razbira
        REFL understands
        'It is understood; of course' (lit. = 'it understands itself')

Examples of enclitic order with non-finite verbs:

9.27   Zemi ja!
        'Take it.' (imperative)

9.28   Zemajći mu   go, počna da   bega.
        taking him-DAT it began COMP run (gerund)
        'Taking it from him, he began to run.'

Interestingly, the tendency for clitics to appear before finite verbs and after non-finite verbs is also found in the Romance languages.[6] Indeed, the Macedonian examples 9.24–9.28 look just like their Italian translations with respect to clitic position.

As clitic pronouns develop a stronger attachment for a particular grammatical category, they begin to look more like (agreement) affixes than free standing syntactic constituents. (This is what we observed for French pronoun clitics in chapter 1.) In Macedonian this impression is strengthened by the fact that a definite direct object, or any indirect object, must be referenced ('reduplicated' in the descriptive literature's terminology) by a clitic pronoun agreeing for person, number and, in the case of 3sg. NPs, gender (Berent, 1980; discussion of this construction can be found in any handbook on Macedonian, such as Lunt, 1952, De Bray, 1980a; see also the discussion in Lyons, forthcoming). Examples are given in 9.29–9.32:[7]

9.29   Mi   ja   dadoa smetka-ta
        1sg.-DAT 3sg.F-ACC gave bill -ART-F
        'He gave me the bill.'

9.30   Dajte mu   ja   košula-ta.
        give 3sg.M-DAT 3sg.F-ACC shirt-ART-F
        'Give him the shirt.'

9.31   Nemu mu   go   dadov.
        to-him 3sg.M-DAT 3sg.M/N-ACC I-gave
        'It was to him that I gave it.'

9.32   Mu   go   dadov pismence -to   nemu a   ne nejze.
        3sg.M-DAT 3sg.M/N I-gave note   -ART-N to-him and not to-her
        'I gave the note to him, not her.'

This sort of thing is not unheard of in more familiar languages, and it has given rise to a great deal of discussion in the syntactic literature under the heading of **clitic doubling**. For instance, in certain South American Spanish dialects we encounter examples such as 9.33 (Jaeggli, 1982, 1986):

9.33   Lo vimos a Juan.
        him I-saw to Juan
        'I saw Juan.'

Here, the clitic 'doubles' the direct object. However, the object NP in these constructions is always associated with a preposition. This has led some observers to propose that the clitic is assigned (abstract) Objective Case and that the full object NP Juan therefore needs to be governed by a preposition in order to receive Case. The descriptive observation that a doubled NP must be assigned Case from a preposition is often referred to as the **Kayne-Jaeggli Generalization**, and a number of theories have been developed to try to explain it (see, for instance, Aoun, 1985, Borer, 1984, Everett, 1986, Jaeggli, 1982, 1986, Suñer, 1988). The Macedonian examples (and other Balkan examples, for instance, from Modern Greek (Joseph, 1988)) show that the Kayne-Jaeggli Generalization is false, at least on its must superficial interpretation. In fact, the clitic doubling phenomenon in Macedonian looks very much like object agreement in a language such as Chukchee.

The third point of interest concerning Macedonian clitics relates to the definition of 'phonological word'. The language has a rather unusual stress system in that, with a handful of exceptions, stress falls on the antepenultimate syllable of a word, or on the first syllable of a disyllabic word (see Hammond, 1989, for some recent discussion). Of interest to us is the fact that the stress rule of Macedonian treats as a word any content word together with its dependent enclitics. For instance, the pronoun clitic used after a kinterm to mark possession will cause stress to be shifted forward from the antepenult of a word with three or more syllables, as in 9.34–9.35 (note that the possessive pronoun is sometimes used with a definite form of the noun):

9.34   a) žéna-ta   b) žená-ta   ti
           wife-ART   wife-ART your
           'the wife'   'your wife'

9.35   a) brátučed   b) bratúčed-ot   c) bratúčed mu
           cousin   cousin -ART   cousin his
                                   'this cousin'   'his cousin'

Likewise, a clitic cluster may shift the stress on a verb in the imperative:[8]

9.36   a) Dájte   mi.   b) Dajté   mi go
           give-pl. me   give-pl. me it
           'Give me.'   'Give it me.'

The same is observed when a pronominal clitic cluster follows a demonstrative, as in 9.37–9.38:

9.37 a) Éve -go!
         there-him
         'There he is!'

   b) Evé -ti -go!
      there-you-him
      'There he is for you!'

9.38 a) Kamó -go?
         where-him
         'Where is he?'

   b) Kamó-ti -go?
      where-you-him
      'Where's he got to?'

   c) Kamo-mí-ti-go?
      where-me-you-him
      'Where's he disappeared to (on me)?!'

With proclitics the stress usually falls on the verb form:

9.39 Mu go dádov.
      him it I-gave
      'I gave it to him.'

However, the negative particle, *ne*, attracts the stress to itself from mono- and disyllabic verb forms. Moreover, a string of proclitics-plus-verb is treated as a phonological word if it is negated:

9.40 a) Né dade.
         not he-gave
         'He didn't give.'
   b) Ne mu gó dade.
      not him it he-gave
      'He didn't give it to him.'

9.41 Ne će sé   venča.
      not FUT REFL they-marry
      'They won't get married.'

Similar behaviour is observed with the words *što* 'what', *koj* 'who', *koga* 'when' (though only when used as genuine interrogatives, not as relative pronouns):

9.42 Štó reče?
      What he-said
      'What did he say?'

9.43 Koj mu gó reče?
      who him it said
      'Who said it to him?'

9.44 Što mú reče?
      what him said
      'What did (he) say to him?'

9.45   Kogá dojde tój?
           when come he
           'When is he coming?'

We can add to these facts the observation that stress shift occurs with lexicalized adjective–noun collocations, as illustrated in 9.46–9.47:

9.46   a) pŕva véčer   b) prvá večer
              first evening   first evening
              'a first evening'   'wedding night'

9.47   a) mála réka   Malá reka
              small river   small river
              'a small river'   '(placename)'

This all goes to suggest that the host plus clitic cluster forms a unit which is more lexical than syntactic. However, what exactly this means isn't entirely clear. Modern Greek has a stress system and a clitic system which bears much resemblance to that of Macedonian. (This is presumably not a coincidence given that Macedonia and Greece border on each other.) Nespor and Vogel (1986: chapter 5) argue at some length, on the basis of the Greek facts, that the theory of Prosodic Phonology must recognize a domain which they call the Clitic Group, over which certain phonological rules, such as stress assignment, must be defined. Moreover, they are at pains to emphasize that this domain is distinct from (and larger than) that of the prosodic word, and distinct from (and smaller than) that of the phonological phrase. If this analysis proves the most satisfactory, then clitics will again fall midway between words and affixes, remaining *sui generis*.

9.1.3 *Portuguese*

In this section we examine the clitic system of European Portuguese. Along the way I shall compare its system with that of a closely related language, (Castilian) Spanish, which differs in a number of intriguing respects. As with Serbo-Croat and Macedonian we shall be looking at the pronominal system and the auxiliary system.[9]

Table 9.3 Pronominal clitics (Portuguese)

		Dir. Obj.	Ind. Obj.	Full
Sg.	1	me	me	mim
	2	te	te	tim
	3M	o	lhe	ele
	3F	a	lhe	ela
Pl.	1	nos	nos	nos
	2	vos	vos	vos
	3M	os	lhes	eles
	3F	as	lhes	elas
Refl.		se		

The pronominal system of Portuguese is summarized in table 9.3 (omitting allomorphy in the 3rd person forms which I discuss later). The full forms are those found as complements to prepositions.

In simple, positive, affirmative sentences the clitics appear as enclitics on the verb. This is unusual in Romance languages. In Spanish, for instance, clitics *precede* the verb, except in non-finite forms (much as in Macedonian). Some examples are given in 9.48–9.50. The (b) examples are Spanish equivalents (taken from the grammar of Vasquez Cuesta and Mendes da Luz, 1961):

9.48   a) via-me   b) me veía
              he-saw me   me he-saw
              'He saw me.'

9.49   a) comprou-me   b) me compró
              he-bought (for) me   me he-bought
              'He bought me (something).'

9.50   a) vejo-o   b) lo veo
              I-see him   him I-see
              'I see him.'

Encliticization triggers certain allomorphic changes both in the pronouns themselves and in the word to which they attach. After a word ending in /r/ or /s/, the 3rd person Direct Object forms (*o, a, os, as*) acquire /l/ to become *lo, la, los, las*, while the /r, s/ of the previous word drops. If the clitic's host ends in a nasalized vowel then the clitic acquires /n/ to become *no, na, nos, nas*. Both these changes can be seen if we conjugate a regular verb such as *levar*, 'to raise', with a 3sg. masc. object, as in *leva-o* 'to raise it' (see table 9.4). (Recall that word final *-Vm* sequences represent a nasalized vowel in Portuguese orthography.)

In a cluster of clitics the Indirect Object form precedes the Direct Object form. Under these circumstances, certain allomorphic changes are observed, summarized in table 9.5.

It will be noticed that the allomorphy with *nos* and *vos* is just a special case of that discussed in the previous paragraph. Some examples of this are:[10]

9.51   a) Mostra-mas   b) enseñamelas
              show me-them (F)   show-me-them (>enseñar)
              'Show them to me.'

Table 9.4 levar 'to raise' *levá-lo* 'to raise it'

Sg.	1	levo	levo-o	
	2	levas	leva-lo	
	3	leva	leva-lo	
Pl.	1	levamos	levamo-lo	
	2	levais	levai-lo	
	3	levam	levam-no	

Table 9.5   Contracted forms
(Portuguese)

me	→ mo, ma, mos, mas
te	→ to, ta, tos, tas
lhe + o, a, os as	→ lho, lha, lhos, lhas
lhes	→ lho, lha, lhos, lhas
nos	→ no-lo, no-la, no-los, no-las
vos	→ vo-lo, vo-la, vo-los, vo-las

9.52   a) Entregaste-lho?   b) ¿Se lo entregaste?
           you-delivered him-it   him it you-delivered
           'Did you deliver it to him?'

Portuguese follows the line of its Romance sisters in clauses containing a WH question word, in negative clauses and in subordinate clauses. Here the pronoun precedes its verb, as seen in 9.53–9.55:

9.53   Não o tenho.
          not it I-have
          'I haven't got it.'

9.54   Quando o vendem?
          When it they-sell
          'When are they selling it?'

9.55   O armazém onde os compra
          the shop where them he-buys
          'the shop where he buys them'

A similar pattern is observed when the subject is a quantified NP in sentence initial position and when the verb is in the infinitive governed by a preposition (except *a*), as in 9.56–9.58:

9.56   a) Ambos se sentiam bem.
              both   REFL they-felt well
           b) Sentiam-se ambos bem.
              'Both felt well.'

9.57   a) Três homens se sentaram à mesa.
              three men   REFL they-sat at table
           b) À mesa sentaram-se três homens.
              'Three men sat down at table.'

9.58   Sem me decidir a interroga-lo não voy.
          without REFL to-decide to ask-him not I-go
          'I'm not going without making up my mind to ask him.'

The reason for this behaviour seems to be that Portuguese clitics retain some of the properties of Wackernagel clitics in migrating to second position in the clause. In most other Romance languages the clitics have shifted completely from Wackernagel's position and appear exclusively as en- or pro-clitics to the verb. This is also shown in the positioning of clitics with respect to auxiliary verbs. In the Spanish example in 9.59b the clitic can appear in sentence initial position and appears as proclitic to the auxiliary, but in the Portuguese equivalent the clitic has to intervene between auxiliary and main verb:

9.59   a) Tinha-o estudado a fundo.   b) Lo había estudiado a fondo.
           I-had it studied in depth   it I-had studied in depth
           'I had studied it in depth.'

However, apart from the absolute ban on sentence initial clitics, the rules governing clitic placement seem to relate more to syntax than to prosody or morphology.

The final peculiarity of Portuguese clitics concerns their interaction with tense markers. Like other Romance languages, Portuguese has developed a synthetic future and conditional form from an original Vulgar Latin analytic construction in which the infinitive was followed by the present or imperfect tense forms of the verb *habere* 'to have'. The similarity between the future and conditional endings and the relevant tense forms of the auxiliary *haver* is still evident, as can be seen from table 9.6.

Lexical phonological rules (e.g. the stress) treat the endings like inflectional affixes,

Table 9.6a *haver* 'to have (aux.)'

		present	imperfect
Sg.	1	hei	havia
	2	hás	havias
	3	há	havia
Pl.	1	havemos	havíamos
	2	haveis	havíeis
	3	hão	haviam

Table 9.6b *levar* 'to raise'

		future	conditional
Sg.	1	levarei	levaria
	2	levarás	levarias
	3	levará	levaria
Pl.	1	levaremos	levaríamos
	2	levareis	levaríeis
	3	levarão	levariam

Table 9.7   *levá-lo* 'to raise it'

		future	conditional
Sg.	1	levá-lo-ei	levá-lo-ia
	2	levá-lo-ás	levá-lo-ias
	3	levá-lo-á	levá-lo-ia
Pl.	1	levá-lo-emos	levá-lo-íamos
	2	levá-lo-eis	levá-lo-íeis
	3	levá-lo-ão	levá-lo-iam

just as in other Romance languages. What is odd about Portuguese is that the pronominal clitics can intervene between the verb stem and the tense/aspect affixes, in effect treating these affixes as though they themselves were clitics. The result is highly reminiscent of the Serbo-Croat future system, except that the auxiliary never migrates away from its host verb. The verbs of table 9.6 are conjugated with a clitic in table 9.7.

Exactly similar behaviour is observed with the future and conditional forms of the auxiliaries in the compound tense. Thus, corresponding to *terei levado* and *teria levado*, 'I shall have raised' and 'I would have raised', we have *te-lo-ei levado* and *te-lo-ia levado*, 'I shall have raised it' and 'I should have raised it'. These tense/aspect forms can be broken up by a clitic cluster as well as just by single pronouns, as seen in 9.60:

9.60   Mostra-no-los-á
          show-us-them-FUT
          'He will show them to us.'

To summarize, we see that the tendency noted in Macedonian for the clitics to cluster around the verb is characteristic of Portuguese (and Romance generally). In other words, the clitic placement rules of the language are defined not so much in terms of the constituent surface structure, as with Wackernagel clitics, but in terms of a lexically defined host. This makes the clitics more reminiscent of affixes than the true Wackernagel clitics are, and in many languages (for example, a number of Bantu languages) it appears that pronominal or agreement affixes have indeed developed out of clitic pronouns.

On the other hand, when we consider the future and conditional tense forms in Portuguese, we see that a process of morphologization which has been completed in other languages of the group has not been taken to its logical conclusion. If it had, and the tense/aspect markers were true suffixes, then we would expect them to appear next to the verb stem and not separated by the person/number markers. As Bybee (1985) points out, there is an overwhelming tendency for person/number agreement markers to be more peripheral than tense/aspect markers. However, it would require a very careful analysis of the syntax and morphology of Portuguese to decide whether the future and conditional markers were 'really' affixes or 'really' clitics, or perhaps something else (akin, for instance, to the particles of English phrasal verbs, such as *put it down*, as opposed to *✶put down it*).

9.1.4 Polish

Polish, like Serbo-Croat and Macedonian, has developed a clitic system from its personal pronouns and its auxiliaries. However, this system is unlike that of other Slav languages in a number of respects, and at the same time it differs from that of the Romance languages exemplified in §9.1.3 by Portuguese and Spanish.

We begin with the pronominals. These are derived, as one would expect, as shortened unaccented forms of the full form pronouns. The latter are used for emphasis and as complements to prepositions. Their forms are shown in table 9.8.[11]

Only the reflexive, 1sg., 2sg. and 3Msg. forms are pure clitics; the others double as full forms.

In Serbo-Croat the distribution of the clitics was governed primarily by Wackernagel's Law. In Portuguese, and Romance generally, the clitics are attached to the verb (before or after). However, as is clear from the description in De Bray (1980b), in Polish the distribution is determined largely by phrase level prosodic considerations. In general, word order in Polish, as in other Slav languages, is very free. Thus, we may find verbs, subject NPs, complement NPs, or adverbials initially, medially or finally in a clause. However, there are a number of constraints governing the position of the clitic pronominals. The most important, inviolable, constraint is that no (true) clitic can begin a clause. In addition, there is a strong stylistic constraint disfavouring clitics at the absolute end of a clause. This means that a clitic will only generally be found felicitous at the end of a clause, if that clause contains only one full lexical word. Moreover, there are certain types of words (for instance, the negative particle, *nie*, and prepositions) which never host clitics.

As a result of these factors we must say, for example, 9.61a, because the clitic *go* can't begin the sentence, whereas when emphasizing the pronoun we can use the full form in initial position, as in 9.61b:

9.61   a) Spotykam go.
         I-meet him
         'I meet him (regularly).'
        b) Jego spotykam (ale nie jej ...)
         him I-meet (but not her ...)
         'HIM, I meet, (but not HER ...)'

Table 9.8 Pronominal clitics (Polish)

		Accusative	Genitive	Dative
Sg.	1	mię	mię	mi
	2	cię	cię	ci
	3M/N	go	go	mu
	3F	ja	jej	jej
Pl.	1	nas	nas	nam
	2	was	was	wam
	3M	ich	ich	im
	3F/N	je	ich	im
	Refl.	się	się	——

Moreover, in 9.62 it's not only possible to place the clitic before the verb, but, indeed, preferred:

9.62   Często go spotykam.
        Often him I-meet
        'I often meet him.'

However, this is not to say that it is impossible to end a sentence with a clitic (contra De Bray). Toman (1981) cites the following examples using the reflexive clitic, *się* (remarking that the (b) and (c) examples sound literary):

9.63   a) Ten stary pan się wczoraj ogolił.
           That old man REFL yesterday shaved
        b) Ten stary pan wczoraj się ogolił.
        c) Ten stary pan wczoraj ogolił się.'
           'That old man shaved himself yesterday.'

The negative participle *nie* always procliticizes to the verb (just as in Serbo-Croat, but not as in Macedonian). This means that the only word order possible for 9.64 is that given:

9.64   Nie spotykam go.
        Not I-meet   him
        'I don't meet him.'

The clitic pronoun can neither begin the sentence, nor intervene between *nie* and the verb. In 9.64, *nie spotykam* effectively forms a prosodic unit equivalent to the single verb *spotykam*. Likewise, the word order in 9.65 is a consequence of the same factors that govern the word order in 9.62, given that *nie spotykam* again forms a prosodic unit:

9.65   Teraz go nie spotykam.
        Nowadays him not I-meet
        'I don't meet him nowadays.'

When we increase the number of phrasal stresses in the clause, the distributional possibilities for the clitic are increased. Thus, in 9.66–9.67 the pronoun has two natural sites (note that Polish has obligatory double negation, which explains the appearance of the pleonastic negative participle in 9.67):

9.66   a) Teraz go często spotykam.
           Nowadays him often I-meet
        b) Teraz często go spotykam.
           'I often meet him nowadays.'

9.67   a) Teraz go nigdy nie spotykam.
           Nowadays him never not I-meet
        b) Teraz nigdy go nie spotykam.
           'I never meet him nowadays.'

The word orders we have seen thus far have been 'unmarked' and hence haven't borne any special emphasis. However, if the verb appears earlier in the clause than the adverb in such cases, it receives a certain degree of extra emphasis. Under these circumstances it is liable to attract its pronoun as an enclitic, as in 9.68 (contrast 9.66):

9.68   Często spotykam go w mieście
          often I-meet him in town
          'I often meet him in town.'

Like the other languages we've seen, Polish imposes the order Dative < Accusative on strings of clitics:

9.69   Daj mi go
          Give 1sg.-DAT 3sgN.-ACC
          'Give me it.'

9.70   Bardzo mi się podoba Ewa.
          Much 1sg.-DAT REFL likes Ewa
          'I like Ewa a lot.'

However, this can't be regarded as a straightforward constraint on the elements of a cluster because it is possible to break up strings of clitics in Polish (unlike the other languages we have seen thus far):

9.71   Teraz mu takie książki się nie podobają.
          Nowadays 3sg.M-DAT such books REFL NEG like
          'He doesn't like such books nowadays.'

Polish pronominal clitics, then, enjoy almost as much freedom as non-clitic pronominals in other languages. However, we again see remnants of the Wackernagel positioning of clitics, in that they are not allowed to occupy absolute initial position. Moreover, we also see remnants of templatic constraints on word order, as a result of which the Dative clitic precedes the Accusative.

In many respects, then, the pronominal clitics behave almost like real words. The main reason for calling them clitics is that they have a somewhat restricted distribution compared with the full form pronominals, which behave just like ordinary nouns. When we turn to the clitics which make up the auxiliary system of Polish we encounter formatives which look much more like affixes.

The past tense of Polish verbs is formed in much the same way as in Serbo-Croat, using a participle ending in *-l* and a reduced form of the verb *to be*. In elementary handbooks of the language the impression is often given that the auxiliary has become a kind of past tense affix, rather in the way that the future and conditional affixes in Romance have developed from an auxiliary verb attached to a non-finite form. Thus, it is typical to see a verb such as *dać*, 'to give', conjugated in the past tense as in table 9.9.

We can analyse these forms morphologically in the following way. The verb stem appears as *dał/dal*, the alternation depending solely on the nature of the following vowel. Then we have a set of subject agreement markers, comprising two parts. The

Table 9.9 Past tense of *dać* 'give'

	Singular			Plural	
	Masc.	Fem.	Neut.	Masc.	Fem./Neut.
1	dałem	dałam	_____	daliśmy	dałyśmy
2	dałeś	dałaś	_____	daliście	dałyście
3	dał	dała	dało	dali	dały

first is a vowel indicating number and gender, as shown in table 9.10a. The second is a person marker, whose forms are given in table 9.10b. This is derived from the auxiliary verb 'to be', as can be seen from comparison with the forms recorded for the language in the fourteenth century, shown in table 9.10c. (In the modern language the verb 'to be' is conjugated in the present tense using the endings of table 9.10b added to the stem *jest-*: *jestem, jesteś, jest, jesteśmy, jesteście, są.*)

There are three principal phonological reasons for wanting to call these formatives affixes rather than clitics. These are summarized in Booij and Rubach's (1987) description of the phenomenon. The first concerns the appearance of the vowel /e/ in the masc. sg. forms. This vowel is not motivated morphologically; instead, its

Table 9.10a Number/gender markers (Polish verb)

Singular			Plural	
Masc.	Fem.	Neut.	Masc.	Fem./Neut.
_____	-a	-o	-i	-y

Table 9.10b Person markers (Polish verb)

	Singular	Plural
1	-m	-śmy
2	-ś	-ście
3	_____	_____

Table 9.10c The verb *być* 'to be' (XIV century)

	Singular	Plural
1	jeśm	jeśmy
2	jeś	jeście
3	je	są

origin is morphophonemic. Polish has a pattern of vowel-zero alternations in which /e/ acts rather like an epenthetic vowel to break up consonant clusters (cf. the discussion of Slavic 'jers' in chapter 4). The alternations are conditioned morphophonemically, however, not phonologically. Booij and Rubach (1987) argue that they are part of the lexical phonology of the language, and that the alternations are part of the cyclic phonology. Since the alternation is triggered by the formatives *-m*, *-ś* and so on, this means that they must be attached in the lexicon, and this strongly suggests they must be affixes.

The second phonological rule is stress assignment. With a handful of exceptions, stress falls on the penultimate syllable in Polish (Hammond, 1989). Stress assignment is generally assumed to be a lexical rule in Polish (though not necessarily cyclic). When we look at polysyllabic verb stems we find that this is still true of the masc. sg. forms which receive an extra vowel. Thus, from the verb *robić* 'to do', we obtain the stress patterns in 9.72 (where the stressed vowel is indicated in boldface):

9.72   a) **robił** 'he did'
        b) ro**bi**łem 'I did'
        c) ro**bi**łeś 'you did'

The fact that the stress shifts in 9.72b, c shows that the *-em*, *-eś* formatives are treated as part of the word at the level of lexical phonology, rather than being syntactically added clitics.

The third rule which interacts with past tense formation is a rule of Vowel Raising applying to stems whose final syllable has /o/ before a voiced consonant. Under certain morphophonologically derived conditions this vowel raises to /u/, orthographically represented as *ó*, when no other vowel follows in the word. Thus, we have alternations such as 9.73:

9.73   a) Ewa mogła.
        Ewa could
        'Ewa could.'

        b) Jan mógł.
        Jan could
        'Jan could.'

As might be expected, the Raising rule fails to apply when the *-em*, *-eś*, formatives are added. This suggests that the rule treats these formatives like affixes, so that the /o/ is no longer the last vowel in the word:

9.73   c) Ja mogłem.
        I could
        'I could.'

Given these facts, we would normally conclude that the Polish clitics had become morphologized, just as has happened with the future and conditional forms of languages such as French and Spanish. However, there is one property of these formatives which prevents us from analysing them as affixes, and that is the fact that, optionally, they may attach to almost any other word in the clause. The major constraints seem to be that they may not attach to the negative particle *nie* or to prepositions, and that they must appear either on the verb itself or somewhere to its left. (Sussex, 1980, provides an interesting summary of these facts, as well as discussion of cases in which the clitics may not move.) Thus, we find examples such as those of 9.74–9.79:

Pronouns:
9.74   a) Ja to robiłem
             I that did-1sg.M
      b) Ja tom robił.
      c) Jam to robił.
         'I did that.'

Complementizers:
9.75   a) Co ty robiłaś?
             What you did-Fsg.
      b) Coś ty robiła?
         'What did you do?'

      c) Czy tam byłeś?
             Question-particle there you-were-Msg.
      d) Czyś tam był?
         'Were you there?'

      e) Myślał, że tam byłem.
             he-thought that there I-was-M.
      f) Myślał, żem tam był.
         'He thought that I was there.'

Conjunctions:
9.76   a) Nie kazali mi ale robiłem.
             not they-told me but I-did-M.
      b) Nie kazali mi alem robił.
         'They didn't tell me to but I did it.'

Adverbs:
9.77   a) Daleko poszła.
             Far   I-went-F
      b) Dalekom poszła.
         'I went a long way.'

Nouns:
9.78   a) W domu to zrobiliście?
             At home it you-did-Mpl.
      b) W domuście to zrobili?
         'Did you make it at home?'

Adjectives/numerals:
9.79   a) Jeden mieliśmy.
             One   we-had-M.
          b) Jedeneśmy mieli.
             'We had one.'

This type of behaviour distinguishes the Polish auxiliary formatives from those of Serbo-Croat or of Portuguese. It would seem that at the time when the analytic past tense forms derived from the *-l* participle and the auxiliary were ousting the older (now defunct) synthetic forms, order of clitic placement was already fairly fluid. Thus, although there was a natural tendency in the fourteenth century to attach the auxiliary to the participle, this was by no means fixed, so that forms such as 9.80 are recorded in medieval Polish documents (Klemensiewicz, 1985: 113):

9.80   Chlebaście nie jedli.
          bread-2pl. not ate-Mpl.
          'You didn't eat bread.'

The fact that the formatives show virtually no selection properties with respect to their hosts strongly indicates that they are clitics and not affixes proper. Again, when they attach to stems other than verbs, the clitics have exactly the phonological effects noted when they attach to verb stems. Booij and Rubach argue that the cliticization must take place in the lexicon, and that the syntactic constraints on the occurrence of clitics must be handled by a surface syntactic filter.

Interestingly, there is one form which is often regarded as a clitic but which seems to behave differently from either the lexical auxiliary clitics or the pronominal clitics. This is the conditional formative *by*. This (like its congener in other Slav languages) is also derived from the verb 'to be'. Booij and Rubach argue, however, that it is a syntactic clitic, on the grounds that it shows none of the phonological behaviour of the lexical clitics. Thus, it doesn't affect stress (9.81) and it doesn't block Raising (9.82):

9.81   a) Protestował.   'He protested.'
          b) Protestowałby.   'He would protest.'

9.82   Mógłby.   'He would be able.'

Moreover, *by* itself can act as host to the auxiliary clitics and it can also appear in initial position in the clause, without any host to encliticize to:

9.83   a) Ja to zrobiłbym.
             I it do-COND-1sg.M
          b) Ja to bym zrobił.
          c) Bym ja to zrobił.
             'I would do it.'

9.84   a) Teraz to zrobiłby.
            Now it do-COND-3sg.M
        b) By teraz to zrobił.
            'He would do it now.'

Booij and Rubach claim that this shows that *by* is a clitic which is moved syntactically from its postverbal position. More likely, however, seems an analysis in which *by* is simply a particle (more specifically, a kind of adverb, cf. Zwicky, 1985b, on this distinction). All of its properties, including its appearance in clause initial position, would then be explained without further stipulation.

There is one final wrinkle to mention. In the standard language the clitics -*śmy*, -*ście*, unlike -*em* and -*eś*, do not cause stress to be shifted forward. Thus, we are supposed to say *robiliśmy* and not *robilíśmy*. Booij and Rubach note that there is a tendency in the colloquial language, however, for the latter (expected) pronunciation to replace the former. Presumably, the reason for the difference in behaviour is that -*śmy* and -*ście* contain their own inherent vowels. It is intriguing that even some five centuries or so after the auxiliary system of Polish first became consolidated, the status of its formatives is not entirely settled.

9.1.5 *Résumé*

Let's take stock of our results. We've seen auxiliary verbs and pronominals losing their status as full words and becoming clitics. In some cases, for instance, the pronominals and the future tense marker in Serbo-Croat, the (nonstressed) clitic is paired with a corresponding free standing (stressable) word, and the clitic can be seen as a morphophonological reduction of that word.

In Serbo-Croat, the pronominal clitics and certain of the auxiliaries, together with the modal (interrogative) particle, *li*, congregate in a particular position in the sentence, the so-called Wackernagel position, or P2. On the other hand, the future auxiliary (derived from the verb 'to want') is in the process of being fused with the infinitive form of the verb, thereby turning into a kind of suffix. In Macedonian, the pronominal clitics attach to the verb itself, as though they were inflectional affixes. This is also true of pronouns in Portuguese (and other Romance languages). Moreover, the future tense auxiliary in these languages, as in Serbo-Croat, became an enclitic historically, and now appears as a genuine inflectional suffix. However, in Portuguese there are interesting remnants of the clitic status of the future marker, in that pronominal clitics can intervene between it and its stem, a rather unusual feature.

The clitics of Serbo-Croat, Macedonian and Portuguese all clearly show the tendency of clitics in clitic clusters to line up in a particular order. In this respect they are highly reminiscent of the affix templates described in chapter 6 for Navajo. This templatic property is true of both the Serbo-Croat clitic cluster, whose distribution is determined by syntax, and the Macedonian and Romance clusters, whose distribution is defined with respect to a single lexical category, the verb.

Syntactically, the pronominal clitics in Serbo-Croat and Portuguese behave like pronouns, in the sense that they 'stand for' a full NP argument. This means that the clitic and the full NP exclude each other.[12] In this respect, they are very different from the pronominal affixes or agreement markers of languages such as Chukchee, in which the affix is an obligatory concomitant of the overt NP argument. However, Macedonian shows one way in which a clitic system can drift into an agreement system for, with definite direct object NPs (including full forms of pronouns), the 'clitic pronouns' are obligatory, just like Chukchee agreement markers.

The last case study, Polish, presented elements of these systems but in a more fluid form. The pronominal forms can be divided morphophonologically into full forms and clitic (nonstressable) forms. However, clitics behave much more like free standing pronouns, in that they are not bound to the verb, but neither are they bound to a particular sentence position. Nonetheless, there are constraints on where pronominal clitics can appear. In particular, they are enclitics, in that they must have a word to their left to 'lean' on. This doesn't hold of the full form, stressed, pronominals. Moreover, when we have a string of clitic pronouns, we find that there is a morphosyntactically defined template ordering (Dative before Accusative), which isn't reflected in the word order of full NPs. The auxiliary clitic system of Polish is particularly fascinating, because morphophonologically the clitics look like affixes, yet they can attach to any word in the sentence (provided that word isn't to the right of the verb). Overall, the Polish clitic systems poses very special problems for a general theory of clitics.

9.2   Definitions of clitics

The situation I've just summarized shows that even within a closely-knit language group like Slavonic there is great variety amongst those things traditionally called clitics. They may or may not have a corresponding, phonologically similar, full form with similar meaning or function; they may or may not be restricted to a particular position in the sentence or to a particular lexical category; and they may or may not undergo/trigger phonologically irregular allomorphy.

Matters become even more complex if we take languages in which the notion of 'clitic' doesn't figure saliently in traditional descriptions. In (spoken) English, for instance, we find reduced forms of auxiliary verbs, particles and pronouns, as illustrated in 9.85–9.91:

9.85   a) Harriet is a linguist.
          b) Harriet [s] a linguist.

9.86   a) Harriet is buying a book.
          b) Harriet [s] buying a book.

9.87   a) Harriet had bought this book.
          b) Harriet [əd] bought this book.

9.88   a) Harriet would buy this book.
          b) Harriet [əd] buy this book.

9.89   a) The man I just phoned up would buy this book.
          b) The man I just phoned up [əd] buy this book.

9.90   a) Put your hands up.
            b) Put[jə] hands up.
            c) Pu[tʃə] hands up.

9.91   a) Give them to me.
            b) Giv[m̩tə] me.

This list is just a handful of relevant cases, of course. What, then, is the relationship between the reduced forms such as *'s, 've, 'd, 'em, tə* and so on and their full forms, *is, has, have, had, would, them, to*? An obvious way to look at them is to say that the reduced forms are essentially phonological reductions, due to a faster and less careful speech style. This view has often been assumed in the past, and is presumably the case with the alternation between full and reduced forms of the preposition and infinitive markers *to*: [tu ~ tə]. However, this can't be the whole story. For instance, *is* gets reduced to [s] in 9.86b, yet *was* is never so reduced, even though both *had* and *would* are reduced to [d]. In other words, the reductions are subject to highly specific lexical conditioning (cf. Kaisse, 1985).

Turning to the data presented in §9.1, can we regard the pronominal clitic forms in our four sample languages as phonologically reduced variants of the full forms? Consider again the Serbo-Croat data from table 9.2. The phonological correspondence is very close except for the 3sg.F which is *je* in the clitic form and *nju* in the full form. Here we seem to have a kind of (partial) suppletion. A similar phenomenon can be seen in the Portuguese pronouns in table 9.3. In other words, the relationship between full form and clitic is governed by lexical allomorphy in certain instances and not purely by phonology. So we would wish to distinguish between the type of phonological clitic illustrated by infinitival *to*, and the more morphological type of clitic illustrated by Serbo-Croat and Portuguese pronominals. A further difference is that the pronominal clitics will still be used in their given forms even in very careful speech, while even highly informal speech still won't turn full forms of the pronouns into the clitic forms (though other genuine phonological reductions may occur). It looks as though we will have to distinguish sharply between the two sorts of clitic. Finally, the clitics represented by Serbo-Croat *li* can't be related to a full form word anyway, so for the existence of this type of clitic we would need an explanation which was independent of phonological reduction.

Reasoning such as this led Zwicky (1977) to propose a classification of clitics into **simple clitics**, **special clitics** and **bound words**. A paradigm example of a simple clitic for Zwicky would be the English reduced pronouns such as illustrated in 9.90–9.91. The form of these seems to be dictated largely by phrase phonology, and can thus be affected by speech rate, level of formality and such like. The special clitics are those which effectively are separate allomorphs of a full form word, such as the Serbo-Croat or Portuguese pronouns. These are not derived from full form equivalents by phrase phonological reduction processes, and therefore aren't dependent on factors such as speaking rate. The bound words are the words which don't correspond to a full form and thus can't possibly be analysed as reductions of 'real' words, but which nevertheless need a host and in some cases are restricted to a particular sentence position, such as Serbo-Croat *li*.

The frequently observed correlations between special clitics and full words can generally be looked upon as a type of allomorphy. It seems reasonable to assume that words which have become simple clitics by fast speech reduction might get reanalysed by a generation of language learners as special clitics. Moreover, if the special clitic always has a host of a particular syntactic category, such as a verb, then it is but a short step from special clitic to affix. In Serbo-Croat this seems to be in the process of happening to the clitic form of the verb 'to want', used as a future marker. In most of the Romance languages this process has gone to completion for the future tense. Nevertheless, we've seen that in Portuguese the auxiliary verb ex-clitic has left relics of its former status, in that pronominal clitics can intervene between it and its host. This is something which bona fide tense inflections don't normally permit (recall the examples in table 9.7 and example 9.60).

This basic typology, while appealing, leaves a number of questions unanswered. It's especially difficult to know exactly what counts as the type of phonological reduction which would give rise to a simple clitic, as opposed to the morphophonological alternation needed to produce a special clitic. In Polish, for instance, which doesn't permit any kind of vowel reduction, the only difference between the monosyllabic full form *nas* 'us' and clitic form *nas* is that the clitic can never be stressed. Yet the 3sg. masc. pronominal does undergo reduction, from disyllabic *jego* to monosyllabic *go*. Does this mean that *go* is a special clitic and *nas* a simple clitic? Presumably not. On the other hand, there are grounds for saying that the alternation between full and reduced forms of auxiliaries in English is dependent on speech rate, level of formality and so on. Yet we know that it would be highly misleading to say that *'s* is a 'reduced' form of *is* (or *has*), especially given that *was* fails to reduce.

Zwicky's original typology didn't attempt a unified characterization of cliticization. Klavans (1982, 1985) argues that a unified theory is possible, however, if we draw certain distinctions. These are presented in the form of parameters along which a clitic system in a language may vary. Different sets of clitics in one and the same language may exhibit different parametrizations.

Klavans argues first that clitics are lexical items with their own morphosyntactic and morphophonological properties. These include syntactic category and also a subcategorization frame. If we think back to the framework of Lieber (1980; see §6.2.2) this in itself doesn't distinguish clitics either from words or from affixes. Klavans claims that what distinguishes clitics from both words and affixes is that clitics are (usually) subcategorized to attach syntactically to a phrase of some sort. This phrase is the domain of cliticization. In this respect clitics are different from affixes, which must attach to word (or stem) level categories. Klavans uses the term **phrasal affix** to refer to clitics in this connection. At the same time clitics don't have the freedom of real words, in that they must show **liaison** with some other word (that is, they must attach phonologically to a host).

Klavans's central proposal is that, for a given clitic system, in addition to specifying the domain of cliticization, we must set the values of three binary parameters, two syntactic, one phonological. The first parameter defines whether the clitic is positioned to the right or the left of its domain, and has values *Initial* and *Final*. The second parameter defines whether the clitic comes *After* or *Before* the peripheral constituent of the domain. The third parameter determines whether the clitic will attach phonologically to a host on its left (Enclitic) or its right (Proclitic). The system is summarized in table 9.11, where I take a schematic ditransitive clause ending in a sentence adverbial (which is therefore not part of the VP) in a hypothetical language

Table 9.11 Klavans's typology of clitics

1	Initial, Before, Enclitic	NP = cl [V NP NP] AP
2	Initial, Before, Proclitic	NP [cl = V NP NP] AP
3	Initial, After, Enclitic	NP [V = cl NP NP] AP
4	Initial, After Proclitic	NP [V cl = NP NP] AP
5	Final, Before, Enclitic	NP [V NP = cl NP] AP
6	Final, Before, Proclitic	NP [V NP cl = NP] AP
7	Final, After, Enclitic	NP [V NP NP = cl] AP
8	Final, After, Proclitic	NP [V NP NP] cl = AP

and illustrate the positioning of clitics in the domain of the VP for each type. I assume that cliticization is defined in terms of constituents and not words.

Notice that there is a tension between the Before/After parameter and the Enclitic/Proclitic parameter. If a clitic has the Before value of P2 but is an enclitic, as 1 or 5, it will have two distinct hosts, one syntactic, the other phonological. The same is true if a proclitic has the After value (as in 4, 8).

According to Klavans it is possible to find examples of all eight, though a number of them are represented by somewhat dubiously attested cases. I shall illustrate examples she provides of Types 1, 2, 3, 5.

We begin with type 2, in which the clitic precedes its host syntactically (Initial, Before) and phonologically (Proclitic). Klavans argues that the definite article in Classical Greek was of this type, where the domain of cliticization is N'.[13] Her example is 9.92, in which the clitic article is preceded by a clitic adverbial, which itself is cliticized to a proclitic preposition:

9.92   en = o:n = te: = pole:
         in = therefore = the = city (clitic = adverb = clitic = noun)
         'In the city, therefore, ...'

Interestingly, some discourse level particles which appear as enclitics on the first word of the sentence may treat articles as hosts. Goodwin (1894) provides an example in which we have string of articles in a recursive possessive construction, the first of which is host to the clitic adverbial *gar* 'for':

9.93   ta = gar = te:s = to:n = pollo:n psukhe:s ommata
         the = for = [of.the = [of.the = cities] soul] eyes

         'For, the eyes of the soul of the cities ...'

Type 1 can be illustrated by NP markers in Kwakwala. Example 9.94 is taken from Anderson (1984b):

9.94

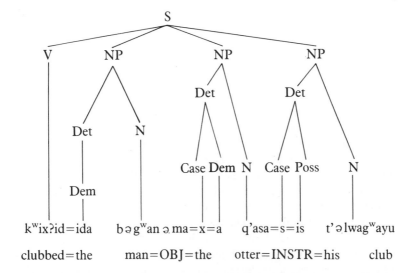

k^wixʔid=ida   bəg^wan ə ma=x=a   q'asa=s=is   t'əlwag^wayu

clubbed=the   man=OBJ=the   otter=INSTR=his   club

It is apparent from this tree diagram that the morphological case markers and the deictic determiners attach themselves as enclitics to the preceding word. We therefore assume that the domain of cliticization for these markers is the NP and that they are attached Initially, Before the first element (in this case the head noun). By analysing such markers as enclitics we are then not committed to the rather startling claim that a verb bears inflectional affixes marking the definiteness of the following noun, or that the object is inflected for the case and possessor of the instrumental adverbial.

The examples in 9.95, from the Australian language Ngiyambaa, show a clitic which attaches to the first word of the sentence:

9.95   a) girbadja = ndu   mamiyi gabira.
         kangaroo = 2NOM catch-PAST yesterday
        b) gabira = ndu mamiya girbidja.
           'You caught a kangaroo yesterday.'

Here we assume that we are dealing with an Enclitic which has the sentence as its domain, and which is attached Initially, but After the first constituent (or word). This characterization corresponds to the classical P2, or Wackernagel position.

Another Australian language, Nganhcara, illustrates Type 5. The clitic *=ngu* cross-references a dative pronoun. It is analysed as a sentence domain Final Enclitic attaching Before the peripheral (hence, final) constituent. Word order in Nganhcara is very free except that the verb is restricted to final position, so the syntactic host will be the verb:

9.96   a) nhila   pama-ng nhingu pukpe-wu kuʔa = ngu wa:
           he/NOM man-ERG him/DAT child-DAT dog-DATsg. give
           'The man gave the dog to the child.'
        b) nhila pama-ng nhingu kuʔa pukpe-wu = ngu wa:
        c) nhila pama-ng kuʔa pukpe-wu nhingu = ngu wa:
        d) kuʔa nhingu pukpe-we nhila pama-ng = ngu wa:
        e) kuʔa nhingu pukpe-wu pama-ng nhila = ngu wa:

The =*ngu* clitic is actually ambiguous syntactically, in that it may also appear After the edge of the sentence domain, i.e. at the very end of the sentence, as in 9.96f:

9.96   f) nhila pama-ng nhingu pukpe-wu ku?a wa: = ngu

While Klavans's approach accounts quite neatly for a number of general features of clitic systems, certain criticisms can be levelled against it. First, two of the theoretically predicted possibilities are at best dubious. These are represented by Types 4, a phrase initial proclitic placed after the first constituent, and 6, a phrase final proclitic placed before the last constituent. However, even if we grant that examination of further languages might unearth decent examples of Type 6, we may have some misgivings about Types 4 and 5.

If we consider all eight Types, then some are more 'iconic' than others. For instance, in Types 2 and 7 we attach the clitic to the peripheral element of the domain, both syntactically and phonologically. In a certain sense this is the most direct location for cliticization because the word which stands at the periphery of the domain is singled out for marking by the clitic. Moreover, the clitics attached to the left of the domain appear to the left of their host, and those attached to the right of the domain appear to the right of their host. However, in Types 1 and 8 the phonological attachment is in the opposite direction to that of the syntactic attachment (an example of a bracketing paradox). Thus, the English reduced auxiliary attaches to the left of the VP syntactically but to the right of the subject NP phonologically. Such constructions undoubtedly exist, so we must ensure our theory doesn't exclude them. Types 3 and 6 also represent a deviation from a straightforward mapping of form and function. Here, the clitic successfully marks the peripheral word of the domain of cliticization, but attaches phonologically to the 'wrong' side of that word. Klavans claims that this is how the Wackernagel position is defined in the case of Type 3 cliticization, but this seems unlikely. The Wackernagel position is generally characterized as the position after the first *constituent* in the sentence, not after the first word, as required by Klavans's account. However, it seems likely that such situations do exist. The Latin conjunction -*que* in its use as sentence coordinator, illustrated in chapter 2 (example 2.6), is a good candidate, attaching Initially to S, After the first word as an Enclitic.

Thus, Types 1–3 and their mirror images, Types 6–8, seem to be the kind of clitic systems we might expect (particularly if we rule out of consideration clitics which attach to specific lexical classes). Admittedly, we might feel that Types 1, 3 and 7 would be more common than the other three types, given that suffixation seems to be more common than prefixation. However, Types 4, 5 should, arguably, be excluded on general grounds unless overwhelming empirical evidence should turn up in their favour. Now, Klavans cites Nganhcara as exemplifying Type 5. However, it seems reasonable to suppose that this case can be analysed differently. Recall that word order is very free in this language, except that the verb must appear finally. If we say that this is the result of a syntactic rule, then we can argue that placement of the =*ngu* clitic is sentence Final, After the last word, but that optionally this placement can occur before the verb placement rule. In other words, we have a Type 7 system. In this way we also account for the data of 9.96f (cf. Sproat, 1988).

Another problem concerns the domain of cliticization. We can regard cliticization as a unitary phenomenon only if we can permit the domain over which it occurs to be either a phrasal category or a lexical one (for instance, a verb). This encounters difficulties with Serbo-Croat P2 clitics, where 'P2' can be defined either as 'after the first constituent' or as 'after the first word' (cf. 9.19 above). In addition to this, some would prefer a more principled difference to be drawn between 'lexical clitics', attaching to a particular word whatever its position in the sentence, and 'phrasal clitics', attaching to a syntactically defined position, irrespective of the category of the host word. Klavans (1985) herself suggests that this might mean that the clitics of Romance languages are actually agreement markers. One reason for adopting this view is that, if a clitic selects a particular lexical category, then the first two (syntactic) parameters are superfluous, and we can define the clitic position solely in terms of the third. The proposal for Romance pronominal clitics is particularly attractive for our Macedonian data, and it's a suggestion I'll be exploring in the next section. But it isn't entirely satisfactory for most (varieties of the) Romance languages, in which the clitics are never 'doubled' by an overt NP, for in such languages the clitic is behaving syntactically much more like a genuine pronominal. Moreover, in French we have clitics *y* and *en* which have an adverbial function (meaning 'there' and 'of it/them' respectively). These, too, presumably can't be analysed as agreement markers.

Finally, Klavans's scheme doesn't directly address the question of the internal structure of clitic clusters, of the kind represented in the 'template' for Serbo-Croat in 9.20 and elsewhere. This doesn't present any serious obstacle in itself for her overall conception. Nonetheless, it seems to be such an integral part of most clitic systems that any theory which fails to account for it appears incomplete.

Zwicky's original classification doesn't provide a hard-and-fast set of criteria for clitichood; rather, it is a descriptive, and essentially pretheoretical, taxonomy. In later work, Zwicky has attempted a more thoroughgoing and motivated classification, which at the same time seeks to distinguish clitics from other things, specifically, free standing words, and inflectional affixes (Zwicky, 1985b, 1987a; Zwicky and Pullum, 1983). The essential idea is that prototypical clitics are syntactically like words, in that they are relatively independent of the words they attach to (that is, they are not specifically selected by their bases), they have a straightforward meaning, they tend not to show idiosyncratic allomorphy themselves, and they do not condition idiosyncratic allomorphy on their hosts. Inflectional affixes, on the other hand, are highly dependent on the bases they attach to, exhibit multiple exponence, and show much allomorphic variation including suppletion. In addition, they frequently condition idiosyncratic allomorphy on the stems to which they attach. Zwicky argues from these properties that cliticization is an essentially syntactic phenomenon, while inflectional affixation is morphological.

These considerations sometimes produce analyses running counter to received wisdom. In Zwicky and Pullum (1983) the criteria are applied to the *n't* negation element in English. This is usually thought of as a contraction of *not*, and hence, presumably, as a simple clitic in Zwicky's (1977) terms. Zwicky and Pullum reason that, in fact, the contracted negative shows pretty well all the signs of being an inflectional affix and none of the properties of a clitic.

Zwicky (1987b) re-examines the English possessive formative, *'s*, which he originally identified as a bound word. He notes that this element has the property of being suppressed by another instance of a morpheme with the same shape (presumably /z/ in underlying form). Thus, we have the data of 9.97:

9.97   a) Katz's reactions   (/katsəz/)
             b) the two cats' reactions   (/kats/)
             c) anyone who hurries'/*hurries's ideas
             d) my two kids'/*kids's ideas
             e) a friend of my two kids'/*kids's's ideas

Example 9.97a shows that possessive 's is pronounced as /əz/ after a noun ending in a sibilant. This forms a minimal pair with 9.97b where the 's formative is dropped after the plural morpheme. Example 9.97c shows the same thing with the 3sg. verb ending, and examples 9.97d, e show that 's can be dropped twice after the plural form.

If the possessive 's is a genuine clitic, then, reasons Zwicky, it will be put in place by syntactic and not morphological rules, just as the 's corresponding to is or has is placed in the syntax. However, unlike the reduced auxiliary verbs, the possessive formative will give us problems if we make this assumption. The zero allomorphy of the possessive after words ending in another /z/ morpheme requires a statement along the lines 'the possessive is /z/ unless its host ends in a morpheme /z/'. This means that (i) the morphological composition of the host has to be visible and (ii) the condition is a statement about when zero allomorphy occurs. Both of these properties are unheard of and arguably should be excluded on general theoretical grounds.

From this, Zwicky concludes that the possessive is an inflectional affix, which is, however, attached to the edge of the phrase rather than to the head of the phrase. Since pretty well any word in the language can end a noun phrase this means that all words in English are given this inflection. The stipulation that the preceding (inflectional) morpheme not itself be /z/ can be recast as something along the lines 'affix /z/ unless the stem already ends in a morpheme /z/'. This kind of thing, effectively a variety of morphological haplology, is not uncommon in inflection. An example which readily springs to mind is that of the Turkish plural morpheme -ler. In the possessive, 'theirs', this takes an affix -i to become -leri. Thus, ev, 'house', gives us evler, 'house', evi, 'his house', and evleri, 'their house' (= [ev + [ler + i]]). This last form can also mean 'his houses' (= [[ev+ler] +i]). However, there is no form *evlerleri to correspond to 'their houses'. Instead, one of the ler formatives drops and we obtain (again) evleri.

From this new vantage point Zwicky also discusses the problem of the Portuguese 'infixed' pronominal forms[14] which I illustrated in §9.1.3. He suggests that the two most plausible analyses are that the pronominal forms and the future/conditional forms are either (i) both clitics or (ii) both inflections. The fact that the Dative and Accusative pronoun forms are fused and the fact that verb stems in /r z s/ undergo special allomorphy argues in favour of the second alternative. However, if the pronoun forms really are inflections, it's hard to see what grammatical function they have, since they can't be used when there's a full NP in direct or indirect object position and hence they can't be used as agreement markers (cf. my remarks earlier about Klavans's difficulties with verb clitics).

To conclude: there seems to be some consensus that it is necessary to separate out the syntactic properties of clitics from their morphophonological properties. The analysis of Kwakwala, for instance, shows that this distinction has to be made. Moreover, this conclusion is consonant with influential views of the morphology-syntax interface which will be reviewed in part IV.[15]

Next, we must ask what kind of things can be clitics. If we set aside the relatively unproblematical case of words which have reduced forms as a result of regular rules of phrase phonology, then we can distinguish two basic sorts of clitic. The first is the type of clitic which seems to have the same morphosyntactic function as full words elsewhere in the language. English auxiliary verbs are an example of this. The second type represents those clitics which don't seem to correspond to a full word. The possessive *'s* is an example of this. There is a tendency to think of the first type as bound words, and the second as phrasal affixes. However, we've seen that Zwicky and Pullum (1983) have argued that *n't*, apparently a short form of *not*, is actually an inflectional ending which only attaches to auxiliaries. Moreover, Zwicky (1987b) has argued that possessive *'s* isn't a clitic, and isn't even a phrasal affix, but rather is an inflectional ending which attaches to the end of phrases.

There's some evidence that unusual inflections such as *n't* aren't so uncommon as might be thought. A curious case concerns reduced auxiliaries. I've said that these must be regarded as separate allomorphs of the full form auxiliaries, because there are no regular phrase phonology rules which could produce, say, /d/ from /had/. However, when we look carefully at the distribution of these elements, it appears as though they behave differently depending on the exact nature of their hosts. Reduced forms of *had*, *would*, *have* and *will/shall* combine directly with pronoun forms, as in 9.98:

9.98   a) She [d] seen it.
          b) I [d] have seen it.
          c) We [v] seen it.
          d) You [l] see it.

However, when such reduced forms attach to full nouns, they have to take the form [əd əv əl] with a schwa, even after vowel final words. Thus, we get 9.99:

9.99   a) Lee [əd] / *Lee [d] seen it.
          b) Bligh [əd] / *Bligh [d] have seen it.
          c) Pru [əl] / *Pru [l] see it.

Moreover, the pronouns themselves can't take the fully reduced form (with schwa) if they're part of a conjoined NP:

9.100   a) Tom and she [əd] / *she [d] see it.
          b) Tom and I [əd] / *I [d] have seen it.
          c) Me and you [əl] / *you [l] see it.

What this suggests (to me, at least) is that the pronouns are inflected for the /d v l/ forms, much as auxiliaries are inflected for negation, and that (i) it is only personal pronouns which can be so inflected and (ii) the inflection is lexical, not phrasal, thus ruling out the schwaless cases in 9.100.

When the question of the nature of clitics and their full word hosts is settled there will remain the question of clitic clusters of the kind exemplified in Serbo-Croat. It remains unclear whether to regard these as a single syntactic constituent (and if so, at what syntactic level). Moreover, though clitic clusters have for some time been recognized as paradigm examples of template morphology (§6.4), there has been rather little discussion of this aspect in the recent literature, and how this might relate to the other issues surrounding the nature of clitics. Nor has there been any serious attempt to relate P2 positioning of clitic clusters to other second-position effects (though Sproat, 1988, has some interesting observations about Warlpiri and Serbo-Croat clitic clusters in this regard).

So, there is much that remains unclear. The Portuguese data still defy adequate analysis. The Polish data pose serious problems for all the theories of cliticization I'm familiar with (and oddly enough, have hardly been discussed anywhere in the published literature on the general problem of clitics). Perhaps most significantly, there is no obvious consensus on the basic typological distinctions that need to be drawn before a deeper theoretical explanation of cliticization phenomena can be attempted. This shouldn't come as any great surprise. After all, we are dealing here with the interface of morphology with both phonology and syntax. It is this, more than anything else, which makes cliticization a challenging area of research.

9.3   Cliticization and agreement

In the introduction to this chapter I mentioned that the study of clitic pronoun systems was of considerable interest in current theories of syntax, especially in Government-Binding theory. One good reason for this is the interaction between cliticization and argument structure. An example of this has been given in chapter 7, where we saw that reflexivization is often signalled by means of a clitic. At the same time, the reflexive formative may have the property of detransitivizing a transitive verb (in a certain sense). Another reason is the inherent importance that any type of pronominal reference system has for syntactic theory. In addition, we know that pronominal clitic systems have often developed historically into agreement systems.

The syntactic literature on clitics is replete with discussion of the basic properties of pronominal clitics and debate as to how linguistic theory should tackle them. The main problem boils down to this: are clitics basically a kind of pronoun with limited syntactic distribution, or are they variety of loosely attached affix signalling syntactic dependencies in the manner of agreement morphology?

The original analysis of pronominal clitics in the transformational literature assumed that they are pronouns which originate in underlying structure in the position usually occupied by complements to the verb. They are then moved by transformation to whatever syntactic position they occupy on the surface. An analysis of this sort was provided (within essentially the Standard Model of generative grammar) for French by Kayne (1975) and for Serbo-Croat by Browne (1974). The rationale for this is straightforward: object clitics are in complementary distribution with full NP objects in these languages. The simplest way of accounting for this distribution, together with the fact that the clitics express the function of objects, is to assume that they are indeed objects underlyingly. Hence, we would assume that the French and Serbo-Croat sentences in 9.101b and 9.102b are derived from sources such as 9.101b and 9.102a (the empty category, [ec], in the (b) examples represents the trace of movement, as is customary in Government-Binding syntax):

9.101 a) Je vois le
b) Je le vois [ec] NP
I him see
'I see him.'

9.102 a) Ja vidim ga
b) Ja ga vidim [ec] NP
I him see
'I see him.'

This means our analysis of cliticization is analogous to that of wh-movement as illustrated in 9.103:

9.103 a) You saw who
b) Who did you see [ec] NP

A further reason for this treatment is the phenomenon of clitic climbing, illustrated earlier in §9.1.1 for Serbo-Croat (see example 9.23). The phenomenon as it occurs in Italian has been discussed from the theoretical point of view by Luigi Rizzi, as part of an argument in favour of a rule of Restructuring, which has the effect of 'fusing' the matrix verb with its complement. (In Relational Grammar, the same effect is accomplished by Clause Union.) The following examples, taken from Rizzi (1978, also published as chapter 1 of Rizzi, 1982), illustrate clitic climbing in Italian. The (b) examples are all optional alternatives to the (a) forms:

9.104 a) Mario vuole risolver = lo da solo.
Mario wants to-solve = it on own
b) Mario lo vuole risolver da solo.
Mario it wants to-solve on own
'Mario wants to solve it on his own.'

9.105 a) Gianni ha dovuto parlar = gli personalmente.
Gianni has had to-speak = to-them personally
b) Gianni gli ha dovuto parlare personalmente.
Gianni to-them has had to-speak personally
'Gianni has had to speak to them personally.'

One way in which such constructions can be understood is by assuming that the clitic moves either from its position in the (a) examples, or from an underlying object position, to the new position in the matrix clause, skipping over the matrix verb (if it belongs to the right verb class).

In order to account for the fact that the verb-clitic combinations in Romance tend to behave phonologically and morphologically like verbs, it is customary to assume a kind of 'noun incorporation' analysis under which the clitic is adjoined to the lexical V node and so the whole complex retains the category V, to give a representation such as 9.106:

9.106   Je [$_V$ le [$_V$ vois]] [ec]$_{NP}$

The question now arises of the identity of the empty NP category in 9.104. Depending on a variety of assumptions, a variety of answers have been given to this question.

In the theory developed by Aoun (1985), the clitic occupies a non-argument (A') position. The empty category is therefore A'-bound. This identifies it as a variable. Aoun also assumes (from his analysis of causative constructions in French amongst other reasons) that the clitic absorbs the verb's theta role. This means that the variable also functions as an anaphor, much like an NP trace. In addition, Aoun assumes that the clitic absorbs the Case which the verb assigns. Since the *ec* is a variable and variables are usually Case marked, this may appear to cause problems but they are illusory. For the variable is no longer theta marked and hence not an argument. In this theory we retain the essential idea from the earlier studies (e.g. Kayne, 1975) that cliticization involves syntactic movement, leaving a trace (in this instance a variable).

Jaeggli (1982, 1986) offers a different analysis. He assumes simply that the clitic absorbs Case. This means that the verb still assigns its theta role to the complement NP position. Jaeggli differs from Aoun in his interpretation of the clitic position. For Jaeggli, this is neither an A position nor an A' position. This determines the nature of the empty category. Since it isn't A'-bound it can't be a variable (*pace* Aoun). Since it isn't A-bound either it can't be an NP trace. The position is governed by the verb (otherwise no theta role could be assigned to it), so that the *ec* can't be PRO. This means that the *ec* must be *pro*.[16]

A similar analysis is presented by Borer (1984a). She assumes with Jaeggli that the complement NP position is an argument position, and hence that the verb theta marks it. She, however, claims that the clitic doesn't so much absorb Case as function as a spell-out or morphological realization of the verb's Case feature. This is possible in part because she assumes that the clitic is adjoined to the verb itself, rather like an affix. (This is an assumption that Jaeggli, 1986, explicitly adopts. It is also the technical basis for Baker's treatment of noun incorporation.) Both Borer's analysis and that of Jaeggli presuppose that the clitics are base generated, for only in this way could we explain how the clitic is coindexed with a pronominal (given the added assumption that empty categories don't change their featural status during a derivation). Thus, their analyses are in a certain sense 'morphological'.

Given this brief background we are in a position to illustrate the two main ways in which analyses of clitics are important for theories of morphosyntax. The crucial constructions are the clitic doubling constructions discussed above in connection with Macedonian. The languages evincing this phenomenon which are most commonly discussed in the literature are Romanian, Hebrew and particularly Latin-American Spanish. The oft-cited Spanish sentence 9.33 (repeated here as 9.107) illustrates the point:

9.107   Lo = vimos a Juan.
          cl we-saw to Juan
          'We saw Juan.'

The clitic *lo* and the direct object *a Juan* are coreferential and hence must be coindexed.

The first point to notice is that these constructions seem to rule out a straight-forward interpretation of cliticization as movement: if the complement NP position is occupied by a lexical NP it could hardly have been occupied by a clitic in D-structure.[17]

Aoun's solution is to regard the doubled NP *a Juan* as a kind of adjunct. In effect, then, this theory says that the Spanish clitic-doubling construction is a species of syntactic antipassive, very much like Baker's analysis of antipassives. Recall that in an antipassive construction a direct object is demoted to oblique status and the verb assigns Case as though it were intransitive. Aoun's analysis is completely parallel to Baker's, except that for Baker the antipassive morpheme is an affix generated in direct object position. The failure of languages like Serbo-Croat, French and Castilian Spanish to exhibit doubling is then, presumably, to do with failure to permit the adjunct phrase to appear, in much the same way that passives in certain languages and antipassives in other languages (e.g. Tzotzil; Aissen, 1987) are unable to license an adjunct *by*-phrase or demoted object. Baker himself doesn't draw any explicit comparison between his analysis of antipassives and Aoun's treatment of cliticization. Equally, Aoun doesn't explicitly point out that he is effectively treating cliticization as a form of antipassive construction (and, hence, doesn't discuss the interesting anomaly of having a productive antipassive in a language which isn't ergative). Nor is it explained why clitic doubling is relatively rare, while it is common for suppressed arguments to appear as adjuncts in passive and antipassive constructions.

There are problems with this analysis (cf. Jaeggli, 1986, Suñer, 1988), in that it fails to predict certain facts concerning extraction possibilities from the doubled NP position, as well as other binding phenomena.[18] Jaeggli (1986) develops an analysis in which the preposition, which is obligatory in Spanish clitic doubling constructions, doesn't itself assign Case, but rather *transmits* the Case assigned by the verb. Jaeggli further assumes a process of *Case Matching* rather than Case assignment, under which the Case assigner, the verb, is matched with either a recipient or a transmitter of Case (e.g. the preposition *a*). This is, in effect, a variant of an idea originally due to Borer (1984a). In a straightforward Verb + Object construction the verb is Case Matched with the object NP. In a Verb + Animate Object construction of the type *vimos a Juan*, 'we saw Juan', without doubling clitic, the verb is Case Matched with *a*, which is itself Case Matched with *Juan*. In the clitic doubled construction we have three Case Matched pairs. The verb is Case Matched with the clitic; the verb is also Case Matched with the preposition; finally, the preposition is Case Matched with the direct object NP. This situation (that of a Case assigner being matched with more than one element) is permitted provided only one of the elements so matched is a nominal. This captures the usual restriction that Case can only be assigned to one NP.

Finally, Suñer (1988) discusses the Porteño variety of River Plate Spanish, which manifests the clitic doubling construction. She argues that the clitic neither absorbs the verb's theta role, nor its Case. With Borer and Jaeggli, she assumes that the clitic is attached to the verb as a kind of affix, though contra Jaeggli she regards this as lexical rather than syntactic affixation. The relation between the verb + clitic complex and the verb's complement is then one of agreement. The coindexing between clitic and complement NP results in a species of chain. To be well-formed, such a chain must be constructed of elements whose morphosyntactic features match. It is a language specific fact about American Spanish (specifically Argentinian Spanish) clitics that they bear the feature [+specific] and must thus be matched with a specific (e.g. definite) NP.

This implies that in the Porteño dialect the preposition *a* is not a Case assigner, for Case is assigned to the complement from the verb. This in turn implies two things: first, we should expect to see clitic doubled constructions in which the complement is not introduced by *a*; second, the preposition must have some function other than Case assignment (or even transmission). Suñer argues that the preposition is a marker of animacy. She points out that in an example such as 9.108 there is no preposition to assign Case to the *pro*:

9.108   Ya las lave todas [*pro*]
          already cl-Fpl. I-washed all-Fpl. *ec*
          'I've already washed them all (e.g. dishes)'

Since it is generally assumed that *pro* must receive Case to be licensed (Chomsky, 1982; Rizzi, 1986),[19] the Case must come from the verb, and therefore can't have been absorbed by the clitic. On the other hand, in example 9.109, the preposition duly appears, this time forcing an animate reading for the complement NP:

9.109   Ya las lave a todas [*pro*]
          'I've already washed them all (e.g. babies)'

Suñer, then, advocates an analysis for these varieties of Latin-American Spanish in which the clitic pronouns have actually become agreement markers of the sort associated with languages like Chukchee or Bantu. She explicitly points out that specificity or definiteness is a common determinant of object agreement, citing Swahili as one of the better-known cases. (Another, less controversial, example from agreement morphology would be Hungarian.) In the light of our discussion in §9.1.2 of this chapter we could draw a parallel with Macedonian, which permits doubling of direct objects only if they are definite. In effect, the only difference between, say, the Porteño dialect of Spanish and other less controversial examples of object agreement inflection is that the clitics (or pronominal affixes?) of Spanish are less fully integrated into the morphological system of the verb. This means that the Spanish object agreement markers, while syntactically agreement formatives, retain (some of) the properties of morphological clitics.[20] This can be thought of as the opposite of the position advanced in the incorporation theory of the passive of Baker et al. (1989). There, we find a formative (the passive morpheme) which is cross-linguistically an affix in the majority of cases, being treated as a kind of syntactic clitic.

Finally, it might be thought that the phenomenon of clitic climbing (exemplified in §9.1, 9.17–9.18) would pose serious problems for an agreement-style analysis. However, it's not clear what the problem is, exactly. This is because the same kind of facts are found in languages which uncontroversially have agreement morphology on the verb, and in which the verb agrees with its direct object. That is, in some languages, we find that a certain restricted class of auxiliary verbs or auxiliary-like elements will take intransitive agreements if the embedded clause is intransitive, but transitive agreements if the embedded clause is transitive, in other words, the matrix verb agrees with the object of the subordinate clause. (We might facetiously refer to this phenomenon as 'Agr climbing'.) This has been reported for Hungarian and Mordvinian, for instance. In 9.110–9.111 we see examples from Chukchee involving the verb *mook* 'to begin':

9.110   ətlon   moo-gʔe   kelitku-k.
         he-ABS begin-PAST/3sg.S study-INF
         'He began to study.'

9.111   ənan   moo-nen   rəgjulew-ək ekək   iwin-ək.
         he-ERG begin-PAST/3sg.S/3sg.O teach-INF   son-ABS hunt-INF
         'He began to teach his son to hunt.'

In 9.110 the matrix verb takes the intransitive agreement marker -*gʔe*, while in 9.111 it takes the transitive marker -*nen* (meaning '3rd sg. subject acts on 3rd sg. object').

Finally, we may note another twist in the tale of pronominal clitics. Fully-fledged pronouns in a language like English appear in so-called *dislocation* constructions, mentioned in passing in Note 12. Here, the pronoun is doubled by a full NP in a non-argument position, usually set off from the rest of the sentence intonationally. In English, we commonly observe **right dislocation**, 9.112, and perhaps less commonly, **left dislocation**, 9.113:

9.112   He teaches linguistics, that man.

9.113   That linguist, he's going to drive me insane.

Chicheŵa, like many other Bantu languages, has a set of prefixes which cross reference subjects and objects. Bresnan and Mchombo (1987) have studied this system and shown that, in the case of objects and, in certain constructions, in the case of subjects, these prefixes function just like the pronouns in examples 9.112, and not like bona fide agreement markers (of the kind we find in, say, Chukchee). For instance, they note that the object markers (OM) are optional (though the subject markers, SM, are obligatory). This is illustrated in examples 9.114–9.115:

9.114   Njûchi zi-ná-lúm-a alenje.
         bees   SM-PAST-bite-INDIC hunters
         'The bees bit the hunters.'

9.115   Njûchi zi-ná-wá-lum-a alenje.
         bees   SM-PAST-OM-bite-INDIC hunters
         'The bees bit them, the hunters.'

They use a variety of syntactic tests, including topicalization, relative clause formation, question formation and various discourse properties, to show that the construction illustrated in 9.115 is actually a type of right dislocation reminiscent of the English example 9.112, and not a case of genuine agreement. One interesting indication of this is the effect of the OM marker on word order possibilities. Without the

OM marker, the object must follow immediately after the verb; any other word order gives ungrammaticality, as shown in 9.116:

9.116   a) SVO   Njûchi zi-ná-lúm-a alenje.
          b) VOS   Zi-ná-lúm-a alenje njûchi.
          c) OVS   ⋆Alenje zi-ná-lúm-a njûchi.
          d) VSO   ⋆Zi-ná-lúm-a njûchi alenje.
          e) SOV   ⋆Njûchi alenje zi-ná-lúm-a.
          f) OSV   ⋆Alenje njûchi zi-ná-lúm-a.

This situation stands in marked contrast to the possibilities found when the OM marker is present. Then, any of the above word orders is grammatical:

9.117   a) SVO   Njûchi zi-ná-wá-lum-a alenje.
          b) VOS   Zi-ná-wá-lum-a alenje njûchi.
          c) OVS   Alenje zi-ná-wá-lum-a njûchi.
          d) VSO   Zi-ná-wá-lum-a njûchi alenje.
          e) SOV   Njûchi alenje zi-ná-wá-lum-a.
          f) OSV   Alenje njûchi zi-ná-wá-lum-a.

Bresnan and Mchombo go on to show that, under certain circumstances, the SM marker, too, behaves like an ordinary pronoun, just like the OM marker. Here, then, we have a situation in which an element which is firmly incorporated into the lexical structure, having the morpholexical properties of an affix, nonetheless behaves like an independent entity syntactically (and, indeed, pragmatically, in discourse structure).

These are important observations, both for our understanding of anaphora, and for the theory of clitics. If the pronominal markers in Chicheŵa can be shown indisputably to be affixes, then we have a very strong form of violation of the Lexicalist Hypothesis. Of course, the issue isn't closed with this one analysis. It might be, for instance (as a number of people have suggested for morphological systems such as this), that we are not dealing here with affixation, but rather with a clitic cluster which happens to have a relatively firm phonological attachment to its verbal host.[21] If that were the case then Chicheŵa would be no more or less problematic than, say, French. But such an observation still wouldn't solve the overall problem, given that students of clitic systems are inclined to say that the French clitic system is, morphologically speaking, a species of affixation.

9.4   Summary and conclusions

In the first section we looked at four 'case studies' of what in Zwicky's (1977) terms would be called 'special clitics'. These systems presented most of the phenomena which have been discussed in the general literature on clitics (plus a few other phenomena which, while no less important, tend to get ignored).

The second section reviewed two influential attempts at a typology of clitics. It is largely agreed that genuine clitics are words which happen to be phonologically dependent on a host. Thus, they are elements which gave the syntactic properties of words, but the phonological properties of affixes. According to Klavans's typology, they are, in fact, affixes which attach to phrases, in accordance with the settings of three parameters. I argued that Klavans's typology isn't without its conceptual and empirical problems. Nonetheless, it represents a significant attempt at making sense of a complex phenomenon.

The section continued with further observations from Zwicky, illustrating how difficult it is to demarcate cliticization and other phenomena, especially inflection. His suggestion that the English possessive might be an inflectional morpheme which attaches to the edge of phrases raises a whole host of questions about the nature of inflection, constituency and wordhood, and the role of heads in morphology (given that the possessive modifies the head semantically while remaining morphologically attached to some other element in the phrase).

Finally, §9.3 reviewed some of the implications that morphological decisions about clitics might have for syntactic theory and vice versa. When we look at pronominal clitics attached to verbs we find that some criteria suggest that these are essentially pronominals, which just happen to have a close morphophonological connection with a lexical head. But other criteria point towards an analysis under which they are more like agreement markers. The controversy remains unresolved, particularly when the 'anaphoric affixes' described for Chicheŵa are taken into consideration.

The kinds of phenomena discussed in this chapter raise a variety of more general questions for linguistic theory. One observation which may prove of importance concerns the notion of 'parameters' for cliticization. In syntax, a parameter is intended to unify a diversity of syntactic surface phenomena. In phonology, however (for example, the phonology of stress systems), what we generally find is that a whole collection of parameters have to be set in order to fix one surface pattern. Klavans's parameters are of the latter type. This is perhaps slightly odd, given that two of them are couched in terms of syntactic domains. However, this may be just another reflection of the fact that we are dealing with the interface between morphology and both syntax and phonology.

One set of technical problems, posed both by agreement-like pronoun clitics, and by cliticized auxiliary elements, concerns recent proposals centering around the notion of **functional categories** (meaning categories like Agr, Comp, Infl, Det and so on). Particularly important are the implications for analyses which posit verb movement (especially the widely adopted Government-Binding assumption that verbs regularly move into the Infl position in order to receive tense/aspect and agreement morphology). If tense, aspect, modality (including negation) and a variety of other verbal categories are to be represented as properties of the Infl system (or perhaps even the Comp-Infl system together), as is currently widely assumed, then we might expect the controversy over the nature of pronominal clitics to be repeated with such elements as auxiliary verbs, negative particles and modal elements of various sorts. This would be a particularly interesting line of inquiry given current syntactic work suggesting that some of these categories might be represented in the syntax as separate fully-fledged X-bar projections (e.g. Pollock, 1989).

However, this line of thinking brings us up against serious conceptual difficulties, which are in urgent need of resolution. The problem is one that I have touched on several times already. If we separate out the morphophonological properties of formatives from their morphosyntactic properties, then we can capture commonalities. For instance, the fact that a notion such as 'perfectivity' or 'causativity' might be sig-nalled by a verb taking a sentential complement, or an auxiliary verb or an affix, or merely some kind of lexical alternation is of no great consequence if we accept the strongest interpretation of Baker's (1988a) UTAH. For in underlying representation we will say that in each case there is some sort of abstract predicate, which may, for instance, condition some sort of head-to-head movement, or incorporation process. Likewise, we can argue, with Baker et al. (1989) that the English Passive involves an abstract 'clitic' generated in Infl position, which is obligatorily assigned the external argument role of the verb and which in turn obligatorily induces an abstract form of incorporation of the verb stem. But if this approach is adopted then we'll need other, non-syntactic, criteria for distinguishing full words from clitics from affixes from other morphological phenomena. In other words, current thinking in GB syntax, at least, implicitly lays a good part of the burden of explaining systematic similarities and differences between languages on the morphology component of grammar. This serves to underline the key role morphology plays in grammatical theory, by virtue of its interface with the other components of grammar.

EXERCISES

9.1   List as many words in English as you can which would plausibly be analysed (in one or other of their forms) as clitics. Group them into simple clitics and special clitics. Are there any properties which all of your candidate clitics have in common?

9.2   (a) Describe in detail which three important phenomena, discussed in this chapter and in chapter 7, are illustrated in the following Serbo-Croat sentence:
Naša se kinematografija može pohvaliti uspjelima dijelima.
'Our cinema industry can be congratulated on its successful work.'
Naša 'our', može 'can (3sg. pres.)', pohvaliti 'to praise', uspjelima dijelima 'suc-cessful work (instr. pl.)'.
    (b) Reanalyse exercise 2.3 (chapter 2) in the light of §9.1.1 of this chapter.

9.3   Bulgarian definite article:
(i) What is the form of the article, and what governs its allomorphy?
(ii) How does it fit into Klavans's scheme?

a) Na masata e červena kniga.
    'On the table is a red book.'
b) Knigata e na masata.
    The book is on the table.'
c) Červenata kniga e na masata.
    'The red book is on the table.'

d) Mojata červena kniga e na masata.
   'My red book is on the table.'
e) Knigite sa na masata.
   'The books are on the table.'
f) Červenite knigi sa na masata.
   'The red books are on the table.'
g) Volət e na poleto.
   'The ox is in the field.'
h) Černət vol e na poleto.
   'The black ox is in the field.'
i) Silnite černi volove sa na poleto.
   'The strong black oxen are in the field.'
j) Volovete sa na poleto.
   'The oxen are in the field.'
k) Na poleto sa silnite černi volove.
   'In the field are the strong black oxen.'

9.4   (a) Write a set of feature co-occurrence rules (redundancy rules) for Klavans's 3-parameter feature system, which would have the effect of ruling out Types 4 and 5.

   (b) It might be thought that we would improve Klavans's system by adopting a different set of binary features. Here is one possibility:

(i)   Initial/Final (as in Klavans)
(ii) Proclitic/Enclitic (as in Klavans)
(iii) Domain attached/Non-domain attached

The third feature is interpreted thus: Domain attached clitics attach to the adjacent word in the domain; Non-domain attached clitics attach in the opposite direction to Domain attached clitics. Thus, the English clitic auxiliaries are Initial (to the domain VP), but are Non-domain attached because they associate to the word before the VP domain, to the left, rather than the first word in the VP, to the right. Show that feature system (i–iii) excludes Types 4 and 5. What are its disadvantages? How might they be overcome? [Hint: for this last part of the question, re-read question 2(a) above.]

★9.5   Carefully consult Zwicky and Pullum (1983) and list the criteria they adduce for analysing a formative as inflectional rather than a clitic. Then, apply these criteria to

(i)   the English 's formative corresponding to *has*;
(ii) the Serbo-Croat pronominal clitics;
(iii) the Polish auxiliary clitics.

[Note: not all the criteria will be applicable to all the cases.]

★9.6   Suppose you wish to investigate the Macedonian clitic doubling construction and determine whether it was a genuine clitic system or an agreement system. What syntactic constructions would you in principle be interested in? Provide English sentences which you might wish to have translated into Macedonian to elicit native speaker informant judgements. (It might help you to know that Macedonian, like other Slav languages, has very free surface word order, but that question words appear in sentence initial position.)

★9.7   Select any good handbook, reference grammar or textbook of Japanese. Collate as much information (phonological, morphological, syntactic) as you can about the 'case' participles *wa*, *ga*, *o*, *no* and *ni*. Are these formatives (i) affixes? (ii) clitics? (iii) words?

PART IV

The Word in Generative Grammar

10

Bracketing Paradoxes

10.1 Introduction: the phenomena

We have already encountered *bracketing paradoxes*, i.e. constructions in which it appears necessary to assign two distinct constituent structures to a word. For example, we noted in chapter 6 that a word such as *ungrammaticality* poses problems for a level ordered theory of morphology because the grammatical restrictions on the affixes *un-* and *-ity* demand a bracketing 10.1a while the level ordering principles demand a bracketing 10.1b:

10.1   a) [[un grammatical] ity]
        b) [un [grammatical ity]

Any theory of morphology aiming at completeness has to have something to say about bracketing paradoxes. In this chapter we will trace the recent history of this set of problems and some of the proposals for tackling it. The bracketing paradoxes don't really constitute a natural kind and hence shouldn't necessarily be given a unified solution. Nonetheless, all of the paradoxes illustrate an important problem in morphological theory construction, that of deciding what a word is. It is for this reason that the various bracketing paradoxes are intrinsically interesting.

Let's begin with some illustrations. In a sense much of the previous chapter was about bracketing paradoxes, since it is frequently the case that a host + clitic combination forms a new word phonologically but behaves as two separate words syntactically. For instance, we might say that a familiar example of simple cliticization as in 10.2 represents a bracketing paradox, as shown in 10.2a, b. In 10.2a we have the phonological bracketing and in 10.2b the syntactic bracketing:

10.2   Tom's a linguist.
        a) [Tom's] a linguist.
        b) [Tom] ['s a linguist].

However, the *ungrammaticality* example shows that the bracketing paradox problem can extend much further than the behaviour of clitics. In 10.3–10.11 I give a number of paradoxes from English which have been discussed in the literature (this list is largely derived from Williams, 1981a):

10.3   hydroelectricity
a) [hydro [electric ity]]
b) [[hydro electric] ity]

10.4   transformational grammarian
a) [transformational [grammarian]]
b) [[transformational grammar] ian]

10.5   atomic scientist
a) [atomic [scientist]]
b) [[atomic science] ist]

10.6   Gödel numbering
a) [Gödel [number ing]]
b) [[Gödel number] ing]

10.7   cross-sectional
a) [cross [sectional]]
b) [[cross section] al]

10.8   white-washed
a) [white [washed]]
b) [[white wash] ed]

10.9   four-legged
a) [four [legged]]
b) [[four legg] ed]

10.10   three-wheeler
a) [three [wheeler]]
b) [[three wheel] er]

10.11   unhappier
a) [un [happy er]]
b) [[un happy] er]

In most of these examples it is fairly clear why we are dealing with a bracketing paradox. The example *hydroelectricity* is paradoxical within a level ordered theory for the same reason that *ungrammaticality* is paradoxical. Semantically the word is derived from *hydroelectric*. However, *hydro-* is either a bound compounded root or a Class II prefix (depending on your analysis). In either case it should be affixed after the Class I affix *-ity*, given level ordering. An atomic scientist is not a scientist who is atomic, rather s/he is a specialist in atomic science. Hence, the meaning demands bracketing 10.5b. Similar remarks hold of *transformational grammarian*. The term *Gödel numbering* refers to a process of assigning a specially constructed number, called a *Gödel number*, to a set as part of a mathematical proof (a technique devised in a famous theorem by Kurt Gödel). In other words, the process does not refer to the number of Gödels, so, again, 10.6b represents the semantic structure of the expression.

The adjective *cross-sectional* means 'pertaining to a cross section', so that the *-al* affix applies to the whole phrase even though it attaches morphologically only to the word *section*. The same reasoning applies to *white-washed, four-legged* and *three-wheller*. The *four-legged* and *three-wheeler* examples are rather interesting, because the semantic sources, *four-leg* and *three-wheel*, don't actually exist (see §10.7 below). These therefore pose a problem for word-based morphology in its stronger form.

The problem with *unhappier* is rather subtle. Semantically, this must have the constituent structure of 10.11b, because it means 'more unhappy' rather than 'not happier'. Phonologically, however, we know that comparative *-er* only attaches to monosyllabic adjectives or those ending in syllabic *l*, *-y* or *-n*, as in *nobler, merrier* or *commoner*. These contrast with impossible comparatives such as *corrupter, *faciler, *curiouser, *tractabler*, and *melancholier*. Thus, to meet the phonological restriction on affixation, *-er* must be attached to *happy* and not to *unhappy*, as in 10.11a.

Some of the paradoxes, like *ungrammaticality* and *hydroelectricity*, are theory internal paradoxes, in the sense that one at least of the bracketings arises out of specific, and often not uncontroversial, theoretical assumptions. In this case the not uncontroversial theoretical assumption is level ordering. A further example of such theory internal paradoxes which we have already seen is the apparently innocuous *truck driver*. This is a bracketing paradox in some theories (e.g. Lieber, Fabb, Sproat) because it is given the constituent structure [[truck drive] er]. In other theories there is no such problem (e.g. Williams).

It must not be thought that the problem is unique to English. Pesetsky (1985) discusses an example from Russian (re-iterated in a number of Slav languages). In 10.12 we see a prefixed verb form in the past tense. The b) and c) forms show two bracketings of the (SPE-style) underlying forms generally ascribed to such forms in generative analyses of Slavic phonology. The # sign represents a 'jer', a lax high vowel which never surfaces in the modern Slavonic languages:

10.12   a) podžog   '(he) set fire to'
          b) [pod # [[[ž#g] l] #]]
            under   burn   PAST-MASC.SG
          c) [[[[pod # ž#g] l] #]

Semantically, we must have the bracketing of 10.12c, because the verb root *ž#g*, 'burn', and the prefix *pod#-*, 'under', form a combination with idiosyncratic meaning which must be lexically listed. However, under usual assumptions about Slavic phonology, in order to get the vowel deletion and lowering rules of Slavic right (basically the rules affecting jers, discussed in §4.1) we must assume the bracketing in 10.12b. This is therefore somewhat reminiscent of the problem with *unhappier*, in that the constituent structure implied by the meaning is at variance with that implied by the phonology. But notice that this, too, is a theory-internal paradox, inasmuch as it only arises given particular assumptions about the underlying phonological representation.

The bracketing paradoxes, then, pose a problem which is essentially that of dual or multiple representations. In this chapter we will look at the significance of the bracketing paradoxes for particular theories of morphology and some of the ways different theoretical approaches have responded to the problem. We conclude with a case study based on the more popular of the paradox types which suggests that some of the paradoxes at least provide evidence for a 'paradigmatic' approach to word formation.

10.2   Bracketing paradoxes in Lexical Phonology

Since a number of the bracketing paradoxes pose special problems for Lexical Phonology we'll start with the response lexical phonologists have made. Kiparsky (1983) pointed out that in English there are two theoretically possible types of bracketing paradox violating level ordering. They are shown in 10.13, where I is a Level 1 affix and II is a Level 2 affix:

10.13   a) I + [Stem + II]   (*in + success + ful)
        b) [II + Stem] + I   (un + grammatical + ity)

Only the second of these occurs. However, there are a large number of cases. One possibility would be to say that some Class II prefixes also belong to Class I, as Selkirk (1982) suggests. However, doubt is cast on the wisdom of this move by the observation that any Class II prefix whatever can be involved. Therefore, it would seem that the 'fault' lies with the Class I suffixes. Yet there is a fairly large number of such suffixes which give rise to paradoxes. Moreover, they may generate paradoxes based on compounds and lexicalized phrases as well as Class II prefixed forms. Some of the examples Kiparsky cites are repeated in 10.14:

10.14   a) [II + Stem] + I
            untruth
            underestimation
            reburial
            decongestant
            arch-ducal
            vice-presidential
        b) set theoretic(al)
            twenty-fifth
            lieutenant-colonelcy
        c) three-dimensional
            double helical

However, these cases, while not infrequent, have been regarded by many as exceptional because it is often impossible to construct such paradoxes from other bases, even using the Class I suffixes found in 10.14. Thus, despite *analysis ~ analytic* we don't have **re-analytic*. Likewise, with *flower ~ floral*, but **wallfloral*, *vision ~ visual* but **tunnel visual*.

If paradoxes are the exception rather than the rule, the problem now centres round the question of why only the second type of paradox (10.13b) arises. Kiparsky's solution was morphological reanalysis. He first assumed that the selectional (or sub-categorization) requirements must be met at every level. Thus, *un-* must be seen to select an adjective, both in underlying representation and in surface representation. Second, he assumed a process of reanalysis under which bracketing can be rearranged freely, providing selectional restrictions aren't violated. The way this can generate *ungrammaticality* is shown in 10.15:

10.15   [[grammatical]$_A$ + ity]$_N$ Level 1
          [un [[grammatical]$_A$ + ity]$_N$]$_N$ Level 2
          [[un + [grammatical]$_A$]$_A$ + ity]$_N$ Reanalysis

Given usual Lexical Phonology assumptions, however, the derivation of 10.15 is impossible. This is because one of the key ideas in Lexical Phonology is that the internal structure of any item forming the output of a level is inaccessible to rules in a subsequent level. This latter property is captured by the Bracket Erasure Convention, which states that brackets are erased from a word when it leaves a morphological level. Hence, there is no way for rules at the next level to distinguish, for instance, monomorphemic words from words which end in a particular sort of affix. The BEC will now correctly rule out the majority of cases where no bracketing paradox is formed, but will not permit the formation of *ungrammaticality*. Therefore, all we need say is that the *ungrammaticality* examples exceptionally fail to undergo bracket erasure.

A number of linguists see the relaxation of the BEC as a serious weakening of the tenets of Lexical Phonology. Zwicky (1987d) also argues that it locates the problem in the wrong place. He says that it is the rule rather than the exception for Class I suffixes to license paradoxes (even very unproductive ones such as *-th*). Moreover, bracketing paradoxes formed on *un-...-ity* and especially *un-...-ability* seem definitely to be the rule rather than the exception. So Kiparsky's BEC approach can at best be regarded as only a partial solution to the problem.

10.3   A prosodic approach (Aronoff and Sridhar)

Aronoff and Sridhar (1983, 1987) deny the validity of level ordering. However, like Selkirk (1982), they note that there are two types of affix in English, Stem affixes and Word affixes, corresponding roughly to Class I and Class II affixes. The Stem affixes attach typically to bound stems or roots, while the Word affixes may attach only to words. They also note that it is commonplace to find that syntactically organized structure, for example, the constituent structure of a sentence as represented in a phrase marker, is distinct from the phonological structure, for instance, the phrasal groupings implied by phrasal stress and intonation. This discrepancy is well known. In SPE (p. 368) it is pointed out that, prosodically speaking, the string *was in an unlikely* behaves like a single word in a sentence such as //*The book* / *was in an unlikely* / *place*// (where the slashes indicate prosodic boundaries).

The importance of prosodic structure in phonology has recently been stressed by a number of phonologists and it's probably fair to say that the majority of phonologists accept that prosodic categories of some sort play a key role in phonology. One important prosodic category is that of the phonological word or **p-word**. This is defined differently for different languages, but in languages with a stress system it will often correspond to a metrical foot, that is, a string of syllables containing exactly one stress. The sentence cited above from SPE would therefore consist of three feet given a normal speaking rate.

Aronoff and Sridhar consider the example of a morphologically complex word, *compartmentalization*, in which we have the Class II (stress-neutral) affixes, *-ment* and *-ize* preceding the Class I affixes, *-al* and *-ation* respectively, in violation of level ordering. What Aronoff and Sridhar suggest is that such cases represent a mismatch between prosodic (phonological) structure and morphological structure. Specifically they claim that the single morphological word ('m-word') consists of three p-words, as in 10.16:

10.16   (compart) (mental) (ization)

For Aronoff and Sridhar, *-al* and *-ation* are both Stem suffixes. Let's assume that a Stem affix must always be contained inside a p-word. This means that the two Word affixes *-ment* and *-ize* must be able to form p-words when they have Stem affixes attached to them. Aronoff and Sridhar suggest that this is possible primarily because the resulting strings are polysyllabic.

Now consider the cases in 10.17, involving Word affixation:

10.17   a) un-able
          b) fear-less
          c) fear-less-ness
          d) random-ize

In these cases we have just a single p-word, for each example consists of just one metrical foot. Phonologically, then, the Word affixes are simply attached to their bases. The other type of element which shows this sort of behaviour is the (phonological) clitic. Thus, we could draw a parallel between examples such as 10.17a, b and examples 10.18:

10.18   a) an apple
          b) fear us

To summarize, then, we have seen that Stem affixes must always be contained within a p-word. Word affixes, on the other hand, can form separate p-words of their own when they themselves are affixed. However, when a word contains just Word affixes and no Stem affixes, the Word affixes behave like phonological clitics whose host is the base to which they are affixed. This means that we can parse complex words into p-words in the following way. A major lexical category (Noun, Verb, Adjective) on its own will constitute a p-word, as will any such category containing just Stem affixes. If a major lexical category contains a Word affix which itself is suffixed by one or more Stem affixes, then the Word affix plus Stem affix complex forms a separate p-word. Any part of a word not thus accounted for will be a clitic, seeking a stressed host.

How does this help us with the bracketing paradoxes? Consider again our old friend *ungrammaticality*. As before, we will consider this to consist of a base, *grammatical*, and the affixes *un-* and *-ity*. We won't assume any level ordering. This means we can say that morphologically speaking the word is formed by taking *ungrammatical* and affixing *-ity*. This gives us the morphological bracketing of 10.19:

10.19   [[un grammatical] ity]

Our p-word parsing principles will analyse this as a major lexical category, *grammatical*, followed by a Stem affix, *-ity*. This will form a p-word. The Word prefix *un-* will then be a clitic. This means that we have a structure which we can represent as 10.20:

10.20   (un (grammaticality))

The adjunction of *un-* to the p-word *grammaticality* in 10.20 is intended to represent cliticization. Now we can see why the example should be regarded as paradoxical. According to Aronoff and Sridhar, this is nothing more alarming than a consequence of the mismatch between morphological and phonological structure, much like the mismatch between syntax and phonology in *the book was in an unlikely place*.

Naturally, this only accounts for a proportion of the constructions which have been branded as bracketing paradoxes in the literature. Nonetheless, it is an approach which has proved popular with a number of researchers, including Lexical Phonologists such as Booij and Rubach (1984), who use the idea of prosodic constituents to handle problems with prefixation in Slavic phonology (see below §10.2.4; cf. also Booij, 1985b, 1987).

10.4   Williams's theory of 'lexical relatedness'

Williams (1981a) provides the first detailed discussion of the bracketing paradoxes. He views the question from the perspective of a concept of relatedness between lexical entries. In his terms, the problem is to explain how to capture the fact that words such as *hydroelectric* and *hydroelectricity* are related to each other and to the words *electric* and *electricity*. It is for this reason that the constructions are sometimes known as 'relatedness paradoxes'.

What the paradoxes show is that it is insufficient simply to take the shorter of two words and derive the longer by affixation. Therefore, Williams offers a more sophisticated way of recording relatedness. According to Williams we want to relate the paradox in 10.21a to 10.21b:

10.21   a) macroeconomist
           b) macroeconomic

We can't do this by simple derivation because, if anything, 10.21a is derived from 10.21b by replacing -*ic* with -*ist*, and not by attaching one of these affixes to the other word (assuming there is no truncation analysis of this case). Williams claims that the rightmost affix is the head of the word. Let's say initially that two words are *lexically related* if they are identical except for their heads. This is illustrated in the tree diagram in 10.22:

10.22

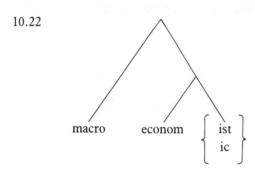

At the same time, argues Williams, we would like to relate *macroeconomist* with *microeconomist*. These differ only in the leftmost portion of the word, which Williams refers to as the 'nonhead', defined as follows (p. 261):

10.23   Nonhead: the highest left branch of a word.

He then proposes the following principle of **lexical relatedness** (p. 261; footnote omitted):

10.24   'X can be related to Y if X and Y differ only in a head position or in the nonhead position.'

This analysis, though the earliest serious attempt to get to grips with the problem, is in many respects one of the more successful. In particular, it can handle many of the more puzzling paradoxes which I shall discuss later and which confound some later theories. However, there are two main difficulties.

First, Strauss (1982a) pointed out that Williams's approach fails to accommodate the subcategorization requirements on affixes. For instance, although it can represent the fact that *grammatical*, *ungrammatical* and *ungrammaticality* are all related, it can't provide a satisfactory bracketing for *ungrammaticality* which reflects the fact that *un*- selects Adjectives and -*ity* selects Nouns.

Hoeksema (1986) enumerates a number of other problems. A particularly serious difficulty is that the theory allows us to relate words which aren't actually related. For example, given the definition of non-head, and the assumption that the regular plural morpheme is the head of its word, we would conclude that all regular plurals of monomorphemic stems (e.g. *brothers* and *sisters*) are lexically related, obviously an absurd result.[1]

By comparing Williams's representational approach to the problem with Kiparsky's later account we can already see an interesting discrepancy in the nature of the data each linguist wishes to explicate. Williams is hard pressed to find an adequate analysis of *ungrammaticality*. On the other hand it is not clear what Kiparsky would say about the *macroeconomist* example, which is the kind of case Williams handles most successfully.

10.5   Pesetsky's 'morphological QR'

Pesetsky (1985) has used some of the bracketing paradoxes to argue that principles of syntax hold of morphological representations. This is a very influential viewpoint nowadays, as we have seen from the work of Fabb, Sproat, Roeper, Baker and several others. While Williams argues that we need to develop a richly structured theory of what it is for lexical items to be related, Pesetsky considerably plays down this notion. Indeed, he claims that his results show that there is really no need for a richly structured lexicon at all: the lexicon is simply a list of idiosyncratic forms, a return to earlier structuralist assumptions. All regularities between words are to be handled by rules (of phonology) or principles (of syntax).

How can we account for the bracketing paradoxes using principles of syntax? Recall that the architecture of the Government-Binding theory of grammar can be represented by the T-model of Figure 10.1. LF represents the interpretive component for semantics. Now, one of the original motivations behind the level of LF was a set of phenomena concerning scope of quantifiers such as *each, all, some, every, no* and so on. For example, a sentence such as 10.25 is ambiguous, with readings 10.25a, b:

10.25   Everybody liked one of the books.
            a) Everybody liked one or other of the books.
            b) One particular book was universally liked.

Logicians (and linguists) have related this ambiguity to the order in which quantifiers such as *everybody* and *one of...* appear. For instance, in a formal theory of semantics

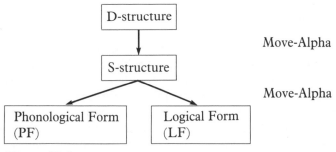

Figure 10.1 The 'T' model of Government-Binding theory

we would relate 10.25 on reading a) to 10.26a and on reading b) to 10.26b:

10.26   a) Everybody, x (one y of the books (x liked y))
           b) One y of the books (everybody, x (x liked y))

To see how the paraphrases of 10.26 bring out the difference in meaning we can read
them as in 10.27:

10.27   a) For every person, x, there was one book y, such that x liked y.
           b) One of the books, y, was such that for every person, x, x liked y.

The point of all this is that the paraphrases in 10.26 and 10.27 can be regarded as
prose renditions of the logical forms of the two readings of 10.25. The logical form
of a sentence is a syntactic representation derived by application of Move-alpha from
the S-structure representation. It is assumed in GB that quantificational elements are
all stacked up at the edge of a sentence form at LF (what mathematical logicians call
the *Prenex Normal Form*). To achieve this we must be able to move quantifier
phrases such as *every person* or *one of the books* and adjoin them to the edge of the
sentence. This may happen in any order, so that we may associate two distinct LF
representations to one sentence in cases such as 10.25. When Move-alpha applies in
this way to reorder quantifier phrases we customarily speak of a rule of **Quantifier
Raising** (because the quantifier is moved higher up the tree). This is often abbreviated to 'QR'. Note that QR is nothing more than a particular type of application
of Move-alpha.

In the original theory, the mapping from S-structure to LF was defined solely for
sentences. Pesetsky's innovation was to suggest that we could view the derivation of
words in the same way. In particular, he argues that the ubiquitous rule of Move-
alpha can apply to parts of words (e.g. bound morphemes) to produce an LF representation of a word which is different from the S-structure (or PF) representation.

Though Pesetsky doesn't cite any such data, it is clear that something like the
analysis he proposes will be necessary in general to handle the facts of language. One
obvious case in which a logical element has to be 'extracted' from a word to form
an LF representation is given by English negative quantifiers. Thus, in order to
represent the fact that sentences 10.28a, b have the same meaning we will need a way
of factoring out the negation element of the word *nobody*, roughly as Pesetsky is
suggesting.

10.28   a) Tom saw nobody.
           b) Tom didn't see anybody.

This type of problem is actually much more widespread. Chukchee furnishes a
particularly interesting illustration. In Chukchee there are three prefixes which are
attached to nouns, *emqən-*, *gemge-*, and *əm-*. These respectively mean (roughly)
'each', 'every, any' and 'all'. An indication that *emqən-* and *gemge-* are prefixes (and
not, say prenominal clitics) is that they undergo vowel harmony, whereby, simplifying somewhat, /i e u/ change to /e a o/ if there is any one of the vowels /e a o/
in the word. Hence we find *emqən-ŋewəsqet* 'each woman' but *amqən-qoraŋə* 'each
reindeer', *gemge-ŋewəsqet* 'every woman' but *gamga-jatjol* 'every fox'. Moreover, all

three can be preceded by the prefix part of the Comitative case inflectional circumfixes, *ge-* and *ga-* (see examples 10.29–10.30), suggesting that we are dealing with a derivational prefix. All this is exemplified in 10.29–10.32:

10.29   Gemge-ŋewəsqet-ək warkən wanenan.
         every-woman-LOC is   sewing-machine.
         'Every woman has a sewing-machine.'

10.30   Amqən-ŋawəsqat-etə gejətlin wanenan.
         each-woman-DAT   they-gave sewing-machine
         'They gave a sewing-machine to each woman.'
         (from *emqən-ŋewəsqet* with the Dative case *-etə* triggering vowel harmony).

10.31   G-emqən-tumg-e nəleqin ənin ŋewʔen.
         COM-each-comrade-COM came his wife
         'Each comrade came accompanied by his wife.'
         (*g-...-e*) is an allomorph of the Comitative case marker *ge-...-te*).

10.32   ətləgən ga-gamga-melgar-ma wanewan niwinigʔin.
         father COM-any-gun-COM not   go-hunting
         'Father doesn't go hunting with (just) any gun.'
         (from *gemge-milger* and the Comitative *ga-...-ma* triggering vowel harmony).

The rule of Quantifier Raising will help to represent, for example, the fact that in 10.29–10.30 we have one sewing machine per woman, rather than a single sewing machine for use by all the women. This means that Chukchee provides good evidence for the application of Quantifier Raising to bound affixes, since otherwise it would be impossible to account for the logical relations in these sentences.

Let's see how Pesetsky's proposals are supposed to work for a concrete case such as *unhappier*. Move-alpha isn't generally involved in the mapping from S-structure to PF so the phonological constituent structure presumably will reflect the S-structure constituency. This means that the S-structure representation will be 10.33a. If we apply Move-alpha as a kind of LF affix movement or 'morphological QR', then we will obtain 10.33b (where we assume that the movement leaves a trace):

10.33   a)   b)

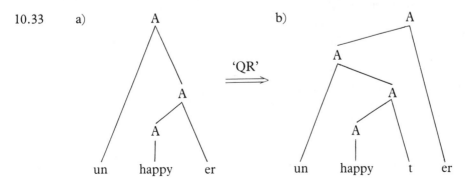

This analysis has some plausibility given that the *-er* affix means 'more' and the *un-* affix means 'not'. Both of these are logical expressions which are involved in scope differences of the kind that syntactic QR was originally designed to handle.

The novelty of Pesetky's approach lies in extending this analysis to all affixes, including the *-ity* suffix of *ungrammaticality*. This is a contentious assumption because such affixes are not usually associated with special logical properties of the sort which motivate QR. Pesetsky's idea is that we first generate a word from its morphemes respecting level ordering restrictions. This gives us the bracketing [un [grammaticality]], diagrammed in 10.34a. However, at the level of LF, it is necessary that *un-* be affixed to a member of the category Adjective, not Noun. Therefore, QR applies to *-ity*, adjoining it to the topmost N node, and leaving a trace. This trace has no syntactic category of its own and hence the resulting constituent [grammatical t] lacks its former head. This former head, *-ity*, is of category N. By Lieber's Percolation Conventions, the syntactic category features of the adjective *grammatical* percolate so that at LF the constituent [grammatical t] is treated as an adjective. It is the constituent [grammatical t] to which *un-* is affixed, so that this prefix is now attached to an adjective, as required. This gives us the LF representation shown in 10.34b:

10.34   a)   b)

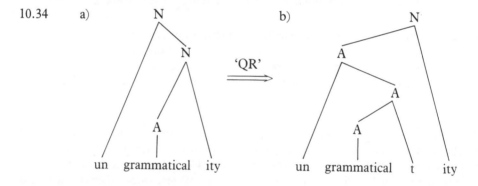

The crucial assumptions here are that morphological constraints such as level ordering hold at the level of PF, while syntactic selection constraints hold of LF alone. (Note that this is in contrast to Kiparsky's assumption mentioned above.) Thus, if there is a mismatch in the syntactic requirements at S-structure this will not matter provided there is a way of patching up the representation by the time we reach LF. Morphological QR, together with the relabelling of nodes in accordance with the Percolation Conventions, is precisely the patching up operation needed. Thus, we may think of 10.34a as the representation generated by the morphology and 10.34b as the representation generated by the syntax.

Pesetsky's theory has been criticized by a number of morphologists (e.g. Sproat, 1985a, b, Hoeksema, 1987, Spencer, 1988c). Hoeksema notes that morphological Quantifier Raising predicts that a greater number of ambiguities would be found than actually are found. For instance, why isn't *unhappier* ambiguous? Also, why does it only affect certain words? We can't say *unfitter* for example, though from Pesetsky's account it's not clear why not. And in general Pesetsky's theory is unconstrained compared with the syntactic version of QR. Although Speas (1984) argued that Pesetsky's approach was needed to account for the tricky problem of prefix ordering in Navajo which we discussed in §6.4, Sproat (1985a, b) has vigorously contested this claim, as well as providing other more general arguments against Pesetsky's theory. Finally, we will see that the morphological QR theory can't handle those of the cases to be discussed in §10.2.7 where there is no affix to move anywhere.

Pesetsky's solution is rather different from Williams's in that it relies on the notion of derivation, while Williams's account is essentially representational. In this respect, Pesetsky is closer to Kiparsky, in that both handle the paradoxes by generating a basic form close to the phonological form and then modifying the result (by morphological QR and rebracketing, respectively). The difference is that Pesetsky regards this as somehow the instantiation of a general process, whereas for Kiparsky it is an exceptional process.

10.6   Sproat's mapping principle

In the introduction to the chapter I mentioned that an example of simple cliticization such as *Tom's a linguist* could be regarded as a kind of bracketing paradox. The way out of the paradox is to say that the *'s* has two types of description, one phonological the other syntactic. Phonologically, we decided that the clitic was rather like an affix. Syntactically, however, it is described as a main verb. Sproat (1984, 1985a, 1985b, 1988) takes this reasoning further and applies it to all cases of (productively formed) bracketing paradox.

Taking *ungrammaticality* as our paradigm case, we have been assuming (simplifying somewhat) that it consists of a stem and two affixes *grammatical*, *un-* and *-ity*. Each has its two principal sets of linguistic properties: phono-morphological properties and syntactico-semantic properties. The phono-morphological properties, say, of the affixes include the information that *un-* is a prefix and does not bear stress, and that *-ity* is a suffix which attracts stress to the previous syllable. The syntactico-semantic properties will include the information that *un-* selects adjectives and means 'not', and that *-ity* creates abstract nouns from adjectives. Any word we construct out of these morphological ingredients, such as *ungrammaticality*, can therefore be thought of in two different ways in that we can assign, broadly speaking, two distinct structural descriptions to the word. Each structural description will be associated with a particular constituent structure, or bracketing. When the morphology is agglutinating and the semantics compositional the two bracketings will coincide. However, given that languages typically admit deviations from strict agglutination and compositionality, this coincidence of structure will not always be in evidence.

When we factor out these two aspects of the representation of word structure it becomes apparent that there are deeper differences between the two sorts of description. At the phono-morphological level hierarchical constituent structure plays relatively little role, as I hinted in §6.1.3. Instead, strict adjacency tends to be much more relevant, so that the linear order of morphemes is more important than which constituent they belong to. On the other hand, at the syntactico-semantic level of description, linear order seems to be less important. What matters here is the hierarchical relationship, or equivalently, sisterhood relationships between morphemes, and this entails that constituent structure is paramount.

We can depict this situation by providing two parallel representations for our example, *ungrammaticality*, in which we write the phono-morphological representation in (very) broad transcription and the syntactico-semantic representation in upper case. The two representations are given in 10.35:

10.35   a) [un [gramatikal iti]]
         b)

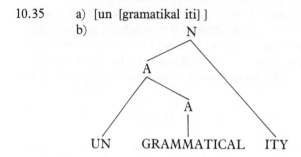

Representation 10.35a reflects the fact that *-ity* is immediately to the right of the stem, and the stress rules of English would be able to compute that the main stress should fall on the /al/ syllable. Similarly, 10.35a informs us that *un-* is a prefix, hence that it appears to the left of the stem. If we accept Aronoff and Sridhar's (1983, 1987) analysis discussed in §10.2.3, we would say that the bracketing in 10.35a is actually a reflection of the prosodic structure of the word, with /gramatikaliti/ being a p-word, which serves as a host to the proclitic /un/.

Representation 10.35b reflects the syntactic restrictions on *un-* by which it selects an element of category A. Another way of saying this is that *un-* is a sister to a node labelled A. Moreover, *un-* itself is a constituent of a category labelled A. Likewise, we can infer that *-ity* is a constituent of a category labelled N, and that it, too, is a sister to a node labelled A. However, since these syntactico-semantic restrictions are couched purely in terms of sisterhood, and since the linear ordering of the morphemes is defined as part of the phono-morphological representation, we could just as well have ignored linear order in representation 10.35b. For instance, we could have decided to write all the affixes first or last, writing 10.35b as 10.36 or 10.37:

10.36

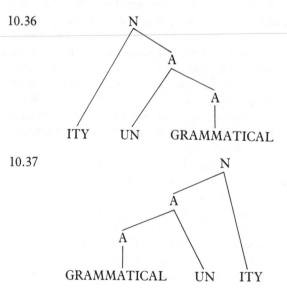

10.37

As far as the relevant information is concerned these three representations would have been equivalent. (Notice that representation 10.36 is almost the same as Pesetsky's (1985) LF representation for *ungrammaticality*.)

If we adopt this line of reasoning, then all we need is a principle or set of principles which will tell us how to relate representations such as 10.35a to those such as 10.35b. The attentive reader who is familiar with my discussion of Marantz's (1984) theory of grammatical relations discussed in chapter 7 will recognize this as similar to the problem Marantz faces in relating l-s structures to s structures. He relied on a simple but effective device which he called Principle M. In his theory of the bracketing paradoxes, Sproat adopts a very similar principle for relating the two parts of a lexical representation.

In essence the idea is that each morpheme has two representations, and the grammar provides for the concatenation of the syntactico-semantic halves to produce the representation 10.35b (or equivalently 10.36 or 10.37). Since linear order is irrelevant for this level of representation, we'll write the result as a pair of unordered sets, as in 10.38 (notice that the second set contains the first as a member, reflecting the hierarchical structure of the representation):

10.38   {GRAMMATICAL, UN}, {ITY, {GRAMMATICAL, UN}}

Now we need to relate this to the phono-morphological form. Sproat assumes that we need to reflect the level ordering restrictions on *un-* and *-ity*, and hence ensure that *-ity* adheres more 'closely' to the stem than does *un-*. However, no additional hierarchical information is of relevance at this level. The main restrictions are on linear order. Therefore, we need a principle which will put the phono-morphological representations of GRAMMATICAL, UN and ITY into the required order. This principle is called the Mapping Principle by Sproat. We'll discuss the technicalities in the Appendix to this chapter. For the present we'll observe that the core of the Mapping Principle is that elements which are sisters in syntactico-semantic representation must be adjacent in phono-morphological representation. Together with linear ordering requirements, this gives us representation 10.39 from 10.38:

10.39   [[un [gramatikal]] iti]

This violates the bracketing required by level ordering, in that *-ity* is external to *un-*. However, we've already observed that hierarchical structure plays no central role in phono-morphological form. Therefore, Sproat so words the Mapping Principle that 10.39 can be rebracketed if morphological principles such as level ordering demand it. (Technically, this hinges on the fact that the species of concatenation defined at this level is *associative*, as explained in the Appendix.) Hence, we are permitted to rewrite 10.39 as 10.40, the required form.

10.40   [un [[gramatikal] iti]]

In summary, Sproat's solution is a little reminiscent of Kiparsky's rebracketing solution. However, whereas for Kiparsky the rebracketing is the result of lexically determined exceptionality, for Sproat it is the result of general principles of grammatical organization. In this, Sproat's approach resembles Pesetsky's, which we saw encountered difficulties because it predicted the existence of paradoxes which don't actually occur. Sproat, however, has an interesting response to this criticism.

Some of the non-existent expressions we might expect to find are illustrated in 10.41:

10.41   a) *symphony orchestrate
          b) *chairpersonify
          c) *white elephantine
          d) *outboard motorize

What is the difference between these and, say, *twenty-fifth*, *cross-sectional* or *transformational grammarian*? Sproat's answer is that, in the acceptable cases, the affix contributes to the meaning of the whole expression in a purely compositional way. Roughly speaking this means that in, say, *twenty-fifth* we have simply the ordinal form of *twenty-five*: the *-th* affix contributes nothing special or idiosyncratic to the meaning. Instead, we are dealing with productive affixation free from lexical idiosyncrasy. In the impossible cases there is an additional, idiosyncratic element of meaning not traceable to the affix. If we do find examples of bracketing paradoxes with idiosyncratic meaning then the entire expression must be stored in the lexicon as an exception. In that case, there is no question of derivation through the Mapping Principle since the whole item is listed along with its meaning.

Turning to the examples of 10.41 we note that each of the affixes which gives rise to the bracketing paradoxes introduces lexical idiosyncrasy. The meaning of *orchestrate* can't be predicted from the meanings of *orchestra* and *-ate*, therefore the whole word has to be lexically listed. If we agree that *-ify* is a productive denominal verb-forming affix, then nonetheless in the verb *personify* we have an idiosyncratic addition to the meaning over and above mere derivation of a verb form. Therefore, this particular case of affixation can't be regarded as productive and no bracketing paradox can be licensed, as we see from 10.41b. The affix *-ine* isn't productive with any meaning, so it can never form bracketing paradoxes. In particular, it could never be affixed to the expression *white elephant* to form a denominal adjective. (Notice that *elephantine* itself doesn't mean simply 'pertaining to an elephant', but rather 'very large (rather like an elephant)'.) Thus, even in *elephantine* the affix is not creating a relational adjective derived from the noun but adding considerably to the meaning of the adjective, too. Therefore, again, the lexicon must contain *elephantine* complete with its idiosyncratic meaning, and *white elephant* (with its idiomatic meaning). Finally, *-ize* is a very productive affix used for forming (causative) verbs from adjectives. However, it is used much more rarely and sporadically to form verbs from nouns as in *motorize*, and the meaning of the resulting verb is not predictable purely from the meaning of the noun. So again, we will not expect *-ize*, when attached to nouns, to license bracketing paradoxes.

This account gets us much closer to a principled explanation for the English bracketing paradoxes. Moreover, it provides the basis for explicitly linking the approach to bracketing paradoxes with the rather more general question of cliticization. Sproat (1988) devotes some attention to this. Marantz (1988a), too, shows how his rather similar mapping principle, together with his operation of Morphological Merger (see chapter 7) can account for bracketing paradoxes and clitics. In both cases the key is to separate the essentially phonological properties of the formatives from their essentially syntactic properties, and handle each by means of separate principles. Thus, the 'mapping principle' type of account of the bracketing paradoxes illustrates rather neatly the importance of specifying very precisely the nature of the two principal interfaces between morphology and other components of grammar: phonology and syntax.

10.7   Bracketing paradoxes and paradigmatic word formation

We close our brief survey of bracketing paradoxes with a recent account of one, significant, subtype. We have seen three different theories which involve some form of rebracketing, those of Kiparsky, Pesetsky and Sproat, and one theory which relies on a non-derivational theory of semantic interpretation. In addition, we've seen a prosodically based account which simply denies that one of the bracketings is morphologically relevant. Now, the rebracketing theories work best with examples like *transformational grammarian* in which we have an affix (more particularly a suffix) that, phonologically, is attached only to the head, but seems to apply to (or 'take scope over') the entire word or phrase. Such theories have a certain difficulty with examples such as Williams's *macroeconomist*. This is because we're not adding an affix and then rebracketing. In fact, given the meaning of this form, I will say that it is derived from the noun *macroeconomics*. However, this means that we are replacing one affix by another rather than merely suffixing and then rebracketing. Williams's theory is designed to handle exactly such cases, of course, but the rebracketing theories need to say something extra about them. Such examples are far from rare. Instances involving a phrasal formation would be *moral philosopher* which has to be derived from *moral philosophy* by substituting the affix *-y* by *-er*, and *marine biolog-ist* from *marine biolog-y*.

There are, however, even more difficult cases for the rebracketing theories. Consider the examples in 10.42:

10.42   a) theoretical linguist
          b) electrical engineer
          c) monumental mason
          d) southern Finn
          e) southern Dane
          f) East German

The reason these are problematical is that they must be derived from 10.43:

10.43   a) theoretical linguistics
          b) electrical engineering
          c) monumental masonry
          d) southern Finland
          e) southern Denmark
          f) East Germany

The direction of derivation can't be the other way, because the expressions of 10.42 all retain semantic idiosyncrasies introduced from the expressions in 10.43. For instance, a theoretical linguist is one who practises a particular brand of linguistics, which we refer to as theoretical linguistics. The same is true of *historical linguist, psycholinguist, applied linguist* and so on. Likewise, electrical (or mechanical or civil) engineers are specifically practitioners of electrical (mechanical, civil) engineering. Monumental masons are people who specialize in carving monuments, i.e. practitioners of 10.43c. Neither southern Finns nor southern Danes are southerners, both come from the north, and an East German only comes from the East by virtue of coming from East Germany.

When we look closely at the constituent structures of 10.43 it becomes evident why they pose grave problems for the rebracketing theories. For in each case the example in 10.42 appears to be derived by *deleting* an affix (or the second member of a compound). Therefore, when we look at the structure of 10.42a, say, and compare it with *transformational grammarian*, there is no affix to rebracket. This is illustrated in 10.44:

10.44   transformational grammar ⇒ [transformational grammar] ian
          electrical [engineer-ing] ⇒ [electrical [engineer-∅]

Examples of this sort cast serious doubts on any kind of rebracketing approach to the paradoxes, including those involving a mapping principle. They can be handled by Williams's theory of lexical relatedness, but we have seen that this theory is descriptively inadequate in other ways, and in any case only allows us to relate 10.42 to 10.43 at the expense of an excessively liberal definition of relatedness. Moreover, even Williams's highly unrestricted theory is unable to cope naturally with examples such as 10.42g, h:

10.42   g) baroque flautist
          h) Modern Linguist

10.43   g) baroque flute
          h) Modern Languages

These last examples are a problem for Williams because the part which changes, namely *flute ~ flaut-* and *language ~ lingu-*, is neither just a head nor just a non-head.

The astute reader may have noticed something interesting about all the examples in this section. They all refer to people who bear some sort of relationship to the source nominal expression. In Spencer (1988c) I refer to these as 'personal nouns'. This subclass forms a small island of productivity in an otherwise exception-ridden area of the English lexicon. It is more or less possible to form a personal noun from a nominal with the right semantics, whatever the allomorphic changes this entails. As an example of the productivity of the process suppose someone devised a form of gymnastics which depends on aerobic exercise, and called this 'aerobic gymnastics'. Then a practitioner of this would be an *aerobic gymnast*. Moreover, any native speaker would be likely to feel happy coining this expression (provided *aerobic gymnastics* was part of his vocabulary), and anyone hearing the expression *aerobic gymnast* being used would assume the existence of a specialism called aerobic gymnastics.

There is an important restriction on the formation of such personal noun bracketing paradoxes. Let's consider an old favourite, *transformational grammarian*, for concreteness. To form this we need in the lexicon three expressions, linked as in 10.45:

10.45

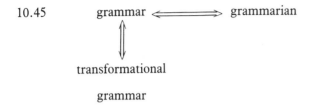

What is important here is that all three expressions be lexicalized, that is, they should all be represented at the same grammatical level, by virtue of being stored in the (permanent) lexicon. It is also necessary that the head have exactly the same meaning in each expression, in other words, we don't allow polysemy. Given these conditions we can 'complete the square' by a process of proportional analogy, as shown in 10.46. This process then constitutes 'personal noun formation':

10.46

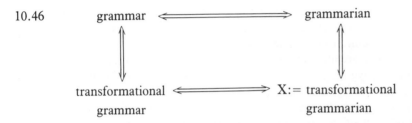

The first prerequisite rules out paradoxes formed from phrasal expressions which haven't been lexicalized, and which therefore haven't been listed in the lexicon. Compare the permissible derivation of *baroque flautist*, shown in 10.47a, with the impermissible derivation of the (extensionally equivalent!) expression ⋆*wooden flautist*, in 10.47b:

10.47

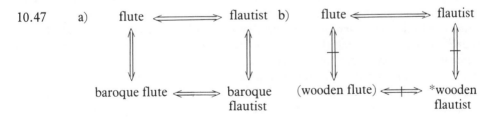

In 10.47b we have tried to form a paradox on an expression which isn't in the lexicon, namely *wooden flute*. Therefore, the derivation can't go through.

The second prerequisite is that the meaning of the individual components be identical. That is, the sense of *grammar* in *grammarian* and *transformational grammar* must be the same, namely something like 'set of rules and representations character-izing a language'. To see the importance of this consider a sociolinguist who makes a scientific study of bad grammar. Here we are using *grammar* in a different sense, namely something like 'set of linguistically defined social conventions relating to language use'. Such a person could not be called a *bad grammarian* (unless, of course he were bad at writing grammars). This is because the sense of *grammar* which licenses *grammarian* and the sense which licenses *bad grammar* are distinct (because *grammar* is polysemous). This is illustrated in 10.48, which shows that we can't complete the square of proportional analogy because the cell for *grammar* contains two distinct entries:

10.48

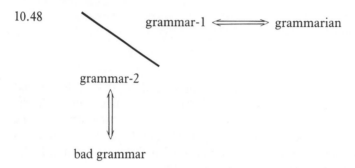

grammar-1 ⟺ grammarian

grammar-2

bad grammar

What we are dealing with here is a type of word formation which is blind to constituent structure (including bracketing paradoxes) and totally cavalier about allomorphy (up to and including suppletion). The word formation rule says, in effect, 'form a personal noun from whatever you can find in the lexicon, provided the requisite expressions are already housed there'. This is interesting because it is the only case of productive word formation discussed in any detail in the literature which involves anything like genuine analogy.

More interesting from the theoretical point of view, however, is the fact that we have here an instance of 'paradigmatic word formation'. This particular word formation process is governed by an abstract linguistic category (and one which is very difficult to pin down semantically), that of 'personal noun related to a nominal expression'. This can be thought of as a grammaticalized lexical category. It is lexical in the sense that it creates new words referring to new concepts. In this it is like, say, the category of 'feminine form of noun', illustrated by *poetess, lioness, she-elephant, bitch, saleswoman, schoolmistress* and so on. However, personal noun formation differs from feminine noun formation, for the latter only applies to a lexically specified subpart of the vocabulary. A great many nouns capable of referring to men lack feminine counterparts in English: *doctor, professor, seaman, chairman, stationmaster*. Most animal terms don't have male-female pairs, either: *wombat, orangutang, frog*. The personal nouns represent a different kind of linguistic relationship, because any nominal which is semantically capable of forming a personal noun will do so. In this respect, personal noun formation is much more akin to, say, plural formation than feminine formation. It's important to stress that this is peculiar to English: there are some languages in which only a handful of nouns have a plural form (e.g. Chinese), so that this represents a (marginal) lexical category, not a grammatical category. On the other hand, in Dutch, it has been argued that feminine formation is so regular and productive that it is a grammaticalized process (van Marle, 1985).

The reason that this type of process is regarded as paradigmatic is because the word formation process relies on the relationship between the items that are currently present in the lexicon, and not on a syntagmatic process of affixation, compounding or whatever. This is a slightly different sense of 'paradigm' from that used in describing inflectional morphology. However, there are significant parallels. The most important of these is that the process should be defined in terms of a network of relationships, such that, if a language has an empty place at some point in the network, that place will (normally) be filled. This corresponds to the idea that, in a verb paradigm for a given language, every normal (non-defective) verb should have, say, a third person singular present indicative form, even if the form itself is suppletive.

There are a number of other plausible candidates for paradigmatic word formation (some of which are discussed in the next chapter, especially §11.2). Andrew Carstairs-McCarthy has pointed out to me that names of important personages (especially heads of state) license relational adjectives, irrespective of allomorphy. Thus, we can qualify the word *limousine* with words referring to royalty (kings, queens, princes and princesses), presidents, bishops and so on, to give the *royal/presidential/episcopal limousine*. In New Zealand, the term *Governor-General* has its own adjective, too: the *vice-regal(!) limousine*. Carstairs (1988) refers to such word formation as 'meaning driven'. Like the personal noun bracketing paradoxes it seems to hinge on a very specific, but covert, semantic category, what Whorf (1956) refers to as a *cryptotype*.

Other cases of paradigmatic word formation involving covert semantic categories (which have not been previously noted as far as I can tell) involve bracketing paradoxes such as *green-eyed* and *quarter-pounder*.

The first type is formed by affixing *-ed* to a phrase consisting of modifier + noun, in which the modifier will typically be a qualitative adjective or numeral, and in which the noun is a body part or 'clothing part'. This seems to be virtually productive (although the obvious examples are set phrases). Some examples (going from top to bottom) are *long-haired, ruddy-cheeked, flat-chested, rosy-fingered, knock-kneed, left-footed* (external body parts), *broad-minded, quick-witted, warm-hearted, lily-livered, cold-blooded* (internal body parts), and *open-necked, double-breasted, short-sleeved* (clothing parts). There are one or two other forms of this type which don't fit the cryptotype, such as *five-pointed, right-angled, six-sided, two-edged, three-cornered, flat-bottomed*. It's possible that the cryptotype is simply more abstract than I've claimed or that these represent a second cryptotype of 'external attribute of geometrical figure, 'inalienable possession' or some such.

The second type is formed by affixing *-er* to an expression formed from a numeral or measure word and a noun referring to a unit of measurement: *three-tonner, five-miler, four-weeker, fifteen-footer*. It seems that these can't be formed if the noun is polysyllabic (*ten-furlonger*), or if it ends in a non-consonant (*two-hourer, *one-yearer, *seven-dayer*). An honorary member of this class appears to be *three-wheeler*. Perhaps a wheel is regarded as a unit of measurement for these purposes.

Of particular interest is the fact that some of these expressions are derived by affixation to an expression which doesn't exist (*lily-livered*) or which (in the case of *five-pointed*) couldn't exist. Like the personal noun bracketing paradoxes, it appears that the source must be (perceived as) a lexicalized phrase.

Appendix: Sproat's formalism

This account is distilled from Sproat (1988). Lexical entries for morphemes have two parts, a 'syntactic half' and a 'phonological half'. The syntactic representation of an affix indicates the syntactic category it attaches to and the syntactic category it forms, as in 10.49 for *un-* and *-ity*:

10.49 $un = \langle UN_{\langle A,O \rangle}, un- \rangle$
          $ity = \langle ITY_{\langle A,N \rangle}, -ity \rangle$

The subscript $\langle A,O \rangle$ on the syntactic half of *un* means 'selects an adjective and effects no change in category'; $\langle A,N \rangle$ means 'derives a noun from an adjective'. The syntactic part of an entry therefore indicates only constituent structure information, while the phonological part encodes only strict adjacency requirements. The idea of separating these two aspects of structure is familiar from syntax. In Generalized Phrase Structure Grammar, for instance (Gazdar, Klein, Pullum and Sag, 1985), Phrase structure rules are factored into two components, the constituent structure rules (Immediate Dominance rules) and linear order rules (Linear Precedence rules). Essentially the same has been advocated for Government-Binding syntax by Zubizarreta and Vergnaud (1982). The formal technique chosen by Sproat for representing immediate dominance and linear precedence information is derived from proposals of Guerssel (1983).

By the Mapping Principle, when the syntactic representations of two morphemes in a word are sisters, then the phonological representations will be adjacent at PF. In concatenative morphologies, 'adjacent to' simply means 'linearly contiguous with', irrespective of any implied bracketing. For non-concatenative morphologies 'adjacent to' will mean 'autosegmentally combined with', so that, in an Arabic verb form such as *katab*, the vocalism, *-a-*, will be adjacent to the triliteral root *k-t-b*. This conception of adjacency means that in *un + grammatical + ity* the morpheme *un-* will be adjacent both to *grammatical* and *grammaticality* while *-ity* will be adjacent to *grammatical* and *ungrammatical*.

Adjacency at PF is represented using the concatenation operator ⋆. Given the syntactic representation of *ungrammaticality* in 10.50, the Mapping Principle delivers PF representation 10.51:

10.50

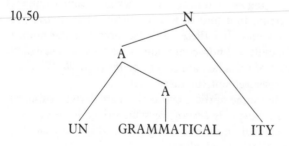

10.51   [[un⋆gramatikal] ⋆iti]

Strictly speaking, 10.51 isn't the phonological form of 10.50, in that linear precedence information isn't yet formally encoded. Recall that the syntactic representation includes no information about linear order. Therefore, we could equally well say that the representations in question are those of 10.52–10.53, with an arbitrary ordering within constituents:

10.52

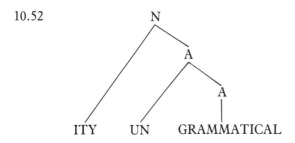

ITY   UN   GRAMMATICAL

10.53   [[gramatikal⋆un] ⋆iti]

Linear order is encoded with the operator ˆ. This is blind to constituent structure (immediate dominance), but sensitive to linear precedence. We assume that there is a further function which maps phonological forms defined using ⋆ into those using ˆ. The representation of *ungrammaticality* will therefore finally take the shape of 10.54a or b.

10.54   a) [[unˆ gramatikal]ˆiti]
        b) [unˆ [gramatikalˆiti]

Either of these two representations will correspond to 10.51 (or, indeed, 10.53). We require 10.54b. How do we ensure this?

We define the operation induced by ⋆ as *commutative* but not *associative*. We speak of commutative concatenation of a and b when (ab) is equivalent to (ba). Hence, ordinary addition is commutative since $2 + 5 = 5 + 2$; however, subtraction isn't commutative because $5 - 2 \neq 2 - 5$. We speak of associative concatenation when ((ab)c) is equivalent to (a(bc)). Hence, again, addition is associative since $((2 + 5) + 3) = (2 + (5 + 3))$ but subtraction isn't, since $((10 - 5) - 2) = 3$ while $(10 - (5 - 2)) = 7$. None of the four operations of school arithmetic is commutative and non-associative, so we'll look at this operator in a little more detail. A representation such as [un⋆grammatical] is equivalent to [grammatical⋆un] by commutativity. Likewise, [[un⋆grammatical] ⋆ity] is equivalent to [ity⋆ [un⋆grammatical]], [[grammatical⋆un] ⋆ity] and [ity⋆ [grammatical⋆un]. However, [[un⋆grammatical] ⋆ity] is not equivalent to [un⋆ [grammatical⋆ity]] because ⋆ isn't an associative operator. To summarize, the ⋆ operator allows us to ignore linear order because it's commutative. On the other hand, it doesn't allow us to rebracket because it isn't associative.

The ˆ operator is associative but not commutative. Thus, aˆ(bˆc) is equivalent to (aˆb)ˆc but neither of these is equivalent to (bˆc)ˆa. It should be apparent that using the ˆ operator allows us to rebracket at will (associativity) but prevents us from altering linear order (non-commutativity). It thus captures linear precedence irrespective of sisterhood.

We are finally in a position to account for our bracketing paradox. Given two otherwise legitimate representations for *ungrammaticality* (i.e. 10.54), we must choose the one which respects the level ordering restriction, namely, 10.54b. We can do this because the ˆ operator is associative and hence permits rebracketing. In other words, by using this property of ˆ we can say that *un-* is syntactically adjacent to (more properly, a sister of) *grammatical* but phonologically adjacent to *grammaticality*, while

-ity is syntactically adjacent to (a sister of) *ungrammatical* and phonologically adjacent to *grammatical*.

Clearly what is crucial about this account is the notion of 'adjacency at PF'. Although Sproat couches his explanation in terms of rebracketing of PF representations, strictly speaking what his formalism does is to eradicate constituent structure from linearized PF representations. This is because it actually makes no sense to talk of 'bracketings' of elements combined using an associative operator. In other words, it is misleading for us to say that both 10.54a and b represent 10.52. The real representation of 10.52 using ˆ is 10.54c, without any brackets:

10.54   c) unˆgramatikalˆiti

This makes it easier to understand why non-concatenative morphologies fall under the same rubric. In these morphologies the linearization rules are slightly different, but otherwise the same principle holds: (morpho-)phonological adjacency makes no reference to constituent structure. Given this interpretation of Sproat's claims, we have an explanation for the bracketing paradoxes which comes very close to that of Aronoff and Sridhar (1983, 1987).

EXERCISES

10.1   Which of the following could be described as bracketing paradoxes? Explain your reasoning

    befell
    ninety-first
    reception
    neuropsychological
    illegibility
    dormice
    postmen
    politico-economic
    Social Democrat

10.2   Investigate the thesis that bracketing paradoxes of the *ungrammaticality* type are exceptional by constructing examples of non-paradoxes (that is, ungrammatical words with the structure of paradoxes) using the Class I suffixes illustrated in 10.14, along the lines of *wallfloral*.

10.3   The following Hungarian expressions represent bracketing paradoxes. Explain why. [Hungarian has a vowel harmony rule under which words have to consist of back vowels or front vowels, with /i e/ being neutral, that is, not under-going vowel harmony, but triggering front vowel harmony in succeeding vowels. Stress falls on the first syllable of a word, indicated by underlining in these examples. ú = [y:], ú = [u:]].

Word list:
alak – 'shape'; eredet – 'origin', kék – 'blue', láb – 'leg', magyar – 'Hungarian', negy – 'four', nyelv – 'language', páratlan – 'unparalleled', szém – 'eye', szépség – 'beauty', szeszélyes – 'strange', vulkanikus – 'volcanic'

kék szému	'blue-eyed'
magyar nyelvú	'pertaining to Hungarian'
negy lábú	'four-legged'
páratlan szépségú	'of unparalleled beauty'
szeszélyes alakú	'strangely shaped'
vulkanikus eredetú	'of volcanic origin'

10.4 Explain exactly how Williams would account for the following examples (it may help to refer to §6.1).

> plastic surgeon
> nuclear physicist
> three hundred and twenty fifth
> vice-presidential
> set-theoretic
> white-washed

10.5 Take the bracketing paradoxes you identified from ex. 10.1. Which can be explained by Sproat's Mapping Principle? How does the explanation work?

⋆**10.6** The word *submariner* means 'one who serves in a submarine'. One pronun-ciation given in dictionaries is stressed on the first syllable and rhymes with 'marina' [ˈsʌbməriːnə]. The pronunciation favoured by naval personnel has the stress on the second syllable to rhyme with 'mariner' [sʌbˈmærinə]. Which of the theories of bracketing paradoxes discussed in this chapter could relate the second pronunci-ation to the word *mariner?*

⋆**10.7** Depending on assumptions about morphology and phonology, the fol-lowing Hungarian verbs may or may not represent instances of bracketing paradoxes. Under what assumptions are they paradoxes, and under what assumptions are they not paradoxes? [See ex. 10.3 for phonological information; also ő = [œ:], ö = [œ], ó = [o:]].

Word list:
ad – ' to give', foglal – 'to occupy', megy – 'to go', nő – 'to grow', old – 'to untie',

össze – 'together', potól – 'to replace', süt – 'to shine', újul – 'to be renewed', ül – 'to sit'.

felold	'to dissolve'
felújul	'to be renewed, revived'
felmegy	'to go up'
kimegy	'to go out'
kipotól	'to compensate for'
kiújul	'to begin again'
összead	'to add together; to marry'
összefoglal	'to summarize'
rámegy	'to go onto'
ránő	'to adhere to'
rásüt	'to illuminate'
ráül	'to sit on'

*10.8   Explain exactly how Kiparsky (1982b: §4.3.2) and Williams (1981a: §6.1) would analyse examples such as *forgave* and *rewrote*. Which of these approaches is compositional, in the sense of assigning a constituent structure (at some level) which matches the semantic structure of the examples?

*10.9   How does Sproat's approach to the bracketing paradoxes help in explaining the structure of synthetic compounds such as *truck driver*, *slum clearance* or *car theft*? (You'll need to consult §8.3.5.2.)

*10.10   Lieber (amongst others) analyses *truck driver* as [[truck drive] er], while Di Sciullo and Williams assume a structure [truck [driver]]. Which of these representations is compatible with the approach advocated by Aronoff and Sridhar (1983, 1987)?

11

The Place of Morphology

Introduction

The central theme which has run through this book is the idea that morphology represents an interface between different components of grammar: the lexicon, syntax, phonology and (though we haven't spoken much of this) semantics. One of the trickiest questions facing those who research at an interface is where one component ends and another begins. On a number of occasions we have seen differences of opinion as to whether a given phenomenon should be regarded as morphological or whether it belongs to some other domain such as phonology or syntax. A corollary of this line of questioning is whether morphology exists as an autonomous component at all. In their preface to the first volume of the *Yearbook of Morphology* (published in 1988) the editors describe morphology as 'a *relatively* autonomous discipline' (emphasis original). But we have seen that some linguists deny the existence of a separate morphological component.

My own view is that it at least makes sense to investigate the extent to which morphology can be viewed as an autonomous discipline, even though many of the more intriguing problems lie on the boundary between morphology and other components. However, this leaves us with another, closely allied, question, succinctly put by Anderson (1982): 'Where's morphology?'.

The answers which have been proposed to this question are many. The main reason for the variety of opinion is the variety of views over what constitutes morphology. For even those who recognize that there is a separate morphology component (or 'module') tend not to agree over what it contains. If we think of morphology rather simplistically in terms of the rules governing the concatenation of morphemes, then for some (e.g. Halle, 1973, Kiparsky, 1982a, Selkirk, 1982, Lieber, 1980) morphology is a part of the lexicon, and the notion of 'lexicon' as a linguistic level of representation therefore has to be enriched over the simple notion of list of idiosyncratic forms. This was a view which came to predominate during the earlier years of the revival of interest in morphology, but it has been challenged in various ways. Others would see morphology as essentially a subcomponent of phonology (in the extended sense of 'phonology' implied by Chomsky's notion of 'Phonological Form' or PF). Sproat (1985a) seems to subscribe to such a view. However, Sproat shares with a number of linguists the opinion that the more syntactic aspects of morphology (particularly those surveyed in chapters 8, 9 and 10) should really be viewed as the morphological aspects of syntax, and not handled by a separate morphology component at all. As we saw in chapter 6, Anderson (1982) regards morphology as split between the lexicon (derivational morphology), and the phonology (inflectional morphology), with the syntactic component intervening between the two. In this chapter, however, we will survey the theoretical underpinnings of a number of proposals to view morphology as an independent component with its own set of principles, representations, and well-formedness conditions.

We begin with a survey of the theoretical position sketched out by Anna-Maria Di Sciullo and Edwin Williams. Their approach is often thought of as 'lexicalist' in as far as it eschews attempts to handle a good many word formation phenomena in terms of purely syntactic principles. However, this is something of a misnomer, since they argue that there is a separate morphology component which is distinct from the lexicon. Indeed, they take what must be regarded as an extreme stance and claim that the lexicon is no more than a list of idiosyncrasies and as such is not of interest to linguistic theory.

Diametrically opposed to this position is that of Robert Beard, surveyed in §11.2. He argues for a separation of morphological form and morphological function, a claim known as the Separation Hypothesis. This denies prior status to the morpheme as a bearer of morphological meaning. It therefore rejects the view that morphology can simply be a question of concatenating morphemes and computing the resultant meaning from the meaning of the parts.

We next look at the overall conception of morphology which has been presented in a number of papers recently by Arnold Zwicky which strongly stress the 'interface' properties of morphology. Many of Zwicky's ideas have already been discussed in some detail, and here I shall in effect tie together these strands and discuss some of the implications of the resulting picture.

Section 4 is devoted to a set of proposals advanced by Jerrold Sadock, under the title of 'Autolexical Syntax'. Sadock argues for an autonomous morphology, with an articulated theory of the interface between morphology and syntax. Along the way he offers analyses of noun incorporation, cliticization, portmanteau morphs in syntax, and an intriguing pattern of agreement in Slavic.

In the next two sections I discuss two recent analyses of compounding processes, the first in Japanese, due to Masayoshi Shibatani and Taro Kageyama (1988), and the second in Hebrew, by Hagit Borer (1988). Although these studies might appear somewhat parochial at first blush, they represent detailed arguments for permitting morphological principles to apply outside the confines of a morphology or lexical component proper. Like Sadock, these authors propose a morphology component which is a separate module of grammar whose function is to define well-formedness conditions for words. Again, like Sadock, but unlike, say, Zwicky or Beard, they claim that this component is not 'ordered' with respect to other components of the grammar. Thus, the well-formedness conditions can be called into play at any (formal) level of linguistic representation, for example, the lexicon, D-structure, S-structure or PF.

I conclude with a speculative attempt to link this debate over the location of morphology in the overall grammatical architecture with the question raised earlier, concerning what constitutes a word.

11.1   Di Sciullo and Williams's definition of 'word'

The theory sketched out in Di Sciullo and Williams's (1987) monograph draws a clear-cut distinction between syntax and morphology.[1] At the same time it provides one of the most thoroughgoing defences of the Lexicalist Hypothesis. Their claim is essentially that syntax and morphology are entirely separate domains of inquiry and that it is therefore incoherent to speak of syntactic rules affecting morphological structures. In other words, lexicalism is not merely a hypothesis about the way language might be organized, it is the only logically possible way in which language could be organized.

Part of the difficulty in understanding the nature of morphology, according to Di Sciullo and Williams, lies in the variety of meanings attached to the notion of 'word' itself. Di Sciullo and Williams provide us with three distinct notions (actually four). The first is that of *morphological object*, constructed out of morphological 'atoms', i.e. morphemes, by (concatenative) processes of affixation and compounding. There is little room here for the view of morphemes as 'processes' rather than as 'things'. The second sense of word is that of a *syntactic atom*, i.e. the indivisible building block of syntax. Since these syntactic words are atomic units with respect to syntax, syntactic rules can't make reference to their subcomponents. Only morphology can refer to parts of words (and then only in the sense of morphological objects). This is a restatement of a strong variety of lexical integrity.

According to Di Sciullo and Williams, morphology and syntax are separate (though related) disciplines (just as history and forestry are separate disciplines, p. 46) so there should be no confusion between morphological objects and syntactic atoms, despite the fact that the two disciplines share a common vocabulary of syntactic categories (Noun, Verb, Adjective and so on). In fact, it is argued, the Lexicalist Hypothesis (or the thesis of the **atomicity of words**) is simply the logical consequence of this division between the two disciplines, and not, for instance, a principle of grammar.[2]

The third conception of word is that of 'listed object', for which Di Sciullo and Williams coin the term **listeme**. Listemes are the linguistic expressions memorized and stored by speakers. According to Di Sciullo and Williams their study belongs to the domain of psychology and not linguistics.[3] The same is true of notions such as productivity. In particular, just because an expression is listed (i.e. specifically memorized) doesn't mean that it is a morphological word (or indeed a word in any sense). There are morphological objects which are formed by perfectly regular and exceptionless processes whose products are not therefore listed. Examples would be abstract deadjectival nouns formed by *-ness* affixation, regular inflections and so on. Likewise, there are syntactic objects, namely idioms such as *take advantage of NP* or *let the cat out of the bag*, which have syntactic structure, and are therefore not simply (syntactic) atoms, but which nonetheless have to be listed.

Now, it is fairly clear that in many cases, if not the majority, morphological words will also be syntactic words. Why, then, is it necessary to distinguish the two? Di Sciullo and Williams argue that a number of phenomena demand this and discuss two classes of examples: Romance compounding and coanalysis. Since I shall be discussing a similar proposal for coanalysis in §11.3 I shall restrict myself to the compounding cases.

Romance compounding, the formation of exocentric compounds found regularly in Romance languages (amongst others), was briefly mentioned in chapter 8. In 11.1–11.2 we see some French examples:

11.1   a) V + N: essuie-glace
                     wipe-window
                     'windscreen wiper'
        b) V + A: gagne-petit
                     gain-small
                     'low wage earner'
        c) V + Adv: couche-tard
                     lie-late
                     'night-owl', 'one who goes to bed late'

11.2   a) trompe-l'oeil
           deceive-the-eye
           'illusion'
        b) boit-sans-soif
           drink-without-thirst
           'heavy drinker'
        c) bon-à-rien
           good-to-nothing
           'good-for-nothing'
        d) homme-de-paille
           man-of-straw
           'stooge'
        e) hors-la-loi
           outside-the-law
           'outlaw'

These compounds and others mentioned earlier all have the distribution of nouns, that is X^0 level elements. In this they contrast with other types of listed syntactic objects, namely idioms, which have the category of maximal projection (typically VP). Amongst idioms, Di Sciullo and Williams include cases such as *timbres-poste* 'postage stamps' (literally 'stamps-post'), on the grounds that they have exactly the structure of a syntactic phrase.

What Di Sciullo and Williams propose is that syntactic words such as those of 11.1–11.2 are formed by simply relabelling syntactic constructions as words. Thus, the structure of *essuie-glace* will be 11.3:

11.3

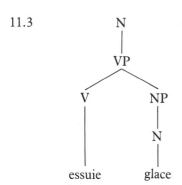

Formations of this sort are considered 'marginal' in the sense of being a marked option in word formation. Since they are not formed by morphological rules (indeed, they have nothing to do with morphology) they don't need to respect morphological principles (such as the Righthand Head Rule). Nor is it necessary to explain the structure of these expressions by assuming that syntactic principles operate in the morphology. For example, we might want to say that the NP *glace* in 11.3 is licensed by receiving (Abstract) Case from the verb, just as in a syntactic VP. However, this is not necessary, because such formations obey syntactic principles already, by virtue of being formed from syntactic objects (maximal projections). This is the only circumstance in which syntactic principles govern the structure of words. A corollary of this line of reasoning is that a language like French probably has no compounding at all.[4]

There are a good many relevant phenomena which Di Sciullo and William's theoretical sketch doesn't address. Although the authors mention the notion of phonological word in passing (to distinguish it from the other three types of word), there is no discussion of the extent to which the morphology module is distinct from phonology. Thus, all the questions about allomorphy which we raised in part II of this book are ignored. Likewise, all the questions which motivated the discussion in chapter 9 on clitics are bypassed. The only discussion of inflectional morphology is a passing reference to Williams's (1981) theory of the paradigm, a proposal which received severe criticism at the hands of Joseph and Wallace (1984) and which doesn't seem to have had much impact on specialists on inflection. These, of course, are questions which subject purely morpheme-based theories to considerable strain.

Di Sciullo and Williams's conception of listedness brings with it radical implications about the nature of the lexicon. For them, the lexicon can be no more than an enumeration of idiosyncrasies. It has no structure of its own, and its only interaction with morphology is to serve as the storage place for the input to and output from morphological rules (i.e. the morphemes and the morphological words). One consequence of this position is the rejection of Aronoff's word-based morphology. Instead, the original Hallean view is espoused according to which word formation is simply the concatenation of morphemes. Now, a prime reason for accepting word-based morphology is that it allows us to explain why a derived word with idiosyncratic meaning retains that idiosyncrasy when further derived. For instance, the word *pluralist* is derived from *plural* but includes an unpredictable semantic element. This element is also found when *pluralist* itself is affixed to give *pluralistic*. Di Sciullo and

Williams appeal to Williams's (1981a) 'constellation' theory of lexical relatedness here, pointing out that a similar problem obtains in relating *pluralist* with *pluralism*. Difficulties with that account have already been discussed in §10.4, in connection with the bracketing paradoxes.

Another challenge to Di Sciullo and Williams's viewpoint is the claim that some word formation may be paradigmatic (or 'meaning-driven'). For this implies that the lexicon as list must play some sort of linguistic role, and not a purely psycholinguistic role. The personal noun formation process and other examples discussed in §10.7 thus casts doubt on the wisdom of Di Sciullo and Williams's point of departure.

The sharpest contrast between the radical lexicalism of Di Sciullo and Williams and other approaches is illustrated by the syntactically based theories of word formation discussed in great detail in chapters 7 and 8. This type of lexicalism is totally incompatible with any attempt to relate valency alternations to incorporation (head-to-head movement), or attempts to account for the structure of compounds in terms of the Projection Principle and Theta Criterion. This has already been illustrated in those earlier chapters, and it is over such constructions that we can expect to see some of the strongest reactions against Di Sciullo and Williams's variety of lexicalism.

11.2   The separation hypothesis

The radical variety of lexicalism espoused by Di Sciullo and Williams brings with it the assumption that morphology is basically agglutinative. Moreover, the 'atoms' which are agglutinated, the morphemes, have a meaning of their own as well as a form. The agglutinating morpheme concept is challenged by Word-and-Paradigm theorists for whom it is important to separate off the morphosyntactic and semantic functions of morphological operations (in inflection, at least) from their physical (phonological and morphological) realization. The primary motivation for this manoeuvre is to handle cases of multiple exponence or many–many mappings between form and function. One example of multiple exponence which we discussed in our initial exposure to morphemics (§2.2.1) concerned a certain ambiguity in the term 'plural morpheme' in English. Are the plural affixes, *-es*, *-en*, *-a*, *-ae*, *-i*, *-im*, and processes such as umlauting (*foot~feet*) all allomorphs of a single plural morpheme, or must we say that these are all different morphemes, complete with their own allomorphy? Simple though this question is, it's not clear whether any of the morpheme based variants of lexicalism we've encountered to date has any principled answer to it.

Similar problems are posed by 'derived' nominalizations, such as those in *-(a)tion*. Many of these can function as nominalizations pure and simple without any additional components of meaning, corresponding roughly to the productive *-ing* nominalizations (but lacking their aspectual nuances for the most part). Thus, in hackneyed examples like *the destruction of the city* we have a phrase meaning simply 'the act or process of destroying the city'. Sproat (1985a) takes these observations to suggest that there is a single NOM morpheme which serves to nominalize verbs and whose exact morphological exponent is a function of the verb stem itself. This is tantamount to saying that there is a [+ Nominalization] feature with exponents such as *-ing*, *-ation* and so on. Likewise, we could take the productive process of personal noun formation discussed in §10.7, as evidence for the existence of a highly abstract personal noun morpheme, call it -ER, realized in a great variety of ways.

Finally, in some languages we find that it is extremely easy to form *relational adjectives* from nouns. These have the general meaning of 'pertaining to Noun'. Thus, in Chukchee a relational adjective is formed by suffixing *-kin* to a noun root. This is used very frequently where in English we would use a prepositional phrase such as 'of the Noun', or a compound noun construction (mentioned in passing in §8.2). For instance, from *weem* 'river' and *wǝkwǝt* 'stones' we can form the expression *weemkin wǝkwǝt* 'the stones in/of the river' (lit. 'fluvial stones'). In the case of Chukchee, not only is this derivational process semantically very regular (in that it simply forms a corresponding adjective from a noun without further semantic change), it is also morphologically very regular.

A very similar process in the Slavonic languages is almost as regular semantically as that of Chukchee (as well as being very productive) but morphologically it shows the same kind of variation in its realization as the English plural or nominalization processes. We see a few examples from Polish in 11.4–11.9 (based on Szymanek, 1985: 141ff):

11.4   a) jagnię   'lamb'   b) jagnięcy 'of a lamb'
         (root: jagnięt-)
         c) skóra jagnięca 'lamb-skin'

11.5   a) ziemniak 'potato'   b) ziemniaczany 'of a potato'
         c) mąka ziemniaczana 'potato flour'
            zaraza ziemniaczana 'potato blight'

11.6   a) żaba   'frog'   b) żabi 'of a frog'
         c) żabi szkrek 'frog spawn'

11.7   a) szkoła   'school'   b) szkolny 'of school'
         c) podręcznik szkolny 'school book'
            budynek szkolny 'school house'
            inspektor szkolny 'school inspector'
            lata szkolne 'school years'

11.8   a) uniwersytet 'university'   b) uniwersytecki 'of a university'
         c) lata uniwersyteckie 'university years'
            studia uniwersiteckie 'university education'

11.9   a) dom   'house'   b) domowy 'of a house'
         c) porządki domowe 'housework'
            przemysl domowy 'cottage industry'
            revizja   domowa 'domiciliary visit'

Here we have six different affixes, each with the basic function of forming a relational adjective. The first of these affixes is perhaps best regarded as a phonological process of palatalization, t > c. The others are *-an, -i, -n, -sk* and *-ow*. Szymanek lists them in this order, which he states is the order of increasing productivity and generality. He claims that it is best to think of the list as a disjunctively ordered set. Any given affix is attached to those roots whose morphology, phonology or semantics demands it (for instance the t > c alternation is characteristic of names of young animals ending in -ęt). In many cases a noun is simply marked in the lexicon for the suffix it takes. However, if no suffix is specified in the lexical entry of a noun, then the last on the list, -ow, is chosen by default. In other words, Szmanek argues that an aspect of derivational morphology is governed by the Elsewhere Condition. For many linguists this is tantamount to saying that there is a derivational paradigm, a claim Szymanek makes explicitly (cf, also van Marle, 1985).

This way of looking at matters is very different from that of a strict morpheme-based approach, in which we would be obliged to say that there were six synonymous but distinct morphemes. In such an approach it would be a coincidence (i) that the morphemes were synonymous and (ii) that almost every noun forms some sort of relational adjective. Moreover, we would simply be failing to capture the fact that in Slavonic (though not in English) there is a morphological *process* of relation adjective formation, irrespective of its morphological realization.

Now, it might be argued that the relational adjective case isn't entirely parallel to an inflectional paradigm proper. For we find that a noun will sometimes take more than one different affix depending on the precise meaning of the resulting adjective. For instance, we see examples 11.10–11.11 from *koń*, 'horse':

11.10   a) konny
         b) gwardia konna 'Horse Guards'
            jazda konna 'horse riding'
            wyścigi konne 'horse race'

11.11   a) koński
         b) grzbiet koński 'horseback'
            giez koński 'horse-fly'
            nawóz końsky 'horse manure'
            końskie mięso 'horse meat'

The adjective in 11.10 seems to mean something like 'involving horses' while that in 11.11 has the meaning 'to do with the body of a horse'. Therefore, it seems to make more sense to say we are dealing with two separate (though similar) affixal morphemes, each with slightly different meanings. Szymanek (citing a different example) states that such cases are rare in Polish, though the phenomenon in general seems well attested for other types of word formation. However, this need not force us to abandon the idea that the process as a whole is paradigmatic. A similar phenomenon is seen in English in the formation of adjectives converted from past participles. For instance, *drunk* is the regular participle form, but there is also a doublet *drunken*, which only has the meaning 'inebriated'. And in more general terms it is actually quite common for complex inflectional systems to permit optional doublets. Even English plural formation permits this, with doublets such as *formulae/formulas*. Furthermore, even in inflectional systems we find that a given inflectional category might be given different realizations with slightly different meaning. This happens in the Russian locative/prepositional singular of certain nouns, where one form (e.g. *sadu* from *sad* 'garden') is used exclusively with the preposition *v* 'in' to express a strictly locational meaning, while the more usual form of this case, *sade*, is found in all other uses.

We are now reaching the position where we might say that we could take something like a Word-and-Paradigm model of inflection (with its separation of form and function) and simply extend it to derivational morphology. This means regarding derivational categories as grammatical categories and not some kind of lexical category. Grammatical categories form a closed class which can be coded by means of a feature system. Thus, we have one part of the grammar which specifies that there are plurals, past tenses, nominalizations, personal nouns, relational adjectives and so on, and another part of the grammar which says that there are affixes and umlauting processes and so on. In addition, there is a set of rules stating that for a given set of lexical items the plural form is realized by such-and-such or that the nominalization is realized by so-and-so. In a WP theory such as Anderson's, inflectional markers do not bear any meaning of their own, rather, they serve as 'cues' for figuring out the morphosyntactic category of the whole word. Likewise, in our extension, no affixes would have any inherent meaning. All of them would be cues for the function of the word in relation to its lexical meaning.

The idea of divorcing the form of both inflectional and derivational affixes from their function is known as the **Separation Hypothesis**. Its most vigorous proponent is Robert Beard (1976, 1981, 1982, 1987, 1988). Szymanek's (1985) monograph also presents a number of arguments in favour of the hypothesis. In Beard's model, 'Lexeme/Morpheme-Based Morphology', we separate out lexical entries, which Beard refers to as *lexemes*, and affixes added to lexemes, which are referred to (in defiance of tradition) as *morphemes*. The grammatical processes of derivation and inflection are effected by L-rules. Processes of affixation or morphophonological operations such as umlaut are M-rules.

These ideas can be illustrated by English plurals. In the words *cats algae, paramecia* and *geese*, we have four lexemes, CAT, ALGA, PARAMECIUM and GOOSE, three plural morphemes *-es, -ae, -a*, two M-rules, one of suffixation and one of umlaut, and one L-rule, that of pluralization. By drawing this distinction between L-rules and M-rules, we can express the fact that the different plural affixes have their own morphological properties (such as exhibiting certain sorts of allomorphy or only attaching to latinate roots), whilst at the same time capturing the fact that they are all exponents of a more generally important morphosyntactic category of 'plural'. It should be apparent that the same solution can be applied to the case of Polish relational adjectives.

Beard contrasts his approach with lexicalist theories such as Lieber's in which affixes are listed as lexical entries. The chief objection is that, for a set of important properties, affixes don't behave like lexical items. The first problem is that there appear to be zero affixes, while there are no entirely uncontroversial cases of zero lexical items. The second problem is that affixes don't themselves seem to undergo derivation. Note that this is different from saying that affixes don't undergo *affixation*. In §10.3, I said that Aronoff and Sridhar (1983, 1987) regard *compartmentalization* as composed of [compart] [mental] [ization], but this is not necessarily to say that the items *ment* and *ize* have undergone lexical derivation (and, indeed, this is not what Aronoff and Sridhar are saying). The third problem is that, properly speaking, lexical items only ever belong to one syntactic (lexical) category (lexical homonymy apart). Where a word appears to belong to more than one category, as when an adjective such as *yellow* is used as a noun or a verb, then we speak about the derivation (by conversion) of one category from another.[5] Affixes are different. It's quite common for a given affix to belong to several totally distinct categories. The *-ing* suffix in English derives words of the categories progressive aspect, gerund, result nominalization and adjective, *inter alia*. In languages with richer morphology this phenomenon is the rule rather than the exception. Finally, lexemes belong to open classes while affixes, being grammatical morphemes, are by definition closed class items.

Beard argues that these four differences pose problems for straightforward lexicalist theories which view affixes as just another type of lexical entry. In particular, if affixes are lexical items then zero morphology poses serious problems. Consider morphological conversion. Lieber's (1981b) account explicitly denies that conversion involves zero affixation. The reason is that some languages have a good many ways of using conversion, so that there would have to be a plethora of zero items all with different grammatical properties. Beard, however, objects to the conversion solution. The main problem with Lieber's account seems to be that she simply lists the stem twice (once as a verb and once as a noun, say) and then writes a redundancy rule saying they are related. But this, argues Beard, fails to explain why stems of identical phonological shape should be thus related to each other rather than arbitrary pairings of stems.

According to the Separation Hypothesis, conversion of *(to) walk* to *(a) walk* is simply using a verb as its own nominalization without specifying any accompanying morphological change. Therefore, conversion still involves a derivational process (that of result nominalization) but happens not to involve any morphological processes. It is difficult to see how the facts of conversion can be captured without assuming some sort of property changing process. The separation of derivation from affixation achieves this quite neatly: conversion is derivation with no affixation.

The converse of conversion is affixation which has no grammatical function. This is not especially uncommon. Beard (1987: 25) cites the well-known phenomenon of German meaningless inflections, illustrated in 11.12:

11.12	Seif-en-blase	frühling-s-haft
	soap-en-bubble	spring-s-like
	'soap bubble'	'spring-like'
	Kalb-s-braten	läch-er-lich
	veal-s-roast	laugh-er-ly
	'roast veal'	'laughable'
	Tag-e-buch	bär-en-haft
	day-e-book	bear-en-like
	'diary'	'bearish'
	Bild-er-buch	
	picture-er-book	
	'picture book'	

The model of morphology Beard proposes then is one in which derivation as well as inflection is viewed in paradigmatic terms, as the formal realization of abstract

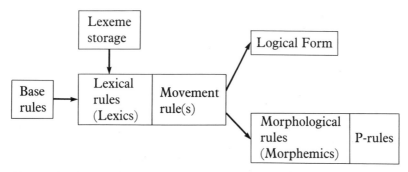

Figure 11.1   Beard's model

grammatical categories. This means that morphological operations are not housed in the lexicon. The lexicon is therefore a storage place for lexemes. These are subject to grammatical processes of derivation (which are lexical rules). They are also subject to the syntactic processes manifested as inflection. Beard refers to such inflectional rules (syntactic affixation) as Movement Rules, on the assumption that they involve either XP movement in the syntax, or feature movement (e.g. as copying). After these processes we have the morphological operations which are exponents of those grammatical processes. This feeds the morphology. The model is diagrammed as in figure 11.1 by Beard (e.g. 1987: 21, 1988: 15). Redrawn and simplified[6] this looks like figure 11.2, which we can compare with the usual T-model of Government-Binding syntax, and particularly with Anderson's EWP model (shown in §6.5.2, figure 6.1).

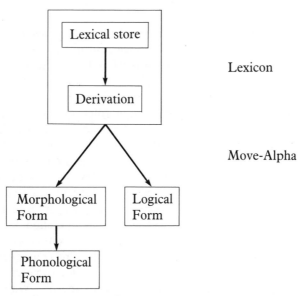

Figure 11.2   Beard's model (redrawn)

11.3   Zwicky's 'interface program'

The theme of morphology representing an autonomous component with rich interfaces with the rest of grammar has been argued perhaps most persuasively by Arnold Zwicky in a series of papers cited at various times during the course of this book. Here I'm relying particularly on the formulation in Zwicky (1986, 1988, 1990). Zwicky's views, which have much in common with those of Beard just reviewed, are diametrically opposed to the radical lexicalism of Di Sciullo and Williams, relying as it does on an ultimately agglutinative, morpheme-based theory of word structure. Zwicky emphasizes the role of processes in morphology, and explicitly sides with Anderson and other Word-and-Paradigm theoreticians in denying the morpheme any privileged status.

We have discussed certain aspects of Zwicky's approach to morphophonemics (§4.6) and clitics (§9.2). Here we examine the crucial role played by the notion of 'interface' in Zwicky's conception of things. The overall model of grammar is shown in 11.13 (Zwicky, 1986):

11.13   SYNTAX < (LIAISON) < SHAPE < MORPHONOLOGY <
         (READJUSTMENT) < AUTOMATIC PHONOLOGY

As indicated, each component on the left strictly precedes each following component. Therefore, no rule of, say, morphonology can feed a rule of shape or syntax.

The Shape component (described in §4.7) comprises the following:

11.14   IMPLICATION / REALIZATION / FORMATION
                        LEXICON
                  SHAPE CONDITIONS

The lexicon is an enumeration of all the word forms of the language (including, for instance, regularly formed inflection). Each such word form has a morphosyntactic description. Thus the lexicon will contain both /kat/ and /kats/ with an indication that the former is singular and the latter plural. Zwicky draws a sharp distinction between inflection and derivation. The rules of Realization are essentially word formation rules for inflection, while the Formation rules are for derivation. The Implication rules are redundancy rules which, for instance, assign lexemes to particular declensional class on the basis of their gender or phonological form.

Zwicky rejects the view that such phenomena as stem allomorphy should be regarded as the result of phonological rules triggered by affixation. Instead, he adopts a form of Separation Hypothesis by distinguishing operations, such as adding an affix, or umlauting a stem vowel, from morphological rules proper. A morphological rule can specify a variety of operations (including no operation at all, as in conversion), some of which may occur in tandem, as when suffixation is accompanied by umlauting of the stem vowel in certain German plurals. One consequence of this view is that, when an operation is blocked from applying for some reason (e.g. a phonological constraint), the result is an apparent zero morph. We've seen an example of this in our discussion of clitics, where Zwicky argues that the failure of a possessive marker to appear on *kids'* in *a friend of my kids'* is due to a general ban on multiple 'Zs', such that the -*Z* affixation process simply fails to apply a second time (i.e. in addition to pluralization). This can't be because of a ban on a plural affix followed by a possessive affix (if only because of the existence of *oxen's*). Instead, it is a constraint on the operation part of the morphological process.

For Zwicky, then, grammar consists of a set of interacting but autonomous modules or components, each with its own set of principles of organization. This means that Zwicky commits himself to a version of the Lexicalist Hypothesis, in the sense that no rule of syntax can be sensitive to purely morphological information (such as the declensional class of a noun, or whether a given plural is formed by suffixation or umlaut). The interface with phonology is given by the Morphonology and Shape components, while the interface with syntax is governed primarily by the rules of inflection. Of interest is that morphology is located as a point in a linear chain (much as in Beard's model). It is part of the rules of interface that syntax must properly precede morphology (and lexical structure) and that morphology must properly precede (phrase, or automatic) phonology.

11.4   Autolexical syntax

In our discussion of Baker's theory of noun incorporation (§7.4) I pointed out that linguistic theory had to find the means to capture the fact that such constructions obey both morphological and syntactic principles. This is the starting point for a theory of the morphology–syntax interface currently being developed by Jerrold Sadock (1985, 1987; see also LaPointe, 1987), which he dubs **autolexical syntax**.

According to Sadock, a well-formed string of the language must be well-formed with respect to the rules and principles of morphology and syntax, but there is no prior ordering of the one with respect to the other. We can therefore simultaneously ask ourselves two independent questions: 'what is the syntactic structure of this string?' and 'what is the morphological structure of this string?' In this respect, Sadock is proposing something distinct from, say, Beard or Zwicky. Rather than making morphological form a level of representation (such as, say, PF in the familiar T-model of Government-Binding theory), Sadock regards morphology as a component or module of grammar, much like Case theory or Theta theory.

Sadock discusses three important aspects of the morphology–syntax interface: cliticization, inflection, and noun incorporation (though inflection is mentioned somewhat tangentially). A simple example of the way his system treats the first two is provided by a sentence such as 11.15a:

11.15   a) Tom's seen that film.

This is given the autolexical representation 11.15b:[7]

11.15   b)

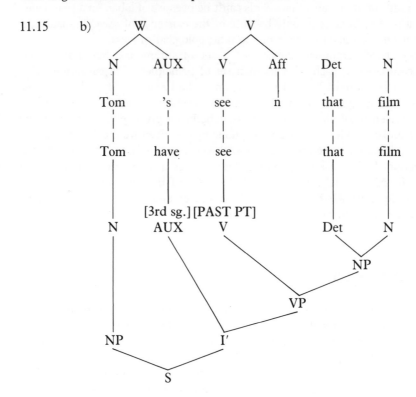

The morphological representation is the top tree and the syntactic representation the lower tree. Here we see that the clitic 's is represented as part of a word morphologically but as an auxiliary verb syntactically. Moreover, the inflectional ending of the past participle is not represented syntactically, since it is merely the morphological spell-out of a feature and not a syntactic element in itself. Another way of thinking of this is to say that the morphology module respresents words in the sense of word forms, while in the syntax module words are represented as morphosyntactic words, in that the units at this level are lexemes together with a featural specification for agreement, government and so on. Much of the point of autolexical representations is to separate the word form from its morphosyntactic description.

Sadock uses this formal mechanism to address the problem of noun incorporation in West Greenlandic (one of the Eskimo languages). Noun incorporation in these languages is very unusual in that the verbs which incorporate their objects are actually affixes ('verbal postbases') and as such can only be found with incorporated noun stems. An example is 11.16:

11.16   Hansi illu-qar-poq.
         Hans (ABS) house-have-3sg.
         'Hans has a house.'

As can be seen from 11.17, the object 'house' is marked in the instrumental case by the syntax because this is the case it would have been in had it not been incorporated (note that *-poq* is an inflectional affix signalling agreement and hence isn't represented in the syntax):

11.17

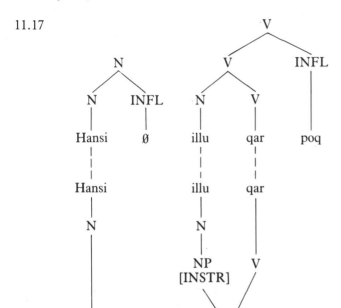

The dual representation in 11.17 illustrates the way that both syntactic requirements (subcategorization frames, word order principles and so on) and morphological requirements (order of affixation, allomorphy and so on) are met simultaneously. In simple cases those phonological strings which are labelled as syntactic words (that is, zero level syntactic categories), such as *Hansi*, are also morphological words. However, this is not always the case: *illu*, 'house', is a syntactic word but morphologically it is an incorporated stem. Nonetheless, we can easily draw two trees for the single string because the linear order of phonemes implied by each representation is identical. In other words, we have a simple case of bracketing paradox, where we need to assign two incompatible constituent structures at different levels of representation.

It is not always the case that linear order is preserved in the two representations, however. We cited West Greenlandic in chapter 7 as a language which permits modifier stranding. A particularly intriguing example of this is shown in 11.18:

11.18   Hansi   ataaseq -nik   qamut-qar-poq.
         Hans-ABS one   -INSTR/PL   sled   -have-3SG/IND
         'Hans has one sled.'

Here, the stem *qamut*, 'sled', is incorporated by the derivational affix *qar* (indicating possession), but the modifier *ataaseq* agrees syntactically with the incorporated element for case and number. Notice that *qamut* is a stem which only ever appears with the plural inflection (rather like English *trousers* or *scissors*). Despite the meaning of the noun phrase, the modifier therefore has to take the plural inflection to agree with the (syntactic) head that it modifies. Now, the grammar of West Greenlandic demands that in syntactic noun phrases a modifier such as *ataaseq* must follow its head noun. However, this is clearly impossible in a sentence such as 11.18 which has undergone noun incorporation. Sadock therefore represents sentence 11.18 with the dual tree structure of 11.19:

11.19

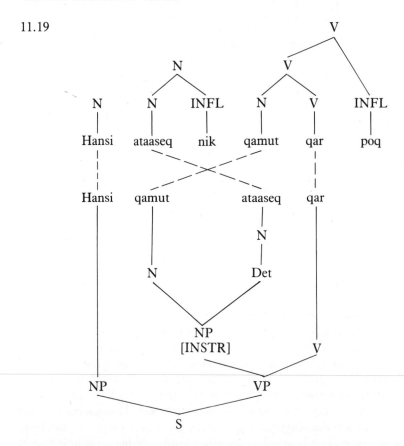

In these phrase markers, the order of elements in the syntactic half of the representation is different from that in the morphological half. This means that the links between morphological words and the corresponding syntactic words have to cross. Such crossing association lines are the equivalent of movement of the noun stem.

It appears that whenever such a clash occurs it is universally the morphological requirements that win out, in the sense that the ordering of the morphemes in the morphology module takes precedence over the ordering of words in the syntax. This is perhaps connected with the fact that syntactic word order variation, even in strict word order languages, is commonplace, while genuinely free (or 'stylistic') variation in morpheme order within words is extremely rare. Sadock therefore assumes a principle under which morphological well-formedness always prevails.

Given that the linear order of elements in the morphological and syntactic representations can be different, we have greatly increased the number of possible mappings between syntax and morphology. Indeed, if nothing further is said, the formalism permits any conceivable morphological arrangement to be linked with any conceivable syntactic arrangement, which is to say that our formalism is so powerful as to be useless. Sadock therefore adds a principle of association, which states that, if crossing lines are unavoidable, the grammatical representation is that in which the fewest lines cross. If there are two distinct representations with this minimum number of crossing lines then both representations are grammatical, other things being equal.

There is a further restriction. In discussing noun incorporation in chapter 7 we observed that it obeys the Head Movement Constraint. This prevents a modifier such as *ataaseq* in 11.18 from being incorporated by a verb stem. Sadock, too, needs such a constraint, which he formulates as his Principle VII'. In simplified form it runs as follows (cf. Sadock, 1985: 423):

11.20   If a lexeme, L, combines syntactically with some X (or X' or XP) it may combine morphologically with a corresponding stem Y, provided that the syntactic equivalent of Y is the head of its phrase (i.e. the head of XP) and that L governs XP.

In example 11.18, the lexeme L would be the verbal postbase *qar*, the X would be the noun *illumik* (the instrumental case of *illu*), and the stem Y would be the stem of that noun, *illu-*. The syntactic equivalent of the morphologically incorporated stem *illu-* is the head of the NP *ataaseq-nik illumik* and the lexeme L (*qar*) does indeed govern the NP in the syntax.

Principle 11.20 does the same kind of work as the Head Movement Constraint, but it is by no means equivalent. This is because the HMC applies only to structures which are analysed as the result of movement in GB syntax. However, 11.20 isn't so restricted and can therefore apply to other types of syntactic dependency. One such dependency is adjective-noun agreement. The autolexical analysis will be useful whenever an agreement process induces a violation of lexical integrity, in other words, whenever a head in the syntax agrees with a proper subpart of another word. A nice example of such a case is provided by possessive adjectives in a number of Slav languages, particularly the two varieties of Sorbian, as described in luxuriant detail by Corbett (1987) (who himself has interesting observations to make on the morphology–syntax interface). In Upper Sorbian possessive forms of nouns referring to people usually take the form of a possessive adjective, derived from the noun by affixation of -(*j*)*ow*. Thus, we have examples such as 11.21–11.22:

11.21   a) wučer 'teacher'   blido 'table' (neut., nom., sg.)
         b) wučerjowe   blido
            teacher-ADJ-N/NOMsg. table
            'the teacher's table'

11.22   a) Jan 'Jan', kniha 'book' (nom., sg., fem.)
         b) Janowa   kniha
            Jan-ADJ-F/NOMsg. book
            'Jan's book'

These constructions are similar to constructions with pronominal possessive adjectives corresponding to 'my', 'his' and so on, which also agree with their head noun in case, number and gender, as shown in 11.23–11.24 (the preposition *k* takes the dative case):

11.23   moje   blido
         my-N/NOMsg. table
         'my table'

11.24   a) dźowkam   'daughter (fem., dat., pl.)'
         b) k našim   dźowkam
            to our-F/DATpl. daughter-F/DATpl.
            'to our daughters'

Within an NP, a possessive adjective itself can be modified by an adjective, for instance, a pronominal possessive adjective, as in 11.25–11.26:

11.25   a) moj 'my', muž 'husband' (masc.),   sotra 'sister' (fem.)
         b) mojeho   mužowa   sotra
            my-M/GENsg. husband-ADJ-F/NOMsg. sister
            'my husband's sister'

11.26   a) k 'to', naš 'our', dźowce 'daughter   (fem., dat., pl.)'
         b) k našeho   wučerjowej   dźowce
            to our-M/GENsg. teacher-ADJ-F/DATsg. daughter
            'to our teacher's daughter'

What is surprising about the constructions in 11.25–11.26 is that the possessive pronouns, *mojeho* and *našeho*, agree with the noun *stem* of the possessive adjective which follows, *muž* and *wučer*. These possessives appear in the genitive case (in effect treating the possessive adjective stems, *mužow-* and *wučerjow-*, as a kind of genitive), and, in addition, agreeing with that stem in (masculine) gender.

This can be thought of as another of our bracketing paradoxes, since one might imagine a structure such as, say, 11.27 for 11.25b at some level of representation (as Corbett himself suggests):

11.27   [[mojeho muž]owa] sotra

Actually, it might be more accurate to say that the structure should be something like 11.28, since the genitive case agreement seems to derive from the possessive force of the possessive adjective affix, *-ow*:

11.28   [[mojeho mužow]a] sotra

In any event, Sadock proposes that an example such as 11.25b should be furnished with a dual representation along the lines of 11.29:

11.29

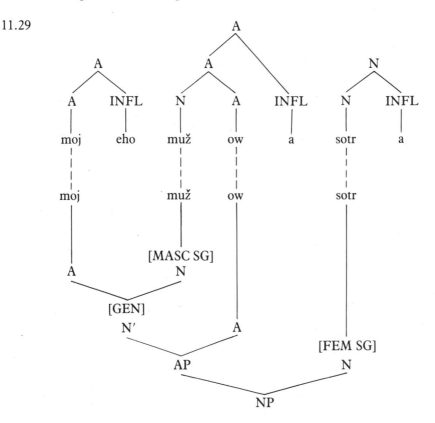

The exotica unearthed by Corbett are potentially very important for theories of the morphology – syntax interface. Baker's transformational account of noun incorporation can't, presumably, be applied to Sorbian agreement. Therefore, if Sadock is right in regarding the Sorbian phenomena as an example of the same kind of thing as noun incorporation then his representational approach to the problem will be preferable to Baker's analysis. The plot thickens when we recall (§9.3) that many linguists have analysed cliticization not as pronoun incorporation (as might be expected within Baker's framework), but as a form of agreement, and that Rosen (1989) has recently argued that the facts which motivated Baker's account of noun incorporation actually support an agreement theory of this phenomenon, too.

11.5 Post-syntactic compounding in Japanese

As is evident from chapters 7 and 8, compounding poses notorious problems for defining wordhood, and for delineating the boundaries between morphology, the lexicon and syntax. Part of the problem for the theoretician lies in identifying where in the grammar compounding takes place. In this and the following section we will review proposals claiming that there may not be a single level of grammatical derivation at which all compounding occurs, but that one and the same set of well-formedness conditions might apply at several, or even all, levels of representation. This claim comes from Shibatani and Kageyama (1988) who argue that, in Japanese, compounds can be formed either in the lexicon (as we might expect), or, much more controversially, can be formed after rules of syntax and postlexical (phrasal) phonology have applied. This latter process they refer to as **post-syntactic compounding**. In essence their argument is that post-syntactic compounds share crucial properties of lexical compounds, making them more like words than like syntactically formed phrases. However, they are constructed after the rules of syntax have applied. Therefore, morphological principles (governing word structure) must have access to the output of the syntax. In effect, compounding occurs at any grammatical level, and the exact form of the compound is determined by properties of the level where it's formed.

Japanese has lexical compounds in abundance. Typical formations are illustrated in 11.30–11.32:

11.30   Nouns:
a) hai-zara
   ash plate   'ashtray'
b) too-isu
   case chair   'cane chair'
c) kaigai-ryokyoo
   overseas travel   'overseas tour'
d) yama-nobori
   mountain climbing   'mountaineering'

11.31   Adjectives:
a) hara-guroi
   stomach black   'black-hearted'
b) darasi-nai
   tidiness non-existent   'slovenly'

11.32   Verbs:
a) yume-miru
   dream see   'to dream'
b) kosi-kakeru
   waist hang   'to sit down'
c) de-kakeru
   go-out hang   'start out'
d) tori-kesu
   take extinguish   'cancel'
e) kaki-naosi
   write repair   'rewrite'
f) yomi-hazimeru
   read begin   'to begin to read'

Shibatani and Kageyama also argue that it is possible to take a syntactically constructed phrase such as 11.34, as found in sentence 11.33, and turn it into a special type of compound, as shown in 11.35 (the colon in *Amerika:hoomon* indicates this special compounding):

11.33   [[Kanai   ga   Amerika o   hoomon] no   ori]   ni wa,
         my-wife NOM America ACC visit   GEN occasion on TOP
         iroiro osewa   ni   narimasita
         much hospitality PTCL received
         'Thank you for your generous hospitality when my wife visited America.'

11.34   [[Amerika o   hoomon] -no   ori]
         America ACC visit   GEN occasion

11.35   [Amerika:hoomon] -no ori

Two crucial facts about this process are that it is fed by the dropping of the syntactic case particle (in this instance *o*), and that the source of the compound is a freely-formed phrase, not necessarily a lexicalized one. The first fact indicates that we are dealing with a compound and not a syntactic phrase. This is because a direct object such as *Amerika* in 11.33–11.34 is obligatorily marked by a case particle such as *o* in genuinely syntactic constructions. Objects can only appear without such a particle in compounds. The second fact, by contrast, indicates that the compound is formed as a result of syntactic processes.

These observations suggest a certain parallel with synthetic compounds in English (of the type *truck driver*), which also share features of lexical compounds and syntactically formed constructions. However, Shibatani and Kageyama adduce arguments that the post-syntactic compounding process is fed not just by syntax but by phrase phonology. Japanese has a pitch accent system. At some point in every word there is exactly one sequence of one or more high toned syllables. This high tone sequence may be preceded or followed by low toned syllables, provided there is exactly one unbroken stretch of high tones. Thus, we find pitch patterns such as 11.36, where the high toned syllables are shown in capitals (think of doubled vowels as constituting two separate syllables, each capable of bearing a high tone):

11.36   a) yaMA   'mountain'
         b) noBORI   'climbing
         c) KAigai   'overseas'
         d) ryoKOO   'travel'
         e) aMERIKA   'America'
         f) yoORROppa   'Europe'

Examples of impossible pitch patterns would be *aMErIKA, where we have two stretches of high tone separated by a low tone, or *amerika, where there are no high tones.

In lexical compounds we find exactly the same kind of pitch patterns (though elements in a compound don't necessarily have the same pitch as they do in isolation):

11.37	a)	yaMA-NObori	'mountaineering'
	b)	kaIGAI-RYOkoo	'overseas tour'
	c)	yoMI-HAZIMEru	'to begin to read'
	d)	yoOROPPA-RYOkoo	'European tour'
	e)	aMERIKA-HOomon	'American visit'

Post-syntactic compounds depart from this model, for they retain essentially the accent pattern of the syntactic phrases to which they correspond. Thus, the phrasal and compound forms respectively of 11.34, 11.35 have the accentuations shown in 11.38, 11.39 (contrasting with 11.37e):

11.38   aMERIKA o hoOMON no ori

11.39   aMERIKA:hoOMON no ori

Since the compound 11.39 has the same accentuation as the corresponding phrase 11.38, Shibatani and Kageyama argue that 11.39 is derived from 11.38 after phonological rules assigning pitch in phrases have applied. Thus, the compounding process must be post-syntactic (rather than, say, a syntactic process).

There are several other respects in which post-syntactic compounds differ from lexical compounds. It is possible for NPs or PPs to modify nouns inside NPs. When this happens the modifying NP or PP must be marked with the postpositive genitive case marker *no*. This is shown in 11.40:

11.40   a) bukka no   zyoosyoo
            price   GEN rise
            'the rise of prices'
         b) sensei to   no   soodan
            teacher with GEN consultation
            'consultation with a teacher'

Provided such a modifier bears the *no* particle it can also modify a compound noun, as shown in 11.41:

11.41   a) kazoku to   no   [Yooroppa-ryokoo]
            family with GEN Europe-travel
            'a European tour with one's family'
         b) *kazoku to [Yooroppa-ryokoo]

However, post-syntactic compounds can't be modified by *no*-phrases of this sort. Thus, 11.41 contrasts with 11.42, in which we have a post-syntactic compound (identifiable by its accentuation, symbolized here by the colon):

11.42   a) kazoku to [Yooroppa:ryokoo]
         b) *kazoku to no [Yooroppa:ryokoo]

It is only in syntactically formed structures that a noun can be modified without requiring a *no*-phrase, so 11.42a provides strong support for an analysis in which the post-syntactic compounds are derived from a syntactic phrase, and not formed in the lexicon.

Another important property distinguishing the post-syntactic from the the lexical compounds concerns anaphoric relations. It is absolutely impossible to refer to the non-head of a lexical compound. In other words, lexical compounds are 'anaphoric islands', a hallmark of words (recall §2.2.2). This is exemplified in 11.43 for the compound *hai-zara* 'ashtray':

11.43   ★[Hai$_i$-zara] o ugokasitara, sore$_i$ ga koboreta.
         ash$_i$-try ACC moved-when, it$_i$ NOM spilled
         'When I moved the ashtray, it (= the ash) spilled.'

This constraint doesn't apply to post-syntactic compounding, however:

11.44   a) Taroo wa   senzitu,   tyuukosya$_i$ o   hanbai no
            Taroo TOP the-other-day used-car$_i$ ACC sell   GEN
            sai   ni,   sorera$_i$ no   itidai o   kowasite simatta.
            occasion PTCL, them$_i$ GEN one-car ACC damage   ended-up
         b) Taroo wa   senzitu,   [tyuukosya$_i$:hanbai] no
            Taroo TOP the-other-day used-car$_i$:sell   GEN
            sai   ni,   sorera$_i$ no   itidai o   kowasite simatta.
            occasion PTCL, them$_i$ GEN one-car ACC damage   ended-up
            'The other day, on the occasion of selling used cars,
            Taroo ended up damaging one of them.'

Given these contrasts between post-syntactic compounds and lexical compounds, and particularly given the fact that the post-syntactic compounds have a pitch pattern characteristic of phrases and not words, we are entitled to ask whether the post-syntactic compounds really are compounds. In fact, there are six respects in which these compounds resemble words rather than phrases.

First, there are no case particles inside the compounds, whereas, in sentences, case particles are in general mandatory for expressing relations such as direct object. Second, verbs inside post-syntactic compounds can't be inflected for tense. This is also true of verbs inside lexical compounds such as *yomihazimeru* illustrated in 11.32. Next, the compounds exhibit morphological integrity, in that they can't be split up by modifiers and the like. For instance, there is no compound 11.46 corresponding to the phrase 11.45:

11.45   Yooroppa o nonbiri ryokoo tyuu ni
         Europe ACC leisurely travel middle in
         'while travelling Europe in a leisurely fashion'

11.46   ★[Yooroppa: nonbiri: ryokoo]-tyuu ni

Fourth, lexical compounds obey a Binary Branching Constraint, which means they may be formed from no more than two elements. This, too, is respected by the post-syntactic compounds.

The post-syntactic compounds obey Roeper and Siegel's (1978) First Sister Principle (see §8.3.1). In particular, it is absolutely forbidden for a post-syntactic compound to be formed from a transitive verb base and its subject. Thus, from 11.47 we can get 11.48a but not 11.48b, on an interpretation in which *Sooseki* is the subject:

11.47   Sooseki ga Syeikusupia o kenkyuu-tyuu ni
            Sooseki NOM Shakespeare ACC study middle in
            'while Sooseki was studying Shakespeare'

11.48   a) Sooseki ga [Syeikusupia:kenkyuu]-tyuu ni
            'while Sooseki was studying Shakespeare'
        b) ⋆Syeikusupia o [Sooseki:kenkyuu]-tyuu ni
            'while Sooseki was studying Shakespeare'

In fact, the compound in 11.48b is possible but only on interpretation 11.48c, in which the non-head of the compound is interpreted as the object of the verb:

11.48   c) [Sooseki-kenkyuu]-tyuu ni
            'while studying Sooseki'

Finally, post-syntactic compounding is lexically governed in the sense that selectional restrictions affecting possible combinations of elements are respected by post-syntactic compounds just as with other types of word. The Japanese vocabulary is divided into native morphemes and non-native morphemes, the latter including a very large number of Chinese words of ancient origin (the Sino-Japanese vocabulary), and a good many Western (chiefly English) words of more recent provenance. The basic rule is that mixed combinations from the two sources are not permitted. For instance, the words *syoseki*, 'book', and *koonyuu*, 'purchase', are from the Sino-Japanese vocabulary, while *hon*, 'book', is a native word. In syntactic phrases either *syoseki* or *hon* can combine with *koonyuu*, as in 11.49a, b, but only *syoseki* forms a post-syntactic compound with *koonyuu*, as in 11.50a:

11.49   a) syoseki o koonyuu no sai
            book ACC purchase GEN occasion
            'when you purchase books'
        b) hon o koonyuu no sai
            book ACC purchase GEN occasion
            'when you purchase books'

11.50   a) [syoseki:koonyuu] no sai
        b) ??[hon:koonyuu] no sai

All this evidence together shows that post-syntactic compounds are words, but that they aren't formed in the lexicon. Rather, they are derived from sentences, by a process which drops the case particle attached to the noun. The pitch pattern of the compound suggests that this process must be *post*-syntactic, rather than an example

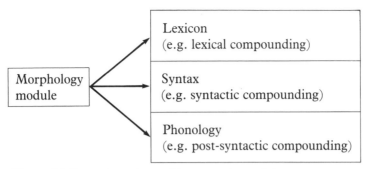

Figure 11.3 Shibatani and Kageyama's model

of syntactic word formation.[8] In this respect, the compounding process resembles, say, the formation of simple clitics discussed in chapter 9. A second reason for rejecting a syntactic analysis is that we don't see any of the transitivity alternations that are common with causatives, applied verbs, possessor raising or noun incorporation, that is, processes which have been argued to be instances of syntactic word formation (see chapter 7). Rather, the arguments left behind after post-syntactic compounding always bear the same case particles that they would have in the original sentence.

On the basis of their detailed analysis of Japanese compounding, Shibatani and Kageyama propose a modular theory of word formation, in which words can be formed in any grammatical component (specifically, the lexicon, the syntax or at the level of PF), and an independent, autonomous morphology module checks that any word formed in any component is well-formed. Their overall model is shown in figure 11.3. The morphology module therefore represents the properties of all words, no matter where formed. Other properties of words will depend on where in the grammar they are derived. For instance, words constructed in the lexicon will obey the Anaphoric Island Constraint and other reflexes of lexical integrity, but this will not necessarily be true of words formed in or after the syntax.

11.6 Parallel morphology

Strictly speaking, what Shibatani and Kageyama have shown is that post-syntactic compounding in Japanese offers support for a morphology module or component which has access to the lexicon and the output of phonology. It is reasonable to suppose that if this model is valid then morphological principles will also have access to the syntax proper. Arguments to precisely this effect have been advanced by Hagit Borer (1988), on the basis of compounding in Hebrew. She, too, observes that there are compound-type constructions which have a character intermediate between syntactically formed phrases and words proper, and concludes that the word-like properties are due to the operation of an independent morphology which has access to the mapping between D-structure and S-structure on the Government-Binding model.

We begin discussion of Borer's claims with a brief survey of compound nouns in

Hebrew, illustrated in 11.51:

11.51   a) beyt xolim
            house sicks   'hospital'
         b) beyt zkenim
            house olds   'retirement home'
         c) beyt sefer
            house book   'school'
         d) beyt safarim
            house books   'library'
         e) gan yeladim
            garden children   'kindergarten'
         f) gan xayot
            garden animals   'zoo'
         g) šomer mitzvot
            guard commandments   'practising Jew'

These consist of N + N with the first N the head. Since these are lexicalized it will
not always be the case that the syntactic head will be a semantic head. For instance,
a kindergarten is not a real garden. The plural of these compounds is formed by
putting the head noun into the plural, e.g. *batey sefer* 'schools'. Notice that the
number marking of the non-head has no syntactic effect whatever on the compound
as a whole, as can be seen by comparing 11.51c, d.

Hebrew nouns can be made definite by prefixing the article *ha-*. In contrast to
plural marking, when a compound is made definite it is the non-head which is given
the definite article. Interestingly, though this makes the compound as a whole
definite, the non-head itself will retain an indefinite interpretation. For example, in
11.52a we have a definite compound which is made plural in 11.52b:

11.52   a) ben ha-melex
            son the-king   'the prince'
         b) bney ha-melex
            sons the-king   'the princes'

The plural form doesn't, however, mean 'the sons of the king', but rather 'the sons
of a (= any) king' or in other words, 'the sons of kings'.

Adjectives agree in definiteness with the nouns they modify, as seen in 11.53:

11.53   a) ha-yeled ha-xadaš/*xadaš higi9a.
            the-boy the-new/new   arrived
            'The new boy arrived.'
         b) yeled xadaš/*ha-xadaš higi9a.
            boy new/the-new   arrived
            'A new boy arrived.'

When an adjective modifies a compound made definite by prefixation of *ha-* to its
non-head, the adjective therefore also takes *ha-*, as though agreeing with the non-
head:

11.54   beyt ha-xolim ha-xadaš
         house the-sicks the-new
         'the new hospital'

Note that the adjective *xadaš* in 11.54 modifies the whole compound, but doesn't modify *ha-xolim* (i.e. 11.54 doesn't have the interpretation 'hospital for new patients').

In addition to compounds of this sort Hebrew has a construction which is superficially very similar known as the **construct state**, shown in 11.55. This has the same meaning as the NP formed from a PP with *šel*, 'of', 11.56:

11.55   cə9if ha-yalda
         scarf the-girl
         'the girl's scarf'

11.56   ha-ca9if šel ha-yalda
         the-scarf of the-girl
         'the scarf of the girl'

In certain respects the construct state nominals behave like compounds. For instance, it is impossible to make the head of a construct state nominal definite by prefixing *ha-* to it (just as in the case of compounds). Instead, we must modify the non-head, thereby making the whole NP definite. Thus, 11.56 can have only the gloss given, it can't, for instance, mean 'the scarf of a girl', and 11.57 is impossible:

11.57   ★ha-cə9if ha-yalda
         the-scarf the-girl
         'the girl's scarf'

Moreover, 11.58 shows that the head can't be directly modified by an adjective (contrast the acceptable formation with *šel*, 11.59):

11.58   ★cə9if (ha-)yafe ha-yalda
         scarf (the-)pretty the-girl
         'the girl's pretty scarf'

11.59   ha-ca9if ha-yafe šel ha-yalda
         the-scarf the pretty of the-girl
         'the girl's pretty scarf'

Another point of similarity between compounds and construct state nominals is phonological: in the full NP 11.56 the head, *ca9if*, retains a full /a/ vowel, while in 11.55 this vowel is reduced. This is because /a/ is reduced if it is not followed by a stressed syllable, and in the construct state form there is only one main stress, which falls on the final syllable of *ha-yalda*.

Because the compounds show lexical idiosyncrasy and word-specific phonological processes it is assumed that they are formed lexically. Given the similarities with construct state nominals we would therefore expect these too to be lexical. However, there are a number of differences between the two constructions.

First, although both compounds and construct state nominals must be made definite by marking the non-head, when the non-head of the construct state nominal is made definite, the interpretation is that *both* the head and the non-head are definite, as in 11.60:

11.60   a) manhig ha-kita
            leader the-class
            'the leader of the class'
         b) manhigey ha-kita
            leaders the-class
            'the leaders of the class' or 'the leaders of a class'

Thus, 11.60b isn't exactly comparable to an English gloss such as 'the class leaders', because in the English compound *class* can be given an indefinite or generic interpretation. This contrasts with compounds such as 11.52 in which the non-head, though marked with *ha-*, is necessarily interpreted as *in*definite.

Second, a construct state nominal can be modified by an adjective, just as a compound can, but the form is ambiguous. The adjective can be read as modifying either the head or its complement, as shown in 11.61:

11.61   cə9if ha-yeled ha-yafe
         scarf the-boy the-pretty
         'the boy's pretty scarf' or 'the pretty boy's scarf'

In a compound it is the whole compound (or equivalently its head) which is modified by the adjective.

Third, construct state nominals permit conjunction in the non-head with *ve-/u-* 'and', as seen in 11.62. This is not found in compounds (e.g. 11.63):

11.62   šomer batim u-mexoniyot
         guard houses and-cars
         'a guard of houses and cars'

11.63   *gan yeladim ve-xayot
         garden children and-animals
         'kindergarten and zoo'

Other differences between compounds and construct state nominals tend to make the construct state construction look syntactic compared with compounding, which is lexical. Thus, while compounding is non-productive and gives rise to non-compositional and idiosyncratic meanings, the construct state nominals are productive and always have a compositional meaning. Moreover, the components of a construct state nominal retain a degree of referentiality, and can be referred to by pronouns (in violation of lexical integrity). This is impossible with compounds, which are, as we would expect, anaphoric islands.

How are we to account for these facts and what are their implications? Borer's argument in summary form is this: in both compounds and construct state nominals the definiteness prefix appears on the 'wrong' noun. To ensure this marker can render the whole NP definite we need to appeal to specifically morphological principles of percolation for each type of construction. Compound formation is lexical. However, certain aspects of the construct state nominals suggest that they are formed by syntactic rules not (lexical) morphological rules. Moreover, the syntactic properties of the construct state nominals suggest that they are formed before the level of S-structure (and not beyond, for instance at a level of PF). Therefore, there is a morphological principle (percolation) which has to apply both to lexically formed constructions (compounds) and syntactically formed constructions (construct state nominals). Hence, morphological principles must be independent of other levels of grammar, in other words, there must be a separate morphology module, which at least has access to the syntax.

The percolation Borer assumes works in the following manner. First, we assume that a construct state nominal consists of a head N followed by an NP, while a compound consists of two nouns. Then, we assume that there is a feature [def] associated with the prefix *ha-*. This percolates as in 11.64–5, to make the whole NP definite:[9]

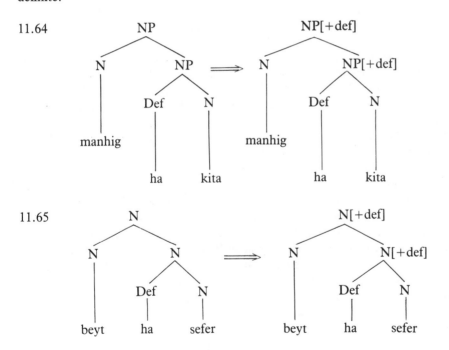

11.64

11.65

The fact that the definiteness feature can be a property of a single noun, as in 11.65, and not just of an NP, distinguishes definiteness in Hebrew from definiteness in European languages such as English. However, we also know that the definiteness marking on *sefer* in 11.65 isn't semantically or syntactically relevant. Thus, *sefer* itself isn't interpreted as definite and a definite adjective agrees in definiteness with the whole compound, not just with *sefer* (cf. example 11.53). Borer argues that secondary percolation of this sort from a complement is characteristic of word formation, not syntax (cf. our discussion of 'relativized heads' in connection with the theories of Williams and of Selkirk in §6.2.1). On the other hand the construct state nominals appear to be syntactically formed (for example, in permitting adjectival modification of the complement, complete with agreement). Therefore, she reasons, at least one word formation process, secondary percolation from a complement, applies in the syntactic formation of a word. From this it is simplest to conclude that all morphological operations can apply either in the lexicon or the syntax.

The demonstration that construct state nominals can be formed no later than the syntax comes from the observation that they are opaque to syntactic processes like WH-extraction, while the *šel* nominals permit this. This can be explained if we assume that construct state nominals become words at or before the level of S-structure, but no later (in particular they can't be formed at PF). Since we have argued that they can't be formed in the lexicon, this means that the only place they could be formed is in the syntactic component (the mapping from D-structure to S-structure).

The model that emerges is spelled out as follows. The notion of the lexicon is reinterpreted in terms of the **Listing Principle** (Borer, 1988: 60):

11.66   The Listing Principle
             a) Words are inserted at D-structure only if they are listed.
             b) Listed words may not be lexically underspecified.

By 'lexical specification' Borer is referring to syntactic category features, argument structure and meaning. In other words, if a word is listed then all these features are fixed. Assuming the Projection Principle this means that none of them can be changed during a derivation in the syntax. Any rule which does change such features (i.e. most derivational morphology) must therefore be pre-syntactic, or lexical. However, if words are not listed, that is, if an item is unspecified for some feature, then it can be inserted after D-structure.

This notion of listedness is distinct from traditional usages and particularly from that of Di Sciullo and Williams (1987). Consider a suppletive plural form such as *teeth*. In a lexically formed compound such as *teeth-marks* we would say that plural formation had taken place 'in the lexicon' (i.e. prior to lexical insertion at D-structure). Therefore, pluralization would be one of the listed features of *teeth* in such a case. On the other hand, in a syntactically relevant context, say, the sentence *Her teeth are white*, we would assume that plural formation had taken place in the syntax, thus making it transparent to syntactic agreement. In other words, listedness is a somewhat abstract notion dependent on our overall conception of grammar.

Borer summarizes her proposals in the diagram of figure 11.4. The word formation

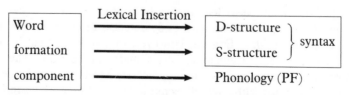

Figure 11.4 Borer's model of Parallel Morphology

component ('morphology module') is then an autonomous component which is responsible for the purely morphological aspects of word structure. Borer's analysis of construct state nominals in Hebrew provides a case study of this module operating in the syntax, while Shibatani and Kageyama's analysis of post-syntactic compounding is an instance of the word-formation module operating at the level of PF.

11.7   Conclusions

We began this chapter by asking 'Where's morphology?' and we've seen a variety of answers, running from 'just in the lexicon', through ' in the lexicon and the syntax', to 'everywhere'. I conclude this discussion with a rephrasing of this question, which will serve as the background to my own answer to it. At various times I've suggested that one of the key unresolved questions in morphology is 'what is a word?'. We can view the various answers to the question 'where's morphology?' as implying answers to this second question.

Recall that in my earlier introduction to the question of wordhood in §2.2, I suggested that there were conflicting criteria for wordhood, and that we should probably distinguish several types of word, including at least the lexeme, word form, morphosyntactic word and phonological word. The radical lexicalist theory of Di Sciullo and Williams draws a rather different set of distinctions centering around a dichotomy between 'morphological object' and 'syntactic atom'. Here, it would seem, it is only word forms that are the proper object of study for the morphologist (though they admit that it might be necessary to distinguish a notion of 'phonological word'). What is crucial to this conception is that all the other linguistic properties of a word, be they phonological, syntactic or semantic, are projected from properties of the component morphemes, and we can't derive them from other components of grammar. Hence, if a derived nominal seems to behave as though it retained the argument assigning properties of its verb stem, this must mean that the word as a whole inherits those properties from that stem by means of morphological principles (e.g. of feature percolation).

One way of weakening the conceptually taut schema of radical lexicalism is to concede that some word formation might take place 'beyond' the lexicon. This was argued for by Borer on the basis of her comparison between Hebrew construct state nominals and lexical compounds. Another example of this is the familiar distinction between (purely lexical) derivation and regular, syntactically determined, inflection. This type of distinction immediately leads to the possibility of a mismatch between form and function. For instance, most verbs in English have a 3 sg. form in /z/, which is subject to at most phonologically conditioned allomorphy. However, the verb *to be* has a suppletive form, *is*. Therefore, we must arrange for the morphological and the syntactic aspects of the agreement process to be separated. This means that we must distinguish minimally between word forms (*is*) and morphosyntactic words ('3sg. form of *be*'). This implies a further conceptual item, the lexeme (though possibly only as a derived notion at this stage). Notice that this isn't to say that a radically lexicalist theory is incapable of accounting for suppletive inflection. It simply means that the lexicalist theory can't regard the disposition of morphosyntactic features as of relevance to morphology.

If we accept the arguments from syntactic affixation and construct state nominals, then the most parsimonious way of locating morphology is in the lexicon and in the syntax (*pace* Sproat, Anderson and others). We have yet to say anything, however, about the phonological word. Thus far, we could allow this to remain a purely phonological concept, the prosodic domain of certain types of phonological rule, related to the morphosyntactic notion of 'word', but not an object of interest to the morphologist (just as an intonational phrase is not necessarily of interest to the phrase structure grammarian). The arguments of Shibatani and Kageyama cast doubt on this judgement. Their Japanese compounding case would seem to indicate that morphological principles are still operative after syntactic rules and rules of phrase phonology have applied to form a post-syntactic compound. However, the resulting type of word can't automatically be identified with the 'phonological word' of the prosodic phonologist. Nonetheless, for the present I'll refer to this as a phonological word, despite the danger of pernicious ambiguity.

All such phonological words will be potential words, in the sense that they are freely formed by general principles and have a compositional interpretation. Is it possible to imagine a listed phonological word? Such an object would have to be formed out of syntactically composed elements which then underwent phonological processes (e.g. reduction processes) to produce an object with wordlike properties. The fact that phonological words are formed by regular syntactic and phonological operations would seem to rule out listing by definition. However, one could argue that certain such constructions might become lexicalized, if the syntactic function they realized were of frequent occurrence and belonged to a well-defined circumscribed syntactic domain. This might be true, for instance, of the negative auxiliaries of the form *won't* and *shan't*, which Zwicky and Pullum (1983) have analysed as a type of inflection.

Finally, there are two senses in which it has been claimed that syntactically formed phrases can enter the lexicon and be treated as what we might call *phrasal words*. The first is the Romance compounding discussed by Di Sciullo and Williams (which has rather more limited reflex in the violations of the No Phrase Constraint in English compounding). Whether we regard this as word formation proper or as some more performance related notion of word creation (cf. van Marle, 1985), we still need to account for its existence and for the fact that it is widespread in some languages and not in others. Such word formation brings us full circle, in the sense that here we have the syntax feeding lexical morphological processes. In effect, it is perhaps best to regard such formations as on a par with the lexicalized phonological words, except that their motivation is purely syntactic and not phonological. In other words, we have something akin to Japanese post-syntactic compounding by simply redefining a phrase as a word.

To summarize, we can view the various answers to the question 'where's morphology?' as implicitly asking 'what is a word?' And the answer to that question turns out to have different answers at different levels of representation. The final picture I've painted is very similar to that of Baker (1988c). That paper is a particularly clear defence of the view of morphology as an *autonomous module*. On this conception, we don't view morphology as a component, or stage, through which all derivations pass on their way from semantic or lexical structure to phonological form. Rather, morphology represents a set of rules and principles which together go to define the well-formedness of words, irrespective of the way in which they are formed.

I've mapped out the final position in some detail in figure 11.5. This illustrates a number of the phenomena discussed in various parts of the book, and how they might be treated on the present model. This diagram is obviously modelled rather closely on those of Shibatani and Kageyama, and of Borer. The morphology module is autonomous of other levels of representation, in that it has its own set of elements and principles of combination, as stressed by Di Sciullo and Williams. It therefore contains information about (lexical) phonological well-formedness and morphological well-formedness. However, it interacts with all other levels of representation, shown in figure 11.5 by the fact that it runs parallel with the rest of the grammatical

Morphology module		Lexicon
Morphological and morphophonological well-formedness principles	Derivational morphology Paradigmatic word formation Lexical compounding Anticausatives etc. Monoclausal causatives Chukchee NI Adjectival passives Synthetic compounds?	List of lexemes, idioms etc. Idiosyncratic word forms
	Regular inflection etc. Hebrew construct state nominals Synthetic compounds? Biclausal causatives Verbal passives Mohawk NI Pronominal clitics	Syntax $\left\{ \begin{array}{l} \text{D structure} \\ \text{S structure} \\ \text{(LF)} \end{array} \right\}$ ECP Binding theory etc.
	Phrasal affixation (including Eng. POSS aux. clitics, a/an) Kwakwala, Polish clitics Post-syntactic compounding	Phonology Prosodic domains Phonotactic constraints Phonological rules

Figure 11.5 The morphology module

derivation. The form this interaction takes is that processes defined over lexical objects, syntactic objects or phonological objects can serve as the input to a word formation process. (Since words ultimately have to be realized in phonological form, this means that there will be no LF processes which feed word formation.)

One way of interpreting figure 11.5 is to imagine that certain aspects of word structure as determined in the morphology module are 'visible' to other components. For instance, the syntactic category of a word is visible to the syntax, and the phonological composition of a word is visible to the phonology. However, in the syntax, we find processes such as agreement, which are defined over morphosyntactic features, manipulated in the syntax. These features are also characteristic of words. In the spirit of separationism (à la Beard, Anderson, or Zwicky) we can distinguish two aspects of, say, an inflected word form. First, we identify the lexeme, then the morphosyntactic feature composition. At the level of syntax, it's the latter which becomes 'visible'. This presupposes that syntactic affixation is defined over features, not actual morphemes. It is only the morphology module that can manipulate morphemes (or word forms).

Since figure 11.5 includes a number of processes which were not mentioned at the beginning of this section, I'll provide a brief annotation, to clarify why certain processes are placed where they are.

There is an interface between the morphology and the lexicon. This means that we follow Di Sciullo and Williams (amongst others) in not identifying the morphology module with the lexicon itself. There are various, often productive, morphological processes which take place at the lexical level, that is, which are defined purely over lexemes or other lexically listed objects. For instance, much of standard derivational morphology is of this character. It also includes lexical compounding, and the 'meaning-driven' paradigmatic word formation processes discussed in chapter 10. I would also claim that monoclausal causative formation occurs at this level. This is incompatible with Baker's analysis, but fully compatible with the view of Booij, and of Zubizarreta. Arguably, it's compatible with a certain interpretation of Marantz's model (though not one Marantz himself would necessarily favour), under which we regard the crucial aspects of his l-s structure as equivalent to Lexico-Conceptual Structure (cf. §8.3.6.2). Similarly, we can treat other types of valency alternation where the syntax is blind to the original valency of the verb stem, such as anticausative formation.

We also find cross-category changes such as the formation of causative or inchoative verbs from adjectives at this level. This type will include adjectival passive formation. However, this doesn't necessarily mean that verbal passive formation has to be a lexical process. This is because the passive word forms themselves are formed in the morphology module, and can thus, in principle, be available for other morphological processes. Such processes can be linked to the lexical level, provided they don't refer crucially to information which is not available till the syntax. Since adjectival passive formation is nothing more than a piece of derivational morphology, this requirement is met. Therefore, adjectival passive formation can be lexical even if verbal passive formation is syntactic. In exactly the same way, inflected forms of words can be subject to lexical processes (such as compounding) provided the inflected forms are interpreted as lexical units and not as the result of a syntactic process (say, of agreement). This allows us to form compounds of the type *systems analyst* in the lexicon. Whether an inflected form is subject to (marginal) word formation in this way seems to be a function of the meaning associated with the form in question.

As an example of lexical compounding I include Chukchee noun incorporation. In Rosen's (1989) analysis, all incorporation is 'lexical'. However, we can say that the morphological properties of incorporation structures are determined in the morphology module, and other properties can be determined elsewhere. Thus, it is a property of Chukchee verbs which incorporate their objects that they become intransitive. We interpret this as meaning that their direct internal theta role is satisfied lexically. Such a thing couldn't happen anywhere but the lexicon, because otherwise it would constitute a violation of the Projection Principle. However, this doesn't prevent different instantiations of noun incorporation from taking place in the syntax or even the phonology.

Finally, how does lexically governed phonological form fit into the picture? Baker (1988c) claims that his model is incompatible with Lexical Phonology, while Borer (1988) claims that her very similar model is compatible with it. In a sense, both are correct. Baker is right to say that our present conception is incompatible with (strict interpretations of) level ordering. However, level ordering creates a good many problems of a purely morphological nature, as we've seen, and there are species of lexical phonology which don't appeal to this. The model presented here is therefore compatible with those approaches to morphophonology which eschew level ordering, including Booij and Rubach's model, Morpholexical Phonology and the approach of Aronoff and Sridhar. The latter two types of approach are perhaps, particularly consonant with our overall model because of the way they permit explicit linking of morphophonemic alternations with particular functions in word formation.

The upshot of this perspective is that the lexicon may be just a list of idiosyncrasies, but that doesn't mean that it has no interesting linguistic properties. On the contrary, by assuming an autonomous morphology module we can retain the more traditional view and claim that a large part of word formation is defined over the lexicon, without committing ourselves to the claim that the word forms which result can be formed *only* at the lexical level.

If word formation at the lexical level takes as its 'raw material' the contents of the lexicon, then at the level of syntax we find word formation defined over material which is not listed in any sense, and which is only defined once it has been created by syntactic processes. This is the crucial distinction drawn by Borer between construct state nominals and lexical compounds in Hebrew. I've followed Roeper (1988) in suggesting that English gerund formation takes place at this level (though not necessarily in exactly the way he proposes). The syntactic properties of biclausal causatives are also accounted for if they are formed in the syntax (what Marantz refers to as s structure). We can account for many of the properties of the verbal passive by assuming that it is formed at this level, too.

The type of noun incorporation illustrated by Mohawk is arguably the result of syntactic processes. This will be true whether we accept Baker's Move-Noun analysis or the alternative in which the noun-verb compound identifies an empty pronoun (pro), rather than a lexical trace. Similarly, the pronominal cliticization phenomena of Romance, Macedonian and other languages will take place here, even though the resulting structures resemble affixed words. The job of accounting for the difference between such formations and true affixation will be the responsibility of the morphology module. At the same time, genuine agreement markers, such as the subject agreement of many Indo-European languages and the subject-object agreement of Chukchee, are also distributed at this level, an instance of what we may regard as syntactic affixation. Such affixation has as its target a specific lexical category (a verb).

The morphology module is also responsible for determining the shape of clitic clusters, such as those described for Serbo-Croat. On the other hand, it is syntactic principles which govern the occurrence and morphosyntactic make-up of such clusters. So, again, the morphology module comes into play only after the syntax has determined various properties of the overall structure of the sentence such as tense/aspect forms, modality and anaphor binding properties. The same goes for the interesting Chicheŵa data cited at the end of chapter 9. If, as some claim, the prefix system of Bantu is actually a type of clitic cluster affixed to the verb, then this case will reduce to something akin to, say, Macedonian, though with slightly different principles licensing the occurrence of NPs. If, on the other hand, we really are dealing with prefixation here, then we'll have a rather unusual case in which true affixes behave like free standing pronouns, a rather serious violation of Strong Lexicalism.

The agreement processes with Slavic possessive adjectives discussed by Corbett will be handled here. On the present model, one way of interpreting such facts would be to say that the possessive adjectives have the morphological form of derived adjectives, but that the process which drives them is syntactic. This means that a form such as Sorbian *wučerjow* 'teacher's' from *wučer* 'teacher' is created morphologically by affixation, but licensed in the syntax, as a kind of spell-out of whatever syntactic features realize the function of a possessive determiner. One corollary of this approach to syntactic affixation (explicitly discussed, for instance, by Corbett, 1987, in respect of the Slavic agreement data) is that there is no unitary distinction to be drawn between inflection and derivation. In syntactic terms the formation of possessive adjectives is inflectional, in that it controls agreement. In morphological terms it is derivational. For example, it changes syntactic category. Much the same can be said about participle and gerund formation. This means that the inflection/derivation dichotomy is a pretheoretic distinction which doesn't correspond to a single phenomenon in our model. If we want to characterize prototypical (pretheoretic) inflectional processes, however, we might try recasting Anderson's (1982) dictum and say that inflectional morphology is the paradigm example of syntax which is relevant to morphology.

Careful scrutiny of figure 11.5 reveals that I have hedged my bets over the locus of synthetic compounding. As should be evident from our discussion in chapter 8 there remain many murky areas surrounding even the English compounds, on which a great deal of attention has been lavished. My suspicion is that ultimately we'll find that in different languages rather similar constructions will turn out to be located at different levels. For the moment I remain agnostic about how best to handle even one variety.

Finally, we come to word formation driven by the phonology component. In addition to post-syntactic compounding in Japanese (which in many respects represents phonologically determined noun incorporation), there are a number of other good candidates for phonologically triggered word formation. Phrasal affixation discussed in chapter 9 is a case in point. The disposition of the possessive *'s* in English is a function of superficial surface syntax, inasmuch as the affix is attached to the last word of a syntactic phrase. Now, in English, the word order in these phrases is determined by syntactic principles. However, this doesn't prevent such phrasal affixation from taking place at the phonological level. In this way we account for the fact that the word formation aspect of possessive formation is concerned solely with linear adjacency, remaining blind to all syntactic aspects of structure. In other languages, in which word order is much freer, it may interact with intonation and rhythm and contribute to the overall degree of emphasis, topicalization or whatever borne by individual constituents. Latin was such a free word order language, and the clitic conjunction -*que*, discussed in §11.4, is therefore an example of a phrasal affix whose placement is arguably determined in the phonology component. Again, in Serbo-Croat, clitics are placed second in their clause. However, we know that this can be interpreted to mean either 'after the first phrase' or 'after the first stressed word'. In the latter case it looks as though clitic placement is again determined by the phonology component. Likewise, Kwakwala clitic placement, illustrated in chapter 9, is constrained only by linear adjacency and should therefore be handled in the phonology.

Finally, by permitting the morphology module access to the post-syntactic, phonological level, we open the way to an understanding of the allomorphic alternations discussed by Zwicky under the heading of Shape Conditions (cf. §4.6). This is illustrated by the choice of the form of the English indefinite article, *a*/*an*. The article forms a (phonological) word with the lexical item to its right, and this happens to be subject to phonologically conditioned allomorphy. Much the same is true of Polish person/number clitics.

Many unanswered questions remain surrounding the composite model I've presented in figure 11.5. The most pressing relates to the way that morphological form matches up with syntactic and phonological form. The existence of bracketing paradoxes and discontinuous dependencies of various sorts shows the mapping is not direct. As we've seen, a number of theoreticians have attacked this problem, proposing a variety of 'mapping principles' (Marantz, Sadock, Sproat, amongst others). Clearly, some set of universal principles is needed, otherwise we couldn't account for the fact that the possible mappings aren't entirely arbitrary. Given that many of the mismatches between form and function are very regular and yet governed by very subtle criteria, we must relate this question to the question of learnability. Hence, whatever principles we propose must not be too parochial. To some extent, ignorance is a problem here: we simply don't know enough about the extent to which mismatches between form and function can occur. This is in part because such mismatches require careful and detailed analysis before we can determine which level word formation takes place at, and what kinds of regularities govern it. It is one of the virtues of the model outlined in figure 11.5 that it encourages us to look for further such cases.

The model of morphology that has emerged over recent years illustrates dramatically the theme that has run through this book, namely, that much of the intellectual challenge posed by morphology for linguistic theory construction lies in the exploration of the interfaces between morphology and the rest of grammar. Age-old questions concerning the nature of words are given novel interpretations, while, at the same time, new phenomena are unearthed, which may well have gone unnoticed under the older perspective. This is precisely what we want of a vigorous and developing branch of study.

Notes

CHAPTER 1 The domain of morphology

1 The word *morpheme* itself is composed of two morphemes, the first *morph*, which comes from the Greek word meaning 'form', and the second *-eme*, also found in *phoneme*, *lexeme* and a number of other terms. The precise meaning of the latter is difficult to characterize outside of linguistic theory. One of the aims of several of the chapters of this book will be to go towards explaining what the *-eme* of *morpheme* means.

2 The reduced vowel of the plural ending, which I represent here as a schwa, is actually pronounced in a variety of different ways depending on accent. For instance, speakers of British 'Received Pronunciation' will pronounce it as /ɪz/.

3 The terminology parallels that in phonology. We have the proportions:

morph	phone
morpheme	phoneme
allomorph (of a morpheme)	allophone (of a phoneme)

4 Appearances may be deceptive here, though, because, on the assumptions of generative phonology (see chapter 4), this would simply be a case of phonologically conditioned allomorphy. For the suffix *-ity* would have a particular effect on the phonological form of roots it attached to, and the allomorphic variation seen in 1.4-5 would then be the result of the application of phonological rules. This illustrates the fact that the proper analysis of a phenomenon depends on the theoretical framework you adopt.

5 At the same time, notice that we also see a case of allomorphy, again conditioned by a particular morpheme (or rather set of morphemes) in the alternations *-ceive ~ -cept*. We know, incidentally, that the correct analysis of words like *conception* is *con-cept-ion* and not *con-cep-tion* because the *-cept* allomorph appears elsewhere in *con-cept*, *con-cept-ual*, *re-cept-ive*, *re-cept-or* and so on.

6 There is a further, syntactic, justification for this arrangement in the grammar of

Russian, namely *agreement*: an adjective which modifies a noun takes on endings corresponding to the gender, number and case of that noun. I shall discuss agreement in §1.4.

7   The transcription here follows Slavicist practice: the symbol t' represents IPA [tʲ], š = [ʃ], č = [tʃ], y = [ɨ].

8   That is, the endings which have a *morphosyntactic* function, of a kind illustrated below in §1.4.

9   A terminological note of caution: many authors use the term 'paradigm' in a rather loose way to mean something like 'subparadigm', or 'the set of inflected forms that I am talking about at the moment', leaving it to the context to specify the extension of the subparadigm. Potentially more confusing for the uninitiated is when morphologists use the term to mean 'tabulated data set arranged so as to illustrate some pattern', a usage which applies to derivational morphology, or even phonology and syntax.

10 I shall try to use the term *root* to refer to a single morpheme which bears the 'core' meaning of a word. The term *stem* will be reserved for that part of a word to which inflectional affixes are added, and *base* for that part to which any other morpheme is added (inflectional, derivational or compound). Unfortunately, this terminology isn't standardized, which is not surprising given that not all linguists admit a distinction between inflection and derivation. You have to be prepared to see these three terms used interchangeably in the literature, or with more narrowly defined meanings than here.

11 English has a somewhat restricted class of infixes, represented by examples such as *abso-bloomin'-lutely*, *fan-bloody-tastic* and other coarser alternatives. This affixation process (which in the early 1970s, when it was first discussed, was called 'Fuckin' Insertion', and which is now coyly referred to as 'Expletive Infixation') forms the basis of an ingenious and extremely interesting argument concerning syllable structure (McCarthy, 1982c).

12 Scalise (1984: 147ff) provides an interesting discussion of the theoretical status of parasynthesis, or circumfixation, in Italian.

13 Structuralist theories of morphology (i.e. the pre-generative theories briefly introduced in chapter 2) also spoke of such things as *replacives* and *subtractives* (as well as zero affixes, mentioned below). I shall briefly discuss these and related concepts in the next chapter.

14 Notice that contrasts such as that between binyan I, *katab*, and binyan III, *kaatab*, provide further illustration of the morphological use of vowel length.

15 An apostrophe after a plosive (e.g. p') indicates aspiration. The hook beneath the letter in t̢ɖɲ indicates a palatal pronunciation. Nivkh has the following uvulars: a voiceless plosive q, voiceless fricative χ and voiced fricative ʁ. The sound r̥ is a voiceless r.

16 The operations just discussed don't exhaust the ways of creating new words. In English new words are formed by *clipping* (e.g. *mike* from *microphone*) and *blending* (e.g. *smog* from *smoke* and *fog*) as well as from acronyms such as *radar* and 'stub' compounds such as *Caltech*. None of these is of any great importance to morphological theory.

   Of greater significance is word formation by analogy as represented by **backformation**. This occurs when word is reanalysed by speakers as though it had a regular derivation even though the base of the derivation didn't previously exist. For instance, from the word *baby-sitter* speakers have coined the verb *to baby-sit*.

   The distinction between these ways of *creating* new words (as opposed to genuine morphological devices used in productive word *formation*) will be touched on in a number of places throughout the book.

17   The bulk of chapter 7 is devoted to recent theories of such phenomena and you can find an expanded account of them at the beginning of that chapter.

18   There are other ways of marking subjects and objects, though the nominative-accusative and the ergative types are the most common. A good source of information on these and other types is Mallinson and Blake (1981).

19   Causatives are also frequently found creating a verb meaning 'cause X to be Adjective' from an adjective.

20   This is not to be confused with the term 'focus', as in 'topic-focus' articulation, also referred to as 'topic-comment', 'functional sentence perspective' and other terms.

21   An introduction to tense can be found in Comrie (1987), and an introduction to aspect in Comrie (1976). Palmer (1986) provides an introduction to mood and modality.

22   The 'y' of the root *yn* is pronounced [ə], otherwise 'y' = [i], 'dd' = [ð], 'ch' = [x], 'f' = [v].

FURTHER READING

Many of the concepts introduced here are discussed in handbooks on structuralist linguistics such as Sapir (1921), Bloomfield (1933), Hockett (1958) or Gleason (1961). A book devoted to morphology which is still well worth reading is Nida (1949). More recent general introductions to linguistics such as Akmajian, Demers and Harnish (1984), Fromkin and Rodman (1988), Atkinson, Kilby and Roca (1988) among others can be consulted for introductory overviews. Lyons (1968) remains a good source. Matthews (1974), Bauer (1988) and Jensen (1990) contain a good deal of information on many of the concepts discussed here (though from a rather different perspective in some cases). Corbett (1990) is an overview of gender, agreement and morphological classes which contains much useful information for morphologists. The chapters in Shopen (ed.) (volume III) provide a very useful discussion to many of the issues I've touched upon in this chapter.

   For details of the morphology of English, in addition to the monumental handbooks of authors such as Jespersen, Poutsma and so on, the reader can consult Adams (1973), Bauer (1983) and Marchand (1969).

CHAPTER 2   Basic concepts and pre-generative approaches

1   This notion of 'deviation' is central to certain theories of inflection, notably those of the Natural Morphologists and the related theory of Carstairs (1987). These are discussed in chapter 6.

2   Phonotactic constraints are syntagmatic restrictions on (surface) phonological representations, in other words, constraints on what ('horizontal') combinations of sounds are permitted by the language. For example, in English, syllables are not permitted to begin with more than three consonants; in a three consonant cluster the first must be /s/; no initial clusters of /tl/ or /dl/ are permitted, and so on. Japanese permits no consonant clusters of any sort, in any position.

   In structuralist morphology we also speak of *morphotactic restrictions*, i.e. the restrictions on the combinations of morphemes. The structuralist literature often referred to these restrictions simply as the 'tactics' of the system (thereby isolating the morpheme implied by the terms *phonotactic*, *morphotactic*, and *syntactic*).

3   A vexed and unresolved question concerns the relationship between the linguist's conception of the lexicon and that of the psycholinguist endeavouring to develop models of language use and acquisition in 'real time'. The lexicon in psycholinguistics is often referred to as the **mental lexicon**. Questions of parsimony of representation, which are important in linguistic theory construction, tend to be subordinated to questions of processing efficiency in psycholinguistic modelling. Many psycholinguists would regard any purely linguistic characterization of the lexicon as superfluous and would claim that only study of the mental lexicon (using psycholinguistic methodology) was legitimate. Reviews of the psycholinguistic literature on the mental lexicon can be found in many places, for instance, Butterworth (1983), Henderson (1985), Harris and Coltheart (1986) and Aitchison (1987).

4   With the growth of generative phonology (see chapter 3) a particular version of the IP approach later became dominant. A common type of analysis (equivalent to solution (3)) would have used an abstract past tense marker in underlying form to trigger a set of phonological rules affecting vowels in specially marked verbs. Other analyses might be best conceived as variants of solution (2) or solution (5). Interestingly, the currently dominant view of vowel alternations of this kind in languages such as those of the Semitic group is effectively a formalization of Hockett's own IA solution (4) (see chapter 5).

5   There is one variety of IA approach to highly agglutinative morphology which seems to require the notion of word (or word form), and that is the analysis by **position class** adopted by certain linguists working on American Indian languages. In this approach a word is analysed as a root plus a string of fixed affix positions. Each position may be occupied by a unique affix or by a set of mutually exclusive affixes (e.g. person and number affixes). Position class analysis is considered in more detail in §6.4.

6   Alternatively, we could adopt the solution suggested earlier and say that the case distinction is neutralized for oblique cases in fem. sg. forms. Given that that solution is a little suspect it's important to observe that such a solution isn't forced on the WP model. However, the neutralization approach is effectively what an IA model is forced into, though that model has to state neutralization rather perversely, as a form of allomorphy.

7   Further discussion of structuralist theories of morphophonemics would have us straying into the field of phonology. A very good and highly readable survey of the issues is provided by Anderson (1985a). A less up-to-date but still valuable review is Fischer-Jørgensen (1975). Phonology textbooks which discuss structuralist theories in some detail include Sommerstein (1977) and Lass (1984). A simple introduction to the principles of phonemics can be found in Hawkins (1984).

FURTHER READING

In addition to the references given in chapter 1 and note 7 above, many of the papers of Joos (1958) will be found interesting. Matthews (1972) gives a detailed but rather technical discussion of inflection and the three models. On wordhood, Brown and Miller (1980) is a good introduction. A very basic initiation to dictionaries from the point of view of lexicography (the art of dictionary writing) is found in Jackson (1988).

CHAPTER 3   Early generative approaches

1   Syntactic accounts of the auxiliary system in generative grammar are very varied. In some versions the auxiliary (Aux) is an immediate constituent of the sentence, in others an immediate constituent of the VP and in still others an immediate constituent of some other node (such as Predicate Phrase, or Infl'). These differences are irrelevant for our purposes. I have chosen a representation found, for instance, in Radford (1981, 1988).

2   A very good example of such work is Dowty (1979). Incidentally, Dowty (1979: 241) rejects McCawley's arguments for decomposing causatives, on the grounds that the alleged ambiguity with *almost* is nothing more than vagueness.

3   The only systematic differences are related ultimately to the interpretation of poorly understood quantifier-type elements in surface structure, and their interaction with 'focus' (or 'functional sentence perspective') Cf. the discussion of the difference between *beavers build dams* and *dams are built by beavers* in Chomsky (1975). Crucially, actives and passives describe the same state of affairs (i.e. they have the same truth conditions).

4   Chomsky left open the question of how it is that inflectional morphology changes the syntactic class of the word in gerunds (and participles).

5   Perhaps I should say 'induce an alteration in the meaning of' in view of the drastic meaning change mentioned in §3.5.3.

6   SPE also uses a = boundary, but this is regarded by most linguists nowadays as simply a notational device for patching up phonological rules. For discussion see Siegel (1980).

7   The extension is largely due to Allen (1978). A useful summary of this area, together with interesting discussion of Italian and Dutch data, is found in Scalise (1984: ch. 5).

8   Aronoff seems to have in mind the incorporation of pronominal clitics onto, say, a verb, rather than the sort of incorporation exhibited by polysynthetic languages like Chukchee.

9   It would appear as if Aronoff spurns here the opportunity to attach a semantic feature such as [+human] onto the output of the word as a function of the WFR. Instead, this information is coded as part of the semantics. The correct choice in such cases obviously depends on one's theory of lexical semantics. Many people would say that features such as [+human] are meaningless anyway and should be discarded for more sophisticated forms of semantic representation, rather than being confounded with syntax.

10   The concept of lexical redundancy is explored in great detail by Jackendoff (1975), who comes to the conclusion that all words have to be listed in the lexicon, and related in all their facets (syntactic, semantic and phonological) by redundancy rules. However, while Aronoff allows his productive WRFs to double as redundancy rules, Jackendoff has his redundancy rules doubling as productive word formation rules to account for novel coinings. Aronoff regards this as a weakness in Jackendoff's theory, because it appears to predict a far greater variety of productive word formation processes than is actually observed.

11   See chapter 1 Note 16 for this term.

12   This is what we would expect given Siegel's observations on the distinction between # (Class II) and + (Class I) affixation.

13   Much more detailed discussion of the phenomenon of blocking is provided in Scalise (1984: 156ff). Aronoff's concept of blocking is criticized by Di Sciullo and Williams (1987: 10ff) but their objections appear to stem from a misreading of Aronoff's book.

FURTHER READING

Introductions to generative syntax which might be found useful background to this chapter include Akmajian and Heny (1975), C. Baker (1978), and Smith and Wilson (1978). Perlmutter and Soames (1979) provides a Generative Semantics orientation. Lyons (1968) gives a useful introduction to the *Aspects* model.

The only text devoted specifically to the material of this chapter is Scalise (1984), which will fill in a good deal of the detail I have left out here. A very good overview of many of the issues raised in the chapter is provided in Booij (1977).

CHAPTER 4 Approaches to allomorphy

1 With sufficient ingenuity we could extend our umlauting rule to cases like *man – men*, or *mouse – mice*.

2 In Czech orthography *č* represents IPA [tʃ], *ch* is a digraph representing IPA [x]; an accent over a vowel indicates length.

3 Solutions along these lines have been proposed by Lightner (1972) for Russian, by Scatton (1975) for Bulgarian and by Gussmann (1980) and Rubach (1984) for Polish.

4 My use of this example shouldn't be taken to imply that phonologists have invariably analysed Velar Softening as a cyclic rule: in Kiparsky (1982b) and in Halle and Mohanan (1985), for instance, it is treated as non-cyclic.

5 There has been extensive discussion of rule ordering in the generative literature. The other two principal types of rule interaction brought about by extrinsic ordering are **bleeding** and **counterbleeding**.

Suppose we have two rules, R1 and R2, such that R1 effects a change B→E before C, while R2 effects a change A→D before B. Either of R1 or R2 could in principle apply to /ABC/ to produce /AEC/ and /DBC/ respectively. If R1 applies before R2, however, R2 won't be able to apply to the new output /AEC/. In this case, we say that R1 bleeds R2. If we apply the rules in the opposite order both can apply and we get /DEC/. This is called a counterbleeding order. Notice that bleeding is in no sense the opposite of feeding (and therefore isn't in any sense equivalent to counterfeeding), and likewise, counterbleeding isn't the same as feeding.

A good textbook discussion of rule interactions in phonology is found in Kenstowicz and Kisseberth (1979).

6 The concept of **distinctness** is that defined in SPE, under which two representations are distinct only if one is given a feature specification [+F], where the other has a specification [−F] for some feature F. This means that if, say, two representations are identical, except that one is specified [+F] while the other has no specification for that feature (or, equivalently, zero specification, [0F]), then the two representations, though different, are not distinct in the technical sense.

7 The Elsewhere Condition is one of a number of conditions that were proposed to predict the order of application of phonological rules (and it is very similar in form to the Proper Inclusion Principle of Koutsoudas, Sanders and Noll, 1974). Zwicky (1986) has a particularly clear discussion of the significance of the notion 'default case' and ways of formalizing it in morphology.

8 For textbook treatments of the metrical approach to stress see Halle and Clements (1983), Hogg and McCully (1987), Goldsmith (1990), and also the overview articles by van der Hulst and Smith (1982c, 1985b).

9 Vol 5, no. 2 of the journal *Phonology* is devoted entirely to the issue of underspecification. See particularly Archangeli's (1988b) paper in that volume.

10   Structure preservation is further discussed by Pulleyblank (1986), and used extensively in a number of recent phonological analyses (e.g. Steriade, 1988b). More
general discussion can be found in Goldsmith (1990). Criticism of the idea has come
from various sources, including Hall (1989), Harris (1987) and Mohanan and
Mohanan (1984).

11   A good many technical proposals have been made for implementing such rules.
Reviews can be found in Kenstowicz and Kisseberth (1977) and especially Zonneveld
(1978).

12   The term 'morpholexical rule' is used in a variety of senses by different authors.
Caveat lector!
    Lieber's morpholexical rules are to all intents and purposes identical to the 'via-
rules' of Natural Generative Phonology.

13   Matters are complicated slightly by the fact that even here there is exceptionality in
that a handful of masculine stems ending in velar consonants select an affix allomorph
−ách, borrowed from the feminine paradigm. This doesn't affect the argument,
however, since the stem allomorph which occurs with the (hard) −ách allomorph is
always itself hard.

14   The distinction between PRs on the one hand and MPRs/AMRs on the other is reminiscent of the distinction between phonological 'processes' and phonological 'rules'
in Natural Phonology.

15   Plank (1984b) discusses a number of cases of this sort, concluding that linguistic
theory needs to countenance 'disagreement' rules. Zwicky (1985c) rebuts this,
pointing out that we can handle the facts at least as well by assuming the allomorphy
solution together with a theory of inflection which allows us to state things like
'the allomorph of *ma* found before a vowel initial word is identical to the masculine
allomorph *mon*'.

FURTHER READING

There are a variety of introductions to the SPE model of phonology. Kenstowicz and
Kisseberth (1979) is particularly good. Hyman (1975) and Sommerstein (1977) can also
be recommended. A more advanced discussion, still of considerable value, is Kenstowicz
and Kisseberth (1977). Introductions which include discussion of Lexical Phonology
include Durand (1990), Katamba (1989) and Goldsmith (1990). Introductions to other
approaches to allomorphy seem to have been lacking until now. A number of the papers
of *Phonology Yearbook* vol. 2 (1985) are devoted to Lexical Phonology (including an
excellent overview article by Kaisse and Shaw).
    From the research literature, Dressler's (1985a) monograph is full of useful facts.
Aronoff's (1976) chapter on allomorphy remains a very useful overview of many of the
issues. Zonneveld (1978) discusses a number of issues of relevance to this chapter.
    The relative paucity of books specially devoted to allomorphy and morphophonology
reflects the view, dominant till recently, that these could be lumped together with
phonology.

CHAPTER 5 Nonlinear approaches to morphology

1   The most up-to-date, authoritative and complete introduction to autosegmental
phonology is Goldsmith (1990). This chapter should be read in conjunction with his
chapter two, especially his §2.3.

2   Some discussion of this hypothesis and ways of implementing can be found in McCarthy (1982b, 1986), and also in the theoretical model advanced in Halle and Vergnaud (1987). A good overview of the implications for autosegmental phonology is given in Goldsmith (1990), chapter 6.

3   This is similar in spirit to the type of rules actually written by Chomsky (1979) in his analysis of essentially the same problems in his Hebrew morphophonemics. Note that, despite the date of publication of this work, it is, in fact, the first real example of generative phonology, being a Masters dissertation which Chomsky wrote in 1949.

4   McCarthy explicitly limits application of this principle to morphological rules proper, and remains agnostic as to whether it should apply to Aronoff's readjustment rules or allomorphy rules.

5   We shall look at further problems with the standard constituent structure view of concatenative morphology in chapter 10 when we discuss so-called bracketing paradoxes (or lexical relatedness paradoxes).

6   Halle and Vergnaud (1987) argue for similar conclusions. A good overview of these issues, and other related questions, is found in Goldsmith (1990)

7   I haven't addressed the still vexed question of the way that phonological rules interact with reduplication. In some cases it seems as though certain phonological rules have to apply before reduplication. This is problematic if reduplication is a morphological operation, and if all morphology has to precede the phonology. In a level ordered morphology, of course, this assumption isn't made, but the problem re-emerges for those who reject level ordering (see §6.1.1). Recall that Lieber (1982) and Marantz (1982) used the relative ordering of reduplication and phonology to argue that certain phonological rules are actually morpholexical relationships in the sense of §4.4.

8   See §4.1 for a detailed account of the morphological functions of umlaut in German, and further information about the phonological characterization of the process.

9   Goldsmith (1990) analyses the morphological function of templates in Sierra Miwok.

10 Alternative solutions are to be found in Spencer (1986), Rubach (1986) and Piotrowski, Roca and Spencer (MS).

11 A survey of the assumptions underlying autosegmental accounts of tone languages can be found in chapter 1 of Goldsmith (1990).

12 Other recent papers which extend or modify some of the proposals reviewed here include Odden and Odden (1985), Aronoff, Arsyad, Basri, and Broselow (1987), Steriade (1988a), Marantz (1987), Aronoff (1988a).

13 This therefore excludes signing systems concocted by educationalists, such as the Paget–Gorman system, which remains in use in some parts of Britain. Such systems may well not be learnable naturalistically, since they include attempts at mimicking the structure of spoken languages which arguably violate universal constraints on the structure of natural sign languages. In this respect they could not be considered natural languages. I am also excluding the signing systems of monks, though it is much more likely that these systems do represent natural languages (even though for sociological reasons it is doubtful that they will ever be learnt by infants!).

FURTHER READING

There is no introductory text which deals specifically with nonconcatenative morphology. Goldsmith (1990) is essential reading for autosegmental approaches to phonology and it includes much useful discussion of the morphology–phonology interface. It is also indispensable reading for tone languages. Other introductory material on nonconcatenative morphology can be found in Atkinson, Kilby and Roca (1988), Durand (1990) and Halle and Clements (1983). Katamba (1989) has an introduction to tonology, while Kaye (1989) provides a very readable and entertaining introduction to the phonological justification for autosegmental representations. From the earlier literature Hyman (1985) contains a helpful discussion of the phonology of African tone and Pike (1948) remains a fascinating source of information on tone languages.

A very simple introduction to signing systems is provided in Fromkin and Rodman (1988). Among the most important and useful references on Sign Language are Klima and Bellugi (1979), Wilbur (1979) and Padden (1988) (ASL, American Sign Language); Deuchar (1984) and Kyle and Woll (1985) (BSL, British Sign Language); and Moody (1983) (LSF, French Sign Language). A recent research monograph on the morphophonology of Sign Language is Sandler (1989), which appeared too late to be incorporated into the text.

CHAPTER 6 Later generative theories

1 This kind of case can't be accounted for so easily by the method by which Di Sciullo and Williams (1987) deal with French compounding (chapter 11), because we are dealing with an endocentric compound in the Germanic case, with just the same structure as ordinary compounds.

   Recently, Lieber (1988) has used such examples to argue that morphology is an entirely syntactic phenomenon.

2 There are a few well-known counterexamples to these claims. For instance, in the word *cannibalistic*, it looks as though we are, after all, adding an idiosyncratic compound suffix -*istic* to a noun or adjective stem, since there is no word **cannibalist* to which to add -*ic*. Booij (1977) discusses similar examples from Dutch.

3 I'm making this assumption simply to clarify what's at stake. Exactly the same sort of argument could be run if we assumed a conversion analysis. Then, we would still have the labelled brackets intervening but no null affixes.

4 While the most frequent use of -*ee*, this is not the only one. Bauer (1983: 243) provides a recent discussion of the functions of this suffix.

5 Carstairs (1987: chapter 4) discusses this question in great detail, under the heading 'systematic inflectional homonymy'.

6 In point of fact there is a good deal of controversy over the status of the aspectual distinction in Slavic and its expression. Comrie (1976: 88) refers to Derived Imperfectives as being formed by a derivational process. However, Zaliznjak's (1977) grammatical dictionary regards the pairs formed by Derived Imperfectivization as the only legitimate type of 'pure' aspectual pairing, implying that there is always some lexical or non-aspectual semantic difference between pairs such as *pisat'* and *napisat'*. This suggests that Derived Imperfectivization might be inflectional and prefixing perfectives derivational. Note, incidentally, that if the prefixed perfectives are inflectional forms, then this is the only case of prefixing inflection in the language except for the formation of superlatives of adjectives (formed by adding *naj-* to the comparative form).

7 Or at least reinterpret it. See for instance the distinction drawn by Carstairs (1988) between 'meaning-driven' and 'expression-driven' morphology.

8 Williams (1981a) tries to reconstruct a notion of paradigm, though this has not been widely taken up and the empirical base of the attempt has been criticized severely by Joseph and Wallace (1984).

9 One of the difficulties in evaluating the split-morphology hypothesis is knowing when

to take claims literally. For instance, it can't literally be the case that real live speakers construct inflected forms of words only when they need that inflected form to express syntactic relations in a sentence. If this were so it's difficult to see how anyone could ever produce an isolated word in an arbitrary inflected form. This is important for Badecker and Caramazza's experiments, for instance, for their argument hinges on the behaviour of a brain-damaged patient failing to repeat accurately inflected words of Italian. At the same time, those who claim that even regular inflection is lexical need to explain what this means in highly inflected languages where every verb might give rise to literally thousands of inflected forms.

10 Fabb argues for some very specific syntactic relations between components of complex words. Some of these are discussed in chapter 8 when we look at compounding.

11 In standard Navajo orthography, b d g represent voiceless unaspirated stops, p t k are aspirated stops, sh is the fricative [ʃ], ł is a voiceless lateral and y represents a palatal glide [j]. The apostrophe ' is the glottal stop, and p' t' k' are ejectives. Vowel doubling represents length, and an accent over a vowel indicates a high tone. The cedilla below a vowel indicates nasalization.

12 Simpson and Withgott are noncommittal about how they would formalize the notion of template. The only formal models I know of which take the notion of template seriously are those of the Soviet linguist Revzin (e.g. Revzin and Juldaševa, 1969) and the model proposed by Grimes (1967, 1983). Grimes's 1983 monograph describes a computer program for expediting the practical task of figuring out position classes.

13 This restriction on selection in 'layered' morphologies is discussed in considerable detail by Carstairs (1987): chapter 5) under the heading of his Peripherality Constraint.

14 It is sometimes argued that there are no affixal template morphologies and that cases of apparent templatic affixation are really cases of cliticization. For example, Joyce McDonough argues this for Navajo in work currently in progress. However, this still leaves us with the problem of characterizing clitic systems, and, in particular, of distinguishing them from affixing systems. §9.3 discusses this in more detail.

15 Anderson (1982) doesn't actually present the data in one place, and doesn't provide all the forms in this paradigm. Table 6.2 has been prepared on the basis of Anderson (1982) and Jensen and Stong-Jensen (1984).

16 A similar idea is adopted in the feature system employed in Generalized Phrase Structure Grammar, where it is developed much more fully and given a formal definition. See Gazdar, Klein, Pullum and Sag (1985) (cf. my remarks in §6.2.1)

17 These rules are based on those given by Anderson (1982), with the ungainly addition of 6.70a to account for the non-appearance of the -t suffix in *xedav* 'thou seest them'. As Jensen and Stong-Jensen (1984) point out, Anderson's (1982) original rules would fail to generate *vxedavt* 'I see them'. As far as I can tell, Anderson's revision of the 1982 rules (Anderson, 1986) would incorrectly predict that 'thou seest them' would come out as *xedavt*.

18 Another aspect of Anderson's proposal which is of interest is the device he suggests for a phenomenon in Georgian grammar known as **inversion**. In certain tense forms, the affixes which normally mark subjects are used to mark direct objects, while the subject gets marked by affixes which elsewhere are used to mark indirect objects. One way of analysing this is to assume a syntactic process in which indirect objects are 'promoted' to subject status and subjects 'demoted' to objects. This is the type of rule favoured by relational grammarians (e.g. Harris, 1984). Anderson suggests handling this by means of a rule operating over morphosyntactic features. Essentially

what this does is to take the outer and inner layer of P/N features and reverse them. It is difficult to see, however, how this rather powerful formalism could be constrained so as to avoid predicting all sorts of unheard of alternations.

19 Anderson devotes little attention to the implications of models of nonconcatenative morphology, such as those discussed in chapter 5. Hammond (1981) has some critical comments on McCarthy's (1982a) analysis of Semitic root-and-pattern morphology, though it seems fair to say that the question of nonconcatenative inflectional systems has not been seriously addressed by protagonists of the EWP approach.

20 The philosophical underpinnings of Natural Morphology lie in the semiotic theories of C. S. Peirce. Unfortunately, we won't have time to discuss these. However, the application of Peircean semiotics to morphology is at a relatively simple level, so little is lost.

FURTHER READING

There is no textbook introduction to the whole of the material covered in this chapter. The most useful overview sources are Bauer (1988) and Di Sciullo and Williams (1987), though the latter is very condensed and is intended as a programmatic research monograph, not as a handbook. The introduction to Hammond and Noonan (1988) provided by the editors is also very helpful. Scalise (1984) has an introduction to some of the earlier work surveyed here (e.g. Lieber).

Introductions to Lexical Functional Grammar can be found in Horrocks (1987), Sells (1985) and Winograd (1983). The theory itself is presented in the collection of papers edited by Bresnan (1982). The Horrocks and Sells textbooks are also good introductions to Generalized Phrase Structure Grammar. Perhaps the most useful discussion devoted specifically to argument structure and theta roles is Jackendoff (1983).

Template morphology is discussed in some of the earlier handbooks of American descriptive linguistics (e.g. Gleason, 1961). Otherwise, there are no introductory accounts. For inflection, there is a classical introduction in Matthews's (1974) textbook. Bauer (1988), too, is very useful. A handy and very readable overview is provided by Anderson (1985b). Anderson (1988b) is a useful summary of Anderson's views, while Anderson (1988a), a lucid summary of morphology, also contains a very readable account of the EWP approach to inflection. After these references a much more thorough account can be found in Carstairs (1987) and Wurzel (1984). Matthews (1972) presents a compendious and minutely argued discussion of earlier work on inflectional systems. A volume edited by Plank (to appear) promises to contain an interesting collection of papers on inflection.

CHAPTER 7 Grammatical relations

1 Usually called -EN, even though its regular allomorph is *-ed*.

2 According to some linguists (e.g. Perlmutter and Postal, 1984, and other references in the Relation Grammar framework) such constructions are fully equivalent to passive constructions involving -EN verbal morphology. However, when we come to discuss middle constructions we will see that there are certain important distinctions to bear in mind.

3 For the present, think of an unaccusative verb as an intransitive verb whose subject is typically a non-voluntary or passive participant. An intransitive verb with a voluntary or active subject will be called 'unergative'.

4 Semantically, causation is related to the rather slippery notion of agentivity. This will be discussed in more detail in §7.5 below.

5 In the GB literature unaccusative verbs are often referred as 'ergative', following a tradition initiated by Burzio in his 1981 PhD thesis. Many linguists find this use of the term 'ergative' rather confusing to the point of being irritating (cf. Dixon, 1987, Pullum, 1988). Given that the term 'unaccusative' is descriptive and not used for other purposes, while 'ergative' is already overworked, and given that many GB linguists seem to prefer the term 'unaccusative', I shall use the latter exclusively.

6 NI is sometimes regarded as 'exotic', but this is only because it is poorly represented in European languages. Explicit descriptions of NI can be found for languages spoken pretty well everywhere except Europe, including Eskimo languages (e.g. Sadock, 1980, 1985), Uto-Aztecan (e.g. Nahuatl: Andrews, 1975, Merlan, 1976), Tanoan (e.g. Southern Tiwa: Allen, Gardner and Frantz, 1984), a number of South American languages (e.g. Derbsyhire and Pullum, 1986), a variety of Polynesian languages (e.g. Niuean: Seiter, 1980), the Chukotkan-Kamchadal group of Paleosiberian languages (Bogoraz, 1922, Comrie, 1981). Ainu, a language isolate of Japan and Sakhalin Island (Shibatani, 1990), a variety of East Cushitic languages (see Sasse, 1984), the Mayan languages (e.g. Jacaltec, Day, 1973; Mam, England 1983), the Caddoan and Iroquoian languages (Chafe, 1976, Baker, 1988a), Tiwi, a language of Australia (Osborne, 1974), Turkish (Özkaragöz, 1986), Takelma, an extinct language of Texas (Sapir, 1922) and a good many more. Overviews of the phenomenon can be found in Mardirussian (1975), Mithun (1984) and Baker (1988a).

7 Presumably the antipassive will be an exception to this.

8 Baker in fact derives (most of) the HMC from the ECP, discussed briefly below.

9 Actually, Chukchee poses an intriguing problem here: the surface case form assumed by the oblique argument may be Dative, Locative or Instrumental, depending on the verb root. This suggests that the antipassive itself is formed lexically rather than syntactically as in Baker's theory.

10 Technically, this is because there would be a violation of the Theta Criterion, which states that every theta role must be assigned to an argument, and every argument must receive a theta role. The Theta Criterion will be discussed in more detail in §8.3.5.1.

11 There is a very interesting parallel here between Rosen's analysis and 'null object' constructions in English and Italian discussed in some detail by Rizzi (1986). In English a verb such as *lead* can be used with or without an object, but when it takes an infinitival complement it must include its direct object. This is illustrated in (i):

(i) a) This leads people to the following conclusion.
   b) This leads _____ to the following conclusion.
   c) This leads people [PRO to conclude the following].
   d) *This leads _____ [PRO to conclude the following].

In Italian, the corresponding verb, *conducere*, permits the direct object to be missing in the equivalent of (i, d).

(ii) a) Questo conduce la gente alla seguente conclusione.
   b) Questo conduce _____ alla seguente conclusione.
   c) Questo conduce la gente a [PRO concludere quanto segue].
   d) Questo conduce _____ a [PRO concludere quanto segue].

Rizzi argues that the missing direct object in the English cases is simply missing syntactically, and that in (i, b) the verb is intransitive. Since an object is required to control the PRO in the infinitival this means (i, d) is impossible. However, in Italian we have a *pro* object in the position of the dash in (ii, b, d) and this syntactically present, though phonetically null, object can hence control the PRO in (ii, d).

Note, also, that Baker himself points out (1988a: 454, note 17) that NI might be lexical compounding in those languages which do not permit stranding of modifiers.

12   Indeed, such a rule would not be expected if, as many linguists assume, the Projection Principle doesn't hold in the lexicon. See chapter 8 for further discussion of this question.

13   Technically, this is a consequence of the Theta Criterion (see note 10), which is discussed in more detail in chapter 8.

14   There is a great deal more one could say about these constructions. In particular, we have not said anything about the fact that in many languages (e.g. English) the passive participle is identical to the perfect participle (see Hoekstra, 1984, for discussion). Nor have we mentioned the fascinating connection between passive participles, adjectival passives, perfect participles and resultatives. This promises to be one of the areas of growth in research on lexical structure.

FURTHER READING

A proper understanding of the material of this chapter presupposes a basic grounding in Government-Binding syntax. Good textbook introductions are Haegeman (1991), Horrocks (1987), Radford (1981, 1988), Sells (1985). A more advanced text is Lasnik and Uriagereka (1988). Perhaps the best introduction from the point of view of this chapter is van Riemsdijk and Williams (1986). McCloskey (1988) provides an article-length overview of recent syntactic theories, particularly GB.

The most convenient source of information on Relational Grammar is Blake (1990). Otherwise, the articles in Perlmutter (1983) and Perlmutter and Rosen (1984) provide a comprehensive overview. (Another volume, edited by Joseph and Perlmutter, is advertised at the time of writing.) *Syntax and Semantics*, vol. 8 (Cole and Sadock, 1977) is devoted to grammatical relations. Other interesting collections are Plank (1984a) and *Syntax and Semantics*, vol. 15, on transitivity (Hopper and Thompson, 1982).

Syntax and Semantics, vol. 6 (Shibatani, 1976) is devoted to causatives. A semantic theory which relies on the relationship between causation and agentivity is presented in Jackendoff (1976, 1983), and, for interesting discussion from a rather different theoretical point of view, see Anderson, J. M. (1971, 1977). More recently, a Parasession of the Chicago Linguistics Society (CLS 24) has been devoted to Causatives and Agentivity.

An excellent collection of articles on resultatives, full of fascinating data, together with a detailed typology of these constructions, is to be found in Nedjalkov (1983).

The syntax of the Italian *si* constructions is discussed by Burzio (1986), and a convenient summary of the issues, together with important theoretical proposals, is to be found in Cinque (1988).

For discussion of ergativity see Comrie (1978), Dixon (1979) and the papers in Plank (1979) (especially Trask's overview), and, more recently, the papers in the special issue of *Lingua*, 1987, edited by Dixon, also published separately. Marantz (1984) offers a particularly interesting theoretical perspective on the notion 'ergative language'.

For references on noun incorporation, see note 6 above.

Marantz (1988b) provides an explicit comparison between his approach and that of Baker.

CHAPTER 8 Compounds

1 Turkish orthography is phonetic, with the following correspondence with IPA: c = [ʤ], ç = [tʃ], ğ indicates a lengthening of the previous vowel (it often alternates with a velar stop). ş = [ʃ], y = [j], ı = [ɨ], ö = [œ], ü = [y]. In transcription, E and I represent vowels which alternate by vowel harmony, respectively a/e and ɨ/i/u/ü.

2 Allen (1978) proposed a theory which distinguishes compounds in terms of the phonological boundaries separating their components. Where a compound is highly lexicalized and undergoes lexical morphophonemic rules, we might adopt a + boundary or a single # boundary, as in *post # man*. Where no lexical processes affect the compound we have a double word boundary, # #, as in *anchor # # man*. With phonological boundaries out of favour, alternatives will involve a separate Stratum (as in Mohanan, 1986) or rules referring to prosodic domains of the kind discussed by Nespor and Vogel (1986).

3 FPC IV will otiose, of course, if, as I've hinted , all *true* (productive) compounding is rightheaded, and the Vietnamese style compounding is really the lexicalization of phrases.

4 Lieber (1983) claims, somewhat controversially, that *truck driver* can also be interpreted as a nonce root compound (say, something with a meaning such as '(taxi) driver who owns a truck'). My own view is that *truck driver* could marginally be interpreted as a root compound, but that this is because *drive* can be interpreted intransitively. A compound formed from an obligatorily transitive verb such as *make*, however, can only be read as a synthetic compound. That is, *coffee maker* can only mean 'person or thing that makes coffee' (cf. Sproat, 1985a).

5 One reason Sproat mentions for assuming that synthetic compounds are formed syntactically is that phrasal chunks can appear inside such compounds, as in the famous *American history teacher*. Interestingly, Fabb uses this fact to argue that phrasal chunks can become lexicalized and thus appear in lexical compounds (such as *American history course*). This illustrates one of the difficulties in finding uncontrovertible criteria for placing processes in the syntax, the lexicon or elsewhere.

6 Granted the need for an inheritance mechanism, it's not entirely clear to me from Sproat's account why a structure such as 8.72 has to be assumed for synthetic compounding. It would seem compatible with Sproat's theory to assign the structure [truck [driving]]. Assuming that *driving* is formed syntactically, the derived nominal would inherit the verb's argument structure. After compounding, the non-head *truck* could then be theta identified with the Theme role in the derived argument structure of the nominalization, just as in *the driving of trucks*. This would bring Sproat's solution closer to that of Di Sciullo and Williams.

7 These assumptions have a number of theoretical consequences and commit Sproat to a number of further assumptions about the syntactic structure of nominalizations, particularly about the nature of the Specifier position in NPs headed by nominalizations. Discussion of these questions is well beyond the scope of a text devoted primarily to morphology. The interested reader can follow some of the debate from recent works such as Chomsky (1986b), Williams (1985, 1987) Lasnik (1988), Safir (1987).

8 Roeper suggests that the NI analysis allows part of the First Sister Principle to fall out from the ECP. However, since Roeper apparently wishes to extend his NI

analysis to examples like *pan-fried* and *well-kept*, it isn't clear how this is to be done. This is because it is a crucial feature of Baker's analysis of NI that incorporation can't extract from Adjuncts, only from theta marked (internal) arguments. This in turn is because any maximal projection which isn't theta marked will be a barrier to (proper) government, so that an incorporated adjunct would leave an ungoverned trace, causing an ECP violation. Roeper doesn't explicitly say he is adopting the *Barriers* framework of Chomsky (1986a), so perhaps he has some other treatment in mind.

9   Roeper actually cites the suffix -*ful*, as in (i):

(i)   *The children are playful of games.

He also mentions that there are exceptions: *resentful of his mother*. What appears to be happening here is that -*ful* attaches preferably to nouns (*sorrowful, painful, soleful*) but also to verbs. In *playful*, we presumably have affixation of a noun, so there is no theta grid to percolate; otherwise, it seems as though -*ful* may permit percolation. Lexicalization muddies the picture, though, as in *mindful of his responsibilities*.

10   One proposal we haven't mentioned is that of Pesetsky (1985), who analyses the inheritance phenomena as the result of the movement of the affix, giving a structure [drive of trucks]er], and permitting the verb to govern its PP complement. We'll discuss the Affix Movement analysis in some detail in chapter 10.

On the other hand, according to Hoekstra (1986) and Hoekstra and van der Putten (1988) there is nothing to explain, and inheritance is simply the result of a misanalysis of the data.

FURTHER READING

Descriptions of English compounding can be found in Adams (1983), Bauer (1983) and Marchand (1969). The stressing of compounds in English is discussed in Hogg and McCully (1967).

The question of productivity and root compounding is discussed in some detail in Bauer (1983). An interesting account is to be found in Downing (1977).

Some of the theoretical issues surrounding root compounding are discussed in Scalise (1984). Botha (1983) provides the most recent overview of synthetic compounding. The notion of argument inheritance was introduced by Randall (1984), who makes a number of interesting observations about the phenomenon. An extended defence of a framework similar to that adopted by Booij for handling inheritance phenomena is given in Zubizarreta (1987). (Readers unfamiliar with recent trends in syntactic theory (especially Government-Binding theory) should consult the references mentioned at the end of chapter 7.)

CHAPTER 9   Clitics

1   The term 'clitic' comes from a Greek root meaning 'to lean'. In addition to the nominalized form 'cliticization', you will sometimes come across the term **clisis**. This is also used in affixed form, so that a language which has enclitics might be said to show 'enclisis'.

2   Serbo-Croat orthography can be taken to be IPA except the following: c = [ts], ć = [tɕ], č = [tʃ], h = [x], ž = [ʒ]. The trilled r can be syllabic. Note the common alternation between -ao/-al and -eo/el (especially in verb forms).

The symbols ` ´ " and ^ in tables 9.1, 2 represent tones. These indicate the position of word stress. They are not marked in the official orthography.

3 Example 9.11 illustrates Croatian usage rather than Serbian, since, in the latter, *je* after *se* is omitted.

4 Strictly speaking, Genitive forms of the pronominal clitics should appear between the Dative and Accusative forms. This is because certain obligatorily reflexive verbs take a Genitive complement. When this surfaces as a pronominal clitic it appears before the Accusative reflexive clitic *se*, as in (i). The Genitive clitic forms, however, are identical in form to the Accusative forms.

(i) Bojim ga se; ja ga se bojim
     I-fear 3sg.M-GEN REFL; I 3sg.M-GEN REFL I-fear
     'I'm afraid of him.'

5 But see §9.3 below for a case of agreement with exactly the properties of clitic climbing.

6 For those who read Italian, an extremely interesting comparison of the development of Romance and Slavic clitics, discussing this aspect in some detail, is presented in Benacchio and Renzi (1987), in which the authors explore Jakobson's (1935) thesis that the loss of Wackernagel's Law in Slavic languages is connected with the development of a moveable stress system.

7 Notice that these examples also illustrate the use of the postpositive definite article *-ot* (masc.), *-ta* (fem.), *-to* (neut.). This is itself a kind of clitic. An interesting discussion of the morphophonological properties of the very similar definite article in Bulgarian is given in Scatton (1980).

8 Lunt (1952: 23) gives an example of stress shift with a gerund form. However, Usikova (1985: 31) explicitly states that gerunds, which exceptionally have stress on the penult, retain this stress pattern even with clitics.

9 The principle vagaries of Portuguese pronunciation and orthography are the following:

   lh = [ʎ] nh = [ɲ].
   Vm = Ṽ = nasalized vowel.
   V́ indicates a stressed vowel; other marks over vowels are purely orthographic.

Note that the clitic systems of Brazilian Portuguese and of many American varieties of Spanish are different from the European varieties of these languages.

10 In the Spanish gloss 9.54b we might have expected the sequence *le lo*, but this is prohibited in Spanish, much as the sequence *je je* is prohibited in Serbo-Croat. Instead, the first of a sequence of 3rd person pronouns is replaced by the reflexive *se*, the so-called Spurious *se* rule.

11 Polish orthography can be taken to be IPA except for the following:

   ą = [õ], ę = [ẽ] ó (= u) = [u], y = [ɨ]
   ł = [w], w = [v], cz = [tʃ], sz = [ʃ], rz = ż = [ʒ].
   Before i: elsewhere:
   c = ć = [tɕ]   c = [ts]
   s = ś = [ɕ]   s = [s]
   z = ź = [ʑ]   z = [z]
   n = ń = [ ]   n = [n]
   Stress almost always falls on the penultimate syllable.

In tables of nominal and participial declension, 'masculine plural' is actually short-hand for 'masculine human plural', the so-called virile gender of Polish.

12   We must be careful to distinguish cases in which the pronominal element excludes an NP argument and **dislocation** structures such as those illustrated in (i, ii):

(i) They're nice, these pears.
(ii) I've seen him before, that chap standing in the corner.

In these sentences, the NP isn't an argument, but rather stands in a 'topic' position, outside the clausal matrix proper. We'll be discussing other cases similar to this in §9.3.

13   This account is something of an oversimplification given NPs of the form *ho ane:r ho sophos* 'the wise man', literally 'the wise the man'.

14   In Zwicky's (1977) descriptive account these would be **endoclitics**, that is, clitics inserted inside inflected words. However, it seems to be generally agreed (e.g. by Zwicky himself, 1987b) that endoclisis should be excluded as a theoretical possibility and putative cases reanalysed.

15   Sproat's Mapping Principle (§10.6) was proposed for just this sort of mismatch, and Sproat (1988) uses it to provide a reanalysis of Klavans's typology of clitics.

16   Recall from chapter 7 that 'small' *pro* is the empty pronominal bearing the feature specifications [+pronominal, -anaphor]. It is most famously represented by the definite null subjects of tensed clauses in null subject ('pro-drop') languages such as Italian and Spanish. In such languages it is frequently the case that the existence of a *pro* subject is associated with verbal subject agreement morphology which identifies the pronominal (gender, person or number) features of the subject. It is therefore a natural step to assume that the same empty category represents the null object in languages with object agreement, and that it also represents the null object in languages in which the object can be expressed as a clitic.

17   Intriguingly, an analogous problem arises in noun incorporation. In Mohawk, for instance, it's possible to 'double' a semantically general incorporated noun (such as 'fish') with an overt NP direct object, provided it has a more specific meaning (e.g. a type of fish). In certain languages, a semantic classifier system has developed in which it is obligatory to incorporate such a general noun as a kind of 'agreement marker' for the more specific NP. The phenomenon is discussed by Baker (1988a), Di Sciullo and Williams (1987) and Rosen (1989). Very curiously, none of these commentators draws any explicit parallel with the equivalent problem posed by pronominal clitics.

18   Not all scholars are sceptical about Aoun's ability to deal with clitic doubling. Everett (1987) discusses very interesting facts from the Brazilian language Pirahã, which has a doubling construction violating the Kayne/Jaeggli generalization. Everett regards this as evidence against the Jaeggli/Borer approach.

19   Jaeggli, of course, also assumes that the empty category in examples such as 9.108 will be *pro* and hence must be licensed by a Case assigner. However, he assumes that if the clitic failed to absorb Case then it would be unable to license the *pro*. This mysterious incompatibility is due to the fact that Jaeggli follows Borer in assuming that the Case feature absorbed by the clitic becomes part of the V + clitic complex. Thus, the Case feature assigned to the clitic comes to be represented on the verb which governs and is indexed with the object position. In this fashion, the verb complex, which as a whole bears the Case feature, is able to license the *pro*.

I find Jaeggli's account a little puzzling here. It would appear that he is actually adopting Borer's thesis that the clitic is a spell-out of Case features; otherwise, he is advocating an odd 'Duke of York' derivation in which the verb assigns Case to the clitic and then the Case feature percolates from the clitic to the verb node dominating the verb + clitic complex, thereby mimicking percolation of that feature from the verbal head.

20 Suñer doesn't wish to claim that all clitic systems showing doubling are necessarily agreement systems. She refers to the case of Modern Hebrew in which clitic doubling is invariably supported by a prepositional Case assigner (Borer, 1984a). Suñer follows Borer in assuming that the Hebrew clitic is a Case absorber, so that the clitic can only be licensed if the verb is not obliged to assign its Case to the lexical NP.

A more radical account of clitic pronouns is offered by Lyons (forthcoming) who argues that all clitic doubling, and by extension all cliticization phenomena, are a species of agreement.

21 Interesting observations in this regard are offered by Myers (1987), discussing Bantu verb morphology.

FURTHER READING

There is no introductory text which includes detailed discussion of the phonology or morphology of clitics. Rather oddly, given the enormous importance of clitic systems in the development of Government-Binding syntax, there is no introductory syntax text which provides an overview of the morphosyntax of clitics, either. In addition to monographs such as Borer (1984a) I can recommend the papers of Borer (1986a) and especially Borer's own succinct introduction to that volume (Borer, 1986b). Still valuable is Perlmutter's (1971) thesis.

The content of §9.3 will be found hard going by those not acquainted with GB approaches to pronominalization. Of the introductions to GB syntax mentioned in chapter 7, perhaps the most useful background to this section would be Lasnik and Uriagereka, (1988).

CHAPTER 10 Bracketing paradoxes

1 Hoeksema proposes to handle Williams's cases (and others he adduces) in terms of rules which are permitted to refer directly to the head of a construction (**Head Operations**). Unfortunately, it would take us too far afield to consider Hoeksema's very interesting proposals. Readers with a basic knowledge of categorial grammar are strongly encouraged to consult Hoeksema's book.

FURTHER READING

There are no textbooks or review monographs which discuss bracketing paradoxes as such.

For §10.3, further information about prosodic domains in phonology can be found in Selkirk (1980, 1986), Kaisse (1985) and Nespor and Vogel (1986).

For §10.5, introductory accounts of those aspects of logic of interest to linguists can be found in books on mathematical linguistics such as Partee (1978) and Wall (1972), in introductions to formal theories of semantics such as Dowty, Wall and Peters (1981),

Fodor (1977) and more specifically in McCawley (1981) and Allwood, Anderson and Dahl (1977). May (1985) is an influential approach to Logical Form in GB theory.

CHAPTER 11 The place of morphology

1 The monograph is given insightful critical reviews by Baker (1988c), and Aronoff (1988b).

2 I confess to being baffled by Di Sciullo and Williams's remarks about the autonomy of scientific disciplines. It is worth noting that Di Sciullo and Williams's view of the philosophy of science is entirely at odds with that usually associated with Generative Grammar (as enunciated, for instance, in Chomsky, 1980, Fodor, 1983). Chomskyan linguists generally assume that in principle any fact from any domain could impinge on inferences drawn in another domain. Indeed, an entertaining, and not very difficult, exercise in the philosophy of science would be to concoct scenarios in which findings in history might influence theory construction in forestry, and vice versa.

3 As Baker (1988c) points out, this radical position seems to be at odds with usual Chomskyan assumptions about the 'psychological reality' of grammar. Perhaps we should therefore interpret the suggestion as the claim that productivity, like word frequency, or the precise content of an individual's mental lexicon, should be regarded as a performance phenomenon and not as part of a competence theory.

4 Notice that the claim that Romance compounds have syntactic structure is mildly overstated. For example, if *essuie-glace* were a real VP then the NP would require a Determiner: *essuie la glace*.

5 It's not obvious to me that this is a very strong criterion. In some languages (Chinese, Chukchee) it's notoriously difficult to decide what the 'real', 'basic' syntactic category of a word or root is since the rules of syntax or morphology frequently don't permit us to define a base form from which other word types are derived. Indeed, this is illustrated by certain English noun-verb pairs: is the noun or the verb basic in *jump, sleep, seat, rain, work* ...? What criteria would allow us to decide?

6 The main simplification in figure 11.2 is that I have ignored Beard's claim that essentially the same kinds of syntactic operations are found in lexical derivation as in syntax proper.

7 Sadock assumes the framework of Generalized Phrase Structure Grammar (Gazdar, Klein, Pullum and Sag, 1985). To make for easier reading, I have altered Sadock's syntactic representations to bring them into line with those used in the rest of this book.

8 This argument requires, of course, that the accentuation be assigned after the syntax, in the phrase phonology, and that it is not possible for the accentuation to be assigned to each component of the compound separately in the lexicon.

9 This type of percolation is highly unusual in that the percolated feature has no effect on the constituent which it marks morphologically. This is different from, say definiteness marking in English possessives: in *the tree's root* both *tree* and the whole NP are definite. (In a compound such as *the tree root* the determiner modifies the compound noun giving a constituent structure [the [tree root]], so this is not comparable to the Hebrew case.) Hebrew definiteness marking therefore constitutes a rather intriguing example of a mismatch between morphological structure and syntactic/semantic structure. It would be interesting to find comparable cases involving different features.

References

Abbreviations

BLS n   *Proceedings of the* nth *Annual Meeting of the Berkeley Linguistics Society,* Berkeley, University of California

CLS n   *Papers from the* nth *Annual Meeting of the Chicago Linguistics Society,* Chicago, University of Chicago

CSLI   Center for the Study of Language and Information

CUP   Cambridge University Press

ESCOL n   *Proceedings of the* nth *Annual Meeting of the East States Society for Computational Linguistics*

IJAL   *International Journal of American Linguistics*

IULC   Indiana University Linguistics Club

JL   *Journal of Linguistics*

Lg   *Language*

LI   *Linguistic Inquiry*

LA   *Linguistic Analysis*

MITWPL   *Massachusetts Institute of Technology Working Papers in Linguistics*

NELS n   *Proceedings of the* nth *Annual Meeting of the North Eastern Linguistics Society*

NLLT   *Natural Language and Linguistic Theory*

OUP   Oxford University Press

TLR   *The Linguistic Review*

WCCFL   *West Coast Conference on Formal Linguistics*

YM   *Yearbook of Morphology*

Adams, V. (1973) *An Introduction to Modern English Word-Formation.* London: Longmans.

Aissen, J. (1987) *Tzotzil Clause Structure.* Dordrecht: Reidel.

Aitchison, J. (1987) *Words in the Mind*. Oxford: Blackwell.

Akmajian, A. and Heny, F. (1975) *Introduction to the Principles of Transformational Syntax*. Cambridge, MA: MIT Press.

Akmajian, A., Demers, R. and Harnish, R. (1984) *Linguistics: an Introduction to Language and Communication* (2nd edn.). Cambridge, MA: MIT Press.

Allen, B., Gardiner, D. and Frantz, D. (1984) Noun incorporation in Southern Tiwa. *IJAL* 50, 292–311.

Allen, M. (1978) *Morphological Investigations*. Phd dissertation, University of Connecticut.

Allwood, J., Andersen, L-G. and Dahl, Ö. (1977) *Logic in Linguistics*. Cambridge: CUP.

Anderson, J. M. (1971) *The Grammar of Case*. Cambridge: CUP

Anderson, J. M. (1977) *A Localist Theory of Case Grammar*. Cambridge: CUP.

Anderson, S. R. (1977) On the formal description of inflection. *CLS* 13, 15–44.

Anderson, S. R. (1982) Where's morphology *LI* 13, 571–612.

Anderson, S. R. (1984a) On representations in morphology: case, agreement and inversion in Georgian. *NLLT* 2, 157–218.

Anderson, S. R. (1984b) Kwakwala syntax and the government-binding theory. In: Cook, E.-D. and Gerdts, D (eds.), *Syntax and Semantics, 16: the Syntax of Native American Languages*. New York: Academic Press.

Anderson, S. R. (1985a) Typological distinctions in word formation. In: Shopen (ed.), Vol. 3.

Anderson, S. R. (1985b) Inflectional morphology. In: Shopen (ed.), Vol. 3.

Anderson, S. R. (1985c) *Phonology in the Twentieth Century: Theories of Rules and Theories of Representations*. Chicago: University of Chicago Press.

Anderson, S. R. (1986) Disjunctive ordering in inflectional morphology. *NLLT* 4, 1–31

Anderson, S. R. (1988a) Morphological theory. In: Newmeyer (ed.), Vol. 1.

Anderson S. R. (1988b) Inflection. In: Hammond and Noonan (eds.).

Anderson, S. R. (1988c) Morphology as a parsing porblem. *Linguistics* 26, 521–44.

Andrews, A. (1988) Lexical structure. In: Newmeyer (ed.). Vol. 1.

Andrews, J. (1975) *Introduction to Classical Nahuatl*. Austin: University of Texas Press.

Aoun, J. (1985) *A Grammar of Anaphora*. Cambridge, MA: MIT Press.

Aoun, J. Hornstein, N., Lightfoot, D. and Weinberg, A. (1987) Two types of locality. *LI* 18, 537–78.

Archangeli, D. (1983) The root CV-template as a property of the affix: evidence from Yawelmani. *NLLT* 1, 347–84.

Archangeli, D. (1988a) *Underspecification in Yawelmani phonology and morphology*. New York: Garland Press. [PhD dissertation, MIT, 1984].

Archangeli, D. (1988b) Aspects of underspecification theory. *Phonology* 5, 183–207.

Aronoff, M. (1976) *Word Formation in Generative Grammar*. Cambridge, MA: MIT Press.

Aronoff, M. (1988a) Head operations and strata in reduplication: a linear treatment. *YM* 1, 1–16.

Aronoff, M. (1988b) Review: Di Sciullo and Williams (1987). *Lg* 64, 766–70.

Aronoff, M. and Sridhar, S. (1983) Morphological levels in English and Kannada; or, Atarizing Reagan. In: *Papers from the Parasession on the Interplay of Phonology, Morphology, and Syntax*. *CLS* 19, 3–16.

Aronoff, M. and Sridhar, S. (1987) Morphological levels in English and Kannada. In: Gussmann (ed.).

Aronoff, M., Arsyad, A., Basri, H. and Broselow, E. (1987) Tier conflation in Macassarese reduplication. In: *Papers from the Parasession on Metrical and Autosegmental Phonology*. *CLS* 23, 1–15.

Ashton, E. (1944) *Swahili Grammar*. London: Longmans.

Atkinson, M., Kilby, D. and Roca, I. (1988) *Fundamentals of General Linguistics* (2nd edn.). London: Unwin.

Bach, E. (1968) Nouns and noun phrases. In: Bach and Harms (eds.).

Bach, E. and Harms, R. (eds.) (1968) *Universals of Grammar*. New York: Holt, Rinehart and Winston.

Badecker, W. and Caramazza, A. (1989) A lexical distinction between inflection and derivation. *LI* 20, 108–16.

Baker, C. (1978) *Introduction to Generative-Transformational Syntax*. Englewood Cliffs, NJ: Prentice-Hall.

Baker, M. (1985a) The Mirror Principle and morphosyntactic explanation. *LI* 16, 373–416.

Baker, M. (1985b) Syntactic affixation and English gerunds. *WCCFL* 4, 1–11.

Baker, M. (1988a) *Incorporation: a Theory of Grammatical Function Changing*. Chicago: University of Chicago Press.

Baker, M. (1988b) Morphology and syntax: an interlocking dependence. In: Everaert et al.

Baker, M. (1988c) Review: Di Sciullo and Williams (1987). *YM* 1, 259–84.

Baker, M., Johnson, K. and Roberts, I. (1989) Passive arguments raised. *LI* 20, 219–52.

Barber, E. (1975) Voice — beyond the passive. *BLS* 1, 16–22.

Bauer, L. (1983) *English Word-formation*. Cambridge: CUP.

Bauer, L. (1988) *Introducing Linguistic Morphology*. Edinburgh: Edinburgh University Press.

Beard, R. (1976) A semantically based model of a generative lexical word-formation rule for Russian adjectives. *Lg* 52, 108–20.

Beard, R. (1981) *The Indo-European Lexicon: a Full Synchronic Theory*. Amsterdam: North-Holland.

Beard, R. (1982) The plural as a lexical derivation. *Glossa* 16, 133–48.

Beard, R. (1987) Morpheme order in a Lexeme/Morpheme based morphology. *Lingua* 72, 1–44.

Beard, R. (1988) On the separation of derivation from morphology: Toward a Lexeme/Morpheme-based morphology. *Quaderni di Semantica* 9, 3–59.

Belletti, A. and Rizzi, L. (1988) Psych-verbs and θ-theory. *NLLT* 6, 291–352.

Benacchio, R. and L. Renzi (1987) *Clitici Slavi e Romanzi*. Padua: CLESP.

Bendor-Samuel, J. T. (1966) Some prosodic features in Terena. In Bazell et al. (eds.) *In memory of J. R. Firth*. London: Longmans; reprinted in Palmer, F. (ed.) (1970) *Prosodic Analysis*. London: OUP.

Berent, G. (1980) On the realization of trace: Macedonian clitic pronouns. In: Chvany and Brecht (eds.).

Blake, B. (1990) *Relational Grammar*. London: Routledge.

Bloch, B. (1941) Phonemic overlapping. *American Speech* 16, 278–84; reprinted in Joos (ed.) (1958).

Bloomfield, L. (1933) *Language*. New York: Holt.

Bloomfield, L. (1939) Menomini morphophonemics. *Travaux du Cercle Linguistique de Prague* 8, 105–15.

Boas, F. (ed.) (1922) *Handbook of American Indian Languages*. Washington: Smithsonian Institution.

Bogoraz, W. (1922) *Chukchee*. In: Boas (ed.).

Booij, G. (1977) *Dutch Morphology: a Study of Word Formation in Generative Grammar*. Dordrecht: Foris.

Booij, G. (1985a) The interaction of phonology and morphology in Prosodic Phonology. In: Gussmann (ed.).

Booij, G. (1985b) Coordination reduction in complex words: a case for Prosodic Phonology. In: van der Hulst and Smith (eds.).

Booij, G. (1987) Lexical Phonology and the organisation of the morphological component. In: Gussmann (ed.).

Booij, G (MS) Morphology, semantics, and argument structure. Amsterdam.

Booij, G. and van Haaften, T. (1988) On the external syntax of derived words: evidence from Dutch. *YM* 1, 29–44.

Booij, G. and Rubach, J. (1984) Morphological and prosodic domains in Lexical Phonology. *Phonology Yearbook* 1, 1–28.

Booij, G. and Rubach, J. (1987) Postcyclic versus postlexical rules in Lexical Phonology. *LI* 18, 1–44.

Borer, H. (1984a) *Parametric Syntax*. Dordrecht: Foris.

Borer, H. (1984b) The Projection Principle and rules of morphology *NELS* 14, 16–33.

Borer, H. (ed.) (1986a) *Syntax and Semantics, 19: the Syntax of Pronominal Clitics*. New York: Academic Press.

Borer, H. (1986b) Introduction. In: Borer (ed.).

Borer, H. (1988) On the parallelism between compounds and constructs. *YM* 1, 45–66.

Botha, R. (1983) *Morphological Mechanisms*. Oxford: Pergamon Press.

Bresnan, J. (1978) A realistic transformational grammar. In: Halle, M., Bresnan, J. and Miller, G. (eds.) *Linguistic Theory and Psychological Reality*. Cambridge, MA: MIT Press.

Bresnan, J. (ed.) (1982) *The Mental Representation of Grammatical Relations*. Cambridge, MA: MIT Press.

Bresnan, J. and Mchombo, S. (1987) Topic, pronoun, and agreement in Chicheŵa. *Lg* 63, 741–82; also in Iida, M., Wechsler, S. and Zec, D. (eds.) *Working Papers in Grammatical Theory and Discourse Structure*. Stanford: CSLI.

Bromberger, S. and Halle, M. (1989) Why phonology is different. *LI* 20, 51–70.

Broselow, E. and McCarthy, J. (1983) A theory of internal reduplication. *TLR* 3, 25–88.

Brown, K. and Miller, J. (1980) *Syntax: an Introduction to Sentence Structure*. London: Hutchinson.

Browne, E. W. (1974) On the problem of enclitic placement in Serbo-Croatian. In Brecht, R. and Chvany, C. (eds.) *Slavic Transformational Syntax*. Ann Arbor: Michigan Slavic Publications.

Burzio, L. (1986) *Italian Syntax: a Government-Binding Approach*. Dordrecht: Reidel.

Butterworth, B. (1983) Lexical representation. In: Butterworth, B. (ed.) *Language Production, Vol. 2*. New York: Academic Press.

Bybee, J. (1985) *Morphology: a Study of the Relation between Meaning and Form*. Amsterdam: Benjamins.

Carlson, G. and Roeper, T. (1980) Morphology and subcategorization: (Case and the unmarked complex verb. In: Hoekstra et al. (eds.).

Carrier, J. (1979) *The Interaction of Morphological and Phonological Rules in Tagalog: a Study in the Relationship between Rule Components in Grammar*. PhD dissertation, MIT.

Carstairs, A. (1987) *Allomorphy in Inflexion*. Beckenham: Croom Helm.

Carstairs, A. (1988) Some implications of phonologically conditioned suppletion. *YM* 1, 67–94.

Chafe, W. (1976) *The Caddoan, Iroquoian, and Siouan Languages*. The Hague: Mouton.

Charette, M. (1989) The Minimality Condition in phonology. *JL* 25, 159–88.

Chomsky, N. (1957) *Syntactic Structures*. The Hague: Mouton.

Chomsky, N. (1965) *Aspects of the Theory of Syntax*. Cambridge, MA: MIT Press.

Chomsky, N. (1970) Remarks on nominalization. In: Jacobs, R. and Rosenbaum, P. (eds.). *Readings in English Transformational Grammar*. Waltham, MA: Blaisdell.

Chomsky, N. (1975) *Reflections on Language*. London: Fontana.

Chomsky, N. (1979) *Hebrew Morphophonemics*. New York: Garland.

Chomsky, N. (1980) *Rules and Representations*. Oxford: Blackwell.

Chomsky, N. (1981) *Lectures on Government and Binding*. Dordrecht: Foris.

Chomsky, N. (1982) *Some Concepts and Consequences of the Theory of Government and Binding*. Cambridge, MA: MIT Press.

Chomsky, N. (1986a) *Barriers*. Cambridge, MA: MIT Press.

Chomsky, N. (1986b) *Knowledge of Language*. New York: Praeger.

Chomsky, N. (MS) Notes on economy of derivation. MIT.

Chomsky, N. and Halle, M. (1968) *The Sound Pattern of English*. New York: Harper and Row.

Chung, S. (1976) An object-creating rule in Bahasa Indonesian. *LI* 7, 41–87; reprinted in Perlmutter, D. (ed.) (1983).

Chvany, C. and Brecht, R. (eds.) (1980) *Morphosyntax in Slavic*. Columbus: Slavica.

Cinque, G. (1988) On *si* constructions and the theory of *Arb*. *LI* 19, 521–82.

Clark, E., Hecht, B. and Mulford, R. (1986) Coining complex compounds in English: affixes and word order in acquisition. *Linguistics* 24, 7–29.

Cole, P. and Sadock, J. (eds.) (1977) *Syntax and Semantics, 8: Grammatical Relations*. New York: Academic Press.

Comrie, B. (1976) *Aspect*. Cambridge: CUP.

Comrie, B. (1977) In defense of spontaneous demotion: the impersonal passive. In: Cole and Sadock (eds.).

Comrie, B. (1978) Ergativity. In: Lehman, W. (ed.) *Syntactic Typology*. Austin: University of Texas Press.

Comrie, B. (1979) Degrees of ergativity. In: Plank (ed.).

Comrie, B. (1981) *Languages of the U.S.S.R.* Cambridge: CUP.

Comrie, B. (1987) *Tense*. Cambridge: CUP.

Corbett, G. (1987) The morphology—syntax interface. *Lg* 63, 299–345.

Corbett, G. (1988) Serbo-Croat. In: Comrie, B. (ed.) *The World's Major Languages*. London: Croom Helm.

Corbett. G. (1990) *Gender*. Cambridge: CUP.

Craig, C. (1977) *The Structure of Jacaltec*. Austin: University of Texas Press.

Day, C. (1973) *The Jacaltec Language*. Bloomington: Indiana University Press.

De Bray, R. (1980a) *Guide to the Slavonic Languages, Vol. 2: South Slavonic*. Ann Arbor: Slavica.

De Bray, R. (1980b) *Guide to the Slavonic Languages, Vol. 3: West Slavonic*. Ann Arbor: Slavica

Derbyshire, D. and Pullum, G. (eds.) (1986) *Handbook of Amazonian Languages*. Berlin: Mouton de Gruyter.

Deuchar, M. (1984) *British Sign Language*. London: Longmans.

Di Sciullo, A.-M. and Williams, E. (1987) *On the Definition of Word*. Cambridge, MA: MIT Press.

Dixon, R. (1979) Ergativity. *Lg* 55, 59–138.

Dixon, R. (1987) Introduction: Lingua special issue on ergativity. *Lingua* 71.

Downing, P. (1977) On the creation and use of English compound nouns. *Lg* 53, 810–42.

Dowty, D. (1979) *Word Meaning and Montague Grammar*. Amsterdam: North-Holland.

Dowty, D., Wall, R. and Peters, S. (1981) *Introduction to Montague Semantics*. Dordrecht: Reidel.

Dressler, W. (1985a) *Morphonology*. Ann Arbor: Karoma.

Dressler, W. (1985b) On the predictiveness of natural morphology. *JL* 21, 321–38.

Durand, J. (1990) *Generative and Non-Linear Phonology*. London: Longmans.

Durie, M. (1988) The so-called passive of Acehnese. *Lg* 64, 104–13.

England, N. (1983) *A Grammar of Mam, a Mayan Language*. Austin: University of Texas.

Everaert, M., Evers, A., Huybregts, R. and Trommelen, M. (eds.) (1988) *Morphology and Modularity*. Dordrecht: Foris.

Everett, D. (1987) Pirahã clitic doubling. *NLLT* 5, 245–76.

Fabb, N. (1984) *Syntactic Affixation*. PhD dissertation, MIT.

Fabb, N. (1988a) English suffixation is constrained only by selectional restrictions. *NLLT* 6, 527–39.

Fabb, N. (1988b) Doing affixation in the GB syntax. In: Everaert et al. (eds.).

Fagan, S. (1988) The English middle. *LI* 19, 181–204.

Fähnrich, H. (1987) *Kurze Grammatik der georgischen Sprache*. Leipzig: VEB Verlag Enzyklopädie.

Feoktistov, A. P. (1966) Mokšanskij jazyk. In: *Jazyki Narodov SSSR, Vol. III*. Moscow: Nauka.

Fischer-Jørgensen, E. (1975) *Trends in Phonological Theory: a Historical Introduction*. Copenhagen: Akademisk Forlag.

Fodor, J. D. (1977) *Semantics*. Hassocks: Harvester Press.

Fodor, J. (1983) *Modularity of Mind*. Cambridge, MA: Bradford Books.

Fromkin, V. and Rodman, R. (1988) *Introduction to Language* (4th edn.). New York: Holt, Rinehart and Winston.

Fujimura, O. (ed.) (1973) *Three Dimensions of Linguistic Theory*. Tokyo: TEC Corporation.

Gazdar, G., Klein, E., Pullum, G. and Sag. I. (1985) *Generalized Phrase Structure Grammar*. Oxford: Blackwell.

Gleason, H. (1961) *An Introduction to Descriptive Linguistics* (rev. ed.) New York: Holt, Rinehart and Winston.

Glossary of Russian Abbreviations and Acronyms (1967). Washington: Library of Congress.

Goldsmith, J. (1979) *Autosegmental Phonology*. New York: Garland.

Goldsmith, J. (1990) *Autosegmental and Metrical Phonology*. Oxford: Blackwell.

Goodwin, W. (1894) *Greek Grammar*. London: Macmillan.

Greenough, J., Kittredge, G., Howard, A. and D'Ooge, B. (eds.) (1983) *Allen and Greenough's New Latin Grammar*. New Rochelle: Caratzas Publishing Co.

Grimes, J. (1967) Positional analysis. *Lg* 43, 437–44.

Grimes, J. (1983) *Affix Positions and Co-occurrence: the PARADIGM Program*. Dallas: Summer Institute of Linguistics.

Grimshaw, J. (1979) Complement selection and the lexicon *LI* 10, 279–326.

Grimshaw, J. (1986) A morphosyntactic explanation for the Mirror Principle *LI* 17, 745–50.

Grunwell, P. (1987) *Clinical Phonology*. Beckenham. Croom Helm.

Guerssel, M. (1983) A lexical approach to word formation in English. *LA* 12, 183–243.

Gussmann, E. (1980) *Studies in Abstract Phonology*. Cambridge, MA: MIT Press.

Gussmann, E. (ed.) (1985) *Phonomorphology*. Lublin: Redakcja Wydawnictw Katolickiego Uniwersytetu Lubelskiego.

Gussmann, E. (ed.) (1987) *Rules and the Lexicon*. Lublin: Redakcja Wydawnictw Katolickiego Uniwersytetu Lubelskiego.

Haegeman, L. (1991) *An Introduction to Generative Syntax*. Oxford: Blackwell.

Hall, T. (1989) Lexical Phonology and the distribution of German [ç] and [x]. *Phonology* 6, 1–18.

Halle, M. (1959) *The Sound Pattern of Russian*. The Hague: Mouton.

Halle, M. (1973) Prolegomena to a theory of word-formation. *LI* 4, 3–16.

Halle, M. and Clements, G. (1983) *Problem Book in Phonology*. Cambridge, MA: MIT Press.

Halle, M. and Mohanan, K. P. (1985) Segmental phonology of Modern English. *LI* 16, 57–116.

Halle, M. and Vergnaud. J.-R. (1987) *An Essay on Stress*. Cambridge MA: MIT Press.

Hammond, M. (1981) Some Vogul morphology: a hierarchical account of multiple exponence. In: Thomas-Flinders (ed.).

Hammond, M. (1988) Templatic transfer in Arabic broken plurals. *NLLT* 6, 247–70.

Hammond, M. (1989) Lexical stresses in Macedonian and Polish. *Phonology* 6, 19–38.

Hammond, M. and Noonan, M. (eds.) (1988) *Theoretical Morphology: Approaches in Modern Linguistics*. Orlando: Academic Press.

Harris, A. (1984) Inversion as a rule of grammar: Georgian evidence. In: Perlmutter and Rosen (eds.).

Harris, James. W. (1969) *Spanish Phonology*. Cambridge, MA: MIT Press.

Harris, James. W. (1983) *Syllable Structure and Stress in Spanish*. Cambridge, MA: MIT Press.

Harris, John (1987) Non-structure-preserving rules in Lexical Phonology. *Lingua* 73, 255–92.

Harris, M. and Coltheart, M. (1986) *Language Processing in Children and Adults*. London: Routledge.

Hawkins, P. (1984) *Introducing Phonology*. London: Hutchinson.

Hayes, B. (1982) Extrametricality and English stress. *LI* 13, 227–76.

Henderson, L. (1985) Towards a psychology of morphemes. In: Ellis, A. (ed.) *Progress in the Psychology of Language, Vol. 1*. London: Lawrence Erlbaum Associates.

Higginbotham, J. (1985) On semantics. *LI* 16, 547–94.

Hockett, C. (1958a) Two models of grammatical description. In: Joos (ed.).

Hockett, C. (1958b) *A Course in Modern Linguistics*. New York: Macmillan.

Hoeksema, J. (1986) *Categorial Morphology*. New York: Garland.

Hoeksema, J. (1987) Relating word structure and logical form. *LI* 18, 119–26.

Hoekstra, T. (1984) *Transitivity: Grammatical Relations in Government-Binding Theory*. Dordrecht: Foris.

Hoekstra, T. (1986) Deverbalization and inheritance. *Linguistics* 24, 549–85.

Hoekstra, T., van der Hulst, H. and Moortgat, M. (eds.) (1980) *Lexical Grammar*. Dordrecht: Foris.

Hoekstra, T. and van der Putten, F. (1988) Inheritance phenomena. In: Everaert et al. (eds.).

Hogg, R. and McCully, C. (1987) *Metrical Phonology: a Coursebook*. Cambridge: CUP.

Hooper, J. (1976) *Introduction to Natural Generative Phonology*. New York: Academic Press.

Hopper, P. and Thompson, S. (1982) *Syntax and Semantics, 15: Studies in Transitivity*. New York: Academic Press.

Horrocks, G. (1987) *Generative Syntax*. London: Longmans.

Huck, G. and Ojeda, A. (eds.) (1987) *Syntax and Semantics, 20: Discontinuous Constituency*. Orlando: Academic Press.

Hudson, G. (1974) The representation of non-productive alternation. In: Anderson, J. and Jones, C. (eds.) *Historical Linguistics, vol. 2*. Amsterdam: North-Holland.

Hudson, G. (1980) Automatic alternations in non-transformational phonology. *Lg* 56, 94–125.

van der Hulst, H. and Smith, N. (eds.) (1982a) *The Structure of Phonological Representations, Part I*. Dordrecht: Foris.

van der Hulst, H. and Smith, N. (eds.) (1982b) *The Structure of Phonological Representations, Part II*. Dordrecht: Foris.

van der Hulst, H. and Smith, N. (1982c) Introduction. In: van der Hulst and Smith (1982a).

van der Hulst, H. and Smith, N. (eds.) (1985a) *Advances in Nonlinear Phonology*. Dordrecht: Foris.

van der Hulst, H. and Smith, N. (1985b) Introduction. In: van der Hulst and Smith (1985a).

Hyman, L. (1975) *Phonology: Theory and Analysis*. New York: Holt, Rinehart and Winston.

Jackendoff, R. (1972) *Semantic Interpretation in Generative Grammar*. Cambridge, MA: MIT Press.

Jackendoff, R. (1975) Morphological and semantic regularities in the lexicon. *Lg* 51, 639–71.

Jackendoff, R. (1976) Towards an explanatory semantic representation. *LI* 7, 89–150.

Jackendoff, R. (1983) *Semantics and Cognition*. Cambridge, MA: MIT Press.

Jackson, H. (1988) *Words and their Meaning*. London: Longmans.

Jakobson, R. (1935) Less enclitiques slaves. *Proceedings of the Congress of Linguists, Rome*, 384–90; reprinted in *Selected Writings, Vol. 2: Word and Language*. (1971) The Hague: Mouton.

Jakobson, R. (1968) *Child Language, Aphasia and Linguistic Universals*. The Hague: Mouton.

Jaeggli, O. (1982) *Topics in Romance Syntax*. Dordrecht: Foris.

Jaeggli, O. (1986) Three issues in the theory of clitics: case, doubled NPs, and extraction. In Borer (ed.).

Jenkins, C. (1984) Some aspects of word formation in a polysynthetic language. *BLS* 10, 104–15.

Jensen, J. (1990) *Morphology*. Amsterdam: Benjamins.

Jensen, J. and Stong-Jensen, M. (1984) Morphology is in the lexicon! *LI* 15, 474–98.

Joos, M. (ed.) (1958) *Readings in Linguistics* (2nd edn.). Chicago: University of Chicago Press.

Joseph, B. (1988) Pronominal affixes in Modern Greek: the case against clisis. *CLS* 24, 203–15.

Joseph, B. and Wallace, R. (1984) Latin morphology: another look. *LI* 15, 319–28.

Kaisse, E. (1985) *Connected Speech: the Interaction of Syntax and Phonology*. Orlando: Academic Press.

Katamba, F. (1989) *An Introduction to Phonology*. London: Longmans.

Kaye, J. (1989) *Phonology: a Cognitive View*. Hillsdale, NJ: Lawrence Erlbaum Associates.

Kaye, J. and Lowenstamm, J. (1981) Syllable structure and markedness theory. In: Belletti, A., Brandi, L. and Rizzi, L. (eds.) *Theory of Markedness in Generative Grammar*. Pisa: Scuola Normale Superiore di Pisa.

Kaye, J., Lowenstamm, J. and Vergnaud, J.-R. (1985) The internal structure of phonological elements: a theory of Charm and Government. *Phonology Yearbook* 2, 305–28.

Kayne, R. (1975) *French Syntax*. Cambridge, MA: MIT Press.

Keenan, E. (1976) Remarkable subjects in Malagasy. In: Li, C. (ed.) *Subject and Topic*. New York: Academic Press.

Keenan, E. and Timberlake, A. (1985) Predicate formation rules in Universal Grammar. *WCCFL* 4, 123–38.

Kenstowicz, M. and Kisseberth, C. (1977) *Topics in Phonological Theory*. New York: Academic Press.

Kenstowicz, M. and Kisseberth, C. (1979) *Generative Phonology: Description and Theory*. New York: Academic Press.

Keyser, S. (ed.) (1978) *Recent Transformational Studies in European Languages*. Cambridge, MA: MIT Press.

Keyser, S. and Roeper, T. (1984) On the middle and ergative constructions in English. *LI* 15, 381–416.

Kibrik, A. E., Kodzasov, S. V., Olovjannikova, I. P. and Samedov, D. S. (1977) *Opyt strukturnogo opisanija arčinskogo jazyka* ['A structural description of Archi'; in Russian]. Moscow: Izdatel'stvo moskovskogo universiteta.

Kiparsky, P. (1973a) 'Elsewhere' in phonology. In Anderson, S. and Kiparsky, P. (eds.) *A Festschrift for Morris Halle*. New York: Holt, Rinehart and Winston.

Kiparsky, P. (1973b) Abstractness, opacity and global rules. In: Fujimura (ed.).

Kiparsky, P. (1982a) From Cyclic Phonology to Lexical Phonology. In van der Hulst and Smith (eds.) (1982a).

Kiparsky, P. (1982b) *Explanation in Phonology*. Dordrecht: Foris.

Kiparsky, P. (1983) Word formation and the lexicon. In: Ingemann, F. (ed.) *Proceedings of the 1982 Mid-America Linguistics Conference*. University of Kansas.

Kiparsky, P. (1985) Some consequences of Lexical Phonology. *Phonology Yearbook* 2, 83–136.

Klavans, J. (1982) *Some Problems in a Theory of Clitics*. Bloomington: IULC.

Klavans, J. (1985) The independence of syntax and phonology in cliticization. *Lg* 61, 95–120.

Klemensiewicz, Z. (1985) *Historia Języka Polskiego* ['The History of Polish'; in Polish]. Warsaw: Państwowe Wydawnictwo Naukowe.

Klima, E. and Bellugi, U. (1979) *The Signs of Language*. Cambridge, MA: Harvard University Press.

Koutsoudas, A., Sanders, G. and Noll, C. (1974) The application of phonological rules. *Lg* 50, 1–28.

Krause, S. (1979) *Topics in Chukchee Phonology and Morphology*. PhD dissertation, University of Illinois.

Kyle, J. and Woll, B (1985) *Sign Language*. Cambridge: CUP.

LaPointe, S. (1981) General and restricted agreement phenomena. In: Moortgat et al. (eds.).

LaPointe, S. (1987) Some extensions of the autolexical approach to structural mismatches. In: Huck and Ojeda (eds.).

Lasnik, H. (1988) Subjects and the θ-Criterion. *NLLT* 6, 1–18.

Lasnik, H. and Saito, M. (1984) On the nature of proper government. *LI* 15, 22–80.

Lasnik, H. and Uriagereka, J. (1988) *A Course in GB Syntax*. Cambridge, MA: MIT Press.

Lass, R. (1984) *Phonology*. Cambridge: CUP.

Lawler, J. (1977) A agrees with B in Achenese: a problem for Relational Grammar. In: Cole and Sadock (eds.).

Lawler, J. (1988) On the question of Acehnese 'passive'. *Lg* 64, 114–17.

Lees, R. (1960) *The Grammar of English Nominalizations*. The Hague: Mouton.

Levin, B. and Rappaport, M. (1986) The formation of adjectival passives. *LI* 17, 623–63.

Levin, J. (MS, 1983) Reduplication and prosodic structure. MIT.

Lewis, G. (1953) *Teach Yourself Turkish*. London: Hodder and Stoughton.

Lewis, G. (1967) *Turkish Grammar*. Oxford: OUP.

Liddell, S. and Johnson, R. (1986) American Sign Language compound formation processes, lexicalization and phonological remnants. *NLLT* 4, 445–513.

Lieber, R. (1980) *The Organization of the Lexicon*. PhD dissertation, MIT. [Distributed by IULC 1981a].

Lieber, R. (1981b) Morphological conversion within a restricted theory of the lexicon. In Moortgat et al. (eds.).

Lieber, R. (1982) Allomorphy. *LA* 10, 27–52.

Lieber, R. (1983) Argument linking and compounding in English. *LI* 14, 251–86.

Lieber, R. (1988) Phrasal compounds in English and the morphology—syntax interface. *Papers from the Parasession on Agreement in Grammatical Theory. CLS* 24, 202–22.

Lightner, T. (1968) On the use of minor rules in Russian phonology. *JL* 4, 69–72.

Lightner, T. (1972) *Problems in the Theory of Phonology*. Edmonton: Linguistic Research.

Lowenstamm, J. and Kaye, J. (1986) Compensatory lengthening in Tiberian Hebrew. In: Wetzels, L. and Sezer, E. (eds.).

Lunt, H. 1952) *A Grammar of the Macedonian Literary Language*. Skopje.

Lyons, C. (forthcoming) Clitics and clitic doubling.

Lyons, J. (1968) *Introduction to Theoretical Linguistics*. Cambridge: CUP.

McCarthy, J. (1979) *Formal Problems in Semitic Phonology and Morphology*. PhD dissertation, MIT. [Distributed by IULC; published by Garland, New York, 1982a].

McCarthy, J. (1982b) Prosodic templates, morphemic templates, and morphemic tiers. In: van der Hulst and Smith (eds.) (1982a).

McCarthy, J. (1982c) Prosodic structure and expletive infixation. *Lg* 58, 574–90.

McCarthy, J. (1986) OCP effects: gemination and antigemination. *LI* 17, 207–64.

McCawley, J. (1968) The role of semantics in a grammar. In: Bach and Harms (eds.).

McCawley, J. (1973) Syntactic and logical arguments for semantic structures. In: Fujimura (ed.).

McCawley, J. (1981) *Everything that Linguists have Always Wanted to Know About Logic★ (but were Ashamed to Ask)*. Oxford: Blackwell.

McCloskey, J. (1988) Syntactic theory. In Newmeyer (ed.).

McDonald, B. (1983) Levels of analysis in sign language research. In: Kyle, J. and Woll, B. (eds.) *Language in Sign: an International Perspective on Sign Language*. London: Croom Helm.

Mallinson, G. and Blake, B. (1981) *Language Typology: Crosslinguistic Studies in Syntax*. Amsterdam: North-Holland.

Manzini, M. R. (1983) On control and control theory. *LI* 14, 421–46.

Manzini, M. R. (1986) On Italian *si*. In: Borer (ed.).

Marantz, A. (1982) Re reduplication. *LI* 13, 483–545.

Marantz, A. (1984) *On the Nature of Grammatical Relations*. Cambridge, MA: MIT Press.

Marantz, A. (1987) Phonologically induced bracketing paradoxes in full morpheme reduplication. *WCCFL* 6, 203–12.

Marantz, A. (1988a) Clitics, morphological merger, and the mapping to phonological structure. In: Hammond and Nooan (eds.).

Marantz, A. (1988b) Apparent exceptions to the Projection Principle. In: Everaert et al. (eds.).

Marchand, H. (1969) *The Categories and Types of Present-Day English Word-Formation.* Munich: C. H. Beck Verlagsbuchhandlung.

Mardirussian, G. (1975) Noun incorporation in universal grammar. *CLS* 11, 383–9.

van Marle, J. (1985) *On the Paradigmatic Dimension of Morphological Creativity.* Dordrecht: Foris.

Mascaró, J. (1976) *Catalan Phonology and the Phonological Cycle.* PhD dissertation, MIT. [Distributed by IULC].

Mascaró, J. (1983) *La Fonologia Catalana i el Cicle Fonologic.* Bellaterra: Universitat Autonoma de Barcelona.

Matthews, P. (1972) *Inflectional Morphology.* Cambridge: CUP.

Matthews, P. (1974) *Morphology.* Cambridge: CUP.

May, R. (1985) *Logical Form.* Cambridge, MA. MIT Press.

Mayerthaler, W. (1981) *Morphologische Natürlichkeit.* Wiesbaden: Athenaion; translated as *Naturalness in Morphology* (1988). Ann Arbor: Karoma.

Menovščikov, G. A. (1975) *Jazyk Naukanskix Èskimosov* ['The language of the Naukan Eskimo'; in Russian] Leningrad: Nauka.

Merlan, F. (1976) Noun incorporation and discourse reference in modern Nahuatl. *IJAL* 42, 177–91.

Mithun, N. (1984) The evolution of noun incorporation. *Lg* 60, 847–94.

Mithun, N. (1986) On the nature of noun incorporation. *Lg* 62, 32–7.

Mohanan, K. (1986) *The Theory of Lexical Phonology.* Dordrecht: Reidel.

Mohanan, K. and Mohanan, T. (1984) Lexical Phonology of the consonant system in Malayalam. *LI* 15, 575–602.

Moody, B. (1983) *La Langue des signes française.* Montpelier.

Moortgat, M., van der Hulst, H. and Hoekstra, T. (eds.) (1981) *The Scope of Lexical Rules.* Dordrecht: Foris.

Mtenje, A. (1987) Tone shift principles in the Chichewa verb: a case for a tone lexicon. *Lingua* 72, 169–209.

Mtenje, A. (1988) On tone and transfer in Chichewa reduplication. *Linguistics* 26, 125–55.

Muysken, P. (1981) Quechua word structure. In: Heny, F. (ed.) *Binding and Filtering.* London: Croom Helm.

Muysken, P. (1988) Affix order and interpretation: Quechua. In: Everaert et al. (eds.).

Myers, S. (1987) *Tone and the Structure of Words in Shona.* PhD dissertation, University of Amherst.

Nash, D. (1980) *Topics in Warlpiri Grammar.* PhD dissertation, MIT. [Published by Garland, New York].

Nedjalkov, V. P. (1976) Diathesen und Satzstruktur im Tschuktschischen. In: Lötsch, R. and Růžička, R. (eds.) *Satzstruktur and Genus Verbi.* Berlin: Akademie Verlag.

Nedjalkov, V. P. (ed.) (1983) *Tipologija rezultativnyx konstrukcij.* Leningrad: Nauka; translated as *Typology of Resultative Constructions* (1987). Amsterdam: Benjamins.

Nespor, M. and Vogel, I. (1986) *Prosodic Phonology.* Dordrecht: Foris.

Newmeyer, F. (1980) *Linguistic Theory in America.* Chicago: University of Chicago Press.

Newmeyer, F. (ed.) (1988) *Linguistics: the Cambridge Survey, Vol. 1: Linguistic Theory: Foundations.* Cambridge: CUP.

Nida, E. (1949) *Morphology: the Descriptive Analysis of Words.* Ann Arbor: University of Michigan Press.

Nykiel-Herbert, B. (1985) The vowel-zero alternation in Polish prefixes. In Gussmann (ed.).

Odden. D. and Odden, M. (1985) Ordered reduplication in Kíhehe. *LI* 16, 497–503.

Osborne, C. (1974) *The Tiwi Language.* Canberra: Australian Institute of Aboriginal Studies.

Öskaragöz, I. (1986) *The Relational Structure of Turkish Syntax.* PhD dissertation, University of California at San Diego.

Padden, C. (1988) Grammatical theory and signed languages. In: Newmeyer, F. (ed.) *Linguistics: the Cambridge Survey, Vol. 2: Linguistic Theory: Extensions and Implications.* Cambridge: CUP.

Padden, C. and Perlmutter, D. (1987) American Sign Language and the architecture of phonological theory. *NLLT* 5, 335–75.

Palmer, F. (1986) *Mood and Modality.* Cambridge: CUP.

Partee, B. H. (1978) *Fundamentals of Mathematics for Linguists.* Dordrecht: Reidel.

Perlmutter, D. (1971) *Deep and Surface Structure Constraints in Syntax.* New York: Holt, Rinehart and Winston.

Perlmutter, D. (1978) Impersonal passives and the Unaccusative Hypothesis. *BLS* 4, 157–89.

Perlmutter, D. (1980) Relational Grammar. In: Moravcsik, E. and Wirth, J. (eds.) *Syntax and Semantics, 13: Current Approaches to Syntax.* New York: Academic Press.

Perlmutter, D. (ed.) (1983) *Studies in Relational Grammar, Vol. 1.* Chicago: University of Chicago Press.

Perlmutter, D. (1988) The split-morphology hypothesis: evidence from Yiddish. In: Hammond and Noonan (eds.).

Perlmutter, D. and Postal, P. (1977) Towards a universal characterization of passivization. *BLS* 3; reprinted in Perlmutter (ed.) (1983).

Perlmutter, D. and Postal, P. (1984) The 1-Advancement Exclusiveness Law. In: Perlmutter and Rosen (eds.).

Perlmutter, D. and Rosen, C. (eds.) (1984) *Studies in Relational Grammar, Vol. 2.* Chicago: University of Chicago Press.

Perlmutter, D. and Soames, S. (1979) *Syntactic Argumentation and the Structure of English.* Berkeley, CA: University of California Press.

Pesetsky, D. (1985) Morphology and Logical Form. *LI* 16, 193–246.

Pike, K. (1948) *Tone Languages.* Ann Arbor: University of Michigan Press.

Piotrowski, M., Roca, I. and Spencer, A. (MS) Polish jers and syllabicity. London/Colchester.

Plank, F. (ed.) (1979) *Ergativity.* New York: Academic Press.

Plank, F. (ed.) (1984a) *Objects.* New York: Academic Press.

Plank, F. (1984b) Romance disagreements: phonology interfering with syntax. *JL* 20, 329–50.

Plank, F. (ed.) (forthcoming) *Paradigms: the Economy of Inflection.* Berlin: Mouton de Gruyter.

Platt, D. (1981) Old Provençal: the balance between regularity and irregularity in verbal inflection. In: Thomas-Flinders (ed.).

Pollock, J.-I. (1989) Verb movement, Universal Grammar, and the structure of IP. *LI* 20, 365–424.

Pulleyblank, D. (1986) *Tone in Lexical Phonology,* Dordrecht: Reidel.

Pullum, G. (1988) Topic … comment: citation etiquette beyond thunderdome. *NLLT* 6, 579–88.

Radford, A. (1981) *Transformational Syntax*. Cambridge: CUP.

Radford, A. (1988) *Transformational Grammar*. Cambridge: CUP.

Randall, J. (1984) *Morphological Structure and Language Acquisition*. New York: Garland.

Revzin, I. I. and Juldaševa, G. D. (1969) Grammatika porjadok i ee ispol'zovanija ['Position class analysis and its application'; in Russian]. *Voprosy Jazykoznanija*, 42–56.

Rice, K. (1985) On the placement of inflection. *LI* 16, 155–61.

van Riemsdijk, H. and Williams, E. (1986) *Introduction to the Theory of Grammar*. Cambridge, MA: MIT Press.

Rizzi, L. (1978) A restructuring rule in Italian syntax. In: Keyser (ed.).

Rizzi, L. (1982) *Issues in Italian Syntax*. Dordrecht: Foris.

Rizzi, L. (1986) Null objects in Italian and the theory of *pro*. *LI* 17, 501–57.

Roberts, I. (1987) *The Representation of Implicit and Dethematized Subjects*. Dordrecht: Foris.

Robertson, J. (1980) *The Structure of Pronoun Incorporation in the Mayan Verbal Complex*. New York: Garland.

Robins, R. (1959) In defence of WP. *Transactions of the Philological Society*, 116–44; reprinted in Robins, R. (1970) *Diversions of Bloomsbury*. Amsterdam: North-Holland.

Roeper, T. (1987) Implicit arguments and the head-complement relation. *LI* 18, 267–310.

Roeper, T. (1988) Compound syntax and head movement. *YM* 1, 187–228.

Roeper, T. and Siegel, D. (1978) A lexical transformation for verbal compounds. *LI* 9, 199–260.

Rosen, C. (1984) The interface between semantic roles and initial grammatical relations. In: Perlmutter and Rosen (eds.).

Rosen, S. (1989) Two types of noun incorporation: a lexical analysis. *Lg* 65, 294–317.

Rubach, J. (1984) *Cyclic and Lexical Phonology*. Dordrecht: Foris.

Rubach, J. (1985) On the interaction of word formation and phonological rules. In: Gussmann (ed.).

Rubach, J. (1986) Abstract vowels in three dimensional phonology: the yers *TLR* 5, 247–80.

Růžička, R. (1986) Typologie der Diathese slavischer Sprachen in parametrischen Variationen. *Die Welt der Slaven* 31, 225–74.

Sadock, J. (1980) Noun incorporation in Greenlandic. *Lg* 56, 300–19.

Sadock J. (1985) Autolexical syntax: a proposal for the treatment of noun incorporation and similar phenomena. *NLLT* 3, 379–439.

Sadock, J. (1986) Some notes on noun incorporation. *Lg* 62, 19–31.

Sadock, J. (1987) Discontinuity in autolexical and autosemantic syntax. In: Huck and Ojeda (eds).

Safir, K. (1987) The syntactic projection of lexical theta structure. *NLLT* 5, 561–601.

Sandler, W. (1989) *Phonological Representation of the Sign*. Dordrecht: Foris.

Sapir, E. (1911) The problem of noun incorporation in American languages. *American Anthropologist* 13, 250–82.

Sapir, E. (1921) *Language*. New York: Harcourt, Brace and World.

Sapir, E. (1922) Takelma. In: Boas (ed.).

Sasse, H.-J. (1984) The pragmatics of noun incorporation in Eastern Cushitic languages. In: Plank (ed.).

Scalise, S. (1984) *Generative Morphology*. Dordrecht: Foris.

Scalise, S. (1988) Inflection and derivation. *Linguistics* 26, 561–82.

Scatton, E. (1975) *Bulgarian Phonology*. Cambridge, MA: Slavica.

Scatton, E. (1980) On the shape of the Bulgarian definite article. In: Chvany and Brecht (eds.).

Seiter, W. (1980) *Studies in Niuean Syntax*. New York: Garland.

Selkirk, E. (1980) On prosodic structure and its relations to syntactic structure. Distributed by IULC.

Selkirk, E. (1981) English compounding and the theory of word structure. In: Moortgat et al. (eds.).

Selkirk, E. (1982) *The Syntax of Words*. Cambridge, MA: MIT Press.

Selkirk, E. (1986) On derived domains in sentence phonology. *Phonology Yearbook* 3, 371–405.

Sells, P. (1985) *Lectures on Contemporary Syntactic Theories*. Stanford University: CSLI.

Shibatani, M. (ed.) (1976) *Syntax and Semantics 6: the Syntax of Causative Constructions*. New York: Academic Press.

Shibatani, M. (1985) Passives and related constructions: a prototype analysis. *Lg* 61, 821–48.

Shibatani, M. (1990) *The Languages of Japan*. Cambridge: CUP.

Shibatani, M. and Kageyama, T. (1988) Word formation in a modular theory of grammar: a case of post-syntactic compounds in Japanese. *Lg* 64, 451–84.

Shopen, T. (ed.) (1985) *Language Typology and Grammatical Description, Vol. 3: Grammatical Categories and the Lexicon*. Cambridge: CUP.

Siegel, D. (1977) The Adjacency Condition and the theory of morphology. *NELS* 8, 189–97.

Siegel, D. (1979) *Topics in English Morphology*. New York: Garland.

Siegel, D. (1980) Why there is no = boundary. In: Aronoff, M. and Kean, M.-L. (eds.) *Juncture*. Saratoga, CA: Anma Libri.

Simpson, J. and Withgott, M. (1986) Pronominal clitic clusters and templates. In: Borer (ed.).

Skorik, I. P. (1948) *Očerki po Sintaksisu Čukotskogo Jazyka: Inkorporatsija* ['Outline of Chukchee Syntax: Incorporation'; in Russian] Leningrad: Učpedgiz.

Skorik, I. P. (1961) *Grammatika Čukotskogo Jazyka. Tom 1* ['A Grammar of Chukchee', Vol. 1'; in Russian]. Moscow: Izdatel'stvo Akademii Nauk.

Skorik, I. P. (1977) *Grammatika Čukotskogo Jazyka. Tom 2* ['A Grammar of Chukchee, Vol. 2'; in Russian] Moscow: Izdatel'stvo Akademii Nauk.

Smith, N. and Wilson, D. (1978) *Modern Linguistics*. Harmondsworth: Penguin.

Sobin, N. (1985) Case assignment in Ukrainian morphological passive constructions. *LI* 16, 649–62.

Sommerstein, A. (1977) *Modern Phonology*. London: Arnold.

Speas, M. (1984) Navajo prefixes and word structure typology. *MITWPL* 7, 86–109.

Spencer, A. (1984) A nonlinear analysis of phonological disability. *Journal of Communication Disorders* 17, 325–48.

Spencer, A. (1986) A non-linear analysis of vowel-zero alternations in Polish. *JL* 22, 249–80.

Spencer, A. (1988a) Arguments for morpholexical rules. *JL* 24, 1–30.

Spencer, A. (1988b) Lexical rules and lexical representation. *Linguistics* 26, 619–40.

Spencer, A. (1988c) Bracketing paradoxes and the English lexicon. *Lg* 64, 663–82.

Sproat, R. (1984) On bracketing paradoxes. *MITWPL* 7, 110–30.

Sproat, R. (1985a) *On Deriving the Lexicon*. PhD dissertation, MIT.

Sproat, R. (1985b) A note on rebracketing in morphology. *MITWPL* 6, 199–205.

Sproat, R. (1988) Bracketing paradoxes, cliticization and other topics: the mapping between syntactic and phonological structure. In: Everaert et al. (eds.).

Stampe, D. (1979) *A Dissertation on Natural Phonology*. New York: Garland.

Steriade, D. (1988a) Reduplication and syllable transfer in Sanskrit and elsewhere. *Phonology* 5, 73–155.

Steriade, D. (1988b) Greek accent: a case for preserving structure. *LI* 19, 271–314.

Strauss, S. (1982a) On 'relatedness paradoxes' and related paradoxes. *LI* 13, 695–700.

Strauss, S. (1982b) *Lexicalist Phonology of English and German*. Dordrecht: Foris.

Suñer, M. (1988) The role of agreement in clitic-doubled constructions. *NLLT* 6, 391–434.

Sussex, R. (1980) On agreement, suffixation and enclisis in Polish. In: Chvany and Brecht (eds.).

Szymanek, B. (1985) *English and Polish Adjectives: a Study in Lexicalist Word Formation*. Lublin: Katolicki Uniwersytet Lubelski.

Ter Mors, C. (1983) Affix to X*. *TLR* 3, 275–98.

Thomas-Flinders, T. (ed.) (1981) *Inflectional Morphology: Introduction to the Extended Word-and-Paradigm Theory*. Occasional Papers in Linguistics 4. UCLA Department of Linguistics.

Thompson, L. (1965) *A Vietnamese Grammar*. Seattle: University of Washington Press.

Timberlake, A. (1982) The impersonal passive in Lithuanian. *BLS* 8, 508–23.

Toman, J. (1981) Aspects of multiple wh-movement in Polish and Czech. In: May, R. and Koster, J. (eds.) *Levels of Syntactic Representation*. Dordrecht: Foris.

Travis, L. and Williams, E. (1982) Externalization of arguments in Malayo-Polynesian languages. *TLR* 2, 57–78.

Usikova, R. P. (1985) *Makedonskij Jazyk* ['The Macedonian Language'; in Russian]. Skopje: Makedonska kniga.

Vasqez Cuesta, P. and Mendes da Luz, M. A. (1961) *Gramática Portuguesa*. Madrid: Editorial Gridos.

Vennemann, T. (1972) Rule inversion. *Lingua* 29, 209–42.

Volodin, A. P. (1976) *Itel'menskij Jazyk* ['The Itel'men Language'; in Russian]. Leningrad: Nauka.

Wall, R. (1972) *Introduction to Mathematical Linguistics*. Englewood Cliffs, NJ: Prentice-Hall.

Wasow, T. (1977) Transformations and the lexicon. In: Culicover, P., Wasow, T. and Akmajian, A. (eds.) *Formal Syntax*. New York: Academic Press.

Wetzels, L. and Sezer, E. (eds.) (1986) *Studies in Compensatory Lengthening*. Dordrecht: Foris.

Whorf, B. (1956) *Language, Thought, and Reality* (J. Carroll, ed.). Cambridge, MA: MIT Press.

Wilbur, R. (1973) *The Phonology of Reduplication*. PhD dissertation, MIT. [Distributed by IULC].

Wilbur, R. (1979) *American Sign Language and Signing Systems*. Cambridge, MA: Harvard University Press.

Williams, E. (1980) Predication. *LI* 11, 203–38.

Williams, E. (1981a) On the notions 'lexically related' and 'head of a word'. *LI* 12, 245–74.

Williams, E. (1981b) Argument structure and morphology. *TLR* 1, 81–114.

Williams, E. (1985) PRO in NP. *NLLT* 3, 277–95.

Williams, E. (1987) Implicit arguments, the binding theory, and control. *NLLT* 5, 151–80.

Winograd, T. (1983) *Language as a Cognitive Process, Vol. 1: Syntax*. Reading, MA: Addison-Wesley.

Wurzel, W. (1984) *Flexionsmorphologie und Natürlichkeit*. Berlin: Akademie Verlag; translated as *Inflectional Morphology and Naturalness* (1989). Dordrecht: Reidel.

Xaritonov, L. N. (1963) *Zalogovye formy glagola v jakutskom jazyke* ['Voice Forms of the Verb in Yakuts'; in Russian]. Moscow-Leningrad: Nauka.

Yip, M. (1982) Reduplication and C-V skeleta in Chinese secret languages. *LI* 13, 637–61.

Young, R. and Morgan, W. (1980) *The Navajo Language*. Albuquerque: University of New Mexico Press.

Zaliznjak, A. A. (1977) *Grammatičeskij Slovar' Russkogo Jazyka* ['A Grammatical Dictionary of Russian'; in Russian]. Moscow: Russkij Jazyk.

Zonneveld, W. (1978) *A Formal Theory of Exceptions in Generative Phonology*. Lisse: Peter de Ridder Press.

Zubizarreta, M.-L. (1987) *Levels of Representation in the Lexicon and in Syntax*. Dordrecht: Foris.

Zubizarreta, M.-L. and Vergnaud, J.-R. (1982) On virtual categories. *MITWPL* 4, 293–303.

Žukova, A. N. (1980) *Jazyk Palanskix Korjakov* ['The Language of the Palan Koryak'; in Russian]. Leningrad: Nauka.

Zwicky, A. (1977) *On Clitics*. Bloomington: IULC.

Zwicky, A. (1985a) How to describe inflection. *BLS* 11, 371–86.

Zwicky, A. (1985b) Clitics and particles. *Lg* 61, 283–305.

Zwicky, A. (1985c) Rules of allomorphy and syntax-phonology interactions. *JL* 21, 431–36.

Zwicky, A. (1985d) Heads. *JL* 21, 1–20.

Zwicky, A. (1986) The general case: basic form versus default form. *BLS* 12, 305–14.

Zwicky, A. (1987a) Suppressing the Zs. *JL* 23, 133–48.

Zwicky, A. (1987b) French prepositions: no peeking. *Phonology Yearbook* 4, 211–27.

Zwicky, A. (1987c) Phonological and morphological rule interactions in highly modular grammars. *ESCOL* 3, 523–32.

Zwicky, A. (1987d) Transformational grammarians and their ilk. *MITWPL* 9, 265–79.

Zwicky, A. (1988) Morphological rules, operations and operation types. *ESCOL* 4, 318–34.

Zwicky, A. (1990) Inflectional morphology as a (sub)component of grammar. In: Luschützky, H. (ed.) *Morphologica 1988*. Amsterdam: Benjamins.

Zwicky, A. and Pullum, G. (1983) Cliticization vs. inflection: English *n't*. *Lg* 59, 502–13.

Subject Index

Note: The symbol ~ represents the position of the head word within a complex technical term. For instance, under *clitic*, pronominal~ and ~doubling stand for *pronominal clitic* and *clitic doubling* respectively.

1-Advancement Exclusiveness Law (1-AEX) 243, **261**, 290
ablaut 16, 50, 51, 114, 135
absolutive (case) *See* ergativity
absorption (of theta role) 386
  (of Case) 283, 303, 386, 476n19
Abstract Case *See* Case
Abstract Incorporation [*see also* Reanalysis] 279–80
abstract (segment, analysis) **63**, 99, 103, 104, 106, 125
accidental gap **76**, 90
acronym 85, 461n16
active (voice) **23**
adjacency 409, 418, 420
Adjacency Condition [*see also* Atom Condition, bracket erasure] **185–6**, 188, 202, 213
Adjectival Passive Formation (APF) 301
affix **5**
  phrasal~ **377**, 383, 458–9
  pronominal~ 374
  Stem~ 401–3
  stress neutral~ **79**
  Word~ 401–3
Affix Hopping 200, 206
Affix Ordering Generalization **80**, 179, 199
Affix Rule [Roeper and Siegel] 326
Affix-to-X 155–6
After [Klavans] 377
Agent (θ role) 190

agent defocusing 245
agentive 84, 111, 195
agglutination (agglutinating morphology) **38**, 50, 52, 69, 74, 103, 133, 134, 189, 215, 223, 224, 225, 230, 428, 463n5
'Agr climbing' 389
agreement 10, **21**, 65–6, 374, 384–90, 394, 439, 457–8, 460n5, 462FR, 475n5
  cliticization as, 359–60, 381, 477n20
Aktionsart 33–4, **196**
allomorph(y) **6**, 40–1, 57–8, 66, 86, 103–5, 227, 460n3,4,5
  derived~ 104, 118, 120
  external~ 128, 356
allomorphy rule *See* rule
Allomorphy Rule (AMR) [in Natural Morphology] 126, 127, 466n14
allophone 460n3
allophony 53, 54
alternation (phonological~) **15**
Alternation Condition **106–7**
analytic (construction) **238**
anaphoric island **42**, 445, 450
Anaphoric Island Constraint 447
antipassive **24**, 251, 267, 278, 289, 471n7,9
anticausative **246**, 297, 343, 456
apophony *See* ablaut
applied verb (applicative [*see also* Dative Shift, Preposition Incorporation] **253**, 254, 273–5, 277, 283, 287–9, 307
archiphoneme **55**

Name Index

Language Index